Wonders

Mc
Graw
Hill

Also Available from McGraw Hill

studysync®

TIME for KIDS

mheducation.com/prek-12

Send all inquiries to:
McGraw Hill
1325 Avenue of the Americas.
New York, NY 10019

ISBN: 978-1-26568917-9
MHID: 1-26-568917-2

Printed in the United States of America

3 4 5 6 7 8 9 LMN 26 25 24 23 22 B

Wonders

Welcome to *Wonders*

Designed to support teachers and empower students.

You want all your students to build knowledge while fostering exploration of our world through literacy. Literacy is the key to understanding – across time, across borders, across cultures – and will help students realize the role they play in the world they are creating.

The result: an evidence-based K–5 ELA program, aligned with standards and based on the Science of Reading, that empowers students to take an active role in learning and exploration. Your students will enjoy unparalleled opportunities for student-friendly self-assessments and self-expression through reading, writing, and speaking. By experiencing diverse perspectives and sharing their own, students will expand their learning. Best-in-class differentiation ensures that all your students have opportunities to become strong readers, writers, and critical thinkers.

We're excited for you to get to know *Wonders* and honored to join you and your students on your pathways to success!

Authors and Consultants

With unmatched expertise in English Language Arts, supporting English language learners, intervention, and more, the *Wonders* team of authors is composed of scholars, researchers, and teachers from across the country. From managing ELA research centers, to creating evidence-based classroom practices for teachers, this highly qualified team of professionals is fully invested in improving student and district outcomes.

Authors

Dr. Douglas Fisher
Close Reading and Writing,
Writing to Sources,
Text Complexity

Dr. Diane August
English Language Learners,
Dual Language

Kathy Bumgardner
Instructional Best Practices,
Multi-Sensory Teaching,
Student Engagement

Dr. Vicki Gibson
Small Group Instruction,
Social Emotional Learning,
Foundational Skills

Dr. Josefina V. Tinajero
English Language Learners,
Dual Language

Dr. Timothy Shanahan
Text Complexity,
Reading and Writing,
Oral Reading Fluency,
Close Reading,
Disciplinary Literacy

Dr. Donald Bear
Word Study, Vocabulary,
Foundational Skills

Dr. Jana Echevarria
English Language Learners,
Oral Language Development

Dr. Jan Hasbrouck
Oral Reading Fluency,
Foundational Skills,
Response to Intervention

"My hope for our students is that their teacher can help every student become a skillful reader and writer." - Dr. Jan Hasbrouck

Consultants

Dr. Doris Walker-Dalhouse
Multicultural Literature

Dr. David J. Francis
Assessment, English Language Learners Research

Jay McTighe
Understanding by Design

Dr. Tracy Spinrad
Social Emotional Learning

Dinah Zike
Professional Development, Multi-Sensory Teaching

"My hope for our students including English Learners, is that they will receive outstanding English language arts and reading instruction to allow them to reach their full academic potential and excel in school and in life." - Dr. Josefina V. Tinajero

Developing
Student Ownership
of Learning

Reflect on What You Know	Monitor Learning	Choose Learning Resources	Reflect on Progress	Set Learning Goals

The instructional routines in *Wonders* guide students to understand the importance of taking ownership of their own learning. The **Reading/Writing Companion** Welcome pages introduce students to routines they will be using throughout the year.

AUTHOR INSIGHT

Learning how to identify what they are learning, talk about what they know, figure out what they need more help with, and figure out next steps are all important aspects of taking ownership of learning that students develop in *Wonders*.

\- Dr. Douglas Fisher

Reflect on What You Know

Text Set Goals

Students are introduced to three overarching goals for each text set. Students first evaluate what they know before instruction begins.

Reading and Writing

Students evaluate what they know about reading in a particular genre and writing in response to texts using text evidence.

Build Knowledge Goals

Each text set is focused on building knowledge through investigation of an Essential Question. After an introduction to the Essential Question, students self-evaluate how much they already know about the topic.

Extended Writing Goals

Students also think about their ability to write in a particular genre before instruction begins.

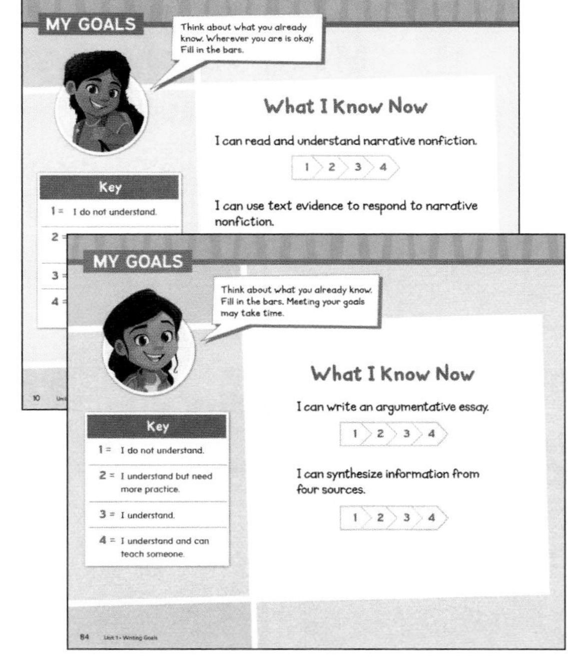

Courtesy of Douglas Fisher

Monitor Learning

Lesson Learning Goals

The journey through a text set and extended writing is made up of a sequence of lessons. The learning goals of these lessons build toward achieving the overarching goals. At the start of each lesson, a targeted learning goal, presented as a "We Can" statement, is introduced to students.

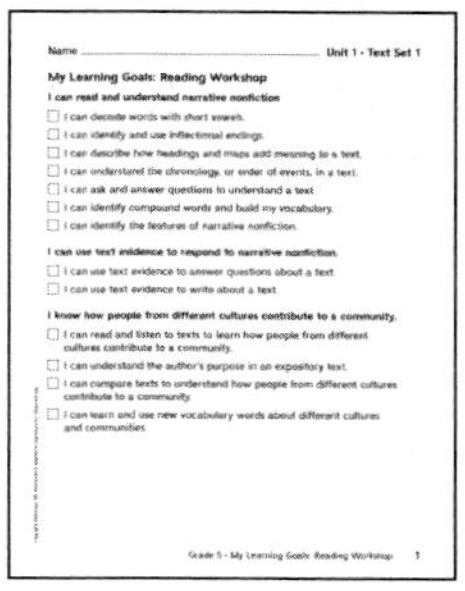

The learning goals are shared with students and parents so that they can track their learning as they work through the lessons.

Check-In Routine

At the end of each lesson, students are asked to self-assess how well they understood the lesson learning goal.

Review

At the end of the lesson, students conference with a partner. They review the lesson learning goal "We Can" statement.

CHECK-IN ROUTINE

Review the lesson learning goal.
Reflect on the activity.
Self-Assess by
- filling in the bars in the Reading/Writing Companion
- holding up 1, 2, 3, or 4 fingers

Share with your teacher.

Reflect

Students take turns self-reflecting on how well they understood the learning goal.

TEACHING TIP

As students develop their ability to reflect on their work, provide sentence frames to support them.

Ask yourself:

Can I ________?

Respond:

I can almost ________.

I am having trouble________.

I need to work on ________.

Self Assess

Students hold up 1, 2, 3 or 4 fingers to self-assess how well they understood the learning goal. When appropriate, they will fill in the bars in the Reading/Writing Companion as well. At the start of the year, review the ratings with students emphasizing that we all learn differently and at a different pace. It is okay to score a 1 or 2. Understanding what they do not know will help students figure out what to do next.

TEACHING TIP

1 I did not understand the learning goal.

2 I understood some things about the learning goal. I need more explanation.

3 I understood how to do the lesson, but I need more practice.

4 I understood the learning goal really well. I think I can teach someone how to do it.

Share

Students share their self-assessments with you by holding up their fingers and sharing the filled-in bars. This lets you know how students think they are doing.

TEACHING TIP

Valuing students' self-assessments is important to enabling students to take ownership of their learning. As students progress throughout the year, they become more adept at self-assessing what they know and what help they need moving forward.

Developing **Student Ownership** of Learning

Reflect on What You Know | Monitor Learning | Choose Learning Resources | Reflect on Progress | Set Learning Goals

Choose Learning Resources

Student-Teacher Conferencing

As students evaluate what they understand, the next step is to think about whether they need more teaching or more practice. The **Reading/Writing Companion** can serve as a powerful conferencing tool. Reviewing their filled-in bars while conferring with each student provides you the opportunity to guide students into identifying what they should do next to improve their understanding.

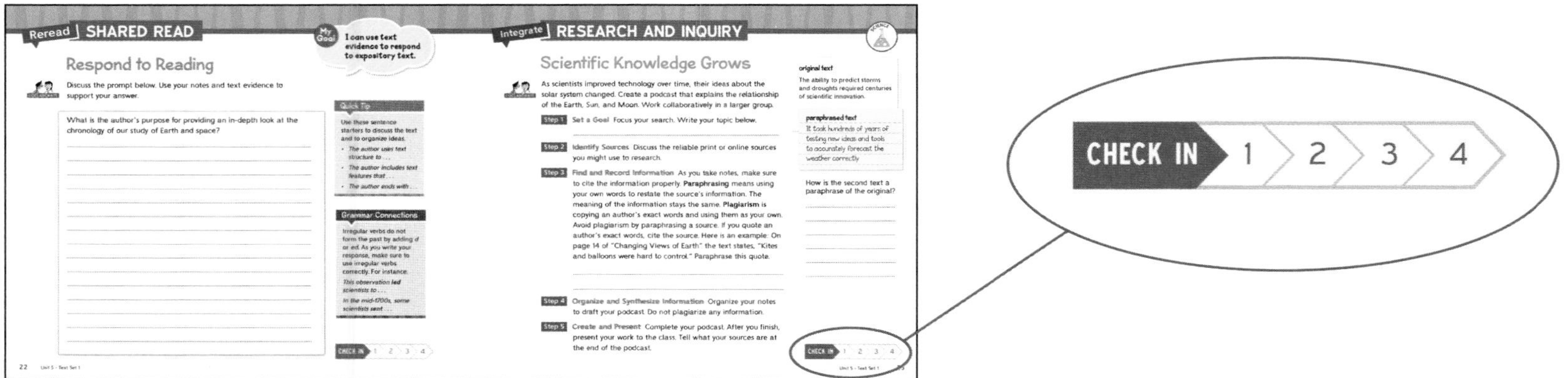

Small Group Teacher-Led Instruction

You and the student may decide that they need more teaching. Student Check-Ins and your observations at the end of each lesson provide timely data that informs the focus for teacher-led small group instruction. Teachers can choose from the small group differentiated lessons provided.

Small Group Independent/Collaborative Work

While meeting with small groups, other students can practice the skills and concepts they have determined they need practice with.

My Independent Work lists options for collaborative and independent practice. Based on student input and your informal observations, you identify "Must Do" activities to be completed. Students then choose activities focused on areas of need and interests they have identified—promoting student choice and voice.

Name ______ Unit 1 • Text Set 1

My Independent Work

	Reading	Phonics/Word Study	Writing
Center Activity Cards	Card: Activity:	Card: Activity:	Card: Activity:
Digital Activities my.mheducation.com	Activity:	Activity:	Activity:
Practice Pages	Content Area Reading:	Practice:	Practice:
Independent Choices	Independent Reading:	Activity:	Self-Selected Writing:

Grade 5 • My Independent Work 1

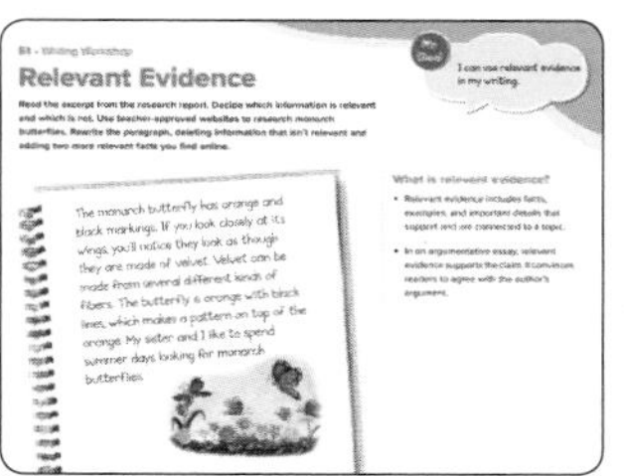

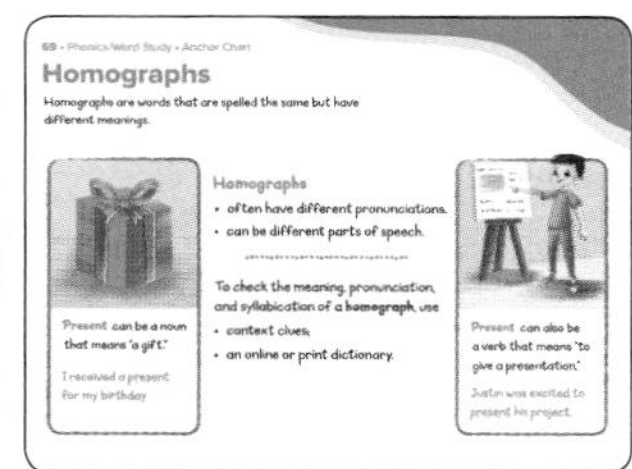

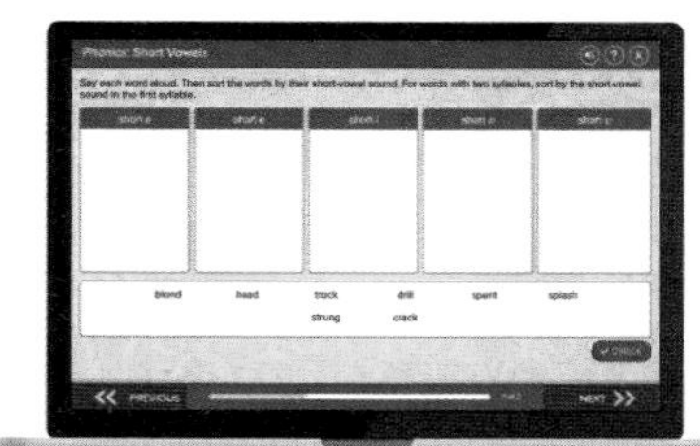

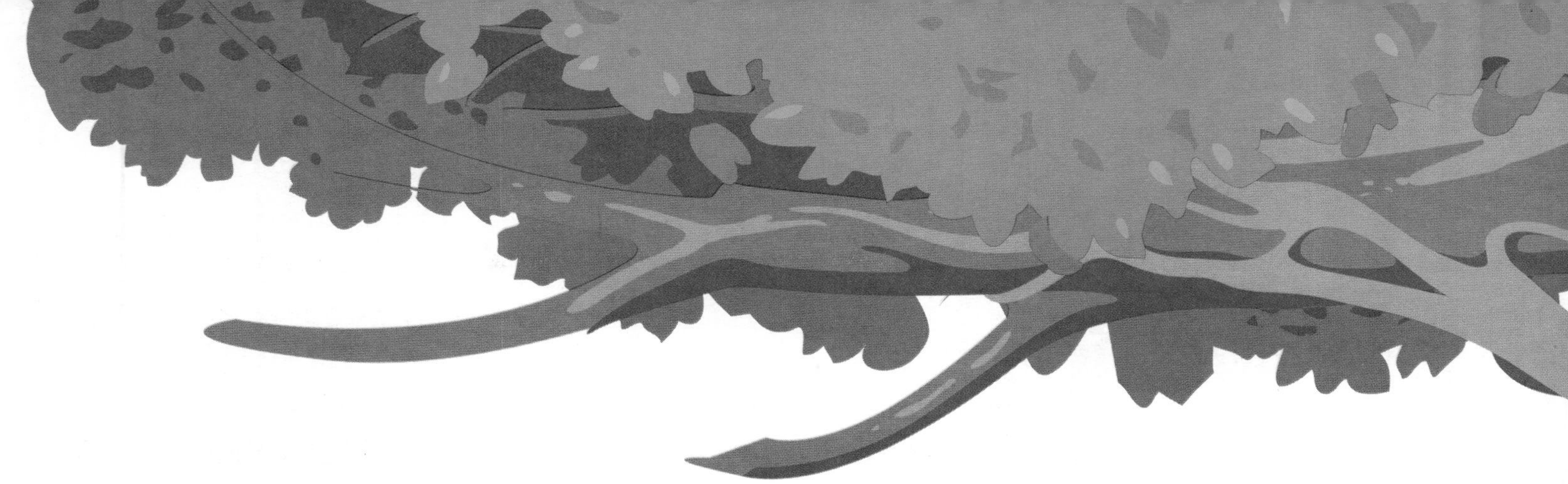

Reflect on Progress

After completing the lessons in the text set and extended writing, students reflect on their overall progress, taking notes to share with their peers and at teacher conferences. The focus of the conversations is on progress made and figuring out next steps to continued progress.

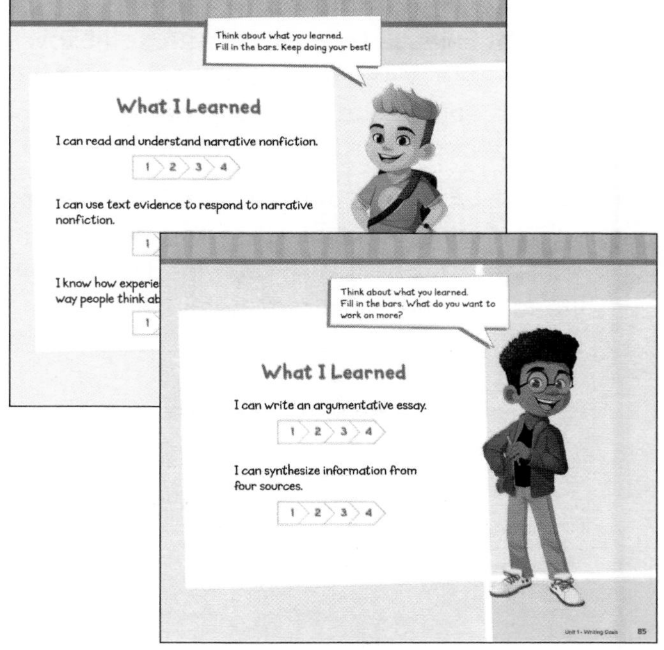

TEACHING TIP

As students discuss their progress, ask them to reflect on the following:

- In what areas did you feel that you made a lot of progress?
- What are some examples?
- What areas do you still need to work on?
- What things can you do to make more progress in these areas?

Set Learning Goals

At the end of the unit, students continue to reflect on their learning. They are also asked to set their own learning goals as they move into the next unit of instruction.

See additional guidance online for supporting students in evaluating work, working toward meeting learning goals, and reflecting on progress.

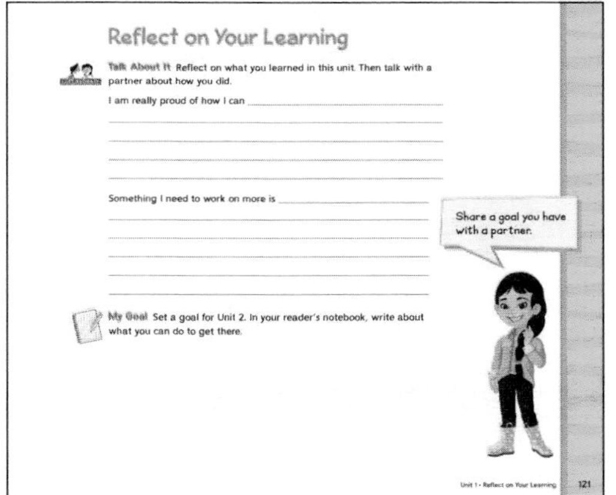

Equity and Access

Differentiated Resources

Every student deserves high-quality instruction. *Wonders* provides high-quality, rigorous instruction that supports access to grade-level content and ELA Skills through equitable, differentiated instruction and resources.

Scaffolded Instruction

Gradual Release Model of Instruction Explicit skills lessons start with teacher explanation and modeling, then move to guided and collaborative practice, then culminate with independent practice with the Your Turn activities.

Access Complex Text The complex features of texts students are asked to read are highlighted. Point-of-use scaffolds are provided to help students to attend to those complex aspects of the text.

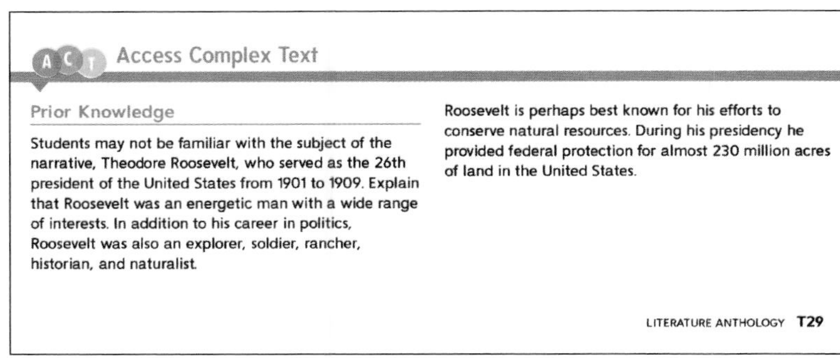

Access Complex Text

Prior Knowledge

Students may not be familiar with the subject of the narrative, Theodore Roosevelt, who served as the 26th president of the United States from 1901 to 1909. Explain that Roosevelt was an energetic man with a wide range of interests. In addition to his career in politics, Roosevelt was also an explorer, soldier, rancher, historian, and naturalist.

Roosevelt is perhaps best known for his efforts to conserve natural resources. During his presidency he provided federal protection for almost 230 million acres of land in the United States.

LITERATURE ANTHOLOGY T29

Data Informed Instruction *Wonders* offers frequent opportunities for informal and formative assessment. The student Check-Ins and teacher Check for Success features provide daily input allowing adjustments for instruction and student practice. The Data Dashboard collects data from online games and activities and the Progress Monitoring assessments.

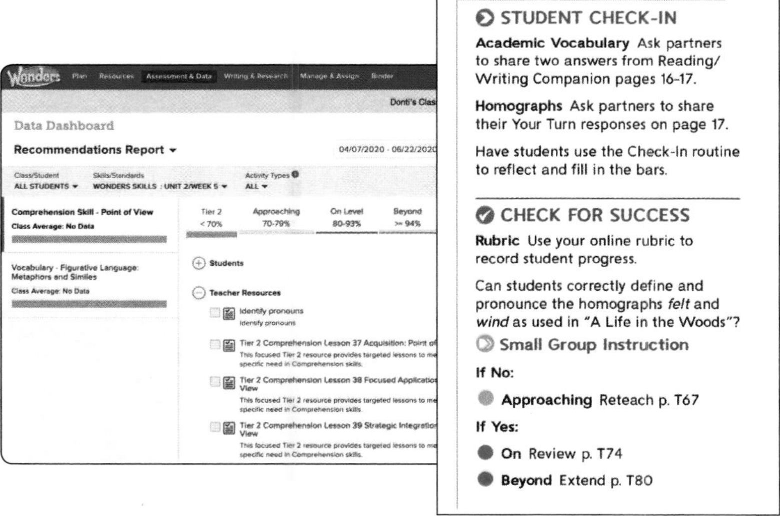

FORMATIVE ASSESSMENT

STUDENT CHECK-IN

Academic Vocabulary Ask partners to share two answers from Reading/Writing Companion pages 16-17.

Homographs Ask partners to share their Your Turn responses on page 17.

Have students use the Check-In routine to reflect and fill in the bars.

CHECK FOR SUCCESS

Rubric Use your online rubric to record student progress.

Can students correctly define and pronounce the homographs *felt* and *wind* as used in "A Life in the Woods"?

Small Group Instruction

If No:

Approaching Reteach p. T67

If Yes:

On Review p. T74

Beyond Extend p. T80

Differentiated Small Group Time

Teacher-Led Instruction Key skills and concepts are supported with explicit differentiated lessons. The Differentiated Genre Passages and Leveled Readers provide a variety of differentiated texts. Literature Small group lessons guide teachers in scaffolding support so all students have access to the same text.

Tier 2 instruction is incorporated into the Approaching level lessons. Additional Tier 2 instruction is available online.

Gifted and Talented activities are also provided for those students who are ready to extend their learning.

Independent/Collaborative Work
A range of choices for practice and extension are provided to support the key skills and concepts taught. Students use this time to work on their independent reading and writing. Resources include the Center Activity Cards, online games, Practice Book, and Content Area Reading blackline masters.

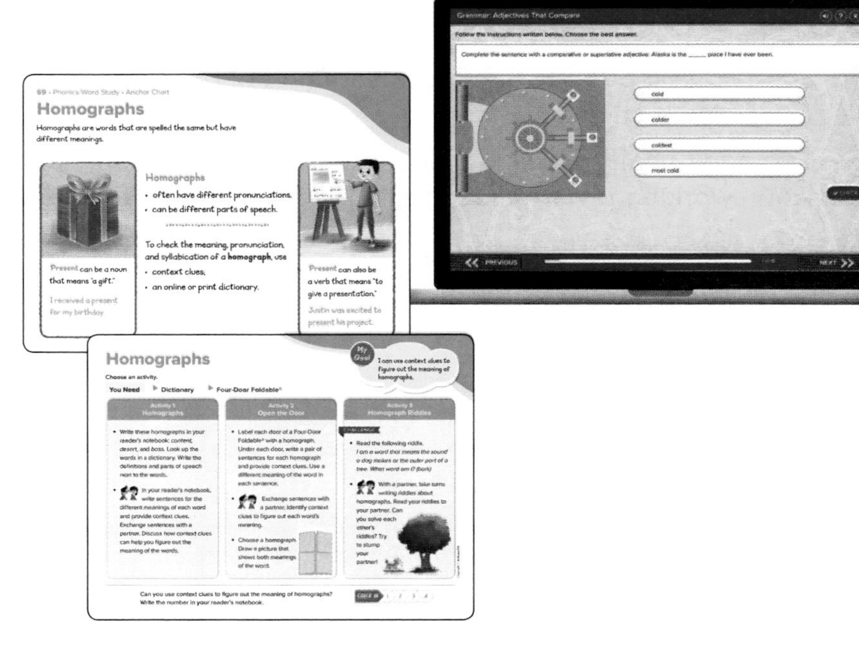

ELL English Language Learners

Access to Grade Level Lessons

English Language Proficiency Levels Targeted support addressing the different English Language Proficiency Levels allows all students to participate.

Spotlight on Language Point-of-use support that highlights English phrases and vocabulary that may be particularly difficult for English Language Learners.

> **ELL English Language Learners**
>
> Use the following scaffolds with **Guided Practice**. For small group support, see the **ELL Teacher's Guide**.
>
> **Beginning**
> Review primary and secondary sources with students. Reread the third sentence in "Cabin Life" with students. Have students point to quotation marks. Remind them that quotation marks show that a person wrote or said this. Ask: *What did Thoreau write?* "I have a great deal of company in my house." *Is this quote from a primary source?* (yes)
>
> **Intermediate**
> Review primary and secondary sources with students. Have students reread the first three sentences of "Cabin Life" and point to the quotation marks. Ask: *What do the quotation marks show?* They show that a person wrote or said this. *Who wrote* "I have a great deal of company in my house"? (Thoreau) Help partners discuss if this quote is from a primary or secondary source using: The words "he wrote" tells me this quote is from a primary source.
>
> **Advanced/Advanced High**
> Have partners take turns reading "Cabin Life" on page 4. Have them identify the quote and tell if it's a primary source. Ask questions to guide them: *Who wrote or said this? How do you know? Why is the primary source unique?*

Multilingual Resources

Home Language Support The following features are available in Spanish, Haitian-Creole, Portuguese, Vietnamese, French, Arabic, Chinese, Russian, Tagalog, and Urdu:

- Summaries of the Shared Read and Anchor Texts.
- School–to-Home Letters that help families support students in their learning goals.
- Multilingual Glossary of key content words with definitions from grade-level texts.
- Spanish and Haitian-Creole Leveled Readers available online.

Strategic Support

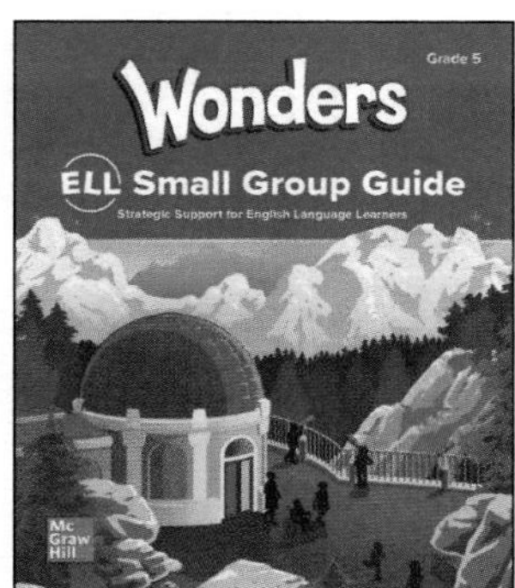

A separate resource is available for small group instruction focused specifically on English Language Learners. The lessons are carefully designed to support the language development, grade level skills, and content. The instruction and resources are differentiated to address all levels of English Language Proficiency and carefully align with the instruction in Reading and Writing.

Additional Resources for Differentiation

Newcomer Kit Instructional cards and practice focused on access to basic, high-utility vocabulary.

Language Development Kit Differentiated instruction and practice for key English grammar concepts.

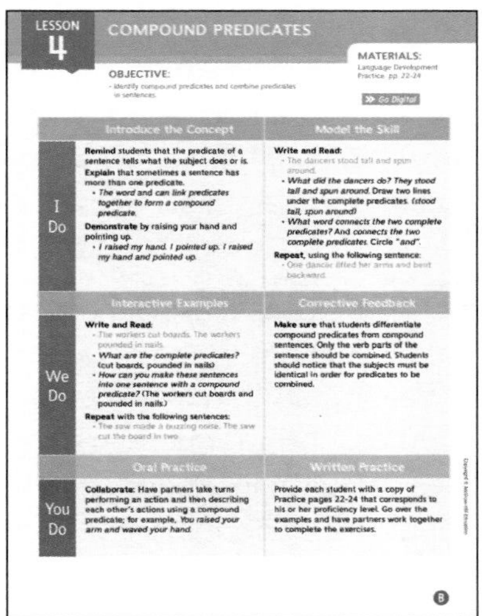

LESSON 4 COMPOUND PREDICATES

OBJECTIVE:
- Identify compound predicates and combine predicates in sentences.

MATERIALS:
Language Development Practice pp. 22-24

Go Digital

	Introduce the Concept	Model the Skill
I Do	**Remind** students that the predicate of a sentence tells what the subject does or is. **Explain** that sometimes a sentence has more than one predicate. • *The word* and *can link predicates together to form a compound predicate.* **Demonstrate** by raising your hand and pointing up. • *I raised my hand. I pointed up. I raised my hand and pointed up.*	**Write and Read:** • The dancers stood tall and spun around. • *What did the dancers do? They stood tall and spun around.* Draw two lines under the complete predicates. *(stood tall, spun around)* • *What word connects the two complete predicates? And connects the two complete predicates.* Circle "*and*". **Repeat**, using the following sentence: • One dancer lifted her arms and bent backward.
	Interactive Examples	**Corrective Feedback**
We Do	**Write and Read:** • The workers cut boards. The workers pounded in nails. • *What are the complete predicates?* (cut boards, pounded in nails) • *How can you make these sentences into one sentence with a compound predicate?* (The workers cut boards and pounded in nails.) **Repeat** with the following sentences: • The saw made a buzzing noise. The saw cut the board in two.	**Make sure** that students differentiate compound predicates from compound sentences. Only the verb parts of the sentence should be combined. Students should notice that the subjects must be identical in order for predicates to be combined.
	Oral Practice	**Written Practice**
You Do	**Collaborate:** Have partners take turns performing an action and then describing each other's actions using a compound predicate; for example, *You raised your arm and waved your hand.*	Provide each student with a copy of Practice pages 22-24 that corresponds to his or her proficiency level. Go over the examples and have partners work together to complete the exercises.

B

Collection of Diverse Literature

The literature in *Wonders* provides a diverse representation of various individuals and cultures. The texts give students the opportunity to see themselves and others within and outside of their communities. As students read, listen to, discuss, and write about texts, they are able to make real-life connections to themselves and the world around them.

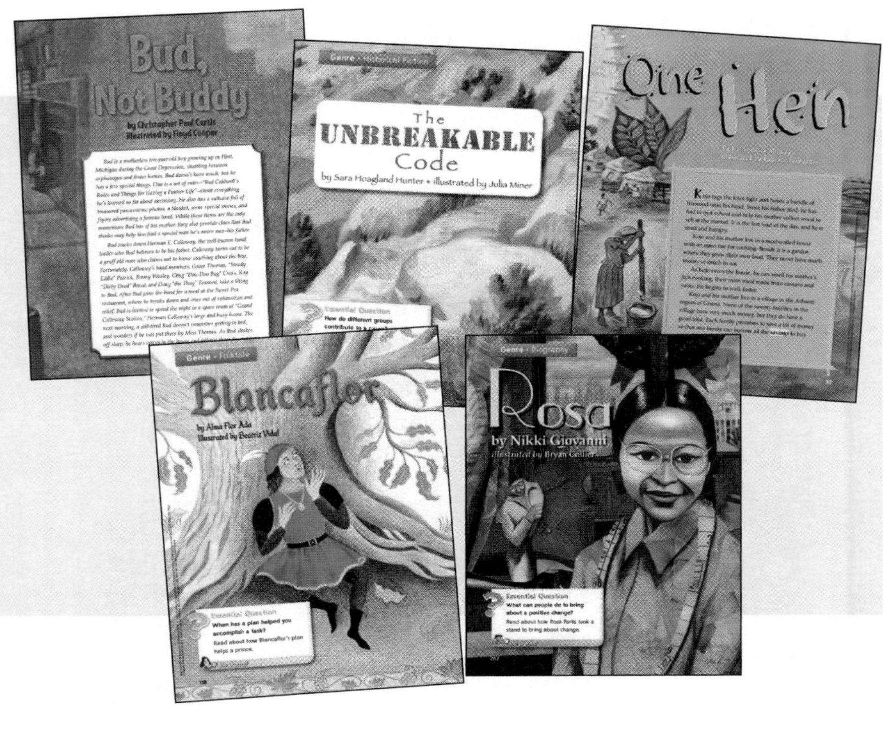

Culturally Responsive Teaching

Drawing from the research, there are a number of factors that support classroom equity and enable the underpinnings of culturally responsive teaching: high academic expectations for all students; a socially and emotionally positive classroom; a safe school climate; authentic and rigorous tasks; inclusive, relevant, and meaningful content; open and accepting communication; drawing from students' strengths, knowledge, culture, and competence; critically and socially aware inquiry practices; strong teaching; and school staff professional support and learning about equity and inclusion (Aronson & Laughter, 2016; Gay, 2010; Krasnoff, 2016; Ladson-Billings, 2006; Morrison, Robbins, & Rose, 2008; NYSED, 2019; Saphier, 2017; Snyder, Trowery & McGrath, 2019; Waddell, 2014). It is important to note the emphasis on developing classrooms and instructional practices that support all students, rather than focusing solely on who the students are and what they bring to school.

Through the high-quality content and research-based best practices of the instructional routines embedded in the program, the *Wonders* curriculum supports all important aspects of culturally responsive teaching.

The Learning Community: providing avenues for the development of a classroom community grounded in collaboration, risk-taking, responsibility, perseverance, and communication. This allows all learners to find a pathway to deep learning and academic success.

Wonders promotes classroom practices that best support meaningful learning and collaboration among peers. Valuing students' voices on what they think about the world around them and what they know allows teachers to build on students' funds of knowledge and adapt instruction and application opportunities. Starting in Kindergarten and progressing through the grades, students develop their ability to engage in focused academic discussions, assisting each other in deep understanding of the texts they read and building knowledge on various topics.

Authentic and Rigorous Learning Tasks: providing multiple methods to learn new material, challenging content for all levels of learners, opportunities to discuss, grapple with, and critique ideas, and space to personally connect to the content. This allows all learners to develop enthusiasm and dedication in their academic endeavors.

In *Wonders*, many of the texts center on relevant issues, examples, and real-world problems, along with prompts and questions that encourage students to engage and think critically about how they would address a similar problem or issue. The Essential Question for each text set introduces the topic that will be explored, culminating in a Show Your Knowledge activity. This allows students to synthesize information they learned analyzing all the texts. Extended writing tasks allow additional opportunities for flexible connections, elaboration of student thinking, and original expression.

Differentiation Opportunities: providing instructional pathways to meet the individual needs of all learners, which creates a more equitable learning experience.

In *Wonders*, clarity around differentiation of instruction, flexibility, adaptability, and choice are some of the key guiding principles on which the resources have been built. In addition to providing a range of differentiated leveled texts, *Wonders* is designed to ensure all students have access to rich, authentic grade-level informational and literary texts. A variety of print and digital resources are provided as options for differentiating practice opportunities.

FatCamera/Getty Images

Evidence of Learning: providing continuous opportunities to gather information about each learner's academic progress through a variety of assessment methods. This allows for timely feedback to learners and supports differentiation for meeting the needs of all learners.

In *Wonders*, students' self-evaluation of their own learning and progress over time is integral to student success. Student Check-In Routines assist students in documenting how well they understand leaning goals and encourage them to reflect on what may have been difficult to understand. Resources such as the Learning Goals Blackline Masters and features in the Reading/Writing Companion assist students in monitoring their progress. Teachers use the results of the Student Check-Ins and their informal observations of students with the Check for Success features in the Teacher's Edition to inform decisions about small group differentiated instruction. A range of innovative tools equip the teacher for assessment-informed instructional decision making, and ensure students are equipped to fully participate in responsive, engaging instruction. This Data Dashboard uses student results from assessments and activities to provide instructional recommendations tailored to the individual needs.

Relevant, Respectful, and Meaningful Content: providing content that represents the lives and experiences of a range of individuals who belong to different racial, ethnic, religious, age, gender, linguistic, socio-economic, and ability groups in equitable, positive, and non-stereotypical ways. This allows all learners to see themselves reflected in the content they are learning.

In *Wonders*, resources have been created and curated to promote literacy and deepen understanding for every student. A commitment to multicultural education and our nation's diverse population is evident in the literature selections and themes found throughout every grade. *Wonders* depicts people from various ethnic backgrounds in all types of environments, avoiding stereotypes. Students of all backgrounds will be able to relate to the texts. The authors of the texts in *Wonders* are also diverse and represent a rich range of backgrounds and cultures, which they bring to their writing.

Shutterstock

Supporting Family Communication: providing open communication avenues for families by developing regular and varied interactions about program content. This provides opportunities for all families to be involved in the academic progress of their learner.

In *Wonders*, the School to Home tab on the ConnectEd Student Workspace provides information to families about what students are learning. The letters introduce the Essential Questions that the students will be investigating in each text set, as well as the key skills and skills. Activities that families can complete with students at home are provided. Access to texts that students are reading is also available through the Student Workspace. Home-to-school letters and audio summaries of student texts are available in multiple languages, including English, Spanish, Haitian-Creole, Portuguese, Vietnamese, French, Arabic, Chinese (Cantonese and Mandarin), Russian, Tagalog, and Urdu.

Professional Learning: providing instructional guidance for administrators and teachers that supports enacting culturally responsive and sustaining pedagogical practices and focuses on asset-based approaches, bias surfacing, cultural awareness, and connections to learner communities, cultures, and resources.

In *Wonders*, a comprehensive set of resources assists administrators and teachers in a successful implementation of the program to ensure teacher and student success. Information embedded in the Teacher's Edition, and targeted components such as the Instructional Routines Handbook, as well as online Professional Learning Videos and resources, provide a wide range of support. Resources focused on helping teachers reflect on their understanding of the different cultures of their students, as well as assisting teachers in facilitating meaningful conversations about texts, are also provided.

Teaching the **Whole Child**

Your students are learning so much more than reading from you. They're learning how to learn, how to master new content areas, and how to handle themselves in and out of the classroom. Research shows that this leads to increased academic success. *Wonders* resources have been developed to support you in teaching the whole child, for success this year and throughout your students' lives.

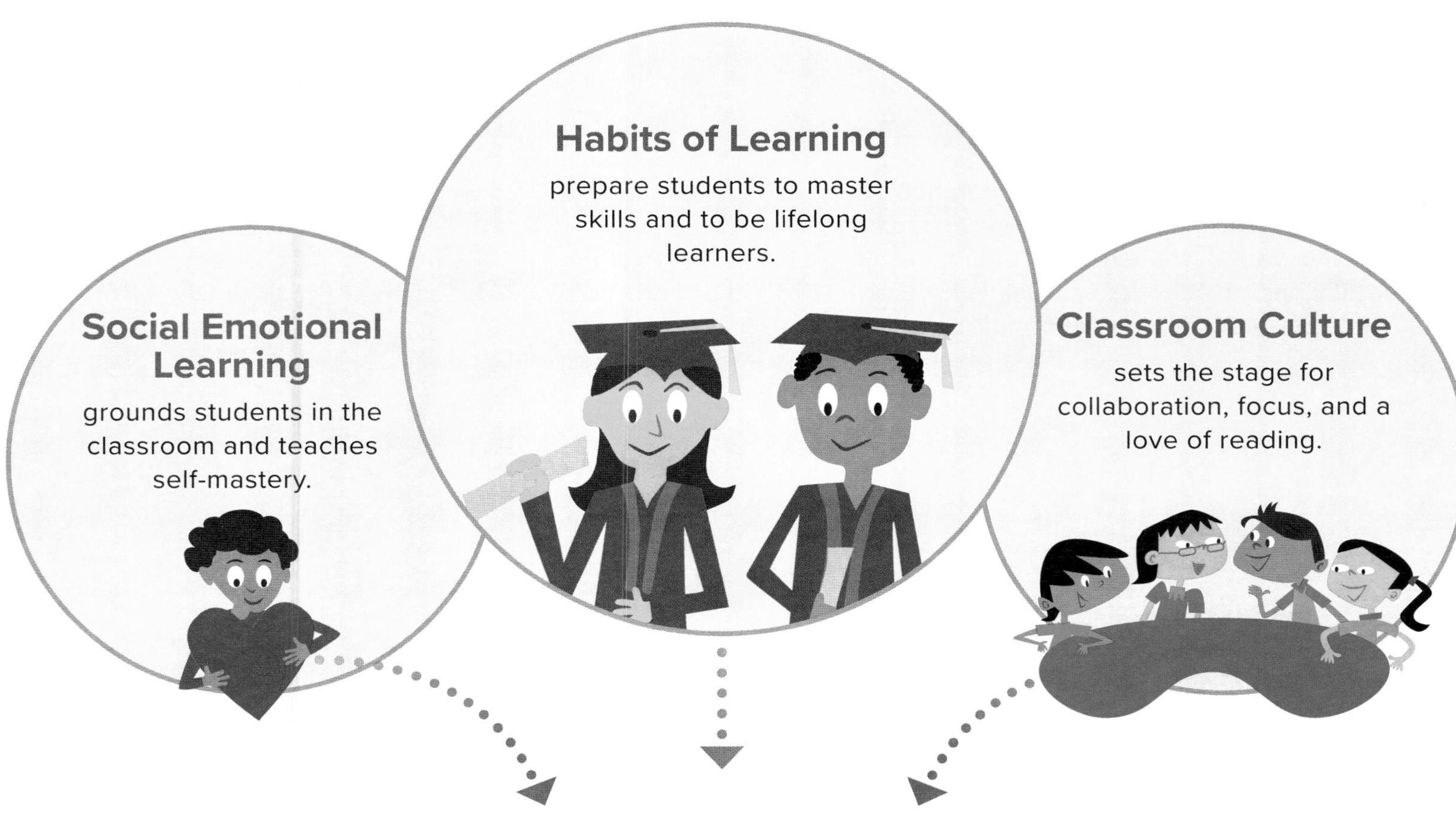

Habits of Learning
prepare students to master skills and to be lifelong learners.
Social Emotional Learning
grounds students in the classroom and teaches self-mastery.
Classroom Culture
sets the stage for collaboration, focus, and a love of reading.

DEVELOPING CRITICAL THINKERS

- Mastery of reading, writing, speaking, and listening
- Knowledge that spans content areas
- College and career readiness
- Strong results this year and beyond

Habits of Learning

I am part of a community of learners.

- ☐ I listen actively to others to learn new ideas.
- ☐ I build upon others' ideas in a conversation.
- ☐ I work with others to understand my learning goals.
- ☐ I stay on topic during discussion.
- ☐ I use words that will make my ideas clear.
- ☐ I share what I know.
- ☐ I gather information to support my thinking.

I use a variety of strategies when I read.

- ☐ I make predictions.
- ☐ I take notes.
- ☐ I think about how a text is organized.
- ☐ I visualize what I'm reading.
- ☐ I think about the author's purpose.

I think critically about what I read.

- ☐ I ask questions.
- ☐ I look for text evidence.
- ☐ I make inferences based on evidence.
- ☐ I connect new ideas to what I already know.

I write to communicate.

- ☐ I think about what I read as models for my writing.
- ☐ I talk with my peers to help make my writing better.
- ☐ I use rubrics to analyze my own writing.
- ☐ I use different tools when I write and present.

I believe I can succeed.

- ☐ I try different ways to learn things that are difficult for me.
- ☐ I ask for help when I need it.
- ☐ I challenge myself to do better.
- ☐ I work to complete my tasks.
- ☐ I read independently.

I am a problem solver.

- ☐ I analyze the problem.
- ☐ I try different ways.

Classroom Culture

We respect and value each other's experiences.

- ☐ We value what each of us brings from home.
- ☐ We work together to understand each other's perspectives.
- ☐ We work with our peers in pairs and in small groups.
- ☐ We use new academic vocabulary we learn when we speak and write.
- ☐ We share our work and learn from others.

We promote student ownership of learning.

- ☐ We understand what our learning goals are.
- ☐ We evaluate how well we understand each learning goal.
- ☐ We find different ways to learn what is difficult.

We learn through modeling and practice.

- ☐ We practice together to make sure we understand.
- ☐ We access many different resources to get information.
- ☐ We use many different tools when we share what we learn.

We foster a love of reading.

- ☐ We create inviting places to sit and read.
- ☐ We read for enjoyment.
- ☐ We read to understand ourselves and our world.

We build knowledge.

- ☐ We investigate what we want to know more about.
- ☐ We read many different types of texts to gain information.
- ☐ We build on what we know.

We inspire confident writers.

- ☐ We analyze the connection between reading and writing.
- ☐ We understand the purpose and audience for our writing.
- ☐ We revise our writing to make it stronger.

Social Emotional Learning

Social emotional learning is one of the most important factors in predicting school success. *Wonders* supports students in social emotional development in the following areas so that they can successfully engage in the instructional routines.

Relationships and Prosocial Behaviors

Engages in and maintains positive relationships and interactions with familiar adults and other students.

Social Problem Solving

Uses basic problem solving skills to resolve conflicts with other students.

Rules and Routines

Follows classroom rules and routines with increasing independence.

Working Memory

Maintains and manipulates distinct pieces of information over short periods of time.

Focus Attention

Maintains focus and sustains attention with minimal teacher supports.

Self Awareness

Recognizes self as a unique individual as well as belonging to a family, community, or other groups; expresses confidence in own skills and perspectives.

Creativity

Expresses creativity in thinking and communication.

Initiative

Demonstrates initiative and independence.

Task Persistence

Sets reasonable goals and persists to complete the task.

Logic and Reasoning

Thinks critically to effectively solve a problem or make a decision.

Planning and Problem Solving

Uses planning and problem solving strategies to achieve goals.

Flexible Thinking

Demonstrates flexibility in thinking and behavior to resolve conflicts with other students.

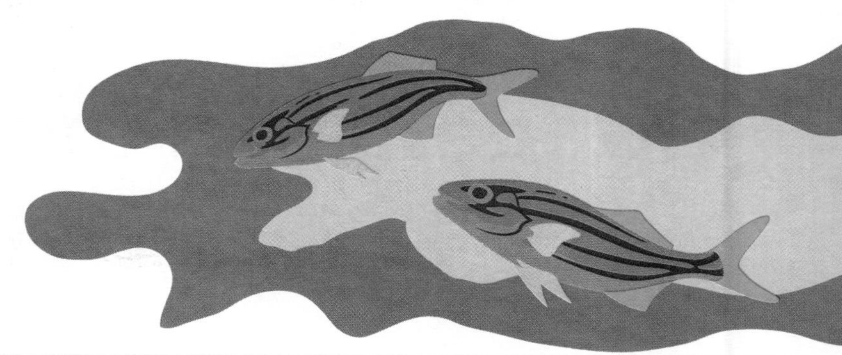

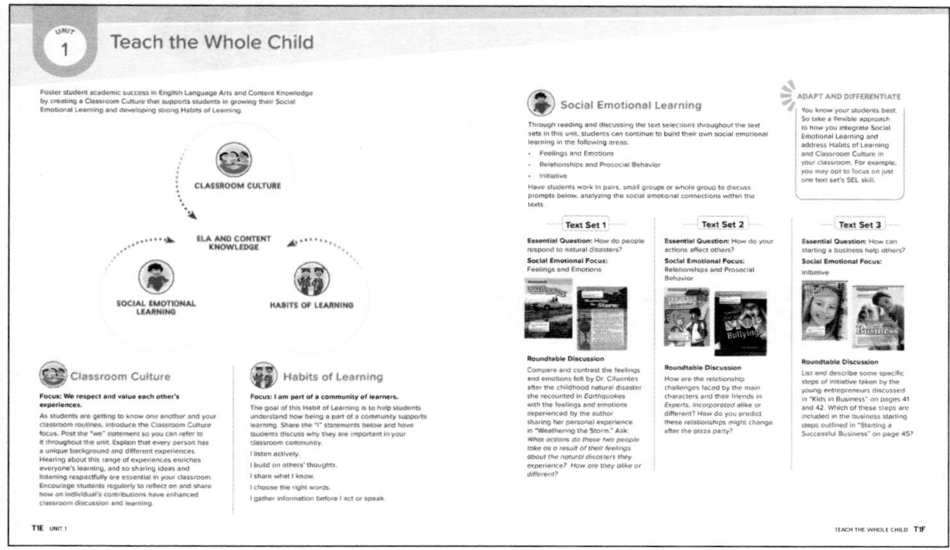

UNIT 1

Teach the Whole Child

Foster student academic success in English Language Arts and Content Knowledge by creating a Classroom Culture that supports students in growing their Social Emotional Learning and developing strong Habits of Learning.

CLASSROOM CULTURE

ELA AND CONTENT KNOWLEDGE

SOCIAL EMOTIONAL LEARNING

HABITS OF LEARNING

Classroom Culture

Focus: We respect and value each other's experiences.

As students are getting to know one another and your classroom routines, introduce the Classroom Culture focus. Post the "we" statement so you can refer to it throughout the unit. Explain that every person has a unique background and different experiences. Hearing about this range of experiences enriches everyone's learning, and so sharing ideas and listening respectfully are essential in your classroom. Encourage students regularly to reflect on and share how an individual's contributions have enhanced classroom discussion and learning.

Habits of Learning

Focus: I am part of a community of learners.

The goal of this Habit of Learning is to help students understand how being a part of a community supports learning. Share the "I" statements below and have students discuss why they are important in your classroom community.

I listen actively.

I build on others' thoughts.

I share what I know.

I choose the right words.

I gather information before I act or speak.

Social Emotional Learning

Through reading and discussing the text selections throughout the text sets in this unit, students can continue to build their own social emotional learning in the following areas:

- Feelings and Emotions
- Relationships and Prosocial Behavior
- Initiative

Have students work in pairs, small groups or whole group to discuss prompts below, analyzing the social emotional connections within the texts.

Text Set 1

Essential Question: How do people respond to natural disasters?

Social Emotional Focus: Feelings and Emotions

Roundtable Discussion

Compare and contrast the feelings and emotions felt by Dr. Cifuentes after the childhood natural disaster she recounted in *Earthquakes* with the feelings and emotions experienced by the author sharing her personal experience in "Weathering the Storm." Ask: *What actions do these two people take as a result of their feelings about the natural disasters they experience? How are they alike or different?*

Text Set 2

Essential Question: How do your actions affect others?

Social Emotional Focus: Relationships and Prosocial Behavior

Roundtable Discussion

How are the relationship challenges faced by the main characters and their friends in *Experts, Incorporated* alike or different? How do you predict these relationships might change after the pizza party?

Text Set 3

Essential Question: How can starting a business help others?

Social Emotional Focus: Initiative

Roundtable Discussion

List and describe some specific steps of initiative taken by the young entrepreneurs discussed in "Kids in Business" on pages 41 and 42. Which of these steps are included in the business starting steps outlined in "Starting a Successful Business" on page 45?

ADAPT AND DIFFERENTIATE

You know your students best. So take a flexible approach to how you integrate Social Emotional Learning and address Habits of Learning and Classroom Culture in your classroom. For example, you may opt to focus on just one text set's SEL skill.

T1E UNIT 1

TEACH THE WHOLE CHILD T1F

For each text set in a unit, a social emotional focus is identified and discussed in the context of the texts students read.

Weekly School-to-Home Communication

Weekly school-to-home family communication letters, ready to send in multiple languages, encourage parents to log on and share resources with their children, including listening to audio summaries of all main selections so they can ask questions. This deepens the connection between community and classroom, supporting social emotional development. This helps ensure that each and every child comes to school engaged, motivated, and eager to learn!

- English
- Spanish
- Chinese
- French
- Portuguese
- Tagalog
- Vietnamese
- Urdu
- Arabic
- Haitian-Creole
- Russian

E-books include audio summaries in the same languages.

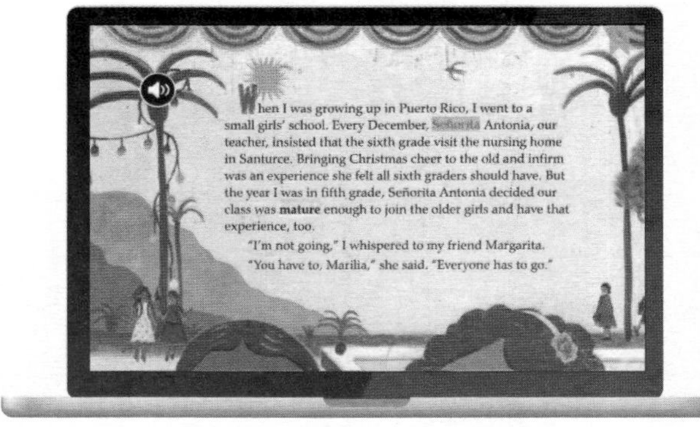

Wonders and the Science of Reading

Dr. Timothy Shanahan

Wonders supports the delivery of high-quality literacy instruction aligned to the science of reading. It provides a comprehensive, integrated plan for meeting the needs of all students. Carefully monitoring advances in literacy research, the program is developed to ensure that lessons focus on teaching the right content at the right time. The right content refers to teaching sufficient amounts of the content that has been proven to deliver learning advantages to students. The right time refers to a carefully structured scope and sequence within a grade and across grades. This ensures that teaching is presented in the most effective and efficient manner, with sound guidance to better support diverse learners.

Foundational Skills

English is an alphabetic language; developing readers must learn to translate letters and spelling patterns to sounds and pronunciations, and to read text accurately, automatically, and with proper expression. When students learn to manage these foundational skills with a minimum of conscious attention, they will have the cognitive resources available to comprehend what they read.

Research shows that the explicit teaching of phonemic awareness, phonics, and text reading fluency are the most successful ways to succeed in foundational skills. *Wonders* presents a sequence of research-aligned learning activities in its grade-level placements, sequences of instruction, and instructional guidance across the following areas:

- Phonemic Awareness
- Phonics/Decoding
- Text Reading Fluency

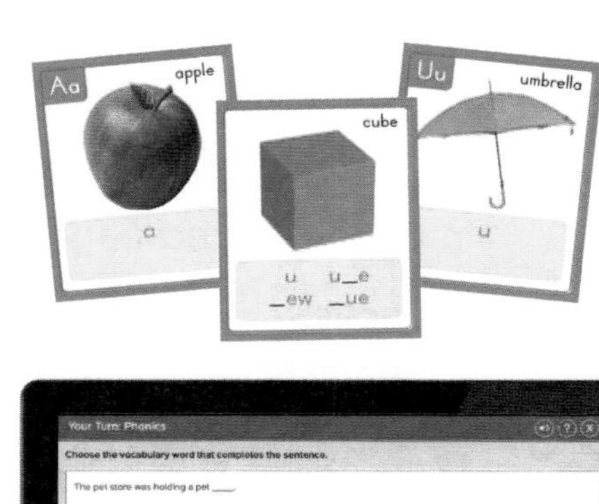

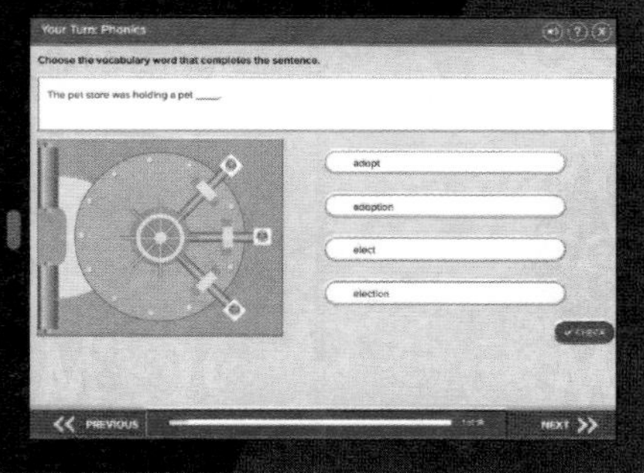

Courtesy of Tim Shanahan

Reading Comprehension

Reading comprehension requires that students extract and construct meaning from text. To comprehend, students must learn to apply the prior knowledge they bring to the text to the information expressed through written language in the text. To accomplish this successfully, readers must do three things. They must:

- expand their knowledge through the reading of high-quality informative texts;
- learn to negotiate increasingly sophisticated and complex written language;
- develop the cognitive abilities to manage and monitor these processes.

Wonders provides lessons built around a high-quality collection of complex literary and informational texts, focused on both the natural and social worlds. Teachers using *Wonders* will find explicit, research-based lessons in vocabulary and other language skills, guidance for high-level, high-quality discussions, and well-designed lessons aimed at building the executive processes that can shift reading comprehension into high gear, including:

- Building Knowledge/Using Knowledge
- Vocabulary and other aspects of written language
- Text complexity
- Executive processes and comprehension strategies

Writing

In the 21st century, it is not enough to be able to read, understand, and learn from the writing of others. Being able to communicate one's own ideas logically and effectively is necessary, too. As with reading, writing includes foundational skills (like spelling and handwriting), as well as higher-order abilities (composition and communication) and the executive processes required to manage the accomplishment of successful writing. Research shows that reading and writing strengthen one another. Focusing writing instruction in the following areas will help students improve their reading:

- Writing foundations
- Quality writing for multiple purposes
- The writing processes
- Writing to enhance reading

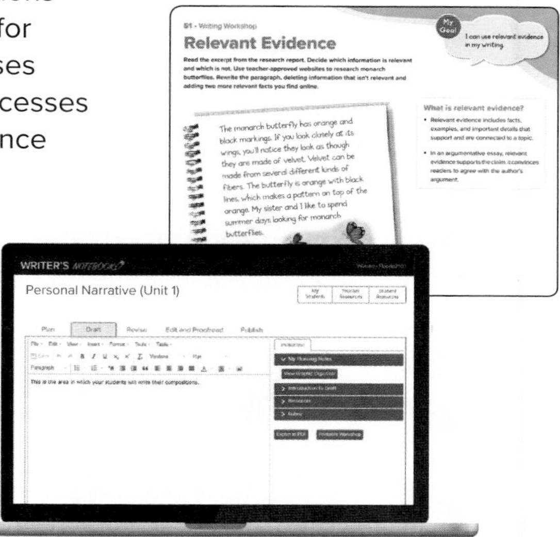

Quality of Instruction

The science of reading is dependent upon the sciences of teaching and learning, as well as on reading research. Reading research has identified specific best practices for teaching particular aspects of literacy. However, research has also revealed other important features of quality instruction that have implications for all learners and that may better support certain student populations. *Wonders* lessons reflect these quality issues in teaching:

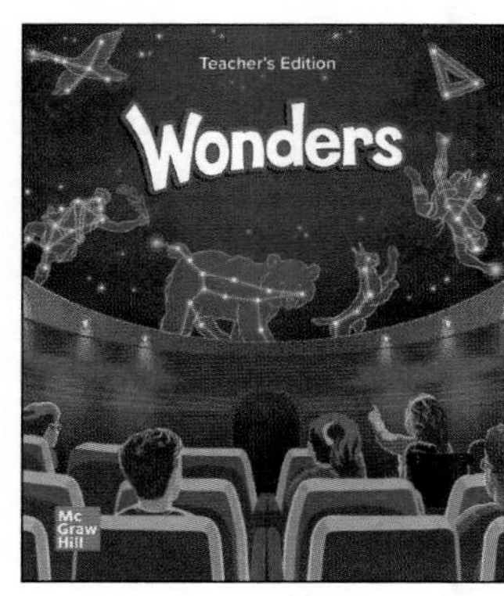

- Lessons with explicit and appropriate purposes
- High-challenge levels
- Appropriate opportunities for review
- Quality discussions promoted by high DOK-level questions
- Ongoing monitoring of learning
- Supports for English language learners
- Connections to social emotional learning

Build Critical Readers, Writers, Communicators, and Thinkers

LISTENING

SPEAKING

READING

Build Knowledge Through a Text Set

- **Investigate** an Essential Question.
- **Read** a variety of texts.
- **Closely read** texts for deeper meaning.
- **Respond** to texts using text evidence.
- **Conduct** research.
- **Share** your knowledge.
- **Inspire** action.

WRITING

Communicate Effectively Through Writing

- **Analyze** mentor texts and student models.
- **Understand** purpose and audience.
- **Plan** writing, using sources as needed.
- **Conference** with peers and teachers.
- **Evaluate** work against a rubric.
- **Improve** writing continuously.
- **Share** your writing.

SMALL GROUP

EXTEND

CONNECT

ASSESS

COLLABORATING

Instruction Aligned to the **Science of Reading**

Reading

Explicit instruction supports students in building knowledge.

- Foundational Reading Skills
  - Phonics/Word Analysis
  - Fluency
- Reading Literature
- Reading Informational Texts
- Comparing Texts
- Vocabulary
- Researching

Writing

Skills-based minilessons support students in developing their writing.

- Writing
  - Narrative
  - Argumentative
  - Expository
- Handwriting
- Speaking and Listening
- Conventions
- Creating and Collaborating

Differentiation

Differentiate resources, instruction, and level of scaffolds.

Small Group Teacher-Led Instruction

- Choose from small group skills lesson options to target instruction to meet students' needs.
- Read texts with scaffolded support.

Independent/Collaborative Work

- Students transfer knowledge of skills to independent reading and practice.
- Students transfer skills to their writing.

Extend, Connect, and Assess

At the end of the unit, students transfer and apply knowledge gained to new contexts.

Demonstrate Understanding

- Extend knowledge through online reading and Reader's Theater.
- Connect ELA skills to content area reading with science and social studies texts.
- Assess learning with program assessments.

Grade 5

Resources

The resources in *Wonders* support skills mastery, differentiated instruction, and the transfer and application of knowledge to new contexts. Teachers will find ways to enhance student learning and ownership through multimodal supports, a strong focus on foundational skills, opportunities to build knowledge, and fostering of expression through writing. All of your *Wonders*-created print resources are available digitally to support a variety of learning environments. The resources shown represent the key instructional elements of your *Wonders* classroom and are a portion of the supports available to you and your students. Login to your **Teacher Workspace** to explore multimedia resources, professional learning, and thousands of resources to meet your students where they are.

Component	Differentiate	Extend, Connect, Assess	Available Digitally
Teacher's Edition	●	●	●
Reading/Writing Companion		●	●
Literature Anthology		●	●
Classroom Library	●		
Classroom Library Lessons	●		●

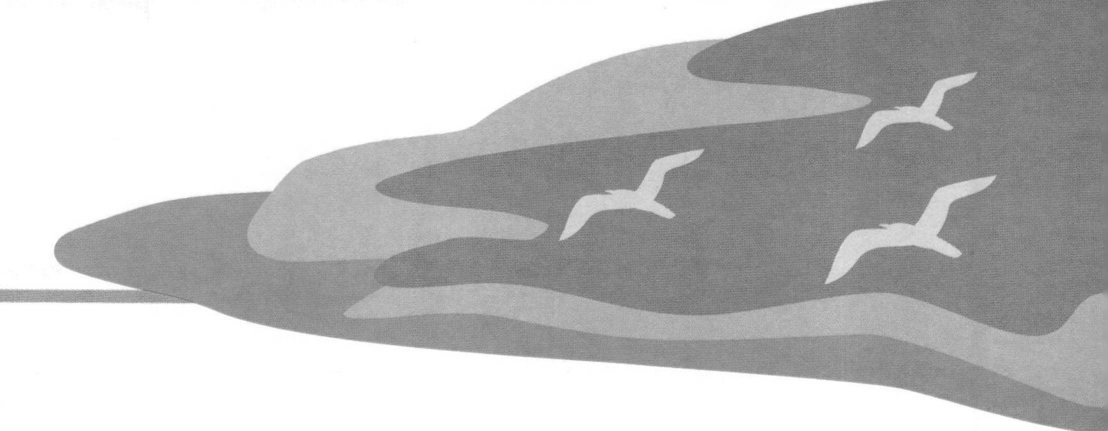

Component	Differentiate	Extend, Connect, Assess	Available Digitally
Leveled Readers & Lesson Cards	●	●	●
Center Activity Cards	●	●	●
ELL Small Group Guide	●		●
Data Dashboard	●	●	●
Progress Monitoring Assessment		●	●
Unit Assessment		●	●
Benchmark Assessments		●	●
Practice Book Blackline Masters		●	●
Inquiry Space		●	●
Online Writer's Notebook		●	●
Foundational Skills Resources: multimodal manipulatives, cards, activities, and games to build key skills	●	●	●
Skills-Based Online Games	●	●	●
Differentiated Genre Passages	●	●	●
Content Area Reading Blackline Masters		●	●

Professional Learning
Every Step of the Way

Get Started Using *Wonders.* Every day of instruction is based on evidence-based classroom best practices, which are embedded into the daily routines to strengthen your teaching and enhance students' learning. Throughout *Wonders*, you'll find support for employing these new routines and making the most of your literacy block.

Use this checklist to access support resources to help you get started with *Wonders* during the first weeks of school. Then refer to this list during the year for ongoing implementation support and to get the most from *Wonders*.

Beginning the Year

We encourage you to review these resources before the first day of school and then use them to support your first weeks of instruction.

In Your Teacher's Edition: Support pages for planning and teaching are embedded throughout your Teacher's Edition to support your big-picture understanding and help you teach effectively.

- ☐ **Start Smart:** In Unit 1 of your Teacher's Edition, Start Smart provides an overview of the instructional lessons and routines within *Wonders* by providing an explanation of the Unit 1 Text Set 1 Teacher's Edition lessons and select other lessons.
- ☐ **Text Set Support:** Each text set is accompanied by an introduction that supports your understanding of the content and simplifies instructional planning. These pages include a daily planner, differentiated learning support, guidance for developing student ownership and building knowledge, and more.
- ☐ **Progress Monitoring and Assessment:** Use data to track progress toward mastery of skills-based content, lesson objectives, and student goals.
  The **My Goals Routine** supports continuous self-monitoring and student feedback.

Online Resources: The digital Teacher Dashboard is your access point for key resources to get you up and running with *Wonders*. From the Teacher Dashboard, select *Resources > Professional Development > Overview*

- ☐ ***Wonders* Basics Module:** Set up your classroom, get to know your materials, learn about the structure of *Wonders*, and receive support for placement testing and grouping students for small group learning.
  ▶ Select *Learn to Use Wonders*
- ☐ **Placement and Diagnostic Assessment:** Access assessments, testing instructions, and placement charts that can be used at the beginning of the year to assess and place students in small groups.
  ▶ Select *Assessment & Data*

Ongoing Support

Your online **Teacher Workspace** also includes a wide range of additional resources. Use them throughout the year for ongoing support and professional learning. From the Teacher Dashboard, select *Resources > Professional Development*

- ☐ **Instructional Routines Handbook:** Reference this handbook throughout the year for support implementing the *Wonders* evidence-based routines and understanding the research behind them, and for guidance on what student success looks like.
  ▶ Select *Overview > Instructional Routines*
- ☐ **Small Group Differentiated Learning Guide:** Use the first few weeks of small group time to teach and model routines and establish small group rules and procedures.
  ▶ Select *Overview > Instructional Routines > Managing Small Groups: A How-to Guide PDF*
- ☐ **Suggested Lesson Plans and Pacing Guides:** Adjust your instruction to your literacy block and meet the needs of your classroom with flexible lesson plans and pacing.
  ▶ Select *Overview > Instructional Routines*
- ☐ **Classroom Videos:** Watch *Wonders* teachers model classroom lessons in reading, writing, collaboration, and teaching English language learners.
  ▶ Select *Classroom Videos*
- ☐ **Small Group Classroom Videos:** Watch *Wonders* teachers model small group instruction and share tips and strategies for effective differentiated lessons.
  ▶ Select *Classroom Videos > Small Group Instruction*
- ☐ **Author & Coach Videos:** Watch Dr. Douglas Fisher, Dr. Timothy Shanahan, and other *Wonders* authors as they provide short explanations of best practices and classroom coaching. Also provided are videos from Dr. Sheldon Eakins, founder of the Leading Equity Center, that focus on important aspects of educational equity and cultural responsive teaching.
  ▶ Select *Author & Coach Videos*
- ☐ **Assessment Handbook:** Review your assessment options and find support for managing multiple assessments, interpreting their results, and using data to inform your instructional planning.
  ▶ Select *Overview > Assessment & Data*
- ☐ **Assessment & Data Guides:** Review your assessment resources and get to know your reporting tools.
  ▶ Select *Overview > Assessment & Data*
- ☐ **Digital Help:** Access video tutorials and printable PDFs to support planning, assessment, writing and research, assignments, and connecting school to home.
  ▶ Select *Digital Help*

Explore the Professional Development section in your Teacher Workspace for more videos, resources, and printable guides. Select *Resources > Professional Development*

Notes

UNIT 3

Contents

UNIT 3

Unit Overview

English Language Arts is not a discrete set of skills. Skills work together to help students analyze the meaningful texts. In *Wonders*, skills are not taught in isolation. Rather they are purposefully combined to support student learning of texts they read.

Reading

Text Set 1

Essential Question: What can learning about different cultures teach us?

Phonics and Word Analysis
Open Syllables; Open Syllables (V/V)

Fluency
Intonation; Expression and Phrasing

Reading Literature
✓ Plot: Characterization
✓ Theme

Reading Informational Text
✓ Author's Purpose
Summarize

Compare Texts
Compare and contrast information

Vocabulary
Academic Vocabulary
✓ Context Clues
Adages

Researching
Learning About Different Cultures

Text Set 2

Essential Question: What benefits come from people working as a group?

Phonics and Word Analysis
Vowel Team Syllables; Consonant + *le* Syllables

Fluency
Accuracy and Rate; Rate

Reading Informational Text
✓ Text Structure: Problem and Solution
✓ Central Idea and Relevant Details
✓ Literal and Figurative Language
Summarize

Compare Texts
Compare and contrast information

Vocabulary
Academic Vocabulary
✓ Latin Roots
Similes and Metaphors

Researching
Working Together

Text Set 3

Essential Question: How do we explain what happened in the past?

Phonics and Word Analysis
r-Controlled Vowel Syllables

Fluency
Accuracy and Rate

Reading Informational Text
✓ Text Structure: Compare and Contrast
✓ Author's Claim
✓ Figurative Language
Summarize

Compare Texts
Compare and contrast information

Vocabulary
Academic Vocabulary
✓ Context Clues

Researching
Investigating the Past

Writing

Extended Writing 1

Writing
Handwriting
✓ Argumentative Writing: Write to Sources
Improving Writing: Writing Process

Speaking and Listening
Oral Presentation

Conventions
✓ Grammar: Action Verbs; Verb Tenses; Main and Helping Verbs; Linking Verbs
Spelling: Words with Open Syllables; Open Syllables (V/V); Vowel Team Syllables; Consonant + *le* Syllables

Creating and Collaborating
Writer's Notebook

Extended Writing 2

Writing
Handwriting
✓ Argumentative Writing: Write to Sources
Improving Writing: Writing Process

Speaking and Listening
Oral Presentation

Key

✓ Tested in *Wonders* Assessments

Extend, Connect, and Assess

Extend previously taught skills and connect to new content.

Extend

Reading Informational Text
Reading Digitally

Central Idea and Relevant Details

Conduct Research

Fluency
Reader's Theater

Phrasing and Rate

Connect

Connect to Science

Impact of Environmental Changes on Plants and Animals

Connect to Social Studies

19th-Century Advancements in Transportation and Communication; Development and Impact of Technology

Assess

✓ Unit Assessment Test

Fluency Assessment

Conventions

✓ Grammar: Irregular Verbs

Spelling: Words with *r*-Controlled Vowel Syllables

Creating and Collaborating

Writer's Notebook

Key Skills Trace

Reading Literature

Plot

Introduce: Unit 1 Text Set 2

Review: Unit 2 Text Set 2; Unit 3 Text Set 1; Unit 5 Text Set 2; Unit 6 Text Set 1

Assess: Unit 1, Unit 2, Unit 3, Unit 5, Unit 6

Theme

Introduce: Unit 2 Text Set 2

Review: Unit 2 Text Set 3; Unit 3 Text Set 1; Unit 4 Text Set 3; Unit 6 Text Set 1

Assess: Unit 2, Unit 3, Unit 4, Unit 6

Reading Informational Text

Central Idea and Relevant Details

Introduce: Unit 3 Text Set 2

Review: Unit 5 Text Set 1

Assess: Unit 3, Unit 5

Author's Claim

Introduce: Unit 1 Text Set 3

Review: Unit 3 Text Set 3

Assess: Unit 1, Unit 3

Text Structure

Introduce: Unit 1 Text Set 1

Review: Unit 1 Text Set 2; Unit 2 Text Set 1, Text Set 2; Unit 3 Text Set 2, Text Set 3; Unit 4 Text Set 1; Unit 5 Text Set 2; Unit 6 Text Set 2

Assess: Unit 1, Unit 2, Unit 3, Unit 4, Unit 5, Unit 6

Literal and Figurative Language

Introduce: Unit 3 Text Set 2

Review: Unit 3 Text Set 3; Unit 5 Text Set 1

Assess: Unit 3, Unit 5

Vocabulary

Context Clues

Introduce: Unit 1 Text Set 2

Review: Unit 2 Text Set 1; Unit 3 Text Set 1, Text Set 3; Unit 6 Text Set 2

Assess: Unit 1, Unit 2, Unit 3, Unit 6

Greek and Latin Roots

Introduce: Unit 2 Text Set 2

Review: Unit 3 Text Set 2; Unit 5 Text Set 1, Text Set 3

Assess: Unit 3, Unit 5

Grammar

Verbs

Introduce: Unit 3

Review: Grammar Handbook and Extended Writing: Unit 4, Unit 5, Unit 6

Assess: Unit 3

Extended Writing

Unit 1: Argumentative Writing/Write to Sources

Unit 2: Expository Writing/Write to Sources

Unit 3: Argumentative Writing/Write to Sources

Unit 4: Expository Writing/Write to Sources

Unit 5: Expository Writing, Personal Narrative

Unit 6: Fictional Narrative, Poem

UNIT 3

Independent Reading

Self-Selected Reading Options

Classroom Library Titles

Students can choose from the following titles to read and further investigate text set Essential Questions.

Online Lessons Available

Laugh with the Moon
Shana Burg
Genre Realistic Fiction
Lexile 740L

How Tía Lola Learned to Teach
Julia Alvarez
Genre Realistic Fiction
Lexile 810L

Eight Dolphins of Katrina: A True Tale of Survival
Janet Wyman Coleman
Genre Expository Text
Lexile 710L

Kakapo Rescue: Saving the World's Strangest Parrot
Sy Montgomery
Genre Expository Text
Lexile 950L

More Leveled Readers to Explore

Search the **Online Leveled Reader Library** and choose texts to provide students with additional texts at various levels to apply skills or read about various topics.

Unit Bibliography

Have students self-select independent reading texts related to the text set Essential Question. Titles in the same genre as the Anchor Text as well as titles in different genres are provided. See the online bibliography for more titles.

Text Set 1

Compare Texts

Flores-Galbis, Enrique. *90 Miles to Havana*. Square Fish, 2012. Historical Fiction **Lexile** 790L

Nichols, Catherine. *Early American Culture*. Rourke Educational Media, 2005. Expository Text **Lexile** 960L

More Realistic Fiction

Lord, Bette Bao. *In the Year of the Boar and Jackie Robinson*. HarperCollins, 1986. **Lexile** 730L

Namioka, Lensey. *Half and Half*. Random House, 2004. **Lexile** 800L

Text Set 2

Compare Texts

Fleischman, Paul. *Seedfolks*. HarperTrophy, 2004. Realistic Fiction **Lexile** 710L

Armstrong, Jennifer. *Spirit of Endurance: The True Story of the Shackleton Expedition to the Antarctic*. Crown Books for Young Readers, 2000. Narrative Nonfiction **Lexile** 890L

More Expository Texts

Montgomery, Sy. *Saving the Ghost of the Mountain*. Houghton Mifflin Harcourt, 2012. **Lexile** 840L

Thimmesh, Catherine. *Team Moon: How 400,000 People Landed on the Moon*. Harcourt, 2015. **Lexile** 1060L

Text Set 3

Compare Texts

Logan, Claudia. *The 5,000 Year Old Puzzle: Solving a Mystery of Ancient Egypt*. Farrar, Straus and Giroux, 2002. Historical Fiction **Lexile** 900L

Sloan, Christopher. *Mummies*. National Geographic, 2010. Expository Text **Lexile** 1190L

More Argumentative Texts

Goldenberg, Linda. *Little People and a Lost World*. Twenty-First Century Books, 2006. **Lexile** 1100L

Schanzer, Rosalyn. *George vs. George*. National Geographic Children's Books, 2007. **Lexile** 1120L

UNIT 3

Teach the Whole Child

Foster student academic success in English Language Arts and Content Knowledge by creating a Classroom Culture that supports students in growing their Social Emotional Learning and developing strong Habits of Learning.

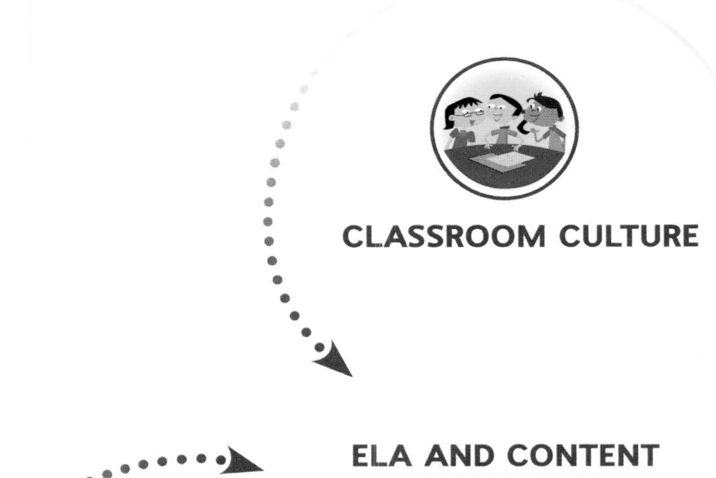

ELA AND CONTENT KNOWLEDGE

Classroom Culture

Focus: We inspire confident writers.

Tell students that the writing lessons and routines in your classroom are designed to help them become confident writers who can communicate effectively. Share and discuss the "we" statements below that explain four ways that your Classroom Culture will help them develop their writing confidence.

We analyze the connection between reading and writing.

We understand the purpose for our writing.

We know the audience for our writing.

We spend time revising our writing to make it stronger.

Habits of Learning

Focus: I write to communicate effectively.

This Habit of Learning can help students understand the power of their own writing to communicate effectively, both in and out of school. Read each statement below and discuss how the tools they describe support students in learning how to write more effectively.

I think about what I read as models for my writing.

I talk with my peers to help make my writing better.

I use rubrics to analyze my own writing.

I use different tools when I write.

Social Emotional Learning

Through reading and discussing the text selections throughout the text sets in this unit, students can continue to build their own social emotional learning in the following areas:

- Identity
- Belonging
- Logic and Reasoning

Have students work in pairs, small groups, or whole group to discuss prompts below, analyzing the social emotional connections within the texts.

ADAPT AND DIFFERENTIATE

You know your students best. So take a flexible approach to how you integrate Social Emotional Learning and address Habits of Learning and Classroom Culture in your classroom. For example, you may opt to focus on just one text set's SEL skill.

Text Set 1

Essential Question: What can learning about different cultures teach us?

Social Emotional Focus: Identity

Roundtable Discussion

What similarities and differences can the reader infer about the ways encountering different cultures changed Mary's and Kim's sense of identities in *They Don't Mean It?*

Text Set 2

Essential Question: What benefits come from people working as a group?

Social Emotional Focus: Belonging

Roundtable Discussion

In both *Winter's Tail* and "Helping Hands," groups with varied expertise work together to solve problems. In the two selections, what are some similar ways people who belong to different groups work together to solve problems?

Text Set 3

Essential Question: How do we explain what happened in the past?

Social Emotional Focus: Logic and Reasoning

Roundtable Discussion

What can we infer about the perspective shared by people who believe that Machu Picchu was a royal estate? How does this compare to the perspective shared by people who feel that it was used as an observatory?

Notes

Text Set 1

Essential Question: What can learning about different cultures teach us?

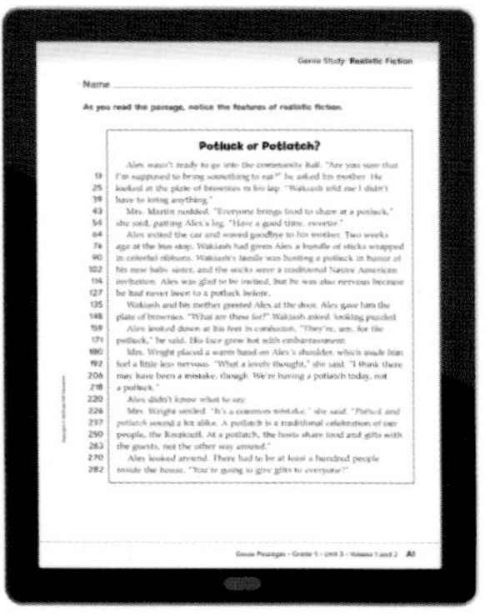

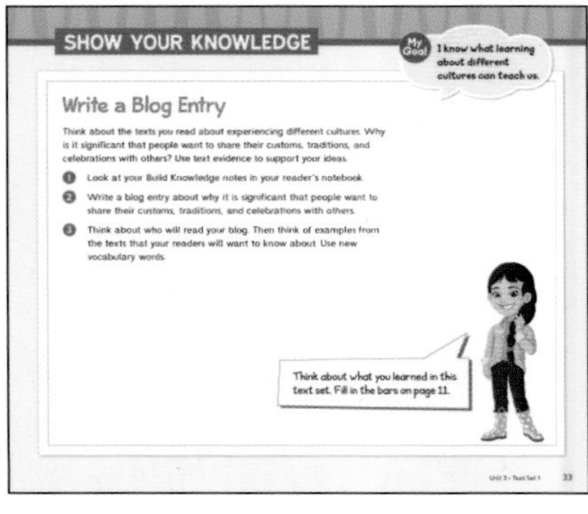

Text Set 2

Essential Question: What benefits come from people working as a group?

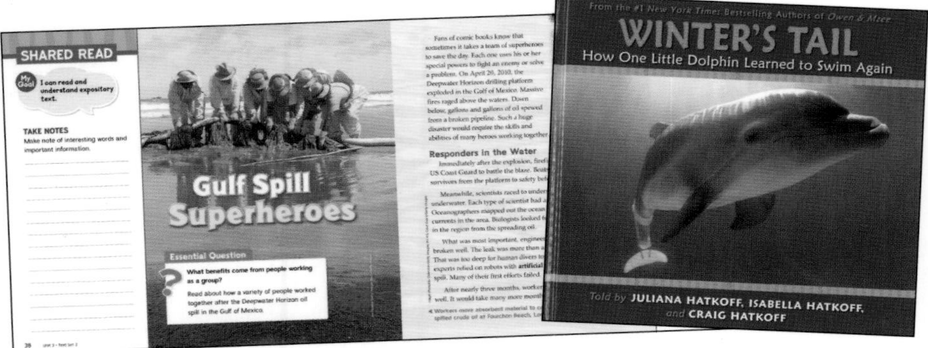

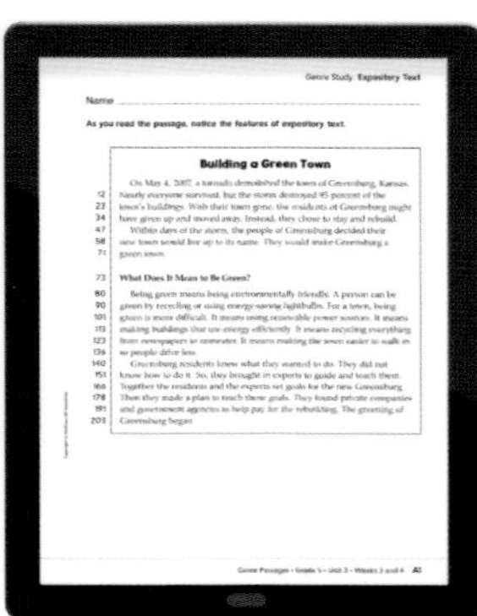

Text Set 3

Essential Question: How do we explain what happened in the past?

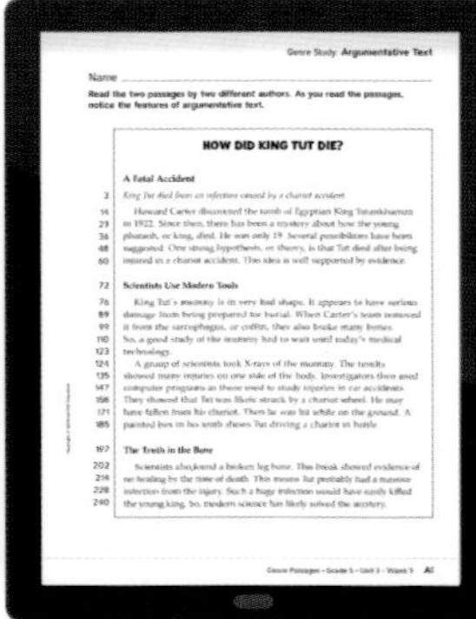

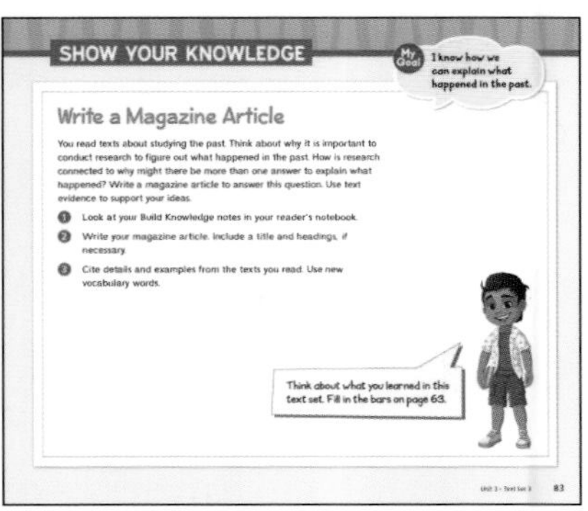

Classroom Library Books

Student Outcomes

✓ Tested in *Wonders* Assessments

FOUNDATIONAL SKILLS

Phonics and Word Analysis

- Decode words with open syllables
- Decode words with open syllables (V/V)

Fluency

- Read grade-level texts with accuracy, appropriate rate, expression, and automaticity

READING

Reading Literature

✓ Analyze how characterization contributes to the plot in a literary text
✓ Explain the development of stated or implied theme(s) throughout a literary text
- Read and comprehend texts in the grades 4–5 text complexity band
- Summarize a text to enhance comprehension
- Write in response to texts

Reading Informational Text

✓ Analyze an author's purpose in an informational text

Compare Texts

✓ Compare and contrast how authors present information on the same topic or theme

COMMUNICATION

Writing

Write to Sources

✓ Write an argumentative essay using precise language, supported with logical reasons and relevant evidence from sources
- With guidance and support from peers and adults, develop and strengthen writing as needed by planning, revising, and editing

Speaking and Listening

- Report on a topic or text or present an opinion, sequencing ideas; speak clearly at an understandable pace

Conventions

Grammar

✓ Identify action verbs
✓ Identify different verb tenses
✓ Avoid shifting verb tenses
✓ Use correct subject-verb agreement

Spelling

- Spell words with open syllables
- Spell words with open syllables (V/V)

Researching

- Conduct short research projects that build knowledge through investigation of different aspects of the topic

Creating and Collaborating

- Add audio recordings and visual displays to presentations when appropriate
- With some guidance and support from adults, use technology to produce and publish writing

VOCABULARY

Academic Vocabulary

- Acquire and use grade-appropriate academic vocabulary

Vocabulary Strategy

✓ Use context to determine the meaning of multiple-meaning words

CONTENT AREA LEARNING

Civic and Political Participation

- Identify different points of view about an issue, topic, or current event. **Social Studies**
- Discuss ways in which people of different backgrounds have contributed to our national identity. **Social Studies**

ELL Scaffolded supports for English Language Learners are embedded throughout the lessons, enabling students to communicate information, ideas, and concepts in English Language Arts and for social and instructional purposes within the school setting.

See the **ELL Small Group Guide** for additional support of the skills for the text set.

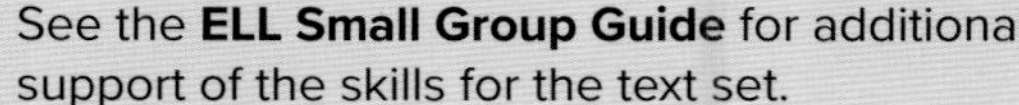

FORMATIVE ASSESSMENT

For assessment throughout the text set, use students' self-assessments and your observations.

Use the Data Dashboard to filter class, group, or individual student data to guide group placement decisions. It provides recommendations to enhance learning for gifted and talented students and offers extra support for students needing remediation.

Develop Student Ownership

To build student ownership, students need to know what they are learning and why they are learning it, and to determine how well they understood it.

Students Discuss Their Goals

READING

TEXT SET GOALS

- I can read and understand realistic fiction.
- I can use text evidence to respond to realistic fiction.
- I know what learning about different cultures can teach us.

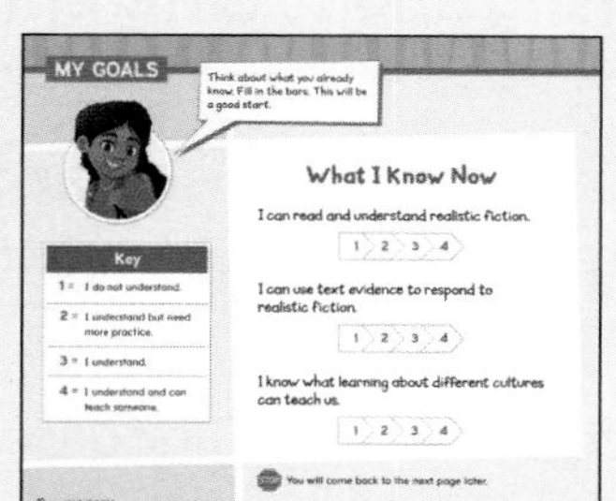

Have students think about what they know and fill in the bars on **Reading/Writing Companion** page 10.

WRITING

EXTENDED WRITING GOALS

Extended Writing 3:

- I can write an argumentative essay.
- I can synthesize information from three sources.

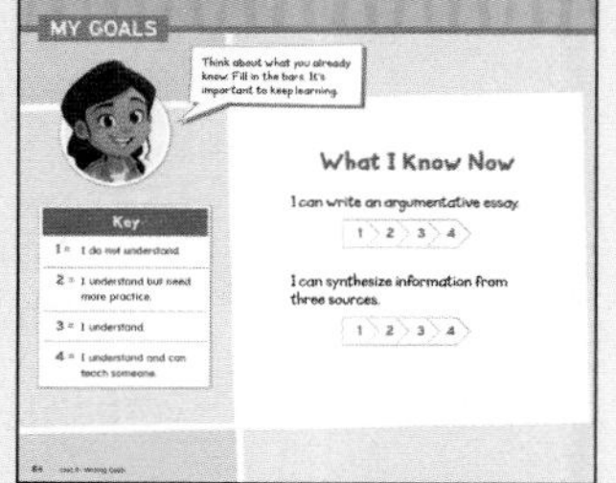

Have students think about what they know and fill in the bars on **Reading/Writing Companion** page 84.

Students Monitor Their Learning

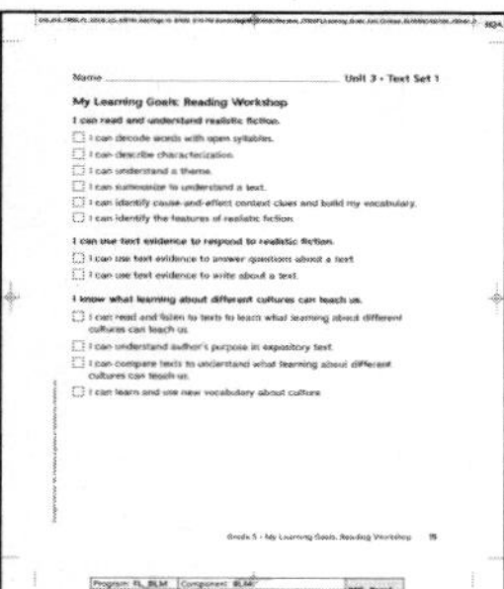

LEARNING GOALS

Specific learning goals identified in every lesson make clear what students will be learning and why. These smaller goals provide stepping stones to help students reach their Text Set and Extended Writing Goals.

CHECK-IN ROUTINE

The Check-In Routine at the close of each lesson guides students to self-reflect on how well they understood each learning goal.

Review the lesson learning goal.
Reflect on the activity.
Self-Assess by

- filling in the bars in the **Reading/Writing Companion**
- holding up 1, 2, 3, or 4 fingers

Share with your teacher.

Students Reflect on Their Progress

READING

TEXT SET GOALS

After completing the Show Your Knowledge task for the text set, students reflect on their understanding of the Text Set Goals by filling in the bars on **Reading/Writing Companion** page 11.

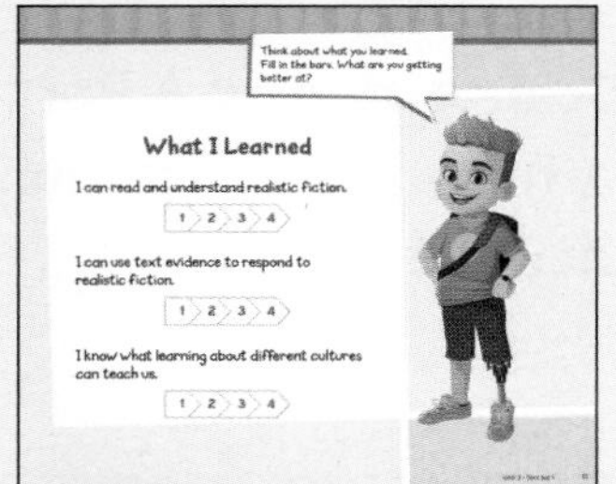

WRITING

EXTENDED WRITING GOALS

After completing both extended writing projects for the unit, students reflect on their understanding of the Extended Writing Goals by filling in the bars on **Reading/Writing Companion** page 85.

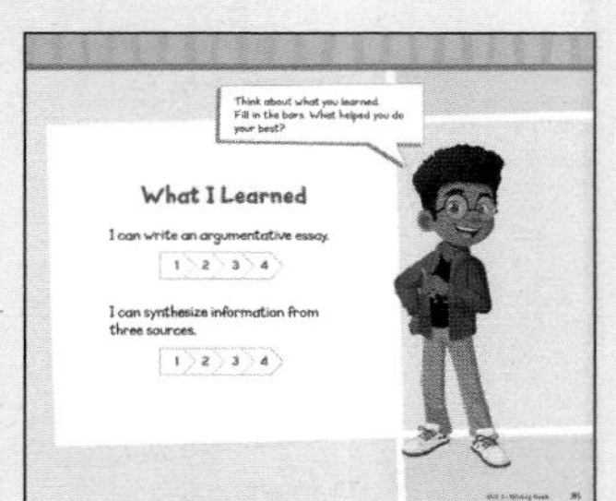

Build Knowledge

Shared Read
Reading/Writing Companion p. 12

Anchor Text
Literature Anthology p. 182

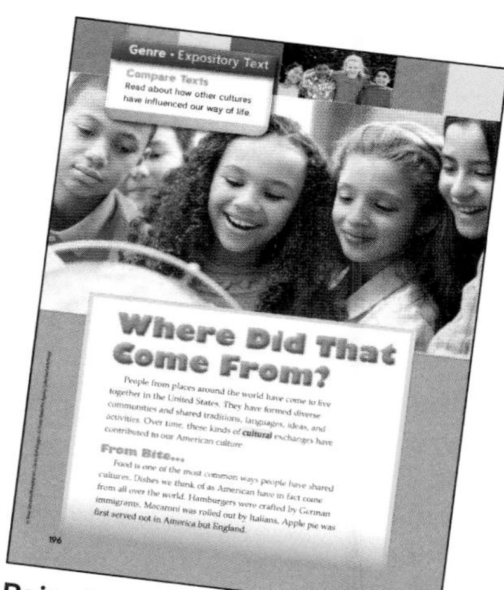

Paired Selection
Literature Anthology p. 196

Essential Question

What can learning about different cultures teach us?

Video Cultures have similarities and differences, but they all have traditions they like to celebrate.

Study Sync Blast Cinco de Mayo is a Mexican holiday that's now celebrated in many different places, including the United States.

Interactive Read Aloud Two friends share similar-looking foods—tamales and dolmade—that come from their different cultures.

Shared Read Though reluctant to visit at first, Paul goes to Argentina where he learns new things. During the trip, his perspective changes.

Anchor Text Chinese, American, and Chinese-American families learn about one another's cultures, including different foods and social customs.

Paired Selection Some things that we might think of as being American culture have actually been adapted from many different cultures.

Make Connections A Portuguese song tells about finding a friend—an experience that happens across many different cultures.

Differentiated Sources

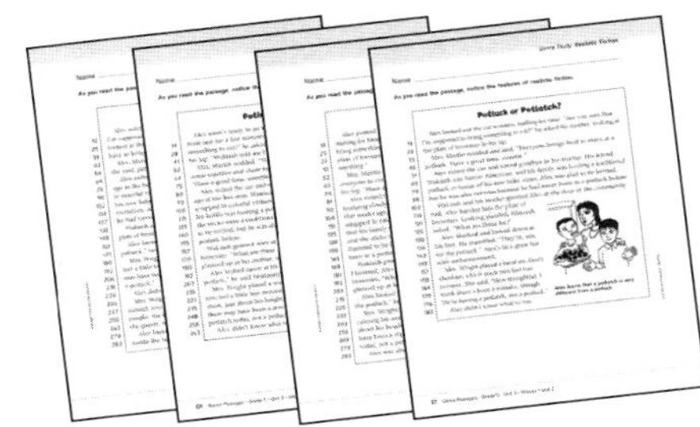

Leveled Readers

All the Way from Europe While traveling abroad, a girl learns that foreign cities are very interesting if you stop to take the time to find out about them.

A Vacation in Minnesota After spending some time in a rural area, a city boy tells his aunt and uncle that he's had fun getting to know the farm.

Dancing the Flamenco A girl's perception of a cultural dance festival changes once she experiences it.

Differentiated Genre Passages

A boy misunderstands the term "potlatch" for "pot luck" and brings food with him to a friend's party. While embarrassed at first, he has a good time learning about his friend's culture and what a potlatch actually is.

Build Knowledge Routine

After reading each text, ask students to document what facts and details they learned to help answer the Essential Question of the text set.

Talk About the source.

Write About the source.

Add to the Class Anchor Chart.

- Add to your Vocabulary List.

Show Your Knowledge

Write a Blog Entry

Have students show how they built knowledge across the text set by writing a blog entry. They should begin by thinking about the Essential Question: *What can learning about different cultures teach us?* Students will write a blog entry about why it is significant that different cultures want to share their customs, traditions, and celebrations with others.

Social Emotional Learning

Identity

Anchor Text: A student with a healthy sense of identity is better able to make positive contributions in the classroom. Ask students to discuss the way the Chinese-American parents contribute to their daughter's sense of identity in *They Don't Mean It!* and how it is different from American parents.

Paired Selection: Have students gather in small groups according to their food, musical, and sporting choices. Discuss how these things are just a small part of their identity and can change over time.

Roundtable Discussion: What similarities and differences can the reader infer about the ways encountering different cultures changed Mary's and Kim's sense of identities in *They Don't Mean It!*?

Explore the Texts

Essential Question: What can learning about different cultures teach us?

Access Complex Text (ACT) boxes throughout the text set provide scaffolded instruction for seven different elements that may make a text complex.

Teacher's Edition	Reading/Writing Companion	Literature Anthology	

"Foods for Thought" Interactive Read Aloud p. T7 Realistic Fiction	**"A Reluctant Traveler"** Shared Read pp. 12–15 Realistic Fiction	***They Don't Mean It!*** Anchor Text pp. 182–193 Realistic Fiction	**"Where Did That Come From?"** Paired Selection pp. 196–197 Expository Text
Qualitative			
Meaning/Purpose Moderate Complexity **Structure** Low Complexity **Language** Moderate Complexity **Knowledge Demands** Moderate Complexity	**Meaning/Purpose** Moderate Complexity **Structure** Low Complexity **Language** Moderate Complexity **Knowledge Demands** Moderate Complexity	**Meaning/Purpose** High Complexity **Structure** Moderate Complexity **Language** Moderate Complexity **Knowledge Demands** Moderate Complexity	**Meaning/Purpose** Moderate Complexity **Structure** Low Complexity **Language** Moderate Complexity **Knowledge Demands** High Complexity
Quantitative			
Lexile 810L	**Lexile** 770L	**Lexile** 870L	**Lexile** 940L
Reader and Task Considerations			
Reader Students should not need extensive background knowledge or cultural experiences to comprehend the text.	**Reader** Students will not need background knowledge to understand the text.	**Reader** Language features will be challenging. Explain idiomatic expressions and that people from different countries may have different customs, ways of celebrating, and table manners.	**Reader** Students will not need background knowledge to understand the text.

Task The questions for the read aloud are supported by teacher modeling. The tasks provide a variety of ways for students to begin to build knowledge and vocabulary about the text set topic. The questions and tasks provided for the other texts are at various levels of complexity, ensuring that all students can interact with the text in meaningful ways.

Additional Texts

Classroom Library
Laugh with the Moon
Genre: Realistic Fiction
Lexile: 740L
How Tia Lola Learned to Teach
Genre: Realistic Fiction
Lexile: 810L
See **Classroom Library Lessons**

Content Area Reading BLMs
Additional online texts related to grade-level Science, Social Studies, and Arts content

Leveled Readers

(A) ***All the Way from Europe***	(O) ***Dancing the Flamenco***	(B) ***A Vacation in Minnesota***	(ELL) ***Dancing the Flamenco***

Qualitative

Meaning/Purpose Moderate Complexity	**Meaning/Purpose** Moderate Complexity	**Meaning/Purpose** Moderate Complexity	**Meaning/Purpose** Moderate Complexity
Structure Low Complexity	**Structure** Low Complexity	**Structure** Low Complexity	**Structure** Low Complexity
Language Low Complexity	**Language** Moderate Complexity	**Language** High Complexity	**Language** Low Complexity
Knowledge Demands Moderate Complexity	**Knowledge Demands** Moderate Complexity	**Knowledge Demands** Moderate Complexity	**Knowledge Demands** Moderate Complexity

Quantitative

Lexile 690L	**Lexile** 790L	**Lexile** 950L	**Lexile** 510L

Reader and Task Considerations

Reader Students might be unfamiliar with the countries in the story. Identify France, German, Belgium, and Italy on a world map.	**Reader** Students will not need background knowledge to understand the story.	**Reader** Students might not understand the distance between Minnesota and New York City. Help by identifying the cities on a map.	**Reader** Students will not need background knowledge to understand the story.

Task The questions and tasks provided for the Leveled Readers are at various levels of complexity, ensuring that all students can interact with the text in meaningful ways.

Differentiated Genre Passages

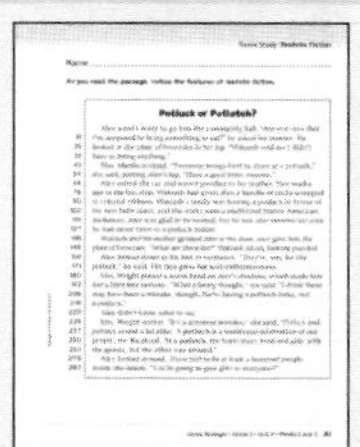		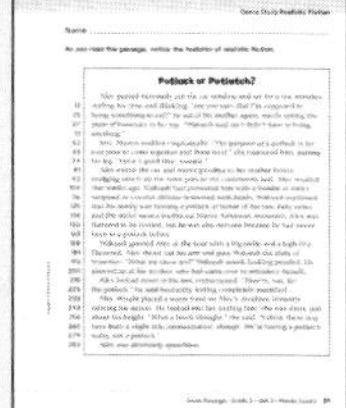	
(A) "Potluck or Potlatch?"	(O) "Potluck or Potlatch?"	(B) "Potluck or Potlatch?"	(ELL) "Potluck or Potlatch?"

Qualitative

Meaning/Purpose Moderate Complexity	**Meaning/Purpose** Moderate Complexity	**Meaning/Purpose** Moderate Complexity	**Meaning/Purpose** Moderate Complexity
Structure Low Complexity	**Structure** Low Complexity	**Structure** Low Complexity	**Structure** Low Complexity
Language Low Complexity	**Language** Moderate Complexity	**Language** Moderate Complexity	**Language** Low Complexity
Knowledge Demands Moderate Complexity	**Knowledge Demands** Moderate Complexity	**Knowledge Demands** High Complexity	**Knowledge Demands** Low Complexity

Quantitative

Lexile 650L	**Lexile** 750L	**Lexile** 810L	**Lexile** 690L

Reader and Task Considerations

Reader Students will not need background information to understand the story.	**Reader** Students will not need background information to understand the story.	**Reader** Students will not need background information to understand the story.	**Reader** Students will not need background information to understand the story.

Task The questions and tasks provided for the Differentiated Genre Passages are at various levels of complexity, ensuring that all students can interact with the text in meaningful ways.

Week 1 Planner

Customize your own lesson plans at
my.mheducation.com

60+ mins **Reading Suggested Daily Time**

READING LESSON GOALS

- **I can read and understand realistic fiction.**
- **I can use text evidence to respond to realistic fiction.**
- **I know what learning about different cultures can teach us.**

SMALL GROUP OPTIONS The designated lessons can be taught in small groups. To determine how to differentiate instruction for small groups, use Formative Assessment and Data Dashboard.

30+ mins **Writing Suggested Daily Time**

WRITING LESSON GOALS

I can write an argumentative essay.

Lesson 1	Lesson 2
Reading	
Introduce the Concept, T4–T5 Build Knowledge **Listening Comprehension, T6–T7** "Foods for Thought" **Shared Read, T8–T11** Read "A Reluctant Traveler" Quick Write: Summarize **Vocabulary, T12–T13** Academic Vocabulary Context Clues: Cause and Effect **Expand Vocabulary, T52**	**Shared Read, T8–T11** Reread "A Reluctant Traveler" **Minilessons, T14–T21** Summarize Plot: Characterization Theme Craft and Structure **Respond to Reading, T22–T23** **Phonics, T24–T25** Open Syllables **Fluency, T25** Intonation **Research and Inquiry, T26–T27** **Expand Vocabulary, T52**
Writing	
Extended Writing 1: Argumentative Essay	
Writing Lesson Bank: Craft Minilessons, T260–T263	
Teacher and Peer Conferences	
Grammar Lesson Bank, T264 Action Verbs Talk About It **Spelling Lesson Bank, T274** Open Syllables	**Grammar Lesson Bank, T264** Action Verbs Talk About It **Spelling Lesson Bank, T274** Open Syllables

SMALL GROUP

Teacher-Led Instruction

Differentiated Reading

Leveled Readers
- *All the Way from Europe*, T54–T55
- *Dancing the Flamenco*, T64–T65
- *A Vacation in Minnesota*, T70–T71

Differentiated Skills Practice

Approaching Level
Phonics/Decoding, T58
- Decode Words with Open Syllables (Tier 2)
- Practice Words with Open Syllables

Vocabulary, T60
- Review High-Frequency Words (Tier 2)
- Review Academic Vocabulary (Tier 2)

Fluency, T62
- Intonation (Tier 2)

Comprehension, T62–T63
- Theme (Tier 2)
- Self-Selected Reading

Independent/Collaborative Work See pages T3I–T3J.

Reading

Comprehension
- Realistic Fiction
- Theme
- Summarize

Fluency
Independent Reading

Phonics/Word Study

Phonics/Decoding
- Open Syllables

Vocabulary
- Context Clues: Cause and Effect

Writing

Extended Writing 1: Argumentative Writing
Self-Selected Writing
Grammar
- Action Verbs

Spelling
- Open Syllables

Handwriting

ACADEMIC VOCABULARY
appreciation, blurted, complimenting, congratulate, contradicted, critical, cultural, misunderstanding

SPELLING
minus, loser, humor, closet, recent, student, equal, profile, local, comet, vacant, punish, cavern, shiver, decent, linen, legal, panic, smoky, tyrant

Review *valley, fifteen, culture*
Challenge *fatigue, fugitive*
See pages T274–T275 for Differentiated Spelling Lists.

Reading		
Anchor Text, T28–T41 Read *They Don't Mean It!* Take Notes About Text **Expand Vocabulary, T53**	**Anchor Text, T28–T41** Read *They Don't Mean It!* Take Notes About Text **Expand Vocabulary, T53**	**Anchor Text, T28–T41** Reread *They Don't Mean It!* **Expand Vocabulary, T53**
Writing		
Extended Writing 1, T224–T225 Analyze the Rubric	**Extended Writing 1, T226–T227** Precise Language	**Extended Writing 1, T228–T229** Analyze the Student Model
Writing Lesson Bank: Craft Minilessons, T260–T263		
Teacher and Peer Conferences		
Grammar Lesson Bank, T265 Action Verbs Talk About It **Spelling Lesson Bank, T275** Open Syllables	**Grammar Lesson Bank, T265** Action Verbs Talk About It **Spelling Lesson Bank, T275** Open Syllables	**Grammar Lesson Bank, T265** Action Verbs Talk About It **Spelling Lesson Bank, T275** Open Syllables

On Level
Vocabulary, T68
- Review Academic Vocabulary
- Context Clues: Cause and Effect

Comprehension, T69
- Review Theme
- Self-Selected Reading

Beyond Level
Vocabulary, T74
- Review Domain-Specific Words
- Context Clues: Cause and Effect

Comprehension, T75
- Review Theme
- Self-Selected Reading GIFTED and TALENTED

English Language Learners
See ELL Small Group Guide, pp. 94–105

Content Area Connections

Content Area Reading
- Science, Social Studies, and the Arts

Research and Inquiry
- Learning About Different Cultures

Inquiry Space
- Options for Project-Based Learning

English Language Learners
See ELL Small Group Guide, pp. 94–105

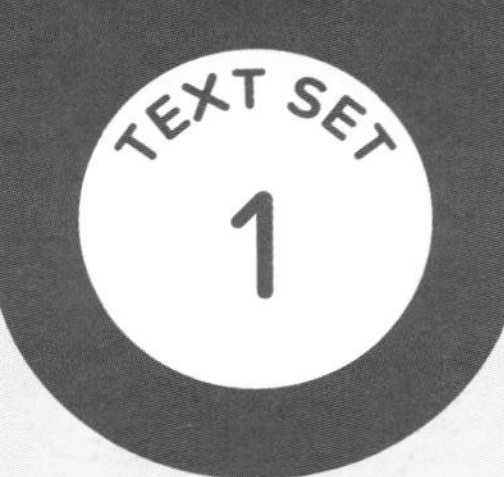

Week 2 Planner

Customize your own lesson plans at **my.mheducation.com**

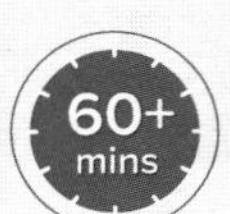

Reading
Suggested Daily Time

READING LESSON GOALS

- I can read and understand realistic fiction.
- I can use text evidence to respond to realistic fiction.
- I know what learning about different cultures can teach us.

SMALL GROUP OPTIONS The designated lessons can be taught in small groups. To determine how to differentiate instruction for small groups, use Formative Assessment and Data Dashboard.

Writing
Suggested Daily Time

WRITING LESSON GOALS

I can write an argumentative essay.

Lesson 6	Lesson 7
Reading	
Anchor Text, T28–T41 Reread *They Don't Mean It!* **Respond to Reading, T42–T43** **Expand Vocabulary, T52**	**Paired Selection, T44–T45** Read "Where Did That Come From?" **Expand Vocabulary, T52**
Writing	
Extended Writing 1, T230–T231 Analyze the Student Model	**Extended Writing 1, T230–T231** Analyze the Student Model
Writing Lesson Bank: Craft Minilessons, T260–T263	
Teacher and Peer Conferences	
Grammar Lesson Bank, T266 Verb Tenses Talk About It **Spelling Lesson Bank, T276** Open Syllables (V/V)	**Grammar Lesson Bank, T266** Verb Tenses Talk About It **Spelling Lesson Bank, T276** Open Syllables (V/V)

Teacher-Led Instruction

Differentiated Reading

Differentiated Genre Passages

- "Potluck or Potlatch?," T56–T57
- "Potluck or Potlatch?," T66–T67
- "Potluck or Potlatch?," T72–T73

Differentiated Skills Practice

Approaching Level

Phonics/Decoding, T59

- Decode Words with Open Syllables (V/V)
- Practice Words with Open Syllables (V/V)

Vocabulary, T61

- Identify Related Words
- Context Clues: Cause and Effect

Fluency, T62

- Expression and Phrasing

Comprehension, T63

- Review Theme
- Self-Selected Reading

Independent/Collaborative Work See pages T3I–T3J.

Reading

Comprehension

- Realistic Fiction
- Theme
- Summarize

Fluency

Independent Reading

Phonics/Word Study

Phonics/Decoding

- Open Syllables (V/V)

Vocabulary

- Context Clues: Cause and Effect

Writing

Extended Writing 1: Argumentative Writing

Self-Selected Writing

Grammar

- Verb Tenses

Spelling

- Open Syllables (V/V)

Handwriting

ACADEMIC VOCABULARY *appreciation, blurted, complimenting, congratulate, contradicted, critical, cultural, misunderstanding*

SPELLING *video, poet, riot, piano, diary, radio, ideas, ruin, diet, patriot, fluid, rodeo, cruel, genuine, casual, trial, fuel, meteor, diameter, meander*

Review *recent, closet, minus*
Challenge *situation, variety*
See pages T276–T277 for Differentiated Spelling Lists.

Reading

Lesson 8	Lesson 9	Lesson 10
Paired Selection, T44–T45 Reread "Where Did That Come From?" **Author's Craft, T46–T47** Author's Purpose **Phonics, T48–T49** Open Syllables (V/V) **Expand Vocabulary, T53**	**Fluency, T49** Expression and Phrasing **Make Connections, T50** **Expand Vocabulary, T53**	**Show Your Knowledge, T51** **Progress Monitoring, T3K–T3L** **Expand Vocabulary, T53**

Writing

Lesson 8	Lesson 9	Lesson 10
Extended Writing 1, T230–T231 Analyze the Student Model		
Writing Lesson Bank: Craft Minilessons, T260–T263		
Teacher and Peer Conferences		
Grammar Lesson Bank, T267 Verb Tenses Talk About It **Spelling Lesson Bank, T277** Open Syllables (V/V)	**Grammar Lesson Bank, T267** Verb Tenses Talk About It **Spelling Lesson Bank, T277** Open Syllables (V/V)	**Grammar Lesson Bank, T267** Verb Tenses Talk About It **Spelling Lesson Bank, T277** Open Syllables (V/V)

On Level
Vocabulary, T68
- Review Academic Vocabulary
- Context Clues: Cause and Effect

Comprehension, T69
- Review Theme
- Self-Selected Reading

Beyond Level
Vocabulary, T74
- Review Domain-Specific Words
- Context Clues: Cause and Effect

Comprehension, T75
- Review Theme
- Self-Selected Reading GIFTED and TALENTED

English Language Learners
See ELL Small Group Guide, pp. 94–105

Content Area Connections

Content Area Reading
- Science, Social Studies, and the Arts

Research and Inquiry
- Learning About Different Cultures

Inquiry Space
- Options for Project-Based Learning

English Language Learners
See ELL Small Group Guide, pp. 94–105

Independent and Collaborative Work

As you meet with small groups, the rest of the class completes activities and projects that allow them to practice and apply the skills they have been working on.

Student Choice and Student Voice

- Print the My Independent Work blackline master and review it with students. Identify the "Must Do" activities.
- Have students choose additional activities that provide the practice they need.
- Remind students to reflect on their learning each day.

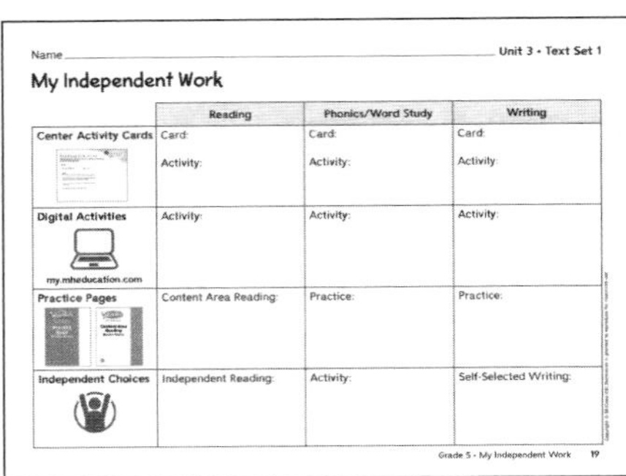

Name ______ Unit 3 • Text Set 1

My Independent Work

	Reading	Phonics/Word Study	Writing
Center Activity Cards	Card: Activity:	Card: Activity:	Card: Activity:
Digital Activities my.mheducation.com	Activity:	Activity:	Activity:
Practice Pages	Content Area Reading:	Practice:	Practice:
Independent Choices	Independent Reading:	Activity:	Self-Selected Writing:

Grade 5 • My Independent Work 19

My Independent Work BLM

Reading

Independent Reading Texts

Students can choose a Center Activity Card to use while they read independently.

Classroom Library
Laugh with the Moon
Genre: Realistic Fiction
Lexile: 740L

How Tía Lola Learned to Teach
Genre: Realistic Fiction
Lexile: 810L

Unit Bibliography
Have students self-select independent reading texts about different cultures.

Leveled Texts Online

- Additional Leveled Readers in the **Leveled Reader Library Online** allow for flexibility.
- Six leveled sets of **Differentiated Genre Passages** in diverse genres are available.
- **Differentiated Texts** offer ELL students more passages at different proficiency levels.

Additional Literature
Literature Anthology
Weslandia, pp. 224–237
Genre: Fantasy

"Plants with a Purpose," pp. 240–241
Genre: Expository Text

Center Activity Cards

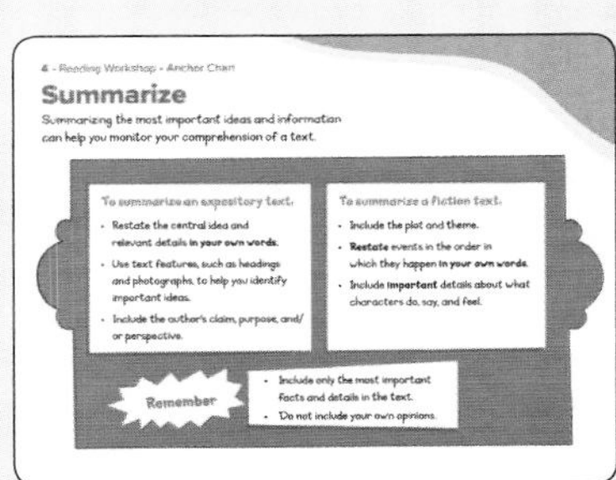

Summarize Card 4

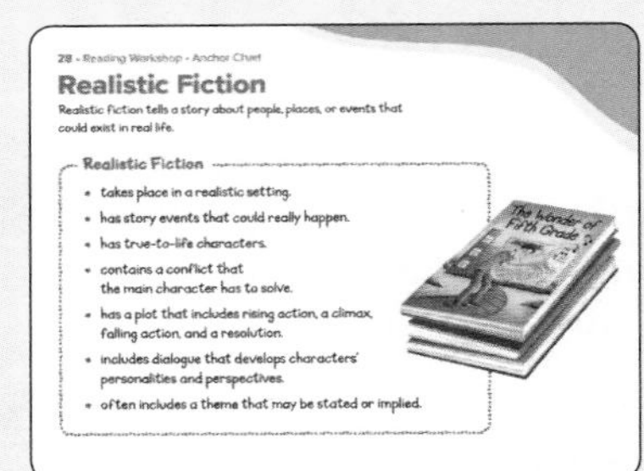

Realistic Fiction Card 28

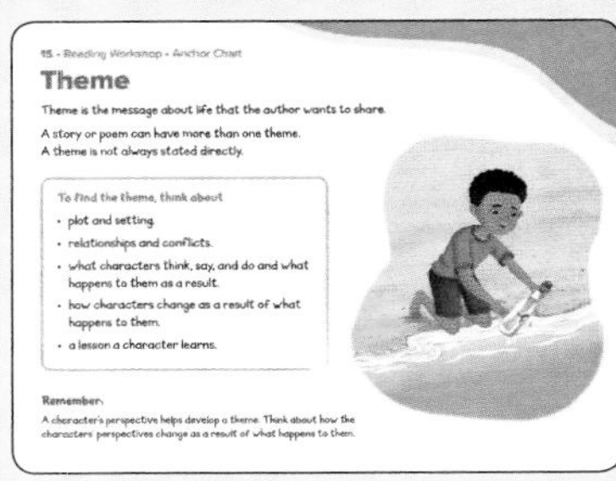

Theme Card 15

Author's Purpose Card 21

Fluency Card 38

Digital Activities

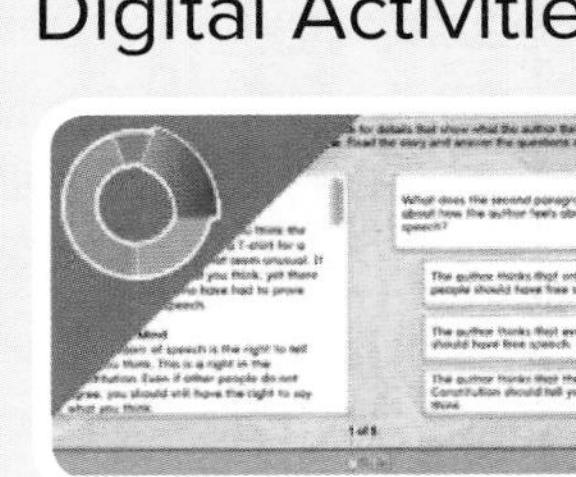

Comprehension

Phonics/Word Study

Center Activity Cards

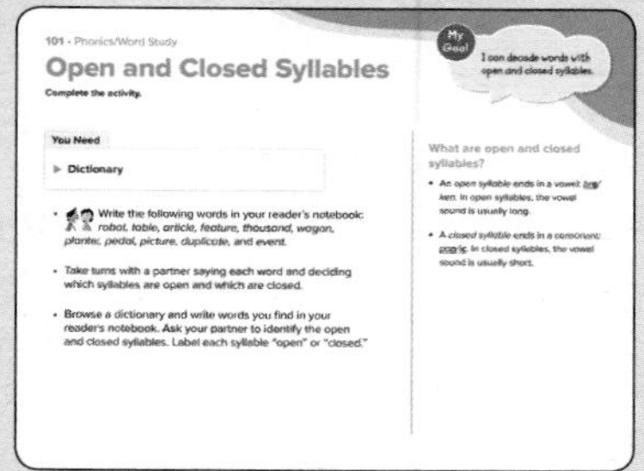

Open and Closed Syllables Card 101

Context Clues Card 71

Practice Book BLMs

Phonics: pages 127–127B, 130, 139–139B, 142

Vocabulary: pages 131–132, 143–144

Digital Activities

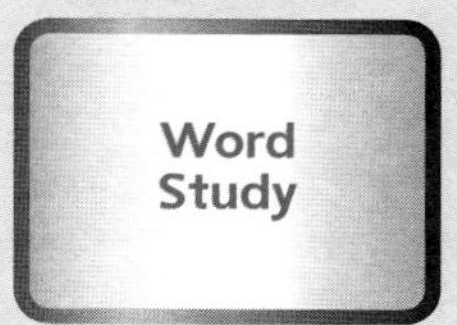

Phonics

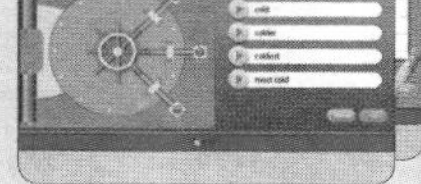

Vocabulary

Writing

Center Activity Cards

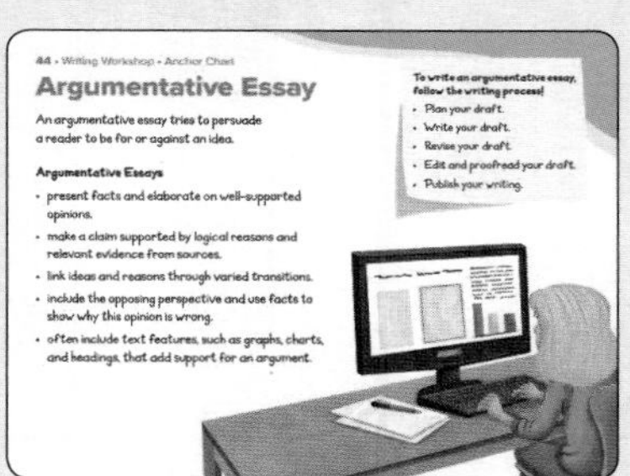

Argumentative Essay Card 44

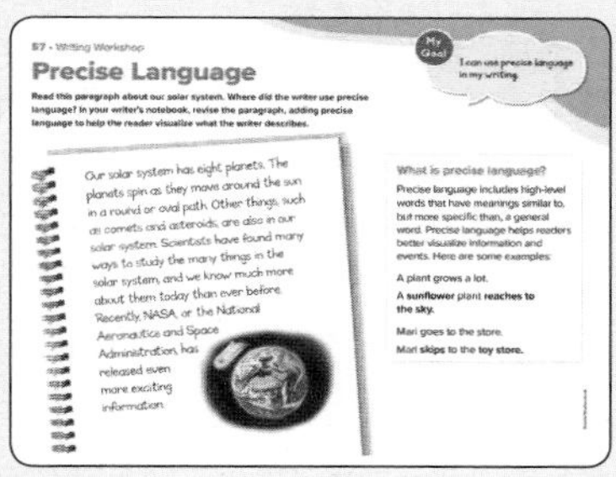

Precise Language Card 57

Self-Selected Writing

Share the following prompts.

- Write about your favorite sport or genre of music. Where did it originate?
- What foreign country would you like to visit? Why does this country interest you?
- Write a story about a kid who moves to a different country and has to get used to new customs.
- Describe one of your favorite dishes. What culture does it come from?
- Write about a holiday celebrated by a different culture. What customs are performed?

Extended Writing

Have students continue developing their **argumentative essays**.

Practice Book BLMs

Grammar: pages 121–125, 133–137

Spelling: pages 126–130, 138–142

Handwriting: pages 361–396

Digital Activities

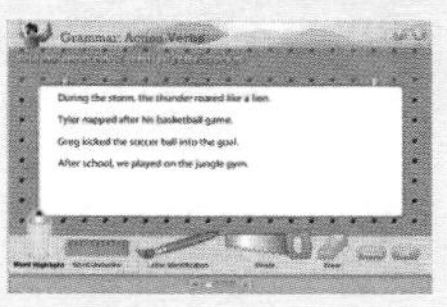

Grammar

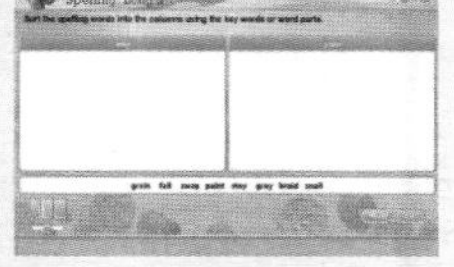

Spelling

Content Area Connections

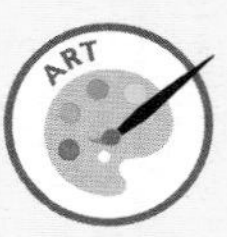

Content Area Reading Blackline Masters

- Additional texts related to Science, Social Studies, and the Arts

Research and Inquiry

- Learning About Different Cultures

Inquiry Space

- Choose an activity

Progress Monitoring

Moving Toward Mastery

FORMATIVE ASSESSMENT
STUDENT CHECK-IN
CHECK FOR SUCCESS

For ongoing formative assessment, use students' self-assessments at the end of each lesson along with your own observations.

Assessing skills along the way . . .

SKILLS	HOW ASSESSED
Comprehension **Vocabulary**	Digital Activities, Rubrics
Text-Based Writing	Reading/Writing Companion: Respond to Reading
Grammar, Mechanics, Phonics, Spelling	Practice Book, Digital Activities including word sorts
Listening/Presenting/Research	Checklists
Oral Reading Fluency (ORF) Fluency Goal: 123–143 words correct per minute (WCPM) Accuracy Rate Goal: 95% or higher	Fluency Assessment

At the end of the text set . . .

SKILLS	HOW ASSESSED
Plot: Characterization **Theme** **Author's Purpose**	Progress Monitoring
Context Clues	

Making the Most of Assessment Results

Make data-based grouping decisions by using the following reports to verify assessment results. For additional student support options refer to the reteaching and enrichment opportunities.

ONLINE ASSESSMENT CENTER

- ***Gradebook***

DATA DASHBOARD

- ***Recommendations Report***
- ***Activity Report***
- ***Skills Report***
- ***Progress Report***
- ***Grade Card Report***

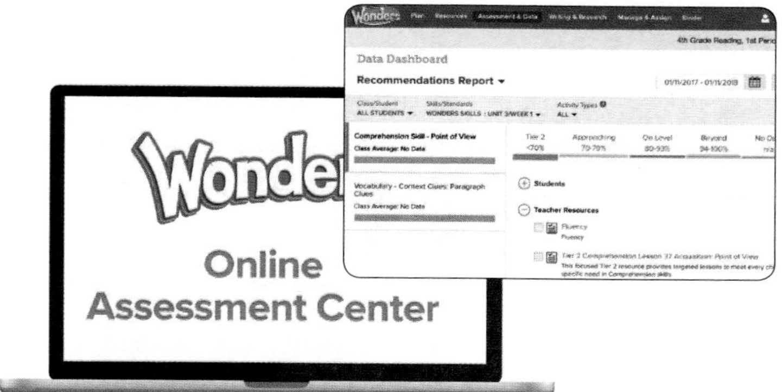

Assign practice pages online for auto-grading.

TIER 2

Reteaching Opportunities with Intervention Online PDFs

IF STUDENTS SCORE . . .	THEN ASSIGN . . .
below 70% in **comprehension** . . .	lessons 25–27 on Character in **Comprehension PDF,** lessons 34–36 on Theme in **Comprehension PDF,** and/or lessons 52–54 on Author's Purpose in **Comprehension PDF**
below 70% in **vocabulary** . . .	lesson 86 on Using Sentence Clues in **Vocabulary PDF**
114–122 WCPM in **fluency** . . .	lessons from Section 1 or 7–10 of **Fluency PDF**
0–113 WCPM in **fluency** . . .	lessons from Sections 2–6 of **Fluency PDF**

Use the* Phonics/Word Study PDF *and* Foundational Skills Kit *for additional reteaching opportunities.
Use the* Foundational Skills Kit *for students who need support with phonemic awareness and other early literacy skills.

Enrichment Opportunities

Beyond Level small group lessons and resources include suggestions for additional activities in these areas to extend learning opportunities for gifted and talented students:

- ***Leveled Readers***
- ***Genre Passages***
- ***Vocabulary***
- ***Comprehension***
- ***Leveled Reader Library Online***
- ***Center Activity Cards***

OBJECTIVES

Engage effectively in a range of collaborative discussions (one-on-one, in groups, and teacher-led) with diverse partners, building on others' ideas and expressing their own clearly.

Pose and respond to specific questions by making comments that contribute to the discussion and elaborate on the remarks of others.

Build background knowledge about different cultures.

ELA ACADEMIC LANGUAGE

- *discuss, understand, narrate*
- Cognates: *discutir, narrar*

DIGITAL TOOLS

Show the images during class discussion. Then play the video.

Discuss Concept

Watch Video

Discuss Images

VOCABULARY

custom (*costumbre*) the way a culture does a particular thing

tradition (*tradición*) when customs are passed down to children

appreciation (*valoración*) value

culture (*cultura*) the customs and traditions of a particular group

exchange (*intercambio*) trade, as in trade ideas

Build Knowledge

Essential Question

What can learning about different cultures teach us?

Read the Essential Question on **Reading/Writing Companion** page 8. Tell students that they will read realistic fiction texts that focus on different cultures and build knowledge about what studying them can teach us. They will learn new words to read, write, and talk about different cultures.

Watch the Video Play the video without sound first. Have partners narrate what they see. Then replay the video with sound as students listen.

Talk About the Video Have partners discuss what learning about different cultures can teach us.

Write About the Video Have students add their ideas to their Build Knowledge pages of their reader's notebooks.

Anchor Chart Begin a Build Knowledge anchor chart. Write the Essential Question at the top of the chart. Have volunteers share what they learned about different cultures and record their ideas. Students will add to the anchor chart after they read each text.

Build Knowledge

Display the photograph with students. Point out that this group of people are engaging in a traditional African dance. Ask: *What can dancing teach us about different cultures? What else can we learn from different cultures?* Have students discuss in small groups.

Build Vocabulary

Model using the graphic organizer to write new words related to what different cultures can teach us. Have partners continue the discussion and add the organizer and new words to their reader's notebooks. Students will add words to the Build Knowledge pages in their notebooks as they read about different cultures throughout the text set.

Collaborative Conversations

Be Open to All Ideas As students engage in partner, small-group, and whole class discussions, remind them

- that all questions and comments are important and should be heard
- to ask relevant questions if something is unclear
- to respect the opinions of others
- to offer opinions, even if they are different from others' viewpoints

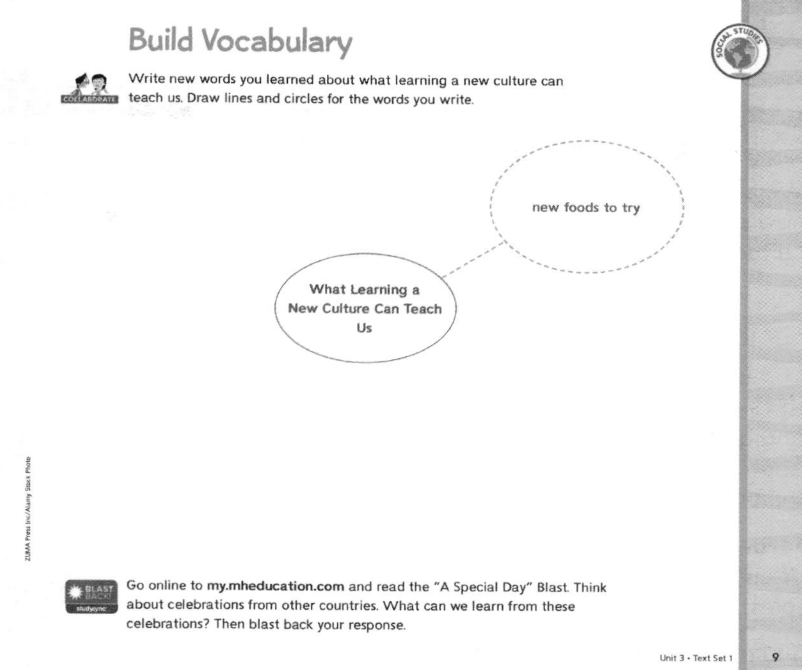
Build Vocabulary

Write new words you learned about what learning a new culture can teach us. Draw lines and circles for the words you write.

What Learning a New Culture Can Teach Us

new foods to try

Go online to **my.mheducation.com** and read the "A Special Day" Blast. Think about celebrations from other countries. What can we learn from these celebrations? Then blast back your response.

Unit 3 • Text Set 1 9

Reading/Writing Companion, pp. 8-9

Share the "A Special Day" Blast assignment with students. Point out that you will discuss their responses about the cultural celebration in the Make Connections lesson at the end of this text set.

English Language Learners

Use the following scaffolds to build knowledge and vocabulary. Teach the ELL Vocabulary, as needed.

Beginning

Describe the photograph with students. Clarify the meaning of *culture*. Ask: *What are the people doing?* (dancing) *Are they learning about an African culture?* (yes) Help students generate a list of words and phrases to describe what they can learn from different cultures. Then have partners discuss using: We can learn about dancing.

Intermediate

Use the photograph to talk about cultures. Say: *This dance is an African tradition. What can people learn from dancing?* People can learn about African culture. Have partners generate a list of words and phrases to describe what they can learn from different cultures and discuss using: We can learn about traditions, such as dancing.

Advanced/Advanced High

Discuss the photo with students. Have partners describe what people can learn from dancing. Then have them share what others can learn from different cultures using the terms *customs* and *traditions*.

NEWCOMERS

To help students develop oral language and build vocabulary, use **Newcomer Cards 5–9** and the accompanying materials in the **Newcomer Teacher's Guide**. Before using the cards, demonstrate that the directionality of print is from left to right and top to bottom. For thematic connection, use **Newcomer Card 24** with the accompanying materials.

MY GOALS ROUTINE

What I Know Now

Read Goals Have students read the goals on Reading/Writing Companion page 10.

Reflect Review the key. Ask students to reflect on each goal and fill in the bars to show what they know now. Explain they will fill in the bars on page 11 at the end of the text set to show their progress.

LEARNING GOALS

We can actively listen to learn how people from different cultures share experiences.

OBJECTIVES

Compare and contrast stories in the same genre (e.g., mysteries and adventure stories) on their approaches to similar themes and topics.

Follow agreed-upon rules for discussions and carry out assigned roles.

Summarize a written text read aloud or information presented in diverse media and formats, including visually, quantitatively, and orally.

Determine or clarify the meaning of unknown and multiple-meaning words and phrases based on grade 5 reading and content, choosing flexibly from a range of strategies.

Identify characteristics of realistic fiction.

ELA ACADEMIC LANGUAGE

- *realistic fiction, details, characters, dialogue, summarize*
- Cognates: *ficcíon realista, detalles, diálogo*

DIGITAL TOOLS

Read or play the Interactive Read Aloud.

Interactive Read Aloud

FORMATIVE ASSESSMENT

STUDENT CHECK-IN

Have partners discuss how Diego and Taylor learn to appreciate each other's culture. Ask them to reflect using the Check-In routine.

Interactive Read Aloud

Connect to Concept: Cultural Exchange

Explain that people from different cultures can share their traditions while learning more about their own. Tell students that you will be reading aloud a passage that shows how two boys learn to appreciate each other's culture through food.

Preview Realistic Fiction

Anchor Chart Explain that the passage you will read is realistic fiction. Ask students to add the features below to the Realistic Fiction anchor chart. Explain that students may want to add characteristics to the chart as they read more realistic fiction stories.

Discuss the features of realistic fiction:

- tells about characters and events that are like people and events in real life
- takes place in a realistic setting
- includes dialogue and descriptive details

Ask them to think about other texts that you have read aloud or they have read independently that were realistic fiction.

Read and Respond

Read the text aloud to students. Then reread it using the Teacher Think Alouds and Student Think Alongs on page T7 to build knowledge and model comprehension and the vocabulary strategy Context Clues.

Summarize Have students summarize the plot and theme of "Foods for Thought." Then have them share their summary with a partner to enhance their comprehension.

Build Knowledge: Make Connections

Talk About the Text Have partners discuss how people from different cultures contribute to a community.

Write About the Text Have students add their ideas to their Build Knowledge pages of their reader's notebooks.

Anchor Chart Record any new ideas on the Build Knowledge anchor chart.

Add to the Vocabulary List Have students write down any words they learned about different cultures in their reader's notebooks.

Foods for Thought

"Score!" Taylor threw his arms up as the ball hit the back of the net. It was the same gesture he made when he made a touchdown, but he and his friend Diego were playing fútbol, not American football.

"Nice shot," Diego said as he picked up the ball and headed toward the house. "Here comes my sister Ramona with my favorite tamales," he said.

The boys thanked Ramona as she set a platter down on the patio table. To Taylor, the tamales looked like little pillows made of leaves. When Diego put one on his plate, Taylor cautiously lifted it up to take a bite.

Diego laughed. "You don't eat the corn husk! That's just to hold in the cheesy deliciousness!" Diego demonstrated how to eat the tamale by spreading apart the husk, after which he added a large dollop of salsa. "I like mine extra spicy," he explained, "but they're just as tasty without any salsa at all."

Taylor followed Diego's example and took a bite of his tamale, then said, "It tastes like a grilled cheese sandwich." (1)

"But it's not grilled," Diego replied. "The dough and cheese are steamed inside the husk."

"This gives me an idea," Taylor said. "Come over to my house later, and I'll have a surprise for you!"

When Diego arrived at Taylor's house later that day, a delicious smell hovered in the air. Inside the kitchen, Taylor and his father had made a platter of snack rolls that looked like dark oblong tamales. "They're called dolmade," Taylor explained. "My Greek grandmother used to make them all the time." (2)

Diego's mouth watered as he began to unwrap one of the rolls on his plate. "No," Taylor said, "you don't unwrap these! The rice and vegetables will fall out. You can eat the grape leaves that are holding all the goodness together!"

Diego laughed and then took a bite of his dolmade. "This is a great way to learn about world cultures," he said. "I can't wait to make these over at our house for dinner some night . . . but with extra spices!" (3)

(1) Teacher Think Aloud

As I read the first paragraph, I will pay attention to the most important details. I read that two friends, Taylor and Diego, are playing fútbol. I know that "fútbol" is "soccer" to many people around the world.

Student Think Along

Listen as I read the next four paragraphs. Pay attention to how Diego shares a cultural experience with Taylor. Turn and tell a partner how Taylor responds.

(2) Teacher Think Aloud

I'm not sure what it means for food to be "steamed." I will use context clues and background knowledge to determine the meaning of "steamed." I know steam occurs when water is heated. Also, Diego uses the word "grilled," and that's a form of cooking, so I can infer that "steamed" refers to a kind of cooking that involves heating water.

Student Think Along

As I reread, pay attention to the word *oblong*. Use context clues and any background knowledge to determine its meaning.

(3) Teacher Think Aloud

After I finish reading a text, I can monitor my comprehension by summarizing the story and identifying the theme. I think it is most important to note that Diego's family makes tamales, and tamales remind Taylor of a food his family makes, dolmade.

Student Think Along

Summarize the story. Then tell what learning about different cultures teaches Taylor and Diego. Summarize what they learn with a partner. Then share something that your family likes to cook or eat.

"A Reluctant Traveler"

Lexile 770L

LEARNING GOALS

We can read and understand realistic fiction.

OBJECTIVES

Quote accurately from a text when explaining what the text says explicitly and when drawing inferences from the text.

Explain different characters' perspectives in a literary text.

Determine a theme of a story, drama, or poem from details in the text, including how characters in a story or drama respond to challenges or how the speaker in a poem reflects upon a topic; summarize the text.

Summarize a written text read aloud or information presented in diverse media and formats, including visually, quantitatively, and orally.

By the end of the year, read and comprehend literature, including stories, dramas, and poetry, at the high end of the grades 4–5 text complexity band independently and proficiently.

Read with sufficient accuracy and fluency to support comprehension. Read grade-level text with purpose and understanding.

Close Reading Routine

Read DOK 1–2

- Identify important ideas and details.
- Take notes and summarize.
- Use ACT prompts as needed.

Reread DOK 2–3

- Analyze the text, craft, and structure.
- Use the **Reread minilessons** and **prompts.**

Integrate DOK 3–4

- Integrate knowledge and ideas.
- Make text-to-text connections.
- Use the Integrate lesson.
- Complete the Show Your Knowledge task.
- Inspire action.

Read

SHARED READ

My Goal I can read and understand realistic fiction.

TAKE NOTES

As you read, make note of interesting words and important events.

12 Unit 3 · Text Set 1

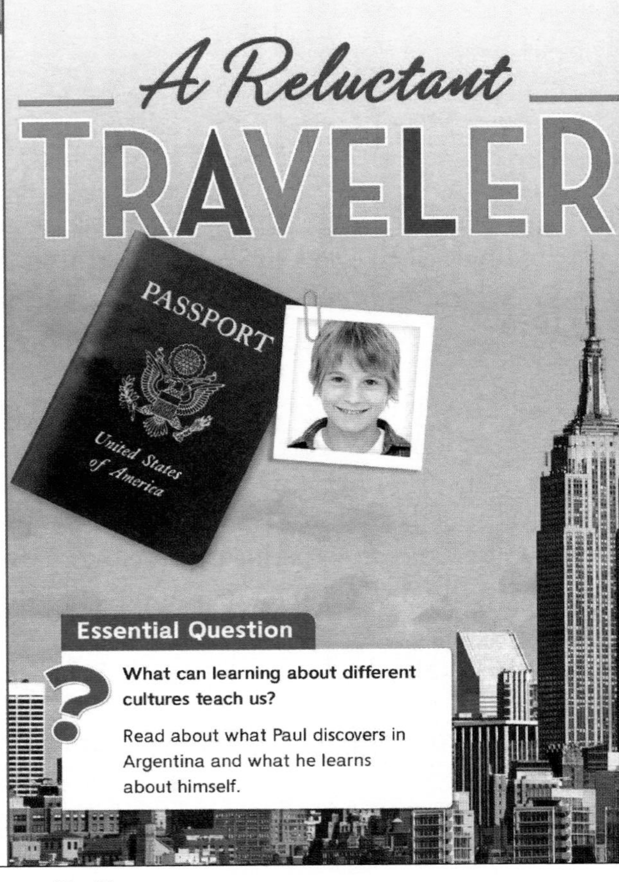

A Reluctant
TRAVELER
PASSPORT
United States of America
Essential Question
What can learning about different cultures teach us?
Read about what Paul discovers in Argentina and what he learns about himself.

Reading/Writing Companion, pp. 12–13

Set a Purpose Have students think about the Essential Question and what they know about different cultures. Then ask them to look at the title and the photos on pages 12–13. Have them generate a question about the story to deepen understanding and then write it in the left column on page 12, along with interesting words and key details from the text.

Focus on the Read prompts now. For additional support, use the extra prompts not included in the **Reading/Writing Companion.** Use the Reread prompts during the Craft and Structure lesson on pages T20–T21. Consider preteaching vocabulary to some students.

DIFFERENTIATED READING

Approaching Level Model and discuss techniques for previewing the text and taking notes. Complete all Read prompts together.

On Level Have partners do the Read prompts before you meet.

Beyond Level Discuss students' responses to the Read prompts. Analyze how setting a purpose helps them focus on the text.

English Language Learners Preteach the vocabulary. Have Beginning and Early-Intermediate ELLs listen to the selection summary, available in multiple languages, and use the **Scaffolded Shared Read**. See also the **ELL Small Group Guide**.

"I think packing winter clothes in August is weird," Paul said, looking from his bedroom window onto West 90th Street. This wasn't going to be a fun vacation. He was sure of it.

His mom **contradicted**, "It's not weird, honey. Argentina's in the Southern Hemisphere, and we're in the Northern Hemisphere, so the seasons are opposite." To Paul, this was just another reason to want to stay in New York City. Paul wanted to spend the rest of his summer break hanging out with his friends, and not with Aunt Lila and Uncle Art in a faraway country.

Paul's parents, Mr. and Mrs. Gorski, were teachers, and this was a chance they couldn't pass up. Their apartment had been covered with travel guides full of **cultural** information ever since Mrs. Gorski's sister and her husband had relocated to Argentina six months ago. The Gorskis had big plans. Paul, on the other hand, wanted to sleep late and play soccer with his friends. They lived in a city already. Why were they going to Buenos Aires?

As their plane took off, Paul's dad said, "Look down there! That's the island of Manhattan. See? You can even see Central Park!" Paul never realized how surrounded by water New York was. Many hours later, as the plane was landing in Buenos Aires, Paul noticed similar outlines of a city on the water, and bright lights, just like home.

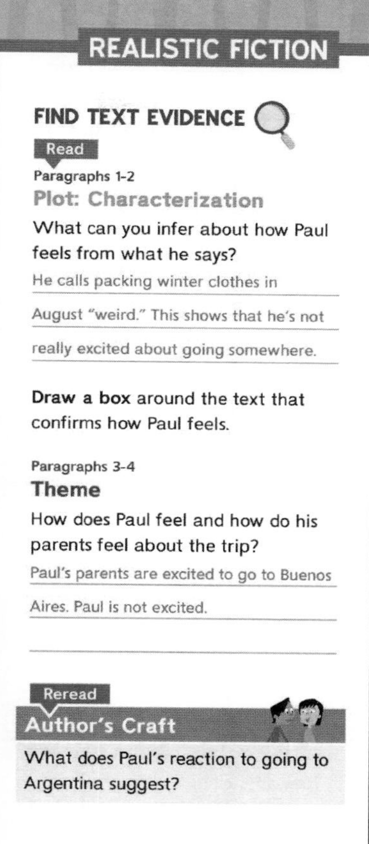

REALISTIC FICTION

FIND TEXT EVIDENCE

Read

Paragraphs 1-2

Plot: Characterization

What can you infer about how Paul feels from what he says?

He calls packing winter clothes in August "weird." This shows that he's not really excited about going somewhere.

Draw a box around the text that confirms how Paul feels.

Paragraphs 3-4

Theme

How does Paul feel and how do his parents feel about the trip?

Paul's parents are excited to go to Buenos Aires. Paul is not excited.

Reread

Author's Craft

What does Paul's reaction to going to Argentina suggest?

Unit 3 • Text Set 1 13

Plot: Characterization DOK 2

Paragraphs 1–2: *How does what Paul says help you infer how he feels?*

Think Aloud The first thing Paul says is "I think packing winter clothes in August is weird." I know that I say something is "weird" when it is not very appealing, so I can infer that Paul is not very excited. The second paragraph confirms this. It explains that his family is going away for the summer, and Paul is not going to be able to see his friends. That must be why he's not very excited. Have students predict how Paul's perspective will affect the trip.

Theme DOK 2

Paragraphs 3–4: *What is the difference between how Paul feels about the trip and how his parents feel about the trip?*

Think Aloud I already know Paul's feelings, so now I'll look for details about his parents' feelings. The text says that it's "a chance they couldn't pass up." I know this means that going now is an opportunity they shouldn't miss. The text also says that their apartment is "covered with travel guides," which tells me they are busy planning. These details confirm they're very excited. Have students predict how this difference might affect what happens on the trip.

Check for Understanding DOK 2

Page 13: Monitor students' understanding of Paul's discoveries about New York City and Buenos Aires. Reread paragraph 2. Ask: *What does Paul learn about seasons in Buenos Aires compared to seasons in New York?* (They are opposite.) Reread paragraph 4. Ask: *In what ways are New York City and Buenos Aires similar?* (Both cities are surrounded by water.) Have students infer how Paul's perspective about the two cities might be changing.

ELL Spotlight on Idioms

Page 13, Paragraph 3 Read the first sentence with students. Clarify the meaning of *pass up.* Explain that when you *pass up* doing something, you say no to an invitation. Clarify with an example: *If you are invited to attend a concert, you don't want to pass up going.* Read the second sentence and then point to the map on page 13. *Talk to your partner about why you think Mr. and Mrs. Gorski don't want to pass up this chance. Tell your partner about something you don't want to pass up.*

Theme DOK 2

Paragraphs 1–3: Read the first three paragraphs. Ask: *How does Paul react to the dinner Uncle Art ordered? What does Paul's reaction tell you about why his mood improves?* (First Paul makes a face. But then he discovers that the food is good. This reaction tells me that his mood improves because he enjoys the food.)

Check for Understanding DOK 2

Paragraph 3: Read the third paragraph and guide students in analyzing how the author characterizes Paul. Ask: *What do you learn by reading Paul's dialogue?* (After biting into an empanada, Paul tells his mother that the food is really good. This tells me that after tasting the unfamiliar food, Paul realizes he likes it.) Discuss how this experience is beginning to change Paul's feelings about being in Buenos Aires.

Context Clues DOK 2

Paragraph 4: Read the fourth paragraph. Point out the word *multilingual* in the last sentence. Ask: *Which words can help you determine the meaning of* multilingual? (The words "had people from all over the world" suggests that because people come from all over the world, they speak different languages. That tells me that *multilingual* means *many languages*.)

Read

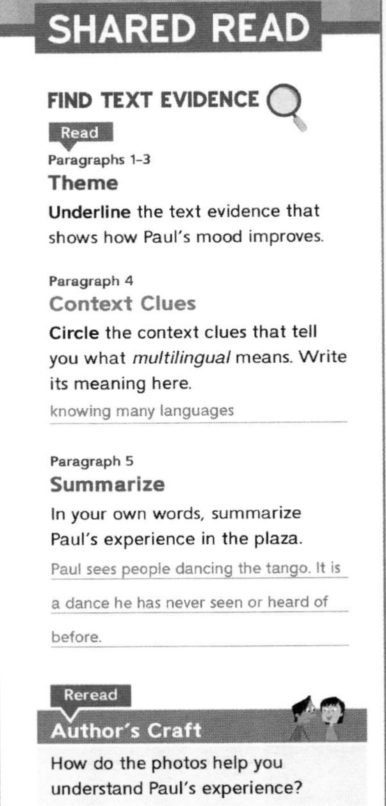
SHARED READ

FIND TEXT EVIDENCE

Read

Paragraphs 1–3

Theme

Underline the text evidence that shows how Paul's mood improves.

Paragraph 4

Context Clues

Circle the context clues that tell you what *multilingual* means. Write its meaning here.

knowing many languages

Paragraph 5

Summarize

In your own words, summarize Paul's experience in the plaza.

Paul sees people dancing the tango. It is a dance he has never seen or heard of before.

Reread

Author's Craft

How do the photos help you understand Paul's experience?

14 Unit 3 • Text Set 1

"We have so much to show you!" Aunt Lila gushed when they met at the airport. They had a late dinner at a restaurant, just as they often did back home. But the smells coming from its kitchen were new. Uncle Art ordered in Spanish for everyone: *empanadas* (small meat pies), followed by *parrillada* (grilled meat), *chimichurri* (spicy sauce), and *ensalada mixta* (lettuce, tomatoes, and onions).

Paul made a face. "Don't be **critical,** Paul," his mom said. "Just take a taste." Though some of the foods were new, the spices and flavors were familiar to Paul.

"Mom, I had something like this at César's house," Paul said, after biting into an empanada. "This is really good." As he was **complimenting** the food, Paul felt his bleak mood improving.

Their first full day in Buenos Aires brought a rush of new sights, sounds, and languages. Paul noticed that like New York, Buenos Aires had people from all over the world. His Aunt Lila remarked, "We speak Spanish, but I really need to be multilingual!"

On a plaza, Paul saw a group of people dancing to music he'd never heard. Paul had seen breakdancing on the street, but never dancing like this. "That's the tango," Uncle Art said. "It's the dance Argentina is famous for! Being a soccer player, Paul, I know you have an **appreciation** for people who move well."

Reading/Writing Companion, pp. 14–15

Summarize DOK 1

Paragraph 5: Read the last paragraph. Ask: *What does Paul observe on the plaza?* (Paul observes a group of people dancing to music he has never heard.) *What kind of dance is Paul familiar with? What important details in Uncle Art's dialogue explain what Paul learns about this unfamiliar dance?* (Paul is familiar with breakdancing. He learns that people in Argentina dance the tango. It is a famous dance.) Have students use the key details to summarize Paul's experience in the plaza. (Paul sees people dancing the tango. He has seen breakdancing before, but has never seen or heard the tango before.)

Access Complex Text

Purpose

Point out that authors of realistic fiction often place fictional characters in real places and situations. Ask: *What real places and situations does the story include?* (New York, Argentina; flying on a plane, change of seasons) *Why does the author include these real details?* (They help show how big and exciting of an experience traveling can be.)

Connection of Ideas

Point out that the title of a story may give a clue to the story's theme. Help students define the word *reluctant. If someone is* reluctant, *he does not feel like doing something. Why is Paul reluctant to travel?* (He doesn't want to be somewhere far away from his friends and the fun he wants to have during the summer.) *How does Paul become less reluctant?* (by enjoying himself on the trip)

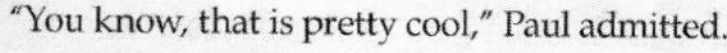

"You know, that is pretty cool," Paul admitted.

Around noon, they piled back into the car and drove to the most unusual neighborhood Paul had seen yet. All the buildings were painted or decorated in yellow and blue. "Soccer season has started here," his Aunt Lila said.

"Huh?" Paul asked, wondering if there had been a **misunderstanding.** "Isn't it too cold for soccer?" he asked.

"It's nearly spring. And," his aunt added, "Boca and River are playing at La Bombonera, the famous stadium, this afternoon." She held out her hand, which held five tickets to see these big teams play. Paul couldn't believe it.

"We're in the neighborhood of La Bombonera," Uncle Art said. "When Boca beats their rival, River, the people decorate their neighborhood in Boca colors!"

"Maybe I could paint my room in soccer team colors!" Paul **blurted.**

His mom smiled. "I **congratulate** you, Paul! You've turned out to be a really great traveler." Paul smiled, too.

Summarize

Use your notes to summarize important details of Paul's trip to Buenos Aires.

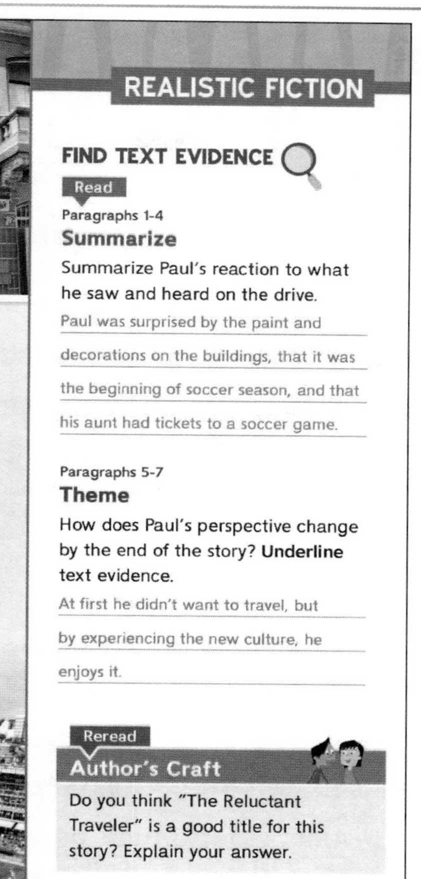

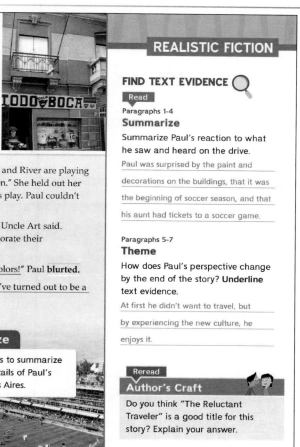

REALISTIC FICTION

FIND TEXT EVIDENCE

Read

Paragraphs 1-4

Summarize

Summarize Paul's reaction to what he saw and heard on the drive.

Paul was surprised by the paint and decorations on the buildings, that it was the beginning of soccer season, and that his aunt had tickets to a soccer game.

Paragraphs 5-7

Theme

How does Paul's perspective change by the end of the story? **Underline** text evidence.

At first he didn't want to travel, but by experiencing the new culture, he enjoys it.

Reread

Author's Craft

Do you think "The Reluctant Traveler" is a good title for this story? Explain your answer.

Unit 3 · Text Set 1 15

Summarize DOK 1

Paragraphs 1–4: Read the first four paragraphs. *Describe what Paul saw in the neighborhood they drove to.* (All the buildings were painted or decorated in yellow and blue.) *What important details explain what surprised Paul the most?* (He was surprised by how the houses were painted, that soccer season was beginning, and that his aunt had tickets to a soccer game.) Have students use the key details to summarize Paul's reaction.

ELL Spotlight on Idioms

Page 14, Paragraph 2: Read the paragraph with students. Clarify the meaning of *made a face*. Explain that if you *made a face* you showed, with your face, that you don't like something. Read the second sentence, and have students make the face they think Paul made. *Talk to your partner about a time you made a face at something you didn't like.*

Context Clues DOK 2

Paragraph 5: Read the fifth paragraph. Ask: *Which words help you determine the meaning of* rival? (Uncle Art says the word *rival* when he's talking about the Boca team beating the *rival* River team. That must mean that the Boca team plays against the River team.) Discuss the meaning of the word *rival.* (*Rival* must mean *opposing team* since River is the rival and that's the team Boca must beat.)

Theme DOK 2

Paragraphs 5–7: Read the last three paragraphs. Ask: *What did Paul say when he saw the painted houses in the La Bombonera neighborhood?* (He said he might paint his own room in soccer team colors.) *What does Paul's reaction tell you about how his perspective has changed?* (At first Paul did not want to travel. But by experiencing the new culture, he enjoys it.) Discuss the overall idea or message about life the author wants the reader to know.

Summarize DOK 2

Quick Write After their initial reads, have student pairs use their notes to orally summarize the selection. Then have them write a summary in their reader's notebooks. Remind them to only include the most important events and details. Have partners read and discuss each other's summary.

FORMATIVE ASSESSMENT

STUDENT CHECK-IN

Have partners share their summaries from Reading/Writing Companion page 15. Ask them to reflect using the Check-In routine.

LEARNING GOALS

- We can use new vocabulary words to read and understand realistic fiction.
- We can use context clues to figure out the meaning of unfamiliar and multiple-meaning words.

OBJECTIVES

Determine or clarify the meaning of unknown and multiple-meaning words and phrases, choosing flexibly from a range of strategies.

Use context (e.g., cause/effect relationships and comparisons in text) as a clue to the meaning of a word or phrase.

ELA ACADEMIC LANGUAGE

- *context, cause, effect*
- Cognates: *contexto, causa, efecto*

DIGITAL TOOLS

Visual Vocabulary Cards

TEACH IN SMALL GROUP

Academic Vocabulary

Approaching Level and **ELL** Preteach the words before students begin the Shared Read.

On Level and **Beyond Level** Have students look up each word in the online **Visual Glossary**.

Reread

Academic Vocabulary

Use the routine on the **Visual Vocabulary Cards** to introduce each word.

People have an **appreciation** for the things they value.

If he **blurted** the answer, he said it suddenly.

If you say something nice about someone, you are **complimenting** them.

Congratulate means to give praise for something that has happened.

The baker's story **contradicted**, or disagreed with, the butcher's story.
Cognate: *contradecir*

A person who is **critical** will find fault with something or someone.

When you research your family's **cultural** past, you learn about your family customs, beliefs, and traditions.
Cognate: *cultural*

When friends have a **misunderstanding**, they fail to understand each other.

Encourage students to use their newly acquired vocabulary in their discussions and written responses about the texts in this text set.

Context Clues

1 Explain

Remind students that they can often figure out the meaning of unknown words by using context clues in a sentence or clues beyond the sentence in a paragraph. Explain that context clues can describe, restate, or define the unknown word. Words and phrases that point to cause-and-effect relationships may also help determine the meaning of words or phrases since they often hint at a word's meaning. Have volunteers add to the context clues anchor chart.

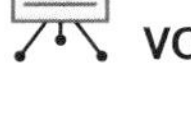

2 Model

Model using context clues to find the meaning of *hemisphere* on **Reading/Writing Companion** page 13. Point out the relationship between seasons and locations above or below the equator.

3 Guided Practice

Help partners use context clues to define *relocated* on page 13 and *bleak* on page 14 of "A Reluctant Traveler." Guide them to go back into the text and use cause-and-effect relationships between words to help them determine each word's meaning.

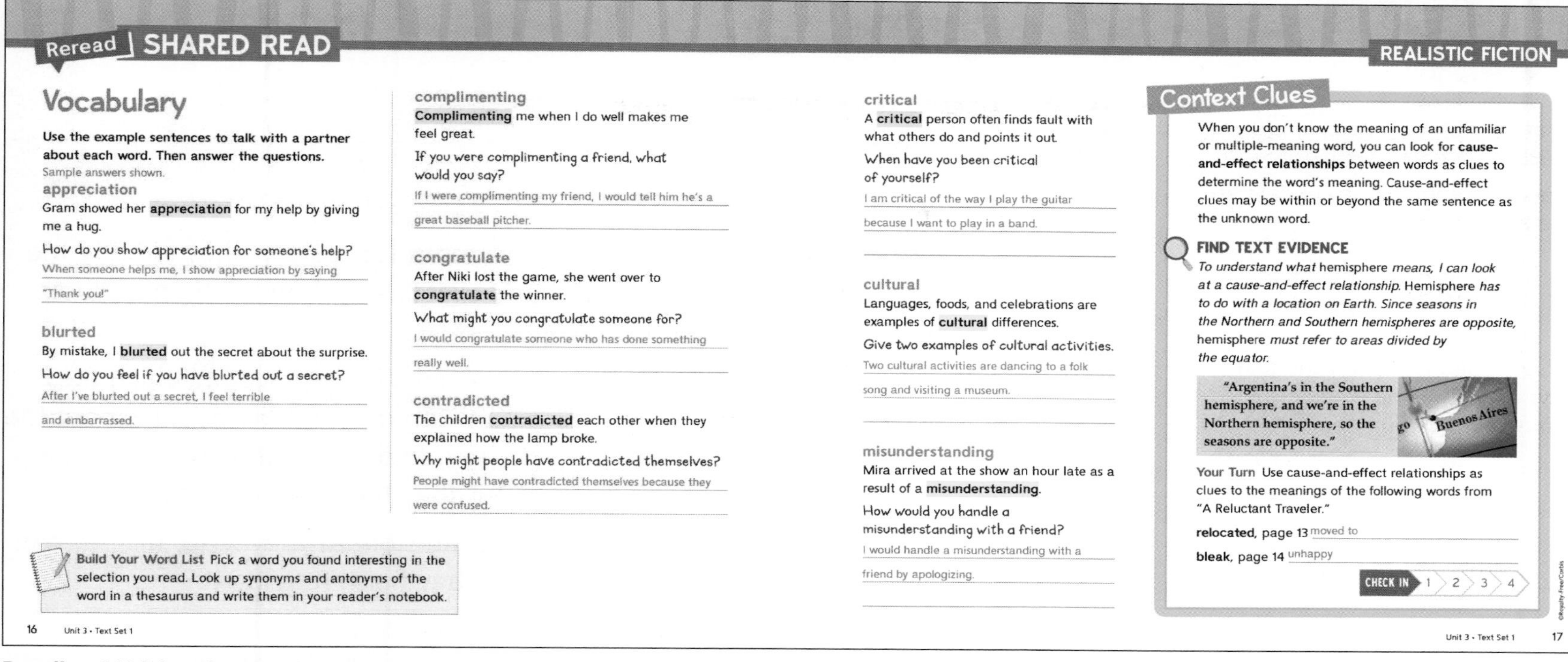
Reread | SHARED READ

REALISTIC FICTION

Vocabulary

Use the example sentences to talk with a partner about each word. Then answer the questions.

Sample answers shown.

appreciation
Gram showed her **appreciation** for my help by giving me a hug.
How do you show appreciation for someone's help?
When someone helps me, I show appreciation by saying "Thank you!"

blurted
By mistake, I **blurted** out the secret about the surprise.
How do you feel if you have blurted out a secret?
After I've blurted out a secret, I feel terrible and embarrassed.

complimenting
Complimenting me when I do well makes me feel great.
If you were complimenting a friend, what would you say?
If I were complimenting my friend, I would tell him he's a great baseball pitcher.

congratulate
After Niki lost the game, she went over to **congratulate** the winner.
What might you congratulate someone for?
I would congratulate someone who has done something really well.

contradicted
The children **contradicted** each other when they explained how the lamp broke.
Why might people have contradicted themselves?
People might have contradicted themselves because they were confused.

critical
A **critical** person often finds fault with what others do and points it out.
When have you been critical of yourself?
I am critical of the way I play the guitar because I want to play in a band.

cultural
Languages, foods, and celebrations are examples of **cultural** differences.
Give two examples of cultural activities.
Two cultural activities are dancing to a folk song and visiting a museum.

misunderstanding
Mira arrived at the show an hour late as a result of a **misunderstanding**.
How would you handle a misunderstanding with a friend?
I would handle a misunderstanding with a friend by apologizing.

Build Your Word List Pick a word you found interesting in the selection you read. Look up synonyms and antonyms of the word in a thesaurus and write them in your reader's notebook.

16 Unit 3 • Text Set 1

Context Clues

When you don't know the meaning of an unfamiliar or multiple-meaning word, you can look for **cause-and-effect relationships** between words as clues to determine the word's meaning. Cause-and-effect clues may be within or beyond the same sentence as the unknown word.

FIND TEXT EVIDENCE
To understand what hemisphere *means, I can look at a cause-and-effect relationship.* Hemisphere *has to do with a location on Earth. Since seasons in the Northern and Southern hemispheres are opposite,* hemisphere *must refer to areas divided by the equator.*

"Argentina's in the Southern hemisphere, and we're in the Northern hemisphere, so the seasons are opposite."

Your Turn Use cause-and-effect relationships as clues to the meanings of the following words from "A Reluctant Traveler."

relocated, page 13 moved to

bleak, page 14 unhappy

CHECK IN 1 2 3 4

Unit 3 • Text Set 1 17

Reading/Writing Companion, pp. 16–17

English Language Learners

Use the following scaffolds with **Guided Practice**. For small group support, see the **ELL Small Group Guide**.

Beginning

Read paragraph 3 on page 13 of "A Reluctant Traveler" with students. Restate sentences as needed. Point to the map. *Mrs. Gorski's sister relocated, or moved.* Help pairs discuss using *relocated: Why does Mrs. Gorksi want to go to Argentina?* Her sister relocated there. Have pairs restate the meaning of relocated: When you relocate you move to a new place.

Intermediate

Have partners read paragraph 3 on page 13 of "A Reluctant Traveler" and look at the map. *What words, phrases, or other clues help you understand* relocated? (travel guides, Argentina, plane on map) *What did Mrs. Gorski's sister do?* (moved) Have pairs define *relocated*: *Relocated* means moved to a new place. *Why does Mrs. Gorski want to go to Argentina?* Her sister relocated there. Repeat with *bleak.*

Advanced/Advanced High

Have partners read the third paragraph on page 13 and describe the events using *relocated.* Guide them to discuss why Mrs. Gorski wants to go to Argentina. Then have them use context clues to define *relocated* and explain how they understood the meaning. Repeat the routine with *bleak*.

BUILD YOUR WORD LIST

Students might choose *outlines* from page 13. Have them use context clues to determine its meaning.

FORMATIVE ASSESSMENT

STUDENT CHECK-IN

Academic Vocabulary Ask partners to share two answers from Reading/Writing Companion pages 16–17.

Context Clues Ask partners to share their Your Turn responses on page 17.

Have students use the Check-In routine to reflect and fill in the bars.

CHECK FOR SUCCESS

Rubric Use your online rubric to record student progress.

Can students use context clues to determine the meaning of *relocated* and *bleak?*

Small Group Instruction

If No:

- **Approaching** Reteach p. T61

If Yes:

- **On** Review p. T68
- **Beyond** Extend p. T74

LEARNING GOALS

We can summarize to understand realistic fiction.

OBJECTIVES

Quote accurately from a text when explaining what the text says explicitly and when drawing inferences from the text.

ELA ACADEMIC LANGUAGE

- *summarize, details, monitor*
- Cognates: *detalles, monitor*

Reread

Summarize

1 Explain

Remind students that when they **summarize** a story, they identify the most important ideas, details, and events and then tell them in their own words.

- Explain that a summary restates events in the order in which they happened in the story. A summary can also include details about the important things characters do, say, and feel. It should not contain students' personal opinions about the characters or events.
- Students can summarize parts of the story as they read, or they can summarize the whole story after they finish reading it.

Point out that summarizing allows students to monitor their own comprehension of ideas and story events and can help them remember and better understand what they have read.

Anchor Chart Begin a summarize anchor chart.

2 Model

Model how summarizing can help you monitor your understanding of important plot events and the development of theme in a story. Reread and summarize the first three paragraphs in "A Reluctant Traveler" on **Reading/Writing Companion** page 13.

3 Guided Practice

Guide students as they work in pairs to recall and summarize events on Paul's first night in Buenos Aires and their effect on him, as described in the first three paragraphs on page 14.

A possible summary might read as follows: *After Paul and his family arrive, Uncle Art and Aunt Lila take them to a restaurant where Paul reluctantly tries new food. Paul ends up liking the empanadas, which remind him of a food he had at a friend's house in New York.*

After partners complete their summaries, have them discuss other sections of "A Reluctant Traveler" that they can summarize to monitor their comprehension of the story.

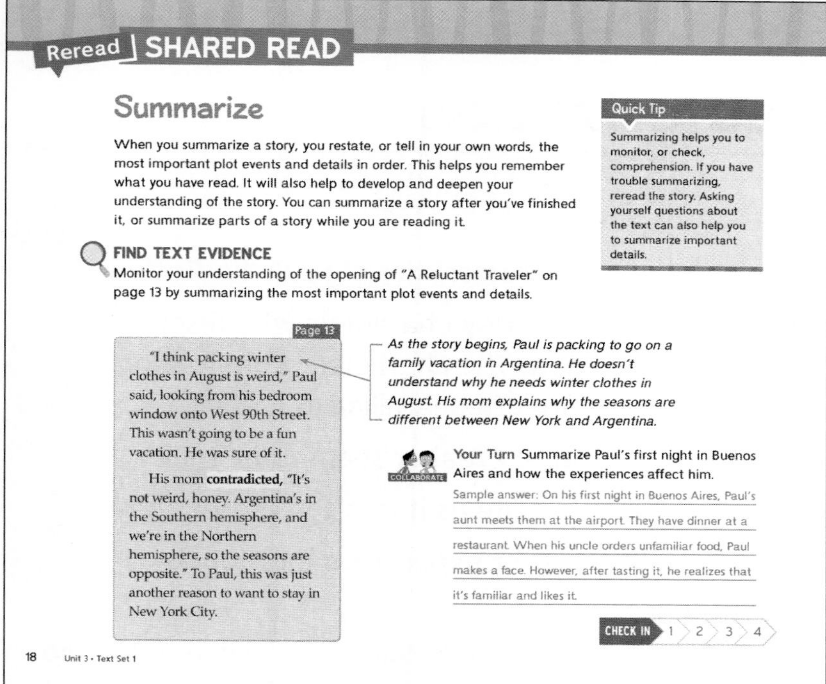

Reread | SHARED READ

Summarize

When you summarize a story, you restate, or tell in your own words, the most important plot events and details in order. This helps you remember what you have read. It will also help to develop and deepen your understanding of the story. You can summarize a story after you've finished it, or summarize parts of a story while you are reading it.

Quick Tip

Summarizing helps you to monitor, or check, comprehension. If you have trouble summarizing, reread the story. Asking yourself questions about the text can also help you to summarize important details.

FIND TEXT EVIDENCE

Monitor your understanding of the opening of "A Reluctant Traveler" on page 13 by summarizing the most important plot events and details.

Page 13

"I think packing winter clothes in August is weird," Paul said, looking from his bedroom window onto West 90th Street. This wasn't going to be a fun vacation. He was sure of it.

His mom **contradicted**, "It's not weird, honey. Argentina's in the Southern hemisphere, and we're in the Northern hemisphere, so the seasons are opposite." To Paul, this was just another reason to want to stay in New York City.

As the story begins, Paul is packing to go on a family vacation in Argentina. He doesn't understand why he needs winter clothes in August. His mom explains why the seasons are different between New York and Argentina.

COLLABORATE

Your Turn Summarize Paul's first night in Buenos Aires and how the experiences affect him.

Sample answer: On his first night in Buenos Aires, Paul's aunt meets them at the airport. They have dinner at a restaurant. When his uncle orders unfamiliar food, Paul makes a face. However, after tasting it, he realizes that it's familiar and likes it.

CHECK IN 1 2 3 4

18 Unit 3 • Text Set 1

Reading/Writing Companion, p. 18

English Language Learners

Use the following scaffolds with **Guided Practice**. For small group support, see the **ELL Small Group Guide**.

Beginning

Read the first three paragraphs on page 14 of "A Reluctant Traveler" with students. Restate sentences as needed. Help partners describe the important events and details to summarize: The family eats dinner at a restaurant, but the food smells new and different. Paul doesn't think he will like the food. Then he tastes the food, and he remembers he likes it. He feels better.

Intermediate

Have partners read the first three paragraphs on page 14 of "A Reluctant Traveler." Ask questions about Paul's first night in Buenos Aires, and guide students to state their answers: *Where does the family go?* They go to a restaurant. *What do they eat? What does Paul do at first?* He makes a face. *What happens next?* (Paul tastes the food, and he likes it. He feels better.) *Work with your partner to summarize these events and their effects on Paul.*

Advanced/Advanced High

Have partners read the first three paragraphs on page 14 and ask and answer questions about Paul's first night in Buenos Aires. Then have partners summarize the events' effects on Paul's mood.

HABITS OF LEARNING

I write to communicate effectively.

Before students write their summaries about Paul's experience in Argentina, explain that talking through ideas with peers will help them make their writing clearer. Remind them to use this strategy—talking about ideas before writing—whether in school or out. Doing so will help them communicate more effectively.

FORMATIVE ASSESSMENT

STUDENT CHECK-IN

Ask partners to share their Your Turn responses on Reading/Writing Companion page 18. Have them use the Check-In routine to reflect and fill in the bars.

CHECK FOR SUCCESS

Do students identify the most important ideas, details, and events in a story? Do they use these to summarize the text in their own words?

Small Group Instruction

If No:

- **Approaching** Reteach p. T54

If Yes:

- **On** Review p. T64
- **Beyond** Extend p. T70

Reread

Plot: Characterization

10 mins

LEARNING GOALS

We can analyze character and plot development in realistic fiction.

OBJECTIVES

Compare and contrast two or more characters, settings, or events in a story or drama, drawing on specific details in the text (e.g., how characters interact).

Quote accurately from a text when explaining what the text says explicitly and when drawing inferences from the text.

By the end of the year, read and comprehend literature, including stories, dramas, and poetry independently and proficiently.

Recognize characteristics of realistic fiction.

ELA ACADEMIC LANGUAGE

- *realistic fiction, dialogue, descriptive details, perspective, characterization*
- Cognates: *ficción realista, diálogo, detalles descriptivos*

1 Explain

Share with students these key characteristics of **realistic fiction**.

- Realistic fiction features present-day characters who resemble people you might actually know. The characters' conflicts, or problems, and relationships are often familiar to readers.
- Events happen in settings that are real or seem to be real.
- Details in realistic fiction reflect life as it is in the present day.
- Descriptive details help the reader experience the story by appealing to the senses.
- Realistic fiction includes dialogue that sounds the way real people speak. Dialogue helps to develop characters and often reveals their perspective, or attitude, toward other characters, relationships, and conflicts.

2 Model

Model identifying realistic elements from "A Reluctant Traveler," such as settings, conflicts, events, and characterization. (New York and Buenos Aires; Paul doesn't want to leave New York to visit relatives; packing, traveling, sightseeing, trying new things; "I think packing winter clothes in August is weird.")

Dialogue Remind students that dialogue appears in quotation marks and is the exact words a character says. A new paragraph is used each time a different character speaks. Reread **Reading/Writing Companion** page 13 and point out examples of dialogue. Ask: *Do you think Paul and his parents speak like real people would? Explain why or why not.* Discuss how the author uses dialogue to reveal Paul's perspective about going to Argentina.

Anchor Chart Have a volunteer add these features to the realistic fiction anchor chart.

3 Guided Practice

Circulate as students work with partners to find and read aloud an example of realistic dialogue in "A Reluctant Traveler." Partners should discuss why each example is realistic and tell what it reveals about the character who is speaking. Provide feedback as necessary. Then have students share their work with the class.

Independent Practice Have students read the online **Differentiated Genre Passage**, "Potluck or Potlatch?"

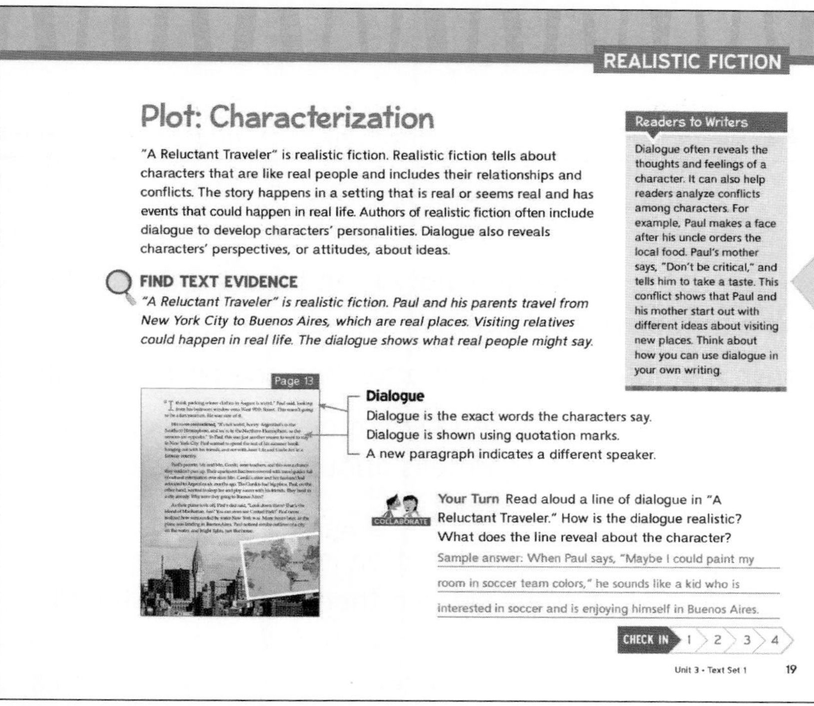

REALISTIC FICTION

Plot: Characterization

"A Reluctant Traveler" is realistic fiction. Realistic fiction tells about characters that are like real people and includes their relationships and conflicts. The story happens in a setting that is real or seems real and has events that could happen in real life. Authors of realistic fiction often include dialogue to develop characters' personalities. Dialogue also reveals characters' perspectives, or attitudes, about ideas.

FIND TEXT EVIDENCE

"A Reluctant Traveler" is realistic fiction. Paul and his parents travel from New York City to Buenos Aires, which are real places. Visiting relatives could happen in real life. The dialogue shows what real people might say.

Page 13

Dialogue

Dialogue is the exact words the characters say.
Dialogue is shown using quotation marks.
A new paragraph indicates a different speaker.

Readers to Writers

Dialogue often reveals the thoughts and feelings of a character. It can also help readers analyze conflicts among characters. For example, Paul makes a face after his uncle orders the local food. Paul's mother says, "Don't be critical," and tells him to take a taste. This conflict shows that Paul and his mother start out with different ideas about visiting new places. Think about how you can use dialogue in your own writing.

COLLABORATE

Your Turn Read aloud a line of dialogue in "A Reluctant Traveler." How is the dialogue realistic? What does the line reveal about the character?

Sample answer: When Paul says, "Maybe I could paint my room in soccer team colors," he sounds like a kid who is interested in soccer and is enjoying himself in Buenos Aires.

CHECK IN 1 2 3 4

Unit 3 • Text Set 1 19

Reading/Writing Companion, p. 19

Readers to Writers

Point out how dialogue can help writers create conflicts among characters. Ask students to reread paragraphs 1–2 on page 13,and then paragraphs 3–4 on page 15. Ask: *How does the dialogue between Paul and his aunt help you understand why Paul was unhappy with his parents at the beginning of the story?* Have students consider how they could add dialogue to their writing.

English Language Learners

Use the following scaffolds with **Guided Practice**. For small group support, see the **ELL Small Group Guide**.

Beginning

Review with students that realistic fiction includes dialogue that sounds the way real people speak. Read the last paragraph on page 14 of "A Reluctant Traveler" with students, pointing to the image of the dancers. Then read the first sentence on page 15 with them. Ask: *Does Paul sound like you or one of your friends?* (yes) *What does Paul say is "pretty cool"?* (tango dancers) Have partners discuss what the dialogue tells them about Paul using: The dialogue shows that Paul likes dancing.

Intermediate

Review with students that realistic fiction includes dialogue that sounds the way real people speak. Have partners read the dialogue in the last paragraph on page 14 and the first sentence on page 15 of "A Reluctant Traveler." Ask: *What causes Paul to say "that is pretty cool"?* Paul thinks the tango dancers are cool. *What does this reveal, or show, about Paul?* It shows that Paul likes dancing.

Advanced/Advanced High

Discuss with students how dialogue helps develop the character. Have partners read the dialogue in the last paragraph on page 14 and the first sentence on page 15. Then have them discuss what the dialogue shows about Paul.

FORMATIVE ASSESSMENT

STUDENT CHECK-IN

Ask partners to share their Your Turn responses on Reading/Writing Companion page 19. Have them use the Check-In routine to reflect and fill in the bars.

CHECK FOR SUCCESS

Are students able to identify the characteristics of realistic fiction in the text? Can they explain what the dialogue reveals about the characters?

Small Group Instruction

If No:

- **Approaching** Reteach p. T56

If Yes:

- **On** Review p. T66
- **Beyond** Extend p. T72

LEARNING GOALS

We can read and understand realistic fiction by identifying the theme.

OBJECTIVES

Determine a theme of a story, drama, or poem from details in the text, including how characters in a story or drama respond to challenges or how the speaker in a poem reflects upon a topic; summarize the text.

Come to discussions prepared, having read or studied required material; explicitly draw on that preparation and other information known about the topic to explore ideas under discussion.

ELA ACADEMIC LANGUAGE

- *theme, paraphrase, inference, perspective*
- Cognates: *tema, parafrasear*

DIGITAL TOOLS

To differentiate instruction for key skills, use the results of the activity.

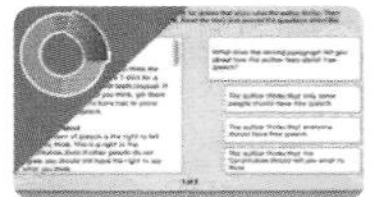

Reread

Theme

1 Explain

Explain to students that a **theme** of a story is an idea or message about life that the author wants to convey to readers.

- A story can have multiple themes and often has one overall theme.
- Remind students that a theme is usually not directly stated; instead, it must be inferred using details about the characters, setting, and plot.
- A character's perspective, or attitude, often leads to the development of a theme. To determine a theme, students should think about what the characters think, say, and do and identify his or her perspective on a conflict, character, or event. Then students should ask themselves what message the author might want to convey to the reader through the character.

Anchor Chart Have a volunteer add to the theme anchor chart.

2 Model

Identify key events in the first paragraph on **Reading/Writing Companion** page 13, such as what characters do and say. (looking from his bedroom window; "I think packing winter clothes in August is weird.") Then read aloud the second paragraph and point out that readers discover what is about to happen to Paul: his family is going to Argentina. Model completing the graphic organizer to identify what Paul thinks, does, and says. Then discuss the impact that traveling to Argentina has on Paul's perspective and on the message the author wants to share with readers.

3 Guided Practice

Have students work in pairs to complete their graphic organizers by recording the most important things Paul thinks, does, and says and then determine his perspective. Discuss each section as students complete their organizers. Remind them to use all of the information they identify to determine the story's theme.

Write About Reading: Summarize Ask pairs of students to work together to summarize the events of "A Reluctant Traveler." Select pairs to share their summaries with the class.

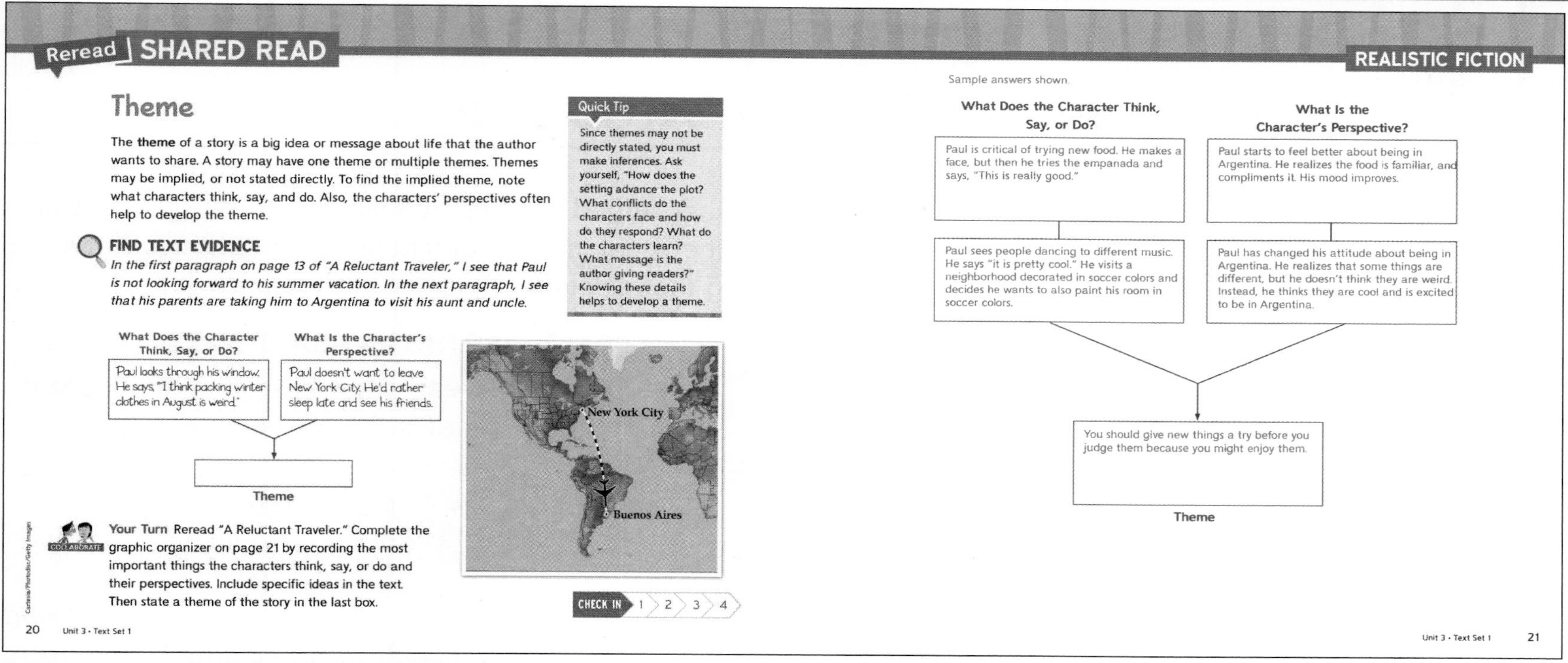
Reread | SHARED READ

REALISTIC FICTION

Theme

The **theme** of a story is a big idea or message about life that the author wants to share. A story may have one theme or multiple themes. Themes may be implied, or not stated directly. To find the implied theme, note what characters think, say, and do. Also, the characters' perspectives often help to develop the theme.

Quick Tip
Since themes may not be directly stated, you must make inferences. Ask yourself, "How does the setting advance the plot? What conflicts do the characters face and how do they respond? What do the characters learn? What message is the author giving readers?" Knowing these details helps to develop a theme.

FIND TEXT EVIDENCE
In the first paragraph on page 13 of "A Reluctant Traveler," I see that Paul is not looking forward to his summer vacation. In the next paragraph, I see that his parents are taking him to Argentina to visit his aunt and uncle.

What Does the Character Think, Say, or Do?	What Is the Character's Perspective?
Paul looks through his window. He says, "I think packing winter clothes in August is weird."	Paul doesn't want to leave New York City. He'd rather sleep late and see his friends.

Theme

COLLABORATE Your Turn Reread "A Reluctant Traveler." Complete the graphic organizer on page 21 by recording the most important things the characters think, say, or do and their perspectives. Include specific ideas in the text. Then state a theme of the story in the last box.

CHECK IN 1 2 3 4

Sample answers shown.

What Does the Character Think, Say, or Do?	What Is the Character's Perspective?
Paul is critical of trying new food. He makes a face, but then he tries the empanada and says, "This is really good."	Paul starts to feel better about being in Argentina. He realizes the food is familiar, and compliments it. His mood improves.
Paul sees people dancing to different music. He says "it is pretty cool." He visits a neighborhood decorated in soccer colors and decides he wants to also paint his room in soccer colors.	Paul has changed his attitude about being in Argentina. He realizes that some things are different, but he doesn't think they are weird. Instead, he thinks they are cool and is excited to be in Argentina.

You should give new things a try before you judge them because you might enjoy them.

Theme

20 Unit 3 • Text Set 1

Unit 3 • Text Set 1 21

Reading/Writing Companion, pp. 20–21

English Language Learners

Use the following scaffolds with **Guided Practice**. For small group support, see the **ELL Small Group Guide**.

Beginning

Review with students how they can determine the theme of a story. Help partners describe what Paul thinks, does, and says during his trip in Argentina to determine his perspective: When he eats the food in Argentina, he says it is really good. Later, Paul says the tango dancers are cool. Ask: *Does Paul enjoy experiencing new things in Argentina?* (yes) Then have partners discuss the theme using: The story's theme is trying new things can be fun.

Intermediate

Review with students how they can determine the theme of a story. Have partners determine Paul's perspective by describing what he thinks, does, and says during his trip in Argentina: When he eats the food in Argentina, he says it is really good. Later, Paul says the tango dancers are cool. Paul enjoys experiencing new things in Argentina. Then have partner discuss the theme using: The story's theme is ____.

Advanced/Advanced High

Discuss with students how to determine the theme of a story. Have pairs use the text to help them describe Paul's perspective about his experiences in Argentina. Then have them discuss the story's theme.

FORMATIVE ASSESSMENT

STUDENT CHECK-IN

Ask partners to share their graphic organizers on Reading/Writing Companion page 21. Have them use the Check-In routine to reflect and fill in the bars.

CHECK FOR SUCCESS

Rubric Use your online rubric to record student progress.

Are students able to identify and record the important things the characters think, do and say and then determine the character's perspective in the graphic organizer? Can they identify a theme in the story?

Small Group Instruction

If No:

- **Approaching** Reteach p. T63

If Yes:

- **On** Review p. T69
- **Beyond** Extend p. T75

Reread

Craft and Structure

LEARNING GOALS

We can reread to analyze craft and structure in realistic fiction.

OBJECTIVES

Quote accurately from a text when explaining what the text says explicitly and when drawing inferences from the text.

Analyze how visual and multimedia elements contribute to the meaning, tone, or beauty of a text (e.g., graphic novel, multimedia presentation of fiction, folktale, myth, poem).

ELA ACADEMIC LANGUAGE

- *author's craft, analyze, technique, conflict*
- Cognates: *analizar, técnica, conflicto*

TEACH IN SMALL GROUP

- **Approaching Level** Use the scaffolded prompts to guide students as they reread "A Reluctant Traveler" and cite evidence for their Reread responses.
- **On Level** Guide partners in completing the Reread prompts and sharing their answers.
- **Beyond Level** Allow pairs to work independently to answer the Reread prompts.
- **ELL** Have Beginning and Early-Intermediate ELLs use the **Scaffolded Shared Read**.

Tell students that as they reread parts of "A Reluctant Traveler," they will look more closely at the visual features and analyze the techniques the author used in writing the selection.

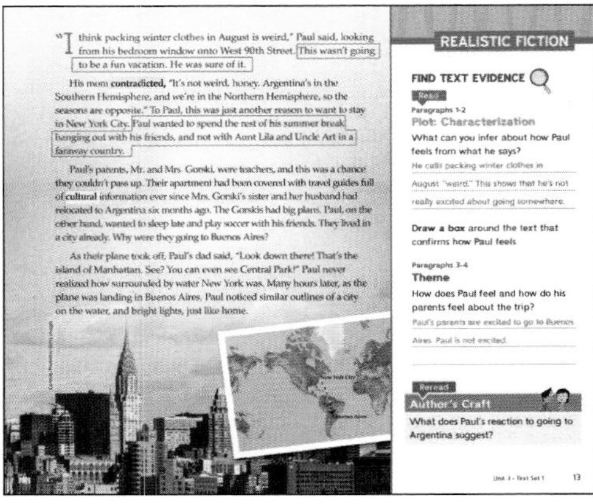

"I think packing winter clothes in August is weird," Paul said, looking from his bedroom window onto West 90th Street. This wasn't going to be a fun vacation. He was sure of it.

His mom **contradicted**, "It's not weird, honey. Argentina's in the Southern Hemisphere, and we're in the Northern Hemisphere, so the seasons are opposite." To Paul, this was just another reason to want to stay in New York City. Paul wanted to spend the rest of his summer break hanging out with his friends, and not with Aunt Lila and Uncle Art in a faraway country.

Paul's parents, Mr. and Mrs. Gorski, were teachers, and this was a chance they couldn't pass up. Their apartment had been covered with travel guides full of **cultural** information ever since Mrs. Gorski's sister and her husband had relocated to Argentina six months ago. The Gorskis had big plans. Paul, on the other hand, wanted to sleep late and play soccer with his friends. They lived in a city already. Why were they going to Buenos Aires?

As their plane took off, Paul's dad said, "Look down there! That's the island of Manhattan. See? You can even see Central Park!" Paul never realized how surrounded by water New York was. Many hours later, as the plane was landing in Buenos Aires, Paul noticed similar outlines of a city on the water, and bright lights, just like home.

REALISTIC FICTION

FIND TEXT EVIDENCE

Paragraphs 1-2

Plot: Characterization

What can you infer about how Paul feels from what he says?

He calls packing winter clothes in August "weird." This shows that he's not really excited about going somewhere.

Draw a box around the text that confirms how Paul feels.

Paragraphs 3-4

Theme

How does Paul feel and how do his parents feel about the trip?

Paul's parents are excited to go to Buenos Aires. Paul is not excited.

Reread

Author's Craft

What does Paul's reaction to going to Argentina suggest?

Unit 3 • Text Set 1 13

Reading/Writing Companion p. 13

AUTHOR'S CRAFT DOK 3

Reread page 13 with students. Ask: *What is the conflict in this story?* (Paul has to go to Argentina with his parents even though he doesn't want to. He would rather stay in New York City, sleep late, and hang out with his friends or play soccer.) *What kind of mood does this create?* (It creates a negative mood.)

ELL *How many cities are labeled on the map?* (two) *Which city is Paul's home? Point to it as you say the name.* (New York City) *Now point to and say the name of the city Paul will visit.* (Buenos Aires) *Why are the two cities connected with a striped line with an airplane on it?* (The line shows the path of the airplane from New York City to Buenos Aires.)

What does Paul's reaction to going to Argentina suggest? (Paul's negative attitude suggests that he is not open to new experiences, and that he is only considering himself and what he wants.)

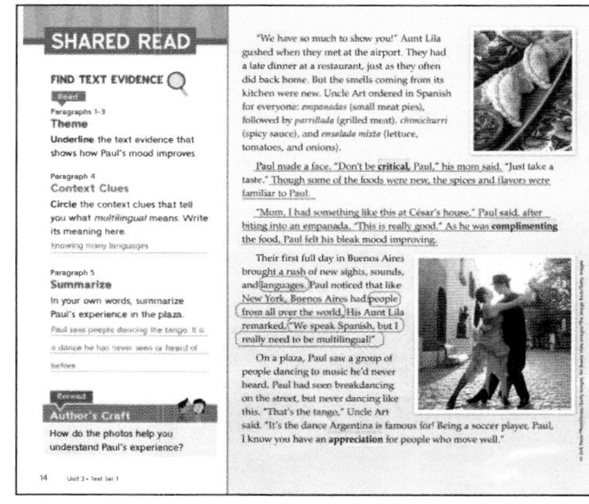

SHARED READ

FIND TEXT EVIDENCE

Read

Paragraphs 1-3

Theme

Underline the text evidence that shows how Paul's mood improves.

Paragraph 4

Context Clues

Circle the context clues that tell you what *multilingual* means. Write its meaning here.

knowing many languages

Paragraph 5

Summarize

In your own words, summarize Paul's experience in the plaza.

Paul sees people dancing the tango. It is a dance he has never seen or heard of before.

Reread

Author's Craft

How do the photos help you understand Paul's experience?

14 Unit 3 • Text Set 1

"We have so much to show you!" Aunt Lila gushed when they met at the airport. They had a late dinner at a restaurant, just as they often did back home. But the smells coming from its kitchen were new. Uncle Art ordered in Spanish for everyone: *empanadas* (small meat pies), followed by *parrillada* (grilled meat), *chimichurri* (spicy sauce), and *ensalada mixta* (lettuce, tomatoes, and onions).

Paul made a face. "Don't be **critical**, Paul," his mom said. "Just take a taste." Though some of the foods were new, the spices and flavors were familiar to Paul.

"Mom, I had something like this at César's house," Paul said, after biting into an empanada. "This is really good." As he was **complimenting** the food, Paul felt his bleak mood improving.

Their first full day in Buenos Aires brought a rush of new sights, sounds, and languages. Paul noticed that like New York, Buenos Aires had people from all over the world. His Aunt Lila remarked, "We speak Spanish, but I really need to be multilingual!"

On a plaza, Paul saw a group of people dancing to music he'd never heard. Paul had seen breakdancing on the street, but never dancing like this. "That's the tango," Uncle Art said. "It's the dance Argentina is famous for! Being a soccer player, Paul, I know you have an **appreciation** for people who move well."

Reading/Writing Companion p. 14

AUTHOR'S CRAFT DOK 2

Reread page 14 with students and look at the two photographs. Ask: *What details from Paul's experience do these photographs show?* (The photo at the top shows *empanadas* like the one Paul tried and liked. The photo on the bottom shows a couple dancing the tango, just like the people Paul saw at the plaza.)

ELL Reread the first and last paragraphs on page 14 aloud. As you read, have students point to the photograph that shows what is being talked about. Ask follow-up questions such as: *What do you see in this photograph?* (empanadas/a couple dancing the tango) *Why are these things important to the story?* (It is a new food Paul tries and likes./It is a new dance Paul sees and enjoys.)

How do the photos help you understand Paul's experience? (The photos help me see what empanadas and dancing the tango look like. The author doesn't describe what these things look like, so seeing pictures allows me to better understand what Paul is seeing in Argentina.)

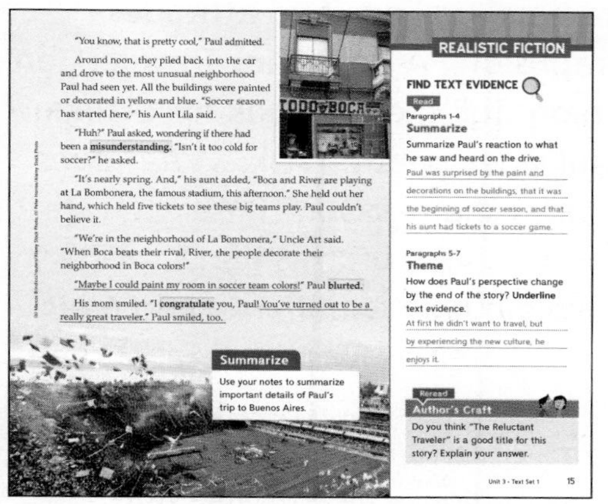

"You know, that is pretty cool," Paul admitted.

Around noon, they piled back into the car and drove to the most unusual neighborhood Paul had seen yet. All the buildings were painted or decorated in yellow and blue. "Soccer season has started here," his Aunt Lila said.

"Huh?" Paul asked, wondering if there had been a **misunderstanding.** "Isn't it too cold for soccer?" he asked.

"It's nearly spring. And," his aunt added, "Boca and River are playing at La Bombonera, the famous stadium, this afternoon." She held out her hand, which held five tickets to see these big teams play. Paul couldn't believe it.

"We're in the neighborhood of La Bombonera," Uncle Art said. "When Boca beats their rival, River, the people decorate their neighborhood in Boca colors!"

"Maybe I could paint my room in soccer team colors!" Paul **blurted.**

His mom smiled. "I **congratulate** you, Paul! You've turned out to be a really great traveler." Paul smiled, too.

Summarize

Use your notes to summarize important details of Paul's trip to Buenos Aires.

REALISTIC FICTION

FIND TEXT EVIDENCE

Read

Paragraphs 1-4

Summarize

Summarize Paul's reaction to what he saw and heard on the drive.

Paul was surprised by the paint and decorations on the buildings, that it was the beginning of soccer season, and that his aunt had tickets to a soccer game.

Paragraphs 5-7

Theme

How does Paul's perspective change by the end of the story? **Underline** text evidence.

At first he didn't want to travel, but by experiencing the new culture, he enjoys it.

Reread

Author's Craft

Do you think "The Reluctant Traveler" is a good title for this story? Explain your answer.

Unit 3 • Text Set 1 15

Reading/Writing Companion p. 15

AUTHOR'S CRAFT DOK 2

Reread the first line of dialogue on page 15. Ask: *What words and phrases tell you that Paul's feelings about the trip are changing?* (The text says that Paul "admitted" that he liked the tango dancing. This makes me think that he didn't expect to like it and was surprised to find that he did.)

ELL *Does Paul like watching the tango dancers?* (Yes.) *Which words tell you that?* (*pretty cool* and *admitted*) *Think back to earlier in the story. Did Paul want to go on the trip?* (No.) *What does that make you think about how Paul feels now?* (He is now enjoying the trip.)

Do you think "The Reluctant Traveler" is a good title for this story? Explain your answer. (Possible response: I think it is a good title for the story because at first Paul was reluctant about leaving New York City and traveling to Argentina. The author explains that he feels this way because he didn't want to leave his friends. Then the author shows that experiencing the culture changes Paul's perspective and makes him stop being a reluctant traveler.)

SYNTHESIZE INFORMATION

Explain that when you synthesize information, you connect ideas in the text in order to create a new understanding. Doing this can help you monitor your own understanding of the important ideas and themes in the text.

Think Aloud In the beginning of "The Reluctant Traveler," I read that Paul did not want to go on the trip. Then while he was on the trip, I read about his positive responses to the things he saw, heard, and ate. I watched him change his perspective from a reluctant traveler to an appreciative traveler who was interested in learning about another culture.

Integrate

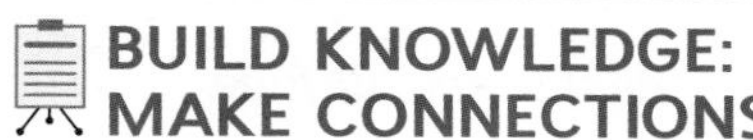

BUILD KNOWLEDGE: MAKE CONNECTIONS

Talk About the Text Have partners discuss how Paul learned to appreciate a different culture.

Write About the Text Have students add their ideas to their Build Knowledge pages of their reader's notebooks.

Anchor Chart Record any new ideas on the Build Knowledge anchor chart.

Add to the Vocabulary List Have students write down any words they learned about experiencing different cultures in their reader's notebooks.

FORMATIVE ASSESSMENT

STUDENT CHECK-IN

Have partners share their responses to one of the Reread prompts on Reading/Writing Companion pages 13-15. Ask them to reflect using the Check-In routine.

Reread

Write About the Shared Read

LEARNING GOALS

We can use text evidence to respond to realistic fiction.

OBJECTIVES

Quote accurately from a text when explaining what the text says explicitly and when drawing inferences from the text.

Explain different characters' perspectives in a literary text.

Determine a theme of a story, drama, or poem from details in the text, including how characters in a story or drama respond to challenges or how the speaker in a poem reflects upon a topic; summarize the text.

ELA ACADEMIC LANGUAGE

- *dialogue, characters, attitude, perspective*
- Cognates: *diálogo, actitud, perspectiva*

TEACH IN SMALL GROUP

Approaching Level Use a graphic organizer to gather and record text evidence students can use to complete the response to the prompt.

On Level Have partners discuss their approaches to the prompt and then write their responses independently.

Beyond Level Have students write their responses independently. Have partners review them and make suggestions for revisions.

ELL Group students of mixed proficiency levels to discuss and respond to the prompt.

Analyze the Prompt DOK 3

Read the prompt aloud: *What does the author want readers to understand about Paul by describing his experience from beginning to end?* Ask: *What is the prompt asking?* (to describe what Paul's experience shows about him) Say: *Let's read to see how the author uses dialogue and descriptions of what Paul thinks, says, and does to reveal his perspective and show how he changed. This will help us make inferences to answer the prompt.*

Analyze Text Evidence

Remind students that dialogue helps the reader know what the characters are thinking and feeling. Descriptions of what the characters think, say, and do help readers understand the characters' feelings and attitudes. Have students reread the first two paragraphs of "A Reluctant Traveler" on page 13 of the **Reading/Writing Companion**. Tell them to look for dialogue and details that help them understand Paul's perspective. Ask: *What does Paul say to his mom about the trip? How does she respond?* (Paul says that packing winter clothes in August is weird. His mom informs him that it's wintertime in Argentina.) *What details explain how Paul thinks and feels about the trip?* (In the first paragraph, the author states that Paul is sure the vacation is not going to be fun. In the second paragraph, the author states that Paul would rather hang out with his friends during the summer.) Have students continue to look for dialogue and details that describe Paul's attitude throughout the story. Tell them to note when and how his attitude changes.

Respond

Direct pairs to the sentence starters on Reading/Writing Companion page 22. Ask: *How does reviewing the dialogue at different points in the story help you understand how Paul's perspective changed? How do Paul's actions at different points in the story indicate a change?* As needed, model a response.

Think Aloud The author opens the story with Paul saying that things about the trip are "weird," so I know that he's not very excited to go. It doesn't seem like he's changed yet as shown on page 14 when he "makes a face" about trying a new food. But once he tries the empanada, he finds that he likes it, and his "bleak mood" improves. This makes me think he is starting to change his attitude about Buenos Aires and what it's like.

Analytical Writing Students should use the sentence starters to form their responses. They should clearly explain how the author's use of dialogue and details helps them see the changes in Paul's perspective. Students may continue their responses on a separate piece of paper.

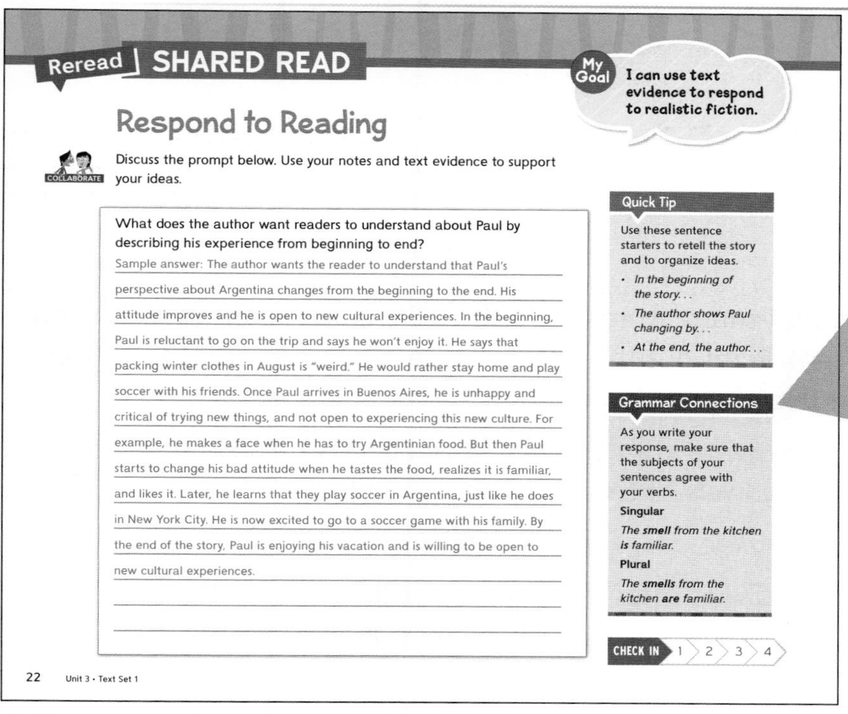

Reread | SHARED READ

My Goal: I can use text evidence to respond to realistic fiction.

Respond to Reading

COLLABORATE: Discuss the prompt below. Use your notes and text evidence to support your ideas.

What does the author want readers to understand about Paul by describing his experience from beginning to end?

Sample answer: The author wants the reader to understand that Paul's perspective about Argentina changes from the beginning to the end. His attitude improves and he is open to new cultural experiences. In the beginning, Paul is reluctant to go on the trip and says he won't enjoy it. He says that packing winter clothes in August is "weird." He would rather stay home and play soccer with his friends. Once Paul arrives in Buenos Aires, he is unhappy and critical of trying new things, and not open to experiencing this new culture. For example, he makes a face when he has to try Argentinian food. But then Paul starts to change his bad attitude when he tastes the food, realizes it is familiar, and likes it. Later, he learns that they play soccer in Argentina, just like he does in New York City. He is now excited to go to a soccer game with his family. By the end of the story, Paul is enjoying his vacation and is willing to be open to new cultural experiences.

Quick Tip

Use these sentence starters to retell the story and to organize ideas.

- *In the beginning of the story. . .*
- *The author shows Paul changing by. . .*
- *At the end, the author. . .*

Grammar Connections

As you write your response, make sure that the subjects of your sentences agree with your verbs.

Singular

*The **smell** from the kitchen **is** familiar.*

Plural

*The **smells** from the kitchen **are** familiar.*

CHECK IN 1 2 3 4

22 Unit 3 • Text Set 1

Grammar Connections

Student can use online **Grammar Handbook** page 459 to review and practice using subject-verb agreement.

Reading/Writing Companion, p. 22

English Language Learners

Use the following scaffolds with **Respond**.

Beginning

Read the prompt with students and discuss what they will write about. Review the meaning of *perspective* with students. Point out the dialogue on pages 14–15 to students. Ask: *Does Paul's perspective about Argentina change from the beginning to the end?* (yes) Help partners discuss Paul's experience from beginning to end using: Paul is not excited to go to Argentina in the beginning. Paul enjoys his time in Argentina in the end.

Intermediate

Read the prompt with students and discuss what they will write about. Have partners reread the dialogue on pages 14–15. Ask: *How does Paul feel about his trip to Argentina in the beginning?* Paul is not excited to go on the trip. *In the end?* Paul enjoys his time in Argentina. Then have partners discuss what Paul's experience shows about him and respond using: Paul's experience shows that his perspective about Argentina changes from the beginning to the end.

Advanced/Advanced High

Review the prompt and sentence starters on page 22 with students. Have partners discuss how Paul's perspective about Argentina changes from beginning to the end. Then have them write their responses using the sentence starters.

NEWCOMERS

Have students listen to summaries of the **Shared Read** in their native language and then in English to help them access the text and develop listening comprehension. Help students ask and answer questions with a partner. Use these sentence frames: How does Paul feel at the beginning of the story? Paul feels ____. Then continue the lessons in the **Newcomer Teacher's Guide**.

FORMATIVE ASSESSMENT

STUDENT CHECK-IN

Ask partners to share their response on Reading/Writing Companion page 22. Have them use the Check-In routine to reflect and fill in the bars.

LEARNING GOALS

- **We can decode words with open syllables.**
- **We can identify and read multisyllabic words.**
- **We can read fluently with intonation.**

OBJECTIVES

Use combined knowledge of all letter-sound correspondences, syllabication patterns, and morphology (e.g., roots and affixes) to read accurately unfamiliar multisyllabic words in context and out of context.

Read grade-level prose and poetry orally with accuracy, appropriate rate, expression, and automaticity on successive readings.

- Rate: 123–143 WCPM

ELA ACADEMIC LANGUAGE

- *syllable, intonation*
- Cognate: *entonación*

TEACH IN SMALL GROUP

Phonics

Approaching Level Use Tier 2 activity on page T58 before teaching the lesson.

On Level As needed, use the Guided Practice section.

Beyond Level As needed, use the Multisyllabic Words section only.

ELL See page 5 in **Language Transfers Handbook** for guidance in identifying sounds and symbols that may not transfer for speakers of certain languages, and support in accommodating those students.

Open Syllables

1 Explain

Tell students that many words have the VCV (vowel-consonant-vowel) syllable pattern. Point out that the syllables in words with this pattern can divide in two ways.

- Syllables can divide after the first vowel (V/CV). These syllables, which end in vowels, are called open syllables.

  bro as in ***broken*** **ra** as in ***radio***

- Syllables can divide after the consonant that follows the first vowel (VC/V). These syllables, which end in consonants, are called closed syllables.

  cab as in ***cabin*** **pan** as in ***panic***

Point out that in open syllables, the vowel sound is usually long. In closed syllables, the vowel sound is usually short.

2 Model

Write the following words on the board. Underline the open syllables. Then model reading the words aloud as you run your finger under the letters in the open syllable.

demand silence profile recent

3 Guided Practice

Write the following syllables and words on the board. Point to the first syllable and word pair. Pronounce both the word part and the word, drawing students' attention to which VCV pattern appears. Emphasize whether the vowel sound is long or short. Have students chorally read the syllables and words.

be	begin	*mi*	minus
mo	motor	*so*	solo
shiv	shiver	*lo*	local

For practice with decoding words with open syllables, use **Practice Book** page 127 or online activities.

Read Multisyllabic Words

Transition to Longer Words Write the following words and word parts on the board. Read aloud the word part in the first column, and identify the first vowel sound as long or short. Then divide the word in the second column into syllables by drawing a slash between them. Have students chorally read each word in the second column. Finally, draw students' attention to the longer word in the third column. Model isolating the VCV syllable pattern in the longer word. Stress that the pattern in the longer word is the same as that in the shorter word in the second column.

la	lazy	laziness
o	over	overcoming
hu	humor	humorous
pho	photo	photography
ro	robot	robotics
pun	punish	punishment

Fluency

Intonation

Explain/Model Remind students that using intonation helps to bring a story to life, and it also helps students better understand and enjoy what they read. Model varying your tone as you read aloud the first two pages of "A Reluctant Traveler," **Reading/Writing Companion** pages 13–14. Change your intonation as you read the dialogue for each new speaker. Remind students that you will be listening for their use of intonation as you monitor their reading during the week.

Practice/Apply Have partners alternate reading paragraphs in the passage, modeling the intonation you used.

Daily Fluency Practice

Automaticity Students can practice reading with accuracy and appropriate rate to develop automaticity using the online **Differentiated Genre Passage**, "Potluck or Potlatch?"

DIGITAL TOOLS

For more practice, use the phonics and fluency activities.

Open Syllables

MULTIMODAL LEARNING

Have students read **Differentiated Genre Passage** "Potluck or Potlatch" and underline sentences that end in a question mark or exclamation point. In pairs, have students take turns reading sections of the passage. Ask students to follow along with their fingers as their partner reads. Remind them that the underlined sentences should be read with expression to convey meaning and the character's emotion.

FORMATIVE ASSESSMENT

STUDENT CHECK-IN

Open Syllables Have partners share three words with open syllables.

Multisyllabic Words Have partners isolate the VCV pattern in three multisyllabic words.

Fluency Have partners read "Potluck or Potlatch?" fluently.

Have partners reflect using the Check-In routine.

CHECK FOR SUCCESS

Can students identify VCV syllable patterns in words? Can they decode words with open syllables? Can students read with intonation?

Small Group Instruction

If No

- **Approaching** Reteach pp. T58, T62
- **ELL** Develop p. T58

If Yes

- **On** Apply p. T64
- **Beyond** Apply p. T70

LEARNING GOALS

- **We can use the research process to make a pamphlet.**
- **We can use an outline to narrow a topic and organize information.**

OBJECTIVES

Analyze multiple accounts of the same event or topic, noting important similarities and differences in the point of view they represent.

Integrate information from several texts on the same topic in order to write or speak about the subject knowledgeably.

Recall relevant information from experiences or gather relevant information from print and digital sources; summarize or paraphrase information in notes and finished work, and provide a list of sources.

Come to discussions prepared, having read or studied required material; explicitly draw on that preparation and other information known about the topic to explore ideas under discussion.

Produce clear and coherent writing in which the development and organization are appropriate to task, purpose, and audience.

Draw evidence from literary or informational texts to support analysis, reflection, and research.

Apply grade 5 Reading standards to informational texts.

ELA ACADEMIC LANGUAGE

- *research, sources, pamphlet, outline*

TEACH IN SMALL GROUP

You may wish to teach the Research and Inquiry lesson during Small Group time. Have groups of mixed abilities complete the page and work on the pamphlet.

Integrate

Learning About Different Cultures

Explain to students that in many countries, people of different cultures have their own customs and traditions and celebrate events differently. Tell students that for the next two weeks they will work with a partner to research one group of people and its celebrations, customs, and traditions. They will create a pamphlet that presents and summarizes the information they gathered about their particular group's customs, traditions, and celebrations. Note the following in regards to pamphlets:

- Readers may be unfamiliar with the culture you are presenting, so it is important to begin your pamphlet with some background information.
- The purpose of a pamphlet is both to inform and to persuade. The pamphlet should encourage readers to want to experience for themselves the celebrations and traditions of the cultural group.
- It is a good idea to provide lots of labels and visual imagery, such as photographs and maps, so that readers can picture the culture. Use sensitivity and be sure that any visuals are accurately representative.

Outline Information Point out the partial outline of a pamphlet on page 23 of the **Reading/Writing Companion** to show how the student categorized her information to help focus her research. Support them as they go through each step in the Research Process as outlined on page 23.

STEP 1 **Set Research Goals** Explain some of the ways groups of people and their customs, traditions, and celebrations vary—size, features, locations, etc. Tell groups to consider these factors as they decide on which cultural group they would like to research. Offer feedback as students generate questions and decide what information to include in their pamphlets. Have students use an **Accordion Book Foldable®**, available online, to take notes.

STEP 2 **Identify Sources** Brainstorm with groups the kinds of digital and print resources they can use for their research. Students may want to include source material from print sources, websites, or people with unique knowledge of their chosen cultural group. Remind them to use valid sources for a formal inquiry. For an informal inquiry, ask and clarify questions.

STEP 3 **Find and Record Information** Review with students how to take notes and cite the sources they use to gather information for their pamphlet.

STEP 4 **Organize and Synthesize Information** Show students how to narrow topics and organize information into an outline. Then guide them in discussing what visuals and labels they will include in their pamphlets.

STEP 5 **Create and Present** Review with students the features they should include in their pamphlets. Discuss options for presenting their work. Model how to present their information on a cultural group's celebrations, customs, and traditions.

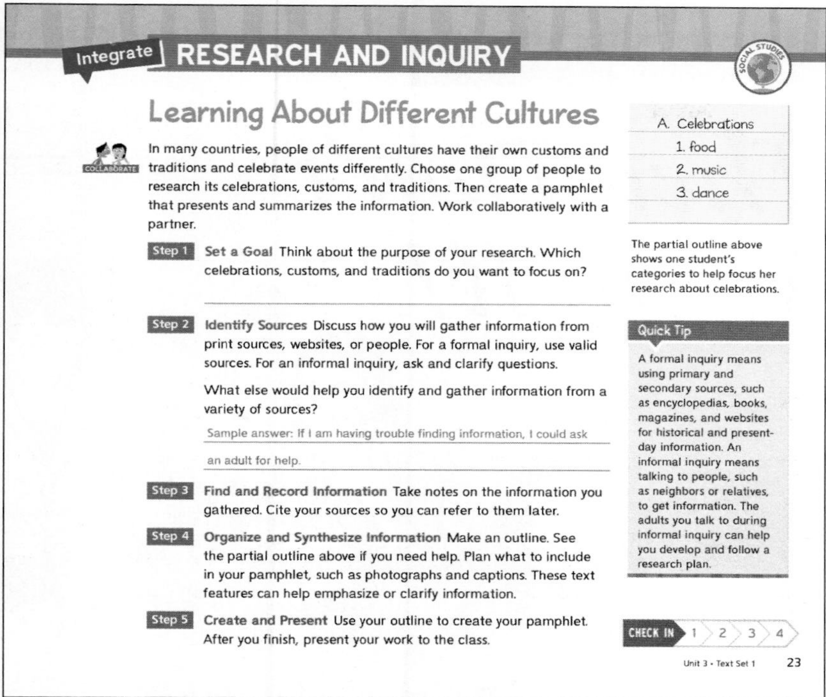

Integrate | RESEARCH AND INQUIRY

Learning About Different Cultures

In many countries, people of different cultures have their own customs and traditions and celebrate events differently. Choose one group of people to research its celebrations, customs, and traditions. Then create a pamphlet that presents and summarizes the information. Work collaboratively with a partner.

A. Celebrations
1. food
2. music
3. dance

The partial outline above shows one student's categories to help focus her research about celebrations.

Step 1 **Set a Goal** Think about the purpose of your research. Which celebrations, customs, and traditions do you want to focus on?

Step 2 **Identify Sources** Discuss how you will gather information from print sources, websites, or people. For a formal inquiry, use valid sources. For an informal inquiry, ask and clarify questions.

What else would help you identify and gather information from a variety of sources?

Sample answer: If I am having trouble finding information, I could ask an adult for help.

Step 3 **Find and Record Information** Take notes on the information you gathered. Cite your sources so you can refer to them later.

Step 4 **Organize and Synthesize Information** Make an outline. See the partial outline above if you need help. Plan what to include in your pamphlet, such as photographs and captions. These text features can help emphasize or clarify information.

Step 5 **Create and Present** Use your outline to create your pamphlet. After you finish, present your work to the class.

Quick Tip

A formal inquiry means using primary and secondary sources, such as encyclopedias, books, magazines, and websites for historical and present-day information. An informal inquiry means talking to people, such as neighbors or relatives, to get information. The adults you talk to during informal inquiry can help you develop and follow a research plan.

CHECK IN 1 2 3 4

Unit 3 • Text Set 1 23

Reading/Writing Companion, p. 23

English Language Learners

Use the following scaffold with **Step 4**.

Beginning

Review the features of a pamphlet with students. Point out the partial outline of a pamphlet on page 23 and model how to organize information into an outline. Help partners organize their information into an outline. Review their outlines and provide feedback. Then help partners discuss what visuals and labels they will include in their pamphlets using: I will include a photograph/map of ___. I will include a label for ___.

Intermediate

Review the features of a pamphlet with students. Guide them on how to organize information into an outline using the example on page 23. Have partners organize their information into an outline. Review their outlines and provide feedback. Then have partners discuss what visuals and labels they will include in their pamphlet using: In my pamphlet, I will include photographs/maps to show ___. I will include labels for ___.

Advanced/Advanced High

Have students review the features of a pamphlet. Use the example on page 23 to show them how to organize information into an outline. Then have partners organize their information into an outline and share what visuals and labels they will include in their pamphlet.

DIGITAL TOOLS

RESOURCE TOOLKIT Take Notes: Print; Organizing Notes

Accordion Book Foldable®

FORMATIVE ASSESSMENT

STUDENT CHECK-IN

Pamphlet Ask students to share their pamphlets.

Outline Information Have students share an example of how they used an outline to organize information.

Have students use the Check-In routine to reflect and fill in the bars on Reading/Writing Companion page 23.

They Don't Mean It!

Lexile 870L

LEARNING GOALS

Read **We can apply strategies and skills to read realistic fiction.**

Reread **We can reread to analyze text, craft, and structure and compare texts.**

Have students apply what they learned as they read.

ACT *What makes this text complex?*

- **Prior Knowledge**
- **Specific Vocabulary**
- **Connection of Ideas**
- **Purpose**

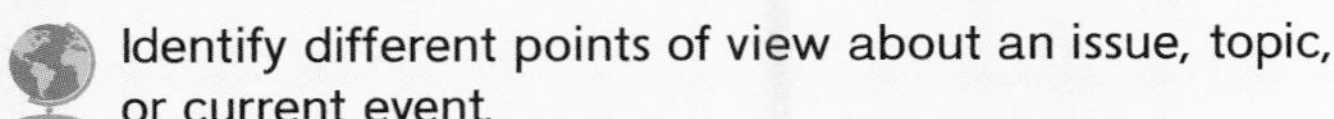

Identify different points of view about an issue, topic, or current event.

Close Reading Routine

Read DOK 1–2

- Identify important ideas and details.
- Take notes and summarize.
- Use ACT prompts as needed.

Reread DOK 2–3

- Analyze the text, craft, and structure.
- Use *Reading/Writing Companion*, pp. 24–26.

Integrate DOK 3–4

- Integrate knowledge and ideas.
- Make text-to-text connections.
- Use the Integrate lesson.
- Complete the Show Your Knowledge task.
- Inspire action.

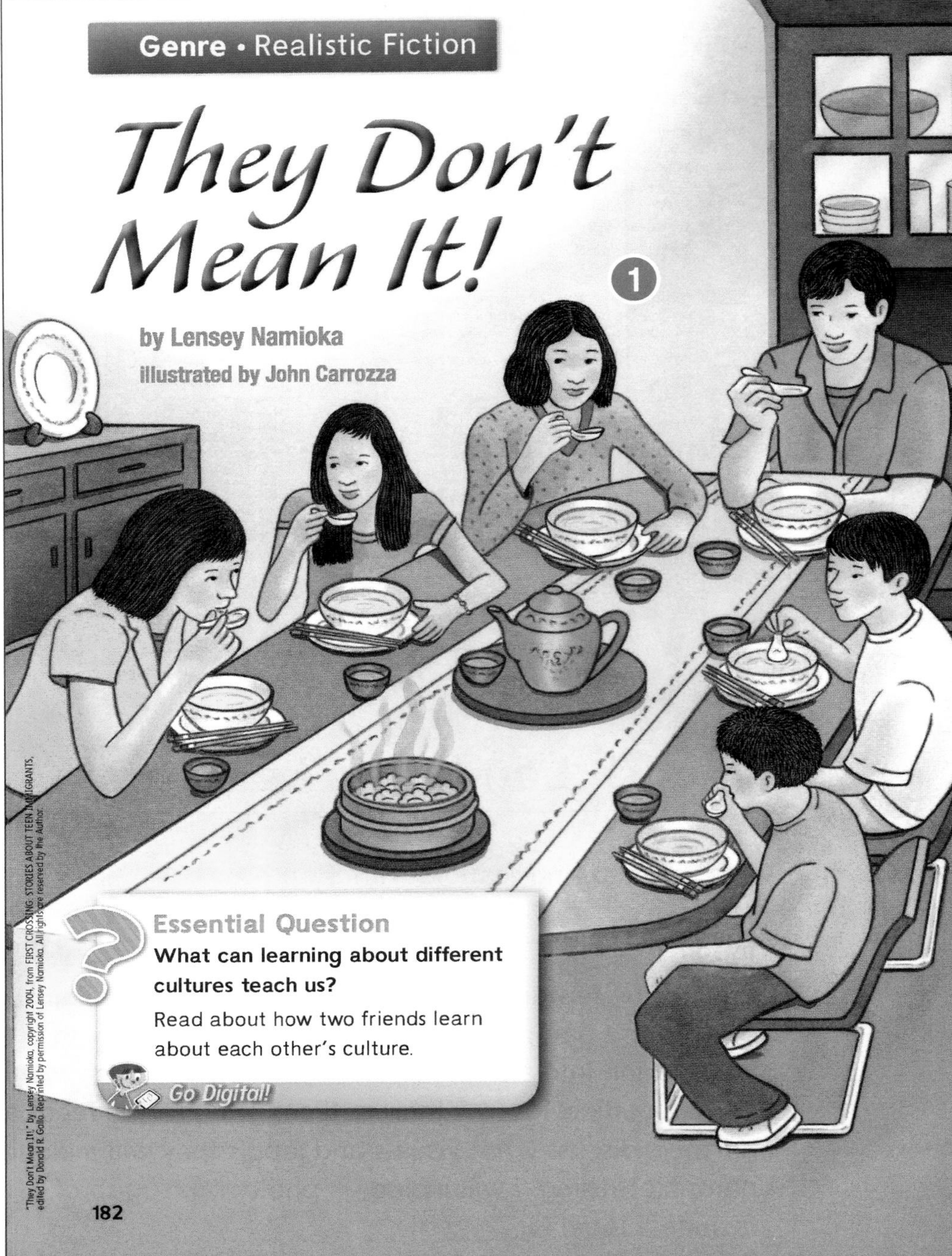

Genre • Realistic Fiction
They Don't Mean It!
1
by Lensey Namioka
illustrated by John Carrozza
Essential Question
What can learning about different cultures teach us?
Read about how two friends learn about each other's culture.
Go Digital!
"They Don't Mean It!," by Lensey Namioka, copyright 2004, from FIRST CROSSING: STORIES ABOUT TEEN IMMIGRANTS, edited by Donald R. Gallo. Reprinted by permission of Lensey Namioka. All rights are reserved by the Author.
182

Literature Anthology, pp. 182–183

DIFFERENTIATED READING

You may wish to read the full selection aloud once with minimal stopping before you use the Read prompts.

Approaching Level Have students listen to the selection summary. Use the Reread prompts during Small-Group time.

On Level and **Beyond Level** Pair students or have them independently complete the Reread prompts on **Reading/ Writing Companion** pages 24–26.

English Language Learners Have ELLs listen to the summary of the selection, available in multiple languages. See also **ELL Small Group Guide.**

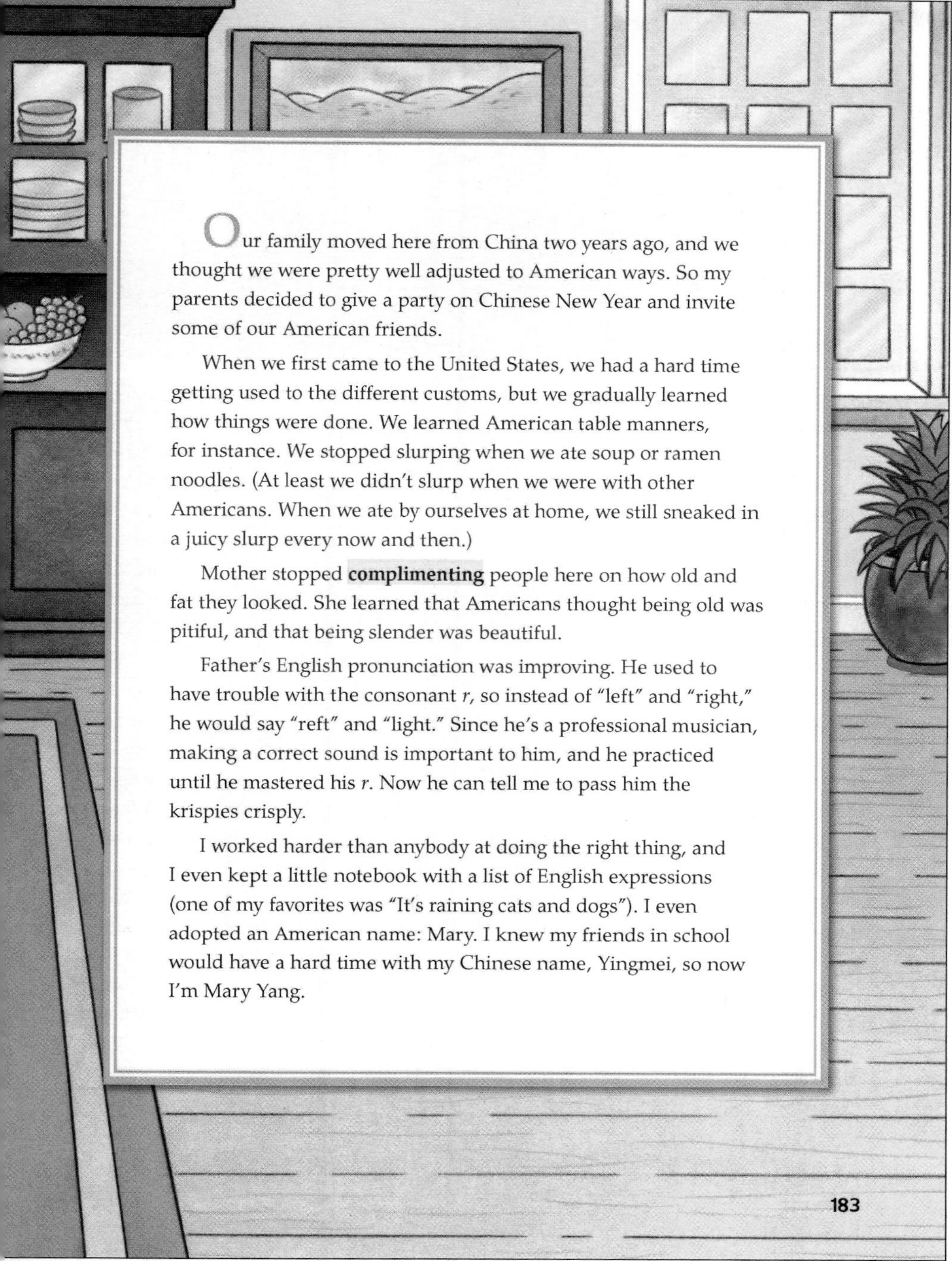

Our family moved here from China two years ago, and we thought we were pretty well adjusted to American ways. So my parents decided to give a party on Chinese New Year and invite some of our American friends.

When we first came to the United States, we had a hard time getting used to the different customs, but we gradually learned how things were done. We learned American table manners, for instance. We stopped slurping when we ate soup or ramen noodles. (At least we didn't slurp when we were with other Americans. When we ate by ourselves at home, we still sneaked in a juicy slurp every now and then.)

Mother stopped **complimenting** people here on how old and fat they looked. She learned that Americans thought being old was pitiful, and that being slender was beautiful.

Father's English pronunciation was improving. He used to have trouble with the consonant *r*, so instead of "left" and "right," he would say "reft" and "light." Since he's a professional musician, making a correct sound is important to him, and he practiced until he mastered his *r*. Now he can tell me to pass him the krispies crisply.

I worked harder than anybody at doing the right thing, and I even kept a little notebook with a list of English expressions (one of my favorites was "It's raining cats and dogs"). I even adopted an American name: Mary. I knew my friends in school would have a hard time with my Chinese name, Yingmei, so now I'm Mary Yang.

183

Read

Set a Purpose Tell students to preview the text and set a purpose for reading. Remind them that setting a purpose can help them monitor their comprehension.

Note Taking: Use the Graphic Organizer

Analytical Writing Remind students to take notes as they read. Distribute copies of online Theme **Graphic Organizer 5**. Have students record the things the characters say and do and what happens to them in each section in the organizer. This information can help them think about the themes of the story.

1 Text Features: Illustration DOK 2

COLLABORATE Look at the illustration on page 182. What is the family doing? How are they feeling? How can you tell? Discuss your answers with a partner. (The illustrations show the family eating and enjoying each other's company.)

Build Vocabulary on page 183

Have students add the Build Vocabulary words to their reader's notebook.

adjusted: used to

gradually: happening little by little

pitiful: causing sorrow or sympathy

ACT Access Complex Text

Prior Knowledge

Explain that people who come from different countries may celebrate different holidays, have different table manners, and have different customs.

- *Reread the second paragraph on page 183. How is eating soup in Chinese culture different than in America?* (It is not uncommon for people in China to slurp soup.)
- *Reread the third paragraph. How are compliments in Chinese culture different?* (It is a compliment to call someone old and fat.)
- Discuss with students other examples of differences in Chinese culture such as the acceptance of holding a rice bowl while eating instead of resting it on the table.

Read

2 Theme DOK 1

On pages 183–185, you learn that the Yang family has made many changes to adjust to American customs, manners, and language. Does Mary feel that her family has adjusted completely? (yes) What does her family decide to do for their American friends? (They invite them to a Chinese New Year celebration.) Add this information to your organizer, and use it to begin thinking about the theme of the story.

What Does the Character Think, Say, and Do?	What is the Character's Perspective?
Mary has made many changes to adjust to American ways. She has worked hard to learn new customs and changed her name.	Mary feels confident about inviting American friends over because of how she and her family have adapted to living in America.

3 Realistic Fiction DOK 2

Reread the third paragraph on page 185. Identify at least two actions or events that show you this story is realistic fiction. (Possible response: Mary and her mother washed and sliced fresh vegetables, and they vacuumed every room.) How are these events examples of realistic fiction? (They could happen in real life. Cooking and cleaning are realistic tasks.)

I really believed that our family had adjusted completely. We had even joined in celebrating American holidays, such as Independence Day, Labor Day, Thanksgiving, Easter, Christmas, and New Year—Western New Year, that is. My
2 parents decided to show our American friends what Chinese New Year was like.

Chinese New Year, which falls in late January or early February, is sometimes called the Lunar New Year because it's based on the phases of the moon. It doesn't always fall on the same day in the solar calendar, but depends on when the first new moon occurs after the winter solstice, or the shortest day of the year. Anyway, in China it's also called the Spring Festival, because by that time you're pretty tired of winter and you're looking forward eagerly to spring.

In China we celebrate the New Year by setting off firecrackers, and we were delighted when we learned that firecrackers were also set off here in Seattle's Chinatown at New Year.

But eating special foods is the most important part of the celebration. So a week before the party, we helped Mother to shop and cook the special New Year dishes. We had to serve fish, since the Chinese word for fish is *yu*, which sounds the same as the word for "surplus." It's good to have a surplus of money and other valuables.

Mother admitted that living in America for two years had made her soft, and she no longer felt like killing a fish with her own hands. These days, she bought dead fish, but she always apologized when she served it to our Chinese guests. When we first came to America, Mother used to keep live fish in the bathtub because that way she knew the fish would be fresh when it came time to cook it. Even for the New Year party, she bought a dead fish, but at least she went to a special store in Chinatown where they had live fish and killed it for you on the spot.

184

Literature Anthology, pp. 184–185

Access Complex Text

Specific Vocabulary

Point out the American holidays the narrator mentions on page 184. Discuss why they are celebrated.

- *How is the Chinese New Year different from the western New Year?* (The Chinese New Year is based on the phases of the moon, whereas the western New Year is always on January 1.)

Point to the words *yu* and *surplus* in paragraph four on page 184. Explain that a surplus is an extra amount of something. *Why do the Yangs serve fish as a special New Year dish?* (The Chinese word for fish, *yu*, sounds the same as the Chinese word for *surplus*. Fish brings luck for extra things, such as money.)

For our New Year dinner we also had to have noodles. We normally eat noodles on birthdays, because the long strands stand for a long life. Why noodles on New Year, then? Because in the old days, instead of having your own special birthday, everybody's birthday was on New Year's Day, no matter what day you were actually born on.

The New Year dish that involves the most work is the ten-vegetable salad. Mother tells us that each of the ten vegetables is supposed to promote health, and eating it on New Year makes you healthy for the whole year. I can understand why some of the vegetables are healthy—things like carrots, bean sprouts, and cabbage, which have lots of vitamins. But the salad also includes things like dried mushrooms and a kind of lichen. When I asked Mother why they were supposed to be healthy, she thought a bit and then admitted that she always included those ingredients because *her* mother and grandmother always included them.

So we got to work. We had to soak the dried ingredients. We had to wash the fresh vegetables and slice them up into thin strips. In addition to all the cooking, we vacuumed every room thoroughly, since we wanted to start the New Year with a really clean house. Mother said that we had to do the cleaning before New Year, because doing it on the day itself was bad luck. It was believed that you'd sweep out good fortune together with the dirt. 3

With all the cooking and the cleaning, I was exhausted by the time our guests arrived at our house for the New Year party.

185

Read

STOP AND CHECK DOK 1

Summarize How does the Yang family adjust to American ways and keep Chinese customs? (The Yangs eat their soup differently when they are at home. Mary changes her name. The family celebrate American holidays but also celebrate Chinese holidays. They cook traditional foods and prepare them the same way their ancestors did. Mother still cooks fish, but she buys them dead instead of live.)

Build Vocabulary on page 185

lichen: an organism made up of a kind of algae and a fungus

Reread

Author's Purpose DOK 2

Reading/Writing Companion, **p. 24**

Reread pages 184–185. How does the author show that Mary's mother does not feel like she is being true to her culture? Cite text evidence in your answer. (Mary's mother "no longer felt like killing a fish with her own hands." She apologized for serving a dead fish, and admits to being soft.) Why is this information important? (Mary's mother is still adjusting to life and the cultural differences in America.)

Evaluate Information DOK 2

Explain: When you evaluate information, you can agree or disagree with it.

Discuss: When someone is "soft," he or she isn't tough anymore. Do you agree that Mother has gone soft about not killing fish with her own hands? (Possible response: Yes; she prefers to buy them already dead.)

Apply: As students continue reading, have them look for additional examples that support their evaluation that Mother is becoming "soft."

ELL Spotlight on Language

Page 185, Paragraph 3 Help students understand the meaning of the phrase *good fortune.* Explain that *good fortune* is the same as *good luck* and is a belief that good things will happen. Have students act out the verb *sweep. What do we usually sweep?* (dirt and dust) *Can you sweep out good fortune?* (no) *According to Mother, why do you have to clean before New Year's?* (cleaning on New Year's day gets rid of good fortune) Have students use the following frame to restate the sentence: If you clean on New Year's day you will throw away your good luck.

Read

4 Theme DOK 1

Turn to a partner and talk about the events on pages 186–187. How does Mary react when her mother says she never makes dessert? (Mary runs to the kitchen and dumps almond cookies on a platter to offer for dessert.) Why does she feel strongly about serving dessert? (She wants to fit in and leave a good impression on her American guests.) Add this information to your organizer.

What Does the Character Think, Say, and Do?	What is the Character's Perspective?
Mary realizes that the American guests will expect dessert, so she hurries to serve cookies.	Mary wants to fit in and leave a good impression on her American guests .

Build Vocabulary on pages 186 and 187

wiggling: moving from side to side in short, sudden movements

buffet: a meal consisting of several dishes from which guests serve themselves

exclaimed: said out loud

complaints: statements that something is wrong

congestion: a very crowded condition

The first of our guests to arrive were the Engs, a Chinese-American family. Paul Eng, their son, was in Eldest Brother's class. Paul and Second Sister were beginning to be interested in each other, although we pretended we didn't notice. I was glad that Second Sister had finally thrown away her Chinese cloth shoes. They had developed big holes, and we could see her toes wiggling around inside. Tonight she was wearing a new pair of sneakers she'd bought with her baby-sitting money.

The O'Mearas arrived next. Kim O'Meara was my best friend in school, and we'd been at each other's house lots of times. The last to arrive were the Conners. My youngest brother's best friend was Matthew Conner, who was a really good violinist and took lessons from my father.

"Happy New Year, Sprout!" Matthew said to Fourth Brother. "Sprout" was my brother's nickname, because for school lunch he used to eat sandwiches filled with stir-fried bean sprouts. Now he eats peanut butter and jelly sandwiches just like his friends, but the nickname stuck.

Because we had too many people to seat around the dining table, we served dinner buffet style, and the guests helped themselves to the food. When they saw all the dishes arranged on the dining table, they exclaimed at how beautiful everything looked.

"Oh, no, it's really plain, simple food," said Mother. "I've only added a few small things for the New Year."

The guests paid no attention to her and began to help themselves. Mrs. Conner wanted to know how Mother had cooked the fish. Mrs. Eng said that she also cooked fish and served noodles on New Year, but she didn't do the ten-vegetable salad. Maybe it wasn't served in the part of China where her family originally came from.

186

Literature Anthology, pp. 186–187

ACT Access Complex Text

Connection of Ideas

Point out the last sentence in the fourth paragraph on page 187. Explain that this sentence connects the reader to the text on page 185 that describes the ingredients in the ten-vegetable salad and why the salad is made.

- *Why does Mary tell the guests that they will be very healthy?* (She tells the guests they will be healthy because they ate the entire ten-vegetable salad. On page 185, the text explained that Mary's mother says that eating the salad on New Year's makes people healthy for the coming year.)

Nobody had complaints about the food, from the way they devoured it and came back for seconds. The kids even ate up the salad. Kim O'Meara laughed when she saw her brother Jason taking a second helping. "Hey, Jason, I thought you hate vegetables!"

Jason's mouth was full, so he just mumbled an answer.

Mrs. O'Meara looked at me and smiled. "I bet you and your mom put a lot of work into making that salad, Mary. Doesn't it hurt to see it disappear in a matter of minutes?"

It *was* a lot of work to make the ten-vegetable salad. I got a blister on my finger from slicing all those celery and carrot sticks. "I'm glad to see how much you people like it," I said. "You'll all be very healthy this coming year!"

Looking at the platters of food getting emptied, I began to worry. "We'd better do something about dessert!" I whispered to Mother. At this rate, our guests would still be hungry after the main courses were finished.

"But I never make dessert!" Mother whispered back. Dessert isn't something Chinese normally eat at the end of a dinner.

So I ran into the kitchen, found a carton of almond cookies, and hurriedly dumped them on a platter. When I put the platter on the dining table, the cookies disappeared before I could say *abracadabra* (*abracadabra* was one of the words in my little notebook).

Since it was a weekday night, people didn't stay long after the last cookie crumb was eaten. There was a congestion at the front door as the guests thanked us for inviting them and showing them what a real Chinese New Year dinner was like.  4

187

Reread

Author's Craft: Word Choice DOK 2

Reread the first sentence on page 187. Why is *devoured* a better word than *ate*? (*Devoured* helps the reader picture how the characters look as they eat. They eat quickly and eagerly without hesitation. It also helps the reader understand how much the guests like the food.)

Author's Craft: Character Perspective DOK 2

Reading/Writing Companion, p. 25

Reread paragraphs 4–6 on page 187. How does the author use dialogue to help you understand Mary's and her mother's different perspectives about American customs? (Possible response: The dialogue helps the reader see that Mary wants to follow American customs and serve dessert. Mary's mother follows Chinese customs and never makes dessert. The author's use of dialogue reveals that Mary is knowledgeable about American customs and that she wants to fit in and be a good hostess to her guests.)

Make Inferences DOK 2

Explain: A character's words and actions can help readers make inferences about what he or she is like.

Model: *Mary doesn't tell Mrs. O'Meara how much work it is to make the salad. When people don't talk about their hard work, they are often being humble. I can infer that Mary is a humble person.*

Apply: As students read pages 188–189, ask: *Why doesn't Mary get angry at her parents for what they said? What inference can you make about Mary?* (Mary is not hurt by her parents' behavior because she understands that they do not like to brag.)

ELL English Language Learners

Non-verbal cues Remind students that they can use non-verbal cues to share information when they are not able to do so verbally. Encourage students to use sounds and gestures. For example, students may use non-verbal cues to demonstrate the meaning of *come back for seconds, mumble, slicing, whispered,* or *dumped.*

Read

5 Make Inferences DOK 2

COLLABORATE Why does Kim gasp and stare at Mary's father and mother? (Kim thinks that Mary's father was being nasty to Mary's mother because he said that she isn't a good cook. She also thinks that Mary's mother was being nasty to Mary because she said the girls did a terrible job slicing the vegetables.)

6 Theme DOK 1

COLLABORATE Turn to a partner and talk about Father's comments about his wife's cooking and Mother's comments about Mary's cut vegetables. What is Kim's reaction? (She thinks Mary's parents were acting "nasty.") How does Kim's reaction affect Mary? (Mary realizes that Chinese parents talk differently because they don't want to look as though they are bragging, and that boasting about family is the same as boasting about yourself.) Add this information to your organizer.

Build Vocabulary on page 188

gasp: a loud breath

"The fish was delicious!" Mrs. Eng said to Father. "I'll have to get the recipe from your wife one of these days. She's a wonderful cook, isn't she?"

"Oh, no, she's not a good cook at all," said Father. "You're just being polite."

I heard a little gasp from my friend Kim. She stared wide-eyed at Father.

"What's the matter, Kim?" I asked.

Instead of answering, Kim turned to look at Mrs. O'Meara, who was saying to my mother, "I *loved* your ten-vegetable salad. Even the kids loved it, and they don't usually eat their vegetables. You and the girls must have spent *hours* doing all that fine dicing and slicing!"

"The girls did the cutting, and I'm sorry they did such a terrible job," said Mother. "I'm embarrassed at how thick those pieces of celery were!"

I heard another little gasp from Kim, who was now staring at Mother. But I didn't get a chance to ask her what the problem was. The O'Mearas were going out the front door, and the rest of the guests followed. 5

Literature Anthology, pp. 188–189

Access Complex Text

Purpose

Remind students that realistic fiction may include details about real places, events, foods, or traditions. In a work of fiction, the main purpose of these details is to show how they affect the characters. Review the story through the bottom of page 189.

- *How have comparisons between Chinese culture and American culture been shown in the story so far?* (Details about food, traditions, and conversations show some differences. Details about the families, including parents and children and the enjoyment of food, show things the cultures have in common.)

"How come your father and your mother were so nasty last night?" asked Kim when we were walking to the school bus stop the next morning.

"What do you mean?" I asked. I didn't remember Father or Mother acting nasty.

"It was when Mrs. Eng was telling your dad what a good cook your mom is," replied Kim.

That's right. Mrs. Eng did say something about Mother being a good cook. "So what's bothering you?" I asked.

Kim stopped dead. "Didn't you hear your dad?" she demanded. "He said that your mom wasn't a good cook at all, and that Mrs. Eng was just being polite!"

I still didn't understand why Kim was bothered. "So what? People are always saying things like that."

But Kim wasn't finished. "And then when my mom said how hard you worked to cut up the vegetables, your mom said she was embarrassed by what a terrible job you did in slicing!"

I had to laugh. "She doesn't mean it! It's just the way she talks."

When the school bus arrived and we got on, Kim began again. "Then why do your parents keep saying these bad things if they don't mean it? I'd be really hurt if my mom said I did a terrible job—after I worked so hard, too."

What Kim said made me thoughtful. I suddenly realized that whenever people said good things about us, my parents always **contradicted** them and said how bad we really were. We kids knew perfectly well that our parents didn't mean it, so our feelings weren't hurt in the least. It was just the way Chinese parents were supposed to talk.

Finally I said to Kim, "I think that if my parents agreed with the compliments, then that would be the same as bragging. It's good manners to contradict people when they compliment your children."

"It's bragging only if you say good things about *yourself*," protested Kim. "It's different when your parents are talking about *you*."

I shook my head. "We Chinese feel it's the same thing. Boasting about our children, or husband, or wife, is the same as boasting about ourselves. People even think it's bad luck." 6

It was Kim's turn to be thoughtful. "So that's why your parents never said what good musicians you were. That would be bragging, right?"

189

Read

7 Summarize DOK 1

Teacher Think Aloud To help me better understand the story, I can **summarize** Kim and Mary's misunderstanding. Kim tells Mary she is upset because she thinks Mary's parents were being mean with the things they said. Mary now understands why Kim was so surprised and explains why her parents respond the way they do. Thanks to Mary's explanation, Kim now understands that in Chinese culture it is important to be modest.

Reread

Author's Craft: Word Choice DOK 2

Reread pages 188–189. Why does the author use the phrases *little gasp* and *stared wide-eyed*? (These phrases convey a feeling of surprise and shock. The author is conveying Kim's surprise that the Yangs are speaking this way about their daughter.) Later, on page 189, the author describes both Mary and Kim as *thoughtful*. Why does the author use this word? (The girls are beginning to understand more about each other's culture, and are learning to respect each other's points of view.)

Spotlight on Language

Page 189, Paragraphs 11–14 Read the paragraphs aloud. *Which sentence helps you understand the meaning of* bragging? (*It's bragging only if...*) Which word or phrase does Kim use to replace *bragging?* (*boasting*) Explain that words that have similar meanings are synonyms and can replace each other. Then have partners write definitions for *bragging* and *boasting.* (complimenting yourself) *Do you agree with Kim's parents that saying good things about your children is bragging or boasting?* Turn to a partner and discuss your response.

Newcomers

Use the **Newcomer Online Visuals** and their accompanying prompts to help students expand vocabulary and language about Family (13a-f) and Community (15-19). Use the Conversation Starters, Speech Balloons, and the Games in the **Newcomer Teacher's Guide** to continue building vocabulary and developing oral and written language.

Read

8 Theme DOK 1

What does Kim notice about how Mary's parents treat their children's musical abilities? (Mary's parents don't tell the truth about their children's talents.) What happens to Kim as a result of Mary's explanation? (She understands Father's reaction at the baseball game.) Add this information to your organizer.

What Does the Character Think, Say, and Do?	What is the Character's Perspective?
Kim learns that Chinese parents don't tell the truth about their children's talents because that would be considered bragging.	Kim sees an example of this at the baseball game and begins to understand Chinese culture.

STOP AND CHECK DOK 1

Summarize What have Kim and Mary learned since the New Year's party? (Kim now understands why Mary's parents contradict compliments. Mary recognizes why Kim might not understand her culture, so she explains it more.)

Build Vocabulary on page 190

overhearing: hearing something that you are not supposed to

Music is the most important thing in our family. My elder brother plays the violin, my second sister plays the viola, and I play the cello. We all practice very hard, and I know Father thinks we are all doing well—only he has never said so to other people.

"The funny thing is," continued Kim, "your kid brother is the only one in your family who isn't a good musician. But I've never heard your parents say anything about how badly he plays."

I thought over what Kim said about Fourth Brother. He is the only one in our family who is no good at all with music. But we don't talk about his terrible ear. Finally I said, "It's like this: We're not hurt when we hear our parents say bad things about us, since we know they're only doing it because it's good manners. We know perfectly well that they don't mean it. But if they say my younger brother has a terrible ear, they'd really be telling the truth. So they don't say anything, because that would hurt his feelings."

Kim rolled her eyes. "Boy, this is confusing! Your parents can't tell the truth about your playing because it would be bragging. And they can't say anything about your brother's playing because that would be telling the truth."

I grinned. "Right! You got it!"

I think Kim understood what I was driving at. She didn't make a face when she heard my mother saying that the cookies Second Sister baked for the PTA bake sale were terrible.

After our Spring Festival party, the days became longer, and cherry trees burst into bloom. The baseball season began, and Fourth Brother's team played an opening game against another school. My brother might have a terrible ear for music, but he was turning out to be a really good baseball player.

In the seventh inning Fourth Brother hit a home run, something he had wanted to do for a long time but had never managed before. All his teammates crowded around to **congratulate** him. "You did it, Sprout! You did it!" shouted Matthew Conner, his best friend.

Mr. Conner turned to Father. "I bet you're proud of the boy!"

"He was just lucky when he hit that home run," said Father.

Overhearing the exchange, Kim turned to me and smiled. "I see what you mean," she whispered.

190

Literature Anthology, pp. 190–191

Access Complex Text

Specific Vocabulary

Point out the idiomatic expressions in the second column on page 190: "driving at" and "a terrible ear for music." Have students reread the expressions.

- *What does Mary mean when she says that Kim understood what she was "driving at?"* (*Kim understands the point Mary is trying to make.*)
- *What does Mary mean when she says her "brother might have a terrible ear for music?"* (She means that he doesn't know when he is playing poorly.)
- Ask students to give examples of other expressions that people might find confusing.

That Easter, the O'Mearas invited our family for dinner. I knew that Easter was a solemn religious holiday, but what I noticed most was that the stores were full of stuffed rabbits and fuzzy baby chicks. Chocolate eggs were everywhere.

For the dinner, Mrs. O'Meara cooked a huge ham. She had also made roast potatoes, vegetables, salad, and the biggest chocolate cake I had ever seen. I had eaten a lot at Thanksgiving dinners, but this time I stuffed myself until I was bursting. The rest of my family did pretty well, too. We all loved ham.

As Mrs. O'Meara started cutting up the cake for dessert, Mother said, "I'm not sure if I can eat one more bite. That was the best ham I've ever tasted!"

"Aw, that ham was terrible," said Kim. "I bet you could do a lot better, Mrs. Yang."

There was a stunned silence around the table. Mrs. O'Meara stared at Kim, and her face slowly turned dark red. 9

I heard a low growl from Mr. O'Meara. "You and I are going to have a little talk later this evening, young lady," he said to Kim.

Our family was speechless with surprise. My parents, my brothers, and sister all stared at Kim. I was the most shocked, because Kim was my best friend, and in the two years since I've known her, I'd never seen her do or say anything mean. How could she say something so cruel about her own mother?

The rest of the evening was pretty uncomfortable. Our family left early, because we could all see that Mr. and Mrs. O'Meara were waiting impatiently to have their "little talk" with Kim as soon as we were gone.

191

ELL Spotlight on Idioms

Page 190, Paragraphs 3-6 Help students understand the meaning of *terrible ear*. Read the second and third sentences in paragraph 3 with them. *Which phrase helps you understand* terrible ear*?* (no good at all with music) Then help students understand why Mary's parents do not say that her Fourth Brother has a terrible ear. *Why don't Mary's parents say bad things about her and her brothers and sisters?* (for good manners) *Why don't the parents say the brother has a terrible ear?* (Even though it's the truth, it will hurt the brother's feelings.)

Read

9 Summarize DOK 1

Teacher Think Aloud I can reread text to **summarize** details that help me understand the story.

Prompt students to apply the strategy in a Think Aloud. Have them turn to a partner to paraphrase what they have read before they summarize. Make sure students summarize specific details to show that they understand the story.

Student Think Aloud At Easter dinner, Mary's mom compliments Mrs. O'Meara's cooking. Kim tries to use what she has learned about Chinese culture by contradicting the compliment, but it just makes her parents upset.

Build Vocabulary on page 191

solemn: serious

stunned: very surprised

Reread

Author's Craft: Characterization DOK 2

Reread page 191. How does the author use realistic elements on this page to further develop the characters and drive the plot forward? (After Kim attempts to follow Chinese custom by criticizing her mother's cooking, Kim's parents react to their daughter's insult the way real parents would. The inclusion of this realistic dialogue creates complications and conflict in the story.)

Read

10 Context Clues: Cause and Effect DOK 2

Cause-and-effect context clues can help you find a word's meaning. What cause-and-effect clue helps you find the meaning of *blurted* on page 193? (Since Mary's mother covered her mouth in embarrassment after she blurted something out, *blurted* must mean "speaking before thinking.")

11 Theme DOK 2

What does Kim say to Mary's mother on page 193? (Kim jokingly says she knows Mrs. Yang didn't mean to compliment Mary.) What does this show about Kim? (Kim now understands Chinese customs.) Use your organizer to help you find the theme. (Learning about cultural differences can help us overcome misunderstandings.)

STOP AND CHECK DOK 1

Reread How does Mary's view of Kim's behavior change? (Mary realizes Kim was trying to be as modest about her mother as Chinese parents are about their children.)

Build Vocabulary on page 192

modest: not thinking too highly of yourself

Next morning at the school bus stop, Kim wouldn't even look at me. Finally I cleared my throat. "What made you talk like that to your mother, Kim?" I asked.

Kim whirled around. She looked furious. "B-but you were the one who t-told me that saying nice things about your own family was the s-same as bragging!" she stuttered. "Last night I was just trying to act modest!"

I finally saw the light. I saw how Kim had misunderstood what I had said. "Listen, Kim," I said, "Chinese *parents* are supposed to say **critical** things about their own *children*, and husbands and wives can say bad things about each other. But *young people* must always be respectful to their *elders*."

The school bus came. "I guess I'll never understand the Chinese," sighed Kim as we sat down. At least we still sat together.

After school I went over to Kim's house and explained to Mrs. O'Meara about how the Chinese were supposed to sound modest about their own children. I told her that Kim had thought I meant children also had to sound modest about their parents. Mrs. O'Meara laughed. Although her laugh sounded a little forced, it was a good sign.

192

Literature Anthology, pp. 192–193

ACT Access Complex Text

Connection of Ideas

Remind students that they learned that in Chinese culture it is normal for parents to contradict compliments about their children. Clarify this concept by having them reread the last two paragraphs on page 193.

- *Why does Mrs. Yang look embarrassed?* (She didn't contradict the compliment that Kim gave Mary about her music.)
- *Why does Kim say, "We all know you didn't mean it?"* (Kim is teasing Mrs. Yang because she now knows why Mary's parents normally contradict compliments instead of giving them.)

I soon forgot about Kim's **misunderstanding**, because I had other things to worry about. Our school orchestra was giving its spring concert, and the conductor asked me to play a cello solo as one of the numbers. Father said I should play a dance movement from one of Bach's unaccompanied cello suites. It was a very hard piece, and I was really scared to play it in public. But Father said we should always try to meet challenges.

I practiced like mad. On the day of the concert, I was so nervous that I was sitting on pins and needles waiting for my turn to play ("sitting on pins and needles" was another expression in my little notebook). My legs were wobbly when it came time for me to walk to the front of the stage. But as I sat down with my cello and actually started playing, I became so wrapped up in the music that I forgot to be nervous.

After the concert, my friends came up to congratulate me. It was the proudest moment of my life. "You were great, Mary, simply great!" said Kim. Her eyes were shining.

Mother's eyes were shining, too. "Yes, she *was* good," she **blurted** out. 10
Then she covered her mouth and looked embarrassed. 11

Kim turned to me and winked. "That's all right, Mrs. Yang. We all know you didn't mean it!" 12

193

Read

12 Summarize DOK 1

Reread page 193. Summarize how Mary feels at first. Paraphrase how she feels at the end.

Student Think Aloud From rereading, I see that Mary was very nervous because her legs were wobbly. After the concert, Mary receives compliments, so she feels proud.

Return to Purpose Review students' purpose for reading. Then ask partners to share how setting a purpose helped them understand the text.

Reread

Author's Craft: Illustrations DOK 2

***Reading/Writing Companion*, p. 26**

Reread paragraph 4 on page 193. Then look at the illustration. How does the author use the illustration to show how Mrs. Yang has changed? (The illustration shows that Mrs. Yang has changed by showing her complimenting her daughter in public. Even though she is a little embarrassed after complimenting Mary, her smile suggests that she is beginning to feel more comfortable with American customs, including showing how proud she is of Mary.)

ELL Spotlight on Idioms

Page 193, Paragraph 2 Point out the phrase "sitting on pins and needles" on page 193. *What words or phrases in the paragraph help you understand the expression?* (I was so nervous; legs were wobbly when it came time) Check for understanding of the literal meanings of *pins* and *needles*. *Why does Mary use this expression to describe feeling nervous?* (When you feel nervous, you might have a physical sensation like pins and needles on your skin.) Have partners discuss times when they felt nervous, using the idiom *pins and needles*.

Read

Meet the Author DOK 2

Lensey Namioka

Have students read the biography of the author. Ask:

- How might Lensey Namioka have used her own experiences as a child to write this story?
- Why might Lensey Namioka write about the Yang family in other books?
- What is a childhood experience you would like to write about?

Author's Purpose DOK 2

To Entertain: Remind students that authors who write to entertain sometimes add funny events and characters to help better understand the story. Students may say that it was funny when Mary described her family sneaking slurps of soup, but it also helped explain something that is typical in Chinese culture.

Reread

Author's Craft: Humor DOK 3

Lensey Namioka uses humor to entertain her readers. What example of humor can you find on page 193? (Kim says, "That's all right, Mrs. Yang. We all know you didn't mean it!") What does this help the reader understand? (It shows that Kim now understands Chinese culture and Mary's family well enough to joke with Mrs. Yang.)

Illustrator's Craft DOK 2

COLLABORATE Have partners look at the illustrations in the story and use these sentence frames to discuss how they reveal what the characters feel:

The characters in this illustration feel . . .

The illustrator shows this by . . .

Use text evidence to support your ideas.

About the Author

Lensey Namioka, like the fictional Yangs, lives in Seattle, Washington and moved from China to the United States. Lensey was nine years old when she made the transition, and remembers what it was like to come to a new country and learn a new language. Several books and short stories she has written, such as "They Don't Mean It!", reflect her experiences.

The Yang family appears in other books by Lensey, such as *Yang the Youngest and His Terrible Ear* and *Yang the Third and Her Impossible Family*. She has also written about Japanese culture in her stories about Japanese warriors called samurai. Lensey continues to write short stories and books for readers of all ages.

Author's Purpose

Authors sometimes have more than one purpose for writing. What was entertaining about the story? What did you learn from it?

Literature Anthology, p. 194

Spotlight on Language

Page 194, Paragraphs 1-2 Reread the information about the author, asking students to identify the types of text Lensey Namioka wrote. Say: *Name two types of text Lensey Namioka has written.* (short stories, books) Point to the titles "They Don't Mean It!" and *Yang the Youngest and His Terrible Ear.* Ask: *What is different about the two titles?* (The first title begins and ends with a quotation mark; the second title is in italics.) Explain that titles of short stories always begin with quotation marks and titles of books always appear in italics.

Read

Summarize

Tell students they will use the details from their Theme Chart to summarize. As I read the selection, I wrote down details about the characters, conflicts, and events in the story. I can use these details to summarize the theme of the story.

Reread

Analyze the Text

After students summarize the selection, have them reread to develop a deeper understanding of the text and answer the questions on **Reading/ Writing Companion** pages 24–26. For students who need support in citing text evidence, use the Reread prompts on pages T31–T40.

Integrate

Build Knowledge: Make Connections

Talk About the Text Have partners discuss what learning about different cultures can teach us.

Write About the Text Have students add their ideas to their Build Knowledge pages of their reader's notebooks.

Anchor Chart Record any new ideas on the Build Knowledge anchor chart.

Add to the Vocabulary List Have students write down any words they learned about experiencing different cultures.

Compare Texts DOK 4

Have students compare how the authors present information on cultures in "A Reluctant Traveler" and *They Don't Mean It!* Ask: *How is Paul's experience similar to that of Mary's? How is it different?*

FORMATIVE ASSESSMENT

STUDENT CHECK-IN

Read Have partners tell each other important details from the text. Then have them reflect using the Check-In routine.

Reread Have partners share responses and text evidence. Then ask them to use the Check in routine to reflect and fill in the bars on Reading/Writing Companion pages 10–11.

LEARNING GOALS

We can use text evidence to respond to realistic fiction.

OBJECTIVES

Quote accurately from a text when explaining what the text says explicitly and when drawing inferences from the text. Explain different characters' perspectives in a literary text.

Determine a theme of a story, drama, or poem from details in the text, including how characters in a story or drama respond to challenges or how the speaker in a poem reflects upon a topic; summarize the text.

Compare and contrast two or more characters, settings, or events in a story or drama, drawing on specific details in the text.

Analyze how visual and multimedia elements contribute to the meaning, tone, or beauty of a text.

By the end of the year, read and comprehend literature, including stories, dramas, and poetry, at the high end of the grades 4–5 text complexity band independently and proficiently.

ELA ACADEMIC LANGUAGE

- *dialogue, illustrations, characterize*
- Cognates: *diálogo, ilustraciones, caracterizar*

TEACH IN SMALL GROUP

Approaching Level and **On Level** Have partners work together to plan and complete the response to the prompt.

Beyond Level Ask students to respond to the prompt independently.

ELL Group students of different proficiency levels to discuss and respond to the prompt.

Reread

Write About the Anchor Text

Analyze the Prompt DOK 3

Read the prompt aloud: *What message does the author want to send by sharing the experiences of different cultures?* Ask: *What is the prompt asking you to write?* (to determine the author's message) Say: *Let's reread to see how word choice, dialogue, and illustrations show how the Yangs and their American friends interact and change. This will help us make inferences to answer the prompt.*

Analyze Text Evidence

Remind students that understanding how characters change and what they learn from their experiences can help readers determine the message of a story. Have students reread **Literature Anthology** page 184. Ask: *In the last paragraph on the page, how does the author reveal Mrs. Yang's perspective about how American culture has affected her?* (The author says that Mrs. Yang felt that living in America had "made her soft" because she now bought dead fish instead of keeping live ones and killing them herself.) Now reread page 186. Ask: *How does Mrs. Yang respond to the compliments about her dinner?* (She contradicts them by saying that the food is "plain" and "simple," with only "a few small things" added because it is a special occasion.) Reread page 186. Ask: *What does Mary's mother say about Mary's performance? What does this suggest?* (She says that Mary's performance was good. By complimenting Mary, it shows that Mary's mother is beginning to use American customs.)

Respond

Review pages 24–26 of the **Reading/Writing Companion**. Have partners or small groups refer to and discuss their completed charts and responses from those pages. Then direct students' attention to the sentence starters on page 27 of the Reading/Writing Companion. Have them use the sentence starters to guide their responses.

Analytical Writing Students should focus on the author's use of dialogue and word choice to reveal the characters' perspectives and develop the theme, along with details in the illustrations. They should explain how these elements show how the members of the Yang family, particularly Mrs. Yang, change over the course of the story. Remind students to vary sentence structure by combining short sentences and adding phrases and clauses to others. Students may use additional paper to complete the assignment if needed.

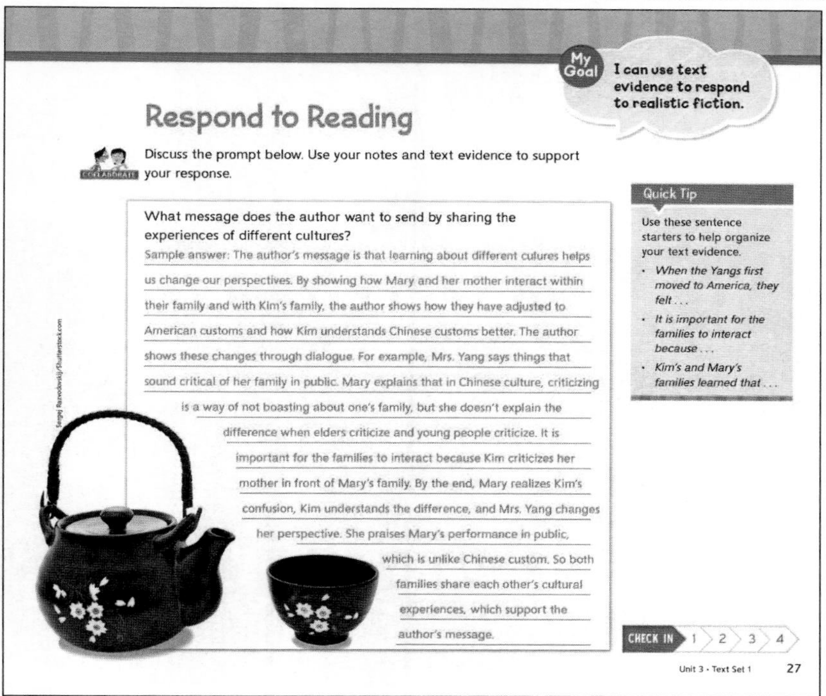
My Goal I can use text evidence to respond to realistic fiction.

Respond to Reading

COLLABORATE Discuss the prompt below. Use your notes and text evidence to support your response.

What message does the author want to send by sharing the experiences of different cultures?

Sample answer: The author's message is that learning about different cultures helps us change our perspectives. By showing how Mary and her mother interact within their family and with Kim's family, the author shows how they have adjusted to American customs and how Kim understands Chinese customs better. The author shows these changes through dialogue. For example, Mrs. Yang says things that sound critical of her family in public. Mary explains that in Chinese culture, criticizing is a way of not boasting about one's family, but she doesn't explain the difference when elders criticize and young people criticize. It is important for the families to interact because Kim criticizes her mother in front of Mary's family. By the end, Mary realizes Kim's confusion, Kim understands the difference, and Mrs. Yang changes her perspective. She praises Mary's performance in public, which is unlike Chinese custom. So both families share each other's cultural experiences, which support the author's message.

Quick Tip

Use these sentence starters to help organize your text evidence.

- *When the Yangs first moved to America, they felt . . .*
- *It is important for the families to interact because . . .*
- *Kim's and Mary's families learned that . . .*

CHECK IN 1 2 3 4

Unit 3 • Text Set 1 27

Reading/Writing Companion, p. 27

English Language Learners

Use the following scaffolds with **Respond**.

Beginning

Read the prompt with students and discuss what they will write about. Review the students' completed charts on **Reading/Writing Companion** pages 24-26. Discuss the meaning of *message* and *perspective* with them. Ask: *Do Kim's and Mary's families learn about each other's culture?* (yes) *perspective ?* (yes) Help partners describe the author's message using: When we learn about different cultures, it helps us change our perspectives.

Intermediate

Read the prompt with students. Have partners review their completed charts on **Reading/Writing Companion** pages 24-26. Ask: *What do characters learn about from sharing each other's cultures?* They learn about American and Chinese customs. *Does this help change their perspectives?* (yes) Have partners describe the author's message using: The author's message is learning about different cultures ____.

Advanced/Advanced High

Review the prompt and sentence starters on page 27 with students. Have them discuss their completed charts on pages 24-26. Guide pairs to describe what the characters learn from sharing each other's cultures. Then have them write their responses using the sentence starters and the terms *cultures, customs,* and *experiences.*

ELL NEWCOMERS

Have students listen to the summaries of the **Anchor Text** in their native language and then in English to help them access the text and develop listening comprehension. Help students ask and answer questions with a partner. Use these sentence frames: What is this story about? This story is about ___. Then have them complete the online **Newcomer Activities** individually or in pairs.

FORMATIVE ASSESSMENT

STUDENT CHECK-IN

Ask partners to share their response on Reading/Writing Companion page 27. Have them reflect using the Check-In routine to fill in the bars.

"Where Did That Come From?"

Lexile 940L

LEARNING GOALS

Read We can apply skills and strategies to read expository text.

Reread We can reread to analyze text, craft, and structure, and to compare texts.

Have students apply what they learned as they read.

ACT *What makes this text complex?*

▶ **Genre**

Discuss ways in which people of different backgrounds have contributed to our national identity.

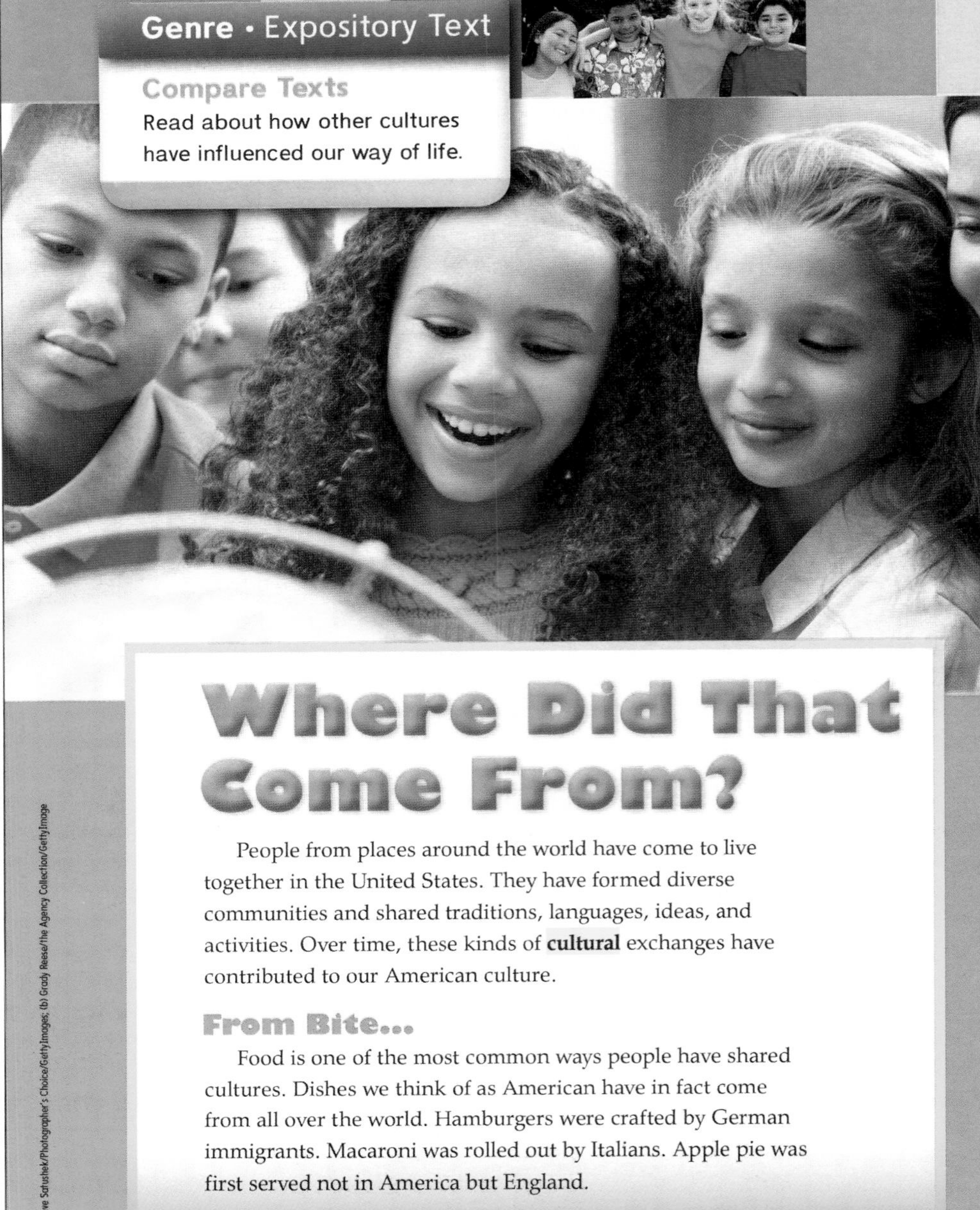

Genre • Expository Text

Compare Texts
Read about how other cultures have influenced our way of life.

Where Did That Come From?

People from places around the world have come to live together in the United States. They have formed diverse communities and shared traditions, languages, ideas, and activities. Over time, these kinds of **cultural** exchanges have contributed to our American culture.

From Bite...

Food is one of the most common ways people have shared cultures. Dishes we think of as American have in fact come from all over the world. Hamburgers were crafted by German immigrants. Macaroni was rolled out by Italians. Apple pie was first served not in America but England.

(t) Steve Satushek/Photographer's Choice/Getty Images; (b) Grady Reese/The Agency Collection/Getty Image

196

Literature Anthology, pp. 196–197

Analytical Writing Compare Texts DOK 4

As students read "Where Did That Come From?," encourage them to think about the Essential Question. Have them discuss how this text compares with *They Don't Mean It!*

Read

1 Text Features: Sidebar DOK 2

Why does the author include the sidebar on page 197? (to illustrate that cultures influence each other by listing shared language)

Build Vocabulary on pages 196-197

diverse: many different types or kinds

enriched: improved

Reread

Author's Craft: Text Features DOK 2

Reading/Writing Companion, p. 30

How do the headings help you understand the influence of other cultures on America? (The headings show the specific ways people across cultures share things.)

ACT Access Complex Text

Genre

Remind students that an expository text is nonfiction that informs readers about a particular topic. Expository texts often have certain text features to indicate that it is informational.

- *What text features indicate this selection is an expository text?* (photographs, captions, section headings, list)
- *How do section headings help readers?* (They organize the text and make it easier to see what topics are being discussed in the selection.)

...To Beat

People from different backgrounds have also drummed distinct sounds into the music we hear today. Hip hop and rap, for example, have been traced to West African and Caribbean storytelling. Salsa music comes from a type of Cuban music called "son," which has been linked to both Spanish and African cultures. These unique genres owe their rhythms to the drum. This instrument can be found in nearly every culture in the world.

United in Sports

Even the sports we play have come from other places. Soccer's origins have been connected with a number of countries, including Italy and China. Tennis likely came from France, but some think it may have even been played in ancient Egypt. While no one may know the exact origin of some of these sports, there is no doubt they are now considered popular American activities.

Our nation has been enriched by a diversity of cultures. Learning the origins of what makes up American culture can lead to a new **appreciation** for the people and places from which they come.

Words from Around the World

Many words used in American English have been "borrowed" from languages around the world.

- chimpanzee: **Kongo (African)**
- chipmunk: **Ojibwa (Native American)**
- bazaar, caravan: **Arabic**
- ketchup: **Chinese**
- voilà, genre: **French**
- kindergarten, dunk: **German**
- bandana, shampoo: **Hindi**
- bravo, magenta: **Italian**
- karaoke, tsunami: **Japanese**
- ranch, mosquito: **Spanish**

1

Soccer is one sport that many cultures share.

Make Connections

What can learning about other cultures teach us? ESSENTIAL QUESTION

How has a character in a story been influenced by American culture? How is this similar to the way other cultures have influenced people in America? TEXT TO TEXT

197

(tl) Ariel Skelley/Blend Images/Getty Images; (tc) 2A Images/Getty Images; (tr) Stocktrek/Digital Vision/Getty Images; (b) Stockbyte/Getty Images

Spotlight on Language

Page 197, Sidebar Support understanding of the "Words from Around the World." Pronounce each word and have students repeat. Elicit other foreign words regularly used in American culture. Ask students if they know English words that might be used in other cultures, including their native languages.

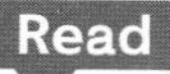
Read

Summarize

Guide students to summarize the selection.

Reread

Analyze the Text

After students read and summarize, have them reread and answer questions on pages 28–30 of the **Reading/Writing Companion**.

Integrate

Build Knowledge: Make Connections

Talk About the Text Have partners discuss what learning about cultures can teach us.

Write About the Text Have students add their ideas to their Build Knowledge pages of their reader's notebooks.

Anchor Chart Record any new ideas on the Build Knowledge anchor chart.

Add to the Vocabulary List Have students write down any words they learned about different cultures in their reader's notebooks.

Compare Texts DOK 4

Text to Text Answer: Both selections show how people adapt to new cultures. Evidence: In *They Don't Mean It!*, Mary starts using American expressions. In "Where Did That Come From?," I read that hip hop music has its roots in West African and Caribbean cultures.

FORMATIVE ASSESSMENT

STUDENT CHECK-IN

Read Ask partners to share their summaries. Then have them reflect using the Check-In routine.

Reread Ask partners to share their responses on Reading/Writing Companion pages 28-30. Then have them use the Check-In routine to reflect and fill in the bars.

LEARNING GOALS

We can identify author's purpose to help us read and understand expository text.

OBJECTIVES

Quote accurately from a text when explaining what the text says explicitly and when drawing inferences from the text.

Identify the author's purpose.

ELA ACADEMIC LANGUAGE

- *author's purpose, inform, persuade, stereotype*
- Cognate: *informar, persuadir, estereotipo*

Reread

Author's Purpose

1 Explain

Have students turn to **Reading/Writing Companion** page 31. Share with students the following key points of author's purpose:

- An author's purpose is his or her reason for writing a text. An author may write to inform, entertain, or persuade.
- Fiction is often written to entertain. Nonfiction is often written to inform or persuade.
- An author can have several purposes for writing. For example, realistic fiction about a person who moves to or visits another country can also inform readers about what that country is like.
- Authors include details that help readers identify and understand their purpose. As you read, think about why the author includes certain details. Ask: *What does the author want me to know? Why?*

2 Model

Model identifying the author's purpose in the first paragraph on page 28. Read the first sentence, identifying key words and phrases the author uses to introduce the topic, for example, "food" and "shared cultures." Then read aloud the next sentence: *Dishes we think of as American have in fact come from all over the world.* Point out that the phrase "in fact" suggests that the author's purpose is to inform—and even surprise—readers who might not be aware that American food comes from other areas of the world. As a group, discuss how the author achieves this purpose while avoiding the use of stereotypes, or unfair beliefs about a group of people.

3 Guided Practice

Now have students reread the first paragraph on page 29. Have partners find key words and phrases that the author uses to introduce the topic. Ask: *What does the author want readers to know about American sports?* (The author wants readers to know that the sports Americans play come from many places.) *What examples does the author provide?* (The author gives examples from Italy, China, France, and Egypt.) Have partners discuss what this indicates about the author's purpose for writing the text.

Allow students time to enter their responses on page 31 of the Reading/Writing Companion.

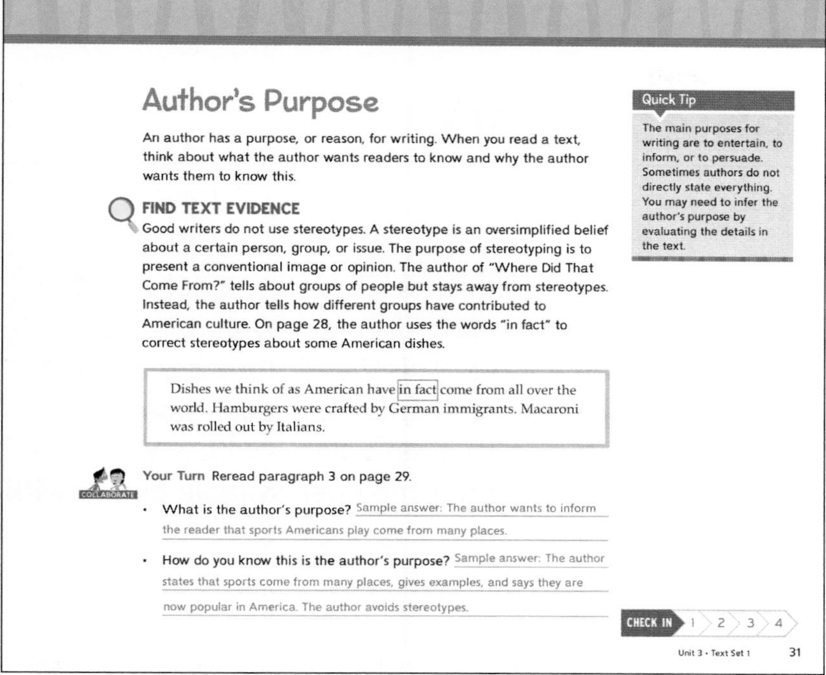

Author's Purpose

An author has a purpose, or reason, for writing. When you read a text, think about what the author wants readers to know and why the author wants them to know this.

FIND TEXT EVIDENCE

Good writers do not use stereotypes. A stereotype is an oversimplified belief about a certain person, group, or issue. The purpose of stereotyping is to present a conventional image or opinion. The author of "Where Did That Come From?" tells about groups of people but stays away from stereotypes. Instead, the author tells how different groups have contributed to American culture. On page 28, the author uses the words "in fact" to correct stereotypes about some American dishes.

> Dishes we think of as American have in fact come from all over the world. Hamburgers were crafted by German immigrants. Macaroni was rolled out by Italians.

Quick Tip

The main purposes for writing are to entertain, to inform, or to persuade. Sometimes authors do not directly state everything. You may need to infer the author's purpose by evaluating the details in the text.

COLLABORATE

Your Turn Reread paragraph 3 on page 29.

- What is the author's purpose? Sample answer: The author wants to inform the reader that sports Americans play come from many places.
- How do you know this is the author's purpose? Sample answer: The author states that sports come from many places, gives examples, and says they are now popular in America. The author avoids stereotypes.

CHECK IN 1 2 3 4

Unit 3 • Text Set 1 31

Reading/Writing Companion, p. 31

English Language Learners

Use the following scaffolds with **Guided Practice**.

Beginning

Review the key point of author's purpose with students. Read the first paragraph on page 29 with students and restate as needed. Act out the sports, pointing to a map to show where each is from. Point out cognates: *unirse, origen, popular, actividades. Where do the sports come from?* (Italy, China, France, Egypt) The author shows that sports come from many different places. These sports are now popular in America.

Intermediate

Review the key points of author's purpose with students. Have partners read the first paragraph on page 29. Elicit them to discuss the author's purpose for writing the text by asking: *Why does the author tell where American sports come from?* The author wants readers to know that American sports come from many places. The author tells that these sports are popular in America.

Advanced/Advanced High

Discuss the key points of author's purpose with students. Have partners read the first paragraph on page 29 and talk about why the author uses the key word *Even* to introduce the topic. *Which details tell about the author's purpose? Explain why you think that.*

FORMATIVE ASSESSMENT

STUDENT CHECK-IN

Ask partners to share their Your Turn responses on Reading/Writing Companion page 31. Then have them use the Check-In routine to reflect and fill in the bars.

LEARNING GOALS

- We can identify and decode words with open syllables.
- We can identify and read multisyllabic words.
- We can read fluently with expression and phrasing.

OBJECTIVES

Use combined knowledge of all letter-sound correspondences, syllabication patterns, and morphology (e.g., roots and affixes) to read accurately unfamiliar multisyllabic words in context and out of context.

Read grade-level prose and poetry orally with accuracy, appropriate rate, expression, and automaticity on successive readings.

- Rate: 123–143 WCPM

ELA ACADEMIC LANGUAGE

- *expression, phrasing*
- Cognates: *expresión, fraseo*

Phonics

Approaching Level Use the Tier 2 activity on page T59 before teaching the lesson.

On Level and **Beyond Level** As needed, use the Read Multisyllabic Words section only.

ELL See page 5 in the **Language Transfers Handbook** for guidance in identifying sounds and symbols that may not transfer for speakers of certain languages and support in accommodating those students.

Open Syllables (V/V)

1 Explain

Review with students that every syllable has only one vowel sound. Write the words *dial* and *ruin* on the board. Point out that in these words, the first syllable ends in a vowel. This means they are open syllables. Then point out that the second syllable in each word also begins with a vowel. Each word has an open syllable with a V/V (Vowel/Vowel) pattern. The syllable after the open syllable begins with a vowel.

2 Model

Write the following words on the board. Underline the open syllables. Then model reading the words aloud as you run your finger under the letters in the open syllable.

sci***ence*** re***al***

Stress that the vowel in each open syllable has the long vowel sound.

3 Guided Practice

Write the following open syllable (V/V) words on the board. Have students underline the open syllable in each word. Then have them chorally read the words.

violin	trial	royal	poem
react	diameter	radio	area
audio	riot	diary	video
poet	being	cereal	rodeo

For practice with decoding and encoding, use **Practice Book** page 139 or online activities.

Read Multisyllabic Words

Transition to Longer Words Write the words below on the board. Have students chorally read a word in the first column. Then point to the related word in the second column. Point out that the vowel pattern in the longer word is the same as that in the shorter one.

As necessary, review the meaning of some common prefixes and suffixes. Explain that knowing the meaning of these added syllables can help students understand the meaning of the longer word.

dial	redialed
quiet	quietly
meteor	meteoric
react	reactive
science	unscientific
lion	lioness
genuine	genuinely
create	creation

Fluency

Expression and Phrasing

Explain/Model Review with students that they can use varied expression, or prosody, and phrasing to create a certain feeling or mood as they read. They can also gain understanding by grouping words into meaningful phrases, using punctuation marks such as commas and periods as clues. Model using appropriate expression and phrasing as you read aloud "A Reluctant Traveler" in the **Reading/Writing Companion** page 12. Remind students that you will be listening for their use of expression and phrasing as you monitor their reading during the week.

Practice/Apply Have partners alternate reading paragraphs in the passage, modeling the expression and phrasing you used.

Daily Fluency Practice

Automaticity Students can practice reading with accuracy and appropriate rate to develop automaticity using the online **Differentiated Genre Passage**, "Potluck or Potlatch?"

DIGITAL TOOLS

For more practice, use the phonics and fluency activities.

Open Syllables (V/V)

MULTIMODAL LEARNING

Write two-syllable words with one open syllable with a V/V pattern, such as *dual, vial,* and *fluent,* on strips of paper or index cards. Have students read the words aloud and then fold the paper or index cards to divide the syllables. Ask students to display their strips or index cards so that only the open syllables with a V/V pattern are visible.

FORMATIVE ASSESSMENT

STUDENT CHECK-IN

Open Syllables (V/V) Have partners share three words with open syllables.

Multisyllabic Words Have partners add prefixes or suffixes to the following words: *meteor, science,* and *genuine.*

Fluency Ask partners to read "Potluck or Potlatch?" fluently.

Have partners reflect using the Check-In routine.

CHECK FOR SUCCESS

Can students decode multisyllabic words with open syllables? Can students read with expression and phrasing?

Small Group Instruction

If No:

- **Approaching** Reteach pp. T59, T62
- **ELL** Develop pp. T59

If Yes:

- **On** Apply p. T64
- **Beyond** Apply p. T70

LEARNING GOALS

We can compare the song with the selections in this text set to build knowledge about what different cultures can teach people.

OBJECTIVES

Determine a theme of a story, drama, or poem from details in the text, including how characters in a story or drama respond to challenges or how the speaker in a poem reflects upon a topic; summarize the text.

Close Reading Routine

Read DOK 1–2

- Identify important ideas and details.
- Take notes and summarize.
- Use ACT prompts as needed.

Reread DOK 2–3

- Analyze the text, craft, and structure.
- Use the ***Reading/Writing Companion.***

Integrate DOK 3–4

- Integrate knowledge and ideas.
- Make text-to-text connections.
- Use the Integrate/Make Connections lesson.
- Use ***Reading/Writing Companion*** p. 32.
- Complete the Show Your Knowledge task.
- Inspire action.

FORMATIVE ASSESSMENT

STUDENT CHECK-IN

Ask partners to share their response. Have them use the Check-In routine to reflect and fill in the bars on Reading/Writing Companion page 32.

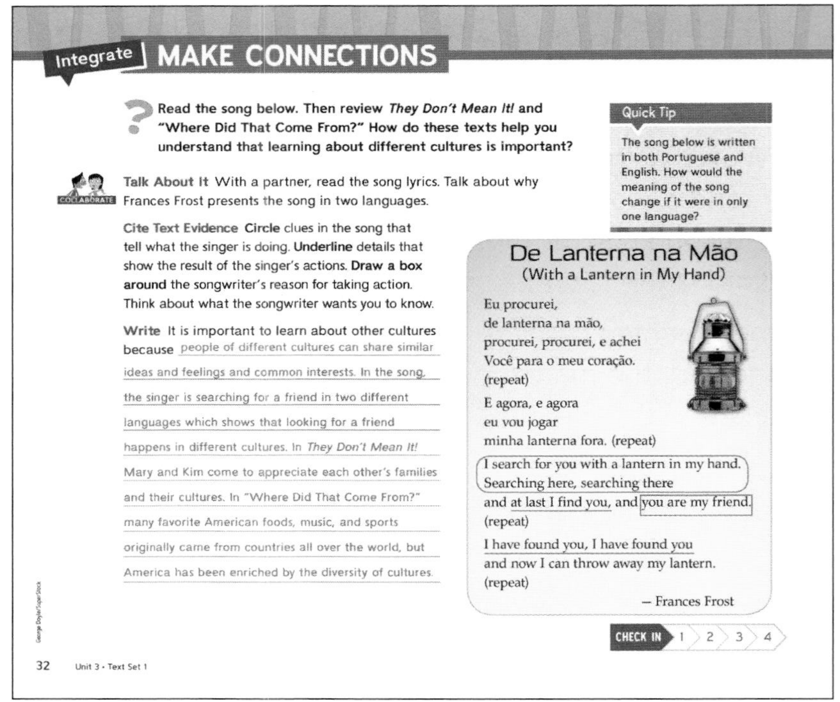

Integrate **MAKE CONNECTIONS**

Read the song below. Then review *They Don't Mean It!* and "Where Did That Come From?" How do these texts help you understand that learning about different cultures is important?

Talk About It With a partner, read the song lyrics. Talk about why Frances Frost presents the song in two languages.

Cite Text Evidence **Circle** clues in the song that tell what the singer is doing. **Underline** details that show the result of the singer's actions. **Draw a box around** the songwriter's reason for taking action. Think about what the songwriter wants you to know.

Write It is important to learn about other cultures because people of different cultures can share similar ideas and feelings and common interests. In the song, the singer is searching for a friend in two different languages which shows that looking for a friend happens in different cultures. In *They Don't Mean It!* Mary and Kim come to appreciate each other's families and their cultures. In "Where Did That Come From?" many favorite American foods, music, and sports originally came from countries all over the world, but America has been enriched by the diversity of cultures.

Quick Tip

The song below is written in both Portuguese and English. How would the meaning of the song change if it were in only one language?

De Lanterna na Mão
(With a Lantern in My Hand)

Eu procurei,
de lanterna na mão,
procurei, procurei, e achei
Você para o meu coração.
(repeat)
E agora, e agora
eu vou jogar
minha lanterna fora. (repeat)
I search for you with a lantern in my hand.
Searching here, searching there
and at last I find you, and you are my friend.
(repeat)
I have found you, I have found you
and now I can throw away my lantern.
(repeat)

— Frances Frost

CHECK IN 1 2 3 4

32 Unit 3 • Text Set 1

Reading/Writing Companion, p. 32

Integrate

Make Connections DOK 4

Talk About It

Share and discuss students' responses to the "A Special Day" blast. Display the Build Knowledge anchor chart. Review the chart and have students read through their notes, annotations, and responses for each text. Then ask them to complete the Talk About It activity on **Reading/Writing Companion** page 32.

Cite Text Evidence

Guide students to see the connections between the song lyrics for "With a Lantern in My Hand" on Reading/Writing Companion page 32 and the different texts. Remind students to read the Quick Tip.

Write

Students should refer to their notes on the chart as they respond to the writing prompt at the bottom of the page. When students have finished, have groups share and discuss their responses.

Build Knowledge: Make Connections

Talk About the Text Have partners discuss what learning about different cultures teaches people.

Write About the Text Have students add their ideas to their Build Knowledge pages of their reader's notebooks.

Anchor Chart Record any new ideas on the Build Knowledge anchor chart.

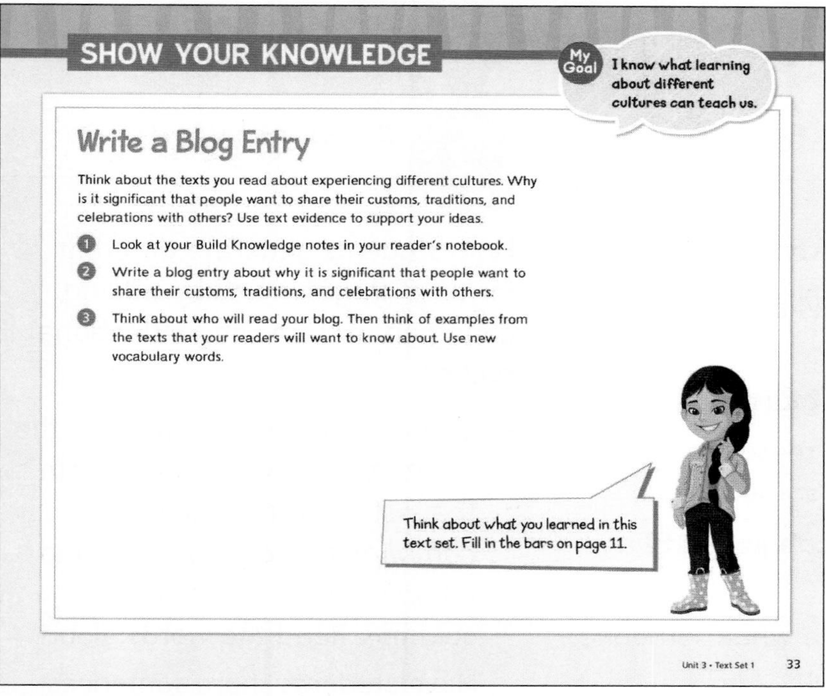

Reading/Writing Companion, p. 33

Integrate

Show Your Knowledge DOK 4

Write a Blog Entry

Explain that students will show how they built knowledge across the text set by writing a blog entry about experiencing different cultures. Display the Build Knowledge anchor chart and ask: *What can learning about different cultures teach us?*

Step 1 Guide partners to review the Build Knowledge anchor chart in their reader's notebook to discuss the prompt.

Step 2 Have students write a blog entry that shares their thoughts about why it is significant that people want to share their customs, traditions, and celebrations with others.

Step 3 Remind students to use evidence from the texts, video, and listening passage to support their ideas. Prompt students to use words from their Build Knowledge vocabulary list in their blogs.

Inspire Action

Share Your Blog Entry Have partners present their blog entries. Ask students in the audience to write down things they found interesting or questions they have for the presenters. Presenters can respond to the comments with sticky notes.

What Are You Inspired to Do? Encourage partners to think of another way to respond to the texts. Ask: *What else do the texts inspire you to do?*

LEARNING GOALS

We can write a blog entry to show the knowledge we built about what different cultures can teach us.

OBJECTIVES

Engage effectively in a range of collaborative discussions with diverse partners, building on others ideas and expressing their own clearly.

Follow agreed-upon rules for discussions and carry out assigned roles.

Report on a topic or text or present an opinion, sequencing ideas logically and using appropriate facts and relevant, descriptive details to support main ideas or themes; speak clearly at an understandable pace.

Include multimedia components and visual displays in presentations when appropriate to enhance the development of main ideas or themes.

ELA ACADEMIC LANGUAGE

- *blog, prompt, discuss*
- Cognate: *discutir*

DIGITAL TOOLS

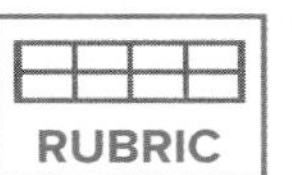

Show Your Knowledge Rubric

ELL ENGLISH LANGUAGE LEARNERS

Provide sentence frames for support. *It is important that people share their customs, traditions, and celebrations with others because ____. Learning about different cultures can teach us ____.*

MY GOALS ROUTINE

What I Learned

Review Goals Have students turn back to page 11 of the Reading/Writing Companion and review the goals for the text set.

Reflect Have students think about the progress they've made toward the goals. Review the key. Then have students reflect and fill in the bars.

LEARNING GOALS

- **We can build and expand on new vocabulary words**
- **We can use context clues to figure out the meaning of unfamiliar words.**
- **We can write using new vocabulary words.**

OBJECTIVES

Use context (e.g., cause/effect relationships and comparisons in text) as a clue to the meaning of a word or phrase.

Use the relationship between particular words (e.g., synonyms, antonyms, homographs) to better understand each of the words.

Expand vocabulary by adding inflectional endings and suffixes.

DIGITAL TOOLS

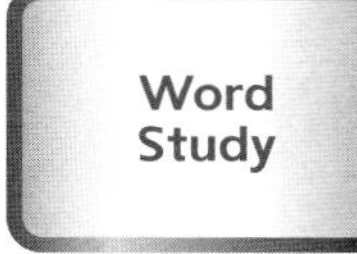

Vocabulary Activities

ELL ENGLISH LANGUAGE LEARNERS

Pair students of different language proficiency levels to practice vocabulary. Have partners discuss different shades of meaning in words with similar meanings, such as *congratulate* and *compliment.*

FORMATIVE ASSESSMENT

STUDENT CHECK-IN

After each lesson, have partners share and reflect using the Check-In routine.

Connect to Words

Practice the target vocabulary.

1. What do you feel **appreciation** for?
2. What have you **blurted** out?
3. What is a good reason for **complimenting** someone?
4. Show how you **congratulate** a friend.
5. Tell about a time when someone **contradicted** you.
6. What might you say to a person who is often **critical**?
7. What special **cultural** traditions do you enjoy?
8. How can people avoid a **misunderstanding**?

OPTION

Related Words

Help students generate different forms of target words by adding, changing, or removing inflectional endings.

- Draw a four-column chart on the board. Write *complimenting* in the last column. Then write *compliment, compliments,* and *complimented* in the other columns. Read the words aloud.
- Have students share sentences using each form of *compliment.*
- Students can fill in the chart for *blurted, congratulate,* and *contradicted,* and then share sentences using the different forms of the words.
- Have students copy the chart in their reader's notebook.

See **Practice Book** page 131.

OPTION

Build Vocabulary

Discuss important academic words.

- Display *phases, similar,* and *style.*
- Define the words and discuss their meanings with students.
- Write *phases* and *phased* on the board. Have partners write other words with the same root and define them. Then have partners ask and answer questions using the words.
- Repeat with *similar* and *style.*

Adages

Remind students that an adage is an old and well-known saying that expresses a truth. Read each adage aloud and have students discuss the meaning.

- *Don't judge a book by its cover.*
- *The early bird catches the worm.*
- *Where there is smoke, there is fire.*

Have students write each adage and its meaning in their reader's notebook. Then have students find and write other adages they like.

See **Practice Book** page 143.

Spiral Review

Reinforce the Words

Review this text set and last text set's vocabulary words. Have students orally complete each sentence stem.

1. We had a misunderstanding about ____.
2. Jeb contradicted Marco when he ____.
3. Nora is complimenting the actors because ____.
4. A good time to congratulate people is ____.
5. "Oh, I'm sorry," Harry blurted out. "I forgot ____."
6. I can be critical when ____.

Have partners ask and answer questions using these vocabulary words from the previous text set: *memorized* and *shuddered*.

See **Practice Book** page 132.

Connect to Writing

- Have students write sentences in their reader's notebooks using the vocabulary from the text set.
- Tell them to write sentences that provide context to show what the words mean.
- ELL Provide the Lesson 3 sentence stems 1–6 for students needing extra support.

Write Using Vocabulary

Have students write something they learned from the words in the text set in their reader's notebook. For example, they might write about how a *misunderstanding* is different from an argument or about some consequences of being *critical*.

Word Squares

Ask students to create Word Squares for each vocabulary word.

- In the first square, students write the word (e.g., *misunderstanding*).
- In the second square, students write their own definition of the word and any related words, such as synonyms (e.g., *mix-up, confusion, mistake*).
- In the third square, students draw a simple illustration that will help them remember the word (e.g., drawing of two people with confused faces and question marks over their heads).
- In the fourth square, students write nonexamples, including antonyms for the word (e.g., *understanding, agreement*).

Have partners discuss their squares.

Context Clues

Remind students to look for cause-and-effect clues to help figure out the meaning of unfamiliar words.

- Display On Level **Differentiated Genre Passage** "Potluck or Potlatch?" Read the second paragraph on page O1. Model using cause-and-effect relationship to define *reassure*.
- Have pairs use context clues to figure out meanings of other unfamiliar words in the passage.
- Partners can confirm meanings in a print or online dictionary.

See **Practice Book** page 144.

Shades of Meaning

Help students generate words related to *contradicted*. Draw a word web and write *contradicted* in the center.

- Have partners generate synonyms to add to the web. Ask students to use a thesaurus.
- Add words not included, such as *opposed, challenged, went against, disagreed with*.
- Ask students to copy the words in their reader's notebook.

Morphology

Draw a T-chart. Write *critical* in the left column. Explain that adding *-al* changes the noun *critic* to an adjective.

- In the right column of the T-chart, write *-ly* and *-ness*.
- Add each suffix to *critical*. Discuss changes to meaning and part of speech.
- Ask partners to list other words with these suffixes.

Write Using Vocabulary

Have students use vocabulary words in their extended writing.

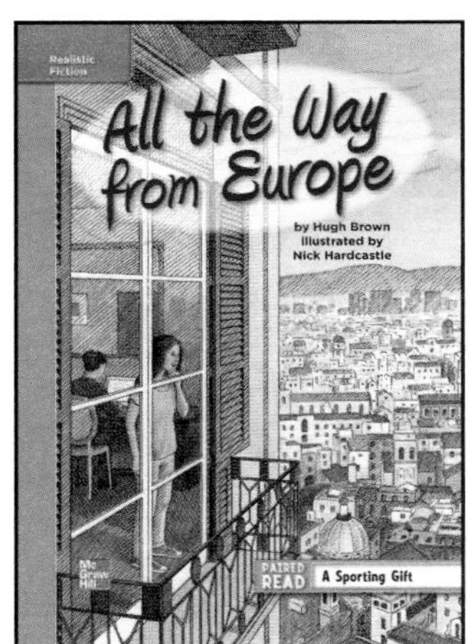

Lexile 690

OBJECTIVES

Determine a theme of a story, drama, or poem from details in the text, including how characters in a story or drama respond to challenges or how the speaker in a poem reflects upon a topic; summarize the text.

Describe how a narrator's or speaker's point of view influences how events are described.

Read grade-level prose and poetry orally with accuracy, appropriate rate, expression, and automaticity on successive readings.

ELA ACADEMIC LANGUAGE

- *realistic fiction, dialogue, theme, summarize, context clues*
- Cognates: *ficción realista, diálogo, tema*

Approaching Level

Leveled Reader: *All the Way from Europe*

Preview and Predict

- Read the Essential Question with students: *What can learning about different cultures teach us?*
- Have students read the title, table of contents, and opening page of *All the Way from Europe* and then preview the illustrations. Have students predict what they think the selection will be about.

Review Genre: Realistic Fiction

Remind students that realistic fiction includes characters, settings, and events similar to those in real life. Realistic fiction also includes dialogue. Have students identify features of realistic fiction in *All the Way from Europe.*

Close Reading

Note Taking Ask students to use a copy of online Theme **Graphic Organizer 5** as they read.

Pages 2–4 *Turn to a partner and summarize the problem that Sarah has.* (She is on a trip to Europe with her mother and is bored with the old buildings.) *What does her mother suggest to help solve Sarah's problem?* (She offers to let Sarah use her laptop to research the cities they visit. She also agrees to do what Sarah wants in the afternoons.)

Pages 5–7 *Reread the paragraphs at the bottom of page 6. What does the word* hesitated *mean?* ("paused" or "waited") *Which context clues help you understand its meaning?* ("looked a bit disappointed" and "but...") Have students add this word in their reader's notebook.

Pages 8–10 *What does Sarah do to make the trip more interesting?* (She researches information about each city she visits.) *How would you describe the theme of the story at this point?* (Foreign cities are very interesting if you stop to take the time to find out about them.)

Pages 11–13 *Reread the third, fourth, and fifth paragraphs on page 13. Which context clues help you determine what* coincidence *means?* (Sarah says that Naples is famous for its pizza, and her mom laughs and says that it also happens to be Sarah's favorite food. A coincidence is when events happen at the same time by accident but seem connected.) Have students add this word in their reader's notebook. *Reread the last paragraph on page 13. How can you tell that Sarah is changing her perspective about and starting to feel more comfortable in Europe?* (She wants to play soccer with a group of kids in a park in Naples.)

Pages 14–15 *Turn to a partner and summarize how Sarah's perspective has changed.* (She now is really interested in the cultures of different countries.) *What lesson about the United States has Sarah learned?* (Many of the things Americans love originally came from other countries.)

Respond to Reading Revisit the Essential Question and ask students to complete the Text Evidence questions on page 16.

Analytical Writing **Write About Reading** Check that students have correctly explained how Sarah's perspective changed after Chapter 1 and how this change connects to the story's theme.

Fluency: Intonation

Model Model reading the fourth and fifth paragraphs on page 2 with appropriate intonation. Next read the paragraphs aloud and have students read along with you.

Apply Have students practice reading with a partner.

Paired Read: "A Sporting Gift"

Make Connections: Write About It

Before reading, ask students to note that the genre of this text is expository text. Then discuss the Essential Question. After reading, ask students to write about connections between *All the Way from Europe* and "A Sporting Gift" to discuss what different cultures can teach us.

Genre Expository Text

Compare Texts
Read about where some sports started.

A SPORTING GIFT

Many sports that we think are as "American as apple pie" actually came from other places.

AMERICAN FOOTBALL

Some say modern American football had its start in 1823 in England. A schoolboy named William Ellis was playing soccer when he picked up the ball and ran with it. That was the beginning of a game called rugby, in which players can carry and throw the ball. Over time, the rugby ball became oval-shaped because that made it easier to carry and pass than a round ball.

In the 1870s, American football was played more like soccer than like rugby. Then schools and universities began to allow players to carry and throw the ball. By the 1880s, these rugby-type rules were popular, and the game that we know as American football was born.

Leveled Reader

Build Knowledge

Talk About the Text Have partners discuss what learning about different cultures can teach us.

Write About the Text Have students add their ideas to the Build Knowledge pages of their reader's notebooks.

FOCUS ON LITERARY ELEMENTS

Students can extend their knowledge of how authors use dialogue to advance the plot by completing the literary elements activity on page 20.

LITERATURE CIRCLES

Ask students to conduct a literature circle using the Thinkmark questions to guide the discussion. You may wish to have a whole-class discussion, using information from both selections in the Leveled Reader, about what learning about different cultures can teach us.

LEVEL UP

IF students read the Approaching Level fluently and answered the questions,

THEN pair them with students who have proficiently read the On Level and have students

- echo read the On Level main selection.
- use self-stick notes to mark at least one new detail that is characteristic of realistic fiction.

ACT Access Complex Text

The On Level challenges students by requiring more **prior knowledge** of different cultures and including more **complex sentence structures**.

"Potluck or Potlatch?"
Lexile 650L

OBJECTIVES

Quote accurately from a text when explaining what the text says explicitly and when drawing inferences from the text. Explain different characters' perspectives in a literary text.

Determine a theme of a story, drama, or poem from details in the text, including how characters in a story or drama respond to challenges or how the speaker in a poem reflects upon a topic; summarize the text.

Compare and contrast two or more characters, settings, or events in a story or drama, drawing on specific details in the text (e.g., how characters interact).

Describe how a narrator's or speaker's point of view influences how events are described.

Compare and contrast stories in the same genre (e.g., mysteries and adventure stories) on their approaches to similar themes and topics.

Determine or clarify the meaning of unknown and multiple-meaning words and phrases based on grade 5 reading and content, choosing flexibly from a range of strategies.

Use context (e.g., cause/effect relationships and comparisons in text) as a clue to the meaning of a word or phrase.

ELA ACADEMIC LANGUAGE

- *realistic fiction, dialogue, theme, culture, celebration*
- Cognates: *ficción realista, diálogo, tema, cultura, celebración*

Approaching Level

Genre Passage: "Potluck or Potlatch?"

Build Background

- Read aloud the Essential Question: *What can learning about different cultures teach us?* Ask students to compare two cultural traditions from texts they have read in this text set. Use the following sentence starters:

  I read that traditions...

  This helps me understand that cultures...

- Explain that the online **Differentiated Genre Passage** "Potluck or Potlatch?" is about two different celebrations. A *potluck* is a meal to which each guest brings something to eat or drink. A *potlatch* is a Native American celebration to celebrate births, marriages, and other important life events. Potlatches are about more than sharing wealth. Accepting the gifts offered at a potlatch means that guests support the event. It is a celebration, an act of generosity, a legal act, and an expression of spirituality.

Review Genre: Realistic Fiction

Remind students that realistic fiction includes characters, settings, and events from the present time. The conflicts and relationships between characters are often familiar. Realistic fiction includes dialogue and descriptive details.

Close Reading

Note Taking As students read the passage the first time, ask them to annotate the text. Have them note central ideas, relevant details, unfamiliar words, and questions they have. Then read again using the following questions.

Genre: Realistic Fiction Read the first two paragraphs on page A1. *What is Alex bringing to the party?* (brownies) *What does Alex's mom call him?* ("sweetie") *How do these details signal that the story is realistic fiction?* (They are all things that people might say or do.)

Context Clues Read paragraph 4 on page A1. *What does Wakiash ask when Alex hands him the brownies? Why?* (He asks what the brownies are for. He doesn't understand why Alex brought the brownies because he had told Alex not to bring anything.) *How does this help you understand what it means to look puzzled?* (It tells me that when you are puzzled, you are confused.)

Literary Elements: Dialogue Read paragraph 1 on page A2. *How do the first two sentences help you understand that Wakiash is excited?* (The sentences end in exclamation points.)

Theme Read the rest of page A2. *What is Alex's perspective on the potlatch? How do you know?* (He feels happy. He says the potlatch is "pretty cool," and he smiles.) *What does his perspective suggest about one of the story's themes?* (It suggests that making a mistake doesn't mean you can't enjoy an event.)

Summarize Have students use their notes to summarize what happens at a potlatch.

Reread

Use the questions on page A3 to guide students' rereading of the passage.

Author's Craft Reread paragraph 5 on page A1. *How does the author help you understand how Alex feels? Why does he feel this way?* (The author writes: "Alex looked down at his feet in confusion" and that "his face grew hot with embarrassment." Alex didn't understand what a potlatch was.)

Author's Craft Reread the eighth paragraph on page A1. *How does the author use dialogue to help you understand what a potlatch is?* (The author has Mrs. Wright tell Alex what happens at a potlatch. This helps the reader know what happens at a potlatch.)

Author's Craft Reread the last paragraph on page A2. *How does the author help you understand that Alex is "having so much fun"?* (Alex loses track of time and doesn't want to go home.)

Integrate

Make Connections Guide students to see the connections between "Potluck or Potlatch?" and "A Reluctant Traveler" on pages 12–15 of the **Reading/Writing Companion**. Have pairs respond to this question: *How do the authors help you understand what learning about a different culture can teach you?*

Compare Texts Draw a Venn diagram with circles labeled *Paul* and *Alex*. Work together to complete it with details that reflect what each character learns.

Build Knowledge

Talk About the Text Have partners discuss what learning about different cultures can teach us.

Write About the Text Have students add their ideas to the Build Knowledge pages of their reader's notebooks.

Differentiate and Collaborate

Be inspired Have students think about "Potluck or Potlatch?" and other selections they have read. Ask: *What do the texts inspire you to do?* Guide students in using the following activities, or have pairs think of a way to respond to the texts.

Plan a Menu Use what you've learned to plan a multicultural lunch menu. Be sure to include foods from several cultures. Share your menu with the school staff of your school's cafeteria.

Create a Visitor's Guide Choose a culture you've read about and create a visitor's guide. Your guide should help visitors decide what to do, see, and eat.

Readers to Writers

Realistic Dialogue Remind students that authors of realistic fiction write dialogue that sounds familiar to readers. Including current expressions and references in dialogue helps an author create characters who seem like people readers might actually know. Have students reread the fifth paragraph on page A1. Ask: *What does the author do to make Alex's dialogue sound like something you or your friends might say?*

LEVEL UP

IF students read the Approaching Level fluently and answered the questions,

THEN pair them with students who have proficiently read the On Level. Have them

- partner read the On Level passage.
- summarize what one character learns by experiencing a different culture.

Approaching Level

Phonics/Decoding

REVIEW WORDS WITH OPEN SYLLABLES

OBJECTIVES

Know and apply grade-level phonics and word analysis skills in decoding words.

Use combined knowledge of all letter-sound correspondences, syllabication patterns, and morphology to read accurately unfamiliar multisyllabic words in context and out of context.

Decode words with open syllables.

I Do

Write the word *remove* on the board, labeling the vowel-consonant-vowel. Explain that syllables in words with the VCV pattern can divide after the first vowel (V/CV). The first syllable in these words ends in a vowel. It is called an **open syllable**. Draw a slash to divide *remove* into syllables: *re/move*. Pronounce the word, running your finger under the letters that spell the open syllable.

We Do

Write the words *nature, polar,* and *sinus* on the board. Say the word *nature* aloud, running your finger under the letters that spell the open syllable. Have volunteers repeat with the words *polar* and *sinus*.

You Do

Add the following examples to the board: *pirate, demand, solar.* Have students chorally read the syllables and words. Repeat several times.

PRACTICE WORDS WITH OPEN SYLLABLES

OBJECTIVES

Know and apply grade-level phonics and word analysis skills in decoding words.

Use combined knowledge of all letter-sound correspondences, syllabication patterns, and morphology to read accurately unfamiliar multisyllabic words in context and out of context.

Practice words with open syllables.

I Do

Write the words *broken, radio,* and *behave* on the board. Read the words aloud, running your finger under the letters that spell the open syllables in the words as you say them. Identify the long vowel sound in each open syllable.

We Do

Write the words *minus, silence,* and *begin* on the board. Model how to say the syllables in the word *minus,* and then say the word itself. Guide students as they repeat the process with the remaining words. As necessary, help them identify the open syllable in each word.

You Do

Afterward, point to each word in random order. Have students chorally say the syllables in each word and then say the word itself.

REVIEW WORDS WITH OPEN SYLLABLES (V/V)

TIER 2

OBJECTIVES

Know and apply grade-level phonics and word analysis skills in decoding words.

Use combined knowledge of all letter-sound correspondences, syllabication patterns, and morphology to read accurately unfamiliar multisyllabic words in context and out of context.

Decode words with open syllables (V/V).

I Do Remind students that every syllable has only one vowel sound. Write the word *diet* on the board, labeling each of the middle vowels with a *V*. Draw a slash to divide the word into syllables: *di/et*. Explain that in this word, the first syllable ends in a vowel. It is an open syllable. The second syllable begins with a vowel. *Diet* has a V/V (Vowel/Vowel) pattern.

We Do Write the word *duet* on the board, drawing a slash between the syllables: *du/et*. Model how to say each syllable in the word *duet* and have students repeat after you. Point out that in this word, as in most words with open syllables, the first vowel sound is long. Write the word *riot* on the board and have students divide it into syllables and pronounce them.

You Do Add the following examples to the board: *fuel, science*. Have students divide the words into syllables and pronounce them.

PRACTICE WORDS WITH OPEN SYLLABLES (V/V)

OBJECTIVES

Know and apply grade-level phonics and word analysis skills in decoding words.

Use combined knowledge of all letter-sound correspondences, syllabication patterns, and morphology to read accurately unfamiliar multisyllabic words in context and out of context.

Decode words with open syllables (V/V).

I Do Write the words *liar* and *area* on the board. Read the words aloud, running your finger under the letters that form the open syllables as you pronounce them. Identify the long vowel sound in each open syllable.

We Do Write the words *ruin, cereal, rodeo, diary, audio,* and *violin* on the board. Model how to decode the first word, and then guide students as they decode the remaining words. As necessary, help them identify the open syllable with the V/V pattern in the word.

You Do Point to the words in random order for students to read chorally.

ELL For **ELL** students who need phonics and decoding practice, define words and help them use the words in sentences, scaffolding to ensure their understanding. See the **Language Transfers Handbook** for phonics elements that may not transfer from students' native languages.

Approaching Level

Vocabulary

REVIEW HIGH-FREQUENCY WORDS

TIER 2

OBJECTIVES

Acquire and use accurately grade-appropriate general academic and domain-specific words and phrases, including those that signal contrast, addition, and other logical relationships (e.g., *however, although, nevertheless, similarly, moreover, in addition*).

I Do Use **High-Frequency Word Cards** 81–100. Display one word at a time, following the routine.

We Do Display the word. Read the word. Then spell the word.

Ask students to state the word and spell the word with you. Model using the word in a sentence and have students repeat the sentence after you.

You Do Display the word. Ask students to say the word, and then spell it. When completed, quickly flip through the word card set as students chorally read the words. Provide opportunities for students to use the words in speaking and writing. For example, provide sentence starters, such as *At the store, I got* ____. Ask students to write each word in their reader's notebook.

REVIEW ACADEMIC VOCABULARY

TIER 2

OBJECTIVES

Acquire and use accurately grade-appropriate general academic and domain-specific words and phrases, including those that signal contrast, addition, and other logical relationships (e.g., *however, although, nevertheless, similarly, moreover, in addition*).

I Do Display each **Visual Vocabulary Card** and state the word. Explain how the photograph illustrates the word. State the example sentence and repeat the word.

We Do Point to the word on the card and read the word with students. Ask them to repeat the word. Engage students in structured partner talk about the image as prompted on the back of the vocabulary card.

You Do Display each visual in random order, hiding the word. Have students match the definitions and context sentences of the words to the visuals displayed.

You may wish to review high-frequency words with ELL students using the lesson above.

UNDERSTAND ACADEMIC VOCABULARY

OBJECTIVES

Acquire and use accurately grade-appropriate general academic and domain-specific words and phrases, including those that signal contrast, addition, and other logical relationships (e.g., *however, although, nevertheless, similarly, moreover, in addition*).

I Do Display the **Visual Vocabulary Card for** *appreciation*. Ask: *Would a person with an appreciation for music enjoy a concert?* Explain that a person who has an appreciation for music would likely enjoy listening to music at a concert.

We Do Ask these questions. Help students respond and explain their answers.

- If you *blurted* something out, did you say it suddenly?
- If someone is *complimenting* you, are they praising you?
- If you *congratulate* a friend, do you express pleasure at her success?

You Do Have student pairs respond to these questions and explain their answers.

- If you *contradicted* someone, did you agree with that person?
- Does a *critical* person give a lot of compliments?
- Is an art festival a *cultural* activity or a sports event?
- Do people who have a *misunderstanding* see things differently?

Have students pick words from their reader's notebook and use an online thesaurus to find synonyms and a dictionary to check their pronunciation.

CONTEXT CLUES

OBJECTIVES

Determine or clarify the meaning of unknown and multiple-meaning words and phrases based on grade 5 reading and content, choosing flexibly from a range of strategies.

Use context (e.g., cause/effect relationships and comparisons in text) as a clue to the meaning of a word or phrase.

I Do Display the Approaching Level of "Potluck or Potlatch?" in the online **Differentiated Genre Passages**. Read aloud the sixth paragraph on page A1. Point to the word *nervous*. Model using cause-and-effect context clues to figure out the meaning of this word.

Think Aloud I notice that Alex felt a little less nervous after Mrs. Wright placed a warm hand on his shoulder. If her comforting gesture made him feel less nervous, then *nervous* must mean "worried."

We Do Ask students to point to the word *confused* (paragraph 2, page A2). With students, discuss how to use the clues in the text to figure out the meaning of the word. Have students write the definition in their reader's notebook.

You Do Have students find the meaning of *startled* (paragraph 5, page A2) using clues from the passage. Then have students write the definition in their reader's notebook. They can use a dictionary to confirm meanings.

Approaching Level

Fluency/Comprehension

FLUENCY

OBJECTIVES

Read grade-level prose and poetry orally with accuracy, appropriate rate, expression, and automaticity on successive readings.

Read fluently with good intonation.

I Do Explain that reading a selection aloud isn't just about reading the words correctly. Readers should change the sound of their voice to help show the meaning of what they read. Read the first paragraph of "Potluck or Potlatch?" in the Approaching Level online **Differentiated Genre Passage** page A1. Tell students to listen for when you raise or lower your voice or place more emphasis on certain words.

We Do Read aloud the rest of page A1 and have students read after you, using the same intonation.

You Do Have partners take turns reading sentences from the passage. Remind them to focus on their intonation. Listen in and provide corrective feedback as needed by modeling proper fluency.

IDENTIFY WHAT CHARACTERS THINK, SAY, AND DO

TIER 2

OBJECTIVES

Determine a theme of a story, drama, or poem from details in the text, including how characters in a story or drama respond to challenges or how the speaker in a poem reflects upon a topic; summarize the text.

I Do Read aloud the first two paragraphs of "Potluck or Potlatch?" in the online Approaching Level **Differentiated Genre Passage** page A1. Ask: *Why does Alex ask if he is supposed to bring food?* Model answering the question: *He is nervous because his friend told him not to bring anything.* Explain that identifying things a character thinks, says, and does can reveal that character's perspective, or attitude, and help reveal the story's theme.

We Do Continue reading the first page of the passage. Ask: *What misunderstanding does Alex have?* Help students recognize that Alex misunderstands the term *potlatch.*

You Do Have students read the rest of the passage and identify important statements the characters make. Review these and discuss possible perspectives and themes the statements might suggest.

REVIEW THEME

OBJECTIVES

Determine a theme of a story, drama, or poem from details in the text, including how characters in a story or drama respond to challenges or how the speaker in a poem reflects upon a topic; summarize the text.

I Do Review that theme is a story's message. Themes are usually not stated directly. Readers can identify themes by identifying what a character thinks, does, and says and determining a character's perspective, or attitude, toward a conflict, character, or event. Then they should consider what message the author is trying to convey through the character.

We Do Read together the first paragraph of "Potluck or Potlatch?" in the online Approaching Level **Differentiated Genre Passage** page A1. Model identifying key things Alex thinks, does, or says. Then work with students to do the same on the rest of the page. Discuss what these details say about Alex's perspective and a possible theme.

You Do Have students identify things Alex thinks, does, or says in the rest of the passage. Have them use these details to summarize important events and determine the theme of the passage.

SELF-SELECTED READING

OBJECTIVES

Determine a theme of a story, drama, or poem from details in the text, including how characters in a story or drama respond to challenges or how the speaker in a poem reflects upon a topic; summarize the text.

Independent Reading

In this text set, students focus on these key aspects of fiction: the development of implied and stated themes and how the author develops a character's perspective. Guide students to transfer what they have learned in this text set as well as in previous lessons as they read independently.

Have students choose a realistic fiction book for sustained silent reading and set a purpose for reading that book. Students can check the online **Leveled Reader Library** for selections. Remind students that:

- theme is a message readers are meant to infer in the story.
- summarizing will help them remember and recall important details in the story.

Have students record what the character does and says and what happens to the character on Theme **Graphic Organizer 5** as they read independently. After they finish, they can conduct a Book Talk about what they read.

- Students should share their organizers and identify different themes as well as their favorite part of the story.
- They should also summarize the story, identifying and describing for others the most important story events and details. Remind students to summarize texts in ways that maintain meaning and logical order.

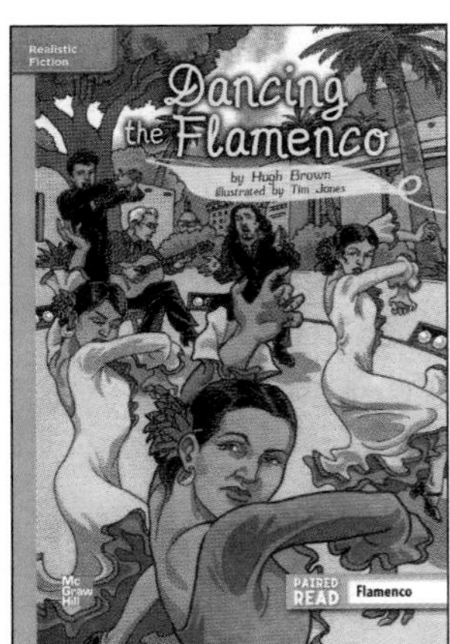

Lexile 790L

OBJECTIVES

Determine a theme of a story, drama, or poem from details in the text, including how characters in a story or drama respond to challenges or how the speaker in a poem reflects upon a topic; summarize the text.

Describe how a narrator's or speaker's point of view influences how events are described.

Read grade-level prose and poetry orally with accuracy, appropriate rate, expression, and automaticity on successive readings.

ELA ACADEMIC LANGUAGE

- *realistic fiction, dialogue, theme, summarize, context clues*
- Cognates: *ficción realista, diálogo, tema*

On Level

Leveled Reader: *Dancing the Flamenco*

Preview and Predict

- Have students read the Essential Question: *What can learning about different cultures teach us?*
- Have students read the title, table of contents, and opening page of *Dancing the Flamenco*. Then preview the illustrations. Have students predict what they think the selection will be about.

Review Genre: Realistic Fiction

Remind students that realistic fiction includes characters, settings, and events similar to those in real life. Realistic fiction also includes dialogue. Have students identify features of realistic fiction in *Dancing the Flamenco*.

Close Reading

Note Taking Ask students to use a copy of online Theme **Graphic Organizer 5** as they read.

Pages 2–3 *Turn to a partner and summarize the beginning of the story.* (Carla's mother drives the family to pick up Aunt Ceci so they can all go somewhere special. Carla hopes they are going shopping, so she is a little disappointed when she finds out they are going to a dance festival.) *What context clues help you understand the meaning of* hosting*?* ("one of Tucson's dance schools"; '"fabulous cultural event!"') Have students add this word in their reader's notebook.

Pages 4–7 *Paraphrase events in the third paragraph on page 4.* (Carla likes watching the dancers' energetic performance and listening to the music.) *Now paraphrase events in the third paragraph on page 6.* (Carla is so fascinated by the dancing that she imitates the dancers' postures.) *What theme might be suggested by this change in Carla's perspective and behavior?* (People's perspectives can change once they experience something new.)

Pages 8–9 *Reread the last four paragraphs on page 8. Which context clues in the dialogue help you understand the meaning of the word* scolded*?* ("Don't be so critical, Mat.") Have students add this word in their reader's notebook. *What happens when the family returns to Aunt Ceci's house?* (Aunt Ceci begins to teach Carla how to dance the flamenco.)

Pages 10–11 *Reread page 10. Turn to a partner and summarize what Carla does after she leaves Aunt Ceci's house.* (She thinks about flamenco dancing and taps her feet in the car. Before bed, she practices again.) *What does Carla want for her birthday?* (flamenco dance lessons)

Pages 12–15 *Summarize events described on pages 12 and 13.* (Carla's mother, Maria, picks Carla up from school and takes her to a dance studio for her first lesson. Maria brings clothes for Carla to wear and gives her a box to open inside. Carla feels nervous.) *What two final surprises does Maria have for Carla?* (Maria is going to take flamenco lessons with her. Carla's present turns out to be flamenco shoes.)

Respond to Reading Revisit the Essential Question and ask students to complete the Text Evidence Questions on page 16.

Analytical Writing **Write About Reading** Check that students have correctly identified the theme the author is trying to convey through Carla's change of perspective after she experiences the flamenco performance.

Fluency: Intonation

Model Model reading page 6 with proper intonation. Then read the passage aloud and have students read along with you.

Apply Have students practice reading with a partner.

Paired Read: "Flamenco"

Make Connections: Write About It

Before reading, ask students to note that the genre of this text is expository text. Then discuss the Essential Question. After reading, have students write connections between *Dancing the Flamenco* and "Flamenco."

Leveled Reader

Build Knowledge

Talk About the Text Have partners discuss what learning about different cultures can teach us.

Write About the Text Have students add their ideas to the Build Knowledge pages of their reader's notebooks.

FOCUS ON LITERARY ELEMENTS

Students can extend their knowledge of how authors use dialogue to advance the plot by completing the literary elements activity on page 20.

LITERATURE CIRCLES

Ask students to conduct a literature circle using the Thinkmark questions to guide the discussion. You may wish to have a whole-class discussion, using information in both selections in the Leveled Reader, regarding what learning about different cultures can teach us.

LEVEL UP

IF students read the On Level fluently and answered the questions,

THEN pair them with students who have proficiently read the Beyond Level and have students

- echo read the Beyond Level main selection.
- identify characteristics of realistic fiction throughout the text.

ACT Access Complex Text

The Beyond Level challenges students by requiring more complicated inferences to **connect ideas** and by including **complex sentence structures**.

"Potluck or Potlatch?"
Lexile 750L

OBJECTIVES

Quote accurately from a text when explaining what the text says explicitly and when drawing inferences from the text. Explain different characters' perspectives in a literary text.

Determine a theme of a story, drama, or poem from details in the text, including how characters in a story or drama respond to challenges or how the speaker in a poem reflects upon a topic; summarize the text.

Compare and contrast stories in the same genre (e.g., mysteries and adventure stories) on their approaches to similar themes and topics.

Compare and contrast two or more characters, settings, or events in a story or drama, drawing on specific details in the text (e.g., how characters interact).

Determine or clarify the meaning of unknown and multiple-meaning words and phrases based on grade 5 reading and content, choosing flexibly from a range of strategies.

Use context (e.g., cause/effect relationships and comparisons in text) as a clue to the meaning of a word or phrase.

ELA ACADEMIC LANGUAGE

- *realistic fiction, dialogue, theme, culture, celebration*
- Cognates: *ficción realista, diálogo, tema, cultura, celebración*

On Level

Genre Passage: "Potluck or Potlatch?"

Build Background

- Read aloud the Essential Question: *What can learning about different cultures teach us?* Ask students to compare two cultural traditions from texts they have read in this text set. Use the following sentence starters:

  I read that traditions...

  This helps me understand that cultures...

- Explain the online **Differentiated Genre Passage** "Potluck or Potlatch?" is about two different types of celebrations. A *potluck* is a meal to which each guest brings something to eat or drink. A *potlatch* is a Native American celebration held to celebrate births, marriages, and other life events. Potlatches are about more than sharing wealth. Accepting the gifts offered at a potlatch means that guests support the event. It is a celebration, an act of generosity, a legal act, and an expression of spirituality.

Review Genre: Realistic Fiction

Remind students that realistic fiction includes characters, settings, and events from the present time. The conflicts and relationships between characters are often familiar to readers. Realistic fiction includes dialogue that reflects the way real people speak, as well as descriptive details that make the story believable.

Close Reading

Note Taking As students read the passage the first time, ask them to annotate the text. Have them note central ideas, relevant details, unfamiliar words, and questions they have. Then read again and use the following questions.

Genre: Realistic Fiction Read paragraphs 1–3 on page O1. *What details help you understand that this selection is realistic fiction?* (Alex brings brownies to a party. He and his mom are in a car. Alex's mom calls him "sweetie.")

Context Clues Read paragraph 5 on page O1. *Why does Alex look at his feet?* (He looks at his feet because he's embarrassed.) *What does this tell you about the meaning of* mortified? (It may mean the same as "embarrassed.")

Theme Read paragraph 6 on page O1. *How does Mrs. Wright react to Alex's mistake?* (She puts her hand on his shoulder and makes Alex feel "a little less nervous" by saying the brownies were "a lovely thought.") *What theme might this suggest?* (It is important to be kind to others even if they make a mistake.)

Literary Elements: Dialogue Read paragraphs 4-5 on page O2. *How does Wakiash's dialogue help you understand more about Wakiash as a character?* (Wakiash says the important part of the potlatch is that the host gives to others. He is generous.)

Theme Read the rest of page O2. *How does Alex's perspective about the potlatch change?* (At first, Alex is nervous and embarrassed. By the end, he realizes a potlatch is fun.) *What theme might this suggest?* (Making a mistake doesn't mean you can't have fun.)

COLLABORATE **Summarize** Have students use their notes to summarize the misunderstanding and how it leads to Alex's change in perspective.

Reread

Use the questions on page O3 to guide students' rereading of the passage.

Author's Craft Read the fifth paragraph on page O1. *How does the author help you understand how Alex is feeling after he gives Wakiash the brownies? Why does Alex feel this way?* (The author shows that Alex feels uncomfortable; he looks down at his feet while talking. He is hesitant and mortified.)

Author's Craft *On page O2, how does the author use dialogue to help readers understand what a potlatch is?* (Mrs. Wright and Wakiash tell Alex what a potlatch is and what happens at one.)

Author's Craft Reread the last paragraph on page O2. *How does the author show that Alex is "having so much fun"?* (Alex is having fun; he loses track of time; isn't ready to go home; and asks to stay.)

Integrate

COLLABORATE **Make Connections** Encourage students to explore the connections between "Potluck or Potlatch?" and "A Reluctant Traveler" on pages 12-15 of the **Reading/Writing Companion.** Have pairs respond to this question: *How do the authors help you understand what learning about a different culture can teach you?*

Compare Texts Have students draw a Venn diagram with circles labeled *Paul* and *Alex*. Tell pairs to work together to complete it with details.

Build Knowledge

Talk About the Text Have partners discuss what learning about different cultures can teach us.

Write About the Text Have students add their ideas to the Build Knowledge pages of their reader's notebooks.

Differentiate and Collaborate

COLLABORATE **Be inspired** Have students think about "Potluck or Potlatch?" and other selections they have read. Ask: *What do the texts inspire you to do?* Use the following activities or have pairs of students think of a way to respond to the texts.

Plan a Menu Use what you've learned to plan a multicultural lunch menu. Be sure to include foods from several cultures. Share your menu with the staff of your school cafeteria.

Create a Visitor's Guide Choose a culture you've read about and create a visitor's guide. Your guide should help visitors decide what to do, see, and eat.

Readers to Writers

Realistic Dialogue Remind students that authors of realistic fiction write dialogue that sounds familiar to readers. Including current expressions and references in dialogue helps an author create characters who seem like people readers might actually know. Have students reread the fifth paragraph on page O1. Ask: *What does the author do to make Alex's dialogue sound like something you or your friends might say?*

LEVEL UP

IF students read the **On Level** fluently and answered the questions,

THEN pair them with students who have proficiently read the **Beyond Level**. Have them

- partner read the **Beyond Level** passage.
- summarize what the potlatch experience teaches both Alex and the Wright family.

On Level

Vocabulary/Comprehension

REVIEW ACADEMIC VOCABULARY

MULTIMODAL

OBJECTIVES

Acquire and use accurately grade-appropriate general academic and domain-specific words and phrases, including those that signal contrast, addition, and other logical relationships (e.g., *however, although, nevertheless, similarly, moreover, in addition*).

I Do Use the **Visual Vocabulary Cards** to review the key selection words *blurted, complimenting, congratulate, contradicted, critical,* and *misunderstanding.* Point to each, read it aloud, and have students repeat.

We Do Ask these questions. Help students explain their answers.

- When have you *blurted* out something?
- How might *complimenting* people make them feel?
- What might you say to *congratulate* someone?

You Do Have student pairs respond to these questions and explain their answers.

- When have you *contradicted* someone?
- Do you think a good coach needs to be *critical*?
- How can you clear up a *misunderstanding*?

Have students pick words from their reader's notebook and use an online thesaurus to find words with similar meanings.

CONTEXT CLUES: CAUSE AND EFFECT

OBJECTIVES

Determine or clarify the meaning of unknown and multiple-meaning words and phrases based on grade 5 reading and content, choosing flexibly from a range of strategies.

Use context (e.g., cause/effect relationships and comparisons in text) as a clue to the meaning of a word or phrase.

I Do Tell students they can often figure out the meaning of an unknown word from cause-and-effect clues within the paragraph. Read aloud the sixth paragraph of "Potluck or Potlatch?" in the On Level online **Differentiated Genre Passage** page O1.

Think Aloud I want to know what the word *nervous* means. When I read the sentence, I see that Mrs. Wright's gesture of placing a warm hand on Alex's shoulder causes him to feel less nervous. This cause-and-effect clue helps me figure out that *nervous* means "to feel worried."

We Do Have students read paragraph four on page O2. Help students figure out the definition of the word *confused* by pointing out the cause-and-effect clue *"so Wakiash explained."*

You Do Have students work in pairs to determine the meaning of the word *startled* in the last paragraph on page O2.

REVIEW THEME

OBJECTIVES

Determine a theme of a story, drama, or poem from details in the text, including how characters in a story or drama respond to challenges or how the speaker in a poem reflects upon a topic; summarize the text.

I Do Review with students that theme is a message about life that the author wishes to convey. You can find it by thinking about what characters say and do and about what happens to them.

We Do Have a volunteer read the first paragraph of "Potluck or Potlatch?" in the On Level online **Differentiated Genre Passage** page O1. Model identifying things the characters do, say, and experience. Then work with students to identify things the characters do, say, and experience in the next three paragraphs.

You Do Have partners identify the characters' words and actions and things that happen to them in the rest of the passage. Then have partners use these details to retell the passage and determine one of its themes.

SELF-SELECTED READING

OBJECTIVES

Determine a theme of a story, drama, or poem from details in the text, including how characters in a story or drama respond to challenges or how the speaker in a poem reflects upon a topic; summarize the text.

Independent Reading

In this text set, students focus on the development of implied and stated themes and how the author develops a character's perspective. Guide students to transfer what they have learned in this text set as well as in previous lessons as they read independently.

Have students choose a realistic fiction book for sustained silent reading. They can check the online **Leveled Reader Library** for selections.

- Before they read, have students preview the book, reading the title and viewing the front and back cover. Have them set a purpose for reading.
- As students read, remind them to summarize.

Encourage students to select books by a variety of authors in order to learn about different writing styles.

- As students read, have them fill in the characters' words, actions, and experiences on Theme **Graphic Organizer 5** and use these details to determine a theme of the book.
- They can use the organizer to help them write a summary of the book.
- Ask students to share their reactions to the book with classmates.

You may want to include ELL students in On Level vocabulary and comprehension lessons. Offer language support as needed.

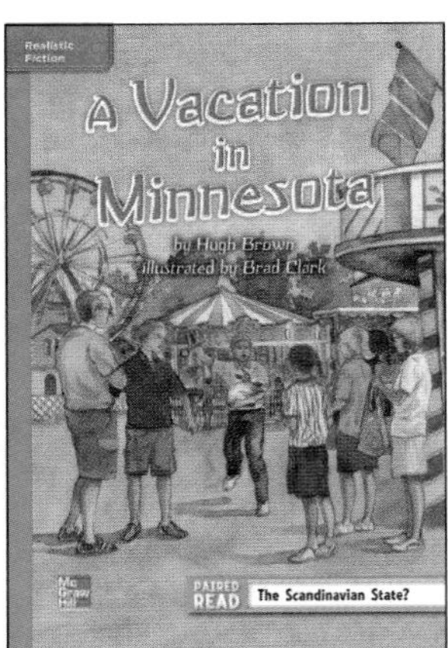

Lexile 950

OBJECTIVES

Determine a theme of a story, drama, or poem from details in the text, including how characters in a story or drama respond to challenges or how the speaker in a poem reflects upon a topic; summarize the text.

Describe how a narrator's or speaker's point of view influences how events are described.

Read grade-level prose and poetry orally with accuracy, appropriate rate, expression, and automaticity on successive readings.

ELA ACADEMIC LANGUAGE

- *realistic fiction, dialogue, theme, summarize, context clues*
- Cognates: *ficción realista, diálogo, tema*

Beyond Level

Leveled Reader: *A Vacation in Minnesota*

Preview and Predict

- Have students read the Essential Question: *What can learning about different cultures teach us?*
- Have students read the title, table of contents, and opening page of *A Vacation in Minnesota* and then preview the illustrations. They should predict what they think the selection will be about. Ask students to discuss and compare their predictions.

Review Genre: Realistic Fiction

Remind students that realistic fiction includes characters, settings, and events similar to those in real life. Realistic fiction also includes dialogue and descriptive details. Have students identify features of realistic fiction in *A Vacation in Minnesota*.

Close Reading

Note Taking Ask students to use a copy of online Theme **Graphic Organizer 5** as they read.

Pages 2–4 *Turn to a partner and summarize important events and ideas described on the first two pages.* (Peter arrives in Minnesota, expecting it to be quieter than New York City. His uncle Gunnar takes him to the family farm, where he meets his aunt and cousins.) *Reread page 3. What does the figurative expression "catch his breath" mean?* ("relax" or "compose oneself") *What context clues help you know what* bustle *means on page 4?* ("around the kitchen"; "Soon Peter had a plate piled high") Have students add this word in their reader's notebook.

Pages 5–8 *This story is about how life is different in different parts of the country. Which details support this theme?* (Peter's cousins joke with him about large mosquitoes. Then they teach him how to skip a stone. They also show him rabbits, which he's never seen.) *What context clues help you understand the meaning of the word* stampeding *on page 7?* ("herd of elephants"; "no way you'll sleep through that") Have students add this word in their reader's notebook. *Reread page 8. How can you tell that Peter is beginning to change his perspective and feel more comfortable on his visit?* (He jokes with his cousins and helps out with their chores. He tells his aunt and uncle that he's had fun getting to know the farm.)

Pages 9–12 *Turn to a partner and summarize the activities described on pages 9 and 10.* (The family visits the fair. The cousins watch monster trucks, play carnival games, and ride bumper cars. Lars wins the rabbit contest. They go home, have a quick swim, do chores, and eat dinner.) *Reread page 12. Has his Minnesota vacation turned out to be as quiet as Peter expected? Explain.* (Minnesota has turned out to be much busier than Peter expected. He is so tired from all the fun activities that he falls asleep on the couch after dinner.)

Pages 13–15 *How does Peter compare Sundays in New York City with Sundays in Minnesota?* (Sundays in New York City are more quiet.) *How do you know that Peter's perspective has changed and he has enjoyed his visit?* (He hopes to be invited back.)

Respond to Reading Revisit the Essential Question and ask students to complete the Text Evidence Questions on page 16.

Analytical Writing **Write About Reading** Check that students have correctly explained how the comparison on page 15 expresses the overall theme.

Fluency: Intonation

Model Model reading aloud page 3 with proper intonation. Then read the passage aloud and have students read along with you.

Apply Have students practice reading with partners.

Paired Read: "The Scandinavian State?"

Make Connections: Write About It

Before reading, ask students to note that the genre of this text is expository text. Then discuss the Essential Question. After reading, ask students to write connections between *A Vacation in Minnesota* and "The Scandinavian State?"

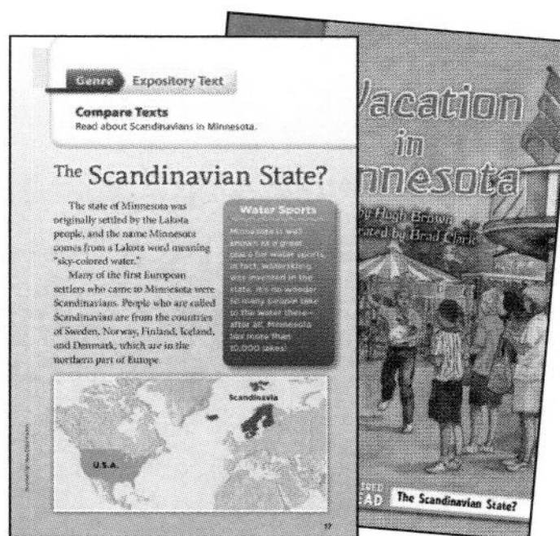

Leveled Reader

Build Knowledge

Talk About the Text Have partners discuss what learning about different cultures can teach us.

Write About the Text Have students add their ideas to the Build Knowledge pages of their reader's notebooks.

FOCUS ON LITERARY ELEMENTS

Students can extend their knowledge of how authors use dialogue to advance the plot by completing the literary elements activity on page 20.

LITERATURE CIRCLES

Ask students to conduct a literature circle using the Thinkmark questions to guide the discussion. You may wish to have a whole-class discussion, using information from both selections in the Leveled Reader, regarding what learning about different cultures can teach us.

GIFTED AND TALENTED

Synthesize Challenge students to list questions and challenges that might arise when being introduced to an unfamiliar culture. Pairs of students should record the initial feelings they might have or difficulties they might encounter during the process, comparing their own experiences with Peter's. Finally, students should use their experiences as well as details in the text to describe the benefits that come from learning about another culture.

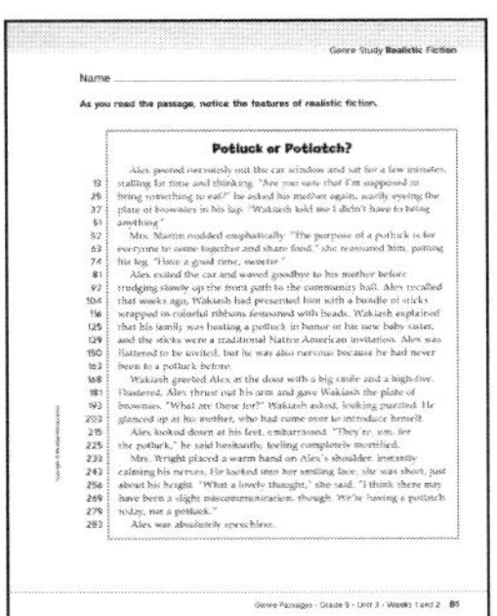

"Potluck or Potlatch?"
Lexile 810L

OBJECTIVES

Quote accurately from a text when explaining what the text says explicitly and when drawing inferences from the text. Explain different characters' perspectives in a literary text.

Determine a theme of a story, drama, or poem from details in the text, including how characters in a story or drama respond to challenges or how the speaker in a poem reflects upon a topic; summarize the text.

Compare and contrast two or more characters, settings, or events in a story or drama, drawing on specific details in the text (e.g., how characters interact).

Determine or clarify the meaning of unknown and multiple-meaning words and phrases based on grade 5 reading and content, choosing flexibly from a range of strategies.

Use context (e.g., cause/effect relationships and comparisons in text) as a clue to the meaning of a word or phrase.

ELA ACADEMIC LANGUAGE

- *realistic fiction, dialogue, theme, culture, celebration*
- Cognates: *ficción realista, diálogo, tema, cultura, celebracíon*

Beyond Level

Genre Passage: "Potluck or Potlatch?"

Build Background

- Read aloud the Essential Question: *What can learning about different cultures teach us?* Ask students to compare two cultural traditions from texts they have read in this text set. Use the following sentence starters:

  I read that traditions...

  This helps me understand that cultures...

- Let students know that the online **Differentiated Genre Passage** "Potluck or Potlatch?" is about two different types of celebrations. A *potluck* is a meal to which each guest brings something to eat or drink. A *potlatch* is a Native American celebration held to celebrate births, marriages, and other important life events. Potlatches are about more than sharing wealth. Accepting the gifts offered at a potlatch means that guests support the event. It is a celebration, an act of generosity, a legal act, and an expression of spirituality.

Review Genre: Realistic Fiction

Remind students that realistic fiction includes characters, settings, and events from the present time. The conflicts and relationships between characters are often familiar to readers. Realistic fiction includes dialogue that reflects the way real people speak, as well as descriptive details that make the story believable.

Close Reading

Note Taking As students read the passage the first time, ask them to annotate the text. Have them note central ideas, relevant details, unfamiliar words, and questions they have. Then read again and use the following questions. Encourage students to cite text evidence from the selection.

Read

Genre: Realistic Fiction Read the first three paragraphs on page B1. *What details help you identify the story as realistic fiction?* (Alex and his mom are in a car. Alex is bringing brownies to a party. Alex's mom calls him "sweetie.")

Context Clues Read paragraph 4 on page B1. *What does Alex do when Wakiash greets him with a big smile and a high-five?* (He puts his arm out and hands him the brownies.) *What does this tell you about the meaning of the word* flustered? (Someone who is flustered may act quickly without thinking clearly.)

Theme Read paragraph 6 on page B1. *How does Mrs. Wright's treatment of Alex hint at a possible theme of the story?* (Mrs. Wright makes Alex feel "a little less nervous" by telling him that the brownies were "a lovely thought." The theme might relate to the idea of being kind to others.)

Literary Elements: Dialogue Read paragraph 3 on page B2. *What does Wakiash's dialogue reveal about his perspective about Alex?* (that he's very excited about helping Alex learn more about the potlatch)

Theme Read the rest of page B2. *Analyze Alex's changing perspective about the potlatch. How does this help you identify a theme?* (Alex is nervous and embarrassed at first. By the end, he realizes how fun a potlatch is. A theme of the story might be that making a mistake doesn't mean you can't enjoy an event.)

COLLABORATE **Summarize** Have students use their notes to summarize how the author uses a misunderstanding to develop Alex's character.

Reread

Use the questions on page B3 to guide students' rereading of the passage.

Author's Craft *How does the author help you understand Alex's perspective as he gives Wakiash the brownies?* (Alex is "flustered" and thrusts out his arm. This shows that he is nervous.)

Author's Craft *On page B2, how does the author help readers understand what a potlatch is?* (Mrs. Wright and Wakiash tell Alex about what happens at a potlatch and why. The author uses dialogue and reports what Alex is told by Wakiash.)

Author's Craft Reread the last paragraph on page B2. *How does the author show that Alex is "having so much fun"?* (Alex loses track of time. He isn't ready to leave, and he can't wait to tell his mother about the potlatch.)

Integrate

COLLABORATE **Make Connections** Have pairs explore the connections between "Potluck or Potlatch?" and "A Reluctant Traveler" on pages 12–15 of the **Reading/Writing Companion** as they respond to this question: *How do the authors help you understand what learning about a different culture can teach you?*

Compare Texts Have pairs draw a Venn diagram labeled *Paul* and *Alex* and complete it with details.

Build Knowledge

Talk About the Text Have partners discuss what learning about different cultures can teach us.

Write About the Text Have students add their ideas to the Build Knowledge pages of their reader's notebooks.

Differentiate and Collaborate

COLLABORATE **Be inspired** Have students think about "Potluck or Potlatch?" and other selections they have read. Ask: *What do the texts inspire you to do?* Use the following activities or have pairs of students think of a way to respond to the texts.

Plan a Menu Use what you've learned to plan a multicultural lunch menu. Be sure to include foods from several cultures. Share your menu with the staff of your school cafeteria.

Create a Visitor's Guide Choose a culture you've read about and create a visitor's guide for an area where that culture is reflected. Your guide should help visitors decide what to do, see, and eat.

Readers to Writers

Realistic Dialogue Remind students that authors of realistic fiction write dialogue that sounds familiar to readers. Including current expressions and references in dialogue helps an author create characters who seem like people readers might actually know. Have students reread the fifth paragraph on page B1. Ask: *What does the author do to make Alex's dialogue sound like something you or your friends might say?*

GIFTED AND TALENTED

Independent Study Have students synthesize their notes and the selections they read to write an essay about a celebration common to their own culture or family. Students should explain how traditions—cultural or otherwise—affect different aspects of the celebration, including what guests bring to the celebration, what they do, and what foods they eat. Encourage students to use their essays as the basis for a presentation on how the celebration came to be and how it has changed over time.

Beyond Level

Vocabulary/Comprehension

REVIEW DOMAIN-SPECIFIC WORDS

MULTIMODAL

OBJECTIVES

Acquire and use accurately grade-appropriate general academic and domain-specific words and phrases, including those that signal contrast, addition, and other logical relationships (e.g., *however, although, nevertheless, similarly, moreover, in addition*).

Model Use the **Visual Vocabulary Cards** to review the meaning of the words *appreciation* and *cultural*. Use each word in a context sentence that gives an example of the word.

Write the words *heritage* and *traditional* on the board and discuss the meanings with students. Then have students write a context sentence for each word that gives an example.

Apply Have partners review the meanings of the words *flustered* and *miscommunication*. Then have partners write sentences using each of the words.

CONTEXT CLUES

OBJECTIVES

Determine or clarify the meaning of unknown and multiple-meaning words and phrases based on grade 5 reading and content, choosing flexibly from a range of strategies.

Use context (e.g., cause/effect relationships and comparisons in text) as a clue to the meaning of a word or phrase.

Model Read aloud the first three paragraphs of "Potluck or Potlatch" in the Beyond Level online **Differentiated Genre Passage** page B1.

Think Aloud I want to know what the word *nervous* in the third paragraph means. When I read the sentence, I see the words "because he had never been to a potluck before." This cause-and-effect clue helps me figure out that *nervous* means "to feel worried or unsure." People often feel worried when they do something new.

With students, read the fourth paragraph on page B2. Help them figure out the meaning of *perplexed*.

Apply Have partners read the rest of the passage. Ask them to use context clues to determine the meaning of *startled* in the last paragraph on page B2.

Independent Study Challenge students to choose an idiom in the text—such as *a warm hand, lost track of time,* and *felt out of place*—and do research to determine its meaning and origin. Have them share their results with the group and explain where they found the information.

Have students pick words from their reader's notebook and use an online thesaurus to find synonyms and a dictionary to check their pronunciation.

REVIEW THEME

OBJECTIVES

Determine a theme of a story, drama, or poem from details in the text, including how characters in a story or drama respond to challenges or how the speaker in a poem reflects upon a topic; summarize the text.

Model Review that theme is a story's message. Readers can identify themes by identifying what a character thinks, does, and says and determining a character's perspective, or attitude, toward a conflict, character, or event.

Have students read the first and second paragraphs of "Potluck or Potlatch?" in the Beyond Level online **Differentiated Genre Passage** page B1. Ask open-ended questions to facilitate discussion, such as What does _____ say? What does he/she do? Why? What is _____'s perspective? What message might this convey? Students should support their responses with details from the selection.

Apply Have students identify things the characters think, do, and say in the rest of the passage and how this reveals their perspectives. Have students fill in a copy of online Theme **Graphic Organizer 102** independently. Then have partners use their work to retell the passage and identify its theme.

SELF-SELECTED READING

OBJECTIVES

Determine a theme of a story, drama, or poem from details in the text, including how characters in a story or drama respond to challenges or how the speaker in a poem reflects upon a topic; summarize the text.

Independent Reading

In this text set, students focus on the development of implied and stated themes and how the author develops a character's perspective. Guide students to transfer what they have learned in this text set as well as in previous lessons as they read independently.

Have students choose a realistic fiction book for sustained silent reading. They can check the online **Leveled Reader Library** for selections. As they choose, they should consider their purpose for reading.

- As students read, have them fill in Theme **Graphic Organizer 5**.
- Remind them to summarize as they read. Students should summarize in ways that maintain meaning and logical order.

Encourage students to keep a reading journal. Ask them to select books by a variety of authors in order to learn about different writing styles.

- Students can write summaries of the books in their journals.
- Ask students to share their reactions to the books with classmates.

You may wish to assign the third Be Inspired! activity from the lesson plan as Independent Study.

Student Outcomes

✓ Tested in *Wonders* Assessments

FOUNDATIONAL SKILLS

Phonics and Word Analysis

- Decode words with vowel team syllables
- Decode words with consonant + *le* syllables

Fluency

- Read grade-level texts with accuracy, appropriate rate, expression, and automaticity

READING

Reading Literature

✓ Explain how the text structure of problem and solution contributes to the overall meaning of a text
✓ Explain how relevant details support the central idea(s), implied or explicit
✓ Analyze how literal and figurative language contributes to meaning in a text
- Read and comprehend texts in the grades 4-5 text complexity band
- Summarize a text to enhance comprehension
- Write in response to texts

Compare Texts

- Compare and contrast how authors present information on the same topic or theme

COMMUNICATION

Writing

Write to Sources

✓ Write an argument with an organizational structure with a logical order, supported by logical reasons and relevant evidence from sources
- With guidance and support from peers and adults, develop and strengthen writing as needed by planning, revising, and editing

Speaking and Listening

- Report on a topic or text or present an opinion, sequencing ideas; speak clearly at an understandable pace

Conventions

Grammar

✓ Identify main and helping verbs
✓ Recognize special helping verbs; contractions; troublesome words
✓ Identify linking verbs
✓ Punctuate titles and product names correctly

Spelling

- Spell words with vowel team syllables
- Spell words with consonant + *le* syllables

Researching

- Conduct short research projects that build knowledge through investigation of different aspects of the topic

Creating and Collaborating

- Add audio recordings and visual displays to presentations when appropriate
- With some guidance and support from adults, use technology to produce and publish writing

VOCABULARY

Academic Vocabulary

- Acquire and use grade-appropriate academic vocabulary

Vocabulary Strategy

✓ Apply knowledge of Latin roots to determine the meaning of unfamiliar words

CONTENT AREA LEARNING

Civic Engagement

- Identify ways in which citizens help to improve government and society. **Social Studies**

Scientists and the History of Science

- Connect grade-level-appropriate science concepts with the history of science, science careers, and contributions of scientists. **Science**

ELL Scaffolded supports for English Language Learners are embedded throughout the lessons, enabling students to communicate information, ideas, and concepts in English Language Arts and for social and instructional purposes within the school setting.

See the **ELL Small Group Guide** for additional support of the skills for the text set.

FORMATIVE ASSESSMENT

For assessment throughout the text set, use students' self-assessments and your observations.

Use the Data Dashboard to filter class, group, or individual student data to guide group placement decisions. It provides recommendations to enhance learning for gifted and talented students and offers extra support for students needing remediation.

Develop Student Ownership

To build student ownership, students need to know what they are learning and why they are learning it, and to determine how well they understood it.

Students Discuss Their Goals

READING

TEXT SET GOALS

- I can read and understand expository text.
- I can use text evidence to respond to expository text.
- I know what benefits come from working as a group.

Have students think about what they know and fill in the bars on **Reading/Writing Companion** page 36.

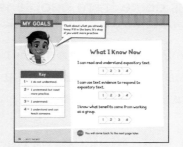

WRITING

EXTENDED WRITING GOALS

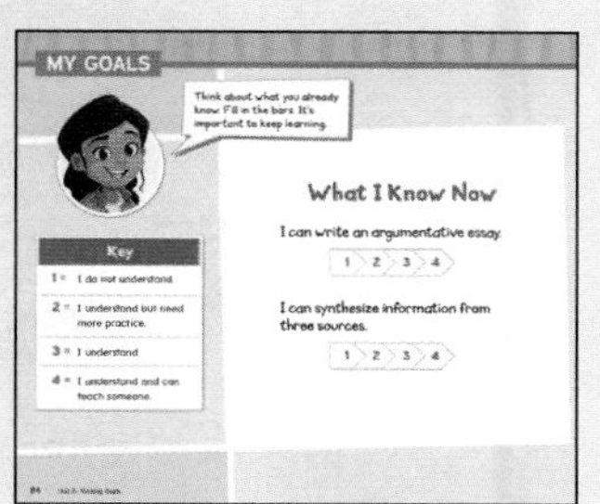

Extended Writing 3:

- I can write an argumentative essay.
- I can synthesize information from three sources.

Have students think about what they know and fill in the bars on Reading/Writing Companion page 84.

Students Monitor Their Learning

LEARNING GOALS

Specific learning goals identified in every lesson make clear what students will be learning and why. These smaller goals provide stepping stones to help students reach their Text Set and Extended Writing Goals.

CHECK-IN ROUTINE

The Check-In Routine at the close of each lesson guides students to self-reflect on how well they understood each learning goal.

Review the lesson learning goal.
Reflect on the activity.
Self-Assess by
- filling in the bars in the Reading/Writing Companion
- holding up 1, 2, 3, or 4 fingers

Share with your teacher.

Students Reflect on Their Progress

READING

TEXT SET GOALS

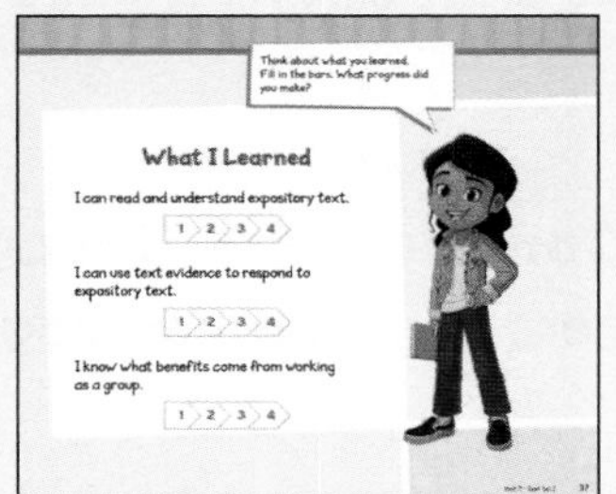

After completing the Show Your Knowledge task for the text set, students reflect on their understanding of the Text Set Goals by filling in the bars on Reading/Writing Companion page 37.

WRITING

EXTENDED WRITING GOALS

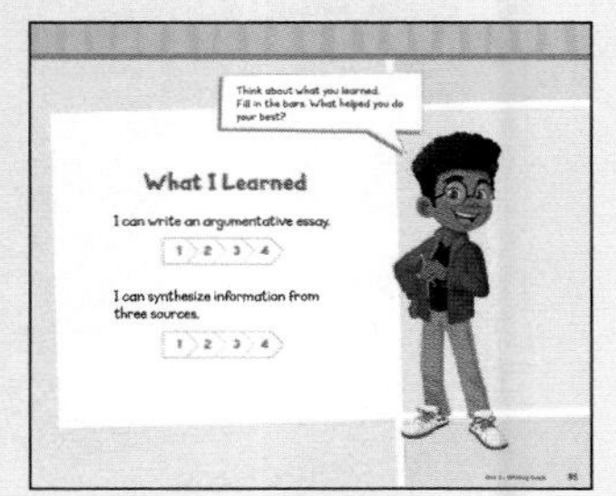

After completing both extended writing projects for the unit, students reflect on their understanding of the Extended Writing Goals by filling in the bars on Reading/Writing Companion page 85.

Build Knowledge

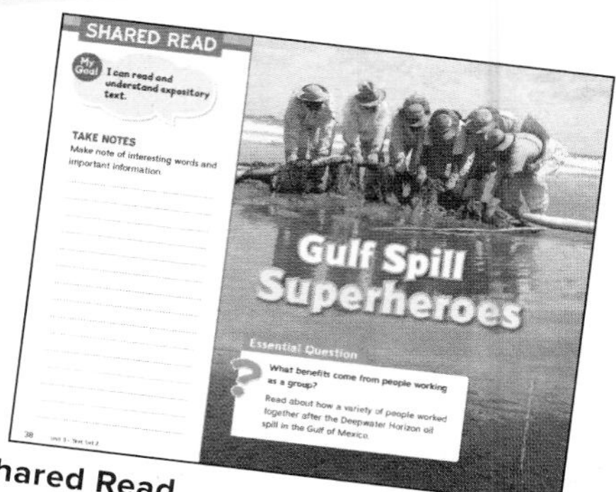

Shared Read
Reading/Writing Companion p. 38

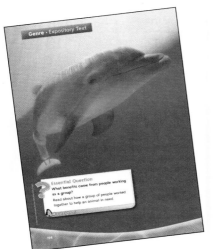

Anchor Text
Literature Anthology p. 198

Paired Selection
Literature Anthology p. 214

Essential Question

What benefits come from people working as a group?

Video People work together to accomplish things in a group, such as painting a mural, performing surgery, and constructing a building.

Study Sync Blast Marie Curie and her husband work together to further scientific research. Dr. Salk and a team of doctors work as a group to develop the polio vaccine.

Interactive Read Aloud Many nations created the International Space Station, which orbits Earth and allows crews from different countries to work together.

Shared Read People with different jobs work together to clean up the mess from the Deepwater Horizon oil spill in the Gulf of Mexico.

Anchor Text A group of people work together to help a dolphin in need, nursing her back to health and creating a prosthetic tail that helps her swim again.

Paired Selection A team of Girl Scouts collaborate and invent a prosthesis that allows a child without fingers to write.

Make Connections Throughout history, firefighters have worked together to help others.

Differentiated Sources

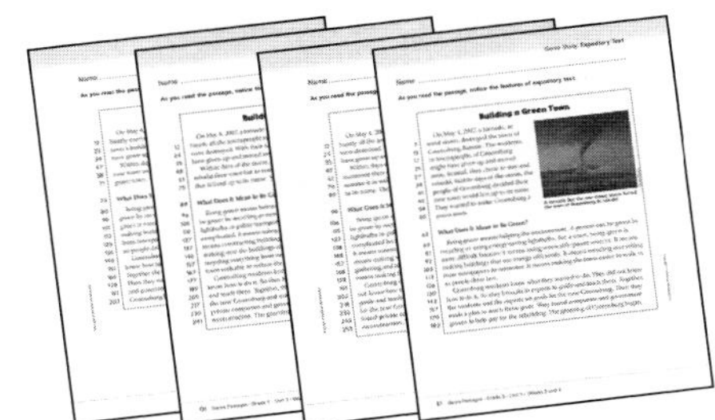

Leveled Readers
Scientists at NASA work together to build and launch robots to explore Mars.

Differentiated Genre Passages
Townspeople work together to rebuild their town after a tornado devastates the area.

Build Knowledge Routine

After reading each text, ask students to document what facts and details they learned to help answer the Essential Question of the text set.

Talk About the source.

Write About the source.

Add to the Class Anchor Chart.

- Add to your Vocabulary List.

Show Your Knowledge

Write a Speech

Have students show how they built knowledge across the text set by writing a speech. They should begin by thinking about the Essential Question: *What benefits come from people working as a group?* Students will write a speech about the qualities that help groups of people successfully work together.

Social Emotional Learning

Belonging

Anchor Text: Belonging a group can make it easier to contribute to important causes. Ask: *How many team members were involved in rehabilitating Winter? What role did each person play?* Have students list the tasks and who was involved in the development or completion of that task. Discuss the importance of needing group involvement.

Paired Selection: Students who feel acceptance within a community will have confidence to fully participate. Ask: *How do you think that working together to help a young girl has affected the girls of the Flying Monkeys?*

Roundtable Discussion: In both *Winter's Tail* and "Helping Hands," groups with varied expertise work together to solve problems. Ask: *What are some similar ways these two groups solved problems?*

Explore the Texts

Essential Question: What benefits come from people working as a group?

ACT: Access Complex Text (ACT) boxes throughout the text set provide scaffolded instruction for seven different elements that may make a text complex.

Teacher's Edition	Reading/Writing Companion	Literature Anthology	
"Teamwork in Space" Interactive Read Aloud p. T83 Expository Text	 **"Gulf Spill Superheroes"** Shared Read pp. 38–41 Expository Text	 ***Winter's Tail: How One Little Dolphin Learned to Swim Again*** Anchor Text pp. 198–211 Expository Text	**"Helping Hands"** Paired Selection pp. 214–217 Expository Text
Qualitative			
Meaning/Purpose Moderate Complexity **Structure** Low Complexity **Language** Low Complexity **Knowledge Demands** Low Complexity	**Meaning/Purpose** Moderate Complexity **Structure** Low Complexity **Language** Moderate Complexity **Knowledge Demands** Low Complexity	**Meaning/Purpose** Moderate Complexity **Structure** Low Complexity **Language** High Complexity **Knowledge Demands** Moderate Complexity	**Meaning/Purpose** Moderate Complexity **Structure** Low Complexity **Language** Moderate Complexity **Knowledge Demands** Moderate Complexity
Quantitative			
Lexile 930L	**Lexile** 860L	**Lexile** 940L	**Lexile** 1040L
Reader and Task Considerations			
Reader Students will need some background knowledge, including information about space travel and about what the Soviet Union was.	**Reader** Students will need background knowledge about oil as an energy source, offshore drilling, and the dangers of extraction and oil spills.	**Reader** The structure and domain-specific vocabulary will be most challenging. Note how authors' word choices can give clues about their purpose for writing.	**Reader** Students will not need background knowledge to understand the text.

Task The questions for the read aloud are supported by teacher modeling. The tasks provide a variety of ways for students to begin to build knowledge and vocabulary about the text set topic. The questions and tasks provided for the other texts are at various levels of complexity, ensuring that all students can interact with the text in meaningful ways.

Additional Texts

Classroom Library

Eight Dolphins of Katrina

Genre: Expository Text

Lexile: 710L

Kakapo Rescue

Genre: Expository Text

Lexile: 950L

See **Classroom Library Lessons**

Content Area Reading BLMs

Additional online texts related to grade-level Science, Social Studies, and Arts content

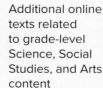

Leveled Readers

 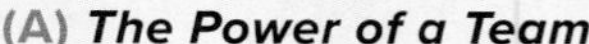 (A) ***The Power of a Team***	 (O) ***The Power of a Team***	 (B) ***The Power of a Team***	 (ELL) ***The Power of a Team***
Qualitative			
Meaning/Purpose Moderate Complexity **Structure** Low Complexity **Language** Low Complexity **Knowledge Demands** Low Complexity	**Meaning/Purpose** Moderate Complexity **Structure** Low Complexity **Language** Low Complexity **Knowledge Demands** Moderate Complexity	**Meaning/Purpose** Moderate Complexity **Structure** Low Complexity **Language** Moderate Complexity **Knowledge Demands** Moderate Complexity	**Meaning/Purpose** Moderate Complexity **Structure** Low Complexity **Language** Low Complexity **Knowledge Demands** Low Complexity
Quantitative			
Lexile 740L	**Lexile** 900L	**Lexile** 1010L	**Lexile** 800L
Reader and Task Considerations			
Reader Students will not need background knowledge to understand the story.	**Reader** Students will not need background knowledge to understand the story.	**Reader** Students will not need background knowledge to understand the story.	**Reader** Students will not need background knowledge to understand the story.

Task The questions and tasks provided for the Leveled Readers are at various levels of complexity, ensuring that all students can interact with the text in meaningful ways.

Differentiated Genre Passages

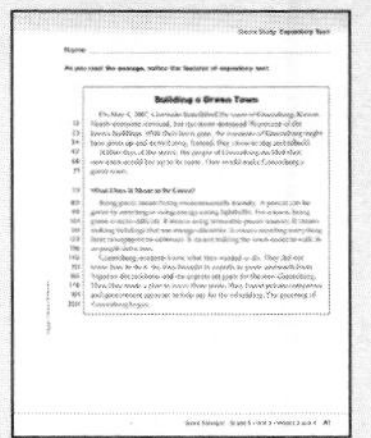 (A) "Building a Green Town"	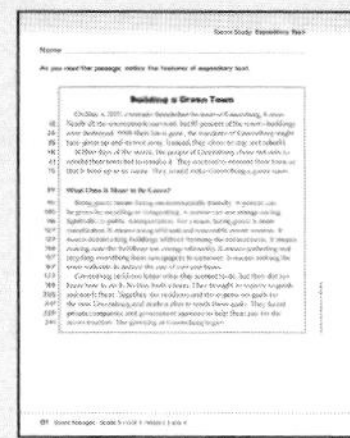 (O) "Building a Green Town"	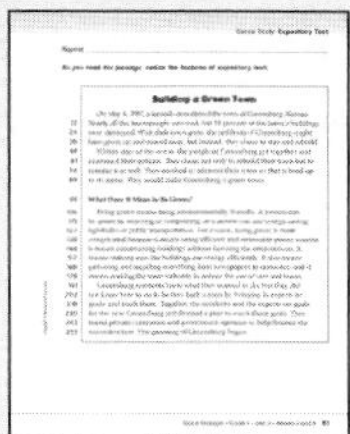 (B) "Building a Green Town"	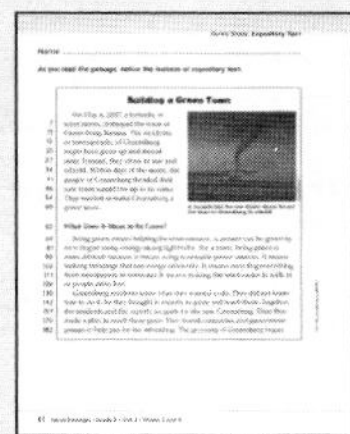 (ELL) "Building a Green Town"
Qualitative			
Meaning/Purpose Mid Complexity **Structure** Low Complexity **Language** Low Complexity **Knowledge Demands** Low Complexity	**Meaning/Purpose** Mid Complexity **Structure** Low Complexity **Language** Low Complexity **Knowledge Demands** Low Complexity	**Meaning/Purpose** Mid Complexity **Structure** Low Complexity **Language** Mid Complexity **Knowledge Demands** Moderate Complexity	**Meaning/Purpose** Mid Complexity **Structure** Low Complexity **Language** Low Complexity **Knowledge Demands** Low Complexity
Quantitative			
Lexile 730L	**Lexile** 800L	**Lexile** 890L	**Lexile** 750L
Reader and Task Considerations			
Reader Students will not need background knowledge to understand the story.	**Reader** Students will not need background knowledge to understand the story.	**Reader** Students will not need background knowledge to understand the story.	**Reader** Students will not need background knowledge to understand the story.

Task The questions and tasks provided for the Differentiated Genre Passages are at various levels of complexity, ensuring that all students can interact with the text in meaningful ways.

Week 3 Planner

Customize your own lesson plans at **my.mheducation.com**

Reading Suggested Daily Time: 60+ mins

READING LESSON GOALS

- **I can read and understand expository text.**
- **I can use text evidence to respond to expository text.**
- **I know what benefits come from working as a group.**

SMALL GROUP OPTIONS The designated lessons can be taught in small groups. To determine how to differentiate instruction for small groups, use Formative Assessment and Data Dashboard.

Writing Suggested Daily Time: 30+ mins

WRITING LESSON GOALS

- **I can write an argumentative essay.**
- **I can synthesize information from three sources.**

Lesson 1	Lesson 2
Reading	
Introduce the Concept, T80–T81 Build Knowledge **Listening Comprehension, T82–T83** "Teamwork" **Shared Read, T84–T87** Read "Gulf Spill Superheroes" Quick Write: Summarize **Vocabulary, T88–T89** Academic Vocabulary Latin Roots **Expand Vocabulary, T132**	**Shared Read, T84–T87** Reread "Gulf Spill Superheroes" **Minilessons, T90–T97** Ask and Answer Questions Text Structure: Problem and Solution Central Idea and Relevant Details Craft and Structure **Respond to Reading, T98–T99** **Phonics, T100–T101** Vowel Team Syllables **Fluency, T100** Accuracy and Rate **Research and Inquiry, T102–T103** **Expand Vocabulary, T132**
Writing	
Extended Writing 1: T232–T233 Analyze the Prompt	**Extended Writing 1, T234–T235** Analyze the Sources
Writing Lesson Bank: Craft Minilessons, T260–T263	
Teacher and Peer Conferences	
Grammar Lesson Bank, T268 Main and Helping Verbs Talk About It **Spelling Lesson Bank, T278** Vowel Team Syllables	**Grammar Lesson Bank, T268** Main and Helping Verbs Talk About It **Spelling Lesson Bank, T278** Vowel Team Syllables

SMALL GROUP

Teacher-Led Instruction

Differentiated Reading

Leveled Readers

- *The Power of a Team,* T134–T135
- *The Power of a Team,* T144–T145
- *The Power of a Team,* T150–T151

Differentiated Skills Practice

Approaching Level
Phonics/Decoding, T138
- Decode Words with Vowel Team Syllables (Tier 2)
- Practice Words with Vowel Team Syllables

Vocabulary, T140
- Review High-Frequency Words (Tier 2)
- Review Academic Vocabulary (Tier 2)

Fluency, T142
- Accuracy and Rate (Tier 2)

Comprehension, T142–T143
- Central Idea and Relevant Details (Tier 2)
- Self-Selected Reading

Independent/Collaborative Work See pages T79G–T79H.

Reading

Comprehension
- Expository Text
- Central Idea and Relevant Details
- Ask and Answer Questions

Fluency
Independent Reading

Phonics/Word Study

Phonics/Decoding
- Vowel Team Syllables

Vocabulary
- Latin Roots

Writing

Extended Writing 1: Argumentative Writing
Self-Selected Writing
Grammar
- Main and Helping Verbs

Spelling
- Vowel Team Syllables

Handwriting

ACADEMIC VOCABULARY
artificial, collaborate, dedicated, flexible, function, mimic, obstacle, techniques

SPELLING
footprint, fairground, although, laughter, appoint, coastal, bleachers, grownup, encounter, grouchy, flawless, lawyer, entertain, applause, faucet, caution, boundary, doubting, southern, roughness

Review *poet, radio, fuel*
Challenge *nowadays, distraught*
See pages T278–T279 for Differentiated Spelling Lists.

Reading

Lesson 3	Lesson 4	Lesson 5
Anchor Text, T104–T119 Read *Winter's Tail* Take Notes About Text **Expand Vocabulary, T133**	**Anchor Text, T104–T119** Read *Winter's Tail* Take Notes About Text **Expand Vocabulary, T133**	**Anchor Text, T104–T119** Reread *Winter's Tail* **Expand Vocabulary, T133**

Writing

Lesson 3	Lesson 4	Lesson 5
Extended Writing 1, T234–T235 Analyze the Sources	**Extended Writing 1, T234–T235** Analyze the Sources	**Extended Writing 1, T236–T237** Plan: Organize Ideas
Writing Lesson Bank: Craft Minilessons, T260–T263		
Teacher and Peer Conferences		
Grammar Lesson Bank, T269 Main and Helping Verbs Talk About It **Spelling Lesson Bank, T279** Vowel Team Syllables	**Grammar Lesson Bank, T269** Main and Helping Verbs Talk About It **Spelling Lesson Bank, T279** Vowel Team Syllables	**Grammar Lesson Bank, T269** Main and Helping Verbs Talk About It **Spelling Lesson Bank, T279** Vowel Team Syllables

On Level
Vocabulary, T148
- Review Academic Vocabulary
- Latin Roots

Comprehension, T149
- Review Central Idea and Relevant Details
- Self-Selected Reading

Beyond Level
Vocabulary, T154
- Review Domain-Specific Words
- Latin Roots

Comprehension, T155
- Review Central Idea and Relevant Details
- Self-Selected Reading 

English Language Learners
See ELL Small Group Guide, pp. 106–117

Content Area Connections

Content Area Reading
- Science, Social Studies, and the Arts

Research and Inquiry
- Working Together

Inquiry Space
- Options for Project-Based Learning

English Language Learners
See ELL Small Group Guide, pp. 106–117

Week 4 Planner

Customize your own lesson plans at **my.mheducation.com**

Reading Suggested Daily Time

READING LESSON GOALS

- **I can read and understand expository text.**
- **I can use text evidence to respond to expository text.**
- **I know what benefits come from working as a group.**

SMALL GROUP OPTIONS The designated lessons can be taught in small groups. To determine how to differentiate instruction for small groups, use Formative Assessment and Data Dashboard.

Writing Suggested Daily Time

WRITING LESSON GOALS

I can write an argumentative essay.

Lesson 6	Lesson 7
Reading	
Anchor Text, T104–T119 Reread *Winter's Tail* **Respond to Reading, T120–T121** **Expand Vocabulary, T132**	**Paired Selection, T122–T125** Read "Helping Hands" **Expand Vocabulary, T132**
Writing	
	Extended Writing 1, T238–T239 Draft: Logical Order
Writing Lesson Bank: Craft Minilessons, T260–T263	
Teacher and Peer Conferences	
Grammar Lesson Bank, T270 Linking Verbs Talk About It **Spelling Lesson Bank, T280** Consonant + *le* Syllables	**Grammar Lesson Bank, T270** Linking Verbs Talk About It **Spelling Lesson Bank, T280** Consonant + *le* Syllables

Teacher-Led Instruction

Differentiated Reading

Differentiated Genre Passages
- "Building a Green Town," T136–T137
- "Building a Green Town," T146–T147
- "Building a Green Town," T152–T153

Differentiated Skills Practice

Approaching Level
Phonics/Decoding, T139
- Decode Words with Consonant + *le* Syllables (Tier 2)
- Practice Words with Consonant + *le* Syllables

Vocabulary, T141
- Identify Related Words
- Latin Roots

Fluency, T142
- Rate (Tier 2)

Comprehension, T143
- Review Central Idea and Relevant Details
- Self-Selected Reading

Independent/Collaborative Work See pages T79G–T79H.

Reading

Comprehension
- Expository Text
- Central Idea and Relevant Details
- Ask and Answer Questions

Fluency
Independent Reading

Phonics/Word Study

Phonics/Decoding
- Consonant + *le* Syllables

Vocabulary
- Latin Roots

Writing

Extended Writing 1: Argumentative Writing
Self-Selected Writing
Grammar
- Linking Verbs

Spelling
- Consonant + *le* Syllables

Handwriting

ACADEMIC VOCABULARY
artificial, collaborate, dedicated, flexible, function, mimic, obstacle, techniques

SPELLING
stable, saddle, table, noble, cattle, stumble, terrible, beetle, kettle, eagle, royal, cripple, hospital, legal, label, vocal, journal, medal, several, sample

Review *entertain, encounter, southern*
Challenge *impossible, people*
See pages T280–T281 for Differentiated Spelling Lists.

Lesson 8	Lesson 9	Lesson 10
Reading		
Paired Selection, T122–T125 Reread "Helping Hands" **Author's Craft, T126–T127** Literal and Figurative Language **Phonics, T128–T129** Consonant + *le* Syllables **Expand Vocabulary, T133**	**Fluency, T129** Rate **Make Connections, T130** **Expand Vocabulary, T133**	**Show Your Knowledge, T131** **Progress Monitoring, T79I–T79J** **Expand Vocabulary, T133**
Writing		
	Extended Writing 1, T240–T241 Revise: Peer Conferences	
Writing Lesson Bank: Craft Minilessons, T260–T263		
Teacher and Peer Conferences		
Grammar Lesson Bank, T271 Linking Verbs Talk About It **Spelling Lesson Bank, T281** Consonant + *le* Syllables	**Grammar Lesson Bank, T271** Linking Verbs Talk About It **Spelling Lesson Bank, T281** Consonant + *le* Syllables	**Grammar Lesson Bank, T271** Linking Verbs Talk About It **Spelling Lesson Bank, T281** Consonant + *le* Syllables

On Level
Vocabulary, T148
- Review Academic Vocabulary
- Latin Roots

Comprehension, T149
- Review Central Idea and Relevant Details
- Self-Selected Reading

Beyond Level
Vocabulary, T154
- Review Domain-Specific Words
- Latin Roots

Comprehension, T155
- Review Central Idea and Relevant Details
- Self-Selected Reading 

English Language Learners
See ELL Small Group Guide, pp. 106–117

Content Area Connections

Content Area Reading
- Science, Social Studies, and the Arts

Research and Inquiry
- Working Together

Inquiry Space
- Options for Project-Based Learning

English Language Learners
See ELL Small Group Guide, pp. 106–117

Independent and Collaborative Work

As you meet with small groups, the rest of the class completes activities and projects that allow them to practice and apply the skills they have been working on.

Student Choice and Student Voice

- Print the My Independent Work blackline master and review it with students. Identify the "Must Do" activities.
- Have students choose additional activities that provide the practice they need.
- Remind students to reflect on their learning each day.

Name ________________ Unit 3 • Text Set 2

My Independent Work

	Reading	Phonics/Word Study	Writing
Center Activity Cards	Card: Activity:	Card: Activity:	Card: Activity:
Digital Activities my.mheducation.com	Activity:	Activity:	Activity:
Practice Pages	Content Area Reading:	Practice:	Practice:
Independent Choices	Independent Reading:	Activity:	Self-Selected Writing:

20 Grade 5 • My Independent Work

My Independent Work BLM

Reading

Independent Reading Texts

Students can choose a Center Activity Card to use while they read independently.

Classroom Library
Eight Dolphins of Katrina: A True Tale of Survival
Genre: Expository Text
Lexile: 710L

Kakapo Rescue: Saving the World's Strangest Parrot
Genre: Expository Text
Lexile: 950L

Unit Bibliography
Have students self-select independent reading texts about people working together to accomplish a goal.

Leveled Texts Online
- Additional Leveled Readers in the **Leveled Reader Library Online** allow for flexibility.
- Six leveled sets of **Differentiated Genre Passages** in diverse genres are available.
- **Differentiated Texts** offer ELL students more passages at different proficiency levels.

Additional Literature
Literature Anthology
The Story of Snow, pp. 242–255
Genre: Expository Text

"Fibonacci's Amazing Find," pp. 258–261
Genre: Expository Text

Center Activity Cards

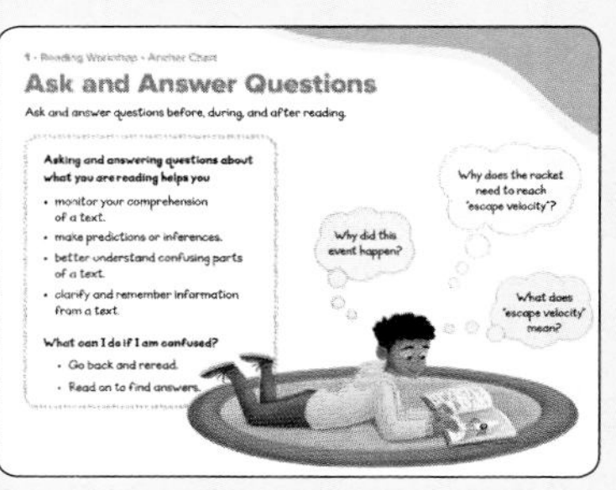

Ask and Answer Questions Card 1

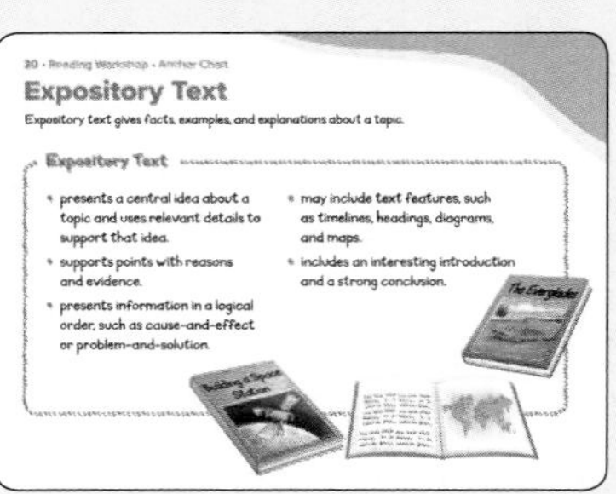

Expository Text Card 30

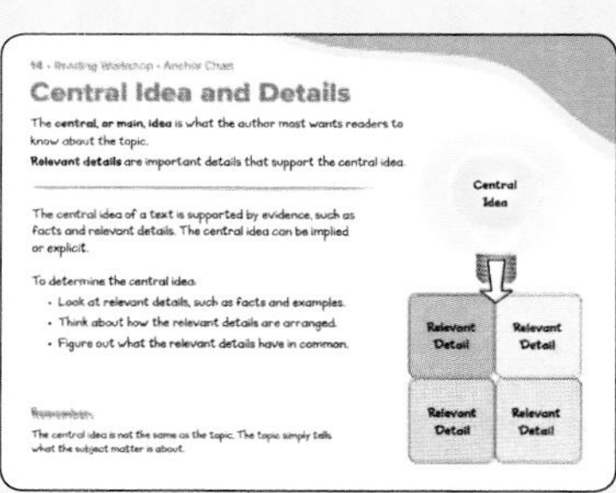

Central Idea and Details Card 14

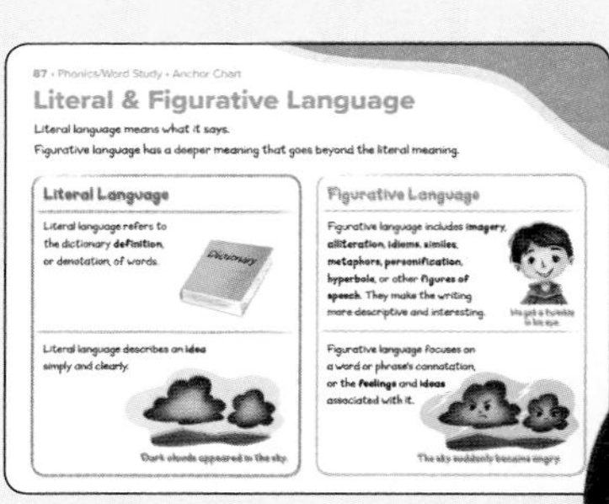

Literal & Figurative Language Card 87

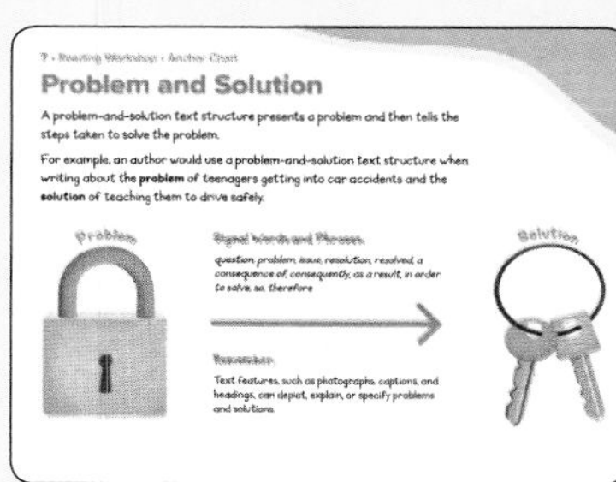

Problem and Solution Card 7

Digital Activities

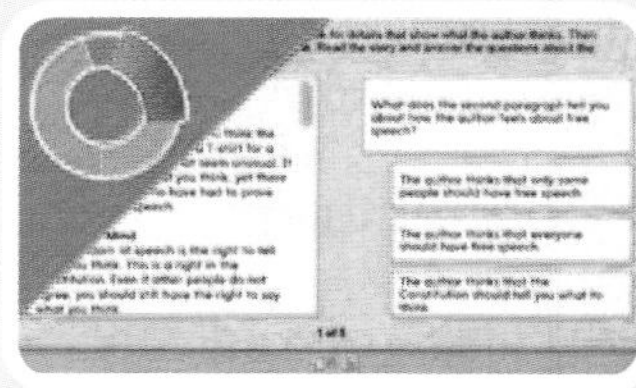

Comprehension

Phonics/Word Study

Center Activity Cards

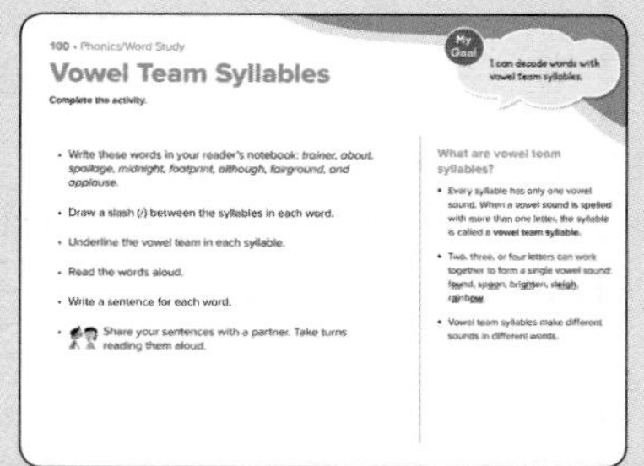

Vowel Team Syllables Card 100

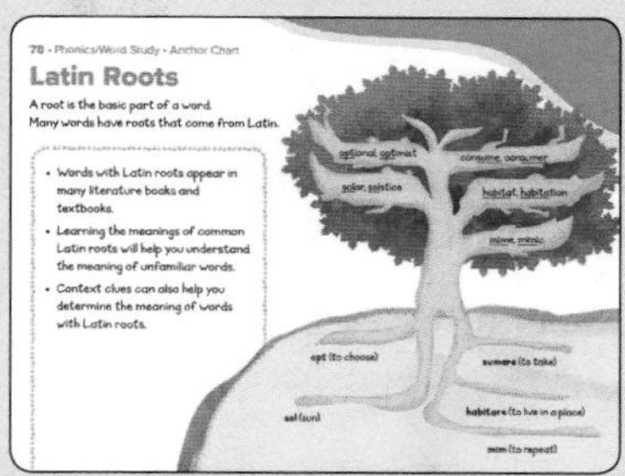

Latin Roots Card 78

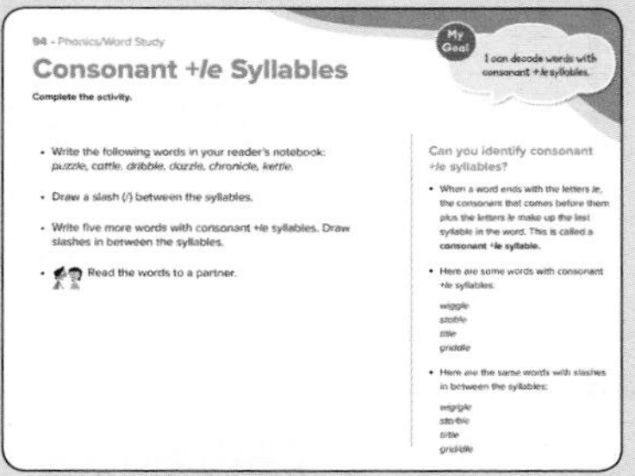

Consonant + *le* Syllables Card 94

Practice Book BLMs

Phonics: pages 151–151B, 154, 163–163B, 166

Vocabulary: pages 155–156, 167–168

Digital Activities

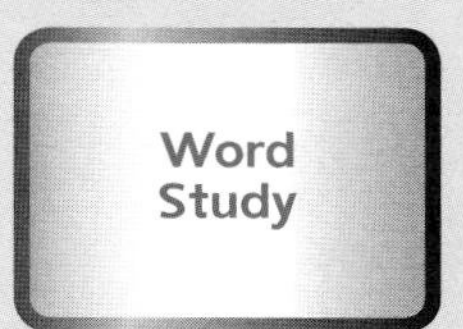

Phonics

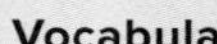

Vocabulary

Writing

Center Activity Cards

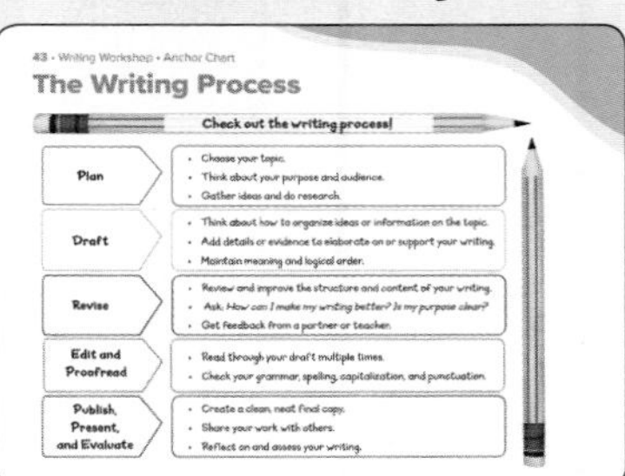

Writing Process Card 43

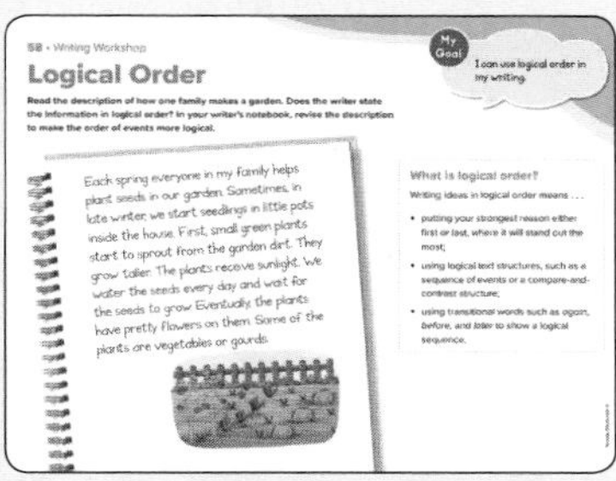

Logical Order Card 58

Self-Selected Writing

Share the following prompts.

- Think of a time when you worked on a group project. What parts of working as a team did you enjoy?
- Describe an issue in your community. How could getting others involved help to fix this issue?
- What traits and qualities does a strong team member have?
- Imagine that you are working on a new invention. Why might it be important to get feedback from others?
- Would you rather work alone or as part of a team? Explain your answer.

Extended Writing

Have students continue developing their **argumentative essays**.

Practice Book BLMs

Grammar: pages 145–149, 157–161
Spelling: pages 150–154, 162–166
Handwriting: pages 361–396

Digital Activities

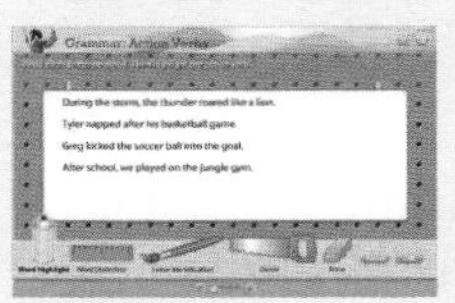

Grammar

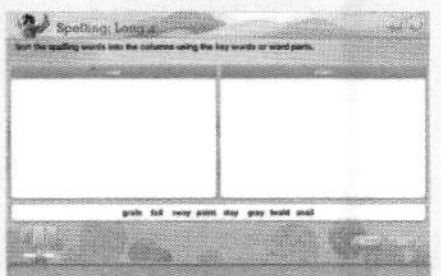

Spelling

Content Area Connections

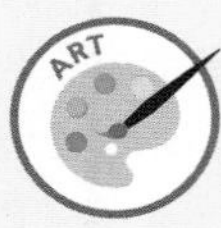

Content Area Reading Blackline Masters
- Additional texts related to Science, Social Studies, and the Arts

Research and Inquiry
- Working Together

Inquiry Space
- Choose an activity

Progress Monitoring

Moving Toward Standards Mastery

FORMATIVE ASSESSMENT
STUDENT CHECK-IN
CHECK FOR SUCCESS

For ongoing formative assessment, use students' self-assessments at the end of each lesson along with your own observations.

Assessing skills along the way . . .

SKILLS	HOW ASSESSED
Comprehension **Vocabulary**	Digital Activities, Rubrics
Text-Based Writing	Reading/Writing Companion: Respond to Reading
Grammar, Mechanics, Phonics, Spelling	Practice Book, Digital Activities including word sorts
Listening/Presenting/Research	Checklists
Oral Reading Fluency (ORF) Fluency Goal: 123–143 words correct per minute (WCPM) Accuracy Rate Goal: 95% or higher	Fluency Assessment

At the end of the text set . . .

SKILLS	HOW ASSESSED
Text Structure: Problem and Solution **Central Idea and Relevant Details** **Literal and Figurative Language**	Progress Monitoring
Latin Roots	

Making the Most of Assessment Results

Make data-based grouping decisions by using the following reports to verify assessment results. For additional student support options refer to the reteaching and enrichment opportunities.

ONLINE ASSESSMENT CENTER

- ***Gradebook***

DATA DASHBOARD

- ***Recommendations Report***
- ***Activity Report***
- ***Skills Report***
- ***Progress Report***
- ***Grade Card Report***

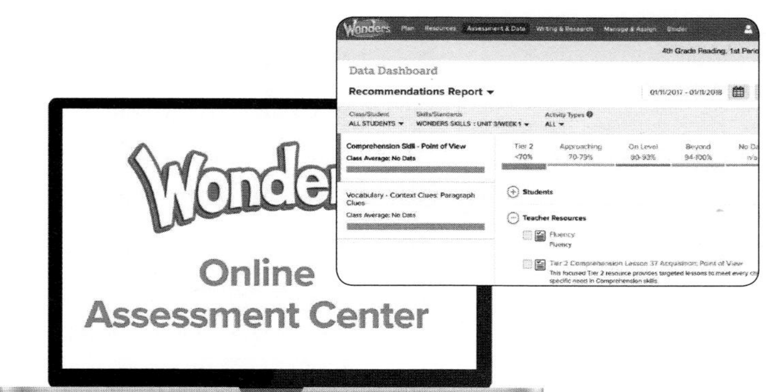

Assign practice pages online for auto-grading.

TIER 2

Reteaching Opportunities with Intervention Online PDFs

IF STUDENTS SCORE . . .	THEN ASSIGN . . .
below 70% in **comprehension** . . .	lessons 83–84 on Problem and Solution in **Comprehension PDF,** lessons 55–57 on Central Idea and Details in **Comprehension PDF,** and/or lesson 130 on Figurative Language in **Comprehension PDF**
below 70% in **vocabulary** . . .	lesson 109 on Greek, Latin, and Other Roots in **Vocabulary PDF**
114–122 WCPM in **fluency** . . .	lessons from Section 1 or 7–10 of **Fluency PDF**
0–113 WCPM in **fluency** . . .	lessons from Sections 2–6 of **Fluency PDF**

Use the* Phonics/Word Study PDF *and* Foundational Skills Kit *for additional reteaching opportunities. Use the* Foundational Skills Kit *for students who need support with phonemic awareness and other early literacy skills.

Enrichment Opportunities

Beyond Level small group lessons and resources include suggestions for additional activities in these areas to extend learning opportunities for gifted and talented students:

- ***Leveled Readers***
- ***Genre Passages***
- ***Vocabulary***
- ***Comprehension***
- ***Leveled Reader Library Online***
- ***Center Activity Cards***

OBJECTIVES

Engage effectively in a range of collaborative discussions (one-on-one, in groups, and teacher-led) with diverse partners, building on others' ideas and expressing their own clearly.

Pose and respond to specific questions by making comments that contribute to the discussion and elaborate on the remarks of others.

Follow agreed-upon rules for discussions and carry out assigned roles.

ELA ACADEMIC LANGUAGE

- *collaboration, clarify*
- Cognates: *colaboración, clarificar*

DIGITAL TOOLS

Show the image during class discussion.

Discuss Concept

Watch Video

VOCABULARY

collaborate (colaborar) to work together

project (proyecto) a plan

community (comunidad) a neighborhood

talent (talento) an ability

inspired (inspirado) the feeling of doing something creative

Build Knowledge

Essential Question

What benefits come from people working as a group?

Read the Essential Question on **Reading/Writing Companion** page 34. Tell students that they will read expository texts to learn about the benefits that come from people working together as a group and build knowledge about the advantages of collaboration. They will use words to read, write, and talk about how people benefit from working together.

Watch the Video Play the video without sound first. Have partners narrate what they see. Then replay the video with sound as students listen.

Talk About the Video Have partners discuss how people benefit from working together.

Write About the Video Have students add their ideas to their Build Knowledge pages of their reader's notebooks.

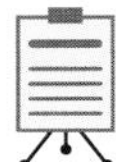

Anchor Chart Begin a Build Knowledge anchor chart. Write the Essential Question at the top of the chart. Have volunteers share what they learned about collaboration and record their ideas. Explain that students will add to the anchor chart after they read each text.

Build Knowledge

Discuss the photograph with students. Focus on how the artists are collaborating on a mural, which is a painting on a wall. Ask: *In what ways is working together beneficial?* Have students discuss in pairs or groups.

Build Vocabulary

Model using the graphic organizer to write down new words related to working together. Have partners continue the discussion and add the graphic organizer and new words to their reader's notebooks. Students will add words to the Build Knowledge pages in their notebooks as they read about the benefits of working together throughout the text set.

Collaborative Conversations

Ask and Answer Questions As students engage in discussions, encourage them to ask and answer questions. Remind students to

- ask questions to clarify ideas or comments.
- wait so that others have a chance to think before responding.
- answer questions thoughtfully and with complete ideas.

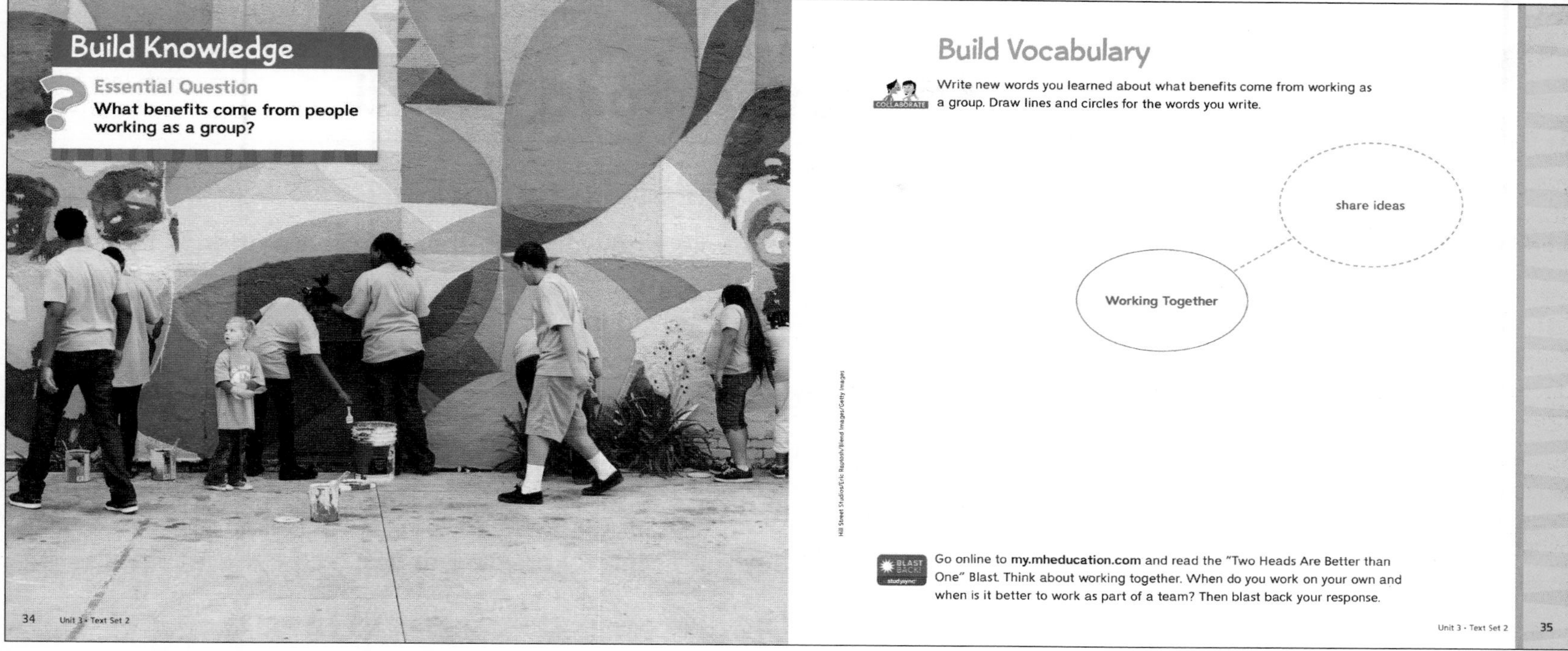

Reading/Writing Companion, pp. 34–35

Share the "Two Heads Are Better Than One" Blast assignment with students. Point out that you will discuss their responses about working together in the Make Connections lesson at the end of this text set.

English Language Learners

Use the following scaffolds to build knowledge and vocabulary. Teach the ELL Vocabulary, as needed.

Beginning

Describe what the people are painting in the photograph with students. Review the meaning of *collaborate*. Ask: *Are the people working alone or collaborating?* They are collaborating. Elicit from students that working together helps to get the project done. Help pairs generate words to describe the benefits of working together.

Intermediate

Use the photograph to discuss the meaning of *collaborate* with students. Ask: *What are the artists collaborating on?* (a mural) Have partners generate a list of words and phrases to describe why working together is beneficial, or helpful. Have them discuss using: Working together helps to ____.

Advanced/Advanced High

Have pairs describe the photograph. *Talk to your partners about what the artists are working on. Explain why you think it's a good idea for them to collaborate.* Have them complete the graphic organizer.

NEWCOMERS

To help students develop oral language and build vocabulary, use **Newcomer Cards 10–14** and the accompanying materials in the **Newcomer Teacher's Guide**. For thematic connection, use **Newcomer Card 15** with the accompanying materials.

MY GOALS ROUTINE

What I Know Now

Read Have students read the goals on page 36 of the Reading/Writing Companion.

Reflect Review the key. Ask students to reflect on each goal and fill in the bars to show what they know now. Explain that they will fill in the bars on page 37 at the end of the text set to show their progress.

LEARNING GOALS

We can actively listen to learn about the benefits of people working together.

OBJECTIVES

Follow agreed-upon rules for discussions and carry out assigned roles.

Summarize a written text read aloud or information presented in diverse media and formats, including visually, quantitatively, and orally.

Use common, grade-appropriate Greek and Latin affixes and roots, or bases, as clues to the meaning of a word (e.g., photograph, photosynthesis).

Listen for a purpose.

Identify characteristics of expository text.

ELA ACADEMIC LANGUAGE

- *expository text, characteristics, teamwork, accomplish*
- Cognate: *texto expositivo*

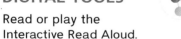

DIGITAL TOOLS

Read or play the Interactive Read Aloud.

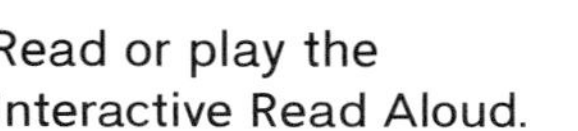

Interactive Read Aloud

FORMATIVE ASSESSMENT

STUDENT CHECK-IN

Have partners share one example of how those involved in the space station were models of teamwork. Ask them to reflect using the Check-In routine.

Interactive Read Aloud

Connect to Concept: Teamwork

Tell students that people who work together as a team often accomplish amazing goals. Let students know that you will be reading aloud a passage about the teamwork involved in space travel and exploration.

Preview Expository Text

Anchor Chart Explain that the text you will read aloud is expository text. Have a volunteer add additional characteristics to the Expository Text anchor chart. Explain that students may want to add more characteristics to the chart as they read other expository texts. Discuss these features of expository text:

- explains a topic
- supports central ideas with relevant facts and examples
- presents information in an order that makes sense

Ask students to think about other texts they have read aloud or they have read independently that were realistic fiction.

Read and Respond

Read the text aloud to students. Then reread it using the Teacher Think Alouds and Student Think Alongs on page T83 to build knowledge and model comprehension and the vocabulary strategy, Latin Roots.

Summarize Have students summarize the central idea and relevant details from "Teamwork in Space" in their own words.

Build Knowledge: Make Connections

Talk About the Text Have partners discuss how people benefit from working together.

Write About the Text Have students add their ideas to their Build Knowledge pages of their reader's notebooks.

Anchor Chart Record any new ideas on the Build Knowledge anchor chart.

Add to the Vocabulary List Have students write down any words they learned about working together in their reader's notebooks.

Teamwork in Space

In the mid-1950s, the dream of space travel was close to becoming a reality. However, the race to be the first nation to put a man in space had turned into a fierce competition between the United States and the Soviet Union. Yet by the beginning of the twenty-first century, the situation had changed. Space exploration had become one of the greatest examples of international teamwork in history!

Early Progress

From the beginning, space travel required teamwork. Scientists, engineers, researchers, computer programmers, maintenance workers, and astronauts had to work together. It was their job to design, construct, launch, care for, and crew for the vehicles that transported humans into space. (1)

Early expeditions showed that humans could survive in space. They could also link vehicles together and walk in space. In 1975, a Soviet spacecraft and an American one docked together. Over the next 25 years, international cooperation in space grew more common.

An International Achievement

Finally, in 2000, the International Space Station was created. The space station was designed to be a research laboratory that orbited Earth. Sixteen nations and thousands of men and women were involved in this amazing project. Teams were responsible for many different tasks. These included research, construction, communications, and operations. Each team contributed its special knowledge to make the project a success. (2)

Crews of men and women have been able to live and work full-time in the International Space Station, far above Earth's surface. In its first decade, the space station's crews conducted research in a variety of areas, from human health to space science. They also engaged in ordinary activities, from brushing their teeth to playing the flute.

From the start, those involved in the space station were models of teamwork. They have shown that people from different nations and cultures could cooperate, not only on Earth but also in space. (3)

(1) Teacher Think Aloud

I read that one of the jobs of the team was to help construct vehicles. I know that the Latin root *struct* means "to build," so this helps me understand that the team worked together to build the vehicles that brought people into space.

Student Think Along

Listen for the word *transported* as I reread this paragraph. What do the Latin roots *trans* and *port* mean? Turn and tell a partner how the Latin roots help you define *transported*.

(2) Teacher Think Aloud

Asking and answering questions as I read can help me monitor my comprehension. I have a question: Why did international cooperation in space become more common? I can reread to see that space travel was once very competitive, but teamwork was essential to make it a reality.

Student Think Along

In what ways does space travel require teamwork? Listen for evidence as I reread these paragraphs. Raise your hand when you can name some jobs that required teamwork.

(3) Teacher Think Aloud

I'm going to ask and answer one final question: What did I learn from reading "Teamwork in Space?" I understand that space exploration relies on the cooperation of people worldwide.

Student Think Along

Before hearing the text again, think of a question that would help you monitor how well you understand the text. Share your question with a partner. Then listen for the answer as I reread the text. Share what you learned about the benefits of people working together.

"Gulf Spill Superheroes"

Lexile 860L

LEARNING GOALS

We can read and understand expository text.

OBJECTIVES

Determine two or more central, or main, ideas of a text and explain how they are supported by relevant, or key, details; summarize the text.

Use context to confirm or self-correct word recognition and understanding, rereading as necessary.

Close Reading Routine

Read DOK 1–2

- Identify important ideas and details.
- Take notes and summarize.
- Use ACT prompts as needed.

Reread DOK 2–3

- Analyze the text, craft, and structure.
- Use the **Reread minilessons** and **prompts.**

Integrate DOK 3–4

- Integrate knowledge and ideas.
- Make text-to-text connections.
- Use the Integrate lesson.
- Complete the Show Your Knowledge task.
- Inspire action.

Read

SHARED READ

My Goal I can read and understand expository text.

TAKE NOTES

Make note of interesting words and important information.

38 Unit 3 • Text Set 2

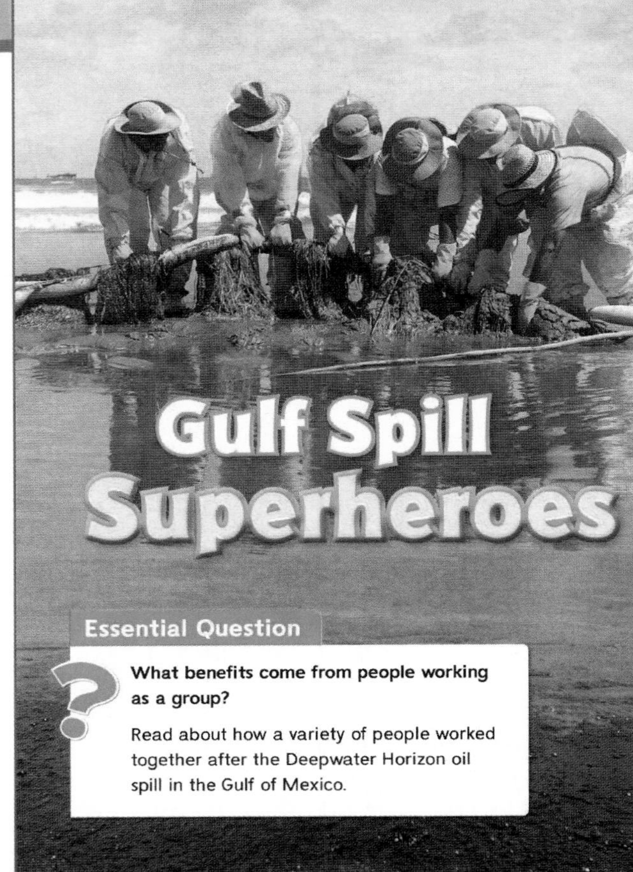

Gulf Spill Superheroes
Essential Question
What benefits come from people working as a group?
Read about how a variety of people worked together after the Deepwater Horizon oil spill in the Gulf of Mexico.

Reading/Writing Companion, pp. 38–39

Set a Purpose Before they begin, have students look at the title and photo on page 38. Connect to the Essential Question by discussing why the people are working as a group. Have students set their purpose for reading. Explain that they should use the left column to record interesting words and key details.

Focus on the Read prompts now. For support, use the extra prompts not included in the **Reading/Writing Companion.** Use the Reread prompts during the Craft and Structure lesson on pages T96–T97. Preteach the vocabulary to some students.

DIFFERENTIATED READING

Approaching Level Model previewing, and use the preview information to form a question. Complete all Read prompts with the group.

On Level Have partners complete the Read prompts.

Beyond Level Ask students to explain how asking questions helps them focus on the expository text.

English Language Learners Preteach the vocabulary. Have Beginning and Early-Intermediate ELLs listen to the selection summary, available in multiple languages, and use the **Scaffolded Shared Read**. See also the **ELL Small Group Guide**.

Fire boats at work at the off shore oil rig Deepwater Horizon.

Fans of comic books know that sometimes it takes a team of superheroes to save the day. Each one uses his or her special powers to fight an enemy or solve a problem. On April 20, 2010, the Deepwater Horizon drilling platform exploded in the Gulf of Mexico. Massive fires raged above the waters. Down below, gallons and gallons of oil spewed from a broken pipeline. Such a huge disaster would require the skills and abilities of many heroes working together.

Responders in the Water

Immediately after the explosion, firefighters worked with the US Coast Guard to battle the blaze. Boats and aircraft transported survivors from the platform to safety before the rig sank.

Meanwhile, scientists raced to understand what was happening underwater. Each type of scientist had a specific **function.** Oceanographers mapped out the ocean floor and charted water currents in the area. Biologists looked for ways to protect animals in the region from the spreading oil.

What was most important, engineers discussed **techniques** to fix the broken well. The leak was more than a mile below the Gulf's surface. That was too deep for human divers to work effectively. For that reason, experts relied on robots with **artificial** arms and special tools to stop the spill. Many of their first efforts failed.

After nearly three months, workers finally plugged up the damaged well. It would take many more months to clean up the mess left behind.

Workers move absorbent material to capture some spilled crude oil at Fourchon Beach, Louisiana.

EXPOSITORY TEXT

FIND TEXT EVIDENCE

Read

Paragraph 1
Central Idea and Relevant Details
Look for details in paragraph 1. **Circle** the central, or main, idea in paragraph 1.

Paragraph 2
Latin Roots
The root *viv* means "to live." What is the meaning of *survivors* in paragraph 2?
Survivors are the people who were still alive after the platform explosion.

Paragraphs 3-5
Ask and Answer Questions
How long did it take for the damaged well to be plugged up?
It took nearly three months.

Reread

Author's Craft
How does the author use descriptive language to help you picture the effects of the accident?

Unit 3 • Text Set 2 39

Central Idea and Relevant Details DOK 2

Paragraph 1: *What is the central idea of the first paragraph? Which details give more information about the central idea?*

Think Aloud: I know that the central, or main, idea of a paragraph is sometimes stated in the text. So, first I read the paragraph and ask: *What is the paragraph mostly about?* It is mostly about a disaster and heroes working together. I read, "On April 20, 2010, the Deepwater Horizon drilling platform exploded in the Gulf of Mexico." This is the central idea. The sentences that follow give relevant details about the explosion. The text says that "massive fires raged" and "gallons of oil spewed from a broken pipeline." Have students use the central idea and relevant details to predict what they will learn about this disaster.

Latin Roots DOK 2

Paragraph 2: Read the second paragraph and point out the word *survivors* in the second sentence. Explain that understanding the meaning of a root word can help you figure out the meaning of the entire word. Ask: *How does knowing* viv *means* "to live" *help you understand what* survivors *means?* (Because *viv* means "to live," I know that boats and aircraft transported people who were still alive after the explosion.) Have students use the word *survivors* in a sentence.

Ask and Answer Questions DOK 1

Paragraphs 3–5: Ask: *How long did it take for the damaged well to be plugged up?*

Think Aloud: I will look for words and phrases in the text that tell me about the time or about how long it took for workers to plug the well. I see that the information I need to answer the question is in the last paragraph. The phrase *After nearly three months* tells me how long it took to plug up the damaged well.

Check for Understanding DOK 2

Page 39: Monitor students' understanding of the central, or main idea. Draw attention to the heading "Responders in the Water." Ask: *How can you use the heading to determine the central idea of the section?* (I can list relevant details that support the heading. Then I can ask myself what the details have in common.) *What are the relevant details?* (Firefighters battled the blaze. Scientists worked to understand what was happening under the water. Engineers worked with robots and special tools to stop the spill a mile under water.) *What is the central idea?* (People with different jobs worked together in the water to plug up the damaged well.)

Spotlight on Idioms

Page 39, Paragraph 1: Read the first two sentences in the paragraph. Explain that *save the day* is an idiom. *When someone saves the day, they solve a big problem.* Read the last two sentences in the paragraph. Then have students look at the photo. *What is the day's big problem in this story?* (drilling platform exploded, fires raged) *Talk to your partner about who you think will* save the day. Then, have partners use the idiom to discuss a time they experienced or saw a big problem: *What was the problem? Who saved the day? How?*

Central Idea and Relevant Details
DOK 2

Paragraphs 1–2: Read the first and second paragraphs. Ask: *What problem did the responders have?* (From the water, it was hard to see where the oil was spreading.) *What did the responders do?* (They collaborated with NASA, meteorologists, pilots, and their crews. These groups looked at the spill from satellites in the sky, studied the weather, and took photographs to see where to send workers.) Have students state the central idea in their own words, based on supporting evidence in the text. (It was hard to track the spread of the oil by looking at it in the water, so responders had to collaborate with many other agencies to see it from the air as well.)

Latin Roots DOK 2

Paragraph 2: Read the second paragraph and draw attention to the word *sensitive*. Explain that the Latin root *sens* means "to feel." Ask: *How can you use the Latin root to figure out the meaning of* sensitive*?* (I know that *sens* means "to feel." *Sensitive* is being used to describe an area, so it can't "feel" in the same way as a person. But I also see that the word *protect* describes what is done to the sensitive areas. That makes me think that in this context, *sensitive* means "easily damaged" or "delicate.") Have students use *sensitive* in a sentence.

Read

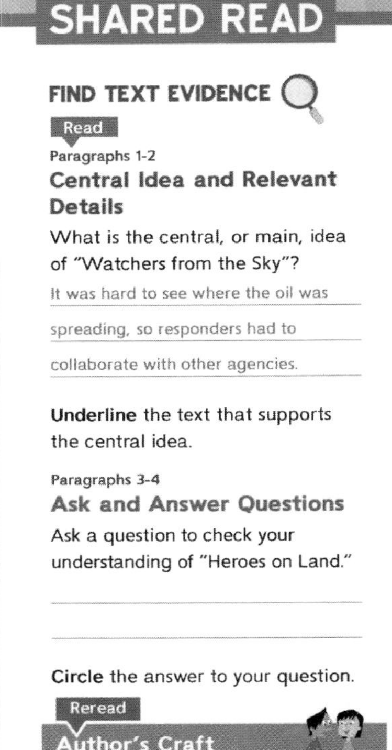
SHARED READ

FIND TEXT EVIDENCE

Read

Paragraphs 1-2

Central Idea and Relevant Details

What is the central, or main, idea of "Watchers from the Sky"?

It was hard to see where the oil was spreading, so responders had to collaborate with other agencies.

Underline the text that supports the central idea.

Paragraphs 3-4

Ask and Answer Questions

Ask a question to check your understanding of "Heroes on Land."

Circle the answer to your question.

Reread

Author's Craft

How does the author help you understand the need for cooperation?

40 Unit 3 • Text Set 2

Watchers from the Sky

From the water, it was hard to see where the oil was spreading. Responders had to **collaborate** with other agencies, such as the NASA space program. Satellites in the sky sent information to scientists on the ground. Meteorologists tracked storms that might pose an **obstacle** to the response teams. Photographs helped team leaders decide how to assign their workers.

Pilots and their crews flew over the Gulf region in helicopters and planes. Some studied how the oil slick moved from place to place. Others directed the placement of floating barriers to protect sensitive areas. Some crews transferred needed supplies back and forth between land and sea.

Heroes on Land

As the oil approached land, new responders leapt into action. Veterinarians **dedicated** their efforts to helping out marine animals, such as pelicans and turtles. They would capture and treat affected animals before returning them to the wild. Naturalists and ecologists cleaned up the animals' habitats. Quite often, these groups' efforts overlapped, and they helped one another. Volunteers also helped out on many tasks.

Biologists catch an oil-soaked brown pelican to clean and return to the wild.

Local fishermen also needed help. They relied on crabs, shrimp, and other seafood for their livelihood. Government officials monitored fishing areas to decide which were safe. Bankers and insurance companies also reached out to the fishermen. They helped find ways to make up for the lost income from seafood sales.

Reading/Writing Companion, pp. 40–41

Ask and Answer Questions DOK 1

Paragraphs 3–4: Read the third and fourth paragraphs. Have students think about details that may be confusing and ask a question about them. (Possible answer: How did government officials help local fishermen?) Ask: *What is the answer to your question? Use text evidence.* (Possible answer: Government officials monitored fishing areas to decide if they were safe.) Explain that as they read, students can write questions they have on sticky notes and then look for text evidence to answer each question.

Access Complex Text

Prior Knowledge

Provide facts about oil and offshore drilling.

- Oil is an important energy source. We use it for fueling our vehicles and heating our homes. Oil is also used to make plastic, paint, and synthetic fibers in our clothing.
- A lot of the world's oil is beneath the floor of the ocean. Offshore rigs are used to drill for it.
- Workers on offshore oil rigs face dangers from explosions, fires, hurricanes, and equipment malfunctions.

As time allows, discuss the ongoing effects of the oil spill. Point out that scientists believe the spill resulted in the deaths of more than 1,400 dolphins and about one million birds. They are still studying the effects on coral and other marine life as the oil drifts further out to sea.

In Florida, experts worked together in a "think tank." They needed to trap floating globs of oil before they ruined area beaches. They created the SWORD, or Shallow-water Weathered Oil Recovery Device. The SWORD was a catamaran with mesh bags hung between its two pontoons. The small craft would **mimic** a pool skimmer and scoop up oil as it moved. Because of its size and speed, the SWORD could be quite **flexible** responding to spills.

Workers place absorbent materials to catch oil in Orange Beach, Alabama.

As we have seen, the Deepwater Horizon accident required heroic efforts of all kinds. In some cases, workers' jobs were quite distinct. In others, their goals and efforts were similar. The success of such a huge mission depended on how well these heroes worked together. The lessons learned will be quite valuable if and when another disaster happens.

Summarize

Use the subheads and your notes to summarize important details about the Gulf oil spill. Then summarize the central idea of "Gulf Spill Superheroes."

EXPOSITORY TEXT

FIND TEXT EVIDENCE

Read

Paragraphs 1-2

Problem and Solution

Underline the problem mentioned in the first paragraph. How do the photo and caption work with the text to help you understand the solution to a problem?

The photo and its caption help you visualize the materials used to catch the oil from the water.

Reread

Author's Craft

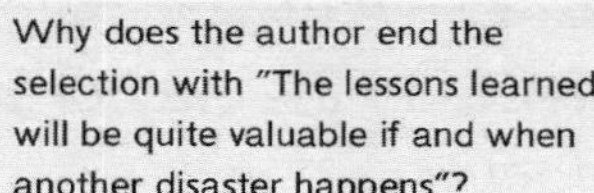

Why does the author end the selection with "The lessons learned will be quite valuable if and when another disaster happens"?

Context Clues DOK 2

Page 41: Draw attention to the photograph and read the caption. Point out the word *absorbent.* Ask: *Which words can help us determine the meaning of* absorbent*?* (The word *catch* is also in the caption. It tells me that the absorbent materials were there to catch oil.) Discuss the meaning of the word *absorbent.* (*Absorbent* must describe something that can catch liquids.)

Summarize

Analytical Writing

Quick Write After their initial reads, have partners summarize the selection orally using their notes. Then have them write a summary in their reader's notebook. Remind them to only include the central ideas and relevant details. Students may decide to digitally record presentations of their summaries.

Problem and Solution DOK 2

Paragraph 1: Read the first paragraph. Ask: *What problem do the scientists have?* (They need to trap floating globs of oil before they ruined beaches.) *How did they solve the problem?* (They created the SWORD device to scoop up oil as it moved.)

Central Idea and Relevant Details DOK 2

Paragraph 2: Read the last paragraph and explain that sometimes an author states the central idea of the entire text in the last paragraph. Have students find the sentence that states the central idea. ("The success of such a huge mission depended on how well these heroes work together.")

Check for Understanding DOK 2

Page 41: Reread the first and second paragraphs and have students use text evidence to describe the SWORD device. (It is a small craft called a catamaran. The catamaran has mesh bags hung between its two pontoons.) *How does the photograph help you understand how the SWORD device worked to solve the problem of scooping up floating globs of oil?* (The photo helps you visualize the mesh bags that the text describes as a solution to scooping up oil from the water.)

ELL Spotlight on Language

Page 41, Paragraph 1: Read the first two sentences of the paragraph. Point out *think tank* and explain the meaning. *Experts and scientists sometimes collaborate, or work together, to solve a problem. This is called a "think tank."* Explain that the quotation marks around *think tank* indicate that this is a special term. Read the rest of the paragraph. Have partners discuss the term: *Why do you think experts working together is called a think tank? Is it a good description?*

FORMATIVE ASSESSMENT

STUDENT CHECK-IN

Have partners share their summaries from Reading/Writing Companion page 41. Ask them to reflect using the Check-In routine.

LEARNING GOALS

- **We can use new vocabulary words to read and understand expository text.**
- **We can use Latin roots, our knowledge of parts of speech, and context clues to find the meaning of unfamiliar words.**

OBJECTIVES

Determine the meaning of words and phrases in a text relevant to a topic or subject area.

Determine the meaning of general academic and domain-specific words and phrases in a text relevant to a grade 5 topic or subject area.

Use context to confirm or self-correct word recognition and understanding, rereading as necessary.

Determine or clarify the meaning of unknown and multiple-meaning words and phrases, choosing flexibly from a range of strategies.

Use common, grade-appropriate Greek and Latin affixes and roots as clues to the meaning of a word (e.g., *photograph, photosynthesis*).

ELA ACADEMIC LANGUAGE

- *routine, unfamiliar, define*
- Cognate: *definir*

DIGITAL TOOLS

Visual Vocabulary Cards

TEACH IN SMALL GROUP

Academic Vocabulary

Approaching Level and **ELL** Preteach the words to the group before beginning the Shared Read.

On Level and **Beyond Level** Have students look up each word in the online **Visual Glossary**.

Reread

Academic Vocabulary

Use the routine on the **Visual Vocabulary Cards** to introduce each word.

Artificial describes a thing not made by nature.
Cognate: *artificial*

When we **collaborate,** we work together.
Cognate: *colaborar*

If the driver **dedicated** his time to volunteer, he gave or devoted his time.
Cognate: *dedicar*

Something **flexible** is able to bend without breaking.
Cognate: *flexible*

To use a tool, you should understand its **function**, or its purpose.
Cognate: *función*

When you **mimic** something, you imitate it.

An **obstacle** stands in the way or blocks progress.
Cognate: *obstáculo*

Techniques are special ways of doing something to achieve a desired result.
Cognate: *técnicas*

Encourage students to use their newly acquired vocabulary in their discussions and written responses about the texts in this text set.

Latin Roots

1 Explain

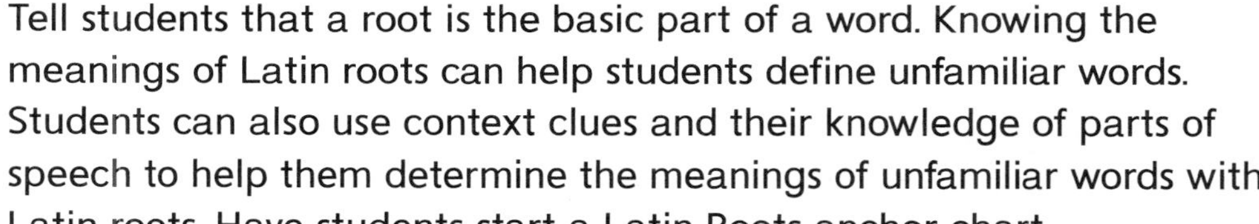

Tell students that a root is the basic part of a word. Knowing the meanings of Latin roots can help students define unfamiliar words. Students can also use context clues and their knowledge of parts of speech to help them determine the meanings of unfamiliar words with Latin roots. Have students start a Latin Roots anchor chart.

2 Model

Model using the Latin root *mar* ("sea"), along with context clues, to define *marine* in the third paragraph of **Reading/Writing Companion** page 40. Point out that knowing *marine* is an adjective can be helpful.

3 Guided Practice

Guide pairs to use context clues and the familiar Latin roots *trans, port, sens,* and *habit* to determine the meaning of *transported, sensitive,* and *habitats*. Have them determine each word's part of speech beforehand to help them.

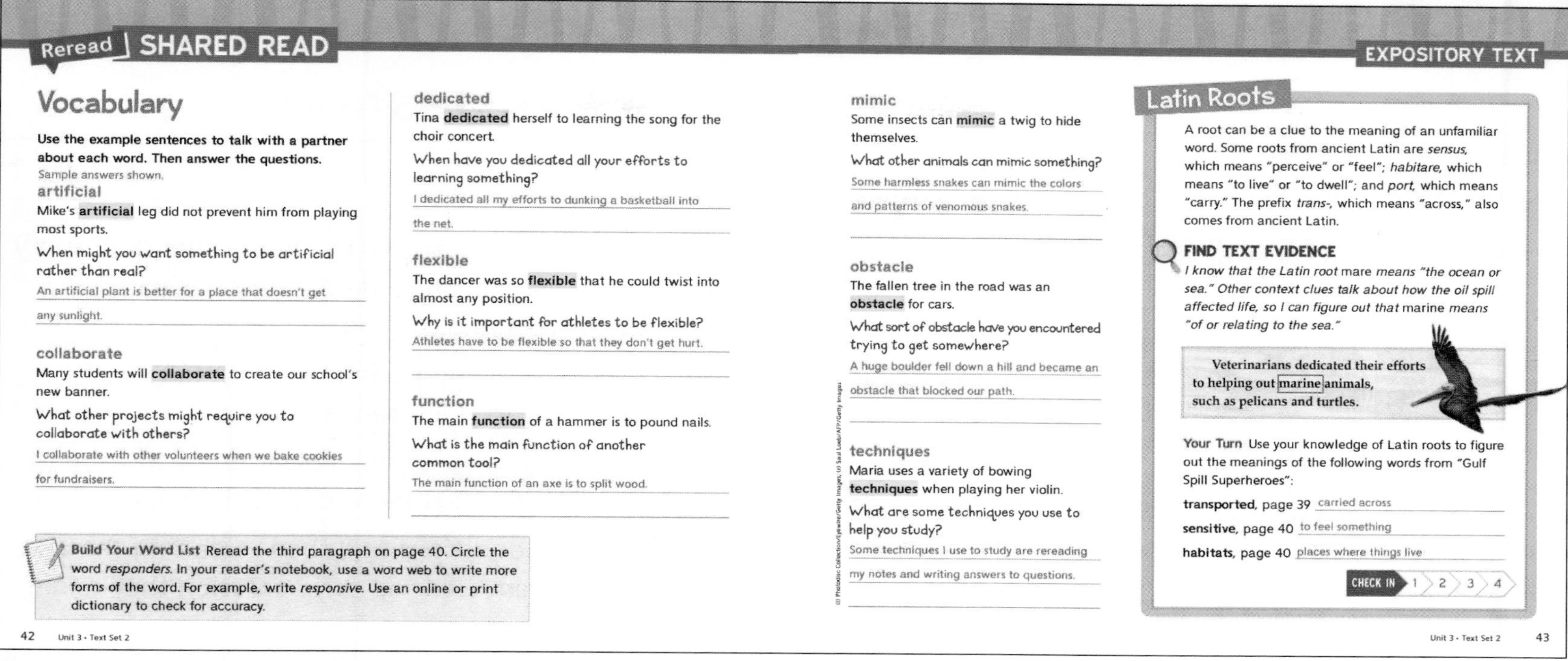

Reread | SHARED READ

EXPOSITORY TEXT

Vocabulary

Use the example sentences to talk with a partner about each word. Then answer the questions.

Sample answers shown.

artificial
Mike's **artificial** leg did not prevent him from playing most sports.
When might you want something to be artificial rather than real?
An artificial plant is better for a place that doesn't get any sunlight.

collaborate
Many students will **collaborate** to create our school's new banner.
What other projects might require you to collaborate with others?
I collaborate with other volunteers when we bake cookies for fundraisers.

dedicated
Tina **dedicated** herself to learning the song for the choir concert.
When have you dedicated all your efforts to learning something?
I dedicated all my efforts to dunking a basketball into the net.

flexible
The dancer was so **flexible** that he could twist into almost any position.
Why is it important for athletes to be flexible?
Athletes have to be flexible so that they don't get hurt.

function
The main **function** of a hammer is to pound nails.
What is the main function of another common tool?
The main function of an axe is to split wood.

mimic
Some insects can **mimic** a twig to hide themselves.
What other animals can mimic something?
Some harmless snakes can mimic the colors and patterns of venomous snakes.

obstacle
The fallen tree in the road was an **obstacle** for cars.
What sort of obstacle have you encountered trying to get somewhere?
A huge boulder fell down a hill and became an obstacle that blocked our path.

techniques
Maria uses a variety of bowing **techniques** when playing her violin.
What are some techniques you use to help you study?
Some techniques I use to study are rereading my notes and writing answers to questions.

Build Your Word List Reread the third paragraph on page 40. Circle the word *responders*. In your reader's notebook, use a word web to write more forms of the word. For example, write *responsive*. Use an online or print dictionary to check for accuracy.

Latin Roots

A root can be a clue to the meaning of an unfamiliar word. Some roots from ancient Latin are *sensus*, which means "perceive" or "feel"; *habitare*, which means "to live" or "to dwell"; and *port*, which means "carry." The prefix *trans-*, which means "across," also comes from ancient Latin.

FIND TEXT EVIDENCE
I know that the Latin root mare *means "the ocean or sea." Other context clues talk about how the oil spill affected life, so I can figure out that* marine *means "of or relating to the sea."*

Veterinarians dedicated their efforts to helping out marine animals, such as pelicans and turtles.

Your Turn Use your knowledge of Latin roots to figure out the meanings of the following words from "Gulf Spill Superheroes":

transported, page 39 carried across
sensitive, page 40 to feel something
habitats, page 40 places where things live

CHECK IN 1 2 3 4

42 Unit 3 • Text Set 2 Unit 3 • Text Set 2 43

Reading/Writing Companion, pp. 42–43

English Language Learners

Use the following scaffolds with **Guided Practice.** For additional support, see the **ELL Small Group Guide**.

Beginning

Point out the word *habitats* in the third paragraph on page 40. Explain that it comes from the Latin root *habitare,* "to live in a place." Help Spanish speakers identify similar words in their home language. (*habitación, habitante*) Point out that the photograph on page 40 gives a clue to the meaning of *habitats.* Ask: *What is the pelican's habitat?* (the water) A habitat is where an animal lives.

Intermediate

Have partners read the second paragraph on page 39. Point out the word *transported.* Explain that *transported* is made up of a Latin prefix and a Latin root. *The prefix* trans- *means "across" and the root* port *means* to carry. Ask: *What does* transported *mean*? *Transported* means carried across a place or a distance.

Advanced/Advanced High

Point out the word *sensitive* in the second paragraph on page 40, and remind students that the Latin root *sensus* means "feel." Point out that sensitive also means "easily hurt" and discuss the context clue *protect* that helps them to figure out the meaning. Guide pairs to write a definition of *sensitive* using the Latin root and the context clue. (answers will vary). Repeat for *transported,* and *habitats.*

BUILD YOUR WORD LIST

Students might choose *created* from page 41. Have them use a dictionary to explore its meaning.

FORMATIVE ASSESSMENT

STUDENT CHECK-IN

Academic Vocabulary Ask partners to share two answers from Reading/Writing Companion pages 42-43.

Latin Roots Ask partners to share their Your Turn responses on page 43.

Have students use the Check-In routine to reflect and fill in the bars.

CHECK FOR SUCCESS

Rubric Use your online rubric to record student progress.

Can students use Latin roots, context clues, and parts of speech to define *transported, sensitive,* and *habitats?*

Small Group Instruction

If No

- **Approaching** Reteach p. T141

If Yes

- **On** Review p. T148
- **Beyond** Extend p. T154

LEARNING GOALS

We can ask and answer questions to understand expository text.

OBJECTIVES

Quote accurately from a text when explaining what the text says explicitly and when drawing inferences from the text.

ELA ACADEMIC LANGUAGE

- *monitor, comprehension, clarify*
- Cognates: *monitor, comprensión, clarificar*

Reread

Ask and Answer Questions

1 Explain

Explain to students that when they read an article or other expository text for the first time, they may encounter details, descriptions, or events that are difficult to understand.

- Explain that when students encounter parts of a text that confuse them, they should pause and ask themselves questions.
- To answer these questions, students should reread the text or read on to see if a later section of the text helps clarify the information.
- Tell students that generating questions and then rereading the text for answers can often help them clear up any confusion they might experience.

Remind students that asking and answering questions is also a good way to monitor their comprehension and check that they have correctly understood the central idea and relevant details in a text.

Anchor Chart Have a volunteer add any additional points about the strategy to the Ask and Answer Questions anchor chart.

2 Model

Reread the two paragraphs under the heading "Watchers from the Sky" on **Reading/Writing Companion** page 40. Model how asking and answering questions can help you understand why pilots and their crews were in charge of placing floating barriers around the oil spill.

3 Guided Practice

Guide partners to ask and answer a question about information in the section "Responders in the Water" on page 39. For example, partners might ask why engineers decided to use robots to fix the broken well. Partners can reread the third paragraph to discover that the leak was too deep for humans to work effectively. Have partners discuss other sections of "Gulf Spill Superheroes" about which they might want to ask and answer questions.

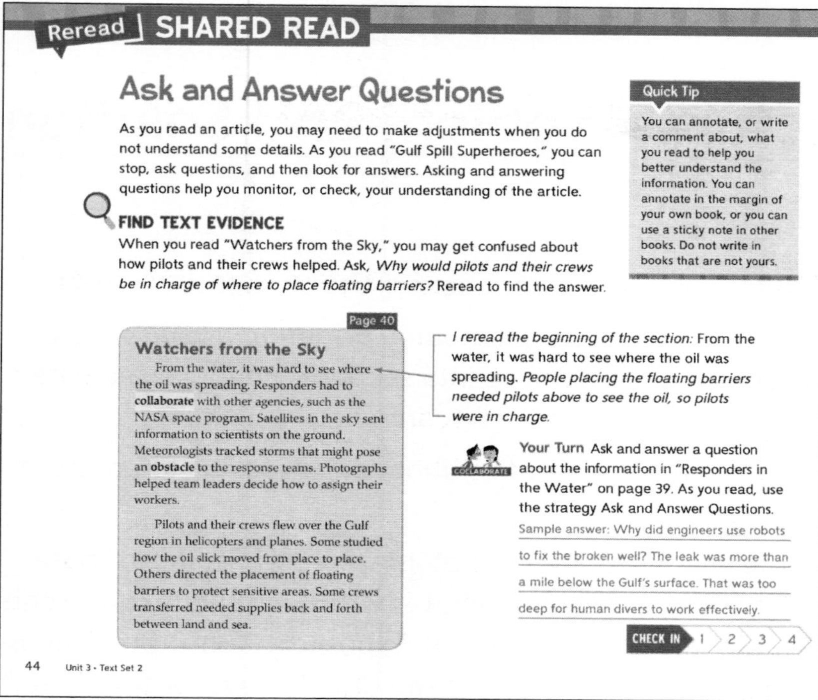

Reread | SHARED READ

Ask and Answer Questions

As you read an article, you may need to make adjustments when you do not understand some details. As you read "Gulf Spill Superheroes," you can stop, ask questions, and then look for answers. Asking and answering questions help you monitor, or check, your understanding of the article.

Quick Tip

You can annotate, or write a comment about, what you read to help you better understand the information. You can annotate in the margin of your own book, or you can use a sticky note in other books. Do not write in books that are not yours.

FIND TEXT EVIDENCE

When you read "Watchers from the Sky," you may get confused about how pilots and their crews helped. Ask, *Why would pilots and their crews be in charge of where to place floating barriers?* Reread to find the answer.

Page 40

Watchers from the Sky

From the water, it was hard to see where the oil was spreading. Responders had to **collaborate** with other agencies, such as the NASA space program. Satellites in the sky sent information to scientists on the ground. Meteorologists tracked storms that might pose an **obstacle** to the response teams. Photographs helped team leaders decide how to assign their workers.

Pilots and their crews flew over the Gulf region in helicopters and planes. Some studied how the oil slick moved from place to place. Others directed the placement of floating barriers to protect sensitive areas. Some crews transferred needed supplies back and forth between land and sea.

I reread the beginning of the section: From the water, it was hard to see where the oil was spreading. *People placing the floating barriers needed pilots above to see the oil, so pilots were in charge.*

COLLABORATE

Your Turn Ask and answer a question about the information in "Responders in the Water" on page 39. As you read, use the strategy Ask and Answer Questions.

Sample answer: Why did engineers use robots to fix the broken well? The leak was more than a mile below the Gulf's surface. That was too deep for human divers to work effectively.

CHECK IN 1 2 3 4

44 Unit 3 • Text Set 2

Reading/Writing Companion, p. 44

English Language Learners

Use the following scaffolds with **Guided Practice**. For small group support, see the **ELL Small Group Guide**.

Beginning

Review with students how asking and answering questions can help them understand the text. Reread sentences 2-4, paragraph 4 on page 39 of "Responders in the Water" with students. Restate sentence as needed. Say: *The engineers use robots to fix the broken well.* Elicit students to ask a question about the engineers and robots using: *Why did the* engineers *use* robots *to fix the broken well?* The leak was too deep.

Intermediate

Review with students how asking and answering questions can help them understand the text. Have partners read paragraph 4 on page 39 of "Responders in the Water." Ask: *How deep below the surface was the leak?* The leak was more than a mile deep. Review question words by eliciting them from students. (who, what, why, where, when, how) Help pairs form a question about the engineers and robots: Why did the _____ use _____ to fix the _____?

Advanced/Advanced High

Have students read the fourth paragraph on page 39. Guide partners as they take turns asking and answering questions about the engineers and robots. Encourage them to use vocabulary from the text and connect questions and answers to text evidence.

HABITS OF LEARNING

I think critically about what I am reading. Understanding how to ask and answer questions about texts helps students learn this key habit of learning. Remind students to ask questions about anything they read, in school and out, such as:

- *Does this make sense?*
- *Does this fit with what I already know?*
- *Is the author's evidence believable?*

FORMATIVE ASSESSMENT

STUDENT CHECK-IN

Ask partners to share their Your Turn responses on Reading/Writing Companion page 44. Have them use the Check-In routine to reflect and fill in the bars.

CHECK FOR SUCCESS

Do students stop and ask questions as they read? Do they reread to find the answers in the text?

Small Group Instruction

If No

- **Approaching** Reteach p. T134

If Yes

- **On** Review p. T144
- **Beyond** Extend p. T150

LEARNING GOALS

We can use photographs, captions, and text structure to understand expository text.

OBJECTIVES

By the end of the year, read and comprehend informational texts, including history/social studies, science, and technical texts independently and proficiently.

Come to discussions prepared, having read or studied required material; explicitly draw on that preparation and other information known about the topic to explore ideas under discussion.

Interpret information presented visually, orally, or quantitatively (e.g., in charts, graphs, diagrams, time lines, animations, or interactive elements on Web pages) and explain how the information contributes to an understanding of the text in which it appears.

ELA ACADEMIC LANGUAGE

- *expository text, organized, photographs, captions, headings*
- Cognates: *texto expositivo, organizar, fotografías*

Reread

Text Structure: Problem and Solution

1 Explain

Share with students the following characteristics of **expository text.**

- An expository text gives readers factual information about a topic. The information is often organized into sections. Headings indicate the kind of information each section contains.
- The text may use a problem-and-solution text structure to organize information.
- An expository text often includes photographs and captions. These features help readers understand what is written in the text and can give readers more information about it. Expository text that includes words and images is an example of a multimodel text, or text that provides information in more than one way.

Explain to students that identifying these features while they read can make reading an expository text easier and more interesting.

2 Model

Model identifying "Gulf Spill Superheroes" as an expository text. Point out passages where the author uses a problem-and-solution text structure to organize information, such as the first three paragraphs on **Reading/Writing Companion** page 39.

Photographs and Captions Remind students that photographs and captions may illustrate something that is described in the text or provide more information about it. Point out the photographs and captions throughout the article. Ask: *How do the photograph and caption provide more information about the problem and solutions described in the text?*

Anchor Chart Have a volunteer add details about photographs and captions to the Expository Text anchor chart.

3 Guided Practice

Circulate as students work with partners to find an example that shows how the author of "Gulf Spill Superheroes" uses a problem-and-solution structure to convey information on page 40. Encourage students to include information from the text and from photographs and captions. Partners should discuss the information they learned from each feature and how the use of the problem-and-solution structure added to their understanding. Have them share their work.

Independent Practice Have students read the online **Differentiated Genre Passage,** "Building a Green Town."

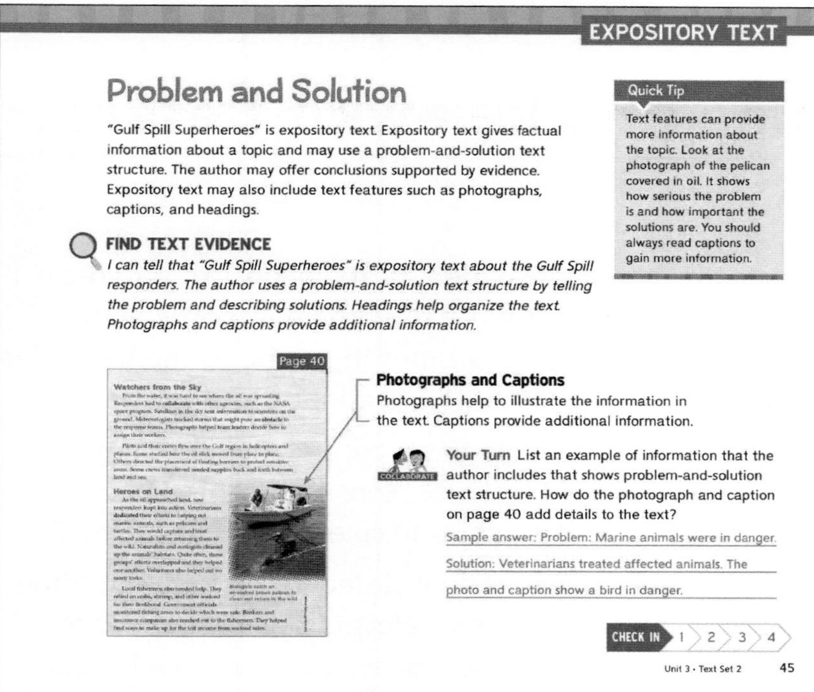
EXPOSITORY TEXT

Problem and Solution

"Gulf Spill Superheroes" is expository text. Expository text gives factual information about a topic and may use a problem-and-solution text structure. The author may offer conclusions supported by evidence. Expository text may also include text features such as photographs, captions, and headings.

FIND TEXT EVIDENCE

I can tell that "Gulf Spill Superheroes" is expository text about the Gulf Spill responders. The author uses a problem-and-solution text structure by telling the problem and describing solutions. Headings help organize the text. Photographs and captions provide additional information.

Quick Tip

Text features can provide more information about the topic. Look at the photograph of the pelican covered in oil. It shows how serious the problem is and how important the solutions are. You should always read captions to gain more information.

Page 40

Photographs and Captions
Photographs help to illustrate the information in the text. Captions provide additional information.

COLLABORATE

Your Turn List an example of information that the author includes that shows problem-and-solution text structure. How do the photograph and caption on page 40 add details to the text?

Sample answer: Problem: Marine animals were in danger. Solution: Veterinarians treated affected animals. The photo and caption show a bird in danger.

CHECK IN 1 2 3 4

Unit 3 • Text Set 2 45

Reading/Writing Companion, p. 45

English Language Learners

Use the following scaffolds with **Guided Practice**. For small group support, see the **ELL Small Group Guide**.

Beginning

Read sentences 1-3, paragraph 3 on page 40 of "Gulf Spill Superheroes" with students. Restate sentences as needed. Explain that pelicans and turtles are examples of *marine animals.* Point to the photo and read the caption with students. Clarify the meaning of *soaked.* Help partners identify the problem and solution by asking: *Is it a problem that the marine animals are soaked in oil?* (yes) *What do the veterinarians do to solve the problem?* The veterinarians treat the marine animals.

Intermediate

Read the third paragraph on page 40 of "Gulf Spill Superheroes" with students. Have partners look at the photo and read the caption on the page. Then help them identify the problem by asking: *Are the marine animals in danger?* (yes) *Why?* The marine animals are soaked in oil. Have them discuss the solution using: The veterinarians treat the marine animals.

Advanced/High Advanced

Have students read the third paragraph on page 40. Have partners discuss the problem and solution about marine animals. Then have them discuss how the photo and caption add details to the text.

FORMATIVE ASSESSMENT

STUDENT CHECK-IN

Ask partners to share their Your Turn responses on Reading/Writing Companion page 45. Have them use the Check-In routine to reflect and fill in the bars.

CHECK FOR SUCCESS

Can students read expository text and identify examples of problem-and-solution text structure? Can they explain how photographs and captions add details to the text?

Small Group Instruction

If No

- **Approaching** Reteach p. T136

If Yes

- **On** Review p. T146
- **Beyond** Extend p. T152

LEARNING GOALS

We can read and understand expository text by identifying the central idea and relevant details.

OBJECTIVES

Determine two or more central, or main, ideas of a text and explain how they are supported by relevant, or key, details; summarize the text.

ELA ACADEMIC LANGUAGE

- *central idea, relevant details, summarize, article, arranged*
- Cognates: *idea central, detalles relevantes, artículo*

DIGITAL TOOLS

To differentiate instruction for key skills, use the results of the activity.

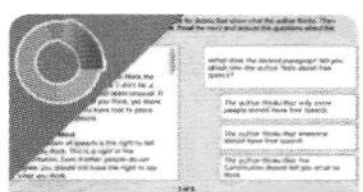

Reread

Central Idea and Relevant Details

1 Explain

Explain to students that the **central idea**, or main idea, of an article such as "Gulf Spill Superheroes" is what the article is mostly about. Remind students that the central idea is not the same as the topic. The topic simply tells what the subject matter is about.

- Explain that the article as a whole has a central idea but that each section of the article has a central idea, too. Each central idea is supported by evidence, such as facts and **relevant, or key, details.**
- Sometimes the central idea is explicitly stated in the text, but often it is implied—readers must look at the relevant details in order to figure out the central idea. Details are often arranged in a logical order—for example, they might be grouped into problems and solutions, or they might be listed from most to least important.
- To determine the central idea, students should identify the relevant details, think about how they are arranged, and figure out what they have in common.

Anchor Chart Begin a Central Idea and Relevant Details anchor chart.

2 Model

Model identifying the relevant details in the section "Heroes on Land" on **Reading/Writing Companion** page 40 and listing them on the graphic organizer. Then model how to use what the details have in common to determine the central idea of the section. (As the oil spill reached land, other responders went to work.)

3 Guided Practice

Guide pairs to complete a graphic organizer for the section "Responders on the Water" on page 39. Encourage students to reread the section for relevant details that point to the central idea. Remind them to look at the order in which the details are arranged and use this information to help them find the central idea. Have partners discuss how different groups of responders worked with and relied on each other to deal with the oil spill.

Analytical Writing **Write About Reading: Summary** Ask pairs to work together to write a summary of the section "Responders on the Water." Have pairs share their summaries with the class. Offer constructive feedback about the effectiveness of the summaries.

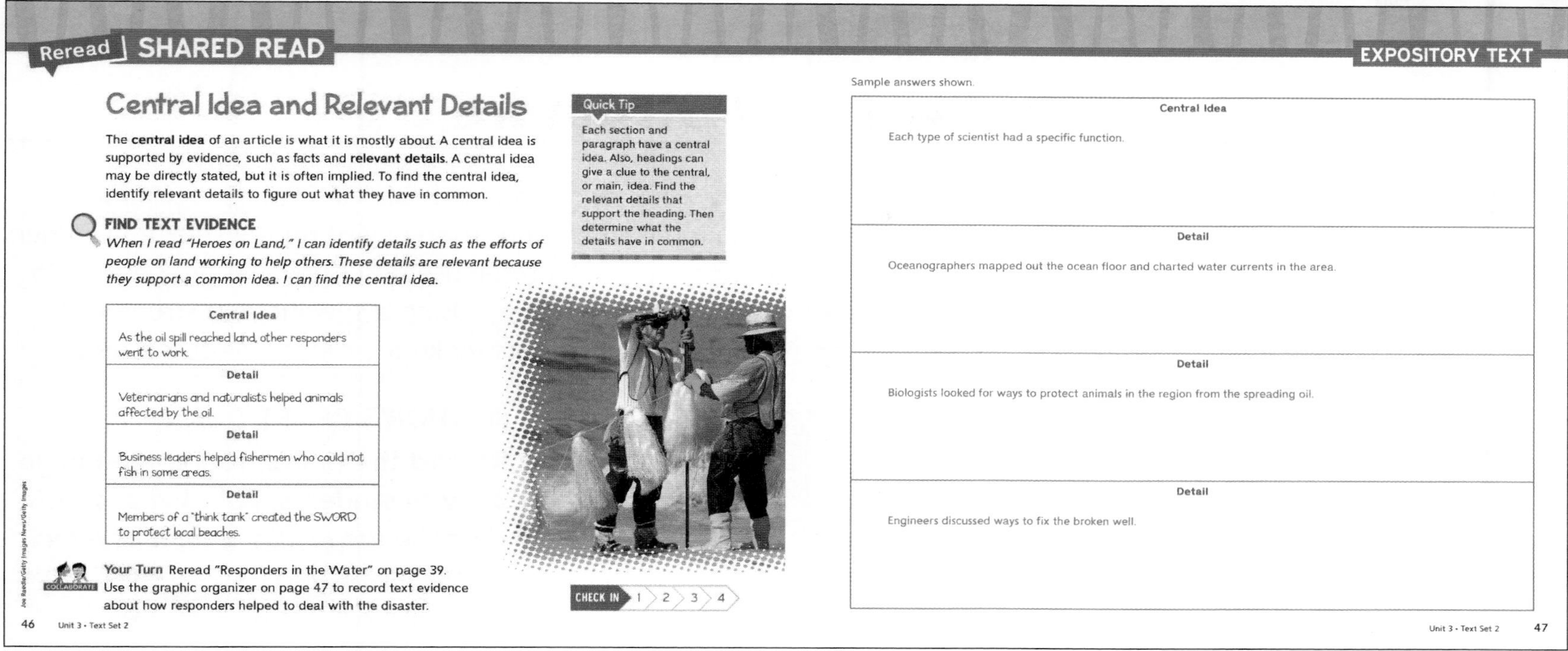

Reread | SHARED READ

EXPOSITORY TEXT

Central Idea and Relevant Details

The **central idea** of an article is what it is mostly about. A central idea is supported by evidence, such as facts and **relevant details**. A central idea may be directly stated, but it is often implied. To find the central idea, identify relevant details to figure out what they have in common.

Quick Tip

Each section and paragraph have a central idea. Also, headings can give a clue to the central, or main, idea. Find the relevant details that support the heading. Then determine what the details have in common.

FIND TEXT EVIDENCE

When I read "Heroes on Land," I can identify details such as the efforts of people on land working to help others. These details are relevant because they support a common idea. I can find the central idea.

Central Idea
As the oil spill reached land, other responders went to work.
Detail
Veterinarians and naturalists helped animals affected by the oil.
Detail
Business leaders helped fishermen who could not fish in some areas.
Detail
Members of a "think tank" created the SWORD to protect local beaches.

COLLABORATE **Your Turn** Reread "Responders in the Water" on page 39. Use the graphic organizer on page 47 to record text evidence about how responders helped to deal with the disaster.

CHECK IN 1 2 3 4

46 Unit 3 • Text Set 2

Sample answers shown.

Central Idea
Each type of scientist had a specific function.
Detail
Oceanographers mapped out the ocean floor and charted water currents in the area.
Detail
Biologists looked for ways to protect animals in the region from the spreading oil.
Detail
Engineers discussed ways to fix the broken well.

Unit 3 • Text Set 2 47

Reading/Writing Companion, pp. 46–47

English Language Learners

Use the following scaffolds with **Guided Practice**. For small group support, see the **ELL Small Group Guide**.

Beginning

Read the third paragraph on page 39 of "Responders on the Water" with students. Restate sentences as needed. Clarify that *oceanographers* and *biologist* are types of scientists. Help them identify relevant details by asking: *Who mapped out the ocean floor and charted water currents?* (oceanographers) *Who looked for ways to protect animals?* (biologists) Have partners discuss the central idea using: The central idea is that each type of scientist had a function.

Intermediate

Read the third paragraph on page 39 of "Responders on the Water" with students. Help partners identify relevant details by asking: *How did the scientists help deal with the disaster?* The oceanographers mapped out the ocean floor and charted the water currents. The biologists looks for ways to protect the animals. Then have them discuss the central idea using: Each type of scientist had a specific function.

Advanced/Advanced High

Have students read the third paragraph on page 39. Then have partners identify relevant details about the scientists and discuss the central idea using the terms *oceanographers, biologist,* and *function*.

FORMATIVE ASSESSMENT

STUDENT CHECK-IN

Ask partners to share their graphic organizers on Reading/Writing Companion page 47. Have them use the Check-In routine to reflect and fill in the bars.

CHECK FOR SUCCESS

Rubric Use your online rubric to record student progress.

Are students able to identify and list on the graphic organizer important details from the text and the central idea?

Small Group Instruction

If No

- **Approaching** Reteach p. T143

If Yes

- **On** Review p. T149
- **Beyond** Extend p. T155

Reread

Craft and Structure

LEARNING GOALS

We can reread to analyze craft and structure in expository text.

OBJECTIVES

Quote accurately from a text when explaining what the text says explicitly and when drawing inferences from the text. Identify the author's purpose.

Compare and contrast the overall structure (e.g., chronology, comparison, cause/effect, problem/solution) of events, ideas, concepts, or information in two or more texts.

Demonstrate understanding of figurative language, word relationships, and nuances in word meanings.

Interpret figurative language, including similes and metaphors, in context.

ELA ACADEMIC LANGUAGE

- *technique, descriptive*
- Cognates: *técnica, descriptivo*

TEACH IN SMALL GROUP

Approaching Level Use the scaffolded prompts to guide students' rereading of "Gulf Spill Superheroes." Have them make notes in the margin to indicate text evidence.

On Level Have partners complete the Reread prompts and share their answers.

Beyond Level Allow pairs to work independently to answer the Reread prompts.

ELL Have Beginning and Early-Intermediate ELLs use the **Scaffolded Shared Read.**

Tell students that they will now reread parts of "Gulf Spill Superheroes" and analyze the techniques the author used in writing the selection. When authors write expository text, they often use descriptive language to help readers picture what happens and why. Using a specific text structure to present information also helps authors make their ideas clear to readers.

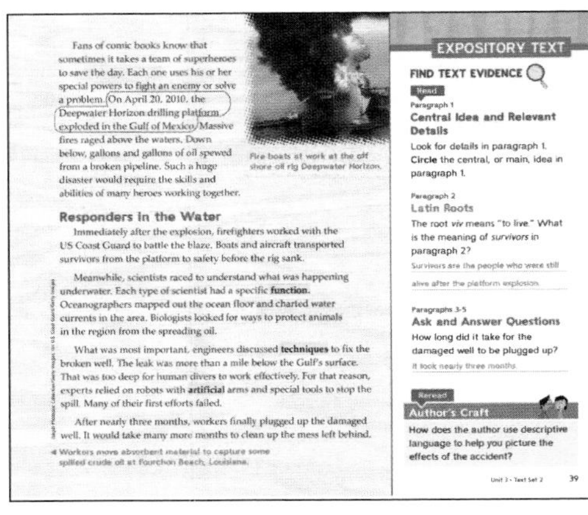

Fans of comic books know that sometimes it takes a team of superheroes to save the day. Each one uses his or her special powers to fight an enemy or solve a problem. On April 20, 2010, the Deepwater Horizon drilling platform exploded in the Gulf of Mexico. Massive fires raged above the waters. Down below, gallons and gallons of oil spewed from a broken pipeline. Such a huge disaster would require the skills and abilities of many heroes working together.

Fire boats at work at the off shore oil rig Deepwater Horizon.

Responders in the Water

Immediately after the explosion, firefighters worked with the US Coast Guard to battle the blaze. Boats and aircraft transported survivors from the platform to safety before the rig sank.

Meanwhile, scientists raced to understand what was happening underwater. Each type of scientist had a specific **function.** Oceanographers mapped out the ocean floor and charted water currents in the area. Biologists looked for ways to protect animals in the region from the spreading oil.

What was most important, engineers discussed **techniques** to fix the broken well. The leak was more than a mile below the Gulf's surface. That was too deep for human divers to work effectively. For that reason, experts relied on robots with **artificial** arms and special tools to stop the spill. Many of their first efforts failed.

After nearly three months, workers finally plugged up the damaged well. It would take many more months to clean up the mess left behind.

Workers move absorbent material to capture some spilled crude oil at Fourchon Beach, Louisiana.

EXPOSITORY TEXT

FIND TEXT EVIDENCE

Read

Paragraph 1
Central Idea and Relevant Details
Look for details in paragraph 1. **Circle** the central, or main, idea in paragraph 1.

Paragraph 2
Latin Roots
The root *viv* means "to live." What is the meaning of *survivors* in paragraph 2?
Survivors are the people who were still alive after the platform explosion.

Paragraphs 3-5
Ask and Answer Questions
How long did it take for the damaged well to be plugged up?
It took nearly three months.

Reread
Author's Craft
How does the author use descriptive language to help you picture the effects of the accident?

Unit 3 • Text Set 2 39

Reading/Writing Companion, p. 39

AUTHOR'S CRAFT DOK 2

Reread the first paragraph on page 39 with students. Ask: *What words describe the explosion and its effects?* (The word "exploded" describes the platform. The words "Massive fires raged" and "oil spewed" describe the effects.) *How did people respond to what happened?* (People worked together to deal with the disaster.) *To whom does the author compare these people?* (comic book superheroes with "special powers")

ELL Provide sentence frames to help students discuss the explosion and its effects: First, the drilling platform exploded. That caused a fire to burn above the water and oil to leak below the water. As a result, many people worked together to respond. Guide partners to point to words used to describe the fire and oil spill (*raged, spilled*) and talk about what these words mean. Then as a group, discuss what students know about comic superheroes and why the author might have chosen to compare them to the responders.

How does the author use descriptive language to help you picture the effects of the accident? (The author says the platform "exploded." The word "exploded" helps me picture the forceful blast. "Massive fires raged" helps me see that there were many out of control fires. The description "gallons and gallons of oil spewed" helps me see how large the spill was. The author also compares the teams of workers to comic superheroes who use their special powers to save people from danger.)

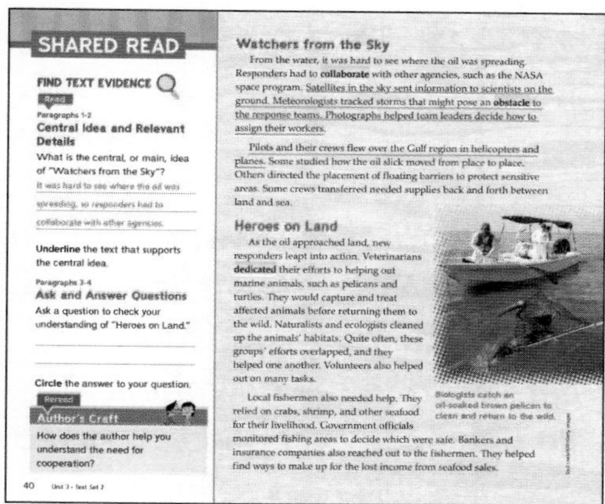

SHARED READ

FIND TEXT EVIDENCE

Read

Paragraphs 1-2

Central Idea and Relevant Details

What is the central, or main, idea of "Watchers from the Sky"?

It was hard to see where the oil was spreading, so responders had to collaborate with other agencies.

Underline the text that supports the central idea.

Paragraphs 3-4

Ask and Answer Questions

Ask a question to check your understanding of "Heroes on Land."

Circle the answer to your question.

Reread

Author's Craft

How does the author help you understand the need for cooperation?

40 Unit 3 • Text Set 2

Watchers from the Sky

From the water, it was hard to see where the oil was spreading. Responders had to **collaborate** with other agencies, such as the NASA space program. Satellites in the sky sent information to scientists on the ground. Meteorologists tracked storms that might pose an **obstacle** to the response teams. Photographs helped team leaders decide how to assign their workers.

Pilots and their crews flew over the Gulf region in helicopters and planes. Some studied how the oil slick moved from place to place. Others directed the placement of floating barriers to protect sensitive areas. Some crews transferred needed supplies back and forth between land and sea.

Heroes on Land

As the oil approached land, new responders leapt into action. Veterinarians **dedicated** their efforts to helping out marine animals, such as pelicans and turtles. They would capture and treat affected animals before returning them to the wild. Naturalists and ecologists cleaned up the animals' habitats. Quite often, these groups' efforts overlapped, and they helped one another. Volunteers also helped out on many tasks.

Biologists catch an oil-soaked brown pelican to clean and return to the wild.

Local fishermen also needed help. They relied on crabs, shrimp, and other seafood for their livelihood. Government officials monitored fishing areas to decide which were safe. Bankers and insurance companies also reached out to the fishermen. They helped find ways to make up for the lost income from seafood sales.

Reading/Writing Companion, p. 40

AUTHOR'S CRAFT DOK 2

Reread the first paragraph on page 40 with students. Ask: *According to the author, what did the meteorologists do?* (They tracked storms.) *How did the NASA space program collaborate with the meteorologists and other scientists?* (The NASA space program used their satellites to send information to the meteorologists.)

ELL *When you* collaborate, *do you work together?* (yes) Review the first paragraph with students, noting words and phrases that signal ways that teams cooperate: *collaborate, sent information to, helped.* Discuss how each supports the idea of working together.

How does the author help you understand the need for cooperation? (The author shows how many people with different skills had to work together on many problems. Individual teams with specific jobs shared information so that each team could do its job better.)

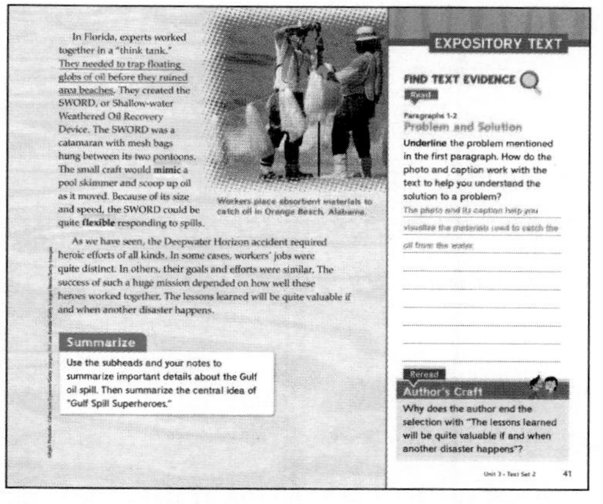

In Florida, experts worked together in a "think tank." They needed to trap floating globs of oil before they ruined area beaches. They created the SWORD, or Shallow-water Weathered Oil Recovery Device. The SWORD was a catamaran with mesh bags hung between its two pontoons. The small craft would **mimic** a pool skimmer and scoop up oil as it moved. Because of its size and speed, the SWORD could be quite **flexible** responding to spills.

Workers place absorbent materials to catch oil in Orange Beach, Alabama.

As we have seen, the Deepwater Horizon accident required heroic efforts of all kinds. In some cases, workers' jobs were quite distinct. In others, their goals and efforts were similar. The success of such a huge mission depended on how well these heroes worked together. The lessons learned will be quite valuable if and when another disaster happens.

Summarize

Use the subheads and your notes to summarize important details about the Gulf oil spill. Then summarize the central idea of "Gulf Spill Superheroes."

EXPOSITORY TEXT

FIND TEXT EVIDENCE

Read

Paragraphs 1-2

Problem and Solution

Underline the problem mentioned in the first paragraph. How do the photo and caption work with the text to help you understand the solution to a problem?

The photo and its caption help you visualize the materials used to catch the oil from the water.

Reread

Author's Craft

Why does the author end the selection with "The lessons learned will be quite valuable if and when another disaster happens"?

Unit 3 • Text Set 2 41

Reading/Writing Companion, p. 41

AUTHOR'S CRAFT DOK 2

Reread page 37 with students. Ask: *What is a "think tank"?* (A group of experts working together to solve a problem.) *What problem did the think tank solve?* (They figured out how to remove oil from the water.)

ELL Explain that an acronym is an abbreviation formed from the first letters of words. Ask: *Does SWORD name a real sword?* (no) *How do you know?* (The letters are all in capital letters.) Elicit the meaning of each word in the acronym and then discuss its meaning.

Why does the author end the selection with "The lessons learned will be quite valuable if and when another disaster happens"? (The author ended with this to show just how important teamwork was to achieve the best possible outcome. Knowing this will help groups be more prepared for another disaster.)

MAKE INFERENCES

Explain that when you make an inference, you use text evidence and what you already know to draw conclusions about details that the author does not state directly. Making inferences can help you to better understand each detail, as well as how several details relate to one another.

Think Aloud The beginning of the article describes a problem: an oil rig has exploded. The text goes on to describe all of the responders' efforts: They stopped the leak, saved animals, and cleaned up the water. I imagine that this must have been a huge job and that the responders spent many hours at work and away from their homes and families. This helps me understand just how important the task was to them and how much they cared about protecting the environment and everything and everyone who depend on it.

Integrate

BUILD KNOWLEDGE: MAKE CONNECTIONS

Talk About the Text Have partners discuss the benefits of people working together after the Deepwater Horizon oil spill.

Write About the Text Have students add their ideas to their Build Knowledge pages of their reader's notebooks.

Anchor Chart Record any new ideas on the Build Knowledge anchor chart.

Add to the Vocabulary List Have students write down any words they learned about the benefits of working as a group in their reader's notebooks.

FORMATIVE ASSESSMENT

STUDENT CHECK-IN

Have partners share their responses to one of the Reread prompts on Reading/Writing Companion pages 39–41. Ask them to reflect using the Check-In routine.

LEARNING GOALS

We can use text evidence to respond to expository text.

OBJECTIVES

Quote accurately from a text when explaining what the text says explicitly and when drawing inferences from the text.

Determine two or more central, or main, ideas of a text and explain how they are supported by relevant, or key, details; summarize the text.

Write in response to text.

ELA ACADEMIC LANGUAGE

- *structure, skim, analyze, evidence*
- Cognates: *estructura, analizar, evidencia*

TEACH IN SMALL GROUP

Approaching Level Have partners work together to plan and complete the response to the prompt.

On Level Have partners discuss their approaches to the prompt before writing their responses independently.

Beyond Level Have students write their responses independently. Have partners review them and recommend any needed revisions.

ELL Group students of mixed proficiency levels to discuss and respond to the prompt.

Reread

Write About the Shared Read

Analyze the Prompt DOK 3

Read the prompt aloud: *How might the outcome of the Deepwater Horizon accident been different if fewer groups responded?* Ask: *What is the prompt asking?* (to describe how the response to the accident would be different with fewer people helping) Say: *Let's read to see how the text uses a problem-and-solution text structure to show how responders worked together. As we do so, we'll note text evidence. This will help us make inferences that will help you write your response.*

Analyze Text Evidence

Remind students that when a text uses a problem-and-solution text structure, as in "Gulf Spill Superheroes," headings can often indicate a description of one problem and its solution. Headings can also be used to indicate central ideas and details that support these relevant ideas. In the **Reading/Writing Companion**, have students skim pages 39–41 of "Gulf Spill Superheroes" to find the section headings. Ask: *What important information do the headings provide about the responders in each section?* (They indicate where the responders worked: in the water, in the sky, and on land.) Next, have students evaluate relevant details in each section to determine the central idea. As students analyze the details, have them infer why teamwork is so important across so many groups.

Respond

Direct student pairs to the sentence starters on Reading/Writing Companion page 48. Ask: *How do the text features and structure help you understand the responders' roles and how important they were?* As needed, model a response.

Think Aloud As I reread each heading and the text that follows, I am reminded about the many different groups of responders and what they did to help after the oil spill. This helps me understand that many groups worked together to respond on the land, in the sea, and in the sky. The text structure emphasizes this collaboration and makes me realize how the outcome would have been different without so much teamwork.

Analytical Writing Students should use the sentence starters to form their responses. Their first paragraph should state the central idea of the response. The following sentences should contain relevant details from both the text and the photographs and captions about the roles the various teams of responders played in the overall effort. Students should use this information to infer how the outcome would have been different with fewer groups helping. They may continue their responses on a separate piece of paper.

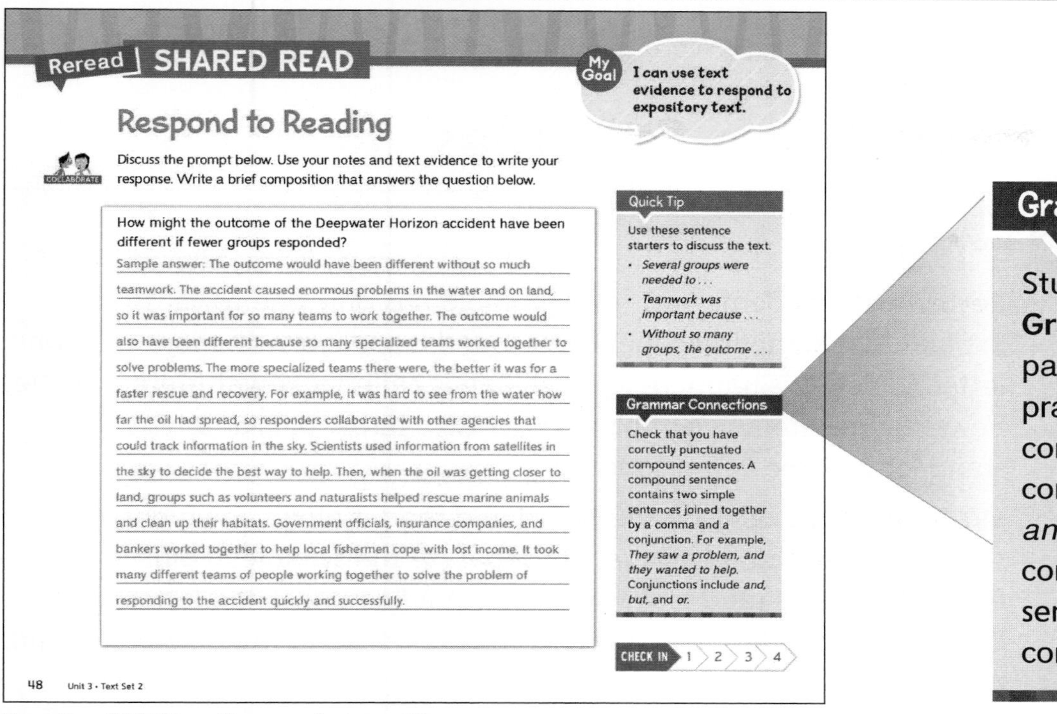

Reread | SHARED READ

My Goal: I can use text evidence to respond to expository text.

Respond to Reading

COLLABORATE: Discuss the prompt below. Use your notes and text evidence to write your response. Write a brief composition that answers the question below.

How might the outcome of the Deepwater Horizon accident have been different if fewer groups responded?

Sample answer: The outcome would have been different without so much teamwork. The accident caused enormous problems in the water and on land, so it was important for so many teams to work together. The outcome would also have been different because so many specialized teams worked together to solve problems. The more specialized teams there were, the better it was for a faster rescue and recovery. For example, it was hard to see from the water how far the oil had spread, so responders collaborated with other agencies that could track information in the sky. Scientists used information from satellites in the sky to decide the best way to help. Then, when the oil was getting closer to land, groups such as volunteers and naturalists helped rescue marine animals and clean up their habitats. Government officials, insurance companies, and bankers worked together to help local fishermen cope with lost income. It took many different teams of people working together to solve the problem of responding to the accident quickly and successfully.

Quick Tip

Use these sentence starters to discuss the text.

- *Several groups were needed to . . .*
- *Teamwork was important because . . .*
- *Without so many groups, the outcome . . .*

Grammar Connections

Check that you have correctly punctuated compound sentences. A compound sentence contains two simple sentences joined together by a comma and a conjunction. For example, *They saw a problem, and they wanted to help.* Conjunctions include *and*, *but*, and *or*.

CHECK IN 1 2 3 4

48 Unit 3 · Text Set 2

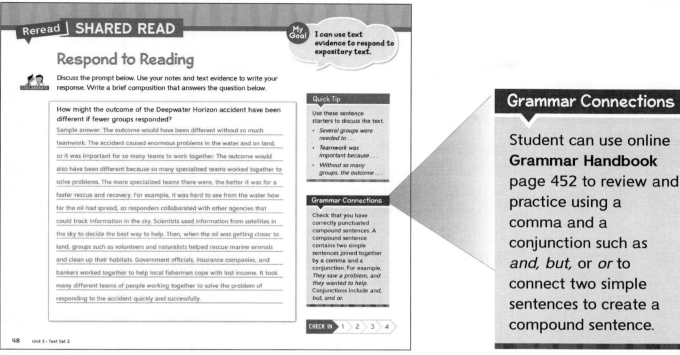

Reading/Writing Companion, p. 48

Grammar Connections

Student can use online **Grammar Handbook** page 452 to review and practice using a comma and a conjunction such as *and, but,* or *or* to connect two simple sentences to create a compound sentence.

English Language Learners

Use the following scaffolds with **Respond**.

Beginning

Read the prompt with students and discuss what they will write about. Clarify the meaning of *outcome* and *fewer*. Point out to them that the text features and structure show that many groups of responders worked together to help with the accident. *Do you think the outcome would have been different if fewer groups responded?* (yes) *Why?* Many groups of people needed to work together to respond to the accident quickly.

Intermediate

Read the prompt with students and discuss what they will write about. Say: *Look at the text features and structure. Does it show that many different groups of responders worked together to help with the accident?* (yes) *What was the outcome when they worked together?* They were able to respond quickly. Then have them answer the prompt using: The people would not have been able to respond to the accident quickly if they did not work together.

Advanced/Advanced High

Review the prompt and sentence starters on page 48 with students. Have partners discuss how the outcome would have been different if fewer groups worked together to respond to the accident. Then have them respond using the sentence starters.

ELL NEWCOMERS

Have students listen to the summaries of the **Shared Read** in their native language and then in English to help them access the text and develop listening comprehension. Help students ask and answer questions with a partner. Use these sentence frames: *How did people respond to the oil spill?* People responded by ____. Then continue the lessons in the **Newcomer Teacher's Guide**.

FORMATIVE ASSESSMENT

STUDENT CHECK-IN

Ask partners to share their response on Reading/Writing Companion page 48. Have them use the Check-In routine to reflect and fill in the bars.

LEARNING GOALS

- We can decode words with vowel team syllables.
- We can identify multisyllabic words with vowel team syllables.
- We can read fluently with accuracy at an appropriate rate.

OBJECTIVES

Use combined knowledge of all letter-sound correspondences, syllabication patterns, and morphology (e.g., roots and affixes) to read accurately unfamiliar multisyllabic words in context and out of context.

Read grade-level text with purpose and understanding.

Use context to confirm or self-correct word recognition and understanding, rereading as necessary.

- Rate: 123–143 WCPM

ELA ACADEMIC LANGUAGE

- *vowel, syllable, accuracy*
- Cognate: *sílaba*

TEACH IN SMALL GROUP

Phonics

Approaching Level and ELL Use Tier 2 activity on page T138 before teaching the lesson.

On Level As needed, use the Guided Practice section.

Beyond Level As needed, use the Multisyllabic Words section only.

ELL See page 5 in the **Language Transfers Handbook** for guidance in identifying sounds and symbols that may not transfer for speakers of certain languages, and support those students.

OPTION 10 mins

Vowel Team Syllables

1 Explain

Review with students that every syllable has only one vowel sound. Explain that sometimes the vowel sound is spelled with more than one letter. When this happens, the syllable is called a **vowel team syllable.** Vowel teams are any combination of two, three, or four letters that stand for a single vowel sound.

Write the word *rainy* on the board and read it aloud. Then draw a slash between the *n* and the *y* to separate the syllables. Point to the first syllable and read it slowly, drawing a line under the letters *ai*. Explain that the letters *a* and *i* work together to form one vowel sound, /ā/.

2 Model

Write the following vowel team syllables and related words on the board. Model how to pronounce each syllable, and then model how to read the related word. Underline the vowel team in each word.

heav as in ***heaven***	**light** *as* in ***delight***
train as in ***trainer***	**neigh** as in ***neighbor***
geal as in ***congeal***	**bout** as in ***about***
low as in ***below***	**spoil** as in ***spoilage***

3 Guided Practice

Write the following words on the board. Have students underline the vowel team syllable in each word. Then have them read the words chorally.

painful	mouthful	beaded
beastly	below	midnight
heavily	monsoon	maybe
yellow	replay	leader

For practice with decoding and encoding, use **Practice Book** page 151 or online activities.

Read Multisyllabic Words

Transition to Longer Words Write on the board the following one-syllable words and related multisyllabic words, each of which contains a vowel team. Have students read the one-syllable words. Then model how to read the longer word. Finally, have students read the words chorally as you point to them. Vary the order of words and the speed at which you move from one to another.

brain	brainy	book	booklet
pay	payment	field	outfield
toe	tiptoe	boy	boyfriend
tree	treetop	ground	grounded
road	roadway	tie	necktie
bowl	bowlful	weigh	weighing

Fluency

Accuracy and Rate

Explain/Model Tell students that good readers are able to correctly pronounce all of the words they read. Explain to them that in order to read words accurately, it may be necessary to read at a slower or faster rate, depending on the kind of text they are reading. Model reading the first page of "Gulf Spill Superheroes," **Reading/Writing Companion** page 39 with accuracy. Remind students that you will be listening for accuracy and rate as you monitor their reading during the week.

Practice/Apply Have partners alternate reading paragraphs in the passage, modeling the rate you used. Encourage them to read accurately and at an appropriate rate.

Daily Fluency Practice

Automaticity Students can practice reading with accuracy and appropriate rate to develop automaticity using the online **Differentiated Genre Passage,** "Building a Green Town."

DIGITAL TOOLS

For more practice, have students use phonics and fluency activities.

Vowel Team Syllables

MULTIMODAL LEARNING

Create a list of words that use vowel team syllables or use the words from Read Multisyllabic Words. Say each word and have students spell it. Then write the vowel team syllable spellings such as *ai, oe, ee,* and *igh* on chart paper and post in different corners of the room. Say random words from the list and have students stand under the chart paper when they hear a word with that vowel team.

FORMATIVE ASSESSMENT

STUDENT CHECK-IN

Vowel Team Syllables Have partners share three words with vowel team syllables.

Multisyllabic Words Have partners read the following words: *payment, grounded,* and *weighing.*

Fluency Ask partners to read "Building a Green Town" fluently.

Have partners reflect using the Check-In routine.

CHECK FOR SUCCESS

Can students read words with vowel team syllables? Can students read fluently with accuracy at an appropriate rate?

Small Group Instruction

If No

- **Approaching** Reteach pp. T138, T142
- **ELL** Develop p. T138

If Yes

- **On** Apply p. T144
- **Beyond** Apply p. T150

Integrate

Working Together

Explain to students that for the next two weeks they will work with a larger group to research an animal rescue group and create a television segment that tells how the group helps animals survive in their own ecosystems.

Formal Inquiry Discuss some of the ways animal rescue groups care for and protect animals. Then have students think about how they might present information about one such group in a television segment. Point out that television segments typically include:

- *Audio clips* that may include opening and closing music, sounds, or voice-overs.
- *Photos* that show the animals, the ecosystem, or the team of people taking care of the animals.
- *Videos* to show the animals or the rescue group at work. Video segments might also include interviews, a title and credit graphics, or commercials.

Have students read the Quick Tip and example box on **Reading/Writing Companion** page 49. Discuss the difference between formal and informal inquiry. Support students as they go through each step in the Research Process as outlined on page 49. If possible, find videos on the Internet related to the topic to share with students.

STEP 1 **Set a Goal** Explain to students that they will generate questions about animal rescue groups that they want to answer with research. Offer feedback as students generate and clarify questions and decide which group to research and feature in their television segments. Have them use an **Accordion Book Foldable®**, available online, to help organize their information.

STEP 2 **Identify Sources** Brainstorm with groups the kinds of digital and print resources they can use for their research. Remind them to use credible sources that are not biased. Discuss the ways in which websites might be biased and how students can determine if a website is trustworthy.

STEP 3 **Find and Record Information** Review with students how to take notes and cite the sources they use to gather information for their television segments. Remind them to write the information they research in their own words to avoid plagiarism.

STEP 4 **Organize and Synthesize Information** Guide students in organizing the information that they want to include in their television segments. Discuss which members of the group will play the part of the rescue group and which members will conduct the interview. Have students determine the audio, video, and photos they plan to include in their segment.

STEP 5 **Create and Present** Review with students the questions, information, and media they should include in their television segments. Discuss options for presenting their segment to the class.

LEARNING GOALS

- **We can use the research process to create a television segment.**
- **We can generate and clarify questions for formal inquiry.**

OBJECTIVES

Conduct short research projects that use several sources to build knowledge through investigation of different aspects of a topic.

Come to discussions prepared, having read or studied required material; explicitly draw on that preparation and other information known about the topic to explore ideas under discussion.

Follow agreed-upon rules for discussions and carry out assigned roles.

Develop a logical research plan.

Include multimedia components (e.g., graphics, sound) and visual displays in presentations when appropriate to enhance the development of main ideas or themes.

ELA ACADEMIC LANGUAGE

- *generate, clarify, source, biased, inquiry*
- Cognates: *generar, clarificar*

TEACH IN SMALL GROUP

You may wish to teach the Research and Inquiry lesson during Small Group time. Have groups of mixed abilities complete the page and work on the television segment.

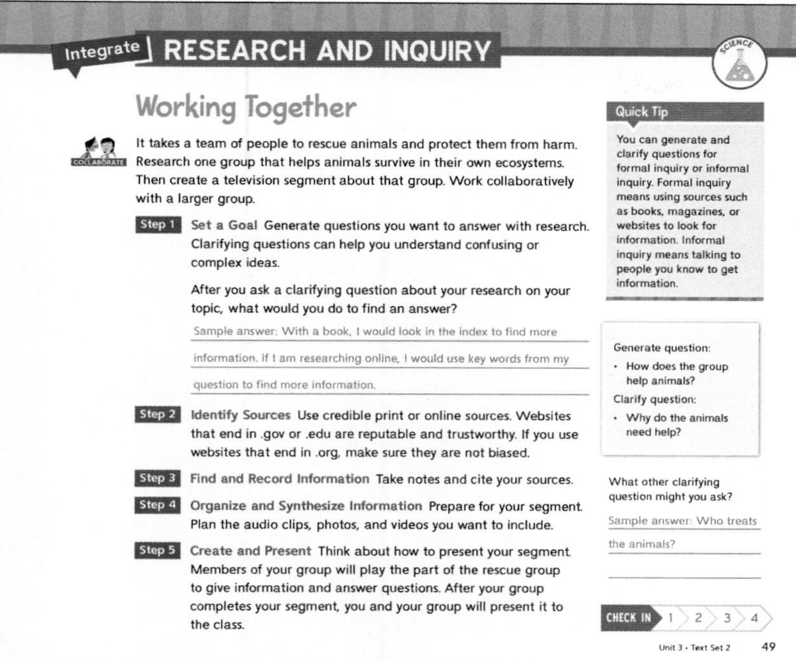

Integrate | RESEARCH AND INQUIRY

SCIENCE

Working Together

COLLABORATE

It takes a team of people to rescue animals and protect them from harm. Research one group that helps animals survive in their own ecosystems. Then create a television segment about that group. Work collaboratively with a larger group.

Step 1 Set a Goal Generate questions you want to answer with research. Clarifying questions can help you understand confusing or complex ideas.

After you ask a clarifying question about your research on your topic, what would you do to find an answer?

Sample answer: With a book, I would look in the index to find more information. If I am researching online, I would use key words from my question to find more information.

Step 2 Identify Sources Use credible print or online sources. Websites that end in .gov or .edu are reputable and trustworthy. If you use websites that end in .org, make sure they are not biased.

Step 3 Find and Record Information Take notes and cite your sources.

Step 4 Organize and Synthesize Information Prepare for your segment. Plan the audio clips, photos, and videos you want to include.

Step 5 Create and Present Think about how to present your segment. Members of your group will play the part of the rescue group to give information and answer questions. After your group completes your segment, you and your group will present it to the class.

Quick Tip

You can generate and clarify questions for formal inquiry or informal inquiry. Formal inquiry means using sources such as books, magazines, or websites to look for information. Informal inquiry means talking to people you know to get information.

Generate question:

- How does the group help animals?

Clarify question:

- Why do the animals need help?

What other clarifying question might you ask?

Sample answer: Who treats the animals?

CHECK IN 1 2 3 4

Unit 3 • Text Set 2 49

Reading/Writing Companion, p. 49

English Language Learners

Use the following scaffolds with **Step 4**.

Beginning

Review what a television segment includes with students. Model how to outline the information they want to include in their television segment. Tell them which members of the group will play the part of the rescue group and which members will conduct the interview. Then have partners discuss the audio, video, and photos they plan to include using: I want to include audio/video/photos of ____.

Intermediate

Review what a television segment includes with students. Guide students to outline the information they want to include in their television segment. Help partners choose which members of the group will play the part of the rescue group and which members will conduct the interview. Then have them discuss the audio, video, and photos they plan to include using: I want to include audio/video/photos of ____ because ____.

Advanced/Advanced High

Have students review what a television segment includes. Guide them to outline the information they want to include in their television segment. Then have partners discuss the audio, video, and photos they plan to include.

DIGITAL TOOLS

Evaluating Sources for Reliability; Organizing Notes

Dinah Zike's FOLDABLES Study Organizer

FOLDABLES

MULTIMODAL

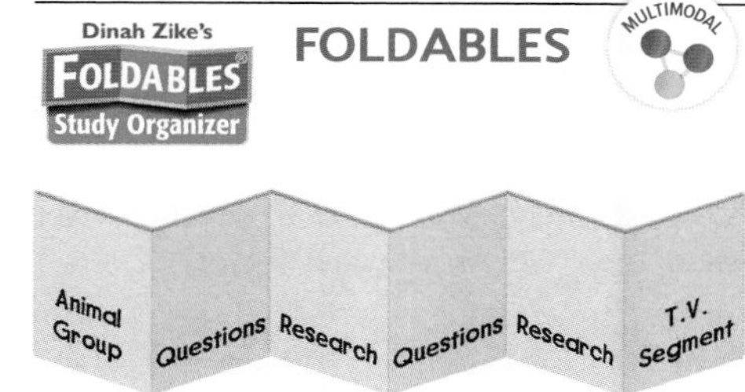

Accordion Book Foldable®

FORMATIVE ASSESSMENT

STUDENT CHECK-IN

Television Segment Ask students to share their TV segments.

Formal Inquiry Have students share one of the questions they generated for their formal inquiry.

Have students use the Check-In routine to reflect and fill in the bars on Reading/Writing Companion page 49.

Winter's Tail

Lexile 940L

LEARNING GOALS

Read We can apply strategies and skills to read expository text.

Reread We can reread to analyze text, craft, and structure, and compare texts.

Have students apply what they learned as they read.

Connect grade-level-appropriate science concepts with the history of science, science careers, and contributions of scientists.

What makes this text complex?

- Organization
- Purpose
- Connection of Ideas
- Specific Vocabulary

Close Reading Routine

Read DOK 1–2

- Identify important ideas and details.
- Take notes and summarize.
- Use ACT prompts as needed.

Reread DOK 2–3

- Analyze the text, craft, and structure.
- Use *Reading/Writing Companion*, pp. 50–52.

Integrate DOK 3–4

- Integrate knowledge and ideas.
- Make text-to-text connections.
- Use the Integrate lesson.
- Complete the Show Your Knowledge task.
- Inspire action.

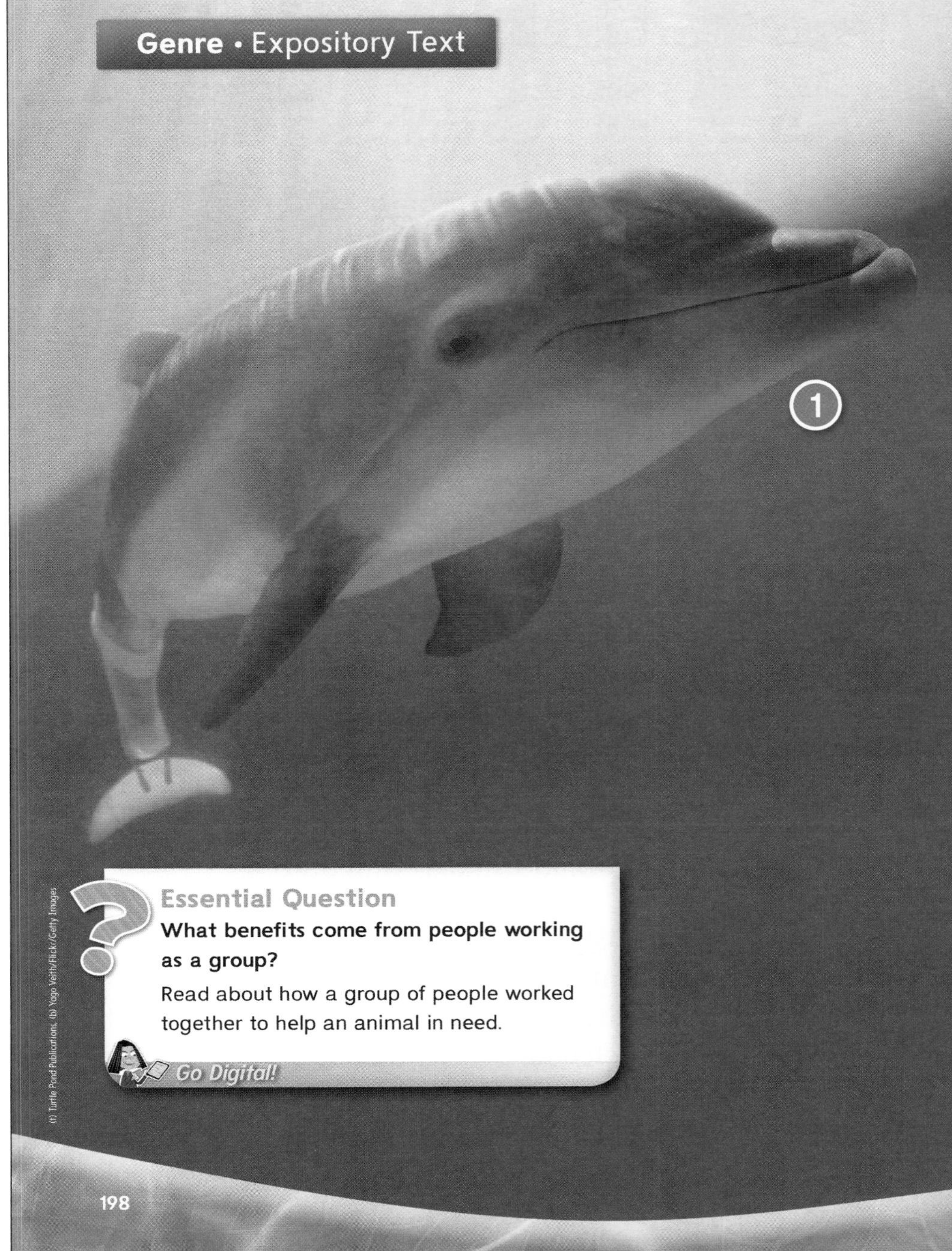

Genre • Expository Text
1
Essential Question
What benefits come from people working as a group?
Read about how a group of people worked together to help an animal in need.
Go Digital!
198

Literature Anthology, pp. 198–199

DIFFERENTIATED READING

You may wish to read the full selection aloud once with minimal stopping before you begin using the Read prompts.

Approaching Level Have students listen to the selection summary. Use the Reread prompts during Small Group time.

On Level and **Beyond Level** Pair students or have them independently complete the Reread prompts on **Reading/ Writing Companion** pages 50–52.

English Language Learners Have ELLs listen to the summary of the selection, available in multiple languages. See also **ELL Small Group Guide**.

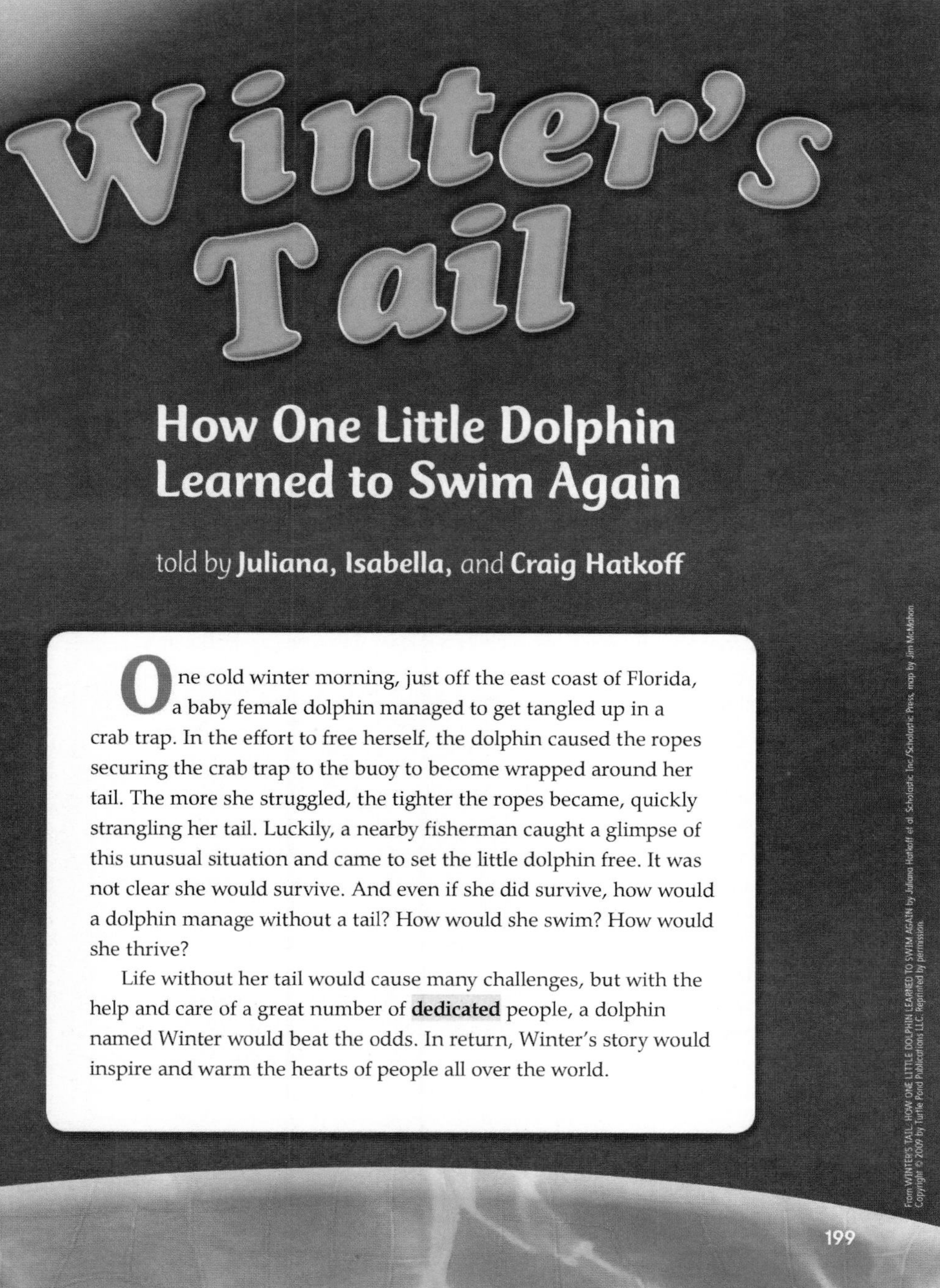

Winter's Tail

How One Little Dolphin Learned to Swim Again

told by **Juliana, Isabella,** and **Craig Hatkoff**

One cold winter morning, just off the east coast of Florida, a baby female dolphin managed to get tangled up in a crab trap. In the effort to free herself, the dolphin caused the ropes securing the crab trap to the buoy to become wrapped around her tail. The more she struggled, the tighter the ropes became, quickly strangling her tail. Luckily, a nearby fisherman caught a glimpse of this unusual situation and came to set the little dolphin free. It was not clear she would survive. And even if she did survive, how would a dolphin manage without a tail? How would she swim? How would she thrive?

Life without her tail would cause many challenges, but with the help and care of a great number of **dedicated** people, a dolphin named Winter would beat the odds. In return, Winter's story would inspire and warm the hearts of people all over the world.

199

Read

Set a Purpose Tell students to preview the text and set a purpose for reading. Remind them that setting a purpose can help them monitor comprehension.

Note Taking: Use the Graphic Organizer

Analytical Writing Remind students to take notes as they read. Distribute copies of online Central Idea and Relevant Details **Graphic Organizer 7.** Have students fill in the organizer with the central idea and relevant details of each section. They can also note words they don't understand and questions they have.

1 Text Features: Photograph DOK 2

Look at the photograph on pages 198–199. Where is the dolphin? What problem do you notice about its tail? (The dolphin is in the water, and its tail is missing. It looks like it has an artificial tail.)

Build Vocabulary on page 199

Have students add the Build Vocabulary words to their reader's notebook.

glimpse: a quick look

thrive: to become healthy and strong

ACT Access Complex Text

Organization

Tell students that this expository text is organized using many text structures, including chronology—explaining events in the order they happened. However, the authors begin with an introduction that summarizes the events, describing the problem and letting readers know how Winter's story ends.

What happens to Winter? (She gets tangled up in a crab trap which strangles her tail.) *What challenge will she face?* (She might not survive, and if she does, how will she live without a tail?) *How does Winter's story turn out?* (With the help of many people, she "beats the odds.") Explain that the rest of the selection will describe how Winter beats the odds and survives.

Read

2 Central Idea and Relevant Details DOK 2

What is the central idea on page 200? (A fisherman found a dolphin struggling while tangled in a rope.) What relevant details support this central idea? (The rope from a crab trap was wrapped around the dolphin's mouth and tail. She couldn't raise her blowhole to breathe normally, and her body was curled like a horseshoe. Jim Savage cut the rope to free the dolphin.) Add the central idea and relevant details to your organizer.

Central Idea
A fisherman named Jim Savage found a dolphin tangled in a rope.
Detail
The rope from a crab trap was wrapped around her mouth and tail. She couldn't breathe normally and she was curled like a horseshoe.
Detail
Jim rescued the dolphin by cutting the rope.

Build Vocabulary on page 200

lagoon: an area of shallow water separated from the sea

idled: operated at a very low speed

rasping: screeching

murky: dark

(t) Jim Savage, (b) Yogo Veith/Flickr/Getty Images

A badly injured Winter in Mosquito Lagoon shortly after being freed.

December 10, 2005, was a chilly Saturday. Jim Savage was the only fisherman braving the bitter wind in Mosquito Lagoon that morning. As Jim steered his boat in the dim light, he noticed a line of crab traps rigged just beneath the water's surface. One trap seemed to be going in a direction opposite from the others. Something was pulling it against the strong wind. Jim idled his boat and steered slowly toward the trap. Even before he could see anything, he heard a harsh, rasping sound over the sound of the waves. When he searched the murky water, Jim found a baby dolphin gasping for breath. She was caught. A rope from the trap was wrapped tightly around both her mouth and tail.

The dolphin was so tangled in the rope that her small body was curled like a horseshoe, her mouth pulled close to her tail. Jim spoke to her, assuring her that he was there to help. He knew he needed to free her head first so she could raise her blowhole out of the water and breathe normally. The dolphin struggled as Jim used his fish-cleaning knife to cut the line that tied her mouth and tail together.

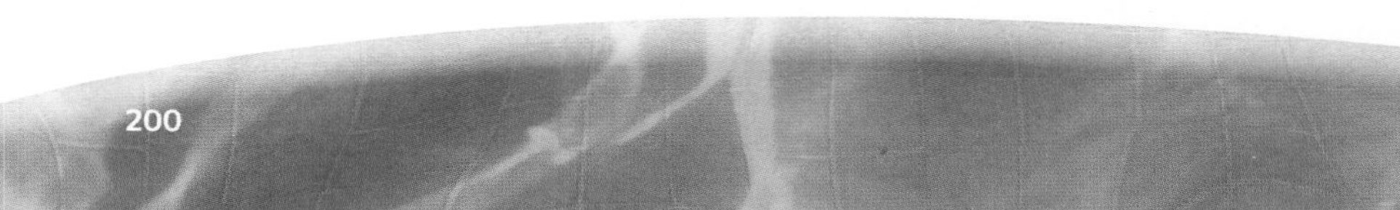

200

Literature Anthology, pp. 200–201

Access Complex Text

Purpose

Remind students that the author's purpose for this text is to explain the benefits that result from a group of people working together to help an animal in need.

- *What details on pages 200–201 describe the help the fisherman gave?* (He spoke to the dolphin. He used his knife to cut the rope. He called for help and stayed with the dolphin until help arrived.)
- *What details describe the help that the rescue team gave?* (Members of the rescue team caught the dolphin, lifted her out of the lagoon, put her in the van, and drove her to the aquarium.)

Several minutes later, Jim pulled off the last of the rope, and the young dolphin swam away from the boat. She kept her distance from the fisherman, but she did not leave the lagoon. After thirty minutes, Jim understood that she was too exhausted, too injured. He called Florida's Fish and Wildlife Conservation Commission. The workers there would know how to take care of a wounded dolphin.

Jim watched over the dolphin until the rescue team arrived a few hours later. As soon as they saw the cuts around the dolphin's tail, they knew they would need to move her somewhere safe so she could heal.

Even though she was injured, the dolphin was not easy to catch. But they finally corralled her. After lifting her from the lagoon, the rescue team tried to help her relax before carrying her to the transport van. They had a long drive ahead of them, all the way across Florida to the Clearwater Marine Aquarium. 3

Teresa, from the Hubbs-SeaWorld Research Institute, tries to keep a shivering, injured Winter warm and calm.

Harbor Branch Oceanographic Institute

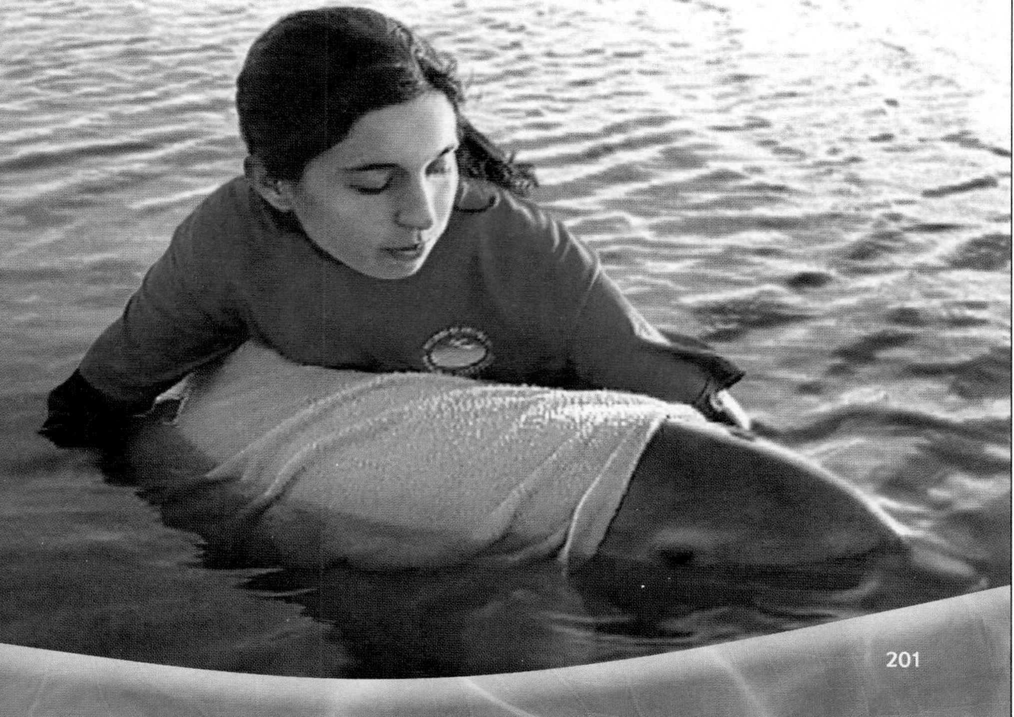

201

Read

3 Ask and Answer Questions DOK 1

Teacher Think Aloud As I read, I ask and answer questions to better understand the text. First I'll ask myself why the dolphin did not leave the lagoon. I read the first paragraph on page 201 and discover she was too tired to swim very far. After I read the second paragraph, I ask myself where the rescue team might take her. When I read the third paragraph, I find the answer: They take her to the Clearwater Marine Aquarium.

Reread

Author's Craft: Text Features DOK 2

Reread the last paragraph on page 201. What information do you learn about the dolphin from the photograph and the caption that you do not learn in the text? Why is this information important? (The worker needed to get right next to the dolphin and wrap her in a blanket to keep her warm and calm. The photograph shows that the plan worked because the dolphin appears calm, even though she had been struggling greatly beforehand.)

English Language Learners

Synonyms and Circumlocution Remind students that they can ask for synonyms to help clarify words or expressions they don't understand, and that they can use the words they know to help express complex ideas. *Remember that you can ask about synonyms or describe the meaning to identify a word you don't know.* Read aloud page 201, paragraph 3. *With a partner, ask about synonyms for words you don't know:* What is a synonym of corralled? Help students generate words and phrases. Then, have partners take turns restating what happened in their own words.

Newcomers

Use the Newcomer Online Visuals and their accompanying prompts to help students expand vocabulary and language about My World (24-a-f). Use the Conversation Starters, Speech Balloons, and the Games in the **Newcomer Teacher's Guide** to continue building vocabulary and developing oral and written language.

Read

4 Genre: Expository Text DOK 1

COLLABORATE Expository texts provide facts and details about a topic. What facts and details do you learn about Winter in this paragraph? Turn to a partner and paraphrase the answer. (Veterinarians, dolphin trainers, and volunteers were there to help, the dolphin had been out of the water for three hours, and it was a cold night.)

5 Make Inferences DOK 2

Does the staff believe that Winter will survive? What evidence supports your inference? (Yes, they knew that Winter's struggling meant she had the heart and energy to protect herself.)

Build Vocabulary on page 202

anxious: eager to do something

evaluated: checked

ordeal: an extremely difficult experience

4 A small, anxious crowd awaited the dolphin's arrival at the aquarium. The group included a veterinarian, dolphin trainers, and volunteers. When the van pulled up, they were all ready to help. It had not been an easy journey. The dolphin had been out of the water for more than three hours. On top of that, the night air was cold. It was so chilly that the group decided to name the dolphin Winter.

The rescue workers carefully moved Winter to a holding tank. Abby, the head dolphin trainer, stood alongside Winter in the tank. Immediately, the veterinarian evaluated Winter's health. It was clear the little dolphin was badly injured. The vet estimated that Winter was only two or three months old. In the wild, baby dolphins drink their mother's milk until they are about two years old. Winter was so young that she would not know how to eat a fish if they offered it to her. But she needed food. The only choice was to gently insert a special feeding tube down her throat. Winter was probably still scared from her ordeal so, although the tube did not hurt, she continued to struggle.

5 Abby and the rest of the aquarium staff knew, however, that it was good that Winter was struggling—it showed she still had the heart and energy to try to protect herself.

(t) Clearwater Marine Aquarium; (b) Diego Verth/Flickr/Getty Images

It would take time for Winter to accept help from all of the many people who were making it possible for her to survive.

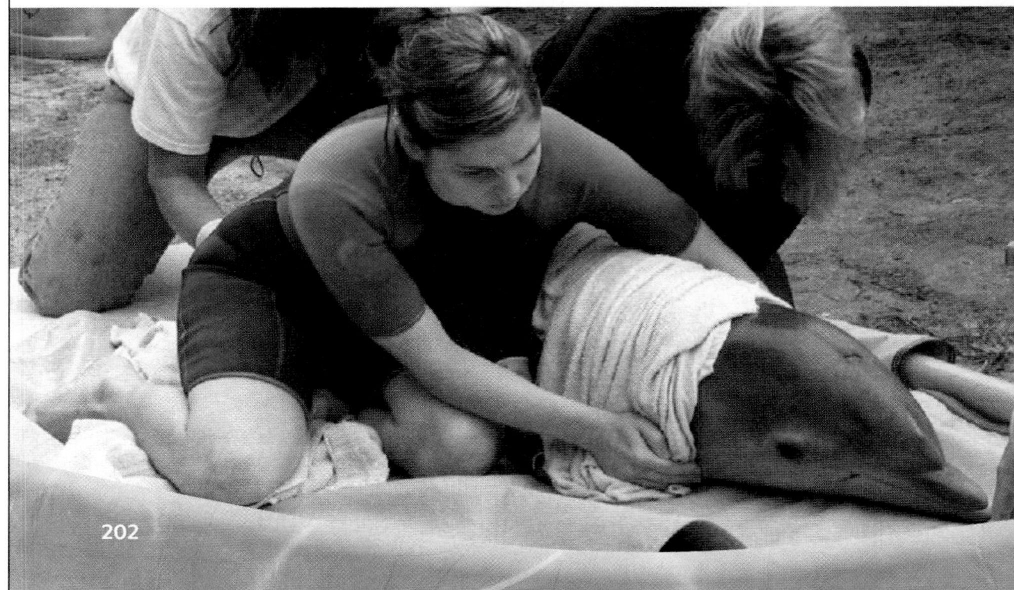

202

Literature Anthology, pp. 202–203

Access Complex Text

Organization

Point out that the authors include specific details about what the helpers do as well as descriptions of how the dolphin reacts to the help.

- *What were the first actions of Abby and the vet?* (Abby stood near the tank. The vet evaluated Winter's health.)
- *How did Abby and the staff make sure Winter got fed?* (At first they fed her through a tube in her throat. Then they showed Winter how to drink from a bottle.)
- *How did Winter respond to the bottle?* (She got used to it and started to gain weight.)

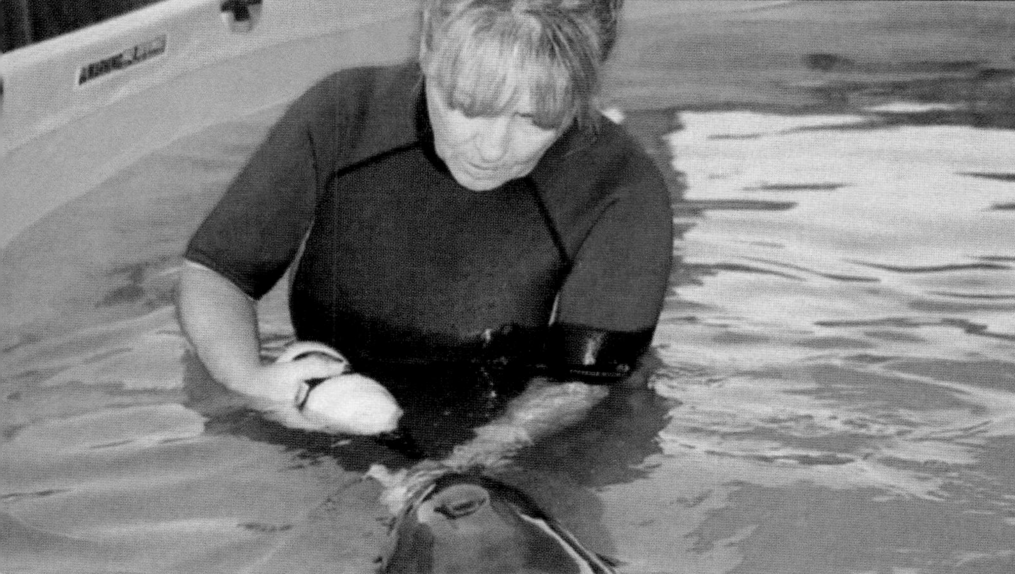

A volunteer coaxes Winter to drink from a bottle.

Clearwater Marine Aquarium

On Winter's second day at the aquarium, Abby showed her a bottle. The bottle contained a milk formula developed for zoo animals. At first, Winter did not know what the bottle was for. It took her a week to get the hang of drinking from it, and then the staff no longer needed to feed her with the tube. Each day, they weighed Winter. She started to gain weight. It was a good sign.

Winter was still very sick. The rope from the trap had been wrapped so tightly around her tail that it had stopped the blood flow. Pieces of her tail were starting to flake off, little by little.

Nonetheless, by the end of the week, Abby and the other trainers no longer felt they had to support Winter in the water. They encouraged her to swim on her own. And then, just as everyone feared, Winter lost her tail. What was left was a fleshy stump that would heal over time.

Would Winter be able to swim without her tail?

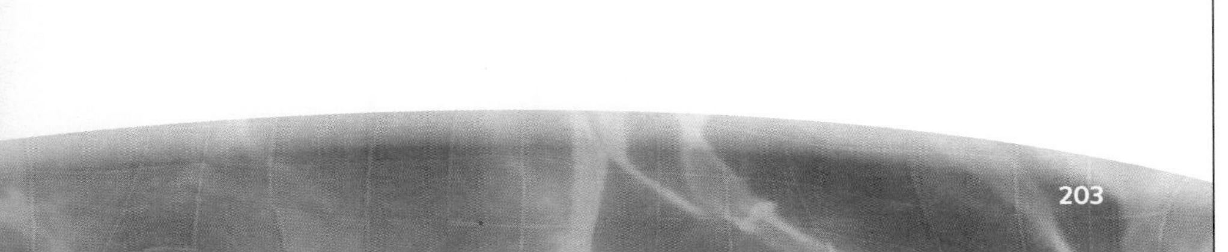

203

STOP AND CHECK **DOK 1**

Ask and Answer Questions How did the aquarium trainers help Winter? (They taught her to drink from a bottle. They supported her in the water and then they encouraged her to swim on her own.)

Reread

Author's Craft: Text Features DOK 2

Reading/Writing Companion, p. 50

Reread pages 202–203. How do you know that the aquarium staff is concerned about Winter? (The aquarium staff devotes a tremendous amount of attention and care to Winter's health and progress. The author emphasizes this by using words like *ready to help, immediately, carefully, gently,* and *encouraged* to show the dedication of Winter's caretakers.) How do the photographs support the text? (The photographs show this devotion in action.)

Author's Purpose DOK 3

How do the authors help you understand that Winter's relationship with the staff is changing? Cite text evidence. (Winter is finally beginning to trust the staff. She allows them to feed her without struggling.) What does their relationship suggest about Winter's future? (Now that Winter feels safe and trusts the staff, her chances of recovery are much better.)

ELL Spotlight on Language

Page 202, Paragraphs 1–2 Explain that a *veterinarian* is a doctor for animals. Have partners read the first three sentences of paragraph 2. *Which words tell you the veterinarian's job with the dolphin?* (evaluated Winter's health) Remind students that they can use the words around an unfamiliar word as context clues to help them figure out the meaning. Have students read the next two sentences and point to the word *vet* in the fifth sentence. *Talk to your partner about what you think vet means.*

Read

6 Text Features: Photograph DOK 2

What does the photograph show? (It shows Winter working with her trainer.) Why is this important? (It means that Winter is continuing to trust her helpers and this will help her improve her condition.)

7 Text Structure: Chronology DOK 1

When did Winter begin daily training lessons with the handlers? (She began training lessons when she was about five months old.) What events happened before Winter was ready to begin her training? (The wound on her tail healed and she got used to her home and her handlers.)

Build Vocabulary on page 204

concerned: worried

handlers: people who assist in training

enthusiastic: excited

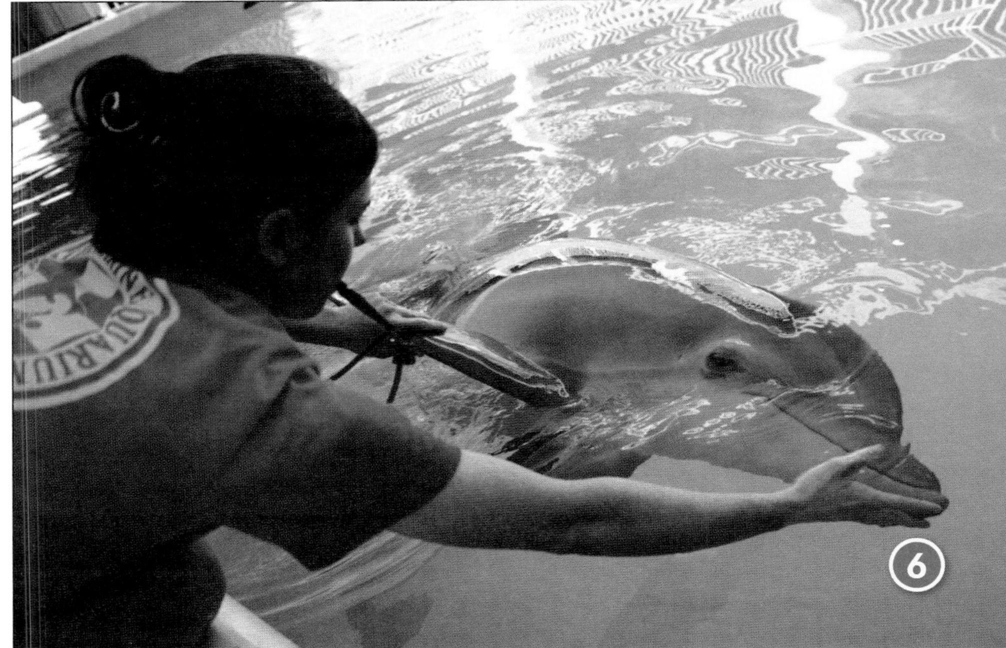

Winter and Abby enjoy their training sessions together.

Winter did start to swim on her own, but she did not swim like other dolphins. Her tail stump swished from side to side, more like the motion of a fish or a shark than the up-and-down tail action of a dolphin. Still, it was amazing! Winter had taught herself an entirely new way to swim! Her trainers were impressed, but they were also concerned that she might damage her backbone by swimming the wrong way.

Although Winter's tail had fallen off, the wound had healed. She was getting used to her new home and her handlers. Whenever someone arrived next to her pool with a bottle, she gave a cheery welcome of clicks and whistles. By the time Winter was about five months old, she began daily training sessions with her handlers. They used training **techniques** similar to those used with the aquarium's other dolphins, and she learned to listen to their signals. Winter was a quick and enthusiastic learner.

204

Literature Anthology, pp. 204–205

Access Complex Text

Connection of Ideas

Tell students that authors often use comparisons to help explain information. Point out that on pages 204 and 205, the author shows ways in which Winter is both like other dolphins and different from other dolphins.

- *How is Winter different from other dolphins?* (She moves her tail side to side, but other dolphins move their tails up and down.)
- *How did the trainers treat Winter compared to other dolphins?* (The trainers used the same techniques and signals.)

Winter had learned to trust the people who cared for her, but she had not seen another dolphin since arriving at the aquarium. Now it was time to meet a new friend. The trainers decided to introduce Winter to Panama, a female dolphin who had been rescued as well. The trainers were not sure how Winter would react to Panama—or how Panama would react to Winter. Would Panama even recognize Winter as a dolphin?

When they first brought Winter to the new tank, Panama kept her distance. Winter stayed by the edge, where she felt safest, and watched the older dolphin swim laps around the pool. But Winter got tired of waiting. If she wanted to make a friend, it was clear she would have to make it happen. Now, whenever Panama passed, Winter swam out to greet her. Panama tried to ignore Winter, but Winter was unfazed. She kept playfully approaching Panama. Finally, after three long days, Panama gave up. She stopped trying to swim away from Winter, and the two dolphins have been together ever since.

Turtle Pond Publications

Panama lets Winter trail just behind her, the way baby dolphins follow their mothers.

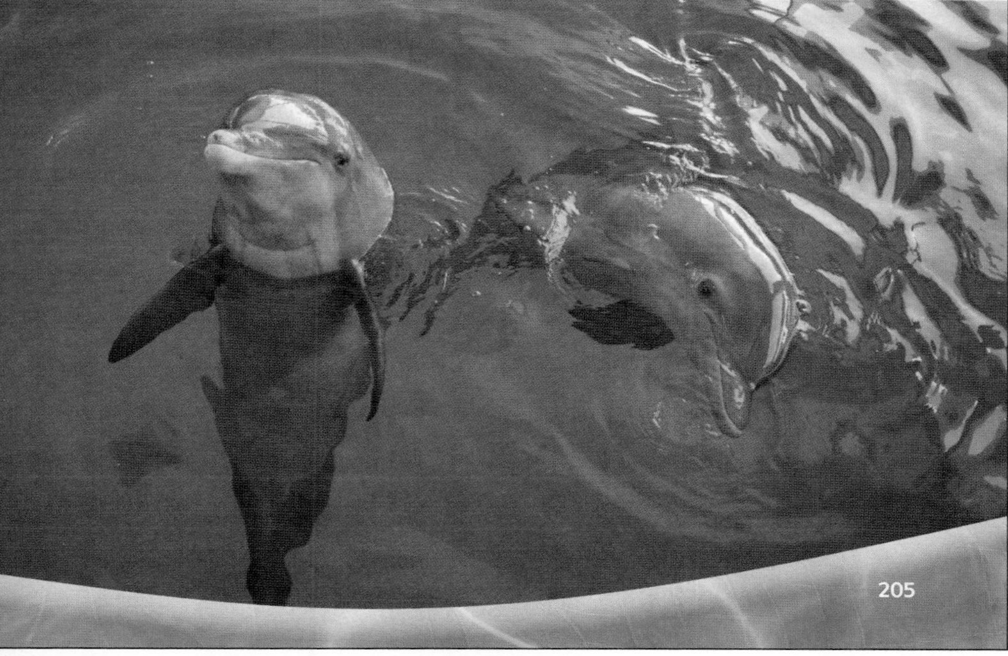

205

Read

8 Central Idea and Relevant Details DOK 2

Paraphrase the relevant details on page 205. (Winter had learned to trust her trainers, but hadn't seen another dolphin. The trainers decided to introduce her to Panama, another rescued dolphin. Winter came out to greet Panama, who tried to ignore her. After three days, Panama stopped swimming away.) Use these details to determine the central idea. (Trainers wondered what would happen when it was time for Winter to meet another dolphin.) Add the central idea and relevant details to your organizer.

Central Idea
Trainers wondered what would happen when Winter met another dolphin, Panama.
Detail
Winter swam out to greet Panama because Panama stayed away from Winter.
Detail
Winter kept approaching Panama.
Detail
After three days, Panama let Winter swim near her.

Build Vocabulary on page 205

unfazed: not bothered

- *Why might Panama have had difficulty recognizing Winter as a dolphin?* (Winter was missing her tail and did not swim like other dolphins.)

Spotlight on Language

Page 204, Paragraph 1 Read the first two sentences aloud. Have students point to the word *swished* and say it several times aloud. Explain that sometimes authors use words that sound like their meaning. *When something* swishes *through water, it makes a* swish *sound.* Have partners brainstorm other words they know that sound like what they mean.

Read

9 Ask and Answer Questions DOK 1

COLLABORATE **Teacher Think Aloud** On page 206, I read about Winter's new popularity. One question I ask myself is, *Why were people so interested?* I can continue reading to find the answer.

Prompt students to apply the strategy in a Think Aloud by asking and answering questions as they read. Have them paraphrase the answer for a partner.

Student Think Aloud Why was Winter popular? As I read the rest of the paragraph, I see that many of Winter's fans were people who had been born without a limb or had a disability or knew someone with a similar problem. I understand now that people were interested in Winter because they could relate to her struggle.

Build Vocabulary on page 206

limb: a part of the body such as an arm or leg

adjusting: getting used to

premier: very talented

9 When Winter was about a year old, NBC's *The Today Show* broadcast a story about her on television. Now the word was out. Winter was famous. People started to come in droves to visit her at the Clearwater Marine Aquarium. The charming young dolphin also started to receive letters from her new fans, including many people who knew someone who had, or had themselves, lost or been born without a limb or had other disabilities. Everyone could relate to Winter.

Winter seemed to be able to overcome any **obstacle**. While her vets and trainers were happy that Winter was adjusting to her new life, they knew she was about to face her biggest challenge. Months of swimming from side to side had taken their toll. Abby helped Winter do special poolside exercises, but Winter's muscles were not as **flexible** and developed as they should have been. Winter needed to be able to swim like a dolphin again.

Luckily, Kevin Carroll heard about Winter on the radio and contacted the aquarium. Kevin was not only a dolphin lover, he was also a premier creator of prostheses—special devices that can help replace a body part such as an arm or a leg. Kevin believed he could help.

Winter helps others understand what it means to have a disability and how people can adapt to almost any circumstance.

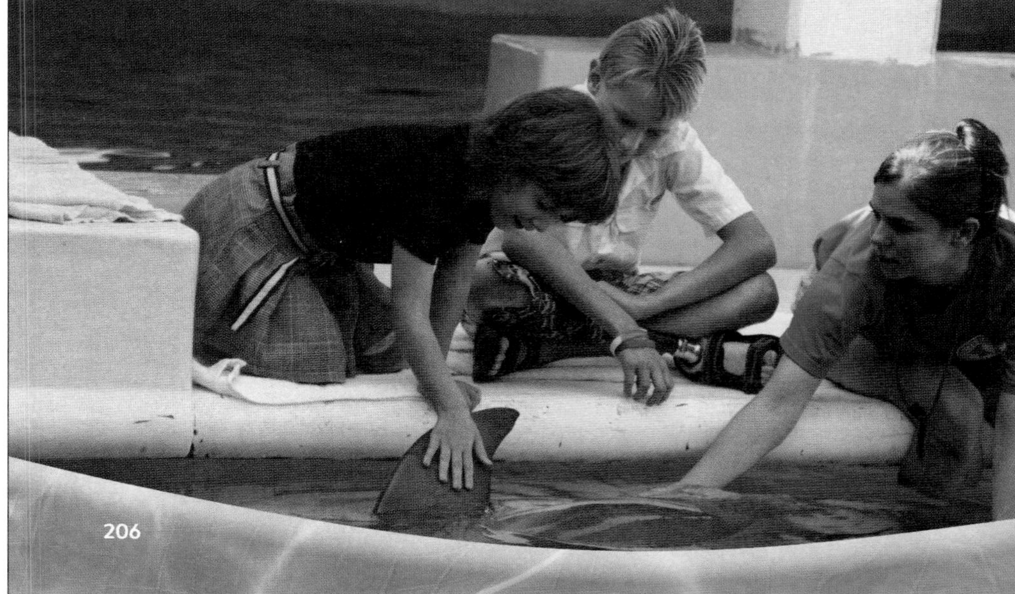

206

Literature Anthology, pp. 206–207

ACT Access Complex Text

Specific Vocabulary

Review strategies students can use to find the meaning of an unfamiliar word, such as using context clues, word parts, or a print or online dictionary.

- *Use the context to figure out the phrase* come in droves. (Winter was on television and became famous. People came in large crowds to see her.)
- Point out the dash in the third paragraph. Explain that a dash is often used to indicate important information about the word before it. *What word does the dash provide information about?* (*prostheses*—the plural form of *prosthesis*)
- *What does the word mean?* ("special devices that help replace a body part such as an arm or leg")

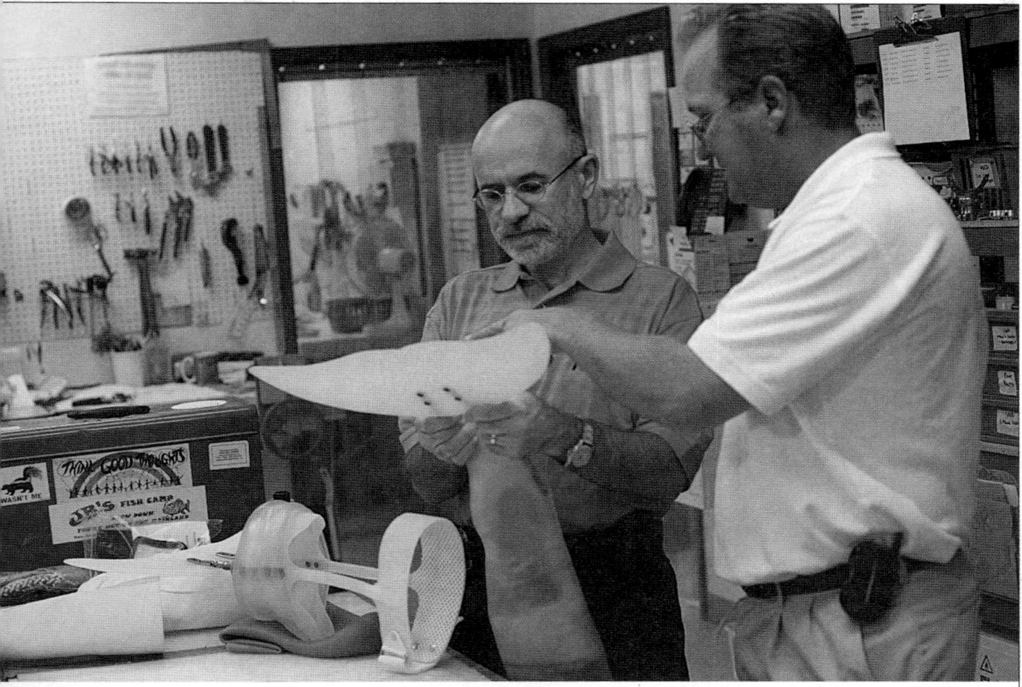

Kevin Carroll (left) and his team face many challenges in devising the perfect tail for Winter.

Being a dolphin, Winter was a special case. Not only would her prosthesis have to work in the water, it would also have to handle the force of each thrust of her tail. A team of experts—including Kevin Carroll, vets, dolphin trainers, and marine mammal researchers—came together to help make Winter's new tail a reality.

Everyone shared ideas about how to create the best prosthesis for Winter. It was something that had never been done before, and there were many obstacles. The first was the fit. Winter did not have a tail joint or any other place for a prosthesis to attach to her body. In addition, dolphins have especially sensitive skin. The team would need to figure out how to connect the tail without causing irritation or discomfort to Winter. The second concern was the tail's **function**. They needed a design that would **mimic** the up-and-down movement of a swimming dolphin. 

207

ELL Spotlight on Idioms

Page 206, Paragraph 1 Read sentences 1-4 of paragraph 1. Which word shows you that a lot of people liked Winter? (famous) Explain that *come in droves* is a way of saying that a lot of people arrived. *Turn to a partner and discuss why people were* coming in droves *to see Winter.* Then, ask pairs to use the idiom to describe other events: People come in droves to _______. Whenever _____, people come in droves.

Read

10 Latin Roots DOK 2

What word can you find in the last sentence on page 207 that has the Latin root *mim-*? (mimic) *Mim-* means "repeat," and the suffix *-ic* means "having the character of." Use the root and the sentence to determine the meaning of *mimic.* (Using the root and the context of the tail's "up-and-down movement," I can determine that *mimic* must mean "to repeat or copy the action of something else.")

Reread

Author's Craft: Text Features DOK 2

Reading/Writing Companion, p. 51

Reread page 207. How do the authors help you visualize what the team had to think about while creating Winter's prosthesis? (The authors point out all of the obstacles in the way of creating a working prosthesis for Winter. They do this so the reader can realize how much of a group effort was needed to create a prosthesis specifically designed for Winter. Without such teamwork, they might not have succeeded.) How does the photograph on page 207 support this? (The photograph shows the teamwork in action.)

Synthesize Information DOK 2

Explain You can synthesize information from other sources to understand new meanings of text.

Model *When I look up the word prosthesis, I see that it's a device that replaces a missing body part. Winter is missing her tail, so I picture the team having to create a part that looks and functions like a real dolphin tail.*

Apply What do the words *tail joint* and *mimic* help you visualize about the team's challenges?

Read

11 Ask and Answer Questions DOK 1

Generate a question of your own about the text on this page and reread to find the answer.

Student Think Aloud I see the word *peduncle* on this page. What does that word mean? The text explains that the team had to create a sleeve for the tail that would fit on Winter's peduncle. The photograph shows her tail, and I can see the parts of the sleeve. I think *peduncle* means the narrow part of Winter's body that leads up to her tail.

STOP AND CHECK DOK 1

Ask and Answer Questions How is Winter's prosthetic tail unique? (On page 207, I read that a prosthetic tail had never been created for a dolphin before. On page 208, I learn that the tail matches the natural motion of a dolphin's tail, using two sleeves that fit on Winter's peduncle to hold the tail in place.)

Build Vocabulary on page 208

unique: one of a kind

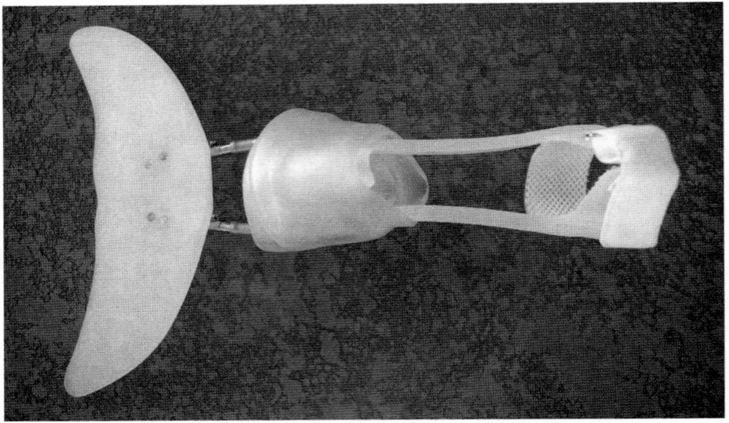

Winter's special tail

Finally, there was a concern for Winter herself. How would she react to wearing the tail? Abby and the other trainers worked tirelessly, preparing Winter. First they needed to help Winter get used to the feel of wearing a prosthesis. Then they could teach her how to swim with her own prosthetic tail.

11 The development team quickly realized they would have to create a sleeve designed specifically to fit Winter. They made a mold of her peduncle so the new sleeve would be a perfect fit. Then Kevin Carroll went one step further. He created a special silicone gel that would be smooth against Winter's skin and would add a cushion to make the prosthesis more comfortable for Winter to wear.

It took several months and several designs for the team to develop a prosthetic sleeve and a tail that matched the natural motion of an actual dolphin tail. They ended up with a unique design. There would be two sleeves. The main silicone sleeve would fit right on Winter's peduncle. A second sleeve would fit on top of the first and would hold the tail and its brace in place.

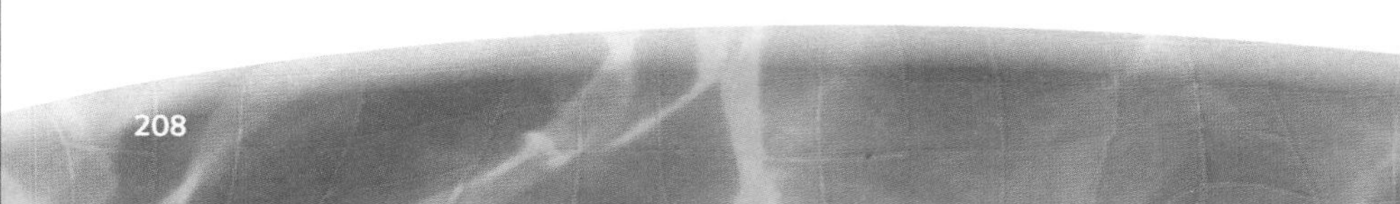
208

Literature Anthology, pp. 208–209

Access Complex Text

Organization

On page 207, the authors present three challenges the team faced. On pages 208–209, they present the solutions to each challenge.

- *On page 207 and the top of 208, use the signal words* first, second, and finally *to identify the challenges.* (attaching the prosthesis, mimicking the motion, and getting Winter used to the tail)
- *Reread pages 208–209. How did the team solve each challenge?* (They created a sleeve that fit on Winter's peduncle, Kevin Carroll created a special gel to make the tail more comfortable, and Abby trained Winter to use the tail.)

Abby spent many hours training Winter how to move her body while wearing the prosthetic tail. Abby needed Winter to understand that, when she was wearing the prosthesis, it was a signal for her to swim by using her tail, not her fins, to move herself forward.

12 Winter seems to like her new tail. She will sometimes swim in circles, chasing it, or show off by swimming right past Panama and flicking her tail in her friend's face. Some days, she doesn't want her trainers to take it off!

13 Winter now wears her tail every day for a short period of time. A trainer is always close by to keep an eye on her. The goal is for Winter to eventually wear the prosthesis a few hours every day, which will be enough to keep her backbone healthy and her body flexible. Even after Winter's first brief outings with the new tail, her trainers could already see an improvement.

Turtle Pond Publications

Winter adjusts like a pro and learns to swim with her new tail.

209

ELL Spotlight on Language

Page 209, Caption Read the caption aloud to support understanding of the term *adjusts like a pro.* Explain that *adjusts* means "get used to something." Also explain that *pro* is short for *professional,* or someone who is an expert at something. Ask: *What did Winter* adjust like a pro *to?* (swimming with her new tail) Guide pairs as they practice using the phrase *like a pro* to describe other people who are very good at something.

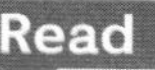

Read

12 Central Idea and Relevant Details DOK 2

What relevant details are in this paragraph? (Winter swims in circles to chase her tail, she shows off by flicking it in Panama's face, and she sometimes doesn't want to take her tail off.) Use these details to determine the central idea. (Winter seems to like her new tail.) Add the central idea and relevant details to your graphic organizer.

13 Text Structure: Problem and Solution DOK 2

COLLABORATE Use what you have read on pages 207–208 to infer why Winter doesn't wear her tail all the time. Share your response with a partner. (On page 207, I learned that dolphins have especially sensitive skin. Even though Kevin Carroll created a special gel to add a cushion, wearing the tail for too long would likely irritate Winter's sensitive skin. This solution to avoid this is to limit how much she wears the tail.)

Build Vocabulary on page 209

flexible: able to bend

Connect to Content

Science and Technology

Scientific investigations are often a matter of trial and error. Researchers repeat experimental trials, collecting and evaluating data and making adjustments until they achieve a successful result. In the case of Winter's tail, researchers assessed the obstacles and applied creative solutions to create the first ever prosthetic tail for a dolphin. Have students read page 208 and then discuss why the team needed to try several different designs before they were successful.

Read

14 Central Idea and Relevant Details DOK 2

What relevant details are included on page 210? (Winter's trainers think she has a special understanding with visitors. A little girl decided to start wearing a hearing aid after meeting her. The technology used to make her tail is helping veterans with prosthetic limbs.) Use these details to determine the central idea. (Winter's success is inspiring many people and helping others.) Add the main idea and details to your graphic organizer.

Central Idea
Winter's success is an inspiration and a help to many people.
Detail
Her trainers think she has a special understanding with visitors.
Detail
One little girl began wearing her hearing aid after she met Winter.
Detail
Kevin Carroll used the gel he developed for Winter on prostheses for Iraq war veterans.

Build Vocabulary on page 210

limb: a body part used for moving or grasping

breakthrough: a development that makes progress possible

Winter had a big party on her third birthday, complete with a cake and candles. Many people came to help her celebrate, and she seemed happy to see them all.

We cannot know what Winter is really thinking, but her trainers admit that she seems to have a special understanding with the people who visit her. The people feel a connection to her as well. From children who have prostheses, to veterans who lost a limb fighting in a war, to one little girl who didn't want to wear a hearing aid until she met Winter, people see how Winter has learned to adapt and are inspired by her story.

With the help of Kevin Carroll, Winter is also sharing her prosthetic technology. After creating the silicone gel for her sleeve, Kevin realized that the same material that made it more comfortable for Winter to wear her prosthetic tail could help people who wear prostheses, too. Kevin put the gel to the test on a veteran of the Iraq war who was having difficulty with his **artificial** legs. The silicone gel created an extra cushion that helped reduce the veteran's discomfort. It was a big breakthrough, making life a little easier for people needing prostheses. 14

Special guests present Winter with her birthday cake!

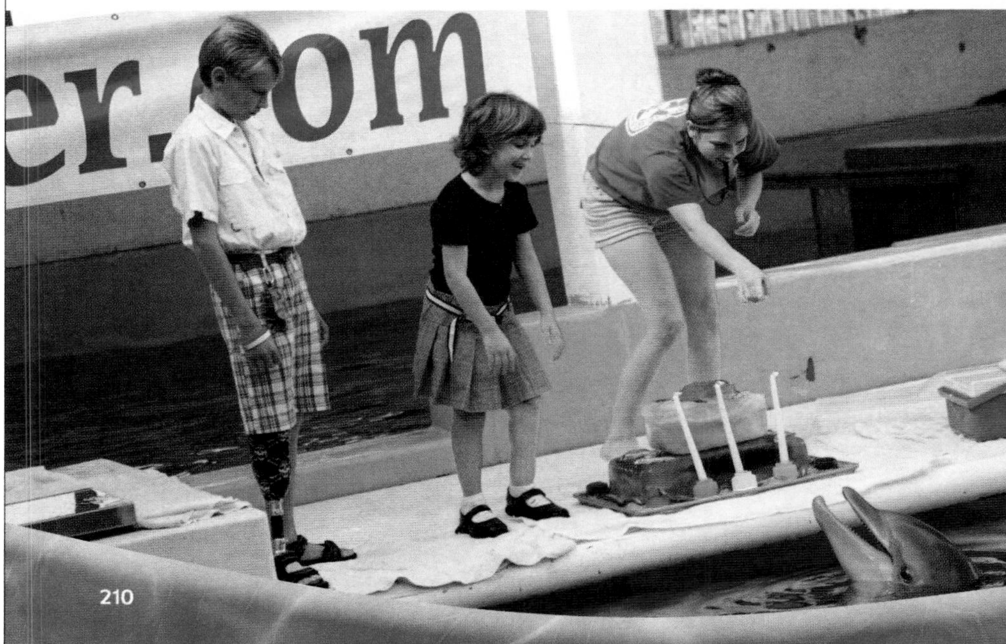

210

Literature Anthology, pp. 210–211

Access Complex Text

Purpose

Point out that authors of expository text may include details to show their perspective about their subject. Help students identify word choices and descriptions that reveal the authors' purpose for writing.

- *What details do the authors include to show how they feel about Winter?* (On page 211, the authors say she has an "uplifting spirit and resilience" which help her make the "most of every situation." They call her a "champion, inspiration, and friend." They want readers to feel inspired, too.)

Winter may have lost her family, her home, and eventually her tail, but she found a new home and family at the Clearwater Marine Aquarium. She found Panama, Abby, and the vets, trainers, and volunteers who take care of her on a daily basis. With the help of all of these people, she also has a new tail. Through these changes, one thing has stayed the same: Winter's uplifting spirit and her resilience have helped her adjust and make the most of every situation.

And her story is far from over. She is still learning all of the things she can do with her special tail, and her trainers and prosthetic designers are still learning how they can help her even more. Every step of the way, they will need to be open to new ideas and be willing to try different solutions. Their shared goal is to help Winter live a long, healthy, and happy life.

As for Winter, she seems ready for any new challenge. As champion, inspiration, and friend, Winter is one little dolphin who gives people hope and shows us that anything is possible.

211

Spotlight on Language

Page 211, Paragraphs 1 and 3 Ask questions to help students understand the tone by explaining vocabulary such as *uplifting, resilience,* and *make the most. How did Winter make the most of situations?* (She learns to swim without a tail and then learns to swim with a new tail.) *If someone is* uplifting *and* shows resilience, *how do you feel about that person? Does the passage give you a positive or negative feeling about Winter? Talk to your partner to answer these questions, using details from the text to help explain your answer.*

Read

STOP AND CHECK **DOK 1**

Summarize How has Winter affected the lives of others? (Winter has inspired people with disabilities. The gel used with her new prosthetic is now being used for people's prostheses, too.)

Return to Purpose Review students' purposes for reading. Then ask partners to share how setting a purpose helped them understand the text.

Reread

Author's Purpose DOK 2

Reading/Writing Companion, p. 52

How do the authors show how Winter will continue to have an impact on the people who have helped her? (The authors explain how Winter brought a group of people together to make a difference. They worked together to solve a problem. This suggests that teamwork will continue to be a theme throughout Winter's life. Winter is the inspiration for that teamwork.)

Make Inferences **DOK 2**

Explain When you make inferences, you use what you know along with text evidence to make a connection.

Model *Winter's team put a lot of time and effort into nursing her back to health and designing a tail that would meet her needs. They care a lot about her, and because of that, I think Winter's team will continue to give Winter the best possible care.*

Apply What additional text evidence suggests that Winter's team will continue to care for her? (They have a shared goal to help Winter live a long, healthy, happy life.)

Read

Meet the Authors DOK 2

Juliana, Isabella, and Craig Hatkoff

Have students read the biography of the authors. Ask:

- Where do the Hatkoffs get ideas for their books?
- Which animal you would like to write about?
- How does teamwork help the Hatkoffs write their books?

Authors' Purpose DOK 2

To Inform: Remind students that the authors use many details to show how Winter's recovery is inspiring. Students may say that Winter is special because of the challenges she faced and the way she survived and inspired others.

Reread

Authors' Craft: Text Structure DOK 2

How did the authors help readers understand Winter's struggle? Cite text evidence to support your answer. (Throughout the text, the authors focused on the problems and solutions Winter and the team continued to encounter. This text structure helped the reader better understand the text. For example, on page 200, the text states that Jim Savage found Winter tangled in a rope, struggling to breathe. Jim cut the rope with his knife to free her. Without his help, Winter wouldn't have survived.)

Authors' Craft: Text Feature DOK 2

How does the photograph on page 200 support the text? Turn to a partner and use this sentence starter to begin the discussion:

The picture shows . . .

Use text evidence to support your ideas.

About the Authors

Juliana, Isabella, and Craig Hatkoff

are a family of authors. Their story began when Juliana Hatkoff was nearly five years old and about to have her tonsils removed. Her father, Craig Hatkoff, suggested that they research the procedure and write about it in a notebook. Soon the Hatkoffs had their first book, *Good-Bye Tonsils!* Later, Juliana's younger sister, Isabella, read a newspaper article about a rescued baby hippo who became close friends with an old tortoise. Isabella thought the story of the hippo and the tortoise would make a good book, too. She was right!

Since then, writing books has become a team activity for this New York City family. Most of their books focus on animals that face difficult circumstances. Dad and daughters work together to do research and craft their stories. The family hopes that books like these will help others find the strength to get through tough times.

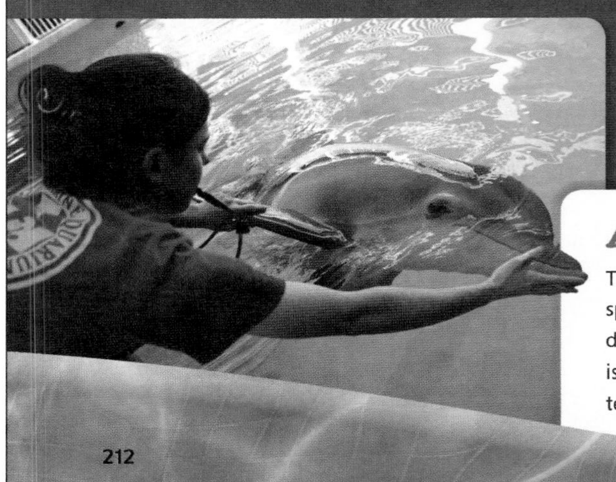

Authors' Purpose

The Hatkoffs like to write about special animals that inspire. How do the authors show that Winter is special? Give examples from the text that support this point.

212

Literature Anthology, pp. 212

ELL Spotlight on Idioms

Page 212, Paragraph 2 Support understanding of the word *circumstances.* (cognate: circunstancias) Ask: *Why did Winter need the team's help?* (She was injured and couldn't swim on her own.) Explain that the situation that led to Winter needing the team's help are *circumstances. Turn to a partner and discuss other circumstances that animals might face that would require help.* Then have pairs use the word *circumstances* to describe whether or not Winter's circumstances were difficult.

Read

Summarize

Tell students they will use information from their Central Idea and Relevant Details chart to summarize the text. As I read *Winter's Tail,* I gathered information about Winter's journey and the processes that helped her swim again. To summarize, I will organize these relevant details in a logical way that helps me understand the text and all the problems Winter and the team overcame.

Reread

Analyze the Text

After students read and summarize the selection, have them reread *Winter's Tail* to develop a deeper understanding of the text by answering the questions on **Reading/Writing Companion** pages 50–52. For students who need support in citing text evidence, use the scaffolded instruction from the Reread prompts on pages T109–T118.

Integrate

Build Knowledge: Make Connections

Talk About the Text Have partners discuss the Essential Question: *What benefits come from people working together as a group?*

Write About the Text Have students add their ideas to their Build Knowledge pages of their reader's notebooks.

Anchor Chart Record any new ideas on the Build Knowledge anchor chart.

Add to the Vocabulary List Have students write down any words they learned about the advantages of working together in their reader's notebooks.

Compare Texts DOK 4

Have students compare how the authors present information on the benefits of collaboration in "Gulf Spill Superheroes" and *Winter's Tail.* Ask: *In what ways did the authors of "Gulf Spill Superheroes" and* Winter's Tail *present information about people working together similarly? What was the purpose in sharing the information this way?*

FORMATIVE ASSESSMENT

STUDENT CHECK-IN

Read Have partners share their graphic organizers and summaries. Have them reflect using the Check-In routine.

Reread Have partners share responses and text evidence on Reading/Writing Companion pages 50–52. Then have them use the Check-In routine to reflect and fill in the bars.

LEARNING GOALS

- **We can use text evidence to respond to expository text.**

OBJECTIVES

Determine two or more central, or main, ideas of a text and explain how they are supported by relevant, or key, details; summarize the text.

Explain how an author uses reasons and evidence to support particular points in a text, identifying which reasons and evidence support which point(s).

Come to discussions prepared, having read or studied required material; explicitly draw on that preparation and other information known about the topic to explore ideas under discussion.

ELA ACADEMIC LANGUAGE

- *central idea, prompt*
- Cognate: *idea central*

TEACH IN SMALL GROUP

Approaching Level and **On Level** Have partners work together to plan and complete the response to the prompt.

Beyond Level Ask students to respond to the prompt independently.

ELL Group students of mixed proficiency levels to discuss and respond to the prompt.

Reread

Write About the Anchor Text

Analyze the Prompt DOK 3

Read the prompt aloud: *In what ways is Winter's story inspiring?* Ask: *What is the prompt asking you to write?* (to describe the ways that Winter's story is inspiring) Say: *Let's reread to see how descriptions, photographs, captions, and specific examples of the obstacles faced by those trying to help Winter show how the dolphin's story inspires people. Doing this will help us answer the prompt.*

Analyze Text Evidence

Remind students that identifying central ideas and relevant details as they gather evidence helps readers understand the most important events, examples, and information in a text. Have students look at **Literature Anthology** page 206. Read the page and ask: *How did Kevin Carroll hear about Winter's story?* (He heard about Winter on the radio and contacted the aquarium.) *What inspired him to respond?* (His job was to create prostheses for people, and he thought he might be able to make a prosthetic tail for Winter.) Now look at the text and photograph on page 207. Ask: *What obstacles did the team making Winter's prosthesis face?* (Winter did not have a tail joint to attach the prosthesis to, she had very sensitive skin, and the prosthesis needed to mimic the up and down movement of a swimming dolphin.) Have students discuss how Winter responded to her injury, treatment, and disability using evidence from the text. Ask: *What does Winter's response say about her?*

Respond

Review pages 50–52 of the **Reading/Writing Companion.** Have partners or small groups refer to and discuss their completed charts and responses from those pages. Then direct students' attention to the sentence starters on page 53 of the Reading/Writing Companion. Have them use the sentence starters to guide their responses.

Analytical Writing Students should focus on the authors' use of examples and relevant details in both the text and photos and explain how they reveal that Winter's story inspired many different people, including the aquarium staff and others who volunteered or visited her. Remind students to vary sentence structure by combining short sentences and adding phrases and clauses to others. Students may use additional paper to complete the assignment if needed.

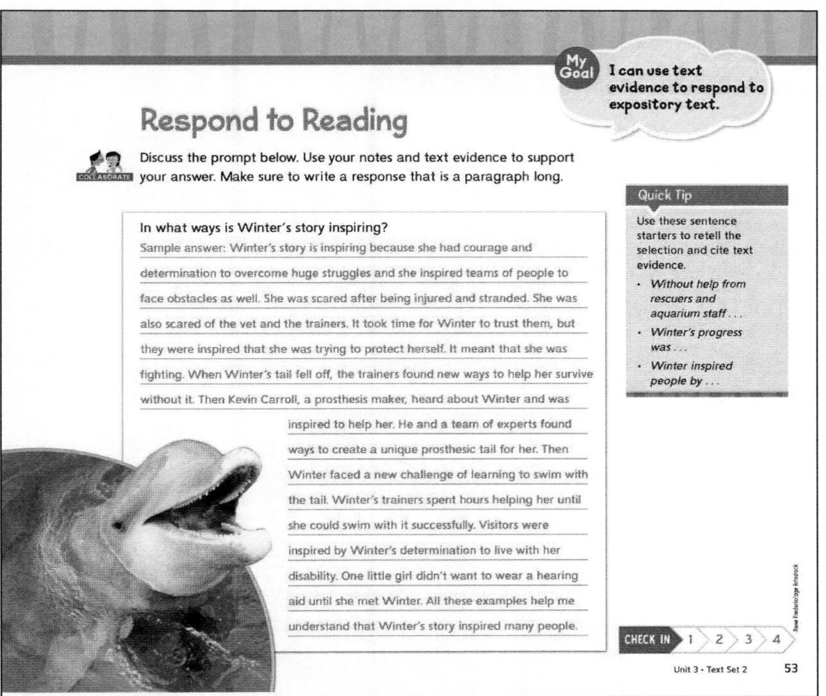

My Goal I can use text evidence to respond to expository text.

Respond to Reading

COLLABORATE Discuss the prompt below. Use your notes and text evidence to support your answer. Make sure to write a response that is a paragraph long.

In what ways is Winter's story inspiring?

Sample answer: Winter's story is inspiring because she had courage and determination to overcome huge struggles and she inspired teams of people to face obstacles as well. She was scared after being injured and stranded. She was also scared of the vet and the trainers. It took time for Winter to trust them, but they were inspired that she was trying to protect herself. It meant that she was fighting. When Winter's tail fell off, the trainers found new ways to help her survive without it. Then Kevin Carroll, a prosthesis maker, heard about Winter and was inspired to help her. He and a team of experts found ways to create a unique prosthesic tail for her. Then Winter faced a new challenge of learning to swim with the tail. Winter's trainers spent hours helping her until she could swim with it successfully. Visitors were inspired by Winter's determination to live with her disability. One little girl didn't want to wear a hearing aid until she met Winter. All these examples help me understand that Winter's story inspired many people.

Quick Tip

Use these sentence starters to retell the selection and cite text evidence.

- *Without help from rescuers and aquarium staff . . .*
- *Winter's progress was . . .*
- *Winter inspired people by . . .*

CHECK IN 1 2 3 4

Rene Frederick/age fotostock

Unit 3 • Text Set 2 53

Reading/Writing Companion, p. 53

English Language Learners

Use the following scaffolds with **Respond**.

Beginning

Read the prompt with students and discuss what they will write about. Review their completed charts on **Reading/Writing Companion** pages 50–52. Say: *When something is inspiring, it makes you want to take action. What happened to Winter's tail?* Winter's tail fell off. *Did Winter learn how to swim again?* (yes) Have partners discuss how Winter's story is inspiring and respond using: Winter lost her tail. Winter got a prosthetic tail and learned how to swim again.

Intermediate

Read the prompt with students. Have partners review their completed charts on **Reading/Writing Companion** pages 50–52. Ask: *What struggles did Winter overcome?* Winter's tail fell off. She got a prosthetic tail and learned how to swim again. Then have partners discuss how Winter's story is inspiring and respond using: Winter's story is inspiring because_____.

Advanced/Advanced High

Review the prompt and sentence starters on page 53 with students. Have partners review their graphic organizers on pages 50–52 and discuss how Winter inspired people. Then have them respond using the sentence starters.

ELL NEWCOMERS

Have students listen to the summaries of the **Anchor Text** in their native language and then in English to help them access the text and develop listening comprehension. Help students ask and answer questions with a partner. Use these sentence frames: *What happens in this text? In this text,* ___. Then have them complete the online **Newcomer Activities** individually or in pairs.

FORMATIVE ASSESSMENT

STUDENT CHECK-IN

Ask partners to share their response on Reading/Writing Companion page 53. Have them reflect using the Check-In routine to fill in the bars.

"Helping Hands"

Lexile 1040L

LEARNING GOALS

Read We can apply strategies and skills to read expository text.

Reread We can reread to analyze text, craft, and structure and compare texts.

Have students apply what they learned as they read.

 Identify ways in which citizens help to improve government and society.

What makes this text complex?

- **Specific Vocabulary**
- **Prior Knowledge**

Analytical Writing Compare Texts DOK 4

As students read "Helping Hands," encourage them to take notes and think about the Essential Question: *What benefits come from people working as a group?* Students should discuss how "Helping Hands" is similar and different from *Winter's Tail.*

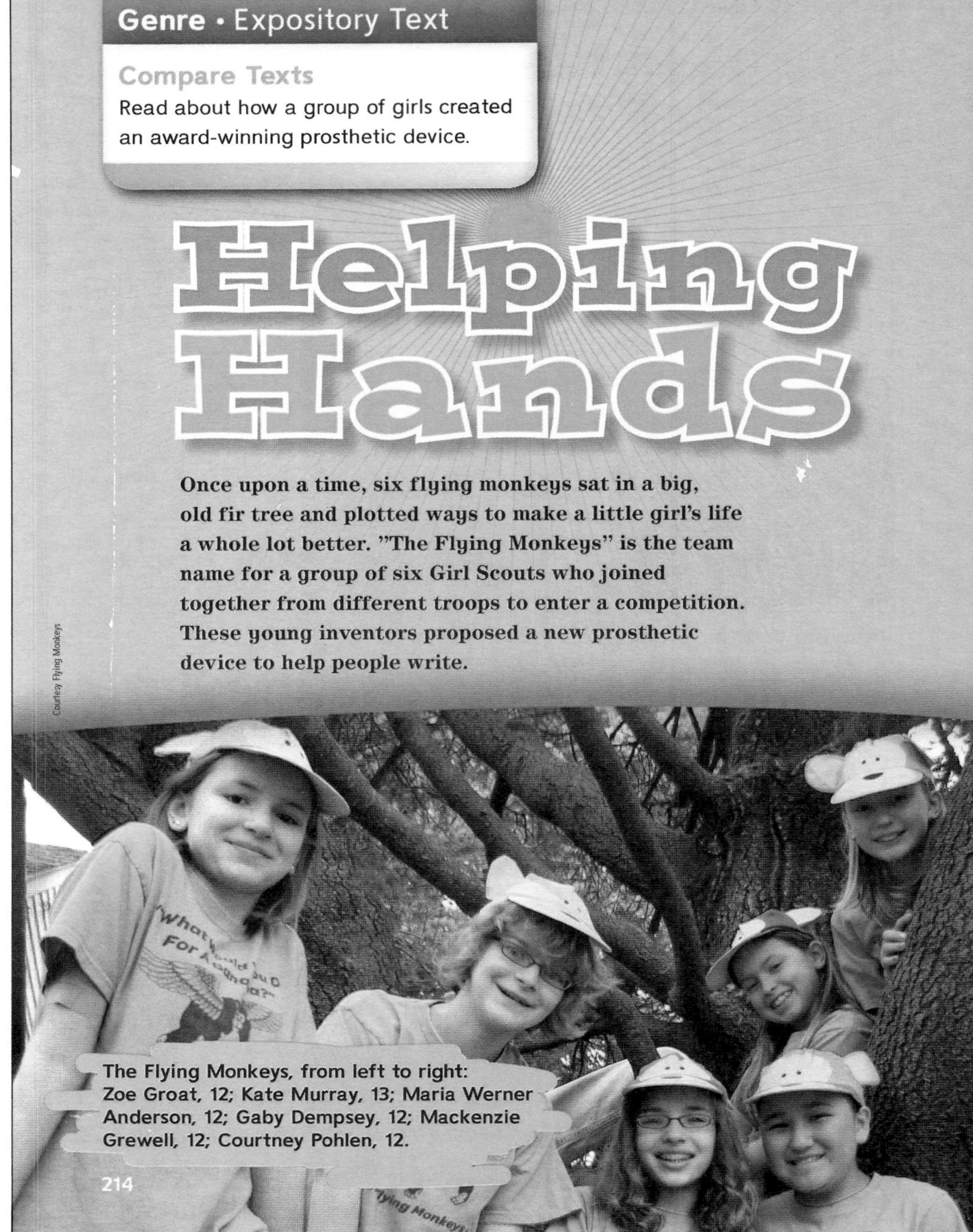

Genre • Expository Text
Compare Texts
Read about how a group of girls created an award-winning prosthetic device.
Helping Hands
Once upon a time, six flying monkeys sat in a big, old fir tree and plotted ways to make a little girl's life a whole lot better. "The Flying Monkeys" is the team name for a group of six Girl Scouts who joined together from different troops to enter a competition. These young inventors proposed a new prosthetic device to help people write.
Courtesy Flying Monkeys
The Flying Monkeys, from left to right: Zoe Groat, 12; Kate Murray, 13; Maria Werner Anderson, 12; Gaby Dempsey, 12; Mackenzie Grewell, 12; Courtney Pohlen, 12.
214

Literature Anthology, pp. 214–215

Access Complex Text

Specific Vocabulary

Point out the second paragraph in the section "Doing the Research." Have students read the last sentence.

- *Which part of the sentence tells you what prototypes are?* (The phrase after the comma, "the first series of creations")
- *Why are prototypes helpful?* (They help the inventors see if their idea works as planned.)
- *How is the word* prototypes *connected to the sentence in the last paragraph on page 215, "Old ideas were cast aside, and new ones began to take shape"?* (The prototypes tested out the girls' new ideas.)

A Need Inspires

The rules of the competition asked participants to come up with new and innovative ways to help heal, repair or improve the human body. One of the group members, Kate Murray, understood the difficulties people with an injury or impairment can face. Kate was born with a left hand that was not fully formed. But that didn't stop Kate from taking part in activities. When she decided she wanted to learn how to play the violin, she and her mother worked with a team of specialists to create a device to allow her to hold a bow. 1

The Flying Monkeys wondered if they could create something similar for the competition. When one of their Girl Scouts coaches learned about Danielle Fairchild, a three-year-old who was born without fingers on her right hand, the Flying Monkeys found their inspiration.

Courtesy Dale Fairchild

Doing the Research

The Flying Monkeys focused on creating a device that would allow Danielle to write with her right hand. But because Danielle lived in Georgia and the girls lived in Iowa, they couldn't work with her directly. What they could do, however, was figure out a way to make a device that would attach a pen or pencil to Danielle's hand. 2

Soon enough, the girls realized that they would need to **collaborate** with experts. Their coaches helped them make contacts. They talked to people who had physical impairments as well as medical experts who created and made prosthetic devices. Old ideas were cast aside, and new ideas began to take shape. The girls made models and tested them before creating their initial prototypes, the first series of creations.

The Flying Monkeys designed a device to help Danielle Fairchild write with her right hand.

215

ELL Spotlight on Idioms

Page 215, Paragraph 3 Read aloud the first sentence. Explain that a *device* is a machine or small object that does a special job. *What job do the girls want the device to do?* (let Danielle write with her right hand) *Read the next two sentences with your partner and describe the device the Flying Monkeys invented.*

Read

1 Ask and Answer Questions DOK 1

How did the girls first get the idea to invent a prosthesis? (They were inspired by one of the girls who had a hand that was not fully formed but was able to play the violin by using a special device that allowed her to hold the bow.)

2 Ask and Answer Questions DOK 1

What specific type of prosthesis did the girls decide to invent? Why? Discuss your answer with a partner. (They invented a prosthesis that would allow a person without fingers to write because they knew of a little girl who was born without fingers on one hand.)

Build Vocabulary on pages 214 and 215

device: a tool that does a certain job

innovative: new and creative

initial: first

Reread

Author's Purpose DOK 3

Reread the introduction on page 214. How does the author start this selection? ("Once upon a time") Why did the author choose to start this selection with these words? (The author does this because the work of the Flying Monkeys is extraordinary, much like the events in fairy tales, which typically start with "Once upon a time.")

Read

3 Context Clues DOK 2

What is the meaning of the word *showcase*? ("to present in a favorable way") What clues help you determine its meaning? (The girls were going to a competition with their invention and hoped to win.)

Build Vocabulary on page 216

portfolio: a collection of the team's work

Reread

Author's Purpose DOK 2

Reading/Writing Companion, p. 56

Reread the first paragraph on page 216. What remark does the author make about the Flying Monkeys' invention? ("Why hadn't anyone thought of creating a device like this before?") Why does the author make this statement? (The remark shows the author's admiration for the Flying Monkey's creativity and practicality.)

Introducing the BOB-1

Before long, the Flying Monkeys settled on a final design for their invention, which they called the BOB-1. They used a **flexible** plastic substance, a pencil grip, and hook-and-eye closures to build it. Everyone involved was impressed by how well the device would fit on Danielle's hand. What's more, it was very simple and inexpensive to make. Why hadn't anyone thought of creating a device like this before?

3 The Flying Monkeys created fliers, a portfolio, and even a skit to take to the competition and showcase their invention. The competition judges were impressed.

The Flying Monkeys won a regional and state-level innovation award. From there, it was on to the global round of the contest, where the BOB-1 would be judged alongside 178 other entries from 16 countries. The winning team would receive $20,000 to further develop the product.

Danielle Fairchild uses the BOB-1.

Courtesy Dale Fairchild

216

Literature Anthology, pp. 216–217

Access Complex Text

Prior Knowledge

Explain that a hook-and-eye closure consists of two surfaces: one has tiny loops, and the other has tiny hooked barbs, like fish hooks. When the two sides are pressed together, the barbs hook onto the loops.

Call attention to the word *patent* in the final paragraph on page 217. Explain that a patent is ownership of the right to make and sell an invention. Patents are granted by the government.

The Flying Monkeys had the chance to meet Danielle at the award ceremony in Washington, D.C.

People from around the world voted online for the project they thought was best and a panel of judges reviewed the top projects. After the **dedicated** team had spent nearly 200 hours developing the BOB-1, the Flying Monkeys were invited to attend the final awards ceremony in Washington, D.C. Their hard work paid off. They won the grand prize!

The best part of their adventure, however, came when the girls finally met Danielle Fairchild in person. Danielle showed the girls how she used the BOB-1 to draw and color with her right hand. The device was a success!

The Flying Monkeys have already revised the BOB-1. They hope to use the prize money to receive a full patent and make the device available to others who might benefit from it. Having more people test the device may even lead to further improvements. When it comes to helping others, these creative young girls aren't just monkeying around!

Make Connections

How did working with others help the girls create an invention? ESSENTIAL QUESTION

How is the Flying Monkeys' work similar to another group's work you've read about? What was the purpose of each effort? TEXT TO TEXT

Courtesy Flying Monkeys

217

Spotlight on Idioms

Page 217, Paragraph 3 Choral read the paragraph. Have partners work together to come up with a definition for *monkeying around.* Explain that monkeys are very silly when they play. *Turn to a partner and describe a time when you were monkeying around, or playing and being silly.* Ask: *Were the girls* monkeying around*? How do you know?* (The text says that the girls "aren't just monkeying around." I know that the girls were very serious and worked hard.)

Read

Summarize

Guide students to summarize the selection.

Reread

Analyze the Text

After students read and summarize, have them reread and answer questions on pages 54–56 of the **Reading/Writing Companion.**

Integrate

Build Knowledge: Make Connections

Talk About the Text Have partners discuss the benefits of working in a group.

Write About the Text Have students add their ideas to their Build Knowledge pages of their reader's notebooks.

Anchor Chart Record any new ideas on the Build Knowledge anchor chart.

Add to the Vocabulary List Have students write down any new words they learned about teamwork in their reader's notebooks.

Compare Texts DOK 4

Text to Text Answer: In both *Winter's Tail* and "Helping Hands," prosthetic devices helped those with impairments. Evidence: Winter was able to swim like other dolphins, and Danielle Fairchild was able to write with a pencil. The group working with Winter and the group working with Danielle both faced problems they solved by using teamwork.

FORMATIVE ASSESSMENT

STUDENT CHECK-IN

Read Ask partners to share their summaries. Then have them reflect using the Check-In routine.

Reread Ask partners to share their responses on Reading/Writing Companion pages 54–56. Then have them use the Check-In routine to reflect and fill in the bars.

Reread

Literal and Figurative Language

LEARNING GOALS

We can identify literal and figurative language to help us read and understand expository text.

OBJECTIVES

Quote accurately from a text when explaining what the text says explicitly and when drawing inferences from the text.

Determine two or more central, or main, ideas of a text and explain how they are supported by relevant, or key, details; summarize the text.

Demonstrate understanding of figurative language, word relationships, and nuances in word meanings.

Interpret figurative language, including similes and metaphors, in context.

ELA ACADEMIC LANGUAGE

- *literal language, figurative language, visualize*
- Cognates: *lenguaje literal, lenguaje figurado, visualizar*

1 Explain

Have students turn to **Reading/Writing Companion** page 57. Share with students the following key points of literal and figurative language.

- Literal language is language that means what it says. For example, in the last sentence on page 214 of the **Literature Anthology**, the author says, "These young inventors proposed a new prosthetic device to help people write." This is literal language because it is a straightforward statement of what the inventors did.
- Figurative language uses words to mean something different or unexpected. In the first sentence on page 214, "six flying monkeys sat in a big, old fir tree" is figurative language. The author is not talking about real monkeys; instead, the author calls the girls "monkeys" to connect with their team name.
- Authors think about their purpose for writing. If they want to describe a complex idea simply and clearly, then they might use literal language. If they want to describe something in an interesting way, then figurative language might be a better choice.

2 Model

Model identifying figurative language on page 217 of the Literature Anthology. Have students reread the last paragraph. Point out the expression "monkeying around." Explain that the author uses this expression because monkeys are known for their mischievous behavior. Ask: *Why did the author choose this expression?* (The girls' team name is The Flying Monkeys, so this is a clever way of saying that the girls are serious about what they are doing and aren't just joking around.)

3 Guided Practice

Now have students identify descriptive words in "Introducing the BOB-1" on **Reading/Writing Companion** page 55 that help better explain what the device looks and feels like. (flexible plastic substance, pencil grip, hook-and-eye closures, fit on Danielle's hand) Ask: *How do these words help you visualize the device?* (They clearly describe what it is made out of, how it works, and how it attaches.)

Have partners discuss why the author chose to use literal language instead of figurative language to describe the device, as well as why both literal and figurative language are useful in an expository text. Allow students time to enter their responses on page 57 of the Reading/Writing Companion.

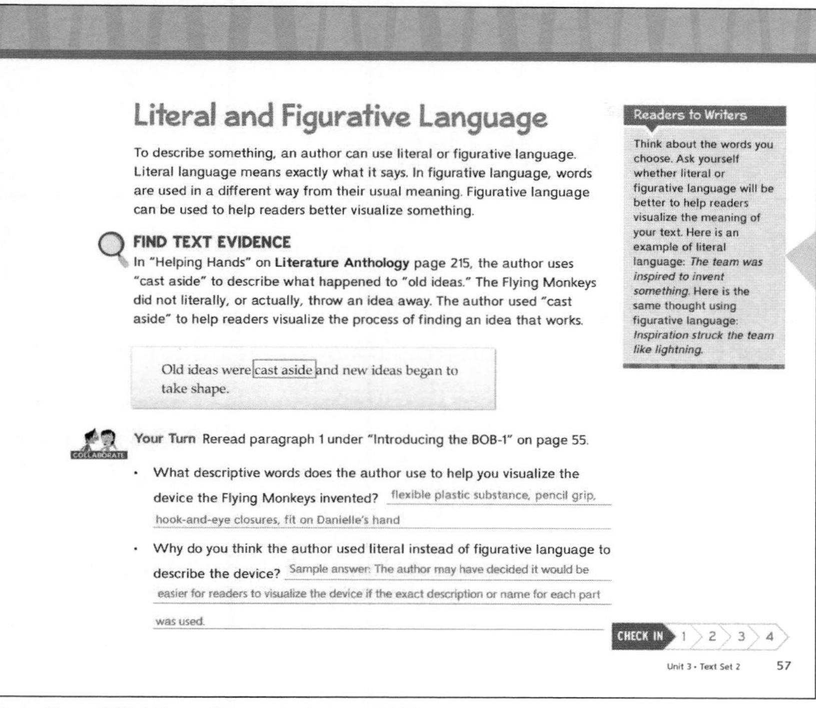

Literal and Figurative Language

To describe something, an author can use literal or figurative language. Literal language means exactly what it says. In figurative language, words are used in a different way from their usual meaning. Figurative language can be used to help readers better visualize something.

FIND TEXT EVIDENCE

In "Helping Hands" on **Literature Anthology** page 215, the author uses "cast aside" to describe what happened to "old ideas." The Flying Monkeys did not literally, or actually, throw an idea away. The author used "cast aside" to help readers visualize the process of finding an idea that works.

Old ideas were cast aside and new ideas began to take shape.

Your Turn Reread paragraph 1 under "Introducing the BOB-1" on page 55.

- What descriptive words does the author use to help you visualize the device the Flying Monkeys invented? flexible plastic substance, pencil grip, hook-and-eye closures, fit on Danielle's hand
- Why do you think the author used literal instead of figurative language to describe the device? Sample answer: The author may have decided it would be easier for readers to visualize the device if the exact description or name for each part was used.

Readers to Writers

Think about the words you choose. Ask yourself whether literal or figurative language will be better to help readers visualize the meaning of your text. Here is an example of literal language: *The team was inspired to invent something.* Here is the same thought using figurative language: *Inspiration struck the team like lightning.*

CHECK IN 1 2 3 4

Unit 3 • Text Set 2 57

Reading/Writing Companion, p. 57

Readers to Writers

Reiterate that authors choose their language carefully to make their ideas clear. Reread the first sentence on page 215 of the **Literature Anthology**. Ask: *Why do you think the author chose literal language to describe the rules of the competition?*

English Language Learners

Use the following scaffolds with **Guided Practice.**

Beginning

Reread the first paragraph on page 55 with students. (cognate: *flexible*) Point out the descriptive words *flexible plastic, pencil grip, fit in Danielle's hand* and use the photograph on page 216 to help them identify the phrases. Ask: *Do these words help you visualize the device?* (yes) Help partners as they take turns describing what the BOB-1 does: I think the BOB-1 _____. Guide them to answer the questions on page 57.

Intermediate

Have partners reread the first paragraph on page 55. Have partners identify descriptive words that help them visualize the BOB-1. (flexible plastic substance, pencil grip, hook-and-eye closures, fit on Danielle's hand) Have them take turns describing what the words tell about: The words *flexible plastic* tell what BOB-1 is _____. The words pencil grip tell what BOB-1 _____. Then have them answer the questions on page 57.

Advanced/Advanced High

Have partners read the first paragraph on page 55. Then have them explain how the descriptive words and phrases help them visualize the BOB-1 device. *Talk to your partner about why you think the author included these descriptive details and respond on page 57.*

FORMATIVE ASSESSMENT

STUDENT CHECK-IN

Ask partners to share their Your Turn responses on Reading/Writing Companion page 57. Then have them use the Check-In routine to reflect and fill in the bars.

LEARNING GOALS

- **We can decode words with consonant + *le* syllables.**
- **We can identify and read multisyllabic words.**
- **We can read fluently at an appropriate rate.**

OBJECTIVES

Use combined knowledge of all letter-sound correspondences, syllabication patterns, and morphology (e.g., roots and affixes) to read accurately unfamiliar multisyllabic words in context and out of context.

Read grade-level text with purpose and understanding.

Read grade-level prose and poetry orally with accuracy, appropriate rate, expression, and automaticity on successive readings.

- Rate: 123–143 WCPM

ELA ACADEMIC LANGUAGE

- *rate, consonant, pronounce*
- Cognates: *ritmo, consonante, pronunciar*

Phonics

Approaching Level Use the Tier 2 activity on page T139 before teaching the lesson.

On Level and **Beyond Level** As needed, use the Read Multisyllabic Words section only.

ELL See page 5 in the **Language Transfers Handbook** to identify sounds and symbols that may not transfer for speakers of certain languages, and help in accommodating them.

Consonant + *le* Syllables

1 Explain

Review with students that every syllable has only one vowel sound. Then write the word *tumble* on the board. Draw a line under the last three letters. Point out that when a word ends with the letters *le*, the consonant that precedes them plus the letters *le* form the last syllable. This is called a **consonant + *le* syllable.** It is one example of a final stable syllable.

Point again to the *ble* in *tumble*, and model how to pronounce the syllable. Then read the word aloud.

2 Model

Write the following consonant + *le* syllable words on the board. Model how to pronounce each final syllable as you run your finger beneath it. Then model how to read the complete word.

humble	wiggle	vehicle
apple	middle	little
beagle	muzzle	shuffle

Briefly review the previously taught syllable types.

Open Syllables, such as *pa* in *paper*, end in a vowel. The vowel sound is usually long.

Closed Syllables, such as *lit* in *little*, end in a consonant. The vowel sound is usually short.

Vowel Team Syllables, such as *fraid* in *afraid*, have two to four letters that spell the single vowel sound.

3 Guided Practice

Write the following words on the board. Have students underline the consonant + *le* syllable in each word. Then have them read the words chorally.

turtle	pickle	topple	bubble
puzzle	uncle	snuggle	article
triple	cattle	dribble	dazzle

For practice with decoding and encoding, use **Practice Book** page 163 or online activities.

Read Multisyllabic Words

Transition to Longer Words Have students read the syllable in the first column. Ask them to identify the syllable as open or closed, and have them use this information to determine the correct pronunciation. Then ask students to underline the consonant + *le* syllable in the longer word in the second column. Model how to read the longer word. Then have students chorally read the words.

man	mantle	ta	table
sad	saddle	ti	title
jig	jiggle	bris	bristle
rat	rattle	fee	feeble
trun	trundle	ca	cable

OPTION 10 mins

Fluency

Rate

Explain/Model Remind students that reading rate is the speed, or pace, with which they read. Explain that using a slower rate can help with reading accurately and with understanding difficult ideas. Point out that changing the reading rate within a selection can also help to build drama or excitement. Model varying your reading rate as you read the second page of "Gulf Spill Superheroes," **Reading/ Writing Companion** page 39. Tell students that you will be listening for their use of an appropriate rate as you monitor their reading during the week.

Practice/Apply Have partners alternate reading paragraphs in the passage, modeling the rate you used.

Daily Fluency Practice

Automaticity Students can practice reading with accuracy and appropriate rate to develop automaticity using the online **Differentiated Genre Passage,** "Building a Green Town."

DIGITAL TOOLS

For more practice, have students use the phonics and fluency activities.

Consonant + *le* Syllables

MULTIMODAL LEARNING

Have partners take turns reading aloud the **Differentiated Genre Passage** "Building a Green Town." Ask them to use **Audio Recorder** to record themselves reading the passage quickly and then reading the same passage slowly. Have students listen to their recording and evaluate the rate. Have them answer the question, *Which reading speed, or rate, is appropriate for the passage?*

FORMATIVE ASSESSMENT

STUDENT CHECK-IN

Consonant + *le* Syllables Have partners share three words with consonant + *le* syllables.

Multisyllabic Words Have partners read the following words: *mantle, bristle,* and *trundle.*

Fluency Ask partners to read "Building a Green Town" fluently.

Have partners reflect using the Check-In routine.

CHECK FOR SUCCESS

Can students read multisyllabic words with consonant + *le* syllables? Can students read fluently?

Small Group Instruction

If No

- **Approaching** Reteach pp. T139, T142
- **ELL** Develop p. T139

If Yes

- **On** Apply p. T144
- **Beyond** Apply p. T150

LEARNING GOALS

We can compare the lithograph with the selections in this text set to build knowledge about the benefits of people working together.

OBJECTIVES

Integrate information from several texts on the same topic in order to write or speak about the subject knowledgeably.

Draw evidence from literary or informational texts to support analysis, reflection, and research.

Close Reading Routine

Read DOK 1–2

- Identify important ideas and details.
- Take notes and summarize.
- Use ACT prompts as needed.

Reread DOK 2–3

- Analyze the text, craft, and structure.
- Use the ***Reading/Writing Companion***.

Integrate DOK 3–4

- Integrate knowledge and ideas.
- Make text-to-text connections.
- Use the Integrate/Make Connections lesson.
- Use ***Reading/Writing Companion***, p. 58.
- Complete the Show Your Knowledge task.
- Inspire action.

FORMATIVE ASSESSMENT

STUDENT CHECK IN

Ask partners to share their responses. Have them use the Check-In routine to reflect and fill in the bars on Reading/Writing Companion page 58.

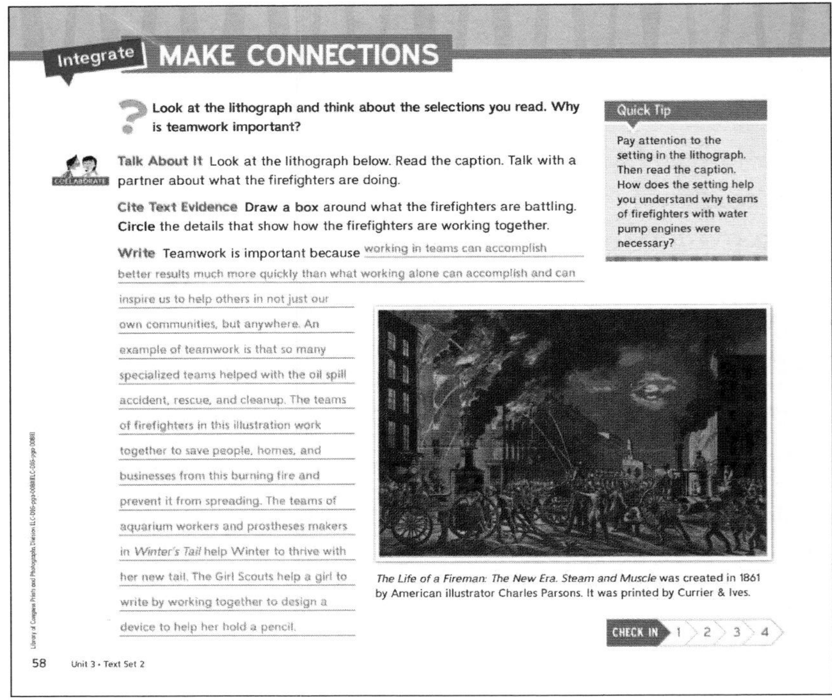

Integrate | MAKE CONNECTIONS

Look at the lithograph and think about the selections you read. Why is teamwork important?

Talk About It Look at the lithograph below. Read the caption. Talk with a partner about what the firefighters are doing.

Cite Text Evidence **Draw a box** around what the firefighters are battling. **Circle** the details that show how the firefighters are working together.

Write Teamwork is important because working in teams can accomplish better results much more quickly than what working alone can accomplish and can inspire us to help others in not just our own communities, but anywhere. An example of teamwork is that so many specialized teams helped with the oil spill accident, rescue, and cleanup. The teams of firefighters in this illustration work together to save people, homes, and businesses from this burning fire and prevent it from spreading. The teams of aquarium workers and prostheses makers in *Winter's Tail* help Winter to thrive with her new tail. The Girl Scouts help a girl to write by working together to design a device to help her hold a pencil.

Quick Tip

Pay attention to the setting in the lithograph. Then read the caption. How does the setting help you understand why teams of firefighters with water pump engines were necessary?

The Life of a Fireman: The New Era. Steam and Muscle was created in 1861 by American illustrator Charles Parsons. It was printed by Currier & Ives.

CHECK IN 1 2 3 4

58 Unit 3 • Text Set 2

Reading/Writing Companion, p. 58

Integrate

Make Connections DOK 4

Talk About It

Share and discuss students' responses to the "Two Heads Are Better Than One" blast. Display the Build Knowledge anchor chart. Review the chart and have students read through their notes, annotations, and responses for each text. Then ask students to complete the Talk About It activity on **Reading/Writing Companion** page 58.

Cite Text Evidence

Guide students to see the connections between the lithograph print on page 58 and the texts. Remind them to read the caption and the Quick Tip.

Write

Students should refer to their notes on the chart as they respond to the writing prompt at the bottom of the page. When students have finished, have groups share and discuss their responses.

Build Knowledge: Make Connections

Talk About the Text Have partners discuss the benefits of people working in a group.

Write About the Text Have students add their ideas to their Build Knowledge pages of their reader's notebooks.

Anchor Chart Record any new ideas on the Build Knowledge anchor chart.

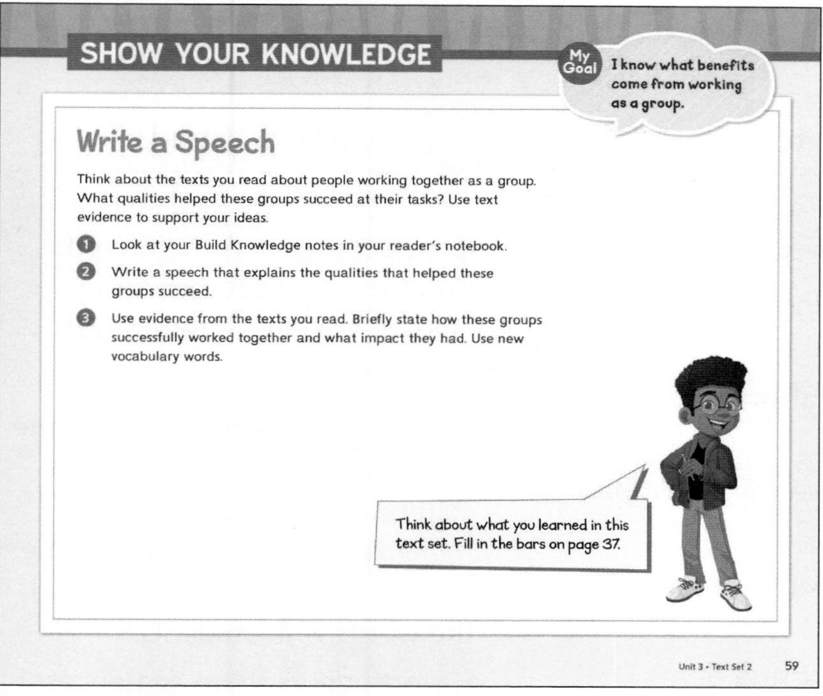

Reading/Writing Companion, p. 59

Integrate

Show Your Knowledge DOK 4

Write a Speech

Explain to students that they will show how they built knowledge across the text set by writing a speech about the qualities that helped groups of people successfully work together. Display the Build Knowledge anchor chart and ask: *What benefits come from people working as a group?*

Step 1 Guide partners to review the Build Knowledge anchor chart in their reader's notebook to discuss the prompt.

Step 2 Have students write a speech that explains the qualities that helped these groups succeed.

Step 3 Remind students to use evidence from the texts, video, and listening passage to support their ideas. Prompt students to use words from their Build Knowledge vocabulary list in their speech.

Inspire Action

Share Your Speech Have partners present their speeches. Ask students in the audience to write down things they found interesting or questions they have for the presenters. After the presentations, students can ask and answer questions about what they heard during the presentations.

What Are You Inspired to Do? Encourage partners to think of another way to respond to the texts. Ask: *What else do the texts inspire you to do?*

LEARNING GOALS

We can write a speech to show the knowledge we built about the benefits that come from people working as a group.

OBJECTIVES

Engage effectively in a range of collaborative discussions (one-on-one, in groups, and teacher-led) with diverse partners, building on others ideas and expressing their own clearly.

Follow agreed-upon rules for discussions and carry out assigned roles.

Report on a topic or text or present an opinion, sequencing ideas logically and using appropriate facts and relevant, descriptive details to support main ideas or themes; speak clearly at an understandable pace.

Include multimedia components (e.g., graphics, sound) and visual displays in presentations when appropriate to enhance the development of main ideas or themes.

ELA ACADEMIC LANGUAGE

- *speech, evidence*
- Cognate: *evidencia*

DIGITAL TOOLS

Show Your Knowledge Rubric

ENGLISH LANGUAGE LEARNERS

Provide sentence frames for support. *Some qualities that helped these groups succeed are ___. When people work as a group ___.*

MY GOALS ROUTINE

What I Learned

Review Goals Have students turn back to Reading/Writing Companion page 37 and review the goals for the text set.

Reflect Have students think about the progress they've made toward the goals. Review the key. Then have students reflect and fill in the bars.

LEARNING GOALS

- **We can build and expand on new vocabulary words.**
- **We can use Latin roots to figure out the meaning of unfamiliar words.**
- **We can write using new vocabulary words.**

OBJECTIVES

Use context (e.g., cause/effect relationships and comparisons in text) as a clue to the meaning of a word or phrase.

Use common, grade-appropriate Greek and Latin affixes and roots as clues to the meaning of a word (e.g., *photograph, photosynthesis*).

Expand vocabulary by adding inflectional endings and suffixes.

DIGITAL TOOLS

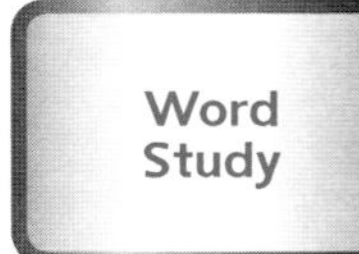

Vocabulary Activities

ENGLISH LANGUAGE LEARNERS

Pair students of different language proficiency levels to practice vocabulary. Have partners write definitions of *simile* and *metaphor:* A simile compares ______. A metaphor compares______. Then ask them to share common similes and metaphors they know, either in English or in their native languages

FORMATIVE ASSESSMENT

STUDENT CHECK-IN

After each lesson, have partners share and reflect using the Check-In routine.

Connect to Words

Practice the target vocabulary.

1. Describe one thing you know that is **artificial.**
2. How do you **collaborate** with others?
3. What things have you **dedicated** yourself to doing?
4. Which sports require you to be **flexible**?
5. Describe the **function** of a machine you use.
6. Which animal sounds can you **mimic**?
7. Tell about an **obstacle** you have faced.
8. What **techniques** do you use when you study?

Related Words

Help students generate different forms of this text set's words by adding, changing, or removing inflectional endings.

- Draw a four-column chart on the board. Write *mimic* in the first column. Then write *mimics, mimicked,* and *mimicking* in the next three columns. Read aloud the words with students.
- Have students share sentences using each form of *mimic.*
- Students can fill in the chart for *collaborate* and *dedicated,* and then share sentences using the different forms of the words.
- Have students copy the chart in their reader's notebook.

See **Practice Book** page 155.

Build Vocabulary

Discuss important academic words.

- Display *region, specific,* and *transported.*
- Define the words and discuss their meanings with students.
- Write *region* and *regional* on the board. Have partners write other words with the same root and define them. Then have partners ask and answer questions using the words.
- Repeat with *specific* and *transported.*

Similes and Metaphors

Remind students of the difference between a simile and a metaphor.

- A simile makes a comparison between two things using *like* or *as. My legs are like jelly.*
- A metaphor does not use *like* or *as* in the comparison. *Life is a roller coaster.*
- Have students write a simile and a metaphor in their reader's notebook.

See **Practice Book** page 167.

Spiral Review

Reinforce the Words

Have students orally complete each sentence stem to review words.

1. One <u>function</u> of a computer is ____.
2. Some <u>techniques</u> for staying flexible are ____.
3. The <u>obstacle</u> on the road is ____.
4. Laney likes <u>artificial</u> flowers because ____.
5. My brother can <u>mimic</u> ____.

Display the previous text set's vocabulary words: *blurted, complimenting, congratulate, contradicted, critical, misunderstanding*. Have partners ask and answer questions using each of the words.

See **Practice Book** page 156.

OPTION

Connect to Writing

- Have students write sentences in their reader's notebook using the target vocabulary.
- Tell them to write sentences that provide context to show what the words mean.
- ELL Provide the Lesson 3 sentence stems 1-5 for students needing extra support.

Write Using Vocabulary

Have students write something they learned from this text set's target words in their reader's notebook. For example, they might write about how being *flexible* can help one play sports or give examples of things that are *artificial*.

OPTION

Word Squares

Ask students to create Word Squares for each vocabulary word.

- In the first square, students write the word (e.g., *collaborate*).
- In the second square, students write their own definition of the word and any related words, such as synonyms (e.g., *partner, join*).
- In the third square, students draw a simple illustration that will help them remember the word (e.g., drawing of three people making a poster).
- In the fourth square, students write nonexamples, including antonyms for the word (e.g., *alone, solo, unaided*).

Have partners discuss their squares.

Latin Roots

Elicit from students what Latin roots are and how they can be helpful.

- Display On Level **Differentiated Genre Passage** "Building a Green Town." Read the first and second paragraphs. Model figuring out the meaning of the word *resolved* in the second paragraph.
- Have pairs use Latin roots to figure out the meanings of other unfamiliar words in the text.
- Partners can confirm meanings in a print or online dictionary.

See **Practice Book** page 168.

OPTION

Shades of Meaning

Help students generate words related to *flexible*. Draw a T-chart with one column labeled "Synonyms" and the other "Antonyms."

- Have small groups use a thesaurus to find synonyms and antonyms for *flexible*.
- Ask groups to write the words on the chart. Have groups share their words with the class.
- Ask groups to copy all the words in their reader's notebook.

OPTION

Morphology

Use *function* to help students learn more words. Draw a word web. Write *function* in the middle.

- In the surrounding circles, write *dis-, mal-, -al, and -less*. Discuss how the affixes change the meaning or part of speech.
- Have students add the affixes to *function*. Review the meaning of the new words.

Write Using Vocabulary

Have students use vocabulary words in their extended writing.

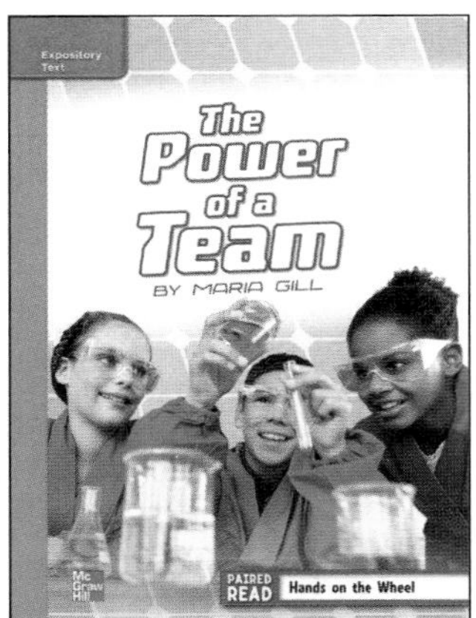

Lexile 740L

OBJECTIVES

Quote accurately from a text when explaining what the text says explicitly and when drawing inferences from the text.

Determine two or more central, or main, ideas of a text and explain how they are supported by relevant, or key, details; summarize the text.

Read grade-level prose and poetry orally with accuracy, appropriate rate, expression, and automaticity on successive readings.

ELA ACADEMIC LANGUAGE

- *expository text, central idea, relevant details*
- Cognates: *texto expositivo, detalles*

Approaching Level

Leveled Reader: *The Power of a Team*

Preview and Predict

- Read the Essential Question: *What benefits come from people working as a group?*
- Have students read the title, table of contents, and opening pages of *The Power of a Team* and preview the photographs to predict what the selection may be about.

Review Genre: Expository Text

Remind students that expository text gives factual information about a topic. The author may draw conclusions that are supported by facts and details. Information within the text may be organized into sections with headings. The text may also include text features, such as photographs and captions that provide additional information. Have students identify features of expository text in *The Power of a Team.*

Close Reading

Note Taking Ask students to use a copy of the online Central Idea and Relevant Details **Graphic Organizer 7** as they read.

Pages 2–6 *How do the relevant details on pages 2 and 3 help you identify the central idea of the introduction?* (The relevant details are all connected to the central idea that scientists often work together in teams to solve problems.) *Paraphrase one detail from pages 4–5 in Chapter 1 that supports this central idea.* (Scientists at NASA worked to build and launch robots to explore Mars.)

Pages 7–8 *What relevant details does page 8 provide about Curiosity? Discuss with your partner.* (It is a robot that left Earth on November 26, 2011. It has tools for collecting and studying rocks and soil.)

Pages 9–11 *The author compares a communication network to the human nervous system. Turn to a partner and discuss how this comparison helps you understand how the two work. What do a communication network and the human nervous system have in common?* (Both send messages through a network or system.)

Page 12 *The Latin root* flex *means "bend." What is the meaning of the word* flexible. ("able to bend") Have students add this word to their reader's notebook. *Explain what the author means in this sentence: "Bell Labs wants to invent flexible networks."* (They want to invent networks that work in different ways to handle lots of signals.)

Pages 13–15 *What question could you ask about the information on page 14?* (How are scientists around the world working on the Miami Project?) *Use relevant details to answer.* (They are testing theories about how to prevent, repair, and help patients recover from spinal cord damage.)

Pages 16–17 *Reread the sidebar on page 16. What is the central idea?* (Dr. James McLurkin wants to send multi-robot swarms to Mars.) *How did he think of this idea?* (seeing honeybees work together)

Respond to Reading Revisit the Essential Question and ask students to complete the Text Evidence questions on page 18.

Analytical Writing **Write About Reading** Check that students have correctly identified the central idea on pages 14–16 and cited one relevant detail that supports it.

Fluency: Accuracy and Rate

Model Model reading page 9 aloud with accuracy and appropriate rate. Then read the page aloud again and have students read along with you.

Apply Have students practice reading the passage with a partner.

Paired Read: "Hands on the Wheel"

Make Connections: Write About It

Before reading, ask students to note that the genre of this text is also expository text. Then discuss the Essential Question. After reading, ask students to write about the connections between *The Power of a Team* and "Hands on the Wheel."

Leveled Reader

Build Knowledge

Talk About the Text Have partners discuss the benefits of working in a group.

Write About the Text Have students add their ideas to the Build Knowledge pages of their reader's notebooks.

FOCUS ON SCIENCE

Students can extend their knowledge of scientific teamwork by developing a product plan on page 24.

LITERATURE CIRCLES

Ask students to conduct a literature circle using the Thinkmark questions to guide the discussion. You may wish to have a whole-class discussion, using information from both selections in the Leveled Reader, about the benefits of teamwork.

LEVEL UP

IF students read the Approaching Level fluently and answered the questions,

THEN pair them with students who have proficiently read the On Level and have students

- echo-read the On Level main selection.
- use self-stick notes to mark ways people benefited from working as a group.

ACT Access Complex Text

The On Level challenges students by requiring more **domain-specific words** and **complex sentence structures.**

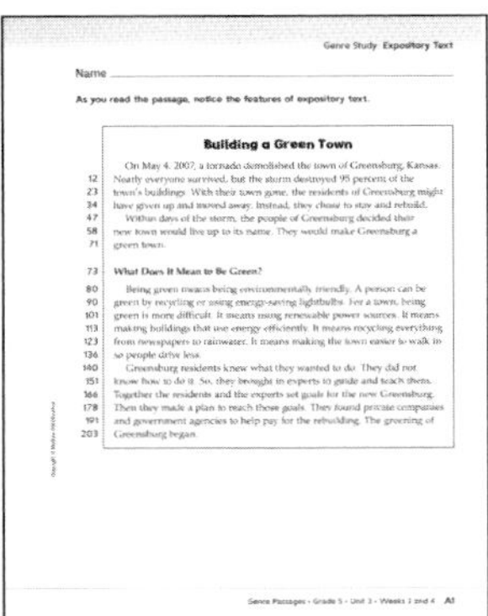

Genre Study Expository Text

Name ______________________

As you read the passage, notice the features of expository text.

Building a Green Town

On May 4, 2007, a tornado demolished the town of Greensburg, Kansas.
12 Nearly everyone survived, but the storm destroyed 95 percent of the
23 town's buildings. With their town gone, the residents of Greensburg might
34 have given up and moved away. Instead, they chose to stay and rebuild.
47 Within days of the storm, the people of Greensburg decided their
58 new town would live up to its name. They would make Greensburg a
71 green town.

73 **What Does It Mean to Be Green?**

80 Being green means being environmentally friendly. A person can be
90 green by recycling or using energy-saving lightbulbs. For a town, being
101 green is more difficult. It means using renewable power sources. It means
113 making buildings that use energy efficiently. It means recycling everything
123 from newspapers to rainwater. It means making the town easier to walk in
136 so people drive less.
140 Greensburg residents knew what they wanted to do. They did not
151 know how to do it. So, they brought in experts to guide and teach them.
166 Together the residents and the experts set goals for the new Greensburg.
178 Then they made a plan to reach those goals. They found private companies
191 and government agencies to help pay for the rebuilding. The greening of
203 Greensburg began.

Genre Passages • Grade 5 • Unit 3 • Weeks 3 and 4 A1

Lexile 730L

OBJECTIVES

Compare and contrast the overall structure (e.g., chronology, comparison, cause/effect, problem/solution) of events, ideas, concepts, or information in two or more texts.

Draw on information from multiple print or digital sources, demonstrating the ability to locate an answer to a question quickly or to solve a problem efficiently.

Determine or clarify the meaning of unknown and multiple-meaning words and phrases based on grade 5 reading and content, choosing flexibly from a range of strategies.

Use common, grade-appropriate Greek and Latin affixes and roots as clues to the meaning of a word (e.g., *photograph, photosynthesis*).

ELA ACADEMIC LANGUAGE

- *expository text, central idea, detail, problem, solution, accomplish, goal*
- Cognates: *texto expositivo, detalles, problema, solución*

Approaching Level

Genre Passage: "Building a Green Town"

Build Background

- Read aloud the Essential Question: *What benefits come from people working as a group?* Ask students to compare two groups they read about in this text set. Use the following questions for starters:

  I read that the group . . .

  This helps me understand that working together . . .

- Before beginning the online **Differentiated Genre Passage** "Building a Green Town," explain the difference between renewable and nonrenewable energy. Oil and gas are nonrenewable because there is a limited supply of them. Renewable sources, such as the sun and wind, are always available.

Review Genre: Expository Text

Remind students that expository text gives facts, examples, and explanations about a topic. It can include features such as photographs and captions. Headings are often used to give information about each section of the text.

Close Reading

Note Taking As students read the passage the first time, ask them to annotate the text. Have them note central ideas and relevant details, unfamiliar words, and questions they have. Then read again and use the following questions. Encourage students to cite text evidence from the selection.

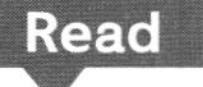

Problem and Solution Read paragraphs 1–2 on page A1. *What is the problem?* (A tornado destroyed Greensburg, Kansas.) *What is the solution?* (The townspeople decided to rebuild and make their new town green.)

Central Idea and Relevant Details Read paragraph 4. *What details explain what Greensburg did to make itself greener?* (They learned more about becoming green from experts. They made a plan and got money from other sources to pay for it.)

Problem and Solution Read paragraph 2 on page A2 and look at the photo and caption. *What is the problem?* (Greensburg wanted to use renewable energy to provide all its power.) *What is the solution?* (The photo shows they built a wind farm.)

Latin Roots *The word* solar *in paragraph 2 on page A2 comes from the Latin root* sol *which means "sun." How does this help you understand what a solar panel is?* (A solar panel gets its energy from the sun.)

Central Idea and Relevant Details Read the last two paragraphs. *Find two details that show how Greensburg became greener.* (New city buildings use 40 percent less energy; new streetlights are 40 percent more energy efficient.) *What is the central idea?* (Greensburg was able to rebuild itself as a green community.)

COLLABORATE **Summarize** Have students use their notes to summarize what Greensburg did to become more environmentally friendly.

Reread

Use the questions on page A3 to guide students' rereading of the passage.

Author's Craft Reread the last two paragraphs on page A1. *Do you think "What Does It Mean to Be Green?" is a good heading for this section? Explain your answer.* (It is a good heading because the section gives details about what a town needs to be a green town. For example, being a green town means using renewable power sources.)

Author's Craft Read paragraph 2 and study the photograph. *What information did you learn from the photo that is not in the text?* (The photo shows what a wind farm looks like.)

Author's Craft *How do you know this is an expository text?* (The author includes facts and a photograph with a caption about Greensburg.)

Integrate

COLLABORATE **Make Connections** Guide students to see connections between "Building a Green Town" and other texts they have read. Help pairs respond to this question: *How do the authors help you understand the benefits of people working together?*

Compare Texts Draw a two-column chart labeled *Renewable* and *Nonrenewable.* Help students complete the chart and discuss the differences.

Build Knowledge

Talk About the Text Have partners discuss the benefits of working in a group.

Write About the Text Have students add their ideas to the Build Knowledge pages of their reader's notebooks.

Differentiate and Collaborate

COLLABORATE **Be Inspired** Have students think about "Building a Green Town" and other selections they have read. Ask: *What do the texts inspire you to do?* Use the following activities or help pairs of students think of a way to respond.

Create a Brochure Choose one of the groups you read about this week. Work with classmates to design a brochure the group could use to raise money to help them with their project.

Write an Interview Script Write a news interview featuring a group you have read about. Include questions and answers about how the group works together to accomplish a specific goal. Perform your interview script.

Readers to Writers

Word Choice Remind students that authors choose words that can reveal their perspective about a topic to readers. Have students reread the last two paragraphs of "Building a Green Town" on page A2. Ask: *How do you think the author feels about what Greensburg was able to accomplish? What words in the text help you understand the author's feelings?*

LEVEL UP

IF students read the Approaching Level fluently and answered the questions,

THEN pair them with students who have proficiently read the On Level. Have them

- partner read the On Level passage.
- summarize one way that the Greensburg residents worked together.

Approaching Level

Phonics/Word Study/Decoding

REVIEW WORDS WITH LONG *e* VOWEL TEAM SYLLABLES

OBJECTIVES

Know and apply grade-level phonics and word analysis skills in decoding words.

Use combined knowledge of all letter-sound correspondences, syllabication patterns, and morphology (e.g., roots and affixes) to read accurately unfamiliar multisyllabic words in context and out of context.

Decode words with long *e* vowel team syllables.

I Do Remind students that each syllable has only one vowel sound. Explain that sometimes the vowel sound is spelled with more than one letter. This syllable is called a **vowel team syllable.** Write the word *heat* on the board. Underline the letters *ea.* Read the word aloud, emphasizing the vowel sound. Point out that the two vowels, *e* and *a,* form one vowel sound: long *e.*

We Do Write *meat* and *indeed* on the board. Model how to decode the word *meat.* Underline the vowel team *ea* and explain that it makes the long *e* sound. Then read the word *indeed* aloud and draw a slash between the *n* and *d* to separate the syllables. Have students identify the vowel team in the second syllable. Explain that both *ea* and *ee* can make the long *e* sound.

You Do Add the following examples to the board: *seat, treat, free, agree.* Have students say each word with you as you point to it. Repeat several times.

PRACTICE WORDS WITH VOWEL TEAM SYLLABLES

OBJECTIVES

Know and apply grade-level phonics and word analysis skills in decoding words.

Use combined knowledge of all letter-sound correspondences, syllabication patterns, and morphology (e.g., roots and affixes) to read accurately unfamiliar multisyllabic words in context and out of context.

Practice words with vowel team syllables.

I Do Write the words *delay* and *neat* on the board. Read the words aloud, running your finger under the letters in the vowel team as you blend them. Identify the vowel teams and the vowel sound each team makes.

We Do Write the words *glowing* and *drainpipe* on the board. Model how to pronounce the first word, and then guide students as they pronounce the remaining word. As necessary, help them identify the vowel team and the sound it makes in the word.

To provide additional practice, write these words on the board. Read aloud the first word and identify the vowel team and the vowel sound it makes.

eastern	flowing	painter	heater
midnight	repay	tried	coaches

You Do Have students read aloud the remaining words. Ask them to identify the vowel team in each word and the vowel sound it makes. Point to the words in random order for students to read chorally.

REVIEW WORDS WITH CONSONANT + *le* SYLLABLE

OBJECTIVES

Know and apply grade-level phonics and word analysis skills in decoding words.

Use combined knowledge of all letter-sound correspondences, syllabication patterns, and morphology (e.g., roots and affixes) to read accurately unfamiliar multisyllabic words in context and out of context.

Decode words with consonant + *le* syllables.

I Do Write the word *dribble* on the board and read the word as you run your finger under the letters. Underline the letters *ble* and repeat the sound the letters make. Explain that when a word ends with the letters *le,* the consonant that comes before them plus the letters *le* make up the last syllable in the word. It is called a **consonant + *le* syllable**.

We Do Write the words *jumble* and *gobble* on the board. Model how to decode the word *jumble.* Underline the letters in the last syllable. Have students repeat the syllable and the word after you. Then have students decode the word *gobble.* Have them identify the consonant + *le* syllable.

You Do Add these words to the board: *beagle, fiddle, puzzle,* and *turtle.* Have students read each word aloud and identify its final syllable.

PRACTICE WORDS WITH CONSONANT + *le* SYLLABLE

OBJECTIVES

Know and apply grade-level phonics and word analysis skills in decoding words.

Use combined knowledge of all letter-sound correspondences, syllabication patterns, and morphology (e.g., roots and affixes) to read accurately unfamiliar multisyllabic words in context and out of context.

Decode words with consonant + *le* syllables.

I Do Write the words *pebble, tackle,* and *sniffle* on the board. Read the words aloud, running you finger under the consonant + *le* syllable in the words as you pronounce them. Model how to read each word and identify the consonant + *le* syllables in each one.

We Do Write the words *possible, freckle,* and *terrible* on the board. Model how to decode the first word. Then guide students as they decode the remaining words. Help students identify the consonant + *le* syllable in each word.

Write these words on the board. Read aloud the first word and identify the consonant + *le* syllable.

wiggle	trickle	wrinkle	title	capable
stable	grumble	waddle	settle	enjoyable
kettle	brittle	griddle	struggle	agreeable

You Do Have students read aloud the remaining words. Have student pairs identify the consonant + *le* syllable in each word. Point to the words in random order for students to read chorally.

ELL For **ELL** students who need phonics and decoding practice, define words and help them use the words in sentences, scaffolding to ensure their understanding. See the **Language Transfers Handbook** for phonics elements that may not transfer from students' native languages.

Approaching Level

Vocabulary

REVIEW HIGH-FREQUENCY WORDS

TIER 2

OBJECTIVES

Acquire and use accurately grade-appropriate general academic and domain-specific words and phrases, including those that signal contrast, addition, and other logical relationships (e.g., *however, although, nevertheless, similarly, moreover, in addition*).

I Do Use **High-Frequency Word Cards** 101–120. Display one word at a time, following the routine: Display the word. Read the word. Then spell the word.

We Do Ask students to state the word and spell the word with you. Model using the word in a sentence and have students repeat it after you.

You Do Display the word. Ask students to say the word then spell it. When completed, quickly flip through the word card set as students chorally read the words. Provide opportunities for students to use the words in speaking and writing. For example, provide sentence starters, such as *On Saturdays I like to* ____. Ask students to write each word in their reader's notebook.

REVIEW ACADEMIC VOCABULARY

OBJECTIVES

Acquire and use accurately grade-appropriate general academic and domain-specific words and phrases, including those that signal contrast, addition, and other logical relationships (e.g., *however, although, nevertheless, similarly, moreover, in addition*).

I Do Display each **Visual Vocabulary Card** and state the word. Explain how the photograph illustrates the word. State the example sentence and repeat the word.

We Do Point to the word on the card and read the word with students. Ask them to repeat the word. Engage students in structured partner talk about the image as prompted on the back of the vocabulary card.

You Do Display each visual in random order, hiding the word. Have students match the definitions and context sentences of the words to the visuals displayed.

You may wish to review high-frequency words with ELL students using the lesson above.

UNDERSTAND ACADEMIC VOCABULARY

OBJECTIVES

Acquire and use accurately grade-appropriate general academic and domain-specific words and phrases, including those that signal contrast, addition, and other logical relationships (e.g., *however, although, nevertheless, similarly, moreover, in addition*).

I Do Display the *artificial* **Visual Vocabulary Card** and ask: *What are artificial flowers made of?* Point out that artificial flowers are often made of plastic or silk.

We Do Display the word card for *obstacle*. Ask: *What obstacle did you overcome in order to achieve a goal?* Have students give detailed examples.

You Do Have student pairs respond to these questions and explain their answers.

- How might you *collaborate* on a school project?
- How can you show that you are *dedicated* to your team?
- Why can a snake's body be described as *flexible?*
- What *function* can you perform with your hands?
- How would a parrot *mimic* your voice?
- Which writing *techniques* do you find most useful?

Have students pick words from their reader's notebook and use an online dictionary to find synonyms and antonyms and to check pronunciations.

LATIN ROOTS

OBJECTIVES

Determine or clarify the meaning of unknown and multiple-meaning words and phrases based on grade 5 reading and content, choosing flexibly from a range of strategies.

Use common, grade-appropriate Greek and Latin affixes and roots as clues to the meaning of a word (e.g., *photograph, photosynthesis*)

I Do Display the Approaching Level of "Building a Green Town" in the online **Differentiated Genre Passage**. Read aloud the second paragraph on page A1. Point to the word *efficiently*. Tell students that they can use their knowledge of a word's root, as well as context clues, to figure out its meaning.

Think Aloud I'm not sure what *efficiently* means. I know that the Latin root *fic* means "to make." I see the surrounding sentences give examples of how a green town makes life better and easier for people. This helps me figure out that *efficiently* means "to make things run more smoothly."

We Do Locate the word *residents* in the first paragraph on page A1. Discuss how to use the Latin root *sedere,* meaning "to sit," along with context clues to figure out the meaning of *residents*. Write the definition of the word.

You Do Have students determine the meaning of solar (page A2, paragraph 2) using the Latin root *sol* ("sun") and context clues. Then have students write all the words and definitions in their reader's notebook.

Approaching Level

Fluency/Comprehension

FLUENCY

MULTIMODAL

TIER 2

OBJECTIVES

Read grade-level prose and poetry orally with accuracy, appropriate rate, expression, and automaticity on successive readings.

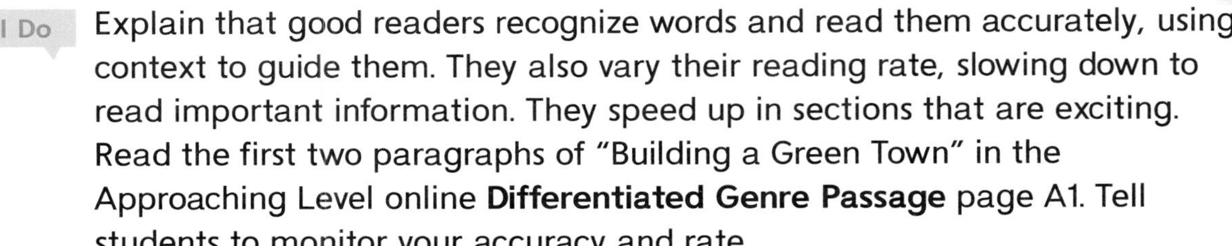

I Do Explain that good readers recognize words and read them accurately, using context to guide them. They also vary their reading rate, slowing down to read important information. They speed up in sections that are exciting. Read the first two paragraphs of "Building a Green Town" in the Approaching Level online **Differentiated Genre Passage** page A1. Tell students to monitor your accuracy and rate.

We Do Read the rest of page A1 aloud. Have students repeat each sentence after you, matching your rate. Explain that you slowed down when you read more difficult text to ensure that you read it accurately, and that you used context clues to correctly identify words.

You Do Have partners take turns reading sentences from the passage. Remind them to focus on their speed. Listen in and, as needed, provide corrective feedback by modeling proper fluency.

IDENTIFY RELEVANT DETAILS

TIER 2

OBJECTIVES

Determine two or more central, or main, ideas of a text and explain how they are supported by relevant, or key, details; summarize the text.

Identify important details.

I Do Read aloud the first paragraph of "Building a Green Town" in the Approaching Level online **Differentiated Genre Passage** page A1. Point out that the paragraph contains details about what happened when a tornado destroyed the town of Greensburg, Kansas. Explain that some details, such as the exact date of the storm, are not as relevant as other details, such as that residents chose to stay and rebuild.

We Do Read the third paragraph on page A1. Ask: *What details does the paragraph give?* Help students identify the most relevant details in the paragraph.

You Do Have students read the rest of the passage. After each paragraph, they should write down the details that seem most relevant. Review their lists with them and help them explain why the details they chose are relevant.

REVIEW CENTRAL IDEA AND RELEVANT DETAILS

OBJECTIVES

Determine two or more central, or main, ideas of a text and explain how they are supported by relevant, or key, details; summarize the text.

I Do Remind students that the central, or main, idea of a passage is what the author most wants readers to know about the topic. Each paragraph may have its own central idea. When it is not directly stated, students can identify it by thinking about what the relevant details have in common.

We Do Read the first paragraph of "Building a Green Town" in the Approaching Level online **Differentiated Genre Passage** page A1 together. Have students name the relevant details they identified earlier. Model connecting the details to determine the central idea. Then work with students to identify the central idea in each paragraph in the passage.

You Do Have students use the central ideas of each paragraph to summarize the passage and identify the central idea in the passage as a whole.

SELF-SELECTED READING

OBJECTIVES

Determine two or more central, or main, ideas of a text and explain how they are supported by relevant, or key, details; summarize the text.

Ask and answer questions to increase understanding of the text.

Independent Reading

Have students choose an expository book or article for independent reading. Students can read a **Classroom Library** book or check the online **Leveled Reader Library** or **Unit Bibliography** for selections. Guide students to transfer what they learned in this text set. Remind them that

- the central idea is the most important point the author makes about the topic. Relevant details support the central idea.
- texts with a problem-and-solution text structure explain how problems arise and how they are resolved.
- photographs, captions, and other text features give important information.

Have students record the central idea and relevant details on Central Idea and Relevant Details **Graphic Organizer 7**. Students can choose activities from Reading **Center Activity Cards** to help them apply skills to the text as they read. After they finish, they can choose a Book Talk activity to talk about the texts they read. Offer assistance and guidance with self-selected assignments.

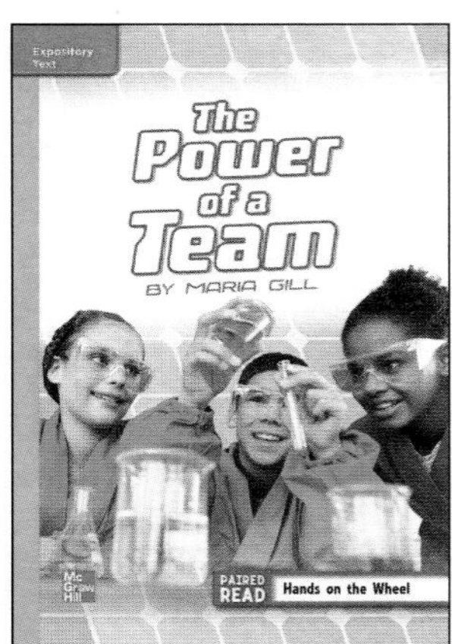

Lexile 900L

OBJECTIVES

Quote accurately from a text when explaining what the text says explicitly and when drawing inferences from the text.

Determine two or more central, or main, ideas of a text and explain how they are supported by relevant, or key, details; summarize the text.

Read grade-level prose and poetry orally with accuracy, appropriate rate, expression, and automaticity on successive readings.

ELA ACADEMIC LANGUAGE

- *expository text, central idea, relevant details*
- Cognates: *texto expositivo, detalles*

On Level

Leveled Reader: *The Power of a Team*

Preview and Predict

- Have students read the Essential Question: *What benefits come from people working as a group?*
- Have students read the title, table of contents, and opening pages of *The Power of a Team* and preview the photographs to predict what the selection may be about.

Review Genre: Expository Text

Remind students that expository text gives factual information about a topic. The author may draw conclusions that are supported by relevant facts and details. Information within the text may be organized into sections with headings. The text may also include text features, such as photographs and captions, that provide additional information. Have students identify features of expository text in *The Power of a Team.*

Close Reading

Note Taking Ask students to use a copy of the online Central Idea and Relevant Details **Graphic Organizer 7** as they read.

Pages 2–3 *What is the central idea of the introduction on pages 2 and 3?* (When scientists share research and ideas, they can reach solutions a lot faster.) *Paraphrase the relevant details in the sidebar "A Team Effort."* (Working together, a team of scientists led by Howard Florey developed penicillin as a cure for many common sicknesses.)

Pages 4–8 *Reread the details on page 4. Why were robots sent to Mars?* (to explore Mars; to scan rocks and soil; to send data back to Earth) *Reread page 6. How did the team on Earth free Spirit when it got stuck?* (They studied a model rover to test possible solutions.) *Discuss with a partner what the presence of silica, churned up by Spirit's wheel, revealed to the team of scientists.* (The silica revealed that there had once been water on Mars.)

Pages 9–12 *Reread the sidebar on page 10. What invention emerged as a result of William Schockley's research?* (the transistor) *Which two details support the idea that his team's work was important?* (They won a Nobel Prize. Transistors are now used in almost all electronic equipment.)

Pages 13–15 *Reread the first paragraph on page 15. What theory do some scientists have about repairing spinal tissue?* (Injecting Schwann cells into a damaged area will help fix the tissue.) *The author includes this simile on page 15: "This wraps around our nerves like insulation around wires." Turn to a partner and identify the two items the author compares and why.* (myelin and insulation; to help readers understand what the myelin does to help the nervous system)

Pages 16–17 *What question might you ask about the sidebar on page 16?* (Why does Dr. McLurkin want to send multi-robot swarms to Mars?) *Use text details to answer.* (He hopes they will function like honeybees, to share information and respond to events as a group.)

Respond to Reading Revisit the Essential Question and ask students to complete the Text Evidence questions on page 18.

Analytical Writing **Write About Reading** Check that students have correctly identified the central idea on pages 14–16 and cited relevant details that support it.

Fluency: Accuracy and Rate

Model Model reading page 9 aloud with accuracy and appropriate rate. Then read the page aloud again and have students read along with you.

Apply Have students practice reading the passage with a partner.

Paired Read: "Hands on the Wheel"

Analytical Writing Make Connections: Write About It

Before reading, ask students to note that the genre of this text is also expository text. Then discuss the Essential Question. After reading, ask students to write connections between the central ideas of *The Power of a Team* and "Hands on the Wheel."

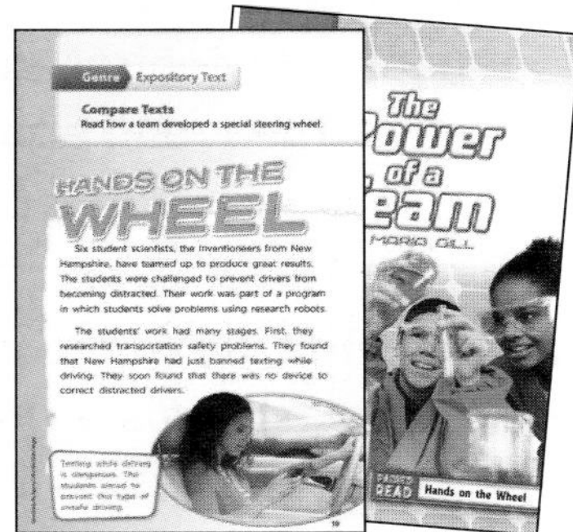

Leveled Reader

Build Knowledge

Talk About the Text Have partners discuss the benefits of working in a group.

Write About the Text Have students add their ideas to the Build Knowledge pages of their reader's notebooks.

FOCUS ON SCIENCE

Students can extend their knowledge of scientific teamwork by developing a product plan on page 24.

LITERATURE CIRCLES

Ask students to conduct a literature circle using the Thinkmark questions to guide the discussion. You may wish to have a whole-class discussion, using information from both selections in the Leveled Reader, about the benefits of teamwork.

LEVEL UP

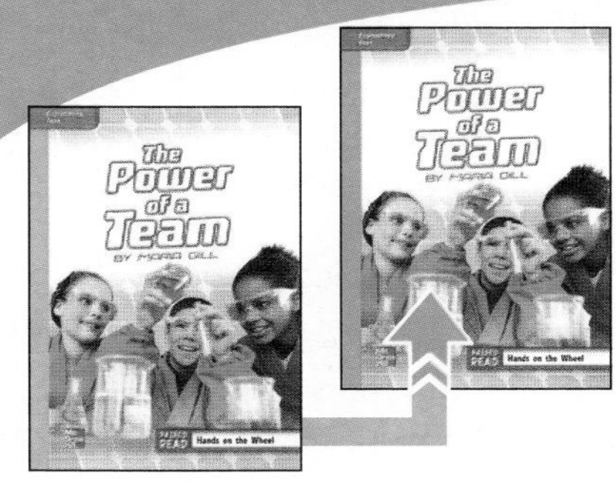

IF students read the On Level fluently and answered the questions,

THEN pair them with students who have proficiently read the Beyond Level and have students

- partner-read the Beyond Level main selection.
- identify the central idea in a section and select at least three relevant details that support it.

ACT Access Complex Text

The Beyond Level challenges students by including more **domain-specific words** and **complex sentence structures.**

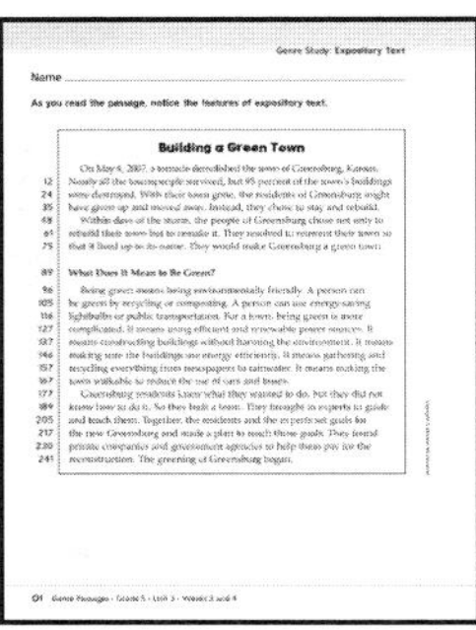

"Building a Green Town"
Lexile 800L

OBJECTIVES

Compare and contrast the overall structure (e.g., chronology, comparison, cause/effect, problem/solution) of events, ideas, concepts, or information in two or more texts.

Draw on information from multiple print or digital sources, demonstrating the ability to locate an answer to a question quickly or to solve a problem efficiently.

Determine or clarify the meaning of unknown and multiple-meaning words and phrases based on grade 5 reading and content, choosing flexibly from a range of strategies.

Use common, grade-appropriate Greek and Latin affixes and roots as clues to the meaning of a word (e.g., *photograph, photosynthesis*).

ELA ACADEMIC LANGUAGE

- *expository text, central idea, relevant detail, problem, solution, accomplish, goal*
- Cognates: *texto expositivo, detalles, problema, solución*

On Level

Genre Passage: "Building a Green Town"

Build Background

- Read aloud the Essential Question: *What benefits come from people working as a group?* Ask students to compare two groups they read about in this text set. Use the following questions for starters to help focus discussion:

  I read that the group . . .

  This helps me understand that working together . . .

- Before beginning the online **Differentiated Genre Passage** "Building a Green Town," explain the difference between renewable and nonrenewable energy. Oil and gas are nonrenewable because there is a limited supply of them. The supply of renewable sources, such as sun and wind, cannot be depleted.

Review Genre: Expository Text

Remind students that expository text gives factual information about a topic. It can include features such as photographs and captions to add information. Headings are used to organize elements and ideas in each section of the text.

Close Reading

Note Taking As students read the passage the first time, ask them to annotate the text. Have them note central ideas and relevant details, unfamiliar words, and questions they have. Then read again and use the following questions.

Read

Problem and Solution Read the first two paragraphs on page O1. *What problem and solution does the author describe?* (In 2007, a tornado destroyed most of Greensburg. Residents decided to rebuild and make Greensburg greener.)

Central Idea and Relevant Details Read paragraph 4 on page O1. *What is the paragraph's central idea?* (The residents of Greensburg worked together to make the town more environmentally friendly.) *How do details in the paragraph support this idea?* (They explain the specific actions residents took, including bringing in experts, making a plan, and getting money from other sources.)

Problem and Solution Read paragraph 2 on page O2 and look at the photo and caption. *What is the problem?* (Greensburg wanted to use renewable energy to provide all its power.) *What is the solution?* (The photo shows they built a wind farm.)

Latin Roots *The word* solar *in paragraph 2 on page O2 comes from the Latin root* sol, *which means "sun." How does this help you understand what a solar panel is?* (A solar panel gets its energy from the sun.)

Central Idea and Relevant Details Read paragraphs 3 and 4. *Summarize the relevant details in paragraph 3.* (Greensburg was able to reduce its energy use and use more renewable energy.) *Use these details to state the central idea.* (Reducing and changing its energy use helped Greensburg rebuild as a green community.)

Summarize Have students use their notes to summarize the ways Greensburg faced and met challenges.

Reread

Use the questions on page O3 to guide students' rereading of the passage.

Author's Craft Reread the last two paragraphs on page O1. *Do you think "What Does It Mean to Be Green?" is a good heading for this section? Explain your answer.* (It is a good heading because the section gives details about how to be a green town. The text explains it means reducing the use of cars and buses.)

Author's Craft Study the photograph and caption on page O2. *What information did you learn from the photo and the caption that was not in the written text?* (I learned what a wind farm like the one in Greensburg looks like.)

Author's Craft *How do you know this is an expository text?* (The author gives factual information about Greensburg building a green town.)

Integrate

Make Connections Have students explore the connections between "Building a Green Town" and other selections. Have them work with a partner to respond to this question: *How do the authors help you understand the benefits of people working together?*

Compare Texts Have pairs make a two-column chart labeled *Renewable* and *Nonrenewable* and complete it. Have them discuss the differences.

Build Knowledge

Talk About the Text Have partners discuss the benefits of working in a group.

Write About the Text Have students add their ideas to the Build Knowledge pages of their reader's notebooks.

Differentiate and Collaborate

Be Inspired Have students think about "Building a Green Town" and other selections they have read. Ask: *What do the texts inspire you to do?* Use the following activities or have pairs of students think of a way to respond to the texts.

Create a Brochure Choose one of the groups you read about this week. Work with classmates to design a brochure the group could use to raise money to help them with their project.

Write an Interview Script Write a news interview featuring a group you have read about. Include questions and answers about how the group works together to accomplish a specific goal. Perform your interview script.

Readers to Writers

Word Choice Remind students that authors often choose words to convey a tone that lets readers know the author's perspective about a topic. Have students reread the last two paragraphs of "Building a Green Town" on page O2. Ask: *What tone does the author convey? What words in the text help you understand how the author feels about Greensburg's accomplishments?*

LEVEL UP

IF students read the On Level fluently and answered the questions,

THEN pair them with students who have proficiently read the Beyond Level. Have them

- partner read the Beyond Level passage.
- summarize how Greensburg became more sustainable by residents working together.

On Level

Vocabulary/Comprehension

REVIEW ACADEMIC VOCABULARY

OBJECTIVES

Use the relationship between particular words (e.g., synonyms, antonyms, homographs) to better understand each of the words.

Demonstrate understanding of figurative language, word relationships, and nuances in word meanings.

I Do Use the **Visual Vocabulary Cards** to review the key selection words *artificial, flexible, function, mimic, obstacle,* and *techniques*. Point to each, read it aloud, and have students repeat.

We Do Read aloud each word set below. Help students identify the word in each set that means almost the same as the first word.

artificial	natural	fake
flexible	limber	stiff
function	decoration	use

You Do Have students work in pairs to identify the word in each set that means almost the same as the first word.

mimic	imitate	innovate
obstacle	aid	hurdle
techniques	problems	methods

Have students pick words from their reader's notebook and use an online thesaurus to find words with similar meanings.

LATIN ROOTS

OBJECTIVES

Determine or clarify the meaning of unknown and multiple-meaning words and phrases based on grade 5 reading and content, choosing flexibly from a range of strategies.

Use common, grade-appropriate Greek and Latin affixes and roots as clues to the meaning of a word (e.g., *photograph, photosynthesis*).

I Do Remind students that they can often determine the meaning of an unknown word by looking for word parts, such as Latin roots. Read aloud the second paragraph of "Building a Green Town" in the On Level online **Differentiated Genre Passage** page O1.

Think Aloud I'm not sure what *efficiently* means. I know that the Latin root *fic* means "to make." I see the surrounding sentences give examples of how a green town makes life better and easier for people. This helps me figure out that *efficiently* means "to make things run more smoothly."

We Do Have students reread paragraph 1. Help them to find the meaning of *residents* using the Latin root *sedere* ("to sit") and context clues.

You Do Have students work in pairs to determine the meaning of *solar* (page O2, paragraph 2) and *consume* (page O2, paragraph 3) using the Latin roots *sol* ("sun") and *sum* ("to take").

REVIEW CENTRAL IDEA AND RELEVANT DETAILS

OBJECTIVES

Determine two or more central, or main, ideas of a text and explain how they are supported by relevant, or key, details; summarize the text.

I Do Remind students that the main, or central, idea of a passage is what the author most wants readers to know about the topic. Each paragraph can have a central idea. When the central idea is not directly stated, students can identify it by thinking about what the relevant details have in common.

We Do Have a volunteer read the first paragraph of "Building a Green Town" in the On Level online **Differentiated Genre Passage** page O1. Have students identify the central idea. Then work with them to identify the central idea in the next paragraph and discuss how the central ideas are related.

You Do Have partners identify the central ideas in each paragraph in the rest of the passage. Then have them summarize the passage and determine the central idea of the passage as a whole.

SELF-SELECTED READING

OBJECTIVES

Determine two or more central, or main, ideas of a text and explain how they are supported by relevant, or key, details; summarize the text.

Ask and answer questions to increase understanding of the text.

Independent Reading

Have students choose an expository book or article for independent reading. Students can read a **Classroom Library** book or check the online **Leveled Reader Library** or **Unit Bibliography** for selections. Guide students to transfer what they learned in this text set. Remind them to

- look for the central idea and relevant details.
- find examples of a problem-and-solution text structure.
- pay attention to photographs, captions, and other text features.

Before they read, have students preview the text, noting photographs, captions, and other text features. Students can choose activities from Reading **Center Activity Cards** to help them apply skills to the text as they read. After they finish, they can choose a Book Talk activity to talk about the texts they read.

You may want to include **ELL** students in On Level vocabulary and comprehension lessons. Offer language support as needed.

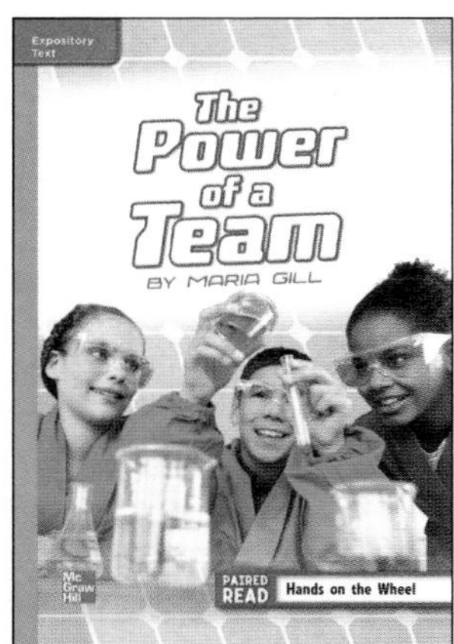

Lexile 1010L

OBJECTIVES

Quote accurately from a text when explaining what the text says explicitly and when drawing inferences from the text.

Determine two or more main ideas of a text and explain how they are supported by key details; summarize the text.

Read grade-level prose and poetry orally with accuracy, appropriate rate, expression, and automaticity on successive readings.

ELA ACADEMIC LANGUAGE

- *expository text, central idea, relevant details*
- Cognates: *texto expositivo, detalles*

Beyond Level

Leveled Reader: *The Power of a Team*

Preview and Predict

- Have students read the Essential Question: *What benefits come from people working as a group?*
- Have students read the title, table of contents, and opening pages of *The Power of a Team* and preview the photographs to predict what the selection may be about.

Review Genre: Expository Text

Remind students that expository text gives factual information about a topic. The author may draw conclusions that are supported by relevant facts and details. Information within the text may be organized into sections with headings. The text may also include text features, such as photographs and captions, which provide additional information. Have students identify features of expository text in *The Power of a Team.*

Close Reading

Note Taking Ask students to use a copy of the online Central Idea and Relevant Details **Graphic Organizer 7** as they read.

Pages 2–3 *What is the central idea of the introduction?* (When scientists collaborate, they are able to make new discoveries faster.) *In the opening paragraph, the author compares a scientific problem to a puzzle. Why?* (To solve a scientific problem or puzzle, it's better to have more people bringing pieces of information together and finding missing pieces.)

Pages 4–8 *Reread page 6. Identify details that explain how the team on Earth kept Spirit going.* (They drove the rover in reverse; They used a model to identify a way to free it when it got stuck.) *What important discovery was made in the process of freeing Spirit?* (Spirit's wheel churned up silica, which confirmed that there had been water on Mars.)

Pages 9–10 *On page 9, what is the central idea in the first paragraph?* (Scientific teams sometimes make unintended discoveries.) *Which relevant details in Chapter 2 support this idea?* (Penzias and Wilson used a microwave antenna to study radio waves in space. Their findings helped scientists at Princeton discover cosmic microwave background radiation.)

Pages 11–15 *Turn to a partner and discuss the purpose of the Miami Project.* (to increase research done on spinal injuries) *Reread the first paragraph on page 15. What theory do some scientists have about repairing spinal tissue?* (Injecting Schwann cells into a damaged area will help repair the tissue.) *Explain why experimental trials are necessary to Schwann cell research.* (They will help scientists determine whether Schwann cell injections work as successfully on humans.)

Pages 16–17 *Turn to your partner and ask a question about the information on page 16 or 17. Discuss possible answers.*

Respond to Reading Revisit the Essential Question and ask students to complete the Text Evidence questions on page 18.

Analytical Writing **Write About Reading** Check that students have correctly identified the central idea on pages 14–16 and cited relevant details from the text that support the central idea.

Fluency: Accuracy and Rate

Model Model reading page 9 with accuracy and appropriate rate. Then read the page aloud again and have students read along with you.

Apply Have partners do repeated readings of the passage.

Paired Read: "Hands on the Wheel"

Make Connections: Write About It

Before reading, ask students to note that the genre of this selection is also expository text. Then discuss the Essential Question. After reading, ask students to write connections between the central ideas in *The Power of a Team* and "Hands on the Wheel."

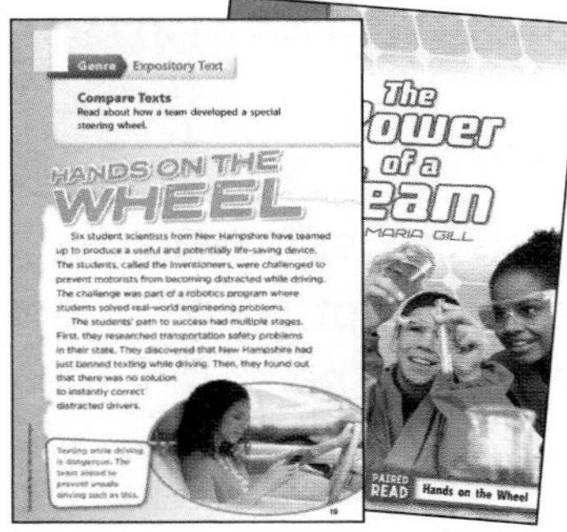

Genre Expository Text
Compare Texts
HANDS ON THE WHEEL
The Power of a Team
MARIO GILL
PAIRED READ Hands on the Wheel

Leveled Reader

Build Knowledge

Talk About the Text Have partners discuss the benefits of working in a group.

Write About the Text Have students add their ideas to the Build Knowledge pages of their reader's notebooks.

FOCUS ON SCIENCE

Students can extend their knowledge of scientific teamwork by developing a product plan on page 24.

LITERATURE CIRCLES

Ask students to conduct a literature circle using the Thinkmark questions to guide the discussion. You may wish to have a whole-class discussion, using information from both selections in the Leveled Reader, about the benefits that come from teamwork.

GIFTED AND TALENTED

Synthesize Lead students to brainstorm a list of problems involving space, communication, medicine, or transportation. Have student pairs research one problem from the list. Provide these focus questions: *Who are the people working on the problem? What kinds of work are the people doing? What benefits come from a team approach to problem-solving?* Have students present their research in the form of web diagrams.

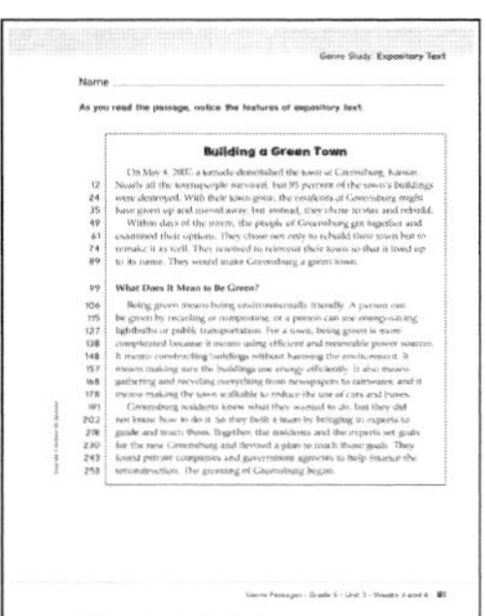

"Building a Green Town"
Lexile 890L

OBJECTIVES

Compare and contrast the overall structure (e.g., chronology, comparison, cause/effect, problem/solution) of events, ideas, concepts, or information in two or more texts.

Draw on information from multiple print or digital sources, demonstrating the ability to locate an answer to a question quickly or to solve a problem efficiently.

Determine or clarify the meaning of unknown and multiple-meaning words and phrases based on grade 5 reading and content, choosing flexibly from a range of strategies.

Use common, grade-appropriate Greek and Latin affixes and roots as clues to the meaning of a word (e.g., *photograph, photosynthesis*).

ELA ACADEMIC LANGUAGE

- *expository text, central idea, relevant detail, problem, solution, accomplish, goal*
- Cognates: *texto expositivo, detalles, problema, solución*

Beyond Level

Genre Passage: "Building a Green Town"

Build Background

- Read aloud the Essential Question: *What benefits come from people working as a group?* Ask students to compare two groups they read about in this text set. Use the following questions for starters to help focus discussion:

  I read that the group . . .

  This helps me understand that working together . . .

- Before beginning the online **Differentiated Genre Passage** "Building a Green Town," explain the difference between renewable and nonrenewable energy. Oil and gas are nonrenewable because there is a limited supply of them. The supply of renewable sources, such as sun and wind, cannot be depleted.

Review Genre: Expository Text

Remind students that expository text gives factual information about a topic. It can include features such as photographs and captions, which help readers understand what is written in the text. Headings are often used to indicate common elements and ideas in each section of the text.

Close Reading

Note Taking As students read the passage the first time, ask them to annotate the text. Have them note central ideas, relevant details, unfamiliar words, and questions they have. Then read again and use the following questions.

Read

Problem and Solution Read the first two paragraphs on page B1. *What problem and solution does the author describe?* (In 2007, a tornado destroyed most of Greensburg. Residents decided to rebuild and make Greensburg greener.)

Latin Roots Read the second paragraph on page B1. *The word* options *contains the Latin root* opt, *which means "to choose." Explain how this adds to your understanding of how the word is used in the text.* (The meaning of the Latin root tells me that *options* means "choices." The word describes the different choices that Greensburg residents had after the tornado.)

Central Idea and Relevant Details Read paragraph 4. *What is the central idea?* (The residents worked together to make the town more environmentally friendly.) *Which relevant details in the paragraph support this idea?* (the residents built a team, brought in experts, came up with a plan, got financing)

Problem and Solution Read paragraph 2 on page B2 and look at the photo and caption. *What is the problem?* (Greensburg wanted to use renewable energy to provide all its power.) *What is the solution?* (The photo shows they built a wind farm.)

Central Idea and Relevant Details Read paragraphs 3 and 4 on page B2. *Use details from paragraph 3 to state the central idea.* (In addition to renewable energy, Greensburg was able to reduce its overall energy usage and become an environmentally friendly town.)

Summarize Have students use their notes to summarize how Greensburg remade itself into a model sustainable community.

Reread

Use the questions on page B3 to guide students' rereading of the passage.

Author's Craft Reread the last two paragraphs on page B1. *Do you think "What Does It Mean to Be Green?" is a good heading for this section? Explain.* (It is a good heading because the section explains what is needed for a town to be "green.")

Author's Craft Study the photo and caption on page B2. *How does the photograph support the text? Why is this helpful?* (The photograph shows what a wind farm looks like. The text did not describe a wind farm.)

Author's Craft *How do you know this is an expository text?* (It gives factual information about Greensburg, and it includes headings and a photo.)

Integrate

Make Connections Encourage students to explore the connections between "Building a Green Town" and other selections they have read. Have them work with a partner to respond to this question: *How do the authors help you understand the benefits of people working together?*

Compare Texts Have pairs make a two-column chart labeled *Renewable* and *Nonrenewable*. Ask them to complete the chart with relevant details. Have them discuss the differences.

Build Knowledge

Talk About the Text Have partners discuss the benefits of working in a group.

Write About the Text Have students add their ideas to the Build Knowledge pages of their reader's notebooks.

Differentiate and Collaborate

Be Inspired Have students think about "Building a Green Town" and other selections they have read. Ask: *What do the texts inspire you to do?* Use the following activities or have pairs of students think of a way to respond to the texts.

Create a Brochure Choose one of the groups you read about this week. Work with classmates to design a brochure the group could use to raise money to help them with their project. In your brochure, explain how the group is helping and how readers' donations would benefit the cause.

Write an Interview Script Write questions and responses for a news interview featuring one of the groups you have read about. Include details about how the group members worked together to accomplish a specific task, as well as how others can become involved in the group. Perform your interview script.

Readers to Writers

Word Choice Remind students that authors often choose words to convey a tone that lets readers know about how the author feels about a topic. Have students reread the last two paragraphs of "Building a Green Town" on page B2. Ask: *What tone does the author convey? What words in the text help you understand how the author feels about Greensburg's accomplishments?*

GIFTED AND TALENTED

Independent Study As they synthesize their notes and the selections they read, have students consider the ways in which people learn how to work together as a team. Then have students design a course that teaches other students how to work cooperatively. Encourage students to consider both behavioral and logistical characteristics important to group work. Have partners evaluate each other's work and make suggestions for revision.

Beyond Level

Vocabulary/Comprehension

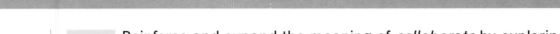

REVIEW DOMAIN-SPECIFIC WORDS

MULTIMODAL

OBJECTIVES

Determine the meaning of general academic and domain-specific words and phrases in a text relevant to a grade 5 topic or subject area.

Acquire and use accurately grade-appropriate general academic and domain-specific words and phrases, including those that signal contrast, addition, and other logical relationships (e.g., *however, although, nevertheless, similarly, moreover, in addition*).

Model Reinforce and expand the meaning of *collaborate* by exploring its word family. Use *collaborate* in a sentence and point out that it is a verb. Then write *collaborative* and *collaborator* on the board, use them in sentences, and identify their parts of speech. Finally, add *-ly* to *collaborative* to make the adverbial form and use it in a sentence.

Display the words *dedicate, dedicated,* and *dedication*. Work with students to determine their parts of speech and write sentences using these words.

Apply Finally, have students work in pairs to review the meanings of the words *renewable* and *efficient* and use them in original sentences.

Have students pick words from their reader's notebook and use an online thesaurus to find words with similar meanings.

LATIN ROOTS

OBJECTIVES

Determine or clarify the meaning of unknown and multiple-meaning words and phrases based on grade 5 reading and content, choosing flexibly from a range of strategies.

Use common, grade-appropriate Greek and Latin affixes and roots as clues to the meaning of a word (e.g., *photograph, photosynthesis*).

Model Read aloud the second paragraph of "Building a Green Town" in the Beyond Level online **Differentiated Genre Passage** page B1.

Think Aloud I'm not sure what *efficiently* means. I know that the Latin root *fic* means "to make." I see the surrounding sentences give examples of how a green town makes life better and easier for people. This helps me figure out that *efficiently* means "to make things run more smoothly."

Have students reread paragraph 1. Help them find the meaning of *residents* using the Latin root *sedere* ("to sit") and context clues.

Apply Have students read the rest of the passage and work in pairs to determine the meaning of *solar* (page B2, paragraph 2) and *consume* (page B2, paragraph 3) using the Latin roots *sol* ("sun") and *sum* ("to take").

Independent Study Challenge students to find words in other texts with the same Latin roots found in *options, efficiently, resident, solar,* and *consume*. Have them combine their lists to create a master list for each root.

Have students pick words from their reader's notebook and use an online dictionary to check their pronunciation and the meaning of Latin roots.

REVIEW CENTRAL IDEA AND RELEVANT DETAILS

OBJECTIVES

Determine two or more central, or main, ideas of a text and explain how they are supported by relevant, or key, details; summarize the text.

Model Remind students that the main, or central, idea of a passage is what the author most wants readers to know about the topic. Each paragraph may have a central idea. When the central idea is not directly stated, students can identify it by noticing what the relevant details have in common.

Have students read the first paragraph of "Building a Green Town" in the Beyond Level online **Differentiated Genre Passage** page B1. Ask open-ended questions to facilitate discussion, such as *What do all the details in this paragraph have in common? What central idea might they support?*

Apply Have students identify the central ideas in each paragraph in the rest of the passage as they independently fill in a copy of the online Central Idea and Details **Graphic Organizer 7.** Then have partners summarize the passage and determine its overall central idea.

SELF-SELECTED READING

OBJECTIVES

Determine two or more central, or main, ideas of a text and explain how they are supported by relevant, or key, details; summarize the text.

Ask and answer questions to increase understanding of a text.

Independent Reading

Have students choose an expository book or article for independent reading. Students can read a **Classroom Library** book or check the online **Leveled Reader Library** or **Unit Bibliography** for selections. Guide students to transfer what they learned in this text set by identifying the central idea and relevant details, finding examples of a problem-and-solution text structure, and paying attention to photographs, captions, and other text features.

Students can choose activities from Reading **Center Activity Cards** to help them apply skills to the text as they read. After they finish, they can choose a Book Talk activity to talk about the texts they read.

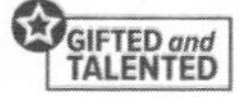

Independent Study Challenge students to discuss how their books relate to the key concept of scientific viewpoints. Then ask students to discuss the different ways that natural events and human activities affect the environment.

Student Outcomes

✓ Tested in *Wonders* Assessments

FOUNDATIONAL SKILLS

Phonics and Word Analysis

- Decode words with *r*-controlled vowel syllables

Fluency

- Read grade-level texts with accuracy, appropriate rate, expression, and automaticity

READING

Reading Informational Text

✓ Explain how the text structure of compare and contrast contributes to the overall meaning of a text
✓ Analyze an author's perspective in an informational text
✓ Track the development of an argument, identifying the specific claim(s), evidence, and reasoning
- Read and comprehend texts in the grades 4-5 text complexity band
- Summarize a text to enhance comprehension
- Write in response to texts

Compare Texts

✓ Analyze how figurative language contributes to meaning in a text
- Compare and contrast how authors present information on the same topic or theme

COMMUNICATION

Writing

Write to Sources

✓ Write an argument with an organizational structure supported by logical reasons, relevant evidence from sources, and a strong conclusion
- With guidance and support from peers and adults, develop and strengthen writing as needed by planning, revising, and editing

Speaking and Listening

- Report on a topic or text or present an opinion, sequencing ideas; speak clearly at an understandable pace

Conventions

Grammar

✓ Use the past tense of irregular verbs correctly
✓ Apply an understanding of correct verb usage

Spelling

- Spell words with *r*-controlled vowel syllables

Researching

- Conduct short research projects that build knowledge through investigation of different aspects of the topic

Creating and Collaborating

- Add audio recordings and visual displays to presentations when appropriate
- With some guidance and support from adults, use technology to produce and publish writing

VOCABULARY

Academic Vocabulary

- Acquire and use grade-appropriate academic vocabulary

Vocabulary Strategy

✓ Use context clues to determine the meaning of multiple-meaning and unknown words and phrases

CONTENT AREA LEARNING

History and Diversity

- Identify different points of view about an issue, topic, or current event. **Social Studies**
- Discuss different cultures of ancient civilizations in the Americas. **Social Studies**

ELL Scaffolded supports for English Language Learners are embedded throughout the lessons, enabling students to communicate information, ideas, and concepts in English Language Arts and for social and instructional purposes within the school setting.

See the **ELL Small Group Guide** for additional support of the skills for the text set.

FORMATIVE ASSESSMENT

For assessment throughout the text set, use students' self-assessments and your observations.

Use the Data Dashboard to filter class, group, or individual student data to guide group placement decisions. It provides recommendations to enhance learning for gifted and talented students and offers extra support for students needing remediation.

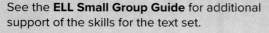

Develop Student Ownership

To build student ownership, students need to know what they are learning and why they are learning it, and to determine how well they understood it.

Students Discuss Their Goals

READING

TEXT SET GOALS

- I can read and understand argumentative text.
- I can use text evidence to respond to argumentative text.
- I know how we can explain what happened in the past.

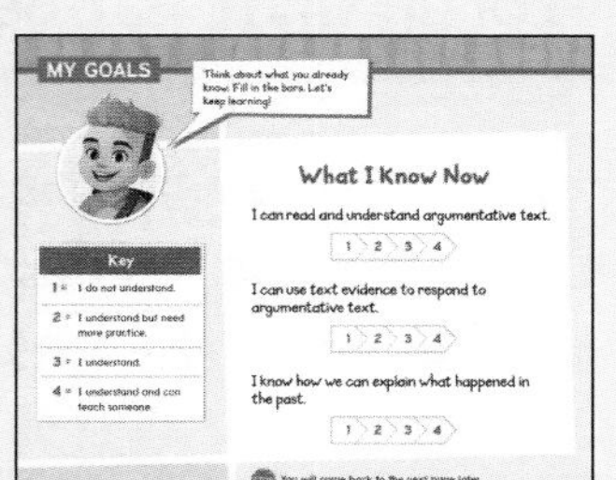

Have students think about what they know and fill in the bars on **Reading/Writing Companion** page 62.

WRITING

EXTENDED WRITING GOALS

Extended Writing 3:

- I can write an argumentative essay.
- I can synthesize information from three sources.

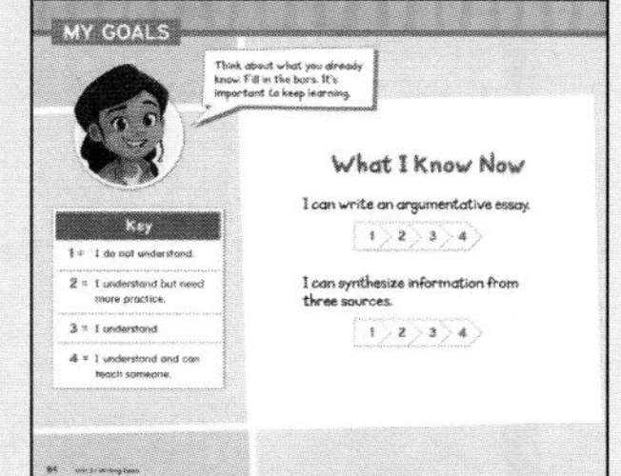

Have students think about what they know and fill in the bars on Reading/Writing Companion page 84.

Students Monitor Their Learning

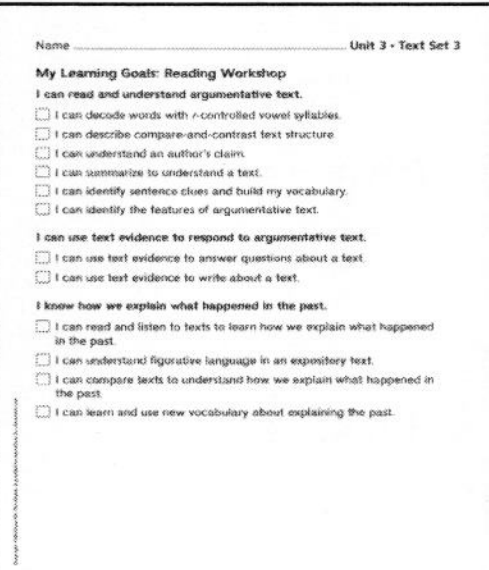

Name ______ Unit 3 • Text Set 3

My Learning Goals: Reading Workshop

I can read and understand argumentative text.

- ☐ I can decode words with r-controlled vowel syllables.
- ☐ I can describe compare-and-contrast text structure.
- ☐ I can understand an author's claim.
- ☐ I can summarize to understand a text.
- ☐ I can identify sentence clues and build my vocabulary.
- ☐ I can identify the features of argumentative text.

I can use text evidence to respond to argumentative text.

- ☐ I can use text evidence to answer questions about a text.
- ☐ I can use text evidence to write about a text.

I know how we explain what happened in the past.

- ☐ I can read and listen to texts to learn how we explain what happened in the past.
- ☐ I can understand figurative language in an expository text.
- ☐ I can compare texts to understand how we explain what happened in the past.
- ☐ I can learn and use new vocabulary about explaining the past.

Grade 5 • My Learning Goals: Reading Workshop 17

LEARNING GOALS

Specific learning goals identified in every lesson make clear what students will be learning and why. These smaller goals provide stepping stones to help students reach their Text Set and Extended Writing Goals.

CHECK-IN ROUTINE

The Check-In Routine at the close of each lesson guides students to self-reflect on how well they understood each learning goal.

Review the lesson learning goal.
Reflect on the activity.
Self-Assess by

- filling in the bars in the Reading/Writing Companion
- holding up 1, 2, 3, or 4 fingers

Share with your teacher.

Students Reflect on Their Progress

READING

TEXT SET GOALS

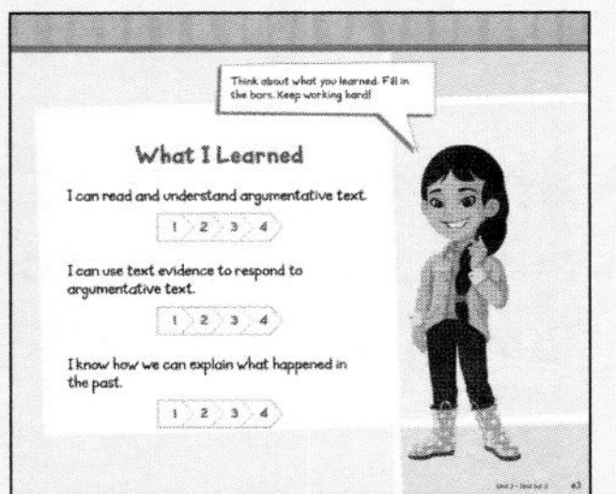

After completing the Show Your Knowledge task for the text set, students reflect on their understanding of the Text Set Goals by filling in the bars on Reading/Writing Companion page 63.

WRITING

EXTENDED WRITING GOALS

After completing both extended writing projects for the unit, students reflect on their understanding of the Extended Writing Goals by filling in the bars on Reading/Writing Companion page 85.

TEXT SET
3

Build Knowledge

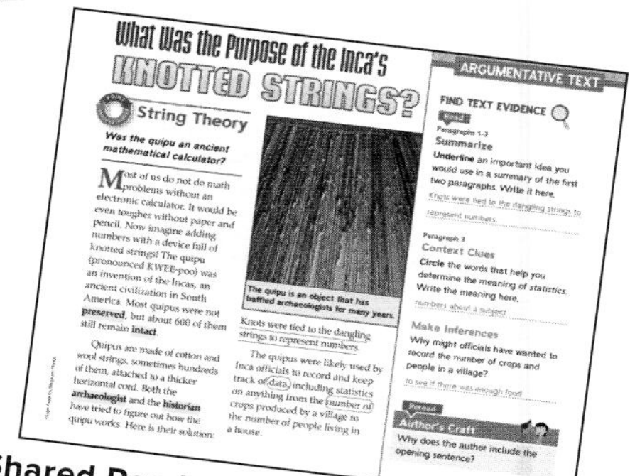

What Was the Purpose of the Inca's KNOTTED STRINGS?

ARGUMENTATIVE TEXT

String Theory

Was the quipu an ancient mathematical calculator?

Most of us do not do math problems without an electronic calculator. It would be even tougher without paper and pencil. Now imagine adding numbers with a device full of knotted strings! The quipu (pronounced KWEE-poo) was an invention of the Incas, an ancient civilization in South America. Most quipus were not **preserved**, but about 600 of them still remain **intact**.

Quipus are made of cotton and wool strings, sometimes hundreds of them, attached to a thicker horizontal cord. Both the **archaeologist** and the **historian** have tried to figure out how the quipu works. Here is their solution: Knots were tied to the dangling strings to represent numbers.

The quipu is an object that has baffled archaeologists for many years.

The quipus were likely used by Inca officials to record and keep track of data, including statistics on anything from the number of crops produced by a village to the number of people living in a house.

FIND TEXT EVIDENCE

Paragraphs 1-2
Summarize
Underline an important idea you would use in a summary of the first two paragraphs. **Write** it here.
Knots were tied to the dangling strings to represent numbers.

Paragraph 3
Context Clues
Circle the words that help you determine the meaning of *statistics*. **Write** the meaning here.
numbers about a subject

Make Inferences
Why might officials have wanted to record the number of crops and people in a village?
to see if there was enough food

Author's Craft
Why does the author include the opening sentence?

65

Shared Read
Reading/Writing Companion p. 65

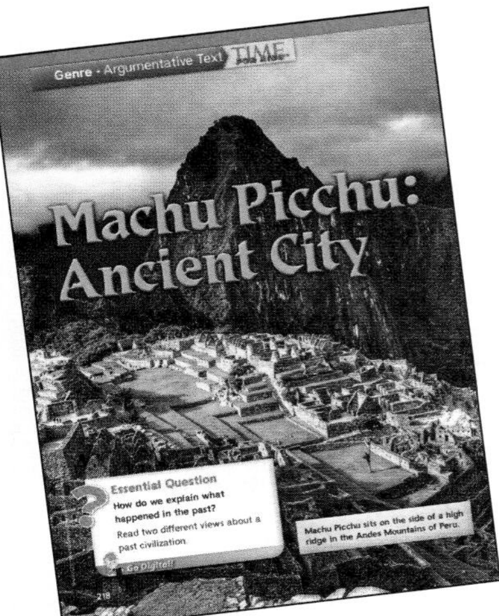
Genre • Argumentative Text
TIME
Machu Picchu: Ancient City
Essential Question
How do we explain what happened in the past?
Read two different views about a past civilization.
Go Digital!
Machu Picchu sits on the side of a high ridge in the Andes Mountains of Peru.
218

Anchor Text
Literature Anthology p. 218

Genre • Expository Text TIME

Compare Texts
Read about how historians use technology to gather information.

Dig This Technology!

In 1911, archaeologists found most of Machu Picchu covered by plants. This growth had to be cut back to see the structures. Artifacts from the site, however, were often harder to reach. At the time, researchers had to rely on a careful process of removing earth to reach artifacts.

New technology has changed that. Archaeologists can now analyze, explore, and even discover **remnants** of the past in other ways.

A big help to researchers of Machu Picchu today is the use of a 3-D scanner. They can use this machine to scan the site with laser beams and **reconstruct** the city as a digital three-dimensional picture.

222

Paired Selection
Literature Anthology p. 222

Essential Question

How do we explain what happened in the past?

Video People study Egyptian tombs, Stonehenge, and other mysterious artifacts to try and understand what happened in the past.

BLAST BACK! studysync

Study Sync Blast Many different theories have been posed about the origin of the Easter Island statues. Recently, archaeologists and scientists have developed a new conclusion based on evidence.

Interactive Read Aloud Stonehenge, a prehistoric stone monument, is a puzzle for historians, archaeologists, and other experts as they try to understand why it was built.

Shared Read Experts have different theories about the purpose of quipus.

Anchor Text Some believe Machu Picchu was once a royal estate because it's too small to be a city. Others believe that it was used as an astronomical observatory because the sun was important to the Incans.

Paired Selection Archaeologists can now analyze, explore, and even discover new remnants of the past, thanks to new technology.

Make Connections The paleontologist Norman Ross reconstructs a skeleton of a baby dinosaur for an exhibit so people can learn about the past.

Differentiated Sources

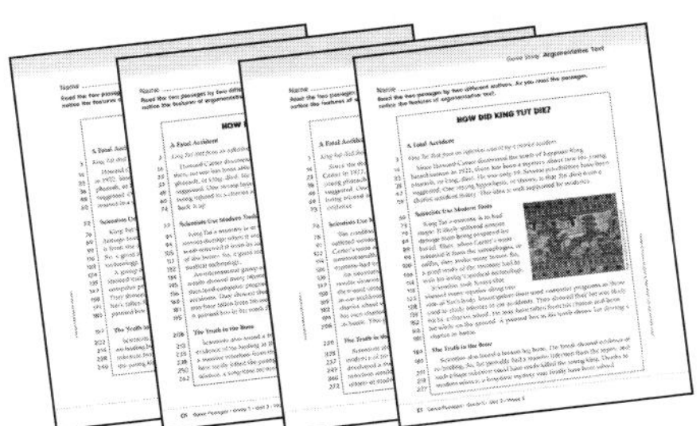

Leveled Readers

Evidence uncovered by archaeologists reveals information on how and where Ancestral Puebloans lived.

Differentiated Genre Passages

Nobody knows for certain how King Tut died, but more than one fact-based theory exists.

Build Knowledge Routine

After reading each text, ask students to document what facts and details they learned to help answer the Essential Question of the text set.

Talk About the source.

Write About the source.

Add to the Class Anchor Chart.

- Add to your Vocabulary List.

Show Your Knowledge

Write a Magazine Article

Have students show how they built knowledge across the text set by writing a magazine article. They should begin by thinking about the Essential Question: *How do we explain what happened in the past?* Students will write a magazine article about the importance of studying the past based on what they read.

Social Emotional Learning

Logic and Reasoning

Anchor Text: A student with strong reasoning skills is able to think critically and make decisions.
Ask: *What reasoning and facts have researchers used to determine Machu Picchu's purpose in the past?*

Paired Selection: Advancements in technology can help with logical thinking through discovery. Ask: *How do you think the use of GPR changed the opinions of experts studying Machu Picchu?*

Roundtable Discussion: What can we infer about the perspective shared by people who believe that Machu Picchu was a royal estate? How does this compare to the perspective shared by people who feel that it was used as an observatory?

Explore the Texts

Essential Question: How do we explain what happened in the past?

> **ACT** Access Complex Text (ACT) boxes throughout the text set provide scaffolded instruction for seven different elements that may make a text complex.

Teacher's Edition	Reading/Writing Companion	Literature Anthology	
	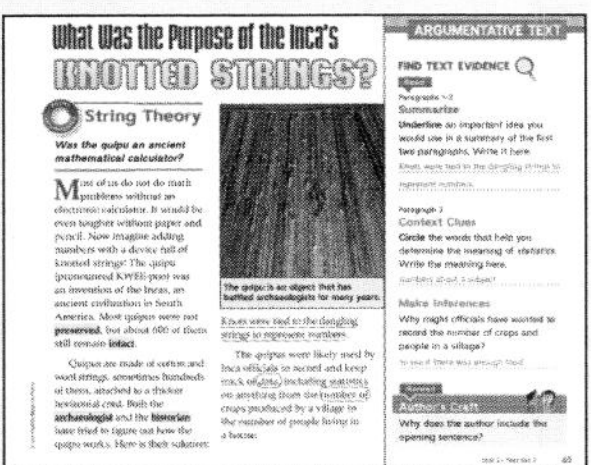		
"Stonehenge: Puzzle from the Past" Interactive Read Aloud p. T163 Argumentative Text	**"What Was the Purpose of Inca's Knotted Strings?"** Shared Read pp. 64–67 Argumentative Text	***Machu Picchu: Ancient City*** Anchor Text pp. 218–221 Argumentative Text	**"Dig This Technology!"** Paired Selection pp. 222–223 Expository Text
Qualitative			
Meaning/Purpose Moderate Complexity **Structure** Moderate Complexity **Language** Low Complexity **Knowledge Demands** Moderate Complexity	**Meaning/Purpose** Moderate Complexity **Structure** Moderate Complexity **Language** Moderate Complexity **Knowledge Demands** Low Complexity	**Meaning/Purpose** Moderate Complexity **Structure** Moderate Complexity **Language** Moderate Complexity **Knowledge Demands** Moderate Complexity	**Meaning/Purpose** Moderate Complexity **Structure** Moderate Complexity **Language** Low Complexity **Knowledge Demands** Moderate Complexity
Quantitative			
Lexile 940L	**Lexile** 920L	**Lexile** 990L	**Lexile** 970L
Reader and Task Considerations			
Reader Students might need some background knowledge to comprehend the mystery surrounding Stonehenge, its formation, and location in England.	**Reader** Explain that many Native American tribes preserve information from generation to generation through oral tradition. Note the difference between the oral tradition and telling a folktale.	**Reader** Students will need background knowledge of the Inca empire and the location of Machu Picchu. Help students recognize the two viewpoints and consider how both could be correct.	**Reader** Students will not need background knowledge to understand the text but may benefit from an overview on Machu Picchu.

Task The questions for the read aloud are supported by teacher modeling. The tasks provide a variety of ways for students to begin to build knowledge and vocabulary about the text set topic. The questions and tasks provided for the other texts are at various levels of complexity, ensuring that all students can interact with the text in meaningful ways.

Additional Texts

Content Area Reading BLMs
Additional online texts related to grade-level Science, Social Studies, and Arts content.

Leveled Readers

 (A) ***The Ancestral Puebloans***	 (O) ***The Ancestral Puebloans***	 (B) ***The Ancestral Puebloans***	 (ELL) ***The Ancestral Puebloans***
Qualitative			
Meaning/Purpose Moderate Complexity **Structure** Low Complexity **Language** Low Complexity **Knowledge Demands** Moderate Complexity	**Meaning/Purpose** Moderate Complexity **Structure** Low Complexity **Language** Moderate Complexity **Knowledge Demands** Moderate Complexity	**Meaning/Purpose** Moderate Complexity **Structure** Moderate Complexity **Language** Moderate Complexity **Knowledge Demands** High Complexity	**Meaning/Purpose** Moderate Complexity **Structure** Low Complexity **Language** Low Complexity **Knowledge Demands** Moderate Complexity
Quantitative			
Lexile 820L	**Lexile** 920L	**Lexile** 990L	**Lexile** 840L
Reader and Task Considerations			
Reader Students may need background knowledge about the location of the cliff houses. Identify Mesa Verde, Colorado.	**Reader** Students may need background knowledge about the location of the cliff houses. Identify Mesa Verde, Colorado.	**Reader** Students may need background knowledge about the location of the cliff houses. Identify Mesa Verde, Colorado.	**Reader** Students may need background knowledge about the location of the cliff houses. Identify Mesa Verde, Colorado.

Task The questions and tasks provided for the Leveled Readers are at various levels of complexity, ensuring that all students can interact with the text in meaningful ways.

Differentiated Genre Passages

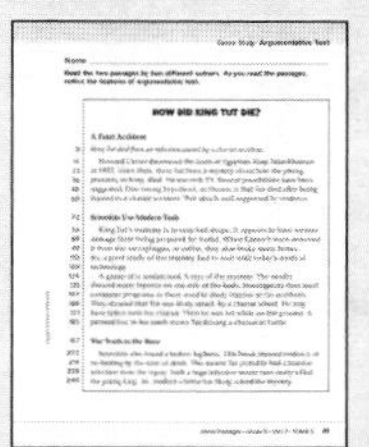 (A) "How Did King Tut Die?"	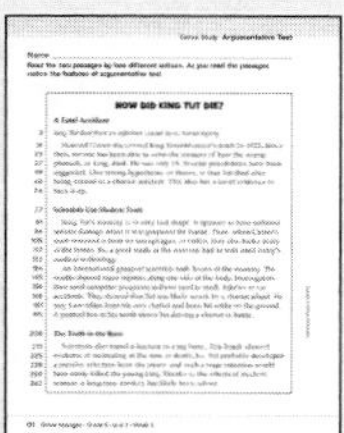 (O) "How Did King Tut Die?"	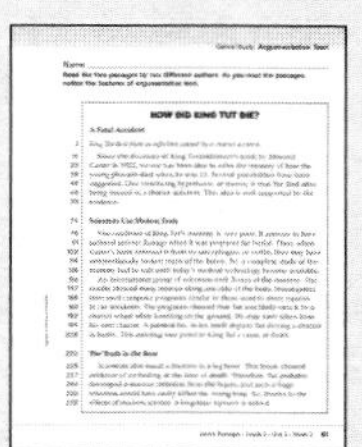 (B) "How Did King Tut Die?"	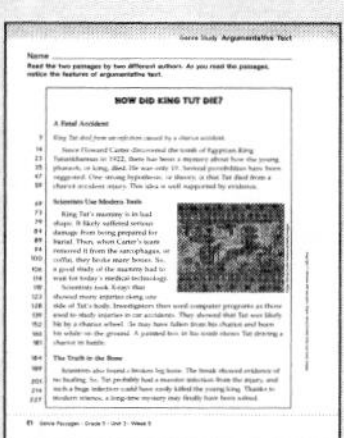 (ELL) "How Did King Tut Die?"
Qualitative			
Meaning/Purpose Moderate Complexity **Structure** Moderate Complexity **Language** Low Complexity **Knowledge Demands** Moderate Complexity	**Meaning/Purpose** Moderate Complexity **Structure** Moderate Complexity **Language** Low Complexity **Knowledge Demands** Moderate Complexity	**Meaning/Purpose** Moderate Complexity **Structure** Moderate Complexity **Language** Moderate Complexity **Knowledge Demands** Moderate Complexity	**Meaning/Purpose** Moderate Complexity **Structure** Moderate Complexity **Language** Low Complexity **Knowledge Demands** Moderate Complexity
Quantitative			
Lexile 750L	**Lexile** 860L	**Lexile** 960L	**Lexile** 830L
Reader and Task Considerations			
Reader Students will need background knowledge about King Tut.	**Reader** Students will need background knowledge about King Tut.	**Reader** Students will need background knowledge about King Tut.	**Reader** Students will need background knowledge about King Tut.

Task The questions and tasks provided for the Differentiated Genre Passages are at various levels of complexity, ensuring that all students can interact with the text in meaningful ways.

Week 5 Planner

Customize your own lesson plans at **my.mheducation.com**

Reading
Suggested Daily Time

READING LESSON GOALS

- **I can read and understand argumentative text.**
- **I can use text evidence to respond to argumentative text.**
- **I know how we can explain what happened in the past.**

SMALL GROUP OPTIONS The designated lessons can be taught in small groups. To determine how to differentiate instruction for small groups, use Formative Assessment and Data Dashboard.

Lesson 1	Lesson 2
Reading	
Introduce the Concept, T160–T161 Build Knowledge **Listening Comprehension, T162–T163** "Stonehenge: Puzzle from the Past" **Shared Read, T164–T167** Read "What Was the Purpose of the Inca's Knotted Strings?" Quick Write: Summarize **Vocabulary, T168–T169** Academic Vocabulary Sentence Clues **Expand Vocabulary, T196**	**Shared Read, T164–T167** Reread "What Was the Purpose of the Inca's Knotted Strings?" **Minilessons, T170–T177** Summarize Text Structure: Compare and Contrast Author's Claim Craft and Structure **Respond to Reading, T178–T179** **Phonics, T180–T181** *r*-controlled Vowel Syllables **Fluency, T180** Accuracy and Rate **Research and Inquiry, T182–T183** **Expand Vocabulary, T196**
Writing	
Extended Writing 2: Argumentative Essay	**Extended Writing 2, T242–T243** Analyze the Rubric
Writing Lesson Bank: Craft Minilessons, T260–T263	
Teacher and Peer Conferences	
Grammar Lesson Bank, T272 Irregular Verbs Talk About It **Spelling Lesson Bank, T282** *r*-controlled Vowel Syllables	**Grammar Lesson Bank, T272** Irregular Verbs Talk About It **Spelling Lesson Bank, T282** *r*-controlled Vowel Syllables

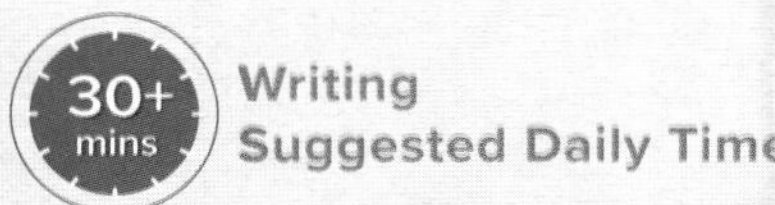

Writing
Suggested Daily Time

WRITING LESSON GOALS

I can write an argumentative essay.

Teacher-Led Instruction

Differentiated Reading

Leveled Readers
- *The Ancestral Puebloans,* T198–T199
- *The Ancestral Puebloans,* T208–T209
- *The Ancestral Puebloans,* T214–T215

Differentiated Genre Passages
- "How Did King Tut Die?," T200–T201
- "How Did King Tut Die?," T210–T211
- "How Did King Tut Die?," T216–T217

Differentiated Skills Practice

Approaching Level

Phonics/Decoding, T202–T203
- Decode and Build *r*-controlled Vowel Syllables 2
- Practice *r*-controlled Vowel Syllables

Vocabulary, T204–T205
- Review High-Frequency Words 2
- Review Academic Vocabulary 2
- Answer Yes/No Questions
- Sentence Clues

Fluency, T206
- Accuracy and Rate 2

Comprehension, T206–T207
- Author's Claim
- Self-Selected Reading

Independent/Collaborative Work See pages T159E–T159F.

Reading

Comprehension
- Argumentative Text
- Author's Claim
- Summarize

Fluency
Independent Reading

Phonics/Word Study

Phonics/Decoding
- *r*-controlled Vowel Syllables

Vocabulary
- Sentence Clues

Writing

Extended Writing 1: Argumentative Essay
Self-Selected Writing
Grammar
- Irregular Verbs

Spelling
- *r*-controlled Vowel Syllables

Handwriting

ACADEMIC VOCABULARY
archaeologist, era, fragments, historian, intact, preserved, reconstruct, remnants

SPELLING
perform, gentler, scissors, founder, director, danger, saucer, labor, peddler, error, crater, pillar, splendor, margin, professor, shatter, governor, vapor, equator, fonder

Review *terrible, legal, journal*
Challenge *refrigerator, remainder*
See pages T282-T283 for Differentiated Spelling Lists.

Reading

Lesson 3	Lesson 4	Lesson 5
Anchor Text, T184–T187 Read and Reread *Machu Picchu: Ancient City* Take Notes About Text **Respond to Reading, T188–T189** **Expand Vocabulary, T197**	**Paired Selection, T190–T191** Read and Reread "Dig This Technology!" **Author's Craft, T192–T193** Figurative Language **Expand Vocabulary, T197**	**Make Connections, T194** **Show Your Knowledge, T195** **Progress Monitoring, T159G–T159H** **Expand Vocabulary, T197**

Writing

Lesson 3	Lesson 4	Lesson 5
Extended Writing 2, T244–T245 Strong Conclusion	**Extended Writing 2, T246–T247** Analyze the Student Model	**Extended Writing 2, T248–T249** Analyze the Student Model
Writing Lesson Bank: Craft Minilessons, T260–T263		
Teacher and Peer Conferences		
Grammar Lesson Bank, T273 Irregular Verbs Talk About It **Spelling Lesson Bank, T283** *r*-controlled Vowel Syllables	**Grammar Lesson Bank, T273** Irregular Verbs Talk About It **Spelling Lesson Bank, T283** *r*-controlled Vowel Syllables	**Grammar Lesson Bank, T273** Irregular Verbs Talk About It **Spelling Lesson Bank, T283** *r*-controlled Vowel Syllables

On Level
Vocabulary, T212
- Review Vocabulary words
- Sentence Clues

Comprehension, T213
- Review Author's Claim
- Self-Selected Reading

Beyond Level
Vocabulary, T218
- Review Domain-Specific Words
- Sentence Clues

Comprehension, T219
- Review Author's Claim
- Self-Selected Reading GIFTED and TALENTED

English Language Learners
See ELL Small Group Guide, pp. 118–129

Content Area Connections

Content Area Reading
- Science, Social Studies, and the Arts

Research and Inquiry
- Investigating the Past

Inquiry Space
- Options for Project-Based Learning

English Language Learners
See ELL Small Group Guide, pp. 118–129

Independent and Collaborative Work

As you meet with small groups, the rest of the class completes activities and projects that allow them to practice and apply the skills they have been working on.

Student Choice and Student Voice

- Print the My Independent Work blackline master and review it with students. Identify the "Must Do" activities.
- Have students choose additional activities that provide the practice they need.
- Remind students to reflect on their learning each day.

Name ______ Unit 3 • Text Set 3

My Independent Work

	Reading	Phonics/Word Study	Writing
Center Activity Cards	Card: Activity:	Card: Activity:	Card: Activity:
Digital Activities my.mheducation.com	Activity:	Activity:	Activity:
Practice Pages	Content Area Reading:	Practice:	Practice:
Independent Choices	Independent Reading:	Activity:	Self-Selected Writing:

Grade 5 • My Independent Work 21

My Independent Work BLM

Reading

Independent Reading Texts

Students can choose a Center Activity Card to use while they read independently.

Classroom Library
Eight Dolphins of Katrina: A True Tale of Survival
Genre: Expository Text
Lexile: 710L

Kakapo Rescue: Saving the World's Strangest Parrot
Genre: Expository Text
Lexile: 950L

Unit Bibliography
Have students self-select independent reading texts about interesting or mysterious things from the past.

Leveled Texts Online
- Additional Leveled Readers in the **Leveled Reader Library Online** allow for flexibility.
- Six leveled sets of **Differentiated Genre Passages** in diverse genres are available.
- **Differentiated Texts** offer ELL students more passages at different proficiency levels.

Additional Literature
Differentiated Genre Passages
Genres: Personal Narrative, Social Studies Article, Fable, Myth, Legend, Tall Tale

Center Activity Cards

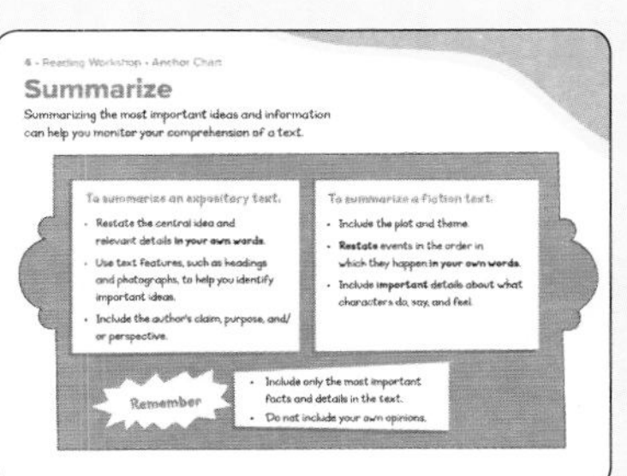

Summarize Card 4

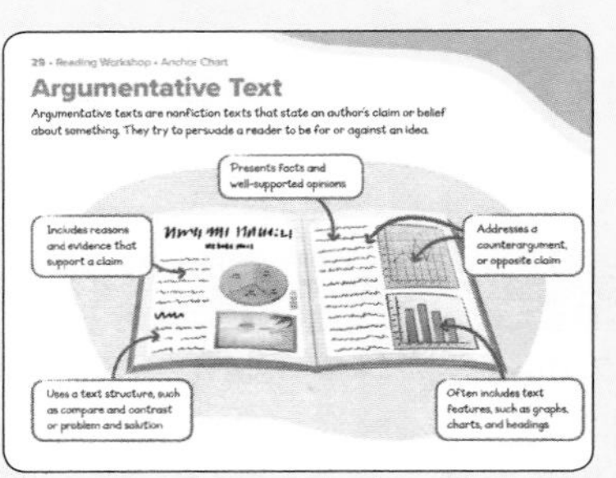

Argumentative Text Card 29

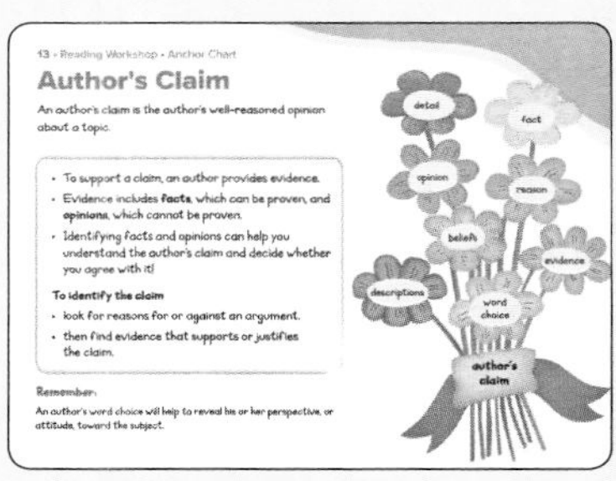

Author's Claim Card 13

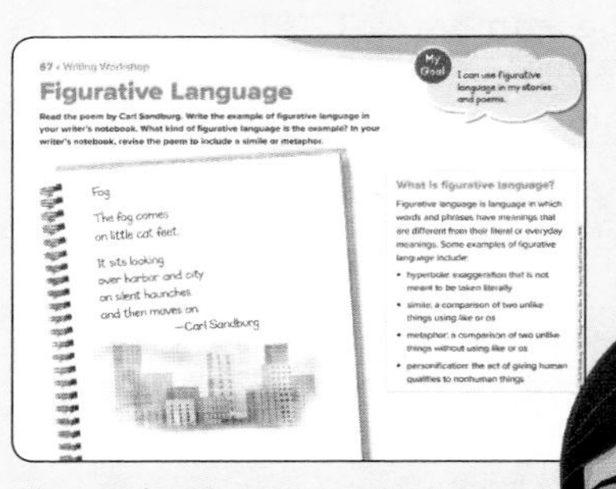

Figurative Language Card 67

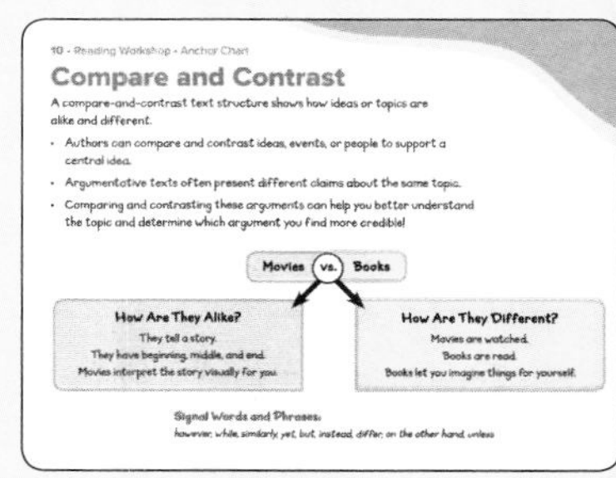

Compare and Contrast Card 10

Digital Activities

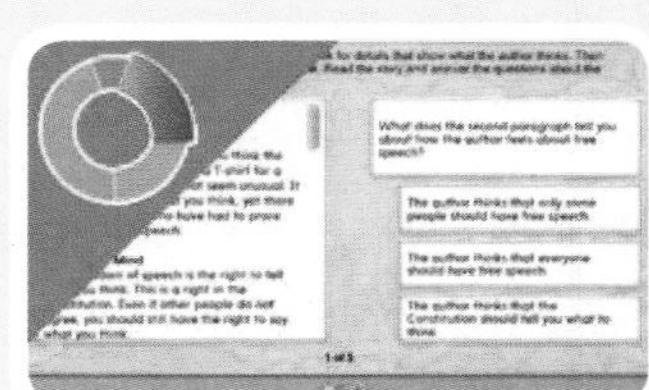

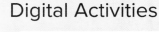

Comprehension

Phonics/Word Study

Center Activity Cards

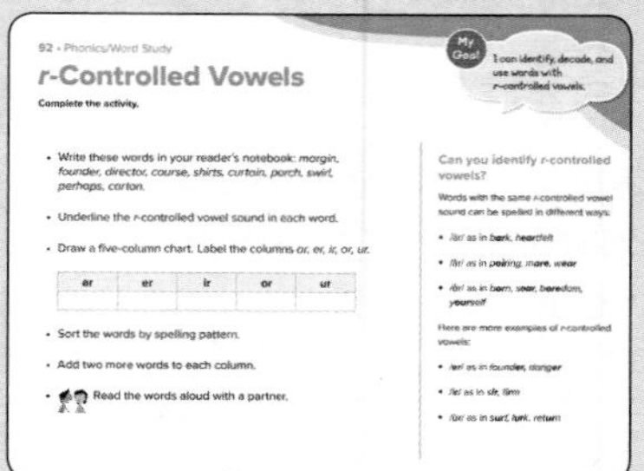
***r*-Controlled Vowels** Card 92

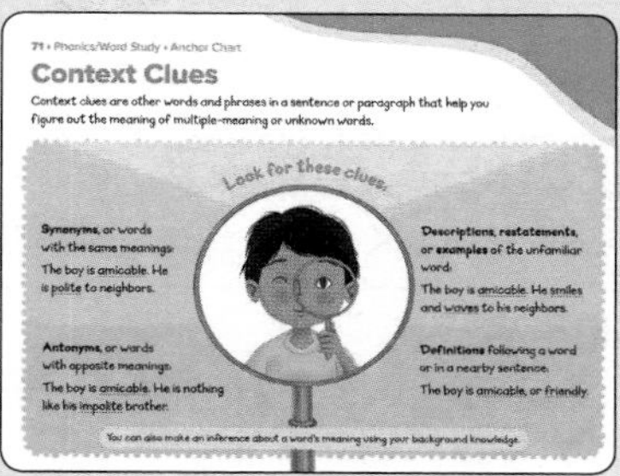
Context Clues Card 71

Practice Book BLMs

Phonics: pages 175–175B, 178

Vocabulary: pages 179–180

Digital Activities

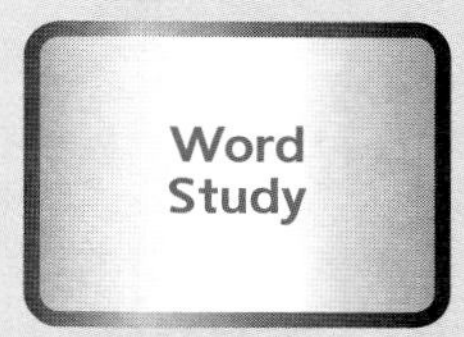

Phonics

Vocabulary

Writing

Center Activity Cards

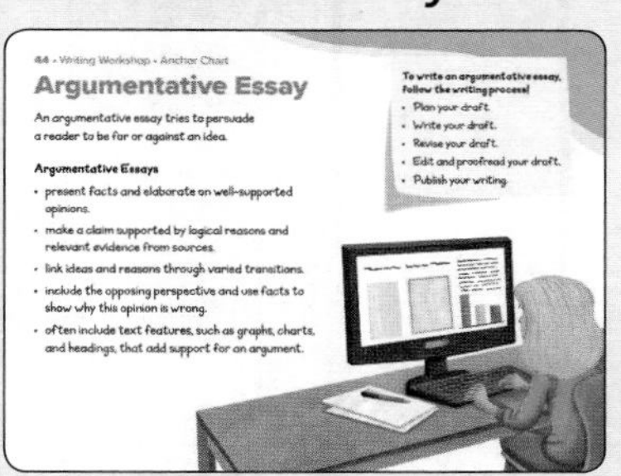
Argumentative Essay Card 44

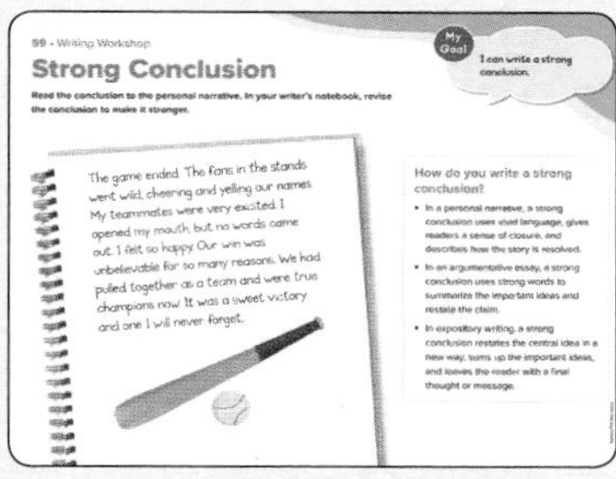
Strong Conclusion Card 59

Self-Selected Writing

Share the following prompts.

- How has an important discovery from the past helped the lives of people today?
- How do you think kids today are different from kids who lived in ancient times?
- Imagine that you lived during a time in the ancient past. Describe a day in your life.
- Describe how you think people who lived during ancient times entertained themselves.
- How do you think people who lived during ancient times expressed their creativity?

Extended Writing

Have students continue developing their **argumentative essays**.

Practice Book BLMs

Grammar: pages 169–173
Spelling: pages 174–178
Handwriting: pages 361–396

Digital Activities

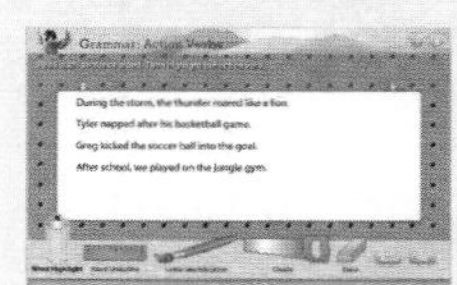
Grammar

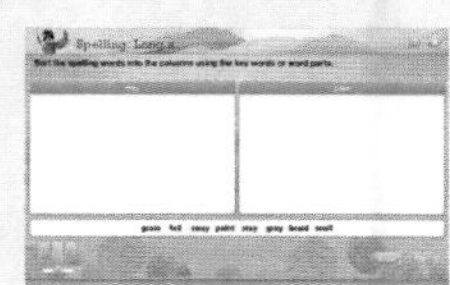
Spelling

Content Area Connections

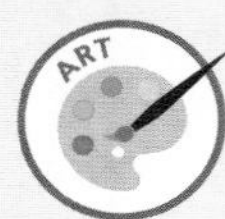

Content Area Reading Blackline Masters

- Additional texts related to Science, Social Studies, and the Arts

Research and Inquiry

- Investigating the Past

Inquiry Space

- Choose an activity

Progress Monitoring

Moving Toward Mastery

FORMATIVE ASSESSMENT
STUDENT CHECK-IN
CHECK FOR SUCCESS

For ongoing formative assessment, use students' self-assessments at the end of each lesson along with your own observations.

Assessing skills along the way . . .

SKILLS	HOW ASSESSED
Comprehension **Vocabulary**	Digital Activities, Rubrics
Text-Based Writing	Reading/Writing Companion: Respond to Reading
Grammar, Mechanics, Phonics, Spelling	Practice Book, Digital Activities including word sorts
Listening/Presenting/Research	Checklists
Oral Reading Fluency (ORF) Fluency Goal: 123–143 words correct per minute (WCPM) Accuracy Rate Goal: 95% or higher	Fluency Assessment

At the end of the text set . . .

SKILLS	HOW ASSESSED
Text Structure: Compare and Contrast **Author's Claim** **Figurative Language**	Progress Monitoring
Context Clues	

Making the Most of Assessment Results

Make data-based grouping decisions by using the following reports to verify assessment results. For additional student support options refer to the reteaching and enrichment opportunities.

ONLINE ASSESSMENT CENTER

- ***Gradebook***

DATA DASHBOARD

- ***Recommendations Report***
- ***Activity Report***
- ***Skills Report***
- ***Progress Report***
- ***Grade Card Report***

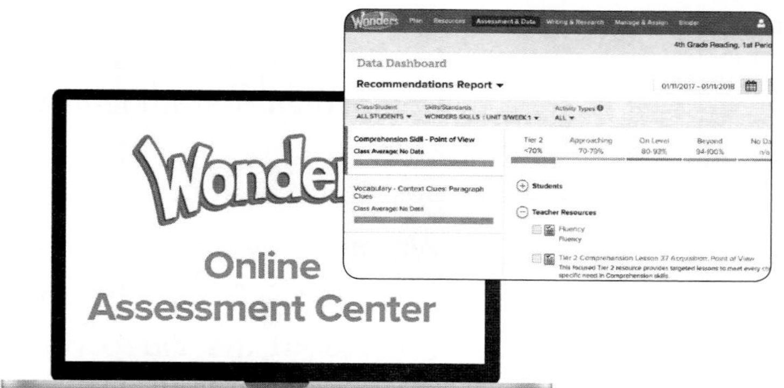

Assign practice pages online for auto-grading.

TIER 2

Reteaching Opportunities with Intervention Online PDFs

IF STUDENTS SCORE . . .	THEN ASSIGN . . .
below 70% in **comprehension . . .**	lessons 79–81 on Compare and Contrast in **Comprehension PDF,** lessons 64–66 on Author's Claim in **Comprehension PDF,** and/or lesson 130 on Figurative Language in **Comprehension PDF**
below 70% in **vocabulary . . .**	lesson 92 on Using Cause and Effect Relationship Clues in **Vocabulary PDF**
114–122 WCPM in **fluency . . .**	lessons from Section 1 or 7–10 of **Fluency PDF**
0–113 WCPM in **fluency . . .**	lessons from Sections 2–6 of **Fluency PDF**

Use the* Phonics/Word Study PDF *and* Foundational Skills Kit *for additional reteaching opportunities. Use the* Foundational Skills Kit *for students who need support with phonemic awareness and other early literacy skills.

Enrichment Opportunities

Beyond Level small group lessons and resources include suggestions for additional activities in these areas to extend learning opportunities for gifted and talented students:

- ***Leveled Readers***
- ***Genre Passages***
- ***Vocabulary***
- ***Comprehension***
- ***Leveled Reader Library Online***
- ***Center Activity Cards***

OBJECTIVES

Engage effectively in a range of collaborative discussions (one-on-one, in groups, and teacher-led) with diverse partners, building on others' ideas and expressing their own clearly.

Follow agreed-upon rules for discussions and carry out assigned roles

Pose and respond to specific questions by making comments that contribute to the discussion and elaborate on the remarks of others.

Build background knowledge on explaining the past.

ELA ACADEMIC LANGUAGE

- *explain, narrate, record, study*
- Cognates: *narrar, estudiar*

DIGITAL TOOLS

Show the image during class discussion.

Discuss Concept

Watch Video

 VOCABULARY

artifacts *(artefacto)* objects made by people long ago

relics *(reliquia)* objects from the past

technology *(tecnología)* the use of science to make things or to solve problems

unearthed *(desenterrado)* dug up from the ground

Build Knowledge

Essential Question

How do we explain what happened in the past?

Read the Essential Question on page 60 of the **Reading/Writing Companion.** Tell students that they will read argumentative texts to learn about events that happened in the past. Point out that scientists study the past to find out how people lived.

Watch the Video Play the video without sound first. Have partners narrate what they see. Then replay the video with sound as students listen.

Talk About the Video Have partners discuss how we explain what happened in the past.

Write About the Video Have students add their ideas to their Build Knowledge pages of their reader's notebooks.

Anchor Chart Begin a Build Knowledge anchor chart. Write the Essential Question at the top of the chart. Have volunteers share what they learned about how we explain what happened in the past and record their ideas. Explain that students will add to the anchor chart after they read each text.

Build Knowledge

Discuss the photograph on the opener with students. Focus on the woman trying to reconstruct the plate. Ask: *Why is this woman trying to put the plate back together? What significance might the plate have?* Have students discuss in pairs or groups.

Build Vocabulary

Model using the graphic organizer to write down new words related to studying the past. Have partners continue the discussion and add the graphic organizer and new words to their reader's notebooks. Students will add words to the Build Knowledge pages in their reader's notebooks as they read about studying the past throughout the text set.

Collaborative Conversations

Take Turns Talking As students engage in partner, small-group, and whole-class discussions, encourage them to follow discussion rules by taking turns speaking. Remind students to

- wait for a person to finish before they speak.
- raise their hand to let others know they would like to speak.
- ask others in the group to share their opinions.

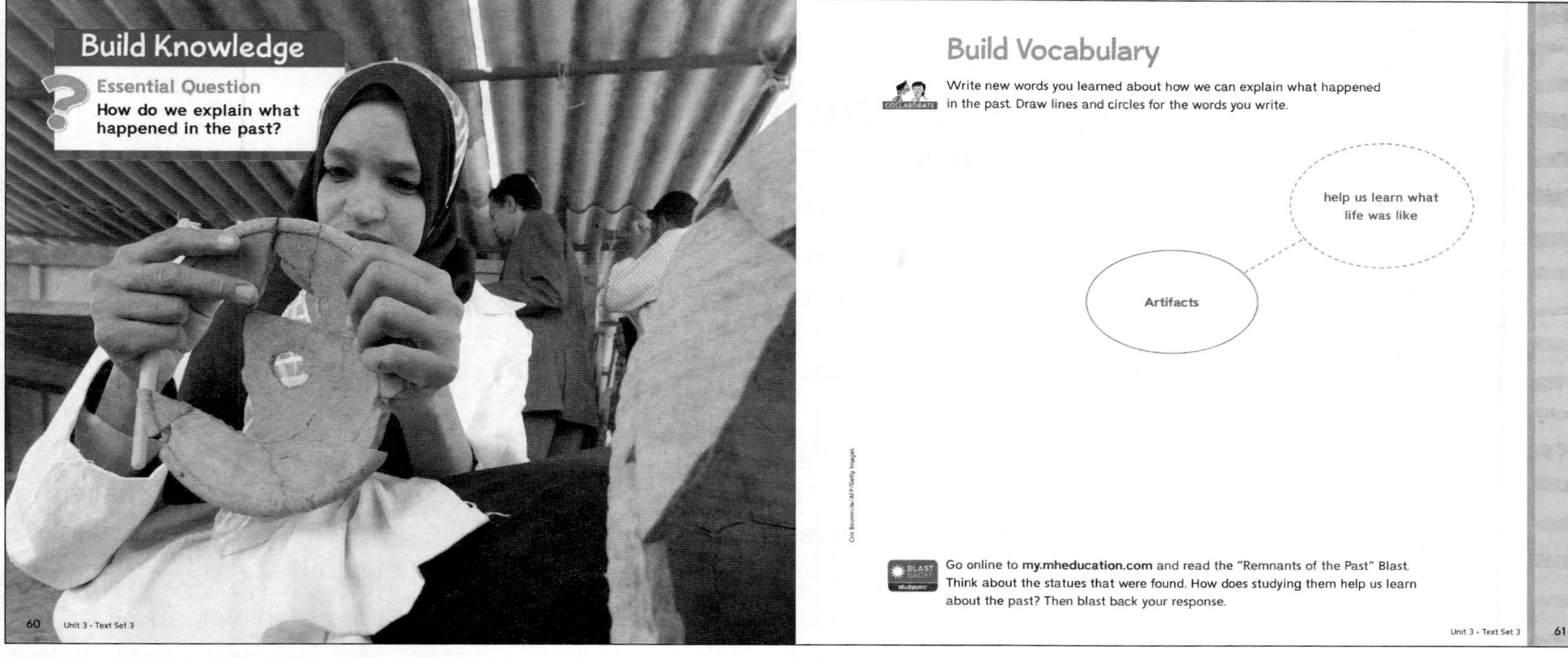

Build Knowledge
Essential Question
How do we explain what happened in the past?
60 Unit 3 • Text Set 3
Build Vocabulary
Write new words you learned about how we can explain what happened in the past. Draw lines and circles for the words you write.
help us learn what life was like
Artifacts
Go online to my.mheducation.com and read the "Remnants of the Past" Blast. Think about the statues that were found. How does studying them help us learn about the past? Then blast back your response.
Unit 3 • Text Set 3 61

Reading/Writing Companion, pp. 60–61

Share the "Remnants of the Past" Blast assignment. Point out that you will discuss their responses about the mystery on Easter Island in the Make Connections lesson at the end of this text set.

English Language Learners

Use the following scaffolds to build knowledge and vocabulary. Teach the ELL Vocabulary, as needed.

Beginning

Point to the artifact in the photograph. *Scientists study old objects, or artifacts. They want to know how people lived in the past.* Help generate a list of words and phrases to describe what the woman is doing. Then have them respond using: She is studying an artifact from the past. The artifact can tell how people lived.

Intermediate

Have students look at the photo. Check understanding of *reconstruct* and *artifact*. Use the following question and frames to help partners ask and answer questions about the photo: *What is the woman doing?* She is studying an artifact. *Why does she study artifacts?* She can reconstruct the artifact to learn about the past.

Advanced/Advanced High

Check understanding of *artifact*. Guide pairs as they brainstorm examples of artifacts. (answers will vary) Have partners describe the photo to confirm understanding of *reconstruct* and *artifact*.

 **NEWCOMERS**

To reinforce students' development of oral language and vocabulary, review **Newcomer Cards 5–14** and the accompanying materials in the **Newcomer Teacher's Guide**. For thematic connection, use **Newcomer Cards 15 and 24** and the accompanying materials.

MY GOALS ROUTINE

What I Know Now

Read Goals Have students read the goals on Reading/Writing Companion page 62.

Reflect Review the key. Ask students to reflect on each goal and fill in the bars to show what they know now. Explain that they will fill in the bars on page 63 at the end of the text set to show their progress.

LEARNING GOALS

We can actively listen to learn how people explain what happened in the past.

OBJECTIVES

Follow agreed-upon rules for discussions and carry out assigned roles.

Summarize a written text read aloud or information presented in diverse media and formats, including visually, quantitatively, and orally.

Determine or clarify the meaning of unknown and multiple-meaning words and phrases based on grade 5 reading and content, choosing flexibly from a range of strategies.

Listen for a purpose.

Identify characteristics of argumentative texts.

ELA ACADEMIC LANGUAGE

- *argumentative text, summarize*
- Cognate: *texto*

DIGITAL TOOLS

Read or play the Interactive Read Aloud.

Interactive Read Aloud

FORMATIVE ASSESSMENT

STUDENT CHECK-IN

Have partners discuss each author's claim about Stone Henge. Ask them to reflect using the Check-In routine.

Interactive Read Aloud

Connect to Concept: Into the Past

Tell students that the past sometimes presents challenging puzzles to solve for historians, archaeologists, and other experts. Let students know that you will be reading aloud a passage about Stonehenge, a prehistoric stone monument, and the efforts to solve the puzzle of why it was built.

Preview Argumentative Text

Anchor Chart Explain that the text you will read aloud is an argumentative text. Have students add characteristics of the genre to their Argumentative Text anchor chart. Review the features of argumentative texts:

- makes a claim, or argument, that clearly states an opinion about a topic. An opinion tells the author's perspective, or attitude, and beliefs about the topic.
- tries to persuade a reader to agree with the author's argument
- support their claims with logical facts, reasons, and evidence from multiple sources
- may include text features, such as diagrams

Ask them to think about other texts that they have read in class or independently that were argumentative texts.

Read and Respond

Read the text aloud to students. Then reread it using the Teacher Think Alouds and Student Think Alongs on page T163 to build knowledge and model comprehension and the vocabulary strategy Sentence Clues.

Summarize Have students summarize the central idea and relevant details from "Stonehenge: Puzzle from the Past." Have them take turns with a partner to restate relevant details in the point and counterpoint articles in ways that maintain meaning and logical order.

Build Knowledge: Make Connections

Talk About the Text Have partners discuss how people explain what happened in the past.

Write About the Text Have students add their ideas to their Build Knowledge pages of their reader's notebooks.

Anchor Chart Record any new ideas on the Build Knowledge anchor chart.

Add to the Vocabulary List Have students write down any words they learned about studying the past in their reader's notebooks.

Stonehenge: Puzzle from the Past

Claim: *Stonehenge is an ancient calendar.*

Constructed of huge stones arranged in a pattern of circles, mysterious Stonehenge is a remarkable prehistoric monument. People built it over several centuries between 3000 BC and 1500 BC. Located in southern England, some historians believe the monument may have been a type of ancient calendar.

A Date Set in Stone?

Why would people go to the effort of building such a complex structure? Some archaeologists have a theory that Stonehenge was created as a calendar in stone.

According to experts, the monument's arrangement of stones allowed people to track events such as the midsummer sunrise and midwinter sunset. This let them predict the changing seasons and to set dates for planting, harvesting, and worship.

Such activities were vitally important to the lives of ancient people. Stonehenge allowed people to plan for these events. (1)

Counterclaim: *Stonehenge is a healing place.*

Built more than 3,500 years ago, Stonehenge is one of the world's most talked about human constructions. The skills needed to build this enormous stone monument were highly sophisticated. Historians today debate the reasons Stonehenge was created.

The Secret Is in the Stone

Stonehenge is made of two kinds of rocks: a local sandstone and bluestone, a type of rock found 150 miles from the site. People went to a great deal of effort to bring the bluestones to the construction site.

Some researchers say that, according to folklore, bluestone has healing powers. Their theory about Stonehenge is that the use of bluestones indicates the monument is where sick people came to be healed. (2)

Stonehenge Burials

Graves discovered in the area are another reason some archaeologists think Stonehenge was a healing site. The skeletons of numerous people buried near the monument show signs of injury or disease. Clearly those traveling to Stonehenge came with the hope of a cure. (3)

(1) Teacher Think Aloud

I can summarize the first paragraph by noting that Stonehenge is a prehistoric monument that some historians believe may have been a type of calendar.

Student Think Along

What evidence suggests that Stonehenge is an ancient calendar? Listen as I reread the section "A Date Set in Stone?". Pay attention to the most important details and summarize them to a partner in your own words.

(2) Teacher Think Aloud

As I read the counterclaim, I notice an unfamiliar word: *sophisticated*. I can use sentence clues to help me determine its meaning. Since Stonehenge is huge and required a certain level of skill to build, I can determine that *sophisticated* means *complex*.

Student Think Along

Use sentence clues to determine the meaning of *theory* in "The Secret Is in the Stone." Raise your hand when you hear the clues.

(3) Teacher Think Aloud

After reading the claim and counterclaim, I can summarize how different historians explain Stonehenge. This will help me understand both arguments and decide which is more convincing.

Student Think Along

Which claim do you think is more convincing? Turn to a partner and summarize the claim that you think is more convincing. Then discuss how people explain what happened in the past.

"What Was the Purpose of the Inca's Knotted Strings?"

Lexile 920L

LEARNING GOALS

We can read and understand argumentative text.

OBJECTIVES

Quote accurately from a text when explaining what the text says explicitly and when drawing inferences from the text. Identify the author's purpose.

Determine two or more central, or main, ideas of a text and explain how they are supported by relevant, or key, details; summarize the text.

Explain how an author uses reasons and evidence to support particular points in a text, identifying which reasons and evidence support which point(s).

Read with sufficient accuracy and fluency to support comprehension. Read grade-level text with purpose and understanding.

 Identify different points of view about an issue, topic, or current event.

Close Reading Routine

Read DOK 1–2

- Identify important ideas and details.
- Take notes and summarize.
- Use ACT prompts as needed.

Reread DOK 2–3

- Analyze the text, craft, and structure.
- Use the **Reread minilessons** and **prompts.**

Integrate DOK 3–4

- Integrate knowledge and ideas.
- Make text-to-text connections.
- Use the Integrate lesson.
- Complete the Show Your Knowledge task.
- Inspire action.

Read

SHARED READ

My Goal I can read and understand argumentative text.

TAKE NOTES

As you read, make note of interesting words and important information.

64 Unit 3 • Text Set 3

Essential Question

How do we explain what happened in the past?

Read two different views about the uses of a fascinating object.

The Inca Empire was centered in what is now Peru. It was taken by Spanish conquest in the middle of the 16th century.

Reading/Writing Companion, pp. 64–65

Set a Purpose Have students first think about the Essential Question, and what they know about how people study the past, and then set a purpose for reading. After students preview titles, subheads, and visuals of both articles, have them write a question about the text in the left column of page 64. As they read, they can list interesting words they learn and record important details.

Focus on the Read prompts now. For additional support, use the extra prompts not included in the **Reading/Writing Companion**. Use the Reread prompts during the Craft and Structure lesson on pages T176–T177. Preteach vocabulary words to students who need support.

DIFFERENTIATED READING

Approaching Level Complete all Read prompts together.

On Level Have pairs read the text and answer Read prompts.

Beyond Level After pairs explain their responses, have them analyze how the photos and diagrams support the prompts.

English Language Learners Preteach the vocabulary. Have Beginning and Early-Intermediate ELLs listen to the summary of the selection, available in multiple languages, and use the **Scaffolded Shared Read**. For small group support, see the **ELL Small Group Guide**.

What Was the Purpose of the Inca's KNOTTED STRINGS?

String Theory

Was the quipu an ancient mathematical calculator?

Most of us do not do math problems without an electronic calculator. It would be even tougher without paper and pencil. Now imagine adding numbers with a device full of knotted strings! The quipu (pronounced KWEE-poo) was an invention of the Incas, an ancient civilization in South America. Most quipus were not **preserved**, but about 600 of them still remain **intact**.

Quipus are made of cotton and wool strings, sometimes hundreds of them, attached to a thicker horizontal cord. Both the **archaeologist** and the **historian** have tried to figure out how the quipu works. Here is their solution:

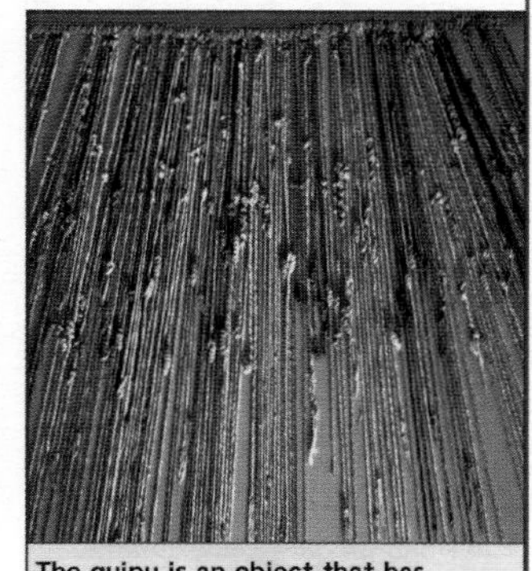

The quipu is an object that has baffled archaeologists for many years.

Knots were tied to the dangling strings to represent numbers.

The quipus were likely used by Inca officials to record and keep track of data, including statistics on anything from the number of crops produced by a village to the number of people living in a house.

ARGUMENTATIVE TEXT

FIND TEXT EVIDENCE 

Read

Paragraphs 1–2
Summarize
Underline an important idea you would use in a summary of the first two paragraphs. Write it here.
Knots were tied to the dangling strings to represent numbers.

Paragraph 3
Context Clues
Circle the words that help you determine the meaning of *statistics*. Write the meaning here.
numbers about a subject

Make Inferences
Why might officials have wanted to record the number of crops and people in a village?
to see if there was enough food

Reread

Author's Craft
Why does the author include the opening sentence?

Unit 3 • Text Set 3 65

Summarize DOK 1

Paragraphs 1–2: *What central idea would you use in a summary of the first two paragraphs?*

Think Aloud: To find the central idea of paragraphs 1 and 2, I will first look for the most important idea in each paragraph. In the first paragraph, I read that the quipu was a tool the Incas used to add numbers. In the second paragraph, I learn that knots tied on the quipu represented numbers. I can combine those two big ideas: Ancient Incas used the quipu to represent and add numbers. Have students discuss how details in paragraph 3 might affect the central idea they generated.

Context Clues DOK 2

Paragraph 3: *Which words help you determine the meaning of* statistics*?*

Think Aloud: The word *including* right before *statistics* tells me that the statistics are part of a larger group. I reread and discover that they were part of the data that Inca officials might have recorded and kept track of. So *statistics* are data, or numbers that people study. When I read on, I learn that the statistics represented numbers of crops and people. Have students discuss how the quipu might have helped keep track of statistical data.

Make Inferences DOK 2

Paragraph 3: Read paragraph 3. Ask: *Why might it be important to keep track of the number of crops an area produces?* (Possible answers: to make sure the area is producing enough food for people to eat; to determine if the area is suitable for farming) *Who might find it useful to have statistics on how many people live in a house?* (Possible answers: someone who designs or builds houses; someone who provides food and supplies to the people in the houses) Discuss how the reasons for collecting and analyzing statistics on crops and population might have changed from the time of the Incas to present day.

Check for Understanding DOK 2

Page 65: Monitor understanding of the role of archaeologists and historians in trying to determine how the quipu works. Ask: *Why might researchers think the quipu was used to represent numbers?* (They know that the Inca didn't use paper or pencils or keep written records. They also know that the Inca empire was large, and there had to be a way to keep track of information. The researchers could use these facts to draw a conclusion about the use of the quipu.) *Why don't they know for sure?* (There aren't any written records, and many of the quipus were probably lost or destroyed.)

Spotlight on Language

Page 65, Paragraph 1 Read the first two sentences with students. Help them clarify what the pronoun *It* in the second sentence refers to. (doing math problems without a calculator) Discuss the clues in the second sentence that help them. (even tougher without paper and pencil) Point to the phrase *even tougher* and explain that we use *even* to indicate that it is tougher than usual.

Context Clues DOK 2

Paragraph 1: Point out the word *power* in paragraph 1. Ask: *How can you tell that the meaning of* power *in this context is not "strength"?* (*Power* is used to describe how groups of knots on the quipu connect to the number 10.) *Use context to determine the correct meaning.* (The next sentence says that knots could stand for ones, tens, hundreds, and thousands. So "a power of 10" is the number of times that 10 is multiplied by itself.)

Author's Claim DOK 2

Paragraphs 1–2: Ask: *How does the author's choice of words in paragraph 2 indicate an opinion about the quipu?* (The author says that it is "clear," or very obvious, that the quipu was an "amazing low-tech calculator.") *What do these words indicate about the author's perspective?* (The author admires the quipu and the Inca's ability to create a simple, yet useful, device.)

Check for Understanding DOK 2

Paragraph 2: Read the information in the diagram and caption. Ask: *How does the information in the diagram make the author's claim more credible?* (The diagram demonstrates how to use the quipu to count and add numbers.)

Read

SHARED READ

FIND TEXT EVIDENCE

Read

Paragraphs 1–2

Author's Claim

Underline the sentence that states the first author's claim about the quipu. Discuss why a quipu was amazing.

The quipu was a low-tech calculator.

Paragraphs 3–4

Summarize

What important idea would connect paragraphs three and four in a summary of "Spinning a Yarn"?

The quipu may have been used by the Incas to keep their empire together.

Reread

Author's Craft

Why does the author of "String Theory" include the illustration?

66 Unit 3 • Text Set 3

TIME KIDS

1	4	0	5
3	1	0	5
2	7	3	2

132 + 417 + 3 = 552

Top Knots = 100s
Middle Knots = 10s
Bottom Knots = 1s

Follow the illustration to understand how to count with a quipu.

Here is how a quipu would work: Each group of knots on a string represents a power of 10. Depending on their position, knots can stand for ones, tens, hundreds, and thousands. Clusters of knots increase in value the higher they are on the string. As a result, Incas with special training could add up the knots on a string to get the sum. They could also add up the total of many strings or even many quipus.

The patterns of the knots show repeating numbers. When you add it all up, it seems clear that the quipu was nothing less than an amazing low-tech calculator.

Spinning a Yarn

The Incas had a 3D language written in thread!

Questions surround the Inca civilization. In its peak **era**—the middle of the 1400s—the Incas built thousands of miles of roads over mountains, and yet they didn't have wheeled vehicles. They made houses of stone blocks that fit together perfectly without mortar, a bonding material. The biggest question may be how the Incas kept their empire together without a written language.

The answer to the last question might be an odd-looking object called a quipu. Only a few hundred of these **remnants** of the Inca culture still exist.

Researchers discuss a quipu.

Reading/Writing Companion, pp. 66–67

Summarize DOK 1

Paragraphs 3–4: Ask: *Which question posed in paragraph 3 is addressed in paragraph 4? Explain.* (Paragraph 4 says that the quipu may solve the "last question" posed in paragraph 3, which is how the Inca empire was able to exist without a written language.) *How does this help you state an important idea that connects the paragraphs?* (Paragraph 4 indicates that the quipu might have been used as a written language that kept the Inca empire together, or allowed it to exist.)

Access Complex Text

Connection of Ideas

Reiterate that many Native American tribes pass down and preserve information through oral tradition. Ask: *How is telling a tribal history different from telling a folktale?* (Native American oral tradition is a recollection of real-life facts about their tribe's history. Folktales are fictional stories meant to teach a lesson.)

How might quipus be related to the oral history of the Incas? (They may have been a visual form of language used to reinforce oral tradition.)

Quipus are made of wool strings that hang from a thick cord. On the strings are groups of knots. Many researchers believe the knots stand for numbers—even though no evidence supports this. But others make a strong case that the knots of the quipu were really language symbols, or a form of language.

Researchers found an identical three-knot pattern in the strings of seven different quipus. They think the order of the knots is code for the name of an Incan city. They hope to **reconstruct** the quipu code based on this and other repeating patterns of knots.

More conclusive proof that the quipu is a language comes from an old manuscript, a series of handwritten pages from the 17th century. It was found in a box holding **fragments** of a quipu. The author of the manuscript says the quipus were woven symbols. The manuscript even matches up the symbols to a list of words.

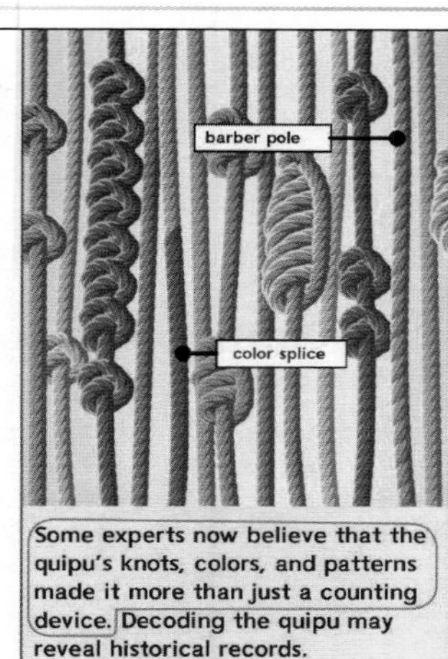

Some experts now believe that the quipu's knots, colors, and patterns made it more than just a counting device. Decoding the quipu may reveal historical records.

The Inca empire covered nearly 3,000 miles. Perhaps the strings of the quipu helped hold it together.

Summarize

Use your notes and the illustrations to orally summarize important details and the central idea of each opinion text.

ARGUMENTATIVE TEXT

FIND TEXT EVIDENCE

Read

Paragraphs 1–4

Author's Claim

Draw a box around the author's claim about quipus in the first paragraph.

Underline the evidence that supports this claim.

Diagrams

Circle information under the illustration that suggests an explanation for the quipu's knots. What does the illustration suggest?

The different knots and colors suggest that the quipu was a form of language.

Reread

Author's Craft

How does the illustration support the author's claim?

Unit 3 • Text Set 3 67

Author's Claim DOK 2

Paragraph 1: Read the first paragraph. Ask: *Does this author make the same claim as the author of "String Theory"? Explain.* (No. The author of "Spinning a Yarn" claims that "no evidence supports" the first author's claim that the quipu was used as a calculator.) *Why do you think this author brings up the claim expressed by the previous author?* (The author wants to first present an existing claim to then respond to it and oppose it.)

Organization

Remind students that text features can help them understand each author's claim. *How do the photos, captions, and diagrams support each claim?* (The photo, caption, and diagram on pages 65 and 66 support the first author's claim that the quipu was an ancient calculator. The photo, caption, and diagram on pages 66 and 67 support the second claim that the quipu was used as a form of language.)

Text Features: Diagram DOK 2

Remind students that a diagram helps readers easily picture and understand details that support an author's claim. Ask: *How does the diagram on page 67 differ from the diagram on page 66?* (It shows the different colors of the quipu; it labels parts of the quipu rather than numbers that the knots might represent.) *How do these differences help the author support a claim?* (The illustration helps readers see the colors and patterns in the quipu, which supports the idea that it was used for language rather than math.)

Summarize

Quick Write After their initial reads, have student pairs summarize the text orally using their notes. Then have them write a summary of the topic and the opposing claims presented in their reader's notebooks. Remind them only to include relevant details about each author's claim. Students may decide to digitally record presentations of their summaries.

ELL Spotlight on Idioms

Page 67, Paragraph 4 Help students understand the author's use of *hold it together.* Read the last sentence. *How big was the Inca empire?* (nearly 3,000 miles) *The Inca had no written language. Would it be easy or difficult for them to communicate?* (difficult) *What does the author mean when he or she says the* quipu *held the empire together?* The quipus helped the Inca communicate across their large empire.

FORMATIVE ASSESSMENT

STUDENT CHECK-IN

Have partners share their summaries from Reading/Writing page 67. Ask them to reflect using the Check-In routine.

LEARNING GOALS

- We can use new vocabulary words to read and understand argumentative text.
- We can use context clues to figure out the meaning of unfamiliar and multiple-meaning words.

OBJECTIVES

Determine the meaning of general academic and domain-specific words and phrases in a text relevant to a grade 5 topic or subject area.

Determine or clarify the meaning of unknown and multiple-meaning words and phrases, choosing flexibly from a range of strategies.

Use context to confirm or self-correct word recognition and understanding, rereading as necessary.

ELA ACADEMIC LANGUAGE

- *context, familiar, multiple*
- Cognates: *contexto, familiar, múltiple*

DIGITAL TOOLS

Visual Vocabulary Cards

TEACH IN SMALL GROUP

Academic Vocabulary

Approaching Level and **ELL** Preteach the words before beginning the Shared Read.

On Level Have students look up the definition of each word in the online **Visual Glossary**.

Beyond Level Ask pairs to write an additional context sentence for each word.

Reread

Academic Vocabulary

Use the routine on the **Visual Vocabulary Cards** to introduce each word.

An **archaeologist** is someone who studies ancient cities and artifacts.

An **era** is a period of time or history.

Fragments are small, broken pieces.

Cognate: *fragmentos*

A **historian** is a person who knows a great deal about history.

Cognate: *historiador(a)*

Something that is **intact** is whole or complete.

Cognate: *intacto*

Something that is **preserved** is protected so that it doesn't get damaged.

When you **reconstruct** something, you put its parts back together.

Cognate: *reconstruir*

Remnants are small pieces or parts of something that are left over.

Encourage students to use their newly acquired vocabulary in their discussions and written responses about the texts in this text set.

Context Clues

1 Explain

Explain that when students come across a word whose meaning they do not know, they can focus on more familiar words, descriptions, or examples within the sentence. These sentence clues can help them determine the meaning of the unfamiliar or multiple-meaning words. Have students add to the Context Clues anchor chart.

2 Model

Use sentence clues to determine the meaning of *calculator* in the first paragraph of "String Theory" on **Reading/Writing Companion** page 65. Point out that *do math problems* and *electronic* point to the meaning of *calculator*: "a mini-computer that solves math problems."

3 Guided Practice

Help student pairs use sentence clues to determine the meanings of *patterns* on page 66 and *manuscript* on page 67. Circulate as partners reread the text and identify context clues that will help them find the meanings of the words. Discuss pairs' findings with the class.

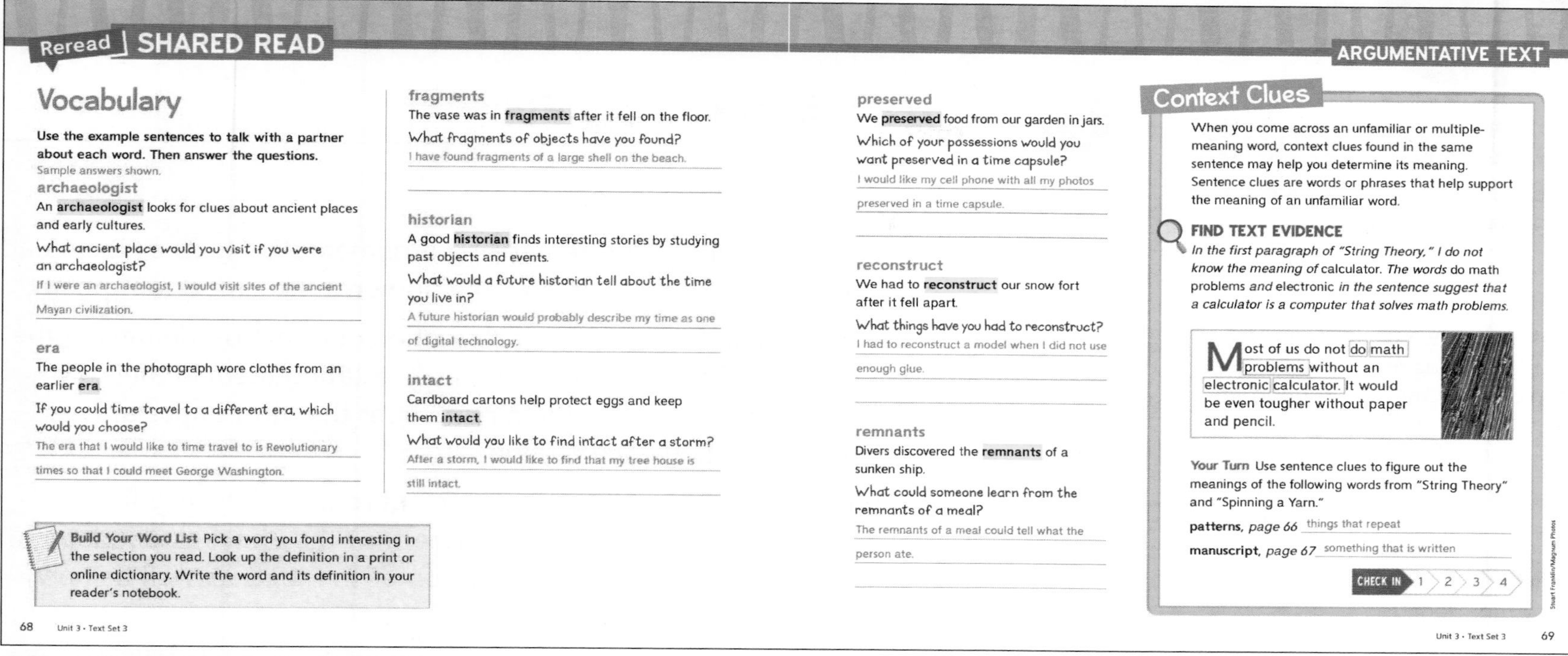
Reread SHARED READ

ARGUMENTATIVE TEXT

Vocabulary

Use the example sentences to talk with a partner about each word. Then answer the questions.

Sample answers shown.

archaeologist

An **archaeologist** looks for clues about ancient places and early cultures.

What ancient place would you visit if you were an archaeologist?

If I were an archaeologist, I would visit sites of the ancient Mayan civilization.

era

The people in the photograph wore clothes from an earlier **era**.

If you could time travel to a different era, which would you choose?

The era that I would like to time travel to is Revolutionary times so that I could meet George Washington.

fragments

The vase was in **fragments** after it fell on the floor.

What fragments of objects have you found?

I have found fragments of a large shell on the beach.

historian

A good **historian** finds interesting stories by studying past objects and events.

What would a future historian tell about the time you live in?

A future historian would probably describe my time as one of digital technology.

intact

Cardboard cartons help protect eggs and keep them **intact**.

What would you like to find intact after a storm?

After a storm, I would like to find that my tree house is still intact.

Build Your Word List Pick a word you found interesting in the selection you read. Look up the definition in a print or online dictionary. Write the word and its definition in your reader's notebook.

68 Unit 3 • Text Set 3

preserved

We **preserved** food from our garden in jars.

Which of your possessions would you want preserved in a time capsule?

I would like my cell phone with all my photos preserved in a time capsule.

reconstruct

We had to **reconstruct** our snow fort after it fell apart.

What things have you had to reconstruct?

I had to reconstruct a model when I did not use enough glue.

remnants

Divers discovered the **remnants** of a sunken ship.

What could someone learn from the remnants of a meal?

The remnants of a meal could tell what the person ate.

Context Clues

When you come across an unfamiliar or multiple-meaning word, context clues found in the same sentence may help you determine its meaning. Sentence clues are words or phrases that help support the meaning of an unfamiliar word.

FIND TEXT EVIDENCE

In the first paragraph of "String Theory," I do not know the meaning of calculator. *The words* do math problems *and* electronic *in the sentence suggest that a calculator is a computer that solves math problems.*

Most of us do not do math problems without an electronic calculator. It would be even tougher without paper and pencil.

Your Turn Use sentence clues to figure out the meanings of the following words from "String Theory" and "Spinning a Yarn."

patterns, *page 66* things that repeat

manuscript, *page 67* something that is written

CHECK IN 1 2 3 4

Unit 3 • Text Set 3 69

Reading/Writing Companion, pp. 68–69

English Language Learners

Use the following scaffolds with **Guided Practice**. For small group support, see the **ELL Small Group Guide**.

Beginning

Read paragraph 3 on page 67 of **Reading/Writing Companion** with students. Have them circle the word *manuscript*. Say: *Let's use clues in the sentence to figure out the meaning of* manuscript. Help partners identify the words *handwritten pages* in the sentence. Then have them discuss the meaning of *manuscript* using: A manuscript is something written. Repeat for *patterns* on page 66.

Intermediate

Have partners read paragraph 3 on page 67 of **Reading/Writing Companion**. Ask: *Which words in the first sentence explain the meaning of manuscript?* (handwritten pages) Have partners identify the two words in *handwritten*. Then have them ask each other questions about manuscripts: How are pages in a manuscript created? The pages are handwritten. What does handwritten mean? People write on the pages by hand. Repeat for *patterns* on page 66.

Advanced/Advanced High

Have students read paragraph 3 on page 67. Have partners point out which words or phrases in the first sentence helps clarify the meaning of *manuscript*. Then have them discuss the meaning of *manuscript*. Repeat for *patterns* on page 66.

BUILD YOUR WORD LIST

Students might choose *dangling* from page 65. Have them use a thesaurus to explore the meaning by locating a synonym or an antonym.

FORMATIVE ASSESSMENT

STUDENT CHECK-IN

Academic Vocabulary Ask partners to share two answers from Reading/Writing Companion pages 68–69.

Context Clues Ask partners to share their Your Turn responses on page 69.

Have students use the Check-In routine to reflect and fill in the bars.

CHECK FOR SUCCESS

Rubric Use your online rubric to record student progress.

Can students identify and use sentence-level context clues to determine the meanings of *patterns* and *manuscript*?

Small Group Instruction

If No

- **Approaching** Reteach p. T205

If Yes

- **On** Review p. T212
- **Beyond** Extend p. T218

Reread

Summarize

LEARNING GOALS

We can summarize to understand argumentative text.

OBJECTIVES

Determine two or more central, or main, ideas of a text and explain how they are supported by relevant, or key, details; summarize the text.

Analyze multiple accounts of the same event or topic, noting important similarities and differences in the point of view they represent.

ELA ACADEMIC LANGUAGE

- *argumentative, summarize, compare, similarity, difference, claim*
- Cognates: *comparar, similaridad, diferencia*

1 Explain

Explain to students that summarizing argumentative texts as they read can help them keep track of how the authors make important points.

- Students should summarize each section of a text by identifying the central ideas and relevant details and restating them in their own words. Doing so will help them remember the most important information within each section.
- Students should also summarize the entire text after they finish reading it. This step will help ensure that they have understood all of the relevant ideas in each section of the text, as well as how the ideas are connected.

Point out that summarizing a text can also help students compare the author's claims, or arguments, presented in different texts on the same topic, such as "String Theory"on pages 65–66 of the **Reading/ Writing Companion** and "Spinning a Yarn" on pages 66–67.

Anchor Chart Have a volunteer add any additional points about the strategy to the Summarize anchor chart.

2 Model

Using "String Theory," model how to summarize the author's claim regarding how the quipu might have been used. Identify relevant details that should be included in the summary, such as what the knots on the strings of the quipu may have represented, what purposes the quipu served, and how the quipu may have worked.

3 Guided Practice

Circulate as pairs of students summarize the claim in "Spinning a Yarn" by rereading each section of the article, identifying the central points the author makes and the relevant details that support those points, and restating these in their own words. Students should then compare and contrast their summaries of the authors' arguments in "Spinning a Yarn" and "String Theory." Ask: *What similarities and differences do you observe in the authors' claims?*

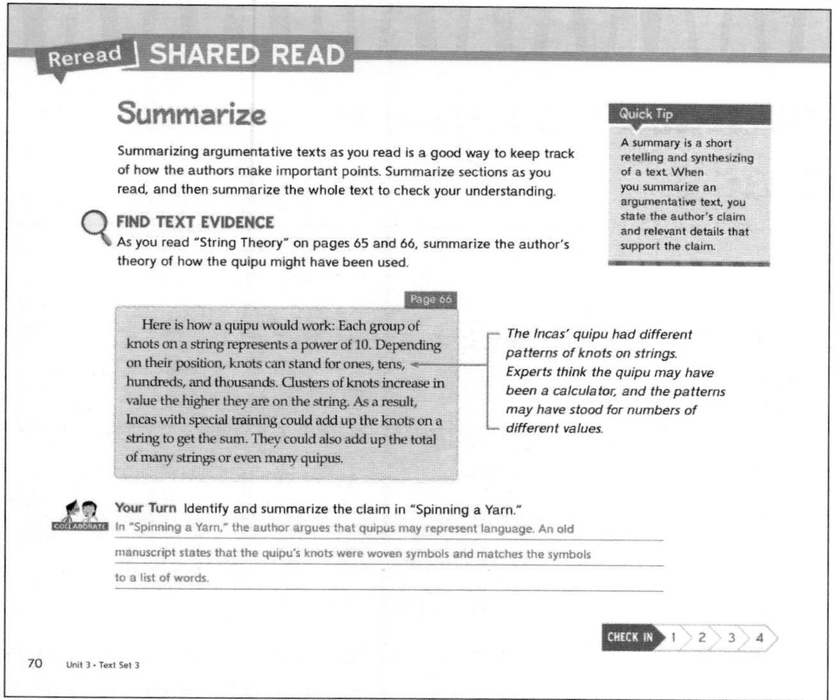

Reread | SHARED READ

Summarize

Summarizing argumentative texts as you read is a good way to keep track of how the authors make important points. Summarize sections as you read, and then summarize the whole text to check your understanding.

FIND TEXT EVIDENCE

As you read "String Theory" on pages 65 and 66, summarize the author's theory of how the quipu might have been used.

Quick Tip

A summary is a short retelling and synthesizing of a text. When you summarize an argumentative text, you state the author's claim and relevant details that support the claim.

Page 66

Here is how a quipu would work: Each group of knots on a string represents a power of 10. Depending on their position, knots can stand for ones, tens, hundreds, and thousands. Clusters of knots increase in value the higher they are on the string. As a result, Incas with special training could add up the knots on a string to get the sum. They could also add up the total of many strings or even many quipus.

The Incas' quipu had different patterns of knots on strings. Experts think the quipu may have been a calculator, and the patterns may have stood for numbers of different values.

COLLABORATE **Your Turn** Identify and summarize the claim in "Spinning a Yarn."

In "Spinning a Yarn," the author argues that quipus may represent language. An old manuscript states that the quipu's knots were woven symbols and matches the symbols to a list of words.

CHECK IN 1 2 3 4

70 Unit 3 • Text Set 3

Reading/Writing Companion, p. 70

English Language Learners

Use these scaffolds with **Guided Practice**. For small group support, see the **ELL Small Group Guide**.

Beginning

Review with students how to summarize. Reread paragraph 3 on page 67 of ""Spinning a Yarn" with students. Restate sentences as needed. Remind them that the author of "Sting Theory" argues that the knots on quipus represent numbers. Ask: *Does the author of* "Spinning a Yarn" *agree?* (no) Then help partners summarize the author's claim in "Spinning a Yarn" using: The author thinks that quipus represent a form of language.

Intermediate

Review with students how to summarize. Have partners reread page 67 of "Spinning a Yarn." Point out that contrast words like *but, however,* and *although* often introduce relevant details. Elicit that the author of "Spinning a Yarn" does not agree with the claim that quipus represent a calculator. Then have them summarize the author's claim in "Spinning a Yarn" using: The author of _______ argues that the knots are ______.

Advanced/Advanced High

Have students discuss how to summarize. Have partners reread page 67 and summarize the author's claim about the quipus. Then have them compare and contrast their summaries of the claim made by "Spinning a Yarn" with the summaries of the claims in "String Theory.

HABITS OF LEARNING

I am a critical thinker and problem solver. Students can gain skill in applying this habit of learning by reflecting on and thinking critically about the process they used to summarize. Have them ask themselves:

- Why is each detail I listed important?
- How does each relevant detail support the central idea?

FORMATIVE ASSESSMENT

STUDENT CHECK-IN

Ask students to share their Your Turn responses on Reading/Writing Companion page 70. Have them use the Check-In routine to reflect and fill in the bars.

CHECK FOR SUCCESS

Can students summarize the claims in "String Theory" and "Spinning a Yarn"? Can they compare and contrast their summaries?

Small Group Instruction

If No

- **Approaching** Reteach p. T198

If Yes

- **On** Review p. T208
- **Beyond** Extend p. T214

LEARNING GOALS

We can identify the text structure used by the author to read and understand argumentative text.

OBJECTIVES

Explain how an author uses reasons and evidence to support particular points in a text, identifying which reasons and evidence support which point(s).

Explain an author's perspective, or point of view, toward an argumentative text.

Interpret information presented visually, orally, or quantitatively (e.g., in charts, graphs, diagrams, time lines, animations, or interactive elements on Web pages) and explain how the information contributes to an understanding of the text in which it appears.

ELA ACADEMIC LANGUAGE

- *argument, claim, compare, contrast, graphic, diagram, perspective*
- Cognates: *comparar, contrastar, gráfico(a), diagrama*

Reread

Text Structure: Compare and Contrast

1 Explain

Share with students the following key characteristics of argumentative text.

- An argumentative text tries to persuade readers to support the author's claim, or argument. The claim clearly states an opinion that reveals the author's perspective.
- Authors of argumentative texts support their claims with logical facts, reasons, and evidence from multiple sources.
- Argumentative texts typically include print features such as headings that help organize information. Graphic features such as diagrams help readers visualize ideas and information related to the text.
- Two argumentative texts may present different claims about the same topic. "String Theory" and "Spinning a Yarn" both focus on the quipu, but each author makes a different claim about its purpose. Comparing and contrasting these claims can help readers better understand the topic and identify the claim they find more credible.

2 Model

Use text evidence and the diagram on **Reading/Writing Companion** page 66, to identify "String Theory" as an argumentative text. Point out that the author's claim is suggested in the heading on page 65. Details within the text about how the quipu worked and how the Incas used it support the author's perspective. Model comparing and contrasting the headings of "String Theory" and "Spinning a Yarn."

Diagrams Remind students that a diagram is a visual representation of an object, place, idea, or event. Diagrams usually include labels that help readers understand how parts within the diagram relate to each other and to the whole. Point out that the diagram on page 66 shows thread from a quipu with knots. Ask: *How do the labels help you interpret and understand the diagram?*

Anchor Chart Have a volunteer add this feature to the Argumentative Text anchor chart.

3 Guided Practice

Guide pairs to give two reasons why the diagram on page 66 supports the author's claim that the Incas used the quipu as a calculator. Then have them compare and contrast the diagram on page 66 with the diagram on page 67. Have students share the similarities and differences with the class.

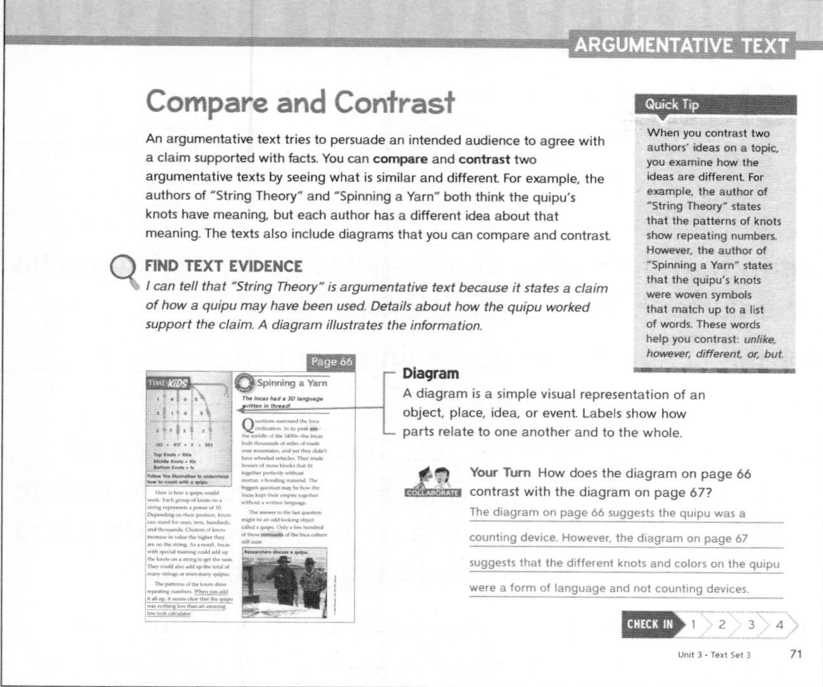

ARGUMENTATIVE TEXT

Compare and Contrast

An argumentative text tries to persuade an intended audience to agree with a claim supported with facts. You can **compare** and **contrast** two argumentative texts by seeing what is similar and different. For example, the authors of "String Theory" and "Spinning a Yarn" both think the quipu's knots have meaning, but each author has a different idea about that meaning. The texts also include diagrams that you can compare and contrast.

FIND TEXT EVIDENCE

I can tell that "String Theory" is argumentative text because it states a claim of how a quipu may have been used. Details about how the quipu worked support the claim. A diagram illustrates the information.

Quick Tip

When you contrast two authors' ideas on a topic, you examine how the ideas are different. For example, the author of "String Theory" states that the patterns of knots show repeating numbers. However, the author of "Spinning a Yarn" states that the quipu's knots were woven symbols that match up to a list of words. These words help you contrast: *unlike, however, different, or, but.*

Page 66

Diagram

A diagram is a simple visual representation of an object, place, idea, or event. Labels show how parts relate to one another and to the whole.

COLLABORATE

Your Turn How does the diagram on page 66 contrast with the diagram on page 67?

The diagram on page 66 suggests the quipu was a counting device. However, the diagram on page 67 suggests that the different knots and colors on the quipu were a form of language and not counting devices.

CHECK IN 1 2 3 4

Unit 3 • Text Set 3 71

Reading/Writing Companion, p. 71

English Language Learners

Use the following scaffolds with **Guided Practice**. For small group support, see the **ELL Small Group Guide**.

Beginning

Review the meaning of *compare* and *contrast* with students. Describe diagrams on **Reading/Writing Companion** pages 66 and 67 with students. Have them point to the labels and read the captions with them. Help partners compare and contrast the diagrams: Both diagrams show quipus with knots. The diagram on page 66 says the knots represent numbers. The diagram on page 67 says the knots represent a form of language.

Intermediate

Review the diagrams on **Reading/Writing Companion** pages 66 and 67 with students. Have partners point to the labels and read the captions. Guide them to compare and contrast what the diagrams show by describing the similarities and differences: Both diagrams show ______. The diagram on page 66 says the knots ______. However, the diagram on page 67 says the knots ______.

Advanced/Advanced High

Have pairs review the diagrams on pages 66 and 67. Have them discuss the labels and captions. Then have them compare and contrast the diagrams and respond using the terms *both* and *however.*

FORMATIVE ASSESSMENT

STUDENT CHECK-IN

Ask partners to share their Your Turn responses on Reading/Writing Companion page 71. Have them use the Check-In routine to reflect and fill in the bars.

CHECK FOR SUCCESS

Can students compare and contrast how the diagrams on pages 66 and 67 support each claim?

Small Group Instruction

If No

- **Approaching** Reteach p. T200

If Yes

- **On** Review p. T210
- **Beyond** Extend p. T216

LEARNING GOALS

We can read and understand argumentative text by identifying the author's claim.

OBJECTIVES

Explain how an author uses reasons and evidence to support particular points in a text, identifying which reasons and evidence support which point(s).

Identify the author's claim.

Determine an author's point of view or purpose in a text and explain how it is conveyed in the text.

ELA ACADEMIC LANGUAGE

- *claim, author, reasons, evidence, convincing*
- Cognates: *autor(a), razones, evidencia, convincente*

DIGITAL TOOLS

To differentiate instruction for key skills, use the results of the activity.

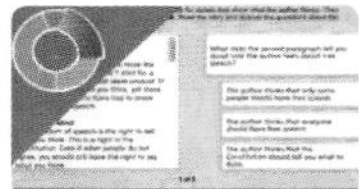

Reread

Author's Claim

1 Explain

Explain to students that the author of an argumentative text states his or her claim, or argument, for or against a topic or idea.

- As support for this claim, the author of an argumentative text provides logical reasons and evidence.
- The author may use details such as facts, figures, examples, and word choice, to develop their claim and persuade readers to find his or her claim credible. The author may also use supporting details to show why another claim is not as convincing as his or hers.
- Point out that examining reasons, evidence, and word choice in argumentative writing can help students track the development of an argument, identify the author's claim, and determine whether or not they agree with it.

Anchor Chart Add these features to the Author's Claim anchor chart.

2 Model

Identify the details that develop the author's claim in "Spinning a Yarn" on **Reading/Writing Companion** pages 66–67, including the heading below the title of the article and different points made throughout the text to support the author's claim. Point out to students that the author ends the heading with an exclamation point to express and create enthusiasm. Then model how to use the details listed in the graphic organizer to determine the author's claim.

3 Guided Practice

Circulate as pairs identify important details in "String Theory" that help them determine the author's claim and then record these details on the graphic organizer. Discuss each section as students complete the graphic organizer. Then have students use the details to determine the author's claim.

Analytical Writing **Write About Reading: Summary** Ask each pair to work together to summarize the reasons and evidence the author of "String Theory" provides to support his or her claim. Then ask partners to tell which article's reasons and evidence they found most convincing and why. Have them share their views in a class discussion.

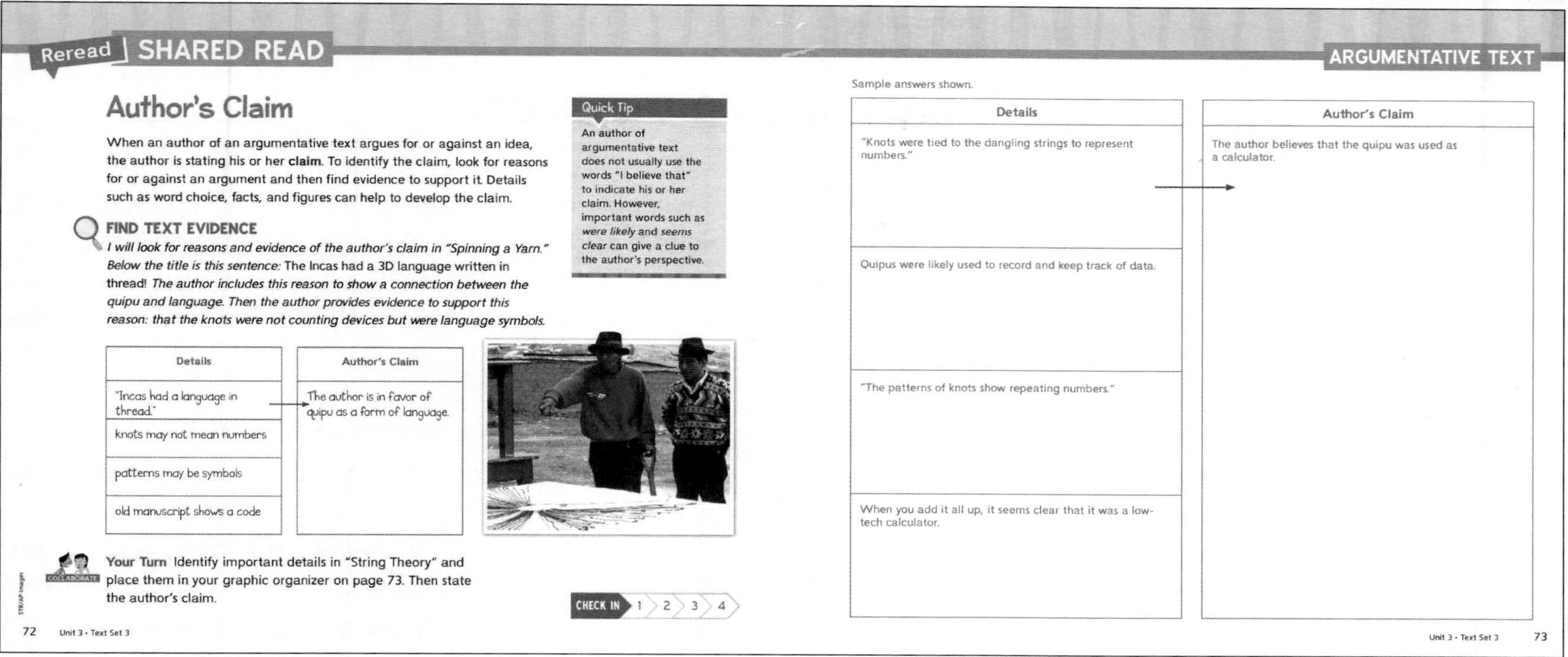

Reread | SHARED READ

ARGUMENTATIVE TEXT

Author's Claim

When an author of an argumentative text argues for or against an idea, the author is stating his or her **claim**. To identify the claim, look for reasons for or against an argument and then find evidence to support it. Details such as word choice, facts, and figures can help to develop the claim.

FIND TEXT EVIDENCE

I will look for reasons and evidence of the author's claim in "Spinning a Yarn." Below the title is this sentence: The Incas had a 3D language written in thread! *The author includes this reason to show a connection between the quipu and language. Then the author provides evidence to support this reason: that the knots were not counting devices but were language symbols.*

Quick Tip

An author of argumentative text does not usually use the words "I believe that" to indicate his or her claim. However, important words such as *were likely* and *seems clear* can give a clue to the author's perspective.

Details	Author's Claim
"Incas had a language in thread."	The author is in favor of quipu as a form of language.
knots may not mean numbers	
patterns may be symbols	
old manuscript shows a code	

Your Turn Identify important details in "String Theory" and place them in your graphic organizer on page 73. Then state the author's claim.

CHECK IN 1 2 3 4

72 Unit 3 • Text Set 3

Sample answers shown.

Details	Author's Claim
"Knots were tied to the dangling strings to represent numbers."	The author believes that the quipu was used as a calculator.
Quipus were likely used to record and keep track of data.	
"The patterns of knots show repeating numbers."	
When you add it all up, it seems clear that it was a low-tech calculator.	

Unit 3 • Text Set 3 73

Reading/Writing Companion, pp. 72–73

English Language Learners

Use the following scaffolds with **Guided Practice**. For small group support, see the **ELL Small Group Guide**.

Beginning

Reread the last paragraph on page 65 of "String Theory" with students. Clarify the words *record* and *data*. Ask: *What is the author's claim about quipus?* The author thinks quipus were used to record data. Have students write *record data* in the graphic organizer. Then have partners discuss the author's claim using: The author believes quipus were calculators used to record data.

Intermediate

Reread the last paragraph on page 65 of "String Theory" with students. Ask: *According to the author, what were quipus used for?* (to record and keep track of data) *Now read paragraph 2 on page 66. What does the author say about the patterns of knots?* (They show repeating numbers.) Have students record the details in the graphic organizer. Then have them discuss the author's claim using: The author believes quipus were calculators used to record data.

Advanced/Advanced High

Have partners reread "String Theory," identify three details, and record them in the graphic organizer. Have students use *detail* and *author's claim* as they determine the author's point of view about quipus.

FORMATIVE ASSESSMENT

STUDENT CHECK-IN

Ask partners to share their graphic organizers on Reading/Writing Companion page 73. Have them use the Check-In routine to reflect and fill in the bars.

CHECK FOR SUCCESS

Rubric Use your online rubric to record student progress.

Are students able to identify important details in an argumentative text and use them to find the author's claim?

Small Group Instruction

If No

- **Approaching** Reteach p. T207

If Yes

- **On** Review p. T213
- **Beyond** Extend p. T219

LEARNING GOALS

We can reread to analyze craft and structure in argumentative text.

OBJECTIVES

Determine two or more central, or main, ideas of a text and explain how they are supported by relevant, or key, details; summarize the text.

Draw on information from multiple print or digital sources, demonstrating the ability to locate an answer to a question quickly or to solve a problem efficiently.

ELA ACADEMIC LANGUAGE

- *techniques, support, illustration, perspective*
- Cognates: *técnicas, ilustración*

TEACH IN SMALL GROUP

Approaching Level Use the Reread prompts and scaffolded questions to help students cite text evidence and connect ideas.

On Level Have partners respond to the Reread prompts. Offer constructive feedback as they share their answers.

Beyond Level After pairs answer the Reread prompts, have them discuss their responses with another pair.

ELL Have Beginning and Early-Intermediate ELLs use the **Scaffolded Shared Read**.

Reread

10 mins

Craft and Structure

Tell students that they will now reread parts of "What Was the Purpose of the Inca's Knotted Strings?" and analyze techniques the authors used in writing the two argumentative texts. Authors of argumentative texts state a claim supported by reasons and evidence that help readers understand the author's perspective on a topic.

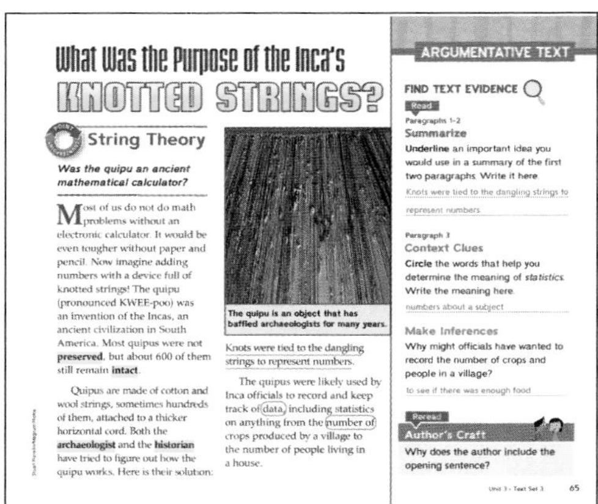

What Was the Purpose of the Inca's KNOTTED STRINGS?

String Theory

Was the quipu an ancient mathematical calculator?

Most of us do not do math problems without an electronic calculator. It would be even tougher without paper and pencil. Now imagine adding numbers with a device full of knotted strings! The quipu (pronounced KWEE-poo) was an invention of the Incas, an ancient civilization in South America. Most quipus were not **preserved**, but about 600 of them still remain **intact**.

Quipus are made of cotton and wool strings, sometimes hundreds of them, attached to a thicker horizontal cord. Both the **archaeologist** and the **historian** have tried to figure out how the quipu works. Here is their solution:

The quipu is an object that has baffled archaeologists for many years.

Knots were tied to the dangling strings to represent numbers.

The quipus were likely used by Inca officials to record and keep track of data, including statistics on anything from the number of crops produced by a village to the number of people living in a house.

ARGUMENTATIVE TEXT

FIND TEXT EVIDENCE

Read

Paragraphs 1-2

Summarize

Underline an important idea you would use in a summary of the first two paragraphs. Write it here.

Knots were tied to the dangling strings to represent numbers.

Paragraph 3

Context Clues

Circle the words that help you determine the meaning of *statistics*. Write the meaning here.

numbers about a subject

Make Inferences

Why might officials have wanted to record the number of crops and people in a village?

to see if there was enough food

Reread

Author's Craft

Why does the author include the opening sentence?

Unit 3 • Text Set 3 65

Reading/Writing Companion, p. 65

AUTHOR'S CRAFT DOK 2

Reread page 65 with students. Ask: *What does the author of "String Theory" believe the knots on a quipu represent?* (numbers) *What does the author believe quipus were used for?* (Incan officials used quipus to record and keep track of data.)

ELL Reread the first sentence of the second paragraph with students. Ask: *Which words or phrases help you visualize a quipu?* (cotton and wool strings; hundreds; attached to a thicker horizontal cord) Then have students identify elements from the sentence in the photograph. Have partners discuss how the text and photograph help them understand the meaning of the words *strings* and *horizontal.*

Why does the author include the opening sentence? (The author wants readers to recognize the difficulty of doing difficult math problems without assistance of some kind. This helps explain the author's perspective on quipus.)

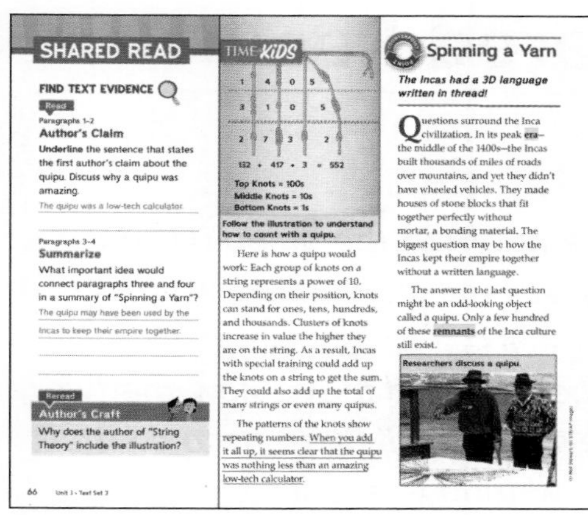
SHARED READ

FIND TEXT EVIDENCE

Read

Paragraphs 1–2

Author's Claim

Underline the sentence that states the first author's claim about the quipu. Discuss why a quipu was amazing.

The quipu was a low-tech calculator.

Paragraphs 3–4

Summarize

What important idea would connect paragraphs three and four in a summary of "Spinning a Yarn"?

The quipu may have been used by the Incas to keep their empire together.

Reread

Author's Craft

Why does the author of "String Theory" include the illustration?

66 Unit 3 • Text Set 3

TIME KIDS

1 4 0 5
3 1 0 5
2 7 3 2
132 + 417 + 3 = 552

Top Knots = 100s
Middle Knots = 10s
Bottom Knots = 1s

Follow the illustration to understand how to count with a quipu.

Here is how a quipu would work: Each group of knots on a string represents a power of 10. Depending on their position, knots can stand for ones, tens, hundreds, and thousands. Clusters of knots increase in value the higher they are on the string. As a result, Incas with special training could add up the knots on a string to get the sum. They could also add up the total of many strings or even many quipus.

The patterns of the knots show repeating numbers. When you add it all up, it seems clear that the quipu was nothing less than an amazing low-tech calculator.

Spinning a Yarn

The Incas had a 3D language written in thread!

Questions surround the Inca civilization. In its peak era—the middle of the 1400s—the Incas built thousands of miles of roads over mountains, and yet they didn't have wheeled vehicles. They made houses of stone blocks that fit together perfectly without mortar, a bonding material. The biggest question may be how the Incas kept their empire together without a written language.

The answer to the last question might be an odd-looking object called a quipu. Only a few hundred of these remnants of the Inca culture still exist.

Researchers discuss a quipu.

Reading/Writing Companion, p. 66

AUTHOR'S CRAFT DOK 2

Reread paragraph 3 on page 66. Ask: *What does each group of knots on a quipu string represent?* (a power of 10) *Why does the position of the knots on a quipu matter?* (The number value changes with the position of the knots.)

ELL *Discuss with students why questions surround the Incas.* Questions surround the Incas because there are many things we don't know about them. Guide students as they identify three accomplishments of the Incas in paragraph 3 and discuss what makes each one mysterious.

Why does the author of "String Theory" include the illustration? (The author wants to include a visual demonstration so readers can understand how a quipu works like a calculator.)

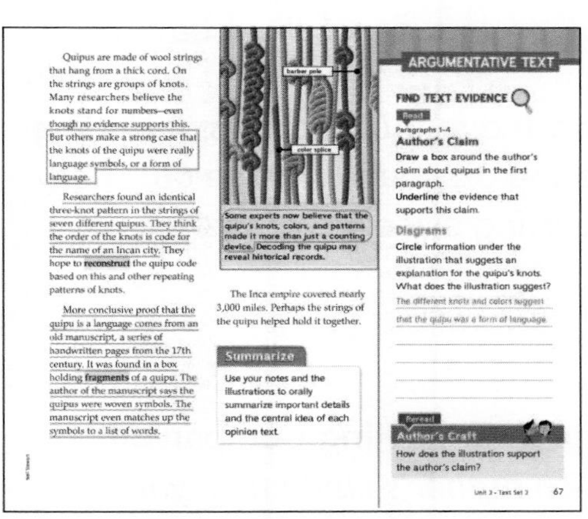
Quipus are made of wool strings that hang from a thick cord. On the strings are groups of knots. Many researchers believe the knots stand for numbers—even though no evidence supports this. But others make a strong case that the knots of the quipu were really language symbols, or a form of language.

Researchers found an identical three-knot pattern in the strings of seven different quipus. They think the order of the knots is code for the name of an Incan city. They hope to reconstruct the quipu code based on this and other repeating patterns of knots.

More conclusive proof that the quipu is a language comes from an old manuscript, a series of handwritten pages from the 17th century. It was found in a box holding fragments of a quipu. The author of the manuscript says the quipus were woven symbols. The manuscript even matches up the symbols to a list of words.

barber pole

color splice

Some experts now believe that the quipu's knots, colors, and patterns made it more than just a counting device. Decoding the quipu may reveal historical records.

The Inca empire covered nearly 3,000 miles. Perhaps the strings of the quipu helped hold it together.

Summarize

Use your notes and the illustrations to orally summarize important details and the central idea of each opinion text.

ARGUMENTATIVE TEXT

FIND TEXT EVIDENCE

Read

Paragraphs 1–4

Author's Claim

Draw a box around the author's claim about quipus in the first paragraph.

Underline the evidence that supports this claim.

Diagrams

Circle information under the illustration that suggests an explanation for the quipu's knots. What does the illustration suggest?

The different knots and colors suggest that the quipu was a form of language.

Reread

Author's Craft

How does the illustration support the author's claim?

Unit 3 • Text Set 3 67

Reading/Writing Companion, p. 67

AUTHOR'S CRAFT DOK 2

Reread paragraphs 1–2 and review the illustration and caption on page 67 with students. Ask: *What purpose does the author think the quipu served?* (The author thinks it was used as a form of language.) *How did it work?* (The knots were symbols that appeared in certain colors and patterns.) *How does the illustration show this?* (It shows a variety of knots and labels that identify different patterns on the strings.)

ELL Restate the caption with students. There are knots on the quipu. They form a pattern. Then have students point to the part of the quipu in the illustration that this might describe. As needed, clarify that a pattern happens when something repeats in a certain order.

How does the illustration support the author's claim? (It supports the author's claim that different patterns make the strings and knots seem more like words by showing the patterns and colors of the strings and knots.)

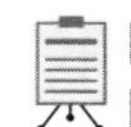

EVALUATE INFORMATION

Explain that when you evaluate information, you think about how helpful or how accurate the information is. Evaluating information in an argumentative text can help you determine if the author provides enough facts, reasons, and evidence to support his or her claim.

Think Aloud The authors of both argumentative texts in "What Was the Purpose of the Inca's Knotted String?" state a clear claim and support their claim with evidence. But the author of "Spinning a Yarn" takes his or her opinion one step further by explaining why the other author's opinion is faulty—because "no evidence" supports it. The fact that the second author anticipated that readers might disagree—and explained why they shouldn't—makes his or her claim slightly more credible.

Integrate

BUILD KNOWLEDGE: MAKE CONNECTIONS

Talk About the Text Have partners discuss the differing opinions about the purpose of quipus.

Write About the Text Have students add their ideas to their Build Knowledge pages of their reader's notebooks.

Anchor Chart Record any new ideas on the Build Knowledge anchor chart.

Add to the Vocabulary List Have students write down any words they learned about studying the past in their reader's notebooks.

STUDENT CHECK-IN

Have partners share their responses to one of the Reread prompts on Reading/Writing Companion pages 65-67. Ask them to reflect using the Check-In routine.

Reread

Write About the Shared Read

LEARNING GOALS

We can use text evidence to respond to argumentative text.

OBJECTIVES

Explain how an author uses reasons and evidence to support particular points in a text, identifying which reasons and evidence support which point(s). Identify the author's claim.

Draw evidence from literary or informational texts to support analysis, reflection, and research.

ELA ACADEMIC LANGUAGE

- *support, claim, evidence, differ*
- Cognate: *evidencia*

TEACH IN SMALL GROUP

Approaching Level Have pairs work together to plan and write a response.

On Level Have pairs discuss how they plan to approach the prompt and then review responses after completing them independently.

Beyond Level Have students review responses in pairs and suggest revisions.

ELL Group students of mixed proficiency levels to discuss and respond to the prompt.

Analyze the Prompt DOK 3

Read the prompt aloud: *Which author's claim about the quipu do you agree with more? In your opinion, what makes the claim more valid?* Ask: *What is the prompt asking?* (to explain why one author's claim is more convincing than the other author's) Say: *Let's reread to see how the two authors support their claims. Noting text evidence will allow us to contrast the claims and make inferences that aid in writing a response.*

Analyze Text Evidence

Remind students that an argumentative text includes a statement of the author's claim, or argument, and supports this claim with reasons and evidence. The author may also include diagrams or photographs to support the claim. Students should begin by identifying statements that convey the claim of each author, and then look for facts, examples, and other details that make an author's claim more credible, or believable. In the **Reading/Writing Companion**, have students reread the second paragraph on page 66. Ask: *Which sentence best conveys the author's perspective about the use of the quipu?* ("When you add it all up, it seems clear that the quipu was nothing less than an amazing low-tech calculator.") *What are some examples the author provides on pages 65–66 to support this idea?* (The author explains how quipus were probably used and how a quipu would work.) Have students look for other support the author provides, including details in the photograph on page 65 and the diagram on page 66. Then have students identify the claim and supporting evidence of the second author on pages 66–67.

Respond

Direct pairs to the sentence starters on **Reading/Writing Companion** page 74 Ask: *How does understanding each author's claim help you identify the evidence that supports it?*

Think Aloud In "String Theory," the author states that the quipu was "an amazing low-tech calculator." I ask myself: *How does the author know this? What makes him or her so sure?* In paragraph 2 on page 65, the author says that archaeologists and historians developed this theory. That tells me that it's not just an idea the author made up—it's one that experts believe. The supporting evidence makes the author's claim more credible to me.

Analytical Writing Students should use the phrases in the sentence starters to summarize each author's claim and supporting evidence. The first part of their response should state the central idea. Specific details about the authors' claims and supporting details should follow. Students may continue their responses on a separate piece of paper.

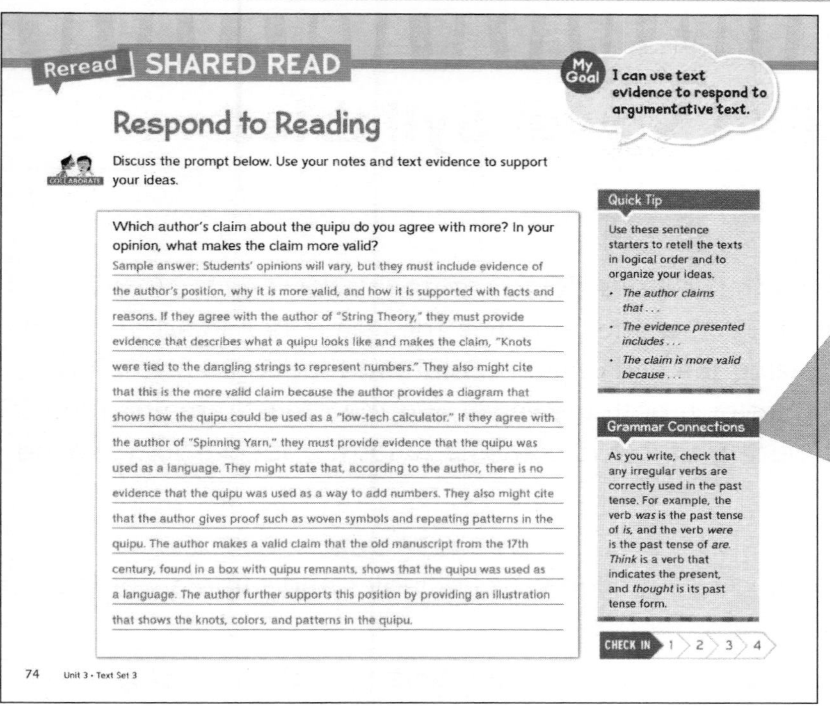

Reread | SHARED READ

My Goal: I can use text evidence to respond to argumentative text.

Respond to Reading

COLLABORATE Discuss the prompt below. Use your notes and text evidence to support your ideas.

Which author's claim about the quipu do you agree with more? In your opinion, what makes the claim more valid?

Sample answer: Students' opinions will vary, but they must include evidence of the author's position, why it is more valid, and how it is supported with facts and reasons. If they agree with the author of "String Theory," they must provide evidence that describes what a quipu looks like and makes the claim, "Knots were tied to the dangling strings to represent numbers." They also might cite that this is the more valid claim because the author provides a diagram that shows how the quipu could be used as a "low-tech calculator." If they agree with the author of "Spinning Yarn," they must provide evidence that the quipu was used as a language. They might state that, according to the author, there is no evidence that the quipu was used as a way to add numbers. They also might cite that the author gives proof such as woven symbols and repeating patterns in the quipu. The author makes a valid claim that the old manuscript from the 17th century, found in a box with quipu remnants, shows that the quipu was used as a language. The author further supports this position by providing an illustration that shows the knots, colors, and patterns in the quipu.

Quick Tip

Use these sentence starters to retell the texts in logical order and to organize your ideas.

- *The author claims that . . .*
- *The evidence presented includes . . .*
- *The claim is more valid because . . .*

Grammar Connections

As you write, check that any irregular verbs are correctly used in the past tense. For example, the verb *was* is the past tense of *is*, and the verb *were* is the past tense of *are*. *Think* is a verb that indicates the present, and *thought* is its past tense form.

CHECK IN 1 2 3 4

74 Unit 3 • Text Set 3

Reading/Writing Companion, p. 74

Grammar Connections

Students can use online **Grammar Handbook** pages 458–459 and 462 to review and practice verb tense and the correct use of irregular verbs in the past tense.

English Language Learners

Use the following scaffolds with **Respond**.

Beginning

Read the prompt with students and discuss what they will write about. Review the meaning of *author's claim* and *valid* with students. Ask: *What does the author of* String Theory *think quipus were used as?* (calculators) *What does the author of* Spinning Yarn *think quipus were used as?* (language) *What do both authors use to support their claims?* (facts and images) Then have partners discuss which author's claim they agree with more and respond using: I agree with the author of "String Theory." The author provides facts that show ____.

Intermediate

Read the prompt with students. Have partners review the author's claim about quipus in "String Theory" and "Spinning Yarn." Ask: *How do the authors show their ideas*? They use facts and images. Then have partners discuss which author's claim they agree with more and respond using: I agree with the author of "String Theory" because ____. The author provides ____ that show ____.

Advanced/Advanced High

Review the prompt and sentence starters on page 74 with students. Have pairs describe the author's claim about the quipu in "String Theory" and "Spinning Yarn" and discuss which claim they agree with more. Have them respond using text evidence and sentence starters.

NEWCOMERS

Have students listen to the summaries of the **Shared Read** in their native language and then in English to help them access the text and develop listening comprehension. Help students ask and answer questions with a partner. Use these sentence frames: What does the author of "String Theory" think the quipu does? This author believes ___. Then continue the lessons in the **Newcomer Teacher's Guide**.

FORMATIVE ASSESSMENT

STUDENT CHECK-IN

Ask partners to share their response on Reading/Writing Companion page 74. Have them use the Check-In routine to reflect and fill in the bars.

LEARNING GOALS

- **We can identify, decode, and use words with *r*-controlled vowel syllables.**
- **We can identify and read multisyllabic words.**
- **We can read fluently and accurately at an appropriate rate.**

OBJECTIVES

Know and apply grade-level phonics and word analysis skills in decoding words.

Use combined knowledge of all letter-sound correspondences, syllabication patterns, and morphology to read accurately unfamiliar multisyllabic words in context and out of context.

Read with sufficient accuracy and fluency to support comprehension.

Read grade-level prose and poetry orally with accuracy, appropriate rate, expression, and automaticity on successive readings.

- Rate: 123–143 WCPM

ELA ACADEMIC LANGUAGE

- *expression, phrasing*
- Cognates: *expresión, fraseo*

TEACH IN SMALL GROUP

Phonics

Approaching Level and **ELL** Use the Tier 2 activity on page T202 before teaching the lesson.

On Level and **Beyond Level** As needed, use Read Multisyllabic Words only.

ELL See page 5 in the **Language Transfers Handbook** for guidance in identifying sounds and symbols that may not transfer for speakers of certain languages.

r-Controlled Vowel Syllables

1 Explain

Remind students that every syllable has one vowel sound. Write the word *party* on the board and underline the letters *par*. Read the word aloud, emphasizing the first syllable. Point out that when a vowel is followed by the letter *r*, both the vowel and the *r* must remain in the same syllable because the two combine to form a special vowel sound.

2 Model

Write the following *r*-controlled vowel syllables and sample words on the board:

gar as in ***garden***	**per** as in ***perfume***	**dir** as in ***dirty***
for as in ***forget***	**pur** as in ***purpose***	**por** as in ***portray***

Read aloud each syllable and sample word, underlining the *r*-controlled vowel sound within the word with your finger.

3 Guided Practice

Write the following words with *r*-controlled vowel syllables on the board. Have students underline the *r*-controlled vowel sound in each word. Then have them chorally read the words.

her	part	third	tarp
port	start	surf	swarm
cart	fern	serve	hurt

Finally, have students make a grid like the one below and sort the words by spelling pattern.

ar	er	ir	or	ur

For practice with decoding and encoding, use **Practice Book** page 175 or online activities.

Read Multisyllabic Words

Transition to Longer Words Help students transition to multisyllabic words with *r*-controlled vowel syllables. Write the following word sets on the board. Have students read the first, one-syllable word. Then model how to read the longer word. Remind students that knowing the meanings of common prefixes and suffixes can help them understand the meanings of longer words.

dark, darkened	fur, refurbish
firm, firmly	sharp, sharpener
for, forwarded	barb, barbecue

After students complete the activity, ask them to write sentences using two of the longer words. Then have them share their sentences with a partner.

Fluency

Accuracy and Rate

Explain/Model Review with students that reading with an appropriate rate can add to accuracy and understanding. Model reading page 65 of "What Was the Purpose of the Inca's Knotted Strings?" in the Reading/Writing Companion. Read aloud with accuracy at an appropriate rate, making sure to slowly and clearly pronounce words that might be unfamiliar to students. Tells students to be mindful of their accuracy when they change their rate.

Practice/Apply Have partners take turns reading the paragraphs on page 65 of the Reading/Writing Companion, modeling the accuracy and rate you used. Remind students that you will be listening for their accuracy and rate as you monitor their reading during the week.

Daily Fluency Practice

Students can practice fluency using the online **Differentiated Genre Passage**, "How Did King Tut Die?"

DIGITAL TOOLS

For more practice, use the phonics and fluency activities.

***r*-Controlled Vowel Syllables**

MULTIMODAL LEARNING

As an alternative to Guided Practice, in groups, have students list words with the *r*-controlled vowels on strips of paper. Make sure that one word is on each strip. Have students sort the word strips into the spelling patterns *ar, er, ir, or,* and *ur*. Check that words have been sorted correctly. Have partners read the words aloud.

FORMATIVE ASSESSMENT

STUDENT CHECK-IN

***r*-Controlled Vowel Syllables** Have partners share three words with *r*-controlled vowel syllables.

Multisyllabic Words Have partners read the following three words: *darkened, refurbish,* and *barbecue*.

Fluency Ask partners to read "How Did King Tut Die?" fluently.

Have partners reflect using the Check-In routine.

CHECK FOR SUCCESS

Do students decode multisyllabic words with *r*-controlled vowel syllables? Can students read accurately and with an appropriate rate?

Small Group Instruction

If No

- **Approaching** Reteach pp. T202, T206
- **ELL** Develop p. T202

If Yes

- **On** Apply p. T208
- **Beyond** Apply p. T214

LEARNING GOALS

- **We can use the research process to create a multimedia presentation.**
- **We can use appropriate audio and text features.**

OBJECTIVES

Conduct short research projects that use several sources to build knowledge through investigation of different aspects of a topic.

Analyze multiple accounts of the same event or topic, noting important similarities and differences in the point of view they represent.

Recall relevant information from experiences or gather relevant information from print and digital sources; summarize or paraphrase information in notes and finished work, and provide a list of sources.

Report on a topic or text or present an opinion, sequencing ideas logically and using appropriate facts and relevant, descriptive details to support main ideas or themes; speak clearly at an understandable pace.

Adapt speech to a variety of contexts and tasks, using formal English when appropriate to task and situation.

ELA ACADEMIC LANGUAGE

- *multimedia, audio, text feature, digital*
- Cognate: *digital*

TEACH IN SMALL GROUP

You may wish to teach the Research and Inquiry lesson during Small Group time. Have groups of mixed abilities complete the page and work on the multimedia presentation.

Investigating the Past

Explain to students that for the next week they will work collaboratively in groups to research an ancestral Native American group and create a multimedia presentation.

Audio and Text Features Explain that a multimedia presentation includes digital features such as audio and text features. This may include audio recordings, videos, illustrations, or photographs. Have students look at the visual of the cliff dwelling on **Reading/Writing Companion** page 75. Discuss why including photographs such as this one will help enhance their presentations.

Support them as they go through each step in the Research Process as outlined on page 75 to make their multimedia presentations.

STEP 1 **Set a Goal** Explain to students that North America had several ancestral Native American groups living in it prior to the arrival of Europeans. Have them consider which group they would like to research. They may wish to research a group that is native to their own region. Offer feedback as students generate questions and decide what details they would like to include on their presentations. Have them use an **Accordion Foldable**®, available online, to help organize their information.

STEP 2 **Identify Sources** Review with students how to locate credible print and online sources. Suggest that students look for books or websites run by official organizations of the Native American groups and discuss why they would be credible. Have students take careful notes and cite the sources they use to gather information for their multimedia presentations.

STEP 3 **Find and Record Information** Brainstorm with groups the kinds of text and audio features they should try to include in their research. Remind them to use valid, historically relevant sources, particularly when using text and audio clips. Note that many Native American groups have their own websites, so they should consider using these in their research. Groups should be sensitive to finding accurate and appropriate depictions of Native Americans.

STEP 4 **Organize and Synthesize Information** Show students how to organize the information that they want to include in their presentations. Help them sketch out the order of how they would like to present information about their chosen Native American group.

STEP 5 **Create and Present** Review with students the details and text and audio features they should include on their multimedia presentations. Discuss options for sharing their presentations. Students may want to designate one person as a narrator or take turns narrating as they go through their presentations.

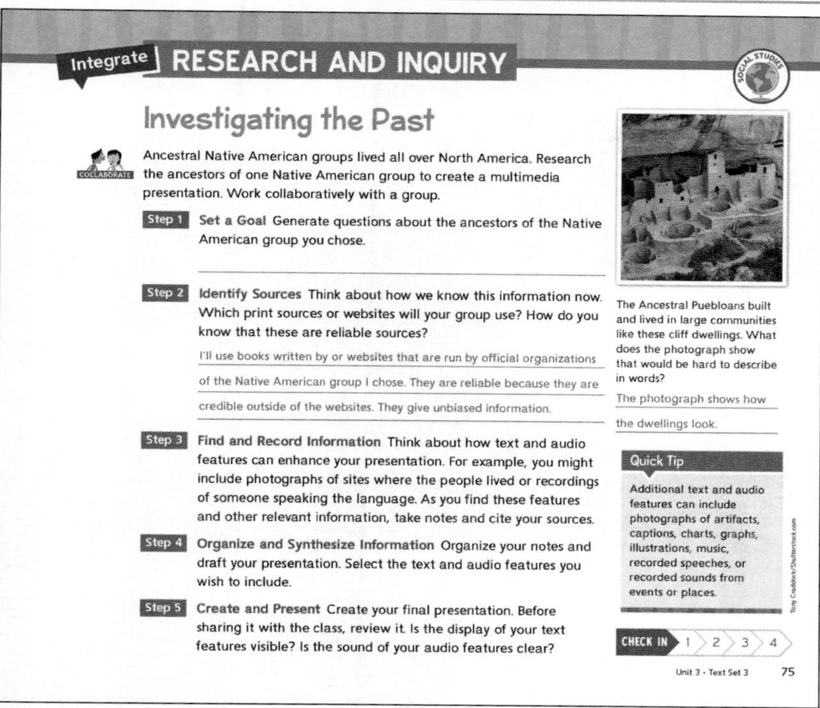

Integrate | RESEARCH AND INQUIRY

SOCIAL STUDIES

Investigating the Past

COLLABORATE

Ancestral Native American groups lived all over North America. Research the ancestors of one Native American group to create a multimedia presentation. Work collaboratively with a group.

Step 1 **Set a Goal** Generate questions about the ancestors of the Native American group you chose.

Step 2 **Identify Sources** Think about how we know this information now. Which print sources or websites will your group use? How do you know that these are reliable sources?

I'll use books written by or websites that are run by official organizations of the Native American group I chose. They are reliable because they are credible outside of the websites. They give unbiased information.

Step 3 **Find and Record Information** Think about how text and audio features can enhance your presentation. For example, you might include photographs of sites where the people lived or recordings of someone speaking the language. As you find these features and other relevant information, take notes and cite your sources.

Step 4 **Organize and Synthesize Information** Organize your notes and draft your presentation. Select the text and audio features you wish to include.

Step 5 **Create and Present** Create your final presentation. Before sharing it with the class, review it. Is the display of your text features visible? Is the sound of your audio features clear?

The Ancestral Puebloans built and lived in large communities like these cliff dwellings. What does the photograph show that would be hard to describe in words?

The photograph shows how the dwellings look.

Quick Tip

Additional text and audio features can include photographs of artifacts, captions, charts, graphs, illustrations, music, recorded speeches, or recorded sounds from events or places.

Tony Craddock/Shutterstock.com

CHECK IN 1 2 3 4

Unit 3 • Text Set 3 75

Reading/Writing Companion, p. 75

English Language Learners

Use the following scaffolds with **Step 3**.

Beginning

Review with students what a multimedia presentation includes. Provide students with a list of the kinds of text and audio features they should include in their research. Guide them to valid, historically relevant sources to find text and audio features for their presentation. Then have partners discuss the audio features they found using: I found an audio clip about ______. Review the students' notes and provide feedback.

Intermediate

Review with students what a multimedia presentation includes. Brainstorm with students a list of the kinds of text and audio features they should include in their research. Guide partners to valid, historically relevant sources to research text and audio features. Then have them discuss the features they found using: I found a text/an audio about ______. I can use this to ______. Review the students' notes and provide feedback.

Advanced/Advanced High

Discuss with students what a multimedia presentation includes. Have partners use valid, historically relevant sources to research text and audio features. Then have them discuss how they will use the features to enhance their presentation.

DIGITAL TOOLS

RESOURCE TOOLKIT Take Notes: Print; Organizing Notes

Dinah Zike's FOLDABLES Study Organizer

FOLDABLES

MULTIMODAL

Who | Where | When | Other Facts | Audio | Visual

Accordion Foldable®

FORMATIVE ASSESSMENT

STUDENT CHECK-IN

Presentation Ask students to share their multimedia presentations.

Audio and Text Features Have students share an example of how incorporating audio and text features helped support their presentation.

Use the Check-In routine to reflect and fill in the bars on Reading/Writing Companion page 75.

"Machu Picchu: Ancient City"

Lexile 990L

LEARNING GOALS

Read **We can apply strategies and skills to read argumentative text.**

Reread **We can reread to analyze text, craft, and structure and compare texts.**

Have students apply what they learned as they read.

Discuss different cultures of ancient civilizations in the Americas.

What makes this text complex?

▶ Prior Knowledge

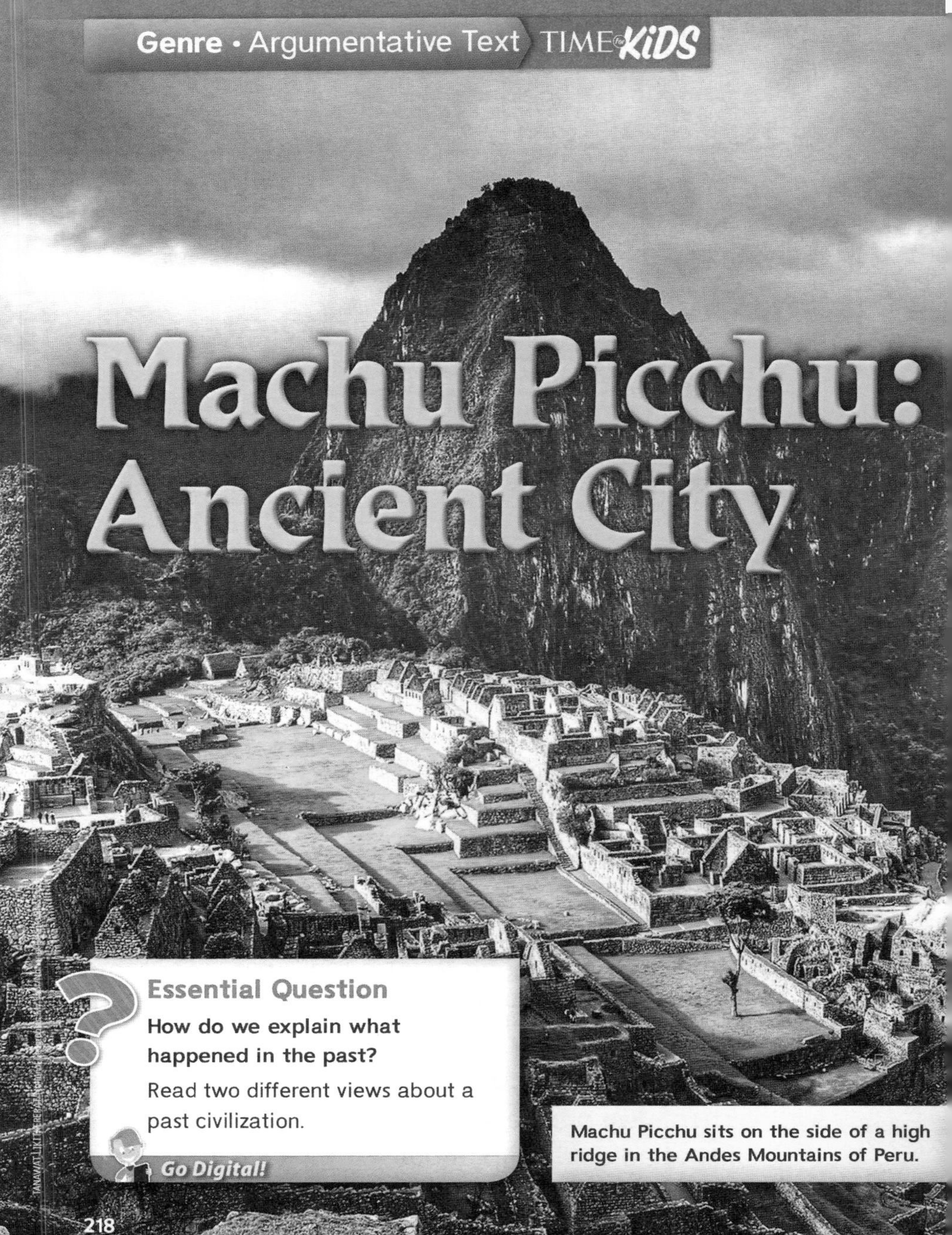

Genre • Argumentative Text TIME KIDS
Machu Picchu: Ancient City
Essential Question
How do we explain what happened in the past?
Read two different views about a past civilization.
Go Digital!
Machu Picchu sits on the side of a high ridge in the Andes Mountains of Peru.
218

Literature Anthology, pp. 218–219

Close Reading Routine

Read DOK 1–2

- Identify important ideas and details.
- Take notes and summarize.
- Use ACT prompts as needed.

Reread DOK 2–3

- Analyze the text, craft, and structure.
- Use *Reading/Writing Companion*, pp. 76–77.

Integrate DOK 3–4

- Integrate knowledge and ideas.
- Make text-to-text connections.
- Use the Integrate lesson.
- Complete the Show Your Knowledge task.
- Inspire action.

DIFFERENTIATED READING

You may wish to read the full selection aloud once with minimal stopping before using the Read prompts.

Approaching Level Have students listen to the selection summary. Use the Reread prompts during Small-Group time.

On Level and Beyond Level Pair students or have them independently complete the Reread prompts on **Reading/ Writing Companion** pages 76–77.

English Language Learners Have ELLs listen to a summary of the selection, available in multiple languages. See also the **ELL Small Group Guide**.

The Royal Treatment

Machu Picchu was a royal estate.

Machu Picchu (pronounced MA-choo PEEK-choo) was a city that was part of the ancient Inca empire, a civilization which once ruled much of western South America. Machu Picchu was built during the reign of the emperor Pachacuti. It was abandoned in the early 1500s. In 1911 an American **historian** named Hiram Bingham came upon the **intact** settlement of stone structures.

Because Machu Picchu was isolated, it was extremely well **preserved**. Though Bingham was not a trained **archaeologist**, he uncovered many remains from the site. Over the years, other archaeologists have studied these objects and structures to learn about the Incas. They have tried to figure out why they built a settlement in this location. Researchers have examined artifacts, such as **fragments** of pottery and metal pins, to find clues about the activities of the people who lived there. Historians have also looked at architectural details. This can help them determine how the buildings were used.

A Reasonable Retreat

Some experts have concluded from these studies that Machu Picchu was built to be an astronomical observatory. They point out structures they believe were used to track the movements of the Sun. However, other strong evidence supports a different view: The site was once a royal estate of the Inca leader.

Historians of this opinion argue that Machu Picchu was too small to be a city. The number of dwellings suggests that only about 750 people ever lived there. The settlement and its objects were also constructed with great care. Moreover, the site was a relatively short distance from the capital city of Cuzco. When it was cold there, the emperor and his family could head for a warmer environment at Machu Picchu. There, he would have hunted, relaxed, and met with noblemen. 1

Given this evidence, it is only reasonable to conclude that Machu Picchu was the emperor's home away from home.

219

Access Complex Text

Prior Knowledge

Use a map or globe to show the location of Machu Picchu in the Andes Mountains. Explain the meaning of "retreat" in the heading "A Reasonable Retreat."

- *A retreat is a quiet, secluded place used for rest and relaxation.*
- *World leaders often have special retreats. The U.S. president uses a retreat called Camp David.*

Read

Set a Purpose Tell students to preview the text and set a purpose for reading. Setting a purpose can help them monitor comprehension.

Use the Graphic Organizer

Analytical Writing Distribute copies of online Author's Claim **Graphic Organizer 3.** Remind students to take notes as they read.

1 Context Clues DOK 2

What is the meaning of *dwellings* in paragraph 4? (homes) Which words in the sentence helped you determine the meaning? ("750 people"; "lived there")

STOP AND CHECK DOK 1

Summarize Why does the author think that Machu Picchu was a royal estate? (Artifacts, structure, size, and proximity to Cuzco suggest it was a vacation retreat.)

Reread

Author's Claim DOK 2

Reading/Writing Companion, **p. 76**

Why does the author address the claim that some experts believe Machu Picchu was an observatory? (The author wants to acknowledge the opposing claim by countering it with what he or she considers a stronger argument.)

Make Inferences DOK 2

Explain Evidence can help readers infer an idea the author doesn't state directly.

Model The author doesn't describe the geography around Machu Picchu, but one theory says it was a royal estate. I can infer that Machu Picchu was in a beautiful area.

Apply Have students infer other ideas about Machu Picchu based on evidence.

Read

2 Author's Claim DOK 1

An argumentative text tries to convince a reader to support the author's perspective. What is the author's claim in "Eyes on the Skies"? (Machu Picchu was an Inca observatory.) Which details support the author's claim? (The Sun was important to Incas; they tracked the movement of planets and stars by creating the structures like the Temple of the Sun to create calendars and mark the winter solstice.) Add the author's claim and supporting details to your graphic organizer.

Reread

Author's Craft: Language DOK 2

Reading/Writing Companion, p. 77

How does the author help you visualize the Temple of the Sun? (The author uses literal, precise language to give a detailed description of the Temple of the Sun, mentioning the "curved walls" and "carved stone," and providing exact details about the location of things.) How does the photograph support the text? (The photograph shows some of the details the author mentions.)

Connect to Content

Primary vs Secondary Sources

To study ancient civilizations, historians rely on primary sources: original objects created at the time of the civilization. The artifacts discussed on page 219 are primary sources. Secondary sources are interpretations of primary sources, such as a scientific article based on research. This article is a secondary source. Have them compare the types of information found in primary and secondary sources.

Eyes on the Skies

Machu Picchu was used as an observatory.

Machu Picchu was a city built on a site more than 7,000 feet high in the Andes Mountains of Peru. This special place was built during the 1400s, the **era** of Pachacuti. He was the ruler of the ancient empire of the Incas at that time. Some archaeologists think that the city was used by Pachacuti as a retreat. But other experts argue that the structures found at Machu Picchu indicate it was an Inca observatory.

Incas and the Sun

Historians have pieced together what they know about Inca life. They have studied explorers' written accounts and **remnants** of Inca settlements. Historians know that the Sun was important to the Inca religion. The Incas believed the movements of the Sun in the sky affected their way of life. The Incas tracked the movements of the Sun and used their observations to create calendars needed by farmers to plant their crops.

Window to the Sky

The fact that religion and agriculture were closely tied to the movements of the Sun has led some experts to look at the structures at Machu Picchu in a new light. They believe the Inca may have built some of these as tools for tracking the Sun, stars, and planets.

One such structure is called the Temple of the Sun. Its curved walls partially enclose a space with a carved stone in the center. This stone appears to point to the center of a window that faces east. Archaeologists have studied these features to try to **reconstruct** how it worked as an observatory. They have found that at a certain time of the year called the winter solstice, light from the rising Sun in the east aligns precisely with the carved stone.

The winter solstice is the shortest day of the year, which occurs in June in South America. Historical accounts of Inca life in other settlements indicate that this date was important to the culture, especially royal families. They would hold a Festival of the Sun, during which they performed ceremonies in honor of the Sun god. Similar ceremonies could have also taken place at Machu Picchu. 2

220

Literature Anthology, pp. 220–221

Spotlight on Language

Page 220, Paragraph 1 Read the paragraph. Discuss the meaning of *retreat* and *observatory.* (cognate: *observatorio*) *Do some archaeologists believe that Machu Picchu was a retreat?* (yes) Discuss the meaning of *observatory* (cognate: *observatorio*). *Which words tell the reason experts think Machu Picchu was an observatory?* (the structures found, indicate)

TIME KIDS

An Ancient Observatory

While other evidence indicates that the royal family used the site as a retreat, the royal family could have traveled here for the winter solstice. The importance of the Sun to the culture and the placement and design of structures like the Temple of the Sun show that it likely was used as an observatory. Machu Picchu helped the Incas keep an eye on the sky.

Respond to the Text

1. Use important details from the selection to summarize. SUMMARIZE
2. What is your opinion about how ancient civilizations used Machu Picchu? Explain why you think your belief offers the stronger argument. WRITE
3. Why is it important to learn about different views of history? Which view of Machu Picchu do you agree with? Why? TEXT TO WORLD

The Temple of the Sun marks the winter solstice.

221

Read

Summarize

Guide students to use the information from the Author's Claim **Graphic Organizer 3** to summarize.

Return to Purpose Review students' purpose for reading. Then ask partners to share how setting a purpose helped them understand the text.

Reread

Analyze the Text

After students read and summarize the selection, have them reread to develop a deeper understanding by answering the questions on pages 76–77 of the **Reading/Writing Companion**.

Integrate

Compare Texts DOK 4

Have students compare and contrast how the authors present information on studying the past in "What Was the Purpose of the Inca's Knotted Strings?" and "Machu Picchu: Ancient City." Ask: *What is similar and different about how the authors explain what happened in the past?*

Integrate

Build Knowledge: Make Connections

Talk About the Text Have partners discuss the Essential Question: *How do we explain what happened in the past?*

Write About the Text Have students add their ideas to their Build Knowledge pages of their reader's notebooks.

Anchor Chart Record any new ideas on the Build Knowledge anchor chart.

Add to the Vocabulary List Have students write down any words they learned about studying the past in their reader's notebooks.

FORMATIVE ASSESSMENT

STUDENT CHECK-IN

Read Have partners share their graphic organizers and summaries. Then have them reflect using the Check-In routine.

Reread Have partners share responses and text evidence on Reading/Writing Companion pages 76–77. Then have them use the Check-In routine to reflect and fill in the bars.

LEARNING GOALS

We can use text evidence to respond to argumentative text.

OBJECTIVES

Quote accurately from a text when explaining what the text says explicitly and when drawing inferences from the text.

Identify the author's purpose.

Explain how an author uses reasons and evidence to support particular points in a text, identifying which reasons and evidence support which point(s).

Identify the author's claim.

Produce clear and coherent writing in which the development and organization are appropriate to task, purpose, and audience.

Draw evidence from literary or informational texts to support analysis, reflection, and research.

Apply grade 5 Reading standards to informational texts.

ACADEMIC LANGUAGE

- *claim, support, prompt*

TEACH IN SMALL GROUP

Approaching Level and **On Level** Have partners work together to plan and complete the response to the prompt.

Beyond Level Ask students to respond to the prompt independently.

ELL Group students of mixed proficiency levels to discuss and respond to the prompt.

Reread

Write About the Anchor Text

Analyze the Prompt DOK 3

Read the prompt aloud: *What is your opinion about how ancient civilizations used Machu Picchu? Explain why you think your belief offers the stronger argument.* Ask: *What is the prompt asking you to write?* (to explain the strength of one argument over the other) Say: *Let's reread to analyze the evidence each author includes in support of his or her claim. This will help us gather evidence to make inferences that will aid us in answering the prompt.*

Analyze Text Evidence

Remind students that authors of argumentative text make a claim, or argument, that clearly states their opinion on a topic. They then use facts, reasons, and relevant evidence to support the claim. Have students look at **Literature Anthology** page 219 and ask: *What evidence does the author of "The Royal Treatment" present about Machu Picchu being used as a retreat?* (The site was too small to be a city; it was not very far from the capital city and was located in a warmer climate.) Turn to page 220 and ask: *What important fact about the Incas helped shape the claim of the author of "Eyes on the Skies"?* (Tracking the movement of the sun was an important part of Inca religion and agriculture.) Encourage students to look for more details that support each author's claim. Then have them craft a short response based on which author they agree with more.

Respond

COLLABORATE

Review pages 76–77 of the **Reading/Writing Companion**. Have partners or small groups refer to and discuss their completed charts and writing responses from those pages. Then direct students' attention to the sentence starters on page 78 of the Reading/Writing Companion. Have them use sentence starters to guide their responses.

Students should focus on the details and evidence each author includes to support his or her perspective on the purpose of Machu Picchu. Students should include specific examples of supporting evidence and explain how it strengthens their opinion. Remind students to vary sentence structure by combining short sentences and adding phrases and clauses to others. Students may use additional paper to complete the assignment if needed.

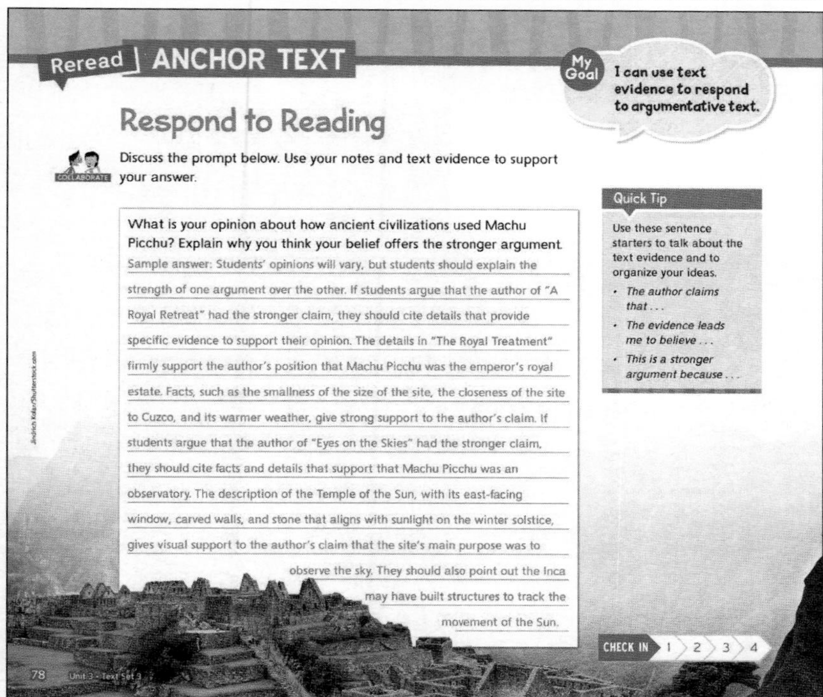
Reread | ANCHOR TEXT

My Goal: I can use text evidence to respond to argumentative text.

Respond to Reading

COLLABORATE Discuss the prompt below. Use your notes and text evidence to support your answer.

What is your opinion about how ancient civilizations used Machu Picchu? Explain why you think your belief offers the stronger argument.

Sample answer: Students' opinions will vary, but students should explain the strength of one argument over the other. If students argue that the author of "A Royal Retreat" had the stronger claim, they should cite details that provide specific evidence to support their opinion. The details in "The Royal Treatment" firmly support the author's position that Machu Picchu was the emperor's royal estate. Facts, such as the smallness of the size of the site, the closeness of the site to Cuzco, and its warmer weather, give strong support to the author's claim. If students argue that the author of "Eyes on the Skies" had the stronger claim, they should cite facts and details that support that Machu Picchu was an observatory. The description of the Temple of the Sun, with its east-facing window, carved walls, and stone that aligns with sunlight on the winter solstice, gives visual support to the author's claim that the site's main purpose was to observe the sky. They should also point out the Inca may have built structures to track the movement of the Sun.

Quick Tip

Use these sentence starters to talk about the text evidence and to organize your ideas.

- *The author claims that . . .*
- *The evidence leads me to believe . . .*
- *This is a stronger argument because . . .*

CHECK IN 1 2 3 4

Jindrich Kolar/Shutterstock.com

78 Unit 3 · Text Set 3

Reading/Writing Companion, p. 78

English Language Learners

Use the following scaffolds with **Respond**.

Beginning

Read the prompt with students and discuss what they will write about. Review the students' completed charts on **Reading/Writing Companion** pages 76-77. Remind them of the authors' claims in "A Reasonable Retreat" and "Eyes in the Skies." Ask: *Do you think Machu Picchu was used a retreat or an observatory?* (retreat/observatory) Have them discuss the arguments and respond using: I think the author of "A Reasonable Retreat" has the stronger argument. The details support the author's claim that Machu Picchu was a retreat.

Intermediate

Read the prompt with students. Have partners review their completed charts on **Reading/Writing Companion** pages 76-77. Ask: *Which author has the stronger argument about Machu Picchu?* I think the author of "A Reasonable Retreat" has the stronger argument. Then have them discuss details that support the author's position using: The facts and details support that Machu Picchu was used as a retreat. One fact/detail is ____.

Advanced/Advanced High

Review the prompt and sentence starters on page 78 with students. Have partners discuss which author has the stronger claim and cite facts and details to support their opinion. Then have them respond using the sentence starters.

ELL NEWCOMERS

Have students listen to the summaries of the **Anchor Text** in their native language and then in English to help them access the text and develop listening comprehension. Help students ask and answer questions with a partner. Use these sentence frames: *What is each author's position on Machu Picchu? The first author believes ____. The second author believes ____.* Then have them complete the online **Newcomer Activities** individually or in pairs.

FORMATIVE ASSESSMENT

STUDENT CHECK-IN

Ask partners to share their response on Reading/Writing Companion page 78. Have them use the Check-In routine to reflect and fill in the bars.

"Dig This Technology!"

Lexile 970L

LEARNING GOALS

Read We can apply strategies and skills to read expository text.

Reread We can reread to analyze text, craft, and structure, and to compare texts.

Have students apply what they learned as they read.

What makes this text complex?

▶ **Genre**

Analytical Writing Compare Texts DOK 4

As students read, have them think about the Essential Question: *How do we explain what happened in the past?* They will compare this text with "Machu Picchu: Ancient City."

Read

1 Compare and Contrast DOK 2

How was Machu Picchu studied in 1911? (The ground had to be dug up to reach the site.) Today? (Researchers use a 3-D scanner.) Explain which method is better. (A 3-D scanner more accurately reconstructs the city.)

2 Author's Perspective DOK 2

What is the author's perspective about the new technology being used at Machu Picchu? (The author thinks it is an improvement over how the site was originally studied. Now researchers do not have to disrupt the site.)

Reread

Author's Craft: Text Features DOK 2

Reading/Writing Companion, p. 80

How does the diagram help you understand how scientists analyze artifacts? (It provides a visualization that shows how GPR works.)

Genre • Expository Text
TIME KIDS
Compare Texts
Read about how historians use technology to gather information.
Dig This Technology!
In 1911, archaeologists found most of Machu Picchu covered by plants. This growth had to be cut back to see the structures. Artifacts from the site, however, were often harder to reach. At the time, researchers had to rely on a careful process of removing earth to reach artifacts.
New technology has changed that. Archaeologists can now analyze, explore, and even discover remnants of the past in other ways.
A big help to researchers of Machu Picchu today is the use of a 3-D scanner. They can use this machine to scan the site with laser beams and reconstruct the city as a digital three-dimensional picture.
222
1

Literature Anthology, pp. 222–223

Access Complex Text

Genre

While the author uses a diagram on page 223 to help readers understand how ground penetrating radar works, readers must visualize the text on page 222 in order to understand the three-dimensional scanner.

- *What two things does a 3-D scanner do?* (It scans the site with laser beams, and it reconstructs the site as a three-dimensional picture.)

The images let researchers study the city from every angle, from a distance, and from so close up you could see details of the stonework. This technology also helps researchers store information about the site. Researchers no longer have to trek up 7,000 feet above sea level to see the site in person. They can study Machu Picchu digitally.

Another tool archaeologists use is a device that looks like a lawn mower. Called "ground penetrating radar" (GPR), it uses radar to locate artifacts under the ground. Radar bounces radio waves off an object to show its location. The diagram below shows how GPR helps archaeologists find artifacts.

These cool tools make the work of uncovering objects from the past a little easier. Moreover, since digging around a site can harm the area, these technologies also help preserve historic sites. Now, archaeologists can dig into the past, without having to lift a shovel. 2

Make Connections

How have new tools helped historians get information about the past? ESSENTIAL QUESTION

Think of a historian's opinion about a place or artifact. How could new tools find evidence to support this point? TEXT TO TEXT

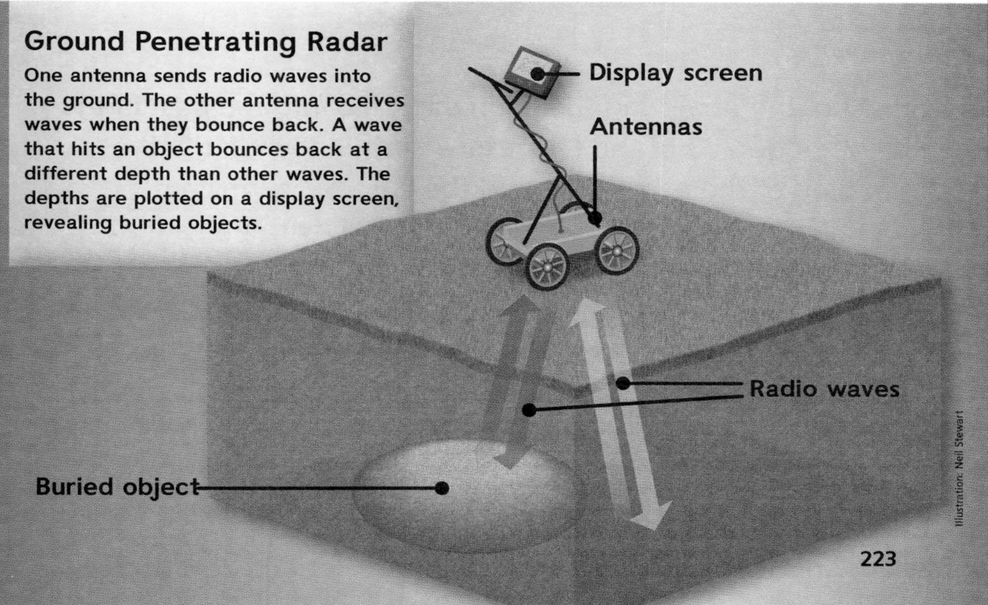

Ground Penetrating Radar
One antenna sends radio waves into the ground. The other antenna receives waves when they bounce back. A wave that hits an object bounces back at a different depth than other waves. The depths are plotted on a display screen, revealing buried objects.
Display screen
Antennas
Radio waves
Buried object
Illustration: Neil Stewart
223

English Language Learners

Build Background Show photos of artifacts and explain that they are human-made objects that have historical or cultural value. *Artifacts can help archaeologists learn about cultures that no longer exist.* Ask: *What kinds of artifacts do you think the researchers found at Machu Picchu?* (pottery, utensils, weapons) *What do you think archaeologists learned from them?* (Possible answers: what people ate with; how people lived; what people used to hunt)

Read

Summarize

Guide students to summarize the selection.

Reread

Analyze the Text

After students read and summarize, have them reread and answer questions on pages 79–80 of the **Reading/Writing Companion.**

Integrate

Build Knowledge: Make Connections

Talk About the Text Have partners discuss how we explain what happened in the past.

Write About the Text Have students add their ideas to their Build Knowledge pages of their reader's notebooks.

Anchor Chart Record any new ideas on the Build Knowledge anchor chart.

Compare Texts DOK 4

Text to Text Answer: Possible response: The author of "Eyes on the Skies" said Machu Picchu's main use was as an observatory. Scientists could use a 3-D scanner to view the site from different angles and see if other structures align with objects in the sky. Evidence: On page 220, I read that the Temple of the Sun at Machu Picchu might be an observatory. On page 222, I read that 3-D images are used to study archaeological sites.

FORMATIVE ASSESSMENT

STUDENT CHECK-IN

Read Ask partners to share their summaries. Then have them reflect using the Check-In routine.

Reread Ask partners to share their responses on Reading/Writing Companion pages 79-80. Then have them use the Check-In routine to reflect and fill in the bars.

LEARNING GOALS

We can identify figurative language to help us read and understand expository text.

OBJECTIVES

Write routinely over extended time frames (time for research, reflection, and revision) and shorter time frames (a single sitting or a day or two) for a range of discipline-specific tasks, purposes, and audiences.

Demonstrate understanding of figurative language, word relationships, and nuances in word meanings. Interpret figurative language, including similes and metaphors, in context.

ELA ACADEMIC LANGUAGE

- *figurative language, literal, context, expression*
- Cognates: *lenguaje figurado, literal, contexto, expresión*

Figurative Language

1 Explain

Have students turn to **Reading/Writing Companion** page 81. Share with students key points of figurative language:

- Figurative language is language that is not used in a literal sense. The words and phrases in figurative language have a nonliteral meaning, or meaning other than their dictionary definitions. Instead, they are used to mean something different or unexpected.
- Authors use figurative language to create interesting mental images. Figurative language can also help an author make a strong point or indicate that an idea is especially important.
- Understanding the context in which figurative language is used can help you determine its meaning.

2 Model

Model identifying and analyzing the expression *dig into the past* in the last sentence on page 223 of the **Literature Anthology**. Clarify the nonliteral meaning of the expression and the context in which it's used. Then point out that archaeologists often work with items that have been buried under the ground for many years. As a group, discuss why the phrase is an effective way to describe how new technology benefits archaeology. Have partners determine whether they think the author would have used this same expression if the article described the ways in which new technology benefited a different profession.

3 Guided Practice

Now guide students as they read the sentence on **Reading/Writing Companion** page 81 and rewrite it using their own examples of figurative language. Ask: *What is something in this sentence that you might be able to describe as something else?* (Possible answer: Since the sentence says that "layers of dirt" are removed using tools, I could think of something else that comes in layers and compare the dirt layers to that.)

Once students have determined how they will approach the revision, have pairs work together to brainstorm examples of nonliteral ways to express a particular idea. Provide questions to focus students' thinking: *Which of your ideas paints the clearest picture in readers' minds? Which helps readers recognize that you are making an important point by using figurative language?*

Allow students time to enter their responses on page 81. Encourage students to use a print or online thesaurus to find descriptive words.

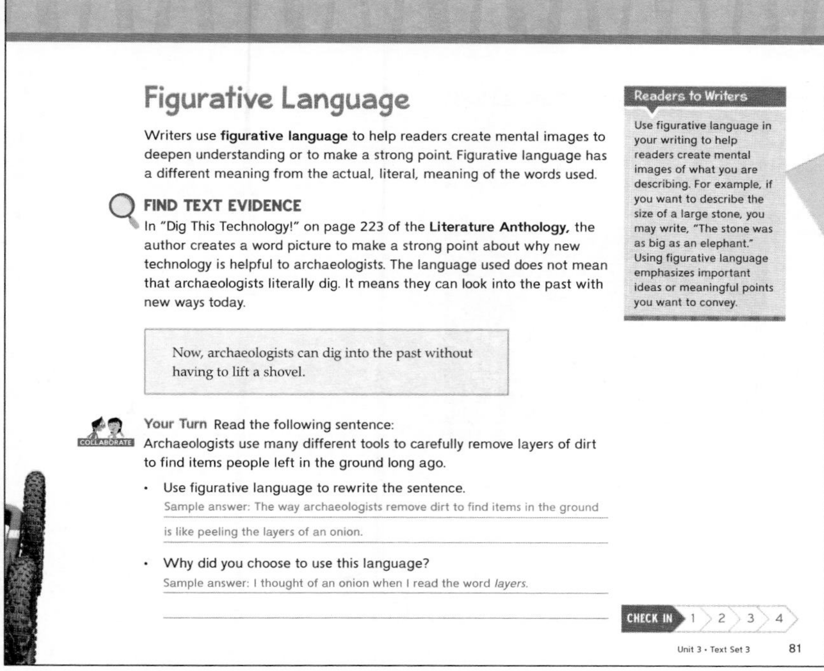

Figurative Language

Writers use **figurative language** to help readers create mental images to deepen understanding or to make a strong point. Figurative language has a different meaning from the actual, literal, meaning of the words used.

FIND TEXT EVIDENCE
In "Dig This Technology!" on page 223 of the **Literature Anthology**, the author creates a word picture to make a strong point about why new technology is helpful to archaeologists. The language used does not mean that archaeologists literally dig. It means they can look into the past with new ways today.

Now, archaeologists can dig into the past without having to lift a shovel.

Readers to Writers
Use figurative language in your writing to help readers create mental images of what you are describing. For example, if you want to describe the size of a large stone, you may write, "The stone was as big as an elephant." Using figurative language emphasizes important ideas or meaningful points you want to convey.

COLLABORATE
Your Turn Read the following sentence:
Archaeologists use many different tools to carefully remove layers of dirt to find items people left in the ground long ago.

- Use figurative language to rewrite the sentence.
  Sample answer: The way archaeologists remove dirt to find items in the ground is like peeling the layers of an onion.
- Why did you choose to use this language?
  Sample answer: I thought of an onion when I read the word *layers*.

CHECK IN 1 2 3 4

Unit 3 • Text Set 3 81

Reading/Writing Companion, p. 81

Readers to Writers

Reiterate that authors often include context to ensure readers understand figurative language and can create mental images. Reread the last sentence of "Dig This Technology" on **Literature Anthology** page 223. Ask: *Why did the author include the phrase "without having to lift a shovel"? How does it help you understand the figurative language in the sentence?*

English Language Learners

Use the following scaffolds with **Guided Practice.**

Beginning

Read with students the sentence from "Dig This Technology!" Have students point to the phrase *layers of dirt.* Using gestures, convey the meaning *of layers.* Ask: *Does a sandwich have layers?* (yes) *What is a vegetable that has layers?* (onion) Have pairs act out this frame: Archaeologists remove layers of dirt like peeling the skin of an onion.

Intermediate

Read with students the sentence from "Dig This Technology!" Ask: *What things do you know that come in layers?* Help students brainstorm layered items. (Possible answers: cake, sandwich, banana, onion) Write the answers on the board. *Which of these would create the strongest image in your reader's mind?* Have students vote and help pairs use the winner to rewrite the sentence.

Advanced/Advanced High

Have students read the sentence from "Dig This Technology!" *What part of this sentence paints an image? What part can you visualize?* (carefully removing layers of dirt) *What things do you know that come in layers?* List students' answers. Model writing a sentence with figurative language. Guide partners as they write another sentence using an option from the list.

FORMATIVE ASSESSMENT

STUDENT CHECK-IN

Ask partners to share their Your Turn responses on Reading/Writing Companion page 81. Then have them use the Check-In routine to reflect and fill in the bars.

LEARNING GOALS

We can compare the photo with the selections in this text set to build knowledge about how people explain what happened in the past.

OBJECTIVES

Draw on information from multiple print or digital sources, demonstrating the ability to locate an answer to a question quickly or to solve a problem efficiently.

Close Reading Routine

Read DOK 1–2

- Identify key ideas and details.
- Take notes and summarize.
- Use ACT prompts as needed.

Reread DOK 2–3

- Analyze the text, craft, and structure.
- Use the ***Reading/Writing Companion***.

Integrate DOK 3–4

- Integrate knowledge and ideas.
- Make text-to-text connections.
- Use the Integrate/Make Connections lesson.
- Use ***Reading/Writing Companion***, p. 82.
- Complete the Show Your Knowledge task.
- Inspire action.

FORMATIVE ASSESSMENT

STUDENT CHECK-IN

Ask partners to share their response. Have them use the Check-In routine to reflect and fill in the bars on Reading/Writing Companion page 82.

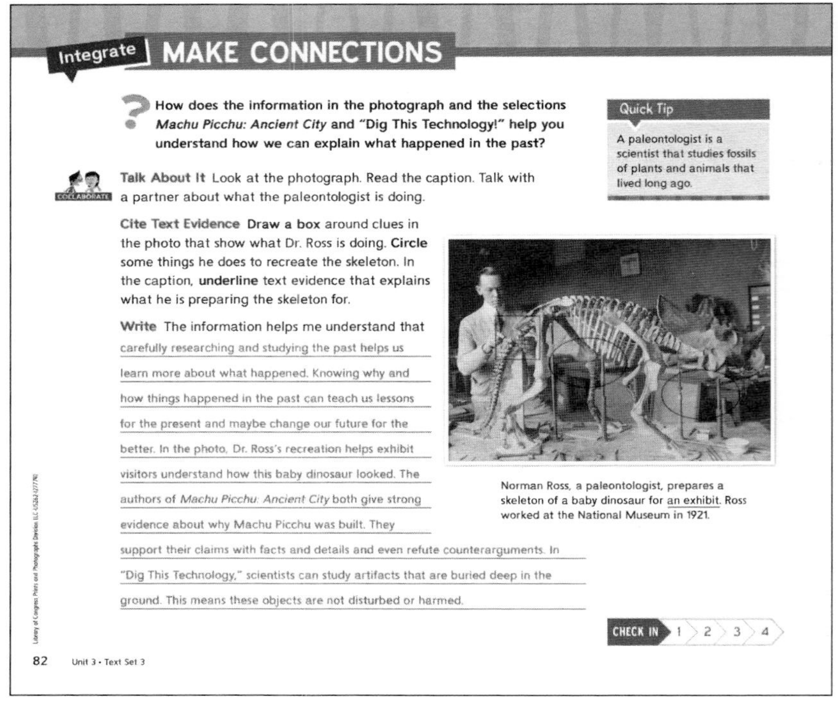

Integrate | MAKE CONNECTIONS

How does the information in the photograph and the selections *Machu Picchu: Ancient City* and "Dig This Technology!" help you understand how we can explain what happened in the past?

Quick Tip

A paleontologist is a scientist that studies fossils of plants and animals that lived long ago.

COLLABORATE

Talk About It Look at the photograph. Read the caption. Talk with a partner about what the paleontologist is doing.

Cite Text Evidence **Draw a box** around clues in the photo that show what Dr. Ross is doing. **Circle** some things he does to recreate the skeleton. In the caption, **underline** text evidence that explains what he is preparing the skeleton for.

Write The information helps me understand that carefully researching and studying the past helps us learn more about what happened. Knowing why and how things happened in the past can teach us lessons for the present and maybe change our future for the better. In the photo, Dr. Ross's recreation helps exhibit visitors understand how this baby dinosaur looked. The authors of *Machu Picchu: Ancient City* both give strong evidence about why Machu Picchu was built. They support their claims with facts and details and even refute counterarguments. In "Dig This Technology," scientists can study artifacts that are buried deep in the ground. This means these objects are not disturbed or harmed.

Norman Ross, a paleontologist, prepares a skeleton of a baby dinosaur for an exhibit. Ross worked at the National Museum in 1921.

CHECK IN 1 2 3 4

82 Unit 3 • Text Set 3

Reading/Writing Companion, p. 82

Integrate

Make Connections DOK 4

Share and discuss students' responses to the "Remnants of the Past" Blast. Then display the Build Knowledge anchor chart. Review the chart. Have students read through their notes, annotations, and responses for each text. Then ask them to complete the Talk About It activity on **Reading/Writing Companion** page 82.

Cite Text Evidence

Guide students to see the connections between the photograph on **Reading/Writing Companion** page 82 and the selections. Remind students to reread the caption under the photograph.

Write

Students should refer to their notes on the chart as they respond to the writing prompt at the bottom of the page. When students have finished writing, have groups share and discuss their responses.

Build Knowledge: Make Connections

Talk About the Text Have partners discuss how people explain what happened in the past.

Write About the Text Have students add their ideas to their Build Knowledge pages of their reader's notebooks.

Anchor Chart Record any new ideas on the Build Knowledge anchor chart.

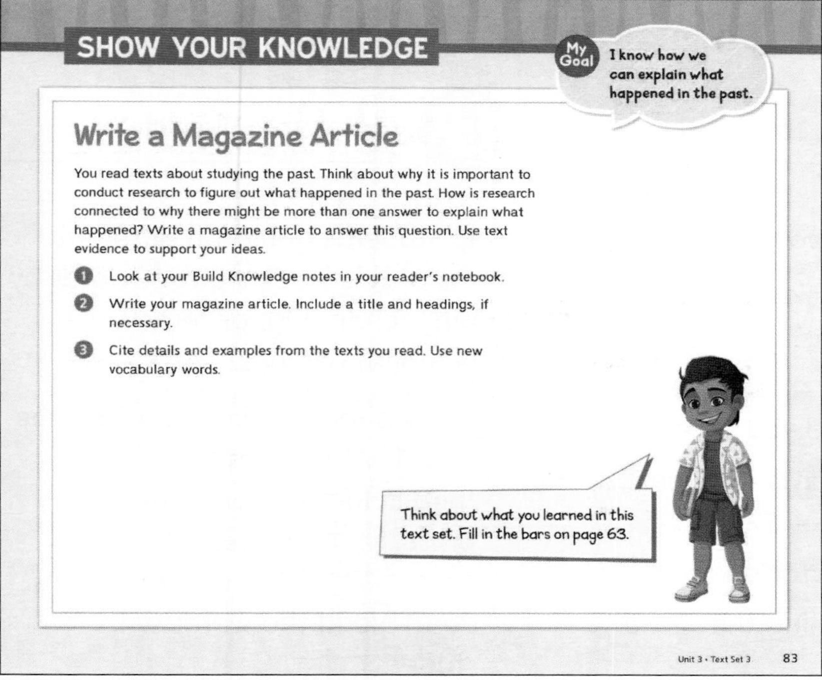

SHOW YOUR KNOWLEDGE

My Goal: I know how we can explain what happened in the past.

Write a Magazine Article

You read texts about studying the past. Think about why it is important to conduct research to figure out what happened in the past. How is research connected to why there might be more than one answer to explain what happened? Write a magazine article to answer this question. Use text evidence to support your ideas.

1. Look at your Build Knowledge notes in your reader's notebook.
2. Write your magazine article. Include a title and headings, if necessary.
3. Cite details and examples from the texts you read. Use new vocabulary words.

Think about what you learned in this text set. Fill in the bars on page 63.

Unit 3 • Text Set 3 83

Reading/Writing Companion, p. 83

Integrate

Show Your Knowledge DOK 4

Write a Magazine Article

Explain to students that they will show how they built knowledge across the text set by writing a magazine article about the importance of studying the past based on what they read. Display the Build Knowledge anchor chart and ask: *How do we explain what happened in the past?*

Step 1 Guide partners to review the Build Knowledge anchor chart in their reader's notebook to discuss the prompt.

Step 2 Discuss the features of a magazine article. Ask students to create a list of reasons about why it is important to study the past. Remind them to include examples from the texts, video, and listening passage. Prompt students to use words from their Build Knowledge vocabulary list in their reader's notebook.

Step 3 Encourage students to think of an interesting title to grab readers' attention. Have them include text features such as photographs, captions, timelines, maps, and more in their articles.

Inspire Action

Share Your Magazine Article Have students present and display their articles. Ask them to use sticky notes to post comments under each article. Presenters can choose to respond to the comments.

What Are You Inspired to Do? Have partners talk about the texts they read this week. Ask: *What else do the texts inspire you to do?*

LEARNING GOALS

We can write a magazine article to show the knowledge we built about how we explain what happened in the past.

OBJECTIVES

Report on a topic or text or present an opinion, sequencing ideas logically and using appropriate facts and relevant, descriptive details to support main ideas or themes; speak clearly at an understandable pace.

Adapt speech to a variety of contexts and tasks, using formal English when appropriate to task and situation.

Demonstrate command of the conventions of standard English grammar and usage when writing or speaking.

ELA ACADEMIC LANGUAGE

- *study, explain, examples, reasons*
- Cognates: *estudiar, ejemplos, razones*

DIGITAL TOOLS

Show Your Knowledge Rubric

ENGLISH LANGUAGE LEARNERS

Provide sentence frames for support. *It is important to study the past because ____. For example, the Incas ____.*

MY GOALS ROUTINE

What I Learned

Review Goals Have students turn back to page 63 of the Reading Writing Companion and review the goals for the text set.

Reflect Have students think about the progress they've made toward the goals. Review the key. Then have students fill in the bars.

LEARNING GOALS

- We can build and expand on new vocabulary words.
- We can use context clues to figure out unfamiliar and multiple-meaning words.
- We can write using new vocabulary words.

OBJECTIVES

Determine the meaning of general academic and domain-specific words and phrases in a text relevant to a grade 5 topic or subject area.

Determine or clarify the meaning of unknown and multiple-meaning words and phrases, choosing flexibly from a range of strategies.

Use context (e.g., cause/effect relationships and comparisons in text) as a clue to the meaning of a word or phrase.

Use common, grade-appropriate Greek and Latin affixes and roots as clues to the meaning of a word (e.g., *photograph, photosynthesis*).

DIGITAL TOOLS

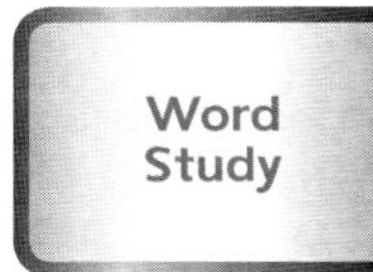

Vocabulary Activities

ENGLISH LANGUAGE LEARNERS

Pair students of different language proficiency levels to practice vocabulary. Guide partners as they repeat the exercise in **Latin Roots** for *preserved* and *reconstruct*. Provide them the following roots: *con-/with, struct-/build, pre-/ before, serv-/protect.*

STUDENT CHECK-IN

After each lesson, have partners share and reflect using the Check-In routine.

Connect to Words

Practice the target vocabulary.

1. What kind of tasks does an **archaeologist** do?
2. If you could visit another **era**, which one would you choose?
3. How are **fragments** different from parts?
4. What does a **historian** do?
5. Describe something that is no longer **intact**.
6. Tell about a souvenir you have **preserved**.
7. What would you do to **reconstruct** a broken vase?
8. Are **remnants** usually big or small?

Build Vocabulary

- Display *calculator, colonies,* and *settlement.*
- Define the words and discuss their meanings with students.
- Write *calculate* under *calculator*. Have partners write other words with the same root and define them. Then have partners ask and answer questions using the words.
- Repeat with *colonies and settlement.*

Content Words

Help students generate different forms of this week's target words by adding, changing, or removing inflectional endings.

- Draw a four-column chart on the board. Write *preserved* in the third column. Then write *preserve, preserves,* and *preserving* in the other columns. Read aloud the words with students.
- Have students share sentences using each form of *preserved.*
- Students should add to the chart for *reconstruct* and then share sentences using different forms of the word.
- Have students copy the chart in their reader's notebook.

See **Practice Book** page 179.

Latin Roots

- Remind students to use Latin roots to help figure out the meaning of unfamiliar words.
- Write *contradict*. Explain that the Latin root *contra-* means "against" and *dict-* means "say, speak."
- Have partners discuss the meaning of *contradict* and determine its part of speech.
- Have students write the word's meaning in their reader's notebook.

Spiral Review

LESSON 3 Reinforce the Words

Review last text set and this text set's vocabulary words. Have students orally complete each sentence stem.

1. The museum preserved the fragments of ____.
2. The historian wrote about the ____ era.
3. An archaeologist found ____.
4. The stunt man's body was surprisingly intact after ____.
5. People make artificial ____ to mimic the real thing.
6. One function of a computer is ____.
7. To be more flexible, you could ____.
8. One obstacle to good health is ____.
9. A doctor's techniques for helping people include ____.

Context Clues

Remind students to use sentence clues to define unknown words.

- Display On Level **Differentiated Genre Passage** "How Did King Tut Die?" Read the first two lines on page O1. Model using context clues to define *fatal* in the subhead.
- Have pairs use context clues to define other unfamiliar words.
- Partners can confirm meanings in print or an online dictionary.

See **Practice Book** page 180.

OPTION LESSON 4 Connect to Writing

- Have students write sentences in their reader's notebook using the target vocabulary.
- Tell them to write sentences that provide context to show what the words mean.
- ELL Provide the Lesson 3 sentence stems 1–9 for students needing extra support.

Write Using Vocabulary

Have students write something they learned from this text set's words in their reader's notebook. For example, they might write about how people *reconstruct* things that have been broken or taken apart or how they study a past *era*.

Shades of Meaning

Help students generate words related to the concept of *era*. Draw a word web and write *era* in the center.

- Have partners generate words and ideas to add to the web, including synonyms.
- Add words and phrases not included, such as *age, epoch, time,* and *period.*
- Ask students to copy the word web in their reader's notebook.

OPTION LESSON 5 Word Squares

MULTIMODAL

Ask students to create Word Squares for each vocabulary word.

- In the first square, students write the word (e.g., *intact*).
- In the second square, students write a definition and any related words, such as synonyms (e.g., *whole, unharmed*).
- In the third square, students draw a simple sketch that will help them remember the word (e.g., an unbroken vase).
- In the fourth square, students write nonexamples, including antonyms for the word (e.g., *broken, damaged, shattered*).

Have partners discuss their squares.

Morphology

Draw a T-chart with the headings *historian* and *suffixes.*

- Discuss how the suffixes *-y, -ical,* and *-ic* change the meaning or part of speech.
- Have students add the suffixes to *historian,* removing *-ian* first. Review the meaning of the new words. Have partners search for other words with these suffixes.

Write Using Vocabulary

Have students use vocabulary words in their extended writing.

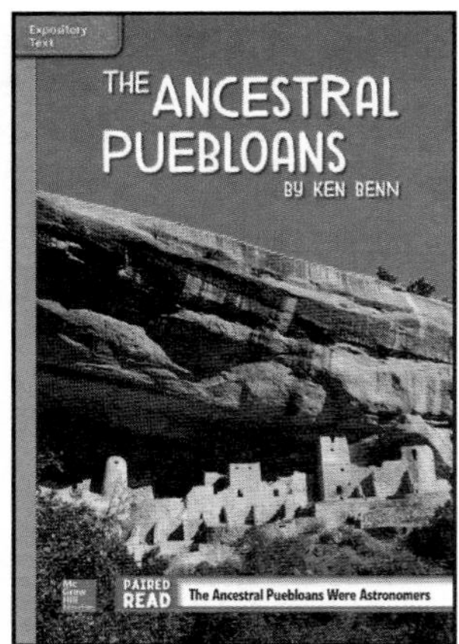

Lexile 820L

OBJECTIVES

Explain how an author uses reasons and evidence to support particular points in a text, identifying which reasons and evidence support which point(s).

Read on-level prose and poetry orally with accuracy, appropriate rate, and expression on successive readings.

ELA ACADEMIC LANGUAGE

- *summarize, evidence, context clues*
- Cognate: *evidencia*

Approaching Level

Leveled Reader: *The Ancestral Puebloans*

Preview and Predict

- Read the Essential Question: *How do we explain what happened in the past?*
- Have students preview the title, table of contents, and first page of *The Ancestral Puebloans.* Students should use information in the text and images to predict what they think the selection will be about.

Review Genre: Expository Text

Tell students that this selection is an expository text that gives factual information. The author may also have an opinion on the topic and support his or her claim with reasons and evidence. Expository texts often contain text features, such as diagrams, maps, charts, and photographs. Have students identify features of expository text in *The Ancestral Puebloans.*

Close Reading

Note Taking Ask students to use a copy of online Author's Claim **Graphic Organizer 3** as they read.

Pages 2–3 *What evidence supports the author's claim that the Ancestral Puebloans were excellent engineers? Summarize information in the text.* (The Ancestral Puebloans built houses into cliffs. Some buildings had hundreds of rooms and were several stories high.)

Pages 4–7 *Look at the map on page 4. In what present-day states did the Ancestral Puebloans live?* (Utah, Colorado, Arizona, New Mexico) *What archaeological evidence supports the idea that the early Ancestral Puebloans were basket makers?* (baskets found in dry rock areas) *Why did the Ancestral Puebloans build their homes near a water source?* (They needed water for farming.)

Pages 8–9 *What do the different baskets and their uses reveal about the Ancestral Puebloans?* (The Ancestral Puebloans built their lives around farming.)

Pages 10–11 *What context clues help you understand the meaning of the word* pueblos*?* (towns) Have students add this word to their reader's notebook. *According to the author, what does the fact that the Ancestral Puebloans brought thousands of logs to the Chaco Canyon tell us about them?* (They worked well together.)

Pages 12–13 *With a partner, summarize the theories about why the Ancestral Puebloans moved away.* (Violence may have caused communities to break up; drought may have made farming hard.)

Pages 14–17 *As a result of archaeological study, what have many people concluded about what happened to the Ancestral Puebloans?* (They merged into other cultures.)

Respond to Reading Revisit the Essential Question and ask students to complete the Respond to Reading section on page 18.

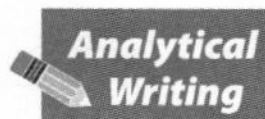

Write About Reading Check that students have correctly identified the author's claim by citing text evidence.

Fluency: Accuracy and Rate

Model Model reading page 10 with accuracy and at an appropriate rate. Next, reread the page aloud and have students read along with you.

Apply Have students practice reading the passage with a partner.

Paired Read: "The Ancestral Puebloans Were Astronomers"

Make Connections: Write About It

Before reading, have students note that this is an argumentative text. Then discuss the Essential Question. After reading both texts, ask students to write connections between the authors' different claims on the Ancestral Puebloans.

Leveled Reader

Build Knowledge

Talk About the Text Have partners discuss how we explain what happened in the past.

Write About the Text Have students add their ideas to the Build Knowledge pages of their reader's notebooks.

FOCUS ON SOCIAL STUDIES

Students can extend their knowledge of Ancestral Puebloan culture by completing the social studies activity on page 24.

LITERATURE CIRCLES

Ask students to conduct a literature circle using the Thinkmark questions to guide the discussion. You may wish to have a whole-class discussion, using information from both selections in the Leveled Reader, about how we explain what happened in the past.

LEVEL UP

IF students read the Approaching Level fluently and answered the questions,

THEN pair them with students who have proficiently read the On Level and have students

- echo-read the On Level main selection.
- use self-stick notes to identify details that show the author's claim.

ACT Access Complex Text

The On Level challenges students by including more **domain-specific words** and **complex sentence structures**.

"How Did King Tut Die?"
Lexile 750L

OBJECTIVES

Quote accurately from a text when explaining what the text says explicitly and when drawing inferences from the text.

Draw on information from multiple print or digital sources, demonstrating the ability to locate an answer to a question quickly or to solve a problem efficiently.

Explain how an author uses reasons and evidence to support particular points in a text, identifying which reasons and evidence support which point(s).

Identify the author's claim.

Determine or clarify the meaning of unknown and multiple-meaning words and phrases based on grade 5 reading and content, choosing flexibly from a range of strategies.

Use context (e.g., cause/effect relationships and comparisons in text) as a clue to the meaning of a word or phrase.

ELA ACADEMIC LANGUAGE

- *compare, contrast, context clues, diagram, claim*
- Cognates: *comparar, contrastar, contexto, diagrama*

Approaching Level

Genre Passage: "How Did King Tut Die?"

Build Background

- Read aloud the Essential Question: *How do we explain what happened in the past?* Ask students to consider the texts they have read in this text set and compare two experiences or discoveries that have taught people something about the past. Use the following sentence starters to help focus discussion:

  Because of this discovery/experience, people learned . . .

  This helped me understand . . .

- The online **Differentiated Genre Passage** "How Did King Tut Die?" references cultural aspects of ancient Egypt. Explain that when an Egyptian pharaoh died, his body would be mummified and placed in a sarcophagus, and then buried in a tomb with his riches. Guide students to consider ways scientists might have tested King Tut's mummy to learn about his death.

Review Genre: Argumentative Text

Review that in argumentative texts, authors use facts, details, and examples to support their claim, or opinion. Diagrams can also support a claim. Note that the two texts that students will read offer different claims on the same topic.

Close Reading

Note Taking As students first read the passage, have them annotate central ideas, relevant details, unfamiliar words, and questions they have. Then read again and use the following questions. Remind students to cite text evidence.

Read

Genre: Argumentative Text Read the first subhead and paragraph 1 on page A1. *How does the subhead help express a claim?* (It suggests a hypothesis for how King Tut died. This hypothesis is the basis for the author's claim.)

Author's Claim Read the last paragraph on page A1. *What does the author believe caused Tut's death?* (The author thinks Tut died from a massive infection after getting injured in a chariot race.) *Why does the author believe this?* (Modern science showed that Tut had a broken bone and an infection.)

Context Clues Read paragraph 1 on page A2. *What phrase tells you why Tut's disorders were* inherited*?* ("From his parents" tells me that Tut's parents passed them on to him.) *What does* inherited *mean?* ("received from your parents")

Text Structure: Compare and Contrast Read the rest of page A2. *What does the second author believe caused Tut's death?* (A genetic disorder made Tut's body weak.) *How does that differ from the first author's claim?* (The first author thinks Tut died from an infection caused by breaking his leg.)

Text Feature: Diagram *What text feature does the author include on page A2?* (a diagram of King Tut's feet) *What does it show?* (It shows how badly formed King Tut's left foot was and how it was turned in.)

COLLABORATE **Summarize** Guide pairs to summarize the authors' claims and evidence and to choose the claim they found more convincing.

Reread

Use the questions on page A3 to guide rereading.

Author's Craft Read the last section on page A1. *Is "The Truth in the Bone" a good heading for this section? Explain.* (Yes, it helps me understand how the author reached his or her conclusion. It tells me that the broken bone is an important piece of evidence.)

Author's Craft *How does the author of the first passage try to persuade you to agree with his or her claim?* (The author uses scientific evidence to persuade readers. The author states that X-rays and computer programs show that King Tut probably died as a result of a chariot accident.)

Author's Craft *How does the diagram of King Tut's feet help you understand the second author's claim?* (The diagram shows King Tut's bone problems. The author thinks that if King Tut had these problems, he could not drive a chariot.)

Integrate

COLLABORATE **Make Connections** Guide students to connect "How Did King Tut Die?" to other selections they have read. Help partners cite evidence and respond to this question: *How has technology affected how we learn about the past?*

Compare Texts Draw a T-chart labeled with titles of texts students considered. Help pairs compare how each text helps readers see the importance of technology in understanding the past.

Build Knowledge

Talk About the Text Have partners discuss how we explain what happened in the past.

Write About the Text Have students add their ideas to the Build Knowledge pages of their reader's notebooks.

Differentiate and Collaborate

COLLABORATE **Be Inspired** Have students think about "How Did King Tut Die?" and other selections they have read. Ask: *What do the texts inspire you to do?* Use the following activities or have pairs of students think of a way to respond to the texts.

Make a Poster Think of what you learned about how scientists and archaeologists study the past and what they learn from their studies. Create a poster to share the passages' examples or other archaeological finds.

Hold a Debate Choose a topic discussed in this text set and organize a debate with classmates. Form two groups and have each group prepare an argument in support of a theory explaining the topic. Have other classmates determine the more convincing argument.

Readers to Writers

Counterargument Reiterate that authors of argumentative texts often use facts, details, and other evidence to refute, or disprove, an opposing claim. Have students reread paragraphs 2–3 on page A2. Ask: *How does this author refute the first author's claim? Does this make the second argument more or less persuasive?*

LEVEL UP

IF students read the Approaching Level fluently and answered the questions,

THEN pair them with students who have proficiently read the On Level. Have them

- partner read the On Level passage.
- summarize both authors' claims.

Approaching Level

Phonics/Decoding

REVIEW WORDS WITH *r*-CONTROLLED VOWEL SYLLABLES

OBJECTIVES

Use combined knowledge of all letter-sound correspondences, syllabication patterns, and morphology (e.g., roots and affixes) to read accurately unfamiliar multisyllabic words in context and out of context.

Decode words with *r*-controlled vowel syllables.

I Do Review with students that every syllable has one vowel sound. Write the word *market* on the board and underline the letters *mar*. Read the word aloud, emphasizing the first syllable. Explain that when a vowel is followed by *r*, both letters must remain in the same syllable because the two combine to form a special vowel sound.

We Do Write the words *argue, cargo,* and *story* on the board. Read the words aloud, and then draw a line under the *r*-controlled vowel syllable in each word.

You Do Add the words *purpose* and *furnace* to the board. Read the words aloud. Have students identify each *r*-controlled vowel syllable. Then have them chorally read the words aloud.

BUILD WORDS WITH *r*-CONTROLLED VOWEL SYLLABLES

TIER 2

OBJECTIVES

Use combined knowledge of all letter-sound correspondences, syllabication patterns, and morphology (e.g., roots and affixes) to read accurately unfamiliar multisyllabic words in context and out of context.

Build words with *r*-controlled vowel syllables.

I Do Explain that students will be building multisyllabic words with *r*-controlled vowel syllables. Display the **Word-Building Cards** *mar, vel, por,* and *tray*. Read each syllable aloud.

We Do Work with students to combine the Word-Building Cards to build words. Have them chorally read the words *marvel* and *portray*. Help students identify the *r*-controlled vowel syllables in the words.

You Do Display the Word-Building Cards *per* and *sur*. Write the syllables *son* and *plus* on the board. Ask students to add the Word-Building Cards to the syllables to build new words. Have them share their words with the class. Write *surplus* and *person* on the board, and ask students to read the words chorally as you point to them.

PRACTICE WORDS WITH *r*-CONTROLLED VOWEL SYLLABLES

OBJECTIVES

Know and apply gradel-evel phonics and word analysis skills in decoding words.

Use combined knowledge of all letter-sound correspondences, syllabication patterns, and morphology to read accurately unfamiliar multisyllabic words in context and out of context.

Decode words with *r*-controlled vowel syllables.

I Do Write these words on the board: *juror, persuade,* and *barley*. Read the words aloud, underlining the letters in the *r*-controlled vowel syllables with your finger as you read.

We Do Write the words *barter, certain,* and *curious* on the board. Model how to pronounce the first word, underlining the letters that form the *r*-controlled vowel syllables with your finger. Then have students pronounce the remaining words. Help them identify the *r*-controlled vowel syllables in the words.

To provide additional practice, write these words on the board. Read aloud the first word and underline the *r*-controlled vowel syllable.

morning	garden	surprise
army	farmer	purpose
formal	order	thirty
border	forgive	forty

You Do Then have students read aloud the remaining words. Ask them to identify the *r*-controlled vowel syllable(s) in each word.

Afterward, point to the words in the list in random order for students to read chorally.

ELL For ELL students who need phonics and decoding practice, define words and help them use the words in sentences, scaffolding to ensure their understanding. See the **Language Transfers Handbook** for phonics elements that may not transfer from students' native languages.

Approaching Level

Vocabulary

REVIEW HIGH-FREQUENCY WORDS

TIER 2

OBJECTIVES

Acquire and use accurately grade-appropriate general academic and domain-specific words and phrases, including those that signal contrast, addition, and other logical relationships (e.g., *however, although, nevertheless, similarly, moreover, in addition*).

Review high-frequency words.

I Do Choose review words from **High-Frequency Word Cards** 81–120. Display one word at a time, following the routine:

Display the word. Read the word. Then spell the word.

We Do Ask students to state the word and spell the word with you. Model using the word in a sentence and have students repeat after you.

You Do Display the word. Ask students to say the word, and then spell it. When completed, quickly flip through the word card set as students chorally read the words. Provide opportunities for students to use the words in speaking and writing. For example, provide sentence starters such as *I laugh when* ____. Ask students to write each word in their reader's notebook.

REVIEW ACADEMIC VOCABULARY

OBJECTIVES

Acquire and use accurately grade-appropriate general academic and domain-specific words and phrases, including those that signal contrast, addition, and other logical relationships (e.g., *however, although, nevertheless, similarly, moreover, in addition*).

I Do Display each **Visual Vocabulary Card** and state the word. Explain how the photograph illustrates the word. State the example sentence and repeat the word.

We Do Point to the word on the card and read the word with students. Ask them to repeat the word. Engage students in structured partner talk about the image as prompted on the back of the vocabulary card.

You Do Display each visual in random order, hiding the word. Have students match the definitions and context sentences of the words to the visuals displayed.

ELL You may wish to review high-frequency words with ELL students using the lesson above.

UNDERSTAND ACADEMIC VOCABULARY

OBJECTIVES

Acquire and use accurately grade-appropriate general academic and domain-specific words and phrases, including those that signal contrast, addition, and other logical relationships (e.g., *however, although, nevertheless, similarly, moreover, in addition*).

I Do Display the *archaeologist* **Visual Vocabulary Card** and ask: *Does an archaeologist study old or new objects?* Explain that an archaeologist studies old objects.

We Do Ask these questions and help students respond and explain their answers.

- Does an *era* refer to a time or a person in history?
- Are *fragments* whole objects or broken pieces?
- Does a *historian* know a little or a lot about history?

You Do Have students work in pairs to respond to these questions and explain their answers.

- If a vase is *intact*, is it whole or broken?
- If you *preserved* a book, would you protect it or throw it out?
- To *reconstruct* something, do you put it together or take it apart?
- Are *remnants* of old dishes whole or in small pieces?

Have students pick words from their reader's notebook and write questions using the words. Have them respond to the questions.

CONTEXT CLUES

OBJECTIVES

Determine or clarify the meaning of unknown and multiple-meaning words and phrases based on grade 5 reading and content, choosing flexibly from a range of strategies.

Use context (e.g., cause/effect relationships and comparisons in text) as a clue to the meaning of a word or phrase.

I Do Read the first paragraph of "How Did King Tut Die?" in the Approaching Level online **Differentiated Genre Passage** page A1. Point to the word *pharaoh* in the second sentence of paragraph 1. Remind students that context clues can be used to determine the meanings of unknown words.

Think Aloud I am not sure of the meaning of *pharaoh*. Right after the word, I see a comma and the words *or king*. This context clue tells me that a pharaoh is a king.

We Do Ask students to point to the word *sarcophagus* in the second paragraph on page A1. Help students identify the context clue that helps them determine the meaning of the word.

You Do Have students use context clues to identify the meanings of *genetic* (page A2, paragraph 4) and *malaria* (page A2, paragraph 4).

Approaching Level

Fluency/Comprehension

FLUENCY

OBJECTIVES

Read grade-level prose and poetry orally with accuracy, appropriate rate, expression, and automaticity on successive readings.

Read fluently with good expression and phrasing.

I Do Explain that when reading a selection out loud, students should read at an appropriate rate for the type and difficulty of the material to ensure reasonable accuracy. Read aloud the first paragraph of "How Did King Tut Die?" in the online Approaching Level **Differentiated Genre Passage** page A1. Tell students to listen for the way you read at an appropriate rate for an argumentative text, as well as for the accuracy of your words.

We Do Read the next three paragraphs aloud, sentence by sentence, and have students repeat each sentence after you, imitating your accuracy and speed. Point out how you grouped words in ways that made sense, emphasized important points, and changed your rate of speaking to convey the text's meaning.

You Do Have partners take turns reading sentences from the passage. Remind them to focus on appropriate rate and accuracy. Listen in. Provide corrective feedback and modeling as needed.

IDENTIFY FACTS AND DETAILS

TIER 2

OBJECTIVES

Explain how an author uses reasons and evidence to support particular points in a text, identifying which reasons and evidence support which point(s).

Identify the author's claim.

Identify important facts.

I Do Remind students that in argumentative texts, the author includes logical reasons and evidence in the form of facts and details to support his or her claim about a topic.

We Do Have students reread the first paragraph of "How Did King Tut Die?" in the online Approaching Level **Differentiated Genre Passage** page A1. Guide students to identify facts and details about King Tut and the hypothesis about the cause of his death.

You Do Have students read the rest of page A1. After each paragraph, have them write down relevant facts about King Tut and the hypotheses about his death. Review their lists with them and help them explain why the facts and details they chose are relevant.

REVIEW AUTHOR'S CLAIM

OBJECTIVES

Explain how an author uses reasons and evidence to support particular points in a text, identifying which reasons and evidence support which point(s).

Identify the author's claim.

Determine an author's point of view or purpose in a text and explain how it is conveyed in the text.

I Do Remind students that the author of an argumentative text gives his or her claim, or argument, for or against a topic or idea and supports it with logical reasons and evidence. Examining reasons and evidence in the text can help readers identify and understand the author's claim.

We Do Display page A1 of "How Did King Tut Die?" in the online Approaching Level **Differentiated Genre Passage**. Refer to the list of facts students have already compiled. Point out that the subhead above the first paragraph contains the author's claim about the cause of King Tut's death. Then read the second paragraph, noting facts as you read. Guide students to use all of these facts and details to determine the author's claim.

You Do Have partners read page A2. Have them use reasons and evidence in the text to identify the author's claim in each section and the entire passage as a whole.

SELF-SELECTED READING

OBJECTIVES

Explain how an author uses reasons and evidence to support particular points in a text, identifying which reasons and evidence support which point(s).

Identify the author's claim.

Determine an author's point of view or purpose in a text and explain how it is conveyed in the text.

Summarize the text to increase understanding.

Independent Reading

In this text set, students focus on this key aspect of nonfiction: how to identify the author's purpose and perspective. Guide students to transfer what they have learned in this text set as well as in previous lessons as they read independently.

Have students choose an argumentative article for sustained silent reading and set a purpose for reading that book. Students can check the online **Leveled Reader Library** for selections. Remind students that

- identifying the reasons and evidence an author includes can help them identify the author's claim.
- as they read, they should identify the most important points the author makes and use them to summarize the text in their own words.

As they read independently, students should use **Graphic Organizer 3** to record details that help them identify the author's claim. After they finish, they can conduct a Book Talk about what they read.

- Students should share their organizers and answer this question: What is the author's claim on the topic?
- They should also relate if there were any sections they summarized to increase their understanding.

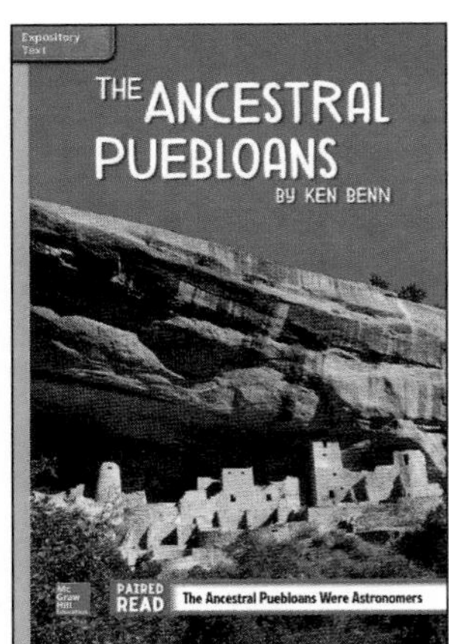

Lexile 920L

OBJECTIVES

Explain how an author uses reasons and evidence to support particular points in a text, identifying which reasons and evidence support which point(s).

Identify the author's claim.

Read grade-level prose and poetry orally with accuracy, appropriate rate, expression, and automaticity on successive readings.

ELA ACADEMIC LANGUAGE

- *summarize, evidence, context clues*
- Cognate: *evidencia*

On Level

Leveled Reader: *The Ancestral Puebloans*

Preview and Predict

- Read the Essential Question with students: *How do we explain what happened in the past?*
- Have students preview the title, table of contents, and first page of *The Ancestral Puebloans.* Students should use information in the text and images to predict what they think the selection will be about.

Review Genre: Expository Text

Tell students that this selection is an expository text that gives factual information. The author may also have an opinion on the topic and support his or her claim with reasons and evidence. Expository texts often contain text features, such as diagrams, maps, charts, and photographs. Have students identify features of expository text in *The Ancestral Puebloans.*

Close Reading

Note Taking Ask students to use a copy of online Author's Claim **Graphic Organizer 3** as they read.

Pages 2–3 *What evidence supports the author's claim that the Ancestral Puebloans were skilled engineers? Summarize information in the text.* (The Ancestral Puebloans built houses into cliffs. They built other structures that were several stories high and had hundreds of rooms. One ceremonial building had a roof that weighed many tons.)

Pages 4–7 *Look at the map on page 4. In what present-day states did the Ancestral Puebloans live?* (Utah, Colorado, Arizona, New Mexico) *What archaeological evidence supports the idea that the Ancestral Puebloans were talented artists and weavers?* (well-preserved baskets found in dry rock sites) *Why did the Ancestral Puebloans build their homes near a water source?* (They needed water for farming.)

Pages 8–9 *For what purposes did the Ancestral Puebloans make baskets?* (They made baskets for carrying babies; gathering seeds, grains, and plants; storing grains; and holding water.) *Which context clues help you understand the meaning of the word* pitch? (*water-proof black substance*) Have students add this word in their reader's notebook.

Pages 10–11 *What archaeological evidence supports the idea that the Ancestral Puebloans were an agricultural people?* (large piles of corncobs and food storage rooms found in the dwellings) *What archaeological evidence supports the claim that the Ancestral Puebloans were very organized and worked together to achieve big goals?* (Analysis of logs in buildings showed that they were cut far away and then transported.)

Pages 12–13 *Identify theories about why the Ancestral Puebloans moved away.* (Violence led communities to break up; drought prevented farming.)

Pages 14–17 *What evidence may support the theory that the Ancestral Puebloans merged into other cultures?* (Modern Pueblo people trace their ancestry from the Ancestral Puebloans and live in similar ways.)

Respond to Reading Revisit the Essential Question and ask students to complete the Respond to Reading section on page 18.

Write About Reading Check that students have correctly identified the author's claim by citing text evidence.

Fluency: Accuracy and Rate

Model Model reading page 10 with accuracy and at an appropriate rate. Next, reread the page aloud and have students read along.

Apply Have students practice reading the passage with a partner.

Paired Read: "The Ancestral Puebloans Were Astronomers"

Make Connections: Write About It

Before reading, ask students to note that this is an argumentative text. Then discuss the Essential Question. After reading, ask students to write connections between the authors' claims.

Leveled Reader

Build Knowledge

Talk About the Text Have partners discuss how we explain what happened in the past.

Write About the Text Have students add their ideas to the Build Knowledge pages of their reader's notebooks.

FOCUS ON SOCIAL STUDIES

Students can extend their knowledge of Ancestral Puebloan culture by completing the social studies activity on page 24.

LITERATURE CIRCLES

Ask students to conduct a literature circle using the Thinkmark questions to guide the discussion. You may wish to have a whole-class discussion, using information from both selections in the Leveled Reader, about how we explain what happened in the past.

IF students read the On Level fluently and answered the questions,

THEN pair them with students who have proficiently read the Beyond Level and have students

- partner-read the Beyond Level main selection.
- identify the author's claim.
- summarize text details that support it.

ACT Access Complex Text

The Beyond Level challenges students by including more **domain-specific words** and **complex sentence structures.**

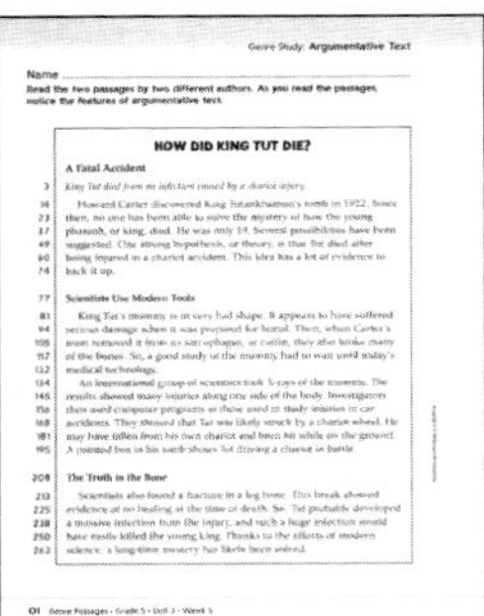

"How Did King Tut Die?"
Lexile 860L

OBJECTIVES

Quote accurately from a text when explaining what the text says explicitly and when drawing inferences from the text.

Draw on information from multiple print or digital sources, demonstrating the ability to locate an answer to a question quickly or to solve a problem efficiently.

Explain how an author uses reasons and evidence to support particular points in a text, identifying which reasons and evidence support which point(s).

Identify the author's claim.

Determine or clarify the meaning of unknown and multiple-meaning words and phrases based on grade 5 reading and content, choosing flexibly from a range of strategies.

Use context (e.g., cause/effect relationships and comparisons in text) as a clue to the meaning of a word or phrase.

ELA ACADEMIC LANGUAGE

- *compare, contrast, context clues, diagram, claim*
- Cognates: *comparar, contrastar, contexto, diagrama*

On Level

Genre Passage: "How Did King Tut Die?"

Build Background

- Read aloud the Essential Question: *How do we explain what happened in the past?* Ask students to consider the texts they have read in this text set and compare two experiences or discoveries that have taught people something about the past. Use the following sentence starters to help focus discussion:

  Because of this discovery/experience, people learned . . .

  This helped me understand . . .

- The online **Differentiated Genre Passage** "How Did King Tut Die?" references cultural aspects of ancient Egypt. Explain that when an Egyptian pharaoh died, his body would be mummified and placed in a sarcophagus, and then buried in a tomb with his riches. Have students consider ways scientists might have tested King Tut's mummy to learn about his death.

Review Genre: Argumentative Text

Review that in argumentative texts, authors use facts, details, and examples to support their claims, or opinions. Diagrams can also support claims. Note that the two texts students will read have different claims about the same topic.

Close Reading

Note Taking As students first read the passage, have them annotate relevant ideas and details, unfamiliar words, and questions they have. Then read again and use the following questions. Remind students to cite evidence from the text.

Read

Genre: Argumentative Text Read the italicized text at the top of page O1. *How do you know this is an argumentative text?* (The author states a claim about how King Tut died.)

Context Clues Read paragraph 1. *What is a* hypothesis? (an explanation that has not been proven correct) *What context clue helped you define the word?* (The sentence indicates that another word for *hypothesis* is *theory*.)

Author's Claim Read the title and introduction on page O2. *How do they reveal this author's claim?* (The title indicates that Tut had genetic weakness and disease. The introduction gives more specific detail and states that these disorders are what caused Tut's death.)

Text Structure: Compare and Contrast Read page O2. *What does the second author believe caused Tut's death?* (a genetic disorder) *How does that differ from the first author's claim?* (The first author thinks Tut died from an infection caused by breaking his leg.)

Text Feature: Diagram *What does the diagram on page O2 show?* (how badly formed Tut's left foot is and how it is turned in) *Why do you think the author included the diagram?* (It provides additional details that support the author's claim.)

Summarize Guide pairs to summarize the claims and evidence and to choose the claim they found more convincing.

Reread

Use the questions on page O3 to guide rereading.

Author's Craft *How does the first author try to persuade you to support a claim?* (The author tells about X-rays and computer programs that show how a chariot accident might have killed King Tut.)

Author's Craft *How does the diagram help you understand the second claim?* (It helps me visualize King Tut's club foot, missing bone, and another badly formed bone. The author thinks that if Tut had these problems, he could not have broken his leg from a fall driving a battle chariot.)

Author's Craft *How does the second author support the claim that Tut had weak bones?* (DNA testing was done on material from Tut's body, showing Tut likely had genetic disorders that caused weak bones.)

Integrate

COLLABORATE **Make Connections** Have students connect "How Did King Tut Die?" to other selections they have read. Ask pairs to cite evidence and respond to this question: *How has technology affected how we learn about the past?*

Compare Texts Have students create a T-chart with two titles they considered and use the chart to compare how each text helps readers see the importance of technology in understanding the past.

Build Knowledge

Talk About the Text Have partners discuss how we explain what happened in the past.

Write About the Text Have students add their ideas to the Build Knowledge pages of their reader's notebooks.

Differentiate and Collaborate

Be Inspired Have students think about "How Did King Tut Die?" and other selections they have read. Ask: *What do the texts inspire you to do?* Use the following activities or have pairs of students think of a way to respond to the texts.

Make a Poster Think of what you learned about how scientists and archaeologists study the past and what they learn from their studies. Create a poster to share the passages' examples or other archaeological finds.

Hold a Debate Choose a topic discussed in this text set and organize a debate with classmates. Form groups and have each group prepare an argument in support of a theory explaining the topic. Have other classmates determine the more convincing argument.

Readers to Writers

Counterargument Reiterate that authors of argumentative texts often use facts, details, and other evidence to refute, or disprove, an opposing claim. Have students reread paragraphs 2–3 on page O2. Ask: *How does this author refute the first author's claim? Does this make the second argument more or less persuasive?*

LEVEL UP

IF students read the **On Level** fluently and answered the questions,

THEN pair them with students who have proficiently read the **Beyond Level**. Have them

- partner read the **Beyond Level** passage.
- summarize both authors' claims.

On Level

Vocabulary/Comprehension

REVIEW ACADEMIC VOCABULARY

OBJECTIVES

Acquire and use accurately grade-appropriate general academic and domain-specific words and phrases, including those that signal contrast, addition, and other logical relationships (e.g., *however, although, nevertheless, similarly, moreover, in addition*).

I Do Use the **Visual Vocabulary Cards** to review the key selection words *archaeologist, era, fragments, historian, intact,* and *preserved.* Point to each word, read it aloud, and have students chorally repeat it.

We Do Ask these questions and help students respond.

- What is one thing that an *archaeologist* might dig up?
- What do you know about an *era* from long ago?
- Why might a bowl be in *fragments*?

You Do Have students work in pairs to respond to these questions.

- How might a *historian* learn about life long ago?
- How can you keep a delicate glass object *intact*?
- How do *preserved* items help you learn about the past?

Have students choose words from their reader's notebooks and use an online thesaurus to find synonyms and antonyms.

CONTEXT CLUES

OBJECTIVES

Determine or clarify the meaning of unknown and multiple-meaning words and phrases based on grade 5 reading and content, choosing flexibly from a range of strategies.

Use context (e.g., cause/effect relationships and comparisons in text) as a clue to the meaning of a word or phrase.

I Do Remind students that they can use context clues within sentences to determine the meanings of words. Read aloud the first paragraph of "How Did King Tut Die?" in the online **Differentiated Genre Passage** page O1.

Think Aloud I'm not sure what the word *pharaoh* means. Right after the word, I see a comma followed by "or king." These words help me to know that a pharaoh is a king.

We Do Have students read the rest of page O1 and determine the meaning of *sarcophagus* (paragraph 2). Have students look for a definition or synonym for the word.

You Do Have pairs identify context clues to determine the meanings of *DNA* (page O2, paragraph 4) and *malaria* (page O2, paragraph 4).

REVIEW AUTHOR'S CLAIM

OBJECTIVES

Explain how an author uses reasons and evidence to support particular points in a text, identifying which reasons and evidence support which point(s).

Identify the author's claim.

Determine an author's point of view or purpose in a text and explain how it is conveyed in the text.

I Do Remind students that the author of an argumentative text gives his or her claim, or argument, for or against a topic or idea and supports it with logical reasons and evidence. Examining reasons and evidence in the text can help readers identify and understand the author's claim.

We Do Have volunteers read the sections titled "A Fatal Accident" and "Scientists Use Modern Tools" on page O1. Guide students to write the most important facts in the paragraphs. Model using facts and relevant details to determine the author's claim regarding King Tut's death.

You Do Have pairs read page O2. Tell them to stop after each section and identify relevant facts and details. When they are finished, have students use the evidence to determine the author's claim.

SELF-SELECTED READING

OBJECTIVES

Explain how an author uses reasons and evidence to support particular points in a text, identifying which reasons and evidence support which point(s).

Identify the author's claim.

Determine an author's point of view or purpose in a text and explain how it is conveyed in the text.

Summarize the text to increase understanding.

Independent Reading

In this text set, students focus on how to identify the author's claim. Guide students to transfer what they have learned in this text set as well as in previous lessons as they read independently.

Have students choose an argumentative text for sustained silent reading. Students can check the online **Leveled Reader Library** for selections.

- Remind them to use facts and details in the text to determine the author's claim.
- Tell students to summarize the text in ways that maintain meaning and logical order.

Encourage students to read different argumentative texts about the same topic to increase their understanding of the issue.

- Have them fill in details, including facts that support an author's claim, on **Graphic Organizer 3**.
- Ask students to share their reactions to the articles with classmates.

You may want to include ELL students in On Level vocabulary and comprehension lessons. Offer language support as needed.

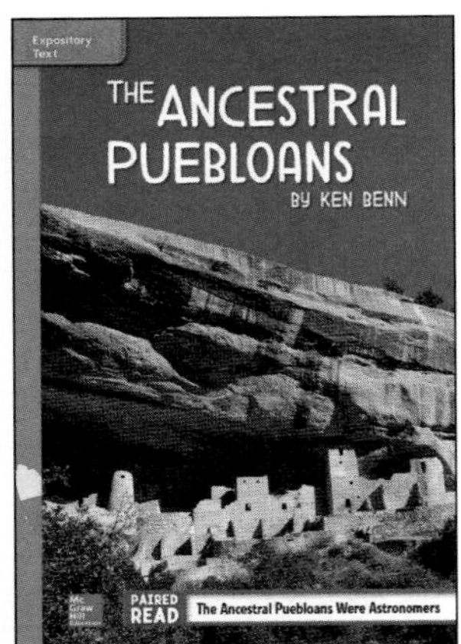

Lexile 990L

OBJECTIVES

Explain how an author uses reasons and evidence to support particular points in a text, identifying which reasons and evidence support which point(s).

Identify the author's claim.

Read grade-level prose and poetry orally with accuracy, appropriate rate, expression, and automaticity on successive readings.

ELA ACADEMIC LANGUAGE

- *summarize, evidence, context clues*
- Cognate: *evidencia*

Beyond Level

Leveled Reader: *The Ancestral Puebloans*

Preview and Predict

- Read the Essential Question with students: *How do we explain what happened in the past?*
- Have students preview the title, table of contents, and first page of *The Ancestral Puebloans.* Students should use images and information in the text to predict what they think the selection will be about.

Review Genre: Expository Text

Tell students that this selection is an expository text that gives factual information. The author may also have an opinion on the topic and support his or her claim with reasons and evidence. Expository texts often contain text features, such as diagrams, maps, charts, and photographs. Have students identify features of expository text in *The Ancestral Puebloans.*

Close Reading

Note Taking Ask students to use a copy of online Author's Claim **Graphic Organizer 3** as they read.

Pages 2–3 *What evidence supports the author's claim that the Ancestral Puebloans were remarkable engineers?* (In addition to cliff dwellings, they built structures that were several stories high and had hundreds of rooms.) *Why do you think there may be different claims about the history of the Ancestral Puebloans? Use text details to draw a conclusion.* (Archaeologists interpret clues found in Ancestral Puebloan artifacts. They also listen to oral histories that have been passed down through generations of Ancestral Puebloan descendants.)

Pages 4–5 *Look at the map on page 4. In what present-day states did the Ancestral Puebloans live?* (Utah, Colorado, Arizona, New Mexico) *According to the sidebar on page 5, where are the most recent artifacts found in an archaeological dig?* (close to the surface)

Pages 6–7 *What evidence supports the idea that Ancestral Puebloan housing became more permanent after 900 C.E.?* (They started to build with stone, mud, and brick. Some stone buildings still exist.) *Why did the Ancestral Puebloans build settlements near water?* (They couldn't depend on regular rainfall.)

Pages 8–11 *What context clues point to the meaning of* pitch? ("black substance; water-proof") Have students add this word in their reader's notebook. *What evidence shows that the Ancestral Puebloans knew how to adapt to changes in climate?* (They built dams, reservoirs, and walls to control water. They moved to other areas with better water resources.) *What evidence supports the claim that the Ancestral Puebloans worked together to achieve huge goals?* (An analysis of logs in their buildings shows that they were cut far away and then transported.)

Pages 12–17 *Summarize the theories regarding the migration of the Ancestral Puebloans. Which theory seems most credible and why.* (They migrated because of a drought or as a result of violence. The drought theory is supported by oral histories and scientific analysis.)

Respond to Reading Revisit the Essential Question and ask students to complete the Respond to Reading section on page 18.

Write About Reading Check that students have correctly identified the author's claim by citing text evidence.

Fluency: Accuracy and Rate

Model Model reading page 10 with accuracy and at an appropriate rate. Then reread the page aloud and have students read along.

Apply Have students practice reading the passage with a partner.

Paired Read: "The Ancestral Puebloans Were Astronomers"

Make Connections: Write About It

Before reading, ask students to note that the genre of this text is argumentative text. Then discuss the Essential Question. After reading, ask students to write connections between the authors' claims in the texts.

Leveled Reader

Build Knowledge

Talk About the Text Have partners discuss how we explain what happened in the past.

Write About the Text Have students add their ideas to the Build Knowledge pages of their reader's notebooks.

FOCUS ON SOCIAL STUDIES

Students can extend their knowledge of Ancestral Puebloan culture by completing the social studies activity on page 24.

LITERATURE CIRCLES

Ask students to conduct a literature circle using the Thinkmark questions to guide the discussion. You may wish to have a whole-class discussion, using information from both selections in the Leveled Reader, about how we explain what happened in the past.

GIFTED AND TALENTED

Synthesize Have partners research information about different Ancestral Puebloan artifacts, including cliff dwellings, baskets, spearheads, tools, clothing, and pottery. Tell students to present their research in the form of a poster. The poster should include five images of different Ancestral Puebloan artifacts. In a caption below each artifact, students should identify the artifact and draw a conclusion about Ancestral Puebloan culture based on that artifact. Make sure students understand that this is one strategy archaeologists use to explain what happened in the past.

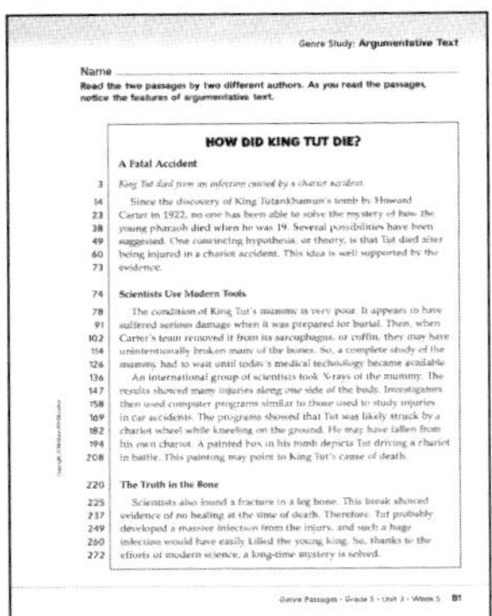

"How Did King Tut Die?"
Lexile 960L

OBJECTIVES

Quote accurately from a text when explaining what the text says explicitly and when drawing inferences from the text.

Draw on information from multiple print or digital sources, demonstrating the ability to locate an answer to a question quickly or to solve a problem efficiently.

Explain how an author uses reasons and evidence to support particular points in a text, identifying which reasons and evidence support which point(s).

Identify the author's claim.

Determine or clarify the meaning of unknown and multiple-meaning words and phrases based on grade 5 reading and content, choosing flexibly from a range of strategies.

Use context (e.g., cause/effect relationships and comparisons in text) as a clue to the meaning of a word or phrase.

ELA ACADEMIC LANGUAGE

- *compare, contrast, context clues, diagram, claim*
- Cognates: *comparar, contrastar, contexto, diagrama*

Beyond Level

Genre Passage: "How Did King Tut Die?"

Build Background

- Read aloud the Essential Question: *How do we explain what happened in the past?* Ask students to consider the texts they have read in this text set and compare two experiences or discoveries that have taught people something about the past. Use the following sentence starters to help focus discussion:

  Because of this discovery/experience, people learned . . .

  This helped me understand . . .

- The online **Differentiated Genre Passage** "How Did King Tut Die?" references cultural aspects of ancient Egypt. Explain that when an Egyptian pharaoh died, his body was mummified, placed in a sarcophagus, and then buried in a tomb with his riches. Have students consider ways scientists might have tested King Tut's mummy to learn about his death, and then read to see if their predictions were correct.

Review Genre: Argumentative Text

Review that in argumentative texts, authors use facts, details, and examples to support their claims. Diagrams can also support claims. Note that the two texts students will read have different claims about the same topic.

Close Reading

Note Taking As students first read the passage, have them annotate relevant ideas and details, unfamiliar words, and questions they have. Then read again and use the following questions. Remind students to cite evidence from the text.

Read

Genre: Argumentative Text Read the italicized text at the top of page B1. *How does it help you identify this text as argumentative text?* (It states the author's claim.)

Context Clues Read paragraph 3 on page B1. *What is an* investigator? *Explain how clues in the sentence help you define the word.* (An investigator finds out more about how something happened. The word "study" helps me understand that investigators are people who must be trying to learn something.)

Author's Claim Read page B2. *What is this author's claim?* (King Tut died of a genetic disorder and a disease.) *How do you know?* (The author indicates the claim in the title and states it in the introduction.)

Text Structure: Compare and Contrast Read page B2. *What does this author believe caused Tut's death? How does this claim differ from that of the first author?* (The first author thinks Tut died from an infection caused by breaking his leg.)

Text Feature: Diagram Look at the diagram on page B2. *How were King Tut's feet different?* (King Tut's left foot was badly formed and turned in. His right foot appeared normal.)

COLLABORATE **Summarize** Guide pairs to summarize the claims and evidence, and then choose the claim they found more convincing.

Reread

Use the questions on page B3 to guide rereading.

Author's Craft *How does the first author try to persuade you to support a claim?* (The author explains how X-rays and a computer program show severe injuries on the side of King Tut's body.)

Author's Craft *How does the diagram help you understand the second author's claim?* (It helps me visualize Tut's club foot, missing toe bone, and another bone problem. These problems show that Tut could not have broken his leg from a fall while driving a battle chariot.)

Author's Craft *How does the second author support the claim that Tut had weak bones?* (The author says that DNA testing was done on material from Tut's body. These tests show that Tut likely had genetic disorders that cause bones in the feet to weaken or collapse.)

Integrate

COLLABORATE **Make Connections** Have students connect "How Did King Tut Die?" to other selections they have read. Ask pairs to cite evidence and respond to this question: *How has technology affected how we learn about the past?*

Compare Genres Have students create a T-chart with two titles and compare how each text helps readers see why technology is helpful in understanding the past.

Build Knowledge

Talk About the Text Have partners discuss how we explain what happened in the past.

Write About the Text Have students add their ideas to the Build Knowledge pages of their reader's notebooks.

Differentiate and Collaborate

COLLABORATE **Be Inspired** Have students think about "How Did King Tut Die?" and other selections they have read. Ask: *What do the texts inspire you to do?* Use the following activities or have pairs of students think of a way to respond to the texts.

Make a Poster Think of what you learned about how scientists and archaeologists study the past and what they learn from their studies. Create a poster that shares examples from the passages you read or from other archaeological finds.

Hold a Debate Choose a topic discussed in this text set and organize a debate with classmates. Form two groups and have each group prepare an argument in support of a theory explaining the topic. Ask a teacher or other classmates to determine the more convincing argument.

Readers to Writers

Counterargument Remind students that authors of argumentative texts often use facts, details, and other evidence to refute, or disprove, an opposing claim. They do this in addition to supporting their own claims. Have students reread paragraphs 2–3 on page B2. Ask: *How does this author refute the first author's claim? Do you think this makes the second argument more or less persuasive?*

GIFTED AND TALENTED

Independent Study Have students synthesize their notes and the selections they read and think about how events from the past can teach us lessons in the present day. Have students write a letter to a class 100 years from now, describing some of the characteristics of our own society and suggesting the lessons that people can learn from those characteristics. Ask them to self-evaluate and revise if necessary.

Beyond Level

Vocabulary/Comprehension

REVIEW DOMAIN-SPECIFIC WORDS

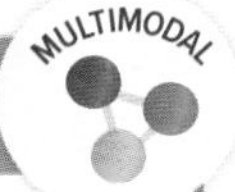

OBJECTIVES

Acquire and use accurately grade-appropriate general academic and domain-specific words and phrases, including those that signal contrast, addition, and other logical relationships.

Model Use the **Visual Vocabulary Cards** to review the meanings of the words *reconstruct* and *remnants*. Write genre-related sentences on the board using the words.

Write the words *connection* and *research* on the board and discuss the meanings with students. Then help students write sentences using these words.

Apply Have students work in pairs to review the meanings of the words *sophisticated* and *intricate*. Then have partners write sentences using these words.

CONTEXT CLUES

OBJECTIVES

Determine or clarify the meaning of unknown and multiple-meaning words and phrases based on grade 5 reading and content, choosing flexibly from a range of strategies.

Use context (e.g., cause/effect relationships and comparisons in text) as a clue to the meaning of a word or phrase.

Model Read aloud the first paragraph of "How Did King Tut Die?" in the online Beyond Level **Differentiated Genre Passage** page B1. Point to the word *hypothesis*.

Think Aloud *I want to understand the meaning of* hypothesis. *I see that the words "or theory" follow* hypothesis. *This context clue tells me that a hypothesis is a theory.*

Read aloud the second paragraph and point out the word *sarcophagus*. Indicate the context clues that help students understand that *sarcophagus* means "coffin."

Apply Have partners read the rest of the passage. Ask them to use context clues to determine the meanings of *chariot* (page B1, paragraph 3), *DNA* (page B2, paragraph 4), and *malaria* (page B2, paragraph 4).

Analyze Challenge students to find other words in the passage that might be difficult to understand. Have them choose three words and write a sentence that contains a context clue for each. Have partners trade papers and determine the meanings using context clues.

Have students repeat the activity by choosing words from their reader's notebooks and finding the definitions in an online dictionary. Then students should write sentences using the words and context clues.

REVIEW AUTHOR'S CLAIM

OBJECTIVES

Explain how an author uses reasons and evidence to support particular points in a text, identifying which reasons and evidence support which point(s). Identify the author's claim.

Determine an author's point of view or purpose in a text and explain how it is conveyed in the text.

Model Remind students that the author of an argumentative text gives his or her claim, or argument, for or against a topic or idea and supports it with logical reasons and evidence. Examining reasons and evidence in the text can help readers identify and understand the author's claim.

Have students reread page B1 of "How Did King Tut Die?" in the Beyond Level online **Differentiated Genre Passage.** Ask discussion questions, such as What relevant facts and details does the author include? How are they connected? Then guide students to use the facts and details to determine the author's claim regarding King Tut's death.

Apply Have students identify relevant facts and details in the passage on a copy of the online Author's Claim **Graphic Organizer 3.** Students should use the information in the organizer to determine the author's claim. Ask partners to discuss how the author's claim in "A Fatal Accident" differs from that in "Genetic Weakness and Disease," and which argument they find more convincing.

SELF-SELECTED READING

OBJECTIVES

Explain how an author uses reasons and evidence to support particular points in a text, identifying which reasons and evidence support which point(s).

Identify the author's claim.

Determine an author's point of view or purpose in a text and explain how it is conveyed in the text.

Summarize the text to increase understanding.

Independent Reading

In this text set, students focus on how to identify the author's claim. Guide students to transfer what they have learned in this text set as well as in previous lessons as they read independently.

Have students choose an argumentative text for sustained silent reading. Students can check the online **Leveled Reader Library** for selections.

- Have them fill in **GraphicOrganizer 3** with reasons and evidence in the form of facts and detailsto determine the author's claim.
- Remind them to use important points in the text to summarize it.

Encourage students to keep a reading journal. Ask them to read argumentative text about the same topic to better evaluate multiple viewpoints.

- Students can write summaries of the articles in their journals.
- Ask students to share their reactions to the articles with classmates.

You may wish to assign the third Be Inspired! activity from the lesson plan as Independent Study.

Notes

Extended Writing 1

Argumentative Essay

Writing to Sources

Writing Prompt: Write an argumentative essay to present to your class. Answer the question: Should students participate in study abroad programs?

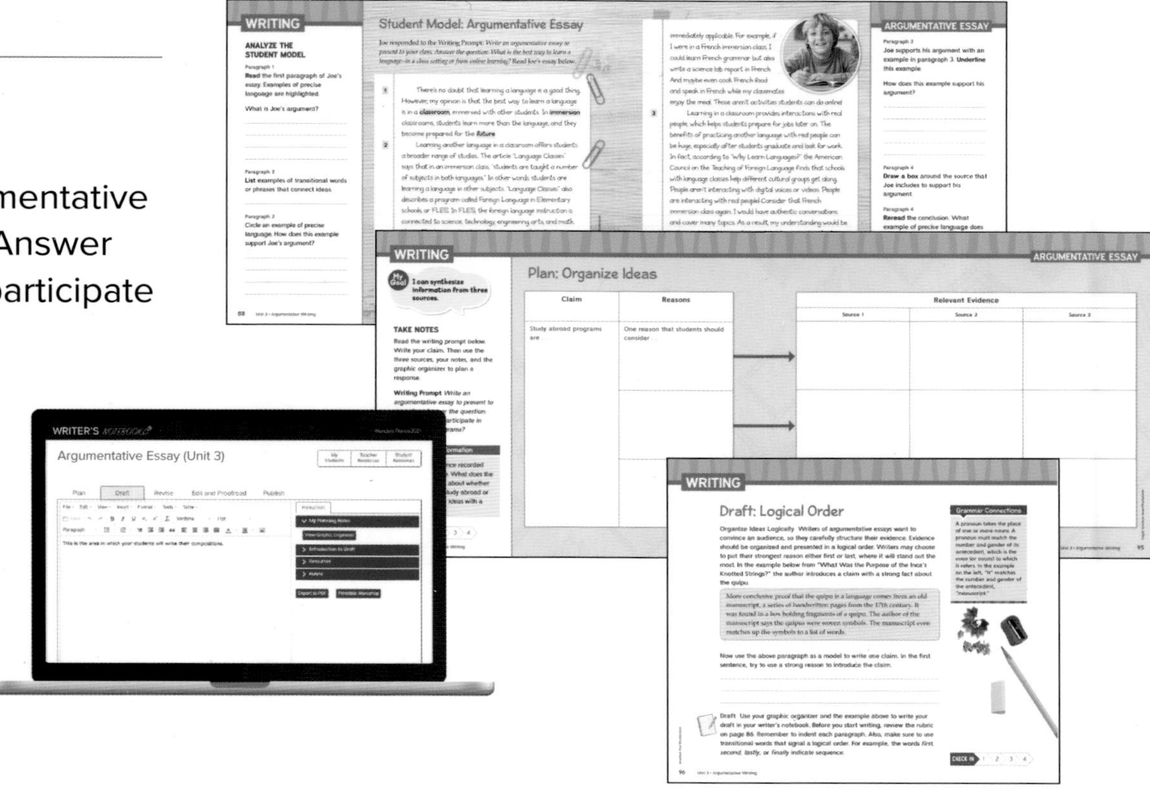

Extended Writing 2

Argumentative Essay

Writing to Sources

Writing Prompt: Write an argumentative essay to present to your class. Answer the question: Why is it important to treat archaeological sites with respect?

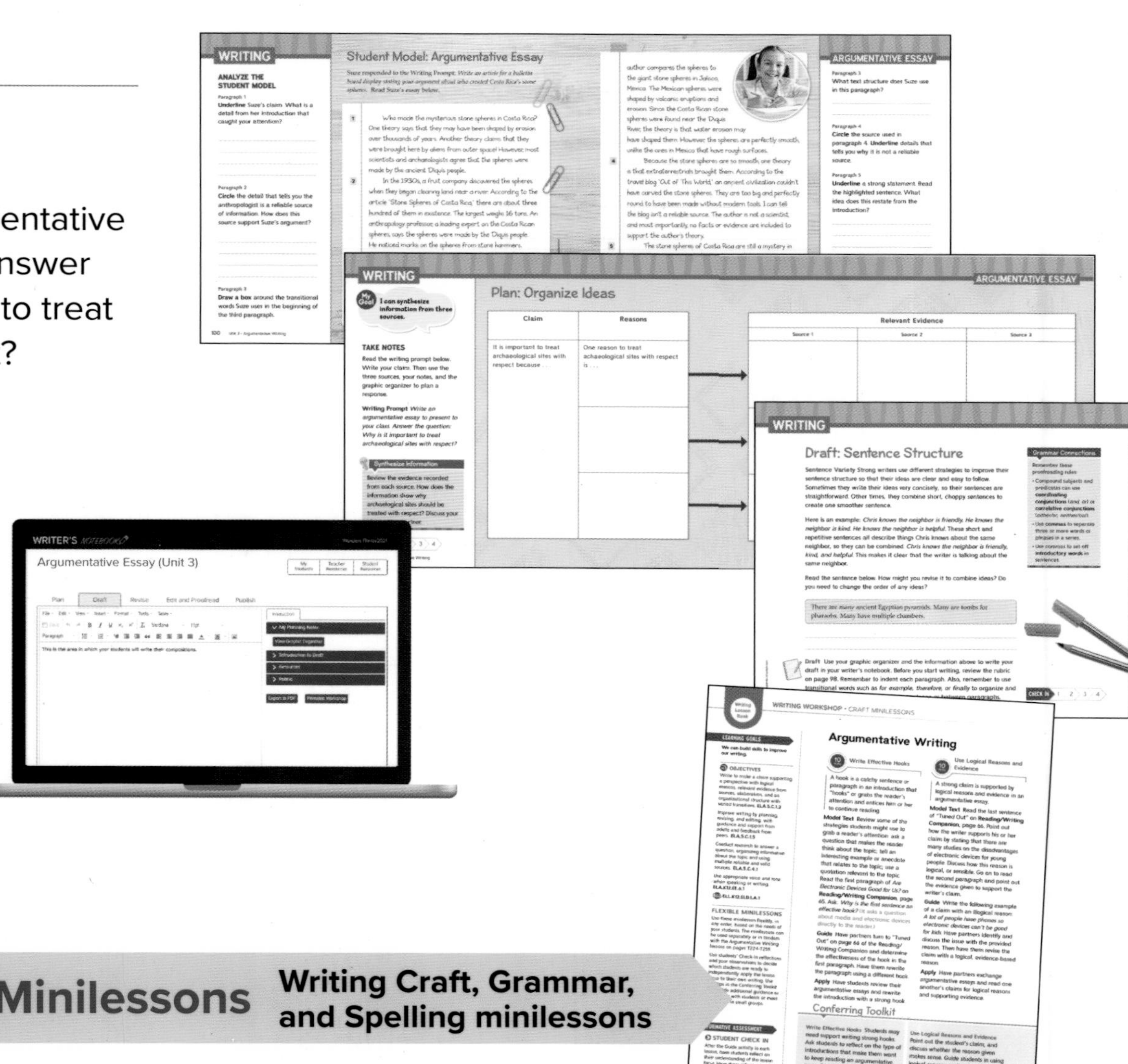

Flexible Minilessons **Writing Craft, Grammar, and Spelling minilessons**

Extended Writing: Write to Sources

Argumentative Essay

Extended Writing Goals

- I can write an argumentative essay.
- I can synthesize information from three sources.

Start off each Extended Writing Project with a Writing Process minilesson, or choose a Craft minilesson from the Writing Craft Lesson Bank. As you confer with students, the rest of your students write independently or collaboratively or confer with peers.

Writing Process Minilessons

During Writing Process minilessons, students first analyze a rubric and student model, and then answer a writing prompt, going through each step of the writing process to develop an argumentative essay.

- Analyze the Rubric
- Precise Language
- Analyze the Student Model
- Analyze the Prompt
- Analyze the Sources
- Plan: Organize Ideas
- Draft: Logical Order
- Revise: Peer Conferences

Independent and Collaborative Writing

- Provide time during writing for students to work collaboratively with partners and independently on their own writing.
- Use this time for teacher and peer conferencing.

Flexible Minilessons

Choose from the following minilessons to focus on areas where your students need support.

Writing Craft Lesson Bank

Write Effective Hooks T260
Use Logical Reasons and Evidence T260
Outline Information T261
Use Parallel Structure T261
Choose Persuasive Words T261
Brainstorm Ideas T262
Integrate Sources T262
Use Formal or Informal Language T263
Add Strong Transitions T263
Use Conjunctions and Commas T263

Grammar Lesson Bank

Action Verbs T264
Subject-Verb Agreement T265
Verb Tenses T266
Avoid Shifting Tenses T267
Main and Helping Verbs T268
Special Helping Verbs; Contractions; Troublesome Words T269
Linking Verbs T270
Punctuating Titles and Product Names T271

Spelling Lesson Bank

Open Syllables T274–T275
Open Syllables (V/V) T276–T277
Differentiated Spelling Lists T274, T276
Vowel Team Syllables T278–T279
Consonant + *le* Syllables T280–T281
Differentiated Spelling Lists T278, T280

Suggested Pacing

Students can develop their writing over four weeks, taking time to deconstruct a student model and then work with sources to write their own argumentative essay. Adjust the pacing to address your students' needs.

Weeks 1–2 ANALYZE A STUDENT MODEL

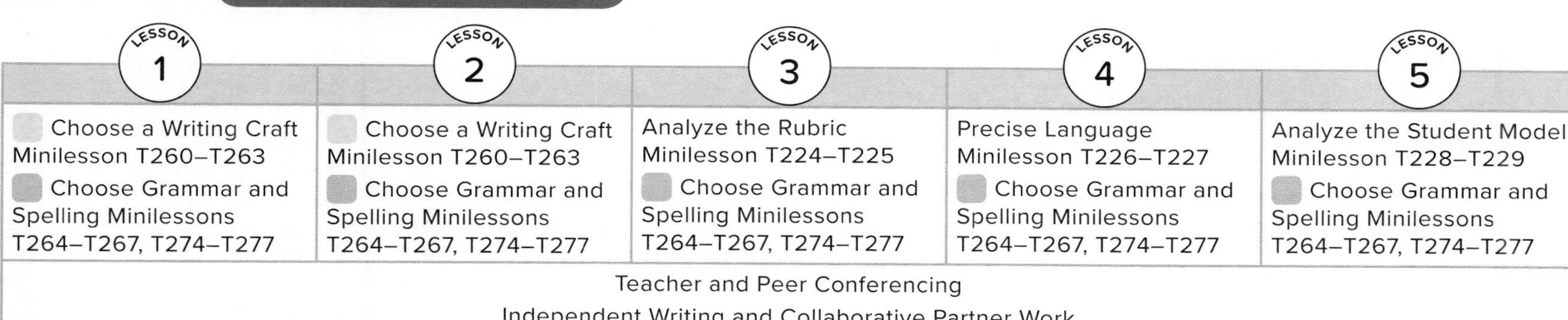

Lesson 1	Lesson 2	Lesson 3	Lesson 4	Lesson 5
Choose a Writing Craft Minilesson T260–T263 Choose Grammar and Spelling Minilessons T264–T267, T274–T277	Choose a Writing Craft Minilesson T260–T263 Choose Grammar and Spelling Minilessons T264–T267, T274–T277	Analyze the Rubric Minilesson T224–T225 Choose Grammar and Spelling Minilessons T264–T267, T274–T277	Precise Language Minilesson T226–T227 Choose Grammar and Spelling Minilessons T264–T267, T274–T277	Analyze the Student Model Minilesson T228–T229 Choose Grammar and Spelling Minilessons T264–T267, T274–T277
Teacher and Peer Conferencing Independent Writing and Collaborative Partner Work				

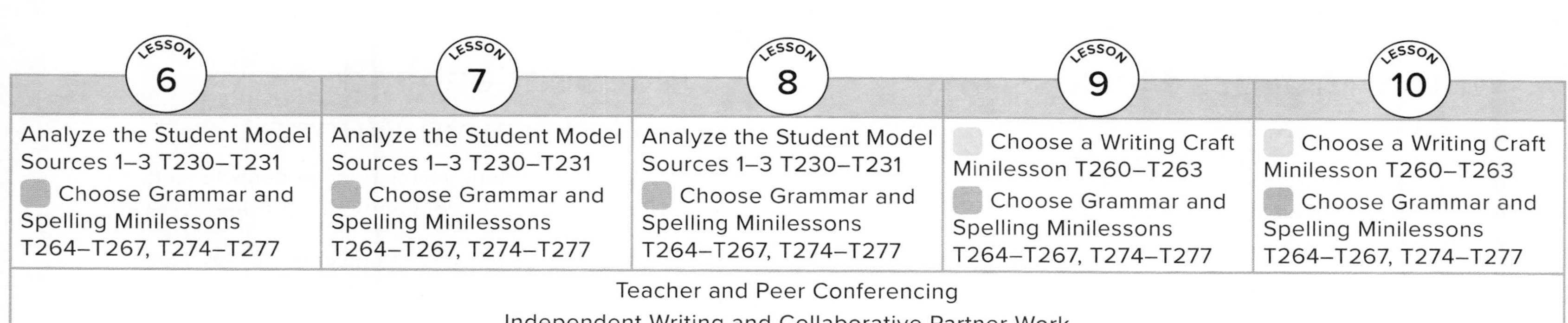

Lesson 6	Lesson 7	Lesson 8	Lesson 9	Lesson 10
Analyze the Student Model Sources 1–3 T230–T231 Choose Grammar and Spelling Minilessons T264–T267, T274–T277	Analyze the Student Model Sources 1–3 T230–T231 Choose Grammar and Spelling Minilessons T264–T267, T274–T277	Analyze the Student Model Sources 1–3 T230–T231 Choose Grammar and Spelling Minilessons T264–T267, T274–T277	Choose a Writing Craft Minilesson T260–T263 Choose Grammar and Spelling Minilessons T264–T267, T274–T277	Choose a Writing Craft Minilesson T260–T263 Choose Grammar and Spelling Minilessons T264–T267, T274–T277
Teacher and Peer Conferencing Independent Writing and Collaborative Partner Work				

Weeks 3–4 DEVELOP ARGUMENTATIVE ESSAYS

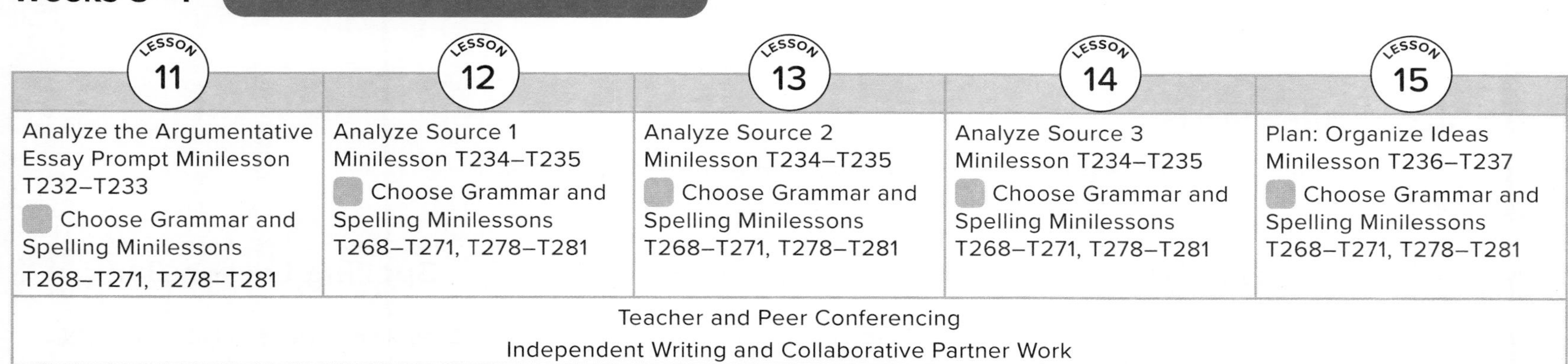

Lesson 11	Lesson 12	Lesson 13	Lesson 14	Lesson 15
Analyze the Argumentative Essay Prompt Minilesson T232–T233 Choose Grammar and Spelling Minilessons T268–T271, T278–T281	Analyze Source 1 Minilesson T234–T235 Choose Grammar and Spelling Minilessons T268–T271, T278–T281	Analyze Source 2 Minilesson T234–T235 Choose Grammar and Spelling Minilessons T268–T271, T278–T281	Analyze Source 3 Minilesson T234–T235 Choose Grammar and Spelling Minilessons T268–T271, T278–T281	Plan: Organize Ideas Minilesson T236–T237 Choose Grammar and Spelling Minilessons T268–T271, T278–T281
Teacher and Peer Conferencing Independent Writing and Collaborative Partner Work				

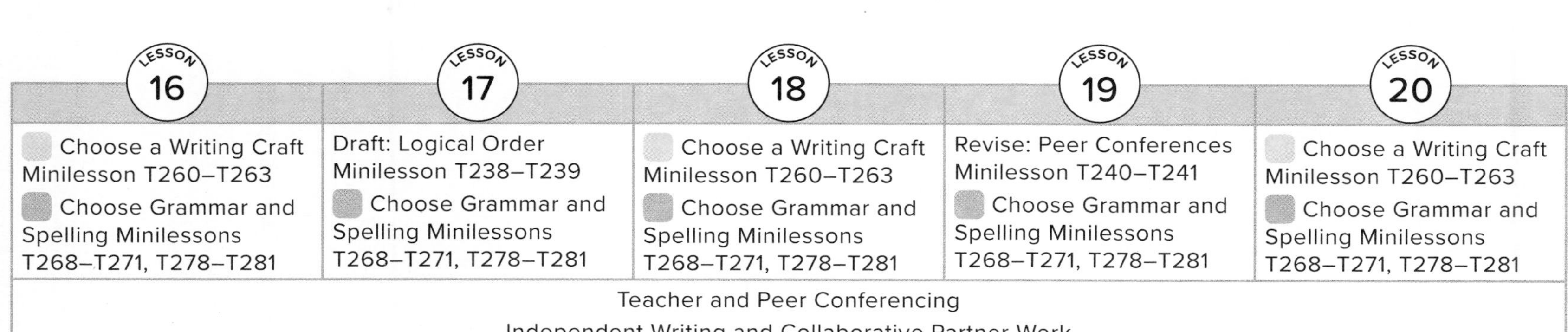

Lesson 16	Lesson 17	Lesson 18	Lesson 19	Lesson 20
Choose a Writing Craft Minilesson T260–T263 Choose Grammar and Spelling Minilessons T268–T271, T278–T281	Draft: Logical Order Minilesson T238–T239 Choose Grammar and Spelling Minilessons T268–T271, T278–T281	Choose a Writing Craft Minilesson T260–T263 Choose Grammar and Spelling Minilessons T268–T271, T278–T281	Revise: Peer Conferences Minilesson T240–T241 Choose Grammar and Spelling Minilessons T268–T271, T278–T281	Choose a Writing Craft Minilesson T260–T263 Choose Grammar and Spelling Minilessons T268–T271, T278–T281
Teacher and Peer Conferencing Independent Writing and Collaborative Partner Work				

Extended Writing: Write to Sources

Argumentative Essay

Extended Writing Goals

- I can write an argumentative essay.
- I can synthesize information from three sources.

Start off each Extended Writing Project with a Writing Process minilesson, or choose a Craft minilesson from the Writing Craft Lesson Bank. As you confer with students, the rest of your students write independently or collaboratively or confer with peers.

Writing Process Minilessons

During Writing Process minilessons, students first analyze a rubric and student model and then answer a writing prompt, going through each step of the writing process to develop an argumentative essay.

- Analyze the Rubric
- Strong Conclusion
- Analyze the Student Model
- Analyze the Prompt
- Analyze the Sources
- Plan: Organize Ideas
- Draft: Sentence Structure
- Revise: Peer Conferences

Independent and Collaborative Writing

- Provide time during writing for students to work on their writing both collaboratively with partners and independently.
- Use this time for teacher and peer conferencing.

Flexible Minilessons

Choose from the following minilessons to focus on areas where your students need support.

Writing Craft Lesson Bank

Write Effective Hooks T260
Use Logical Reasons and Evidence T260
Outline Information T261
Use Parallel Structure T261
Choose Persuasive Words T261
Brainstorm Ideas T262
Integrate Sources T262
Use Formal or Informal Language T263
Add Strong Transitions T263
Use Conjunctions and Punctuation T263

Grammar Lesson Bank

Irregular Verbs T272
Correct Verb Usage T273

Spelling Lesson Bank

r-Controlled Vowel Syllables T282–T283
Differentiated Spelling List T282

Suggested Pacing

Students can develop their writing over two weeks, taking time to deconstruct a student model and then work with sources to write their own argumentative essay. Adjust the pacing to address your students' needs.

Week 5 ANALYZE A STUDENT MODEL

Lesson 1	Lesson 2	Lesson 3	Lesson 4	Lesson 5
Choose a Writing Craft Minilesson T260–T263 Choose Grammar and Spelling Minilessons T272–T273, T282–T283	Analyze the Rubric Minilesson T242–T243 Choose Grammar and Spelling Minilessons T272–T273, T282–T283	Strong Conclusion Minilesson T244–T245 Choose Grammar and Spelling Minilessons T272–T273, T282–T283	Analyze the Student Model Minilesson T246–T247 Choose Grammar and Spelling Minilessons T272–T273, T282–T283	Analyze the Student Model Minilesson T248–T249 Choose Grammar and Spelling Minilessons T272–T273, T282–T283
Teacher and Peer Conferencing Independent Writing and Collaborative Partner Work				

Week 6 DEVELOP ARGUMENTATIVE ESSAYS

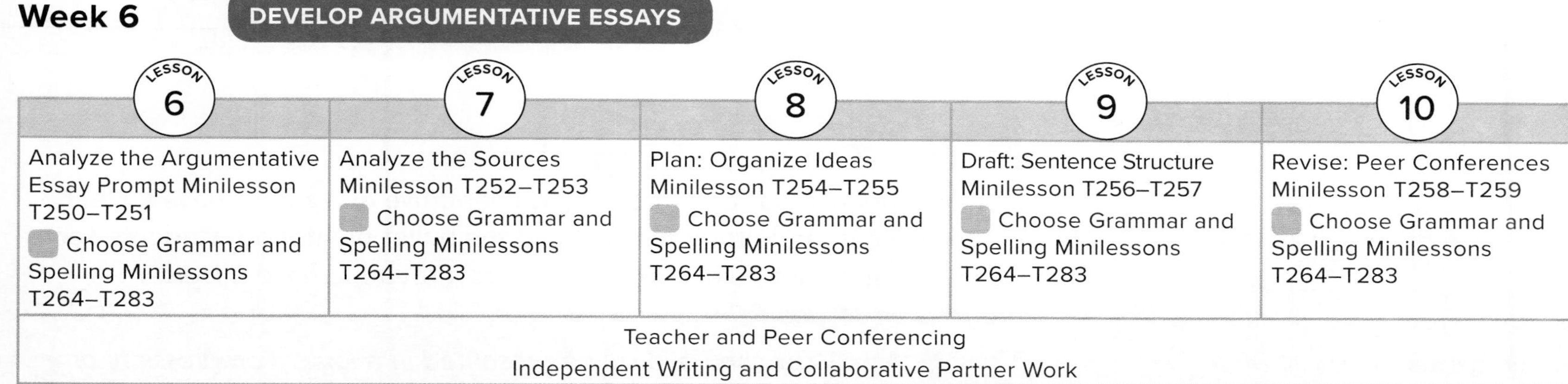

Lesson 6	Lesson 7	Lesson 8	Lesson 9	Lesson 10
Analyze the Argumentative Essay Prompt Minilesson T250–T251 Choose Grammar and Spelling Minilessons T264–T283	Analyze the Sources Minilesson T252–T253 Choose Grammar and Spelling Minilessons T264–T283	Plan: Organize Ideas Minilesson T254–T255 Choose Grammar and Spelling Minilessons T264–T283	Draft: Sentence Structure Minilesson T256–T257 Choose Grammar and Spelling Minilessons T264–T283	Revise: Peer Conferences Minilesson T258–T259 Choose Grammar and Spelling Minilessons T264–T283
Teacher and Peer Conferencing Independent Writing and Collaborative Partner Work				

MY GOALS ROUTINE

What I Know Now

Read Have students read the goals on Reading/Writing Companion page 84.

Reflect Review the key. Ask students to reflect on each goal and fill in the bars to show what they know now. Explain they will fill in the bars on page 85 at the end of the text set to show their progress.

LEARNING GOALS

We can use a rubric to understand what makes a strong argumentative essay.

OBJECTIVES

Explain how an author uses reasons and evidence to support particular points in a text, identifying which reasons and evidence support which point(s).

Identify the author's claim.

Write opinion pieces on topics or texts, supporting a point of view with reasons and information.

Provide logically ordered reasons that are supported by facts and details.

Demonstrate command of the conventions of standard English grammar and usage when writing or speaking.

Analyze a rubric used to evaluate argumentative essays.

ELA ACADEMIC LANGUAGE

- *progression, logical, precise, vocabulary*
- Cognates: *progresión, lógico, preciso, vocabulario*

Analyze the Rubric

Argumentative Writing Rubric

Students will use the Argumentative Writing Rubric first to evaluate a student model and then to write their own argumentative essays. Remind students that a rubric helps them know what to include. Remind students that this section of the rubric shows the highest scores and the criteria for each score. Point out each category and the score of 4 on the rubric on **Reading/Writing Companion** page 86.

Have partners define the terms *purpose, focus,* and *organization* as these words might relate to an argumentative essay. (A *purpose* is a reason for writing an argumentative essay. The purpose of an argumentative essay is to persuade. A *focus* is a topic of the essay. *Organization* is a way that the argumentative essay is put together that makes sense and convinces the readers.)

Purpose, Focus, and Organization

Remind students that an effective argumentative essay must have a clear purpose, focus, and organization. Read the bullet points with students. Focus on the fourth bullet point. Ask: *What does it mean to have a logical progression of ideas?* (Ideas are presented in an order that makes sense.)

Ask: *Why should ideas be presented in a logical progression, or order?* (so readers can easily follow the ideas and details) Have students write their response on page 86. Remind students that a logical progression of ideas helps to support the author's claim, or argument, in an essay. When ideas logically support the claim, readers are more likely to understand and agree with it. Students will examine the organization of an argumentative essay in a student model and then develop their own.

Evidence and Elaboration

Remind students that a strong essay must include evidence and elaboration. This part of the rubric identifies how evidence should be used and what kinds of elaborative techniques can be used. Review all the bullets with students. Then read aloud the highlighted bullet. Ask: *What do you think precise language is?* (language that says exactly what the writer means)

Reread the fourth bullet. Ask: *Why is it important to use precise language?* (Using precise language helps you express your ideas and support more clearly.) Have students write their response on page 86. Remind students that precise language can make clear how the evidence and elaboration in an argumentative essay support the claim. Students will examine the use of precise language in a student model and then use precise language in their essays to support a claim.

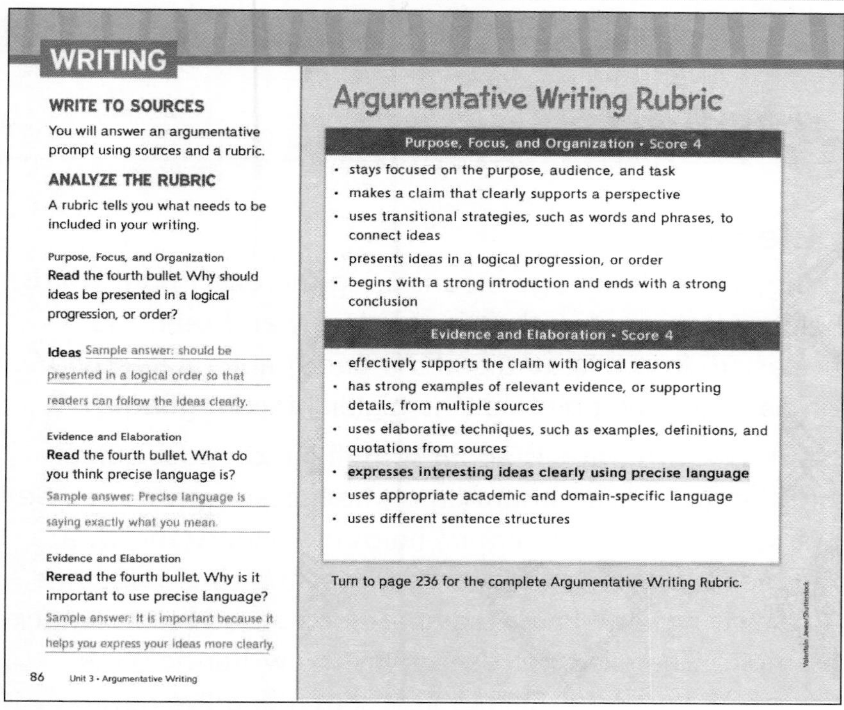

WRITING

WRITE TO SOURCES

You will answer an argumentative prompt using sources and a rubric.

ANALYZE THE RUBRIC

A rubric tells you what needs to be included in your writing.

Purpose, Focus, and Organization
Read the fourth bullet. Why should ideas be presented in a logical progression, or order?

Ideas Sample answer: should be presented in a logical order so that readers can follow the ideas clearly.

Evidence and Elaboration
Read the fourth bullet. What do you think precise language is?

Sample answer: Precise language is saying exactly what you mean.

Evidence and Elaboration
Reread the fourth bullet. Why is it important to use precise language?

Sample answer: It is important because it helps you express your ideas more clearly.

Argumentative Writing Rubric

Purpose, Focus, and Organization • Score 4

- stays focused on the purpose, audience, and task
- makes a claim that clearly supports a perspective
- uses transitional strategies, such as words and phrases, to connect ideas
- presents ideas in a logical progression, or order
- begins with a strong introduction and ends with a strong conclusion

Evidence and Elaboration • Score 4

- effectively supports the claim with logical reasons
- has strong examples of relevant evidence, or supporting details, from multiple sources
- uses elaborative techniques, such as examples, definitions, and quotations from sources
- expresses interesting ideas clearly using precise language
- uses appropriate academic and domain-specific language
- uses different sentence structures

Turn to page 236 for the complete Argumentative Writing Rubric.

86 Unit 3 • Argumentative Writing

Reading/Writing Companion, p. 86

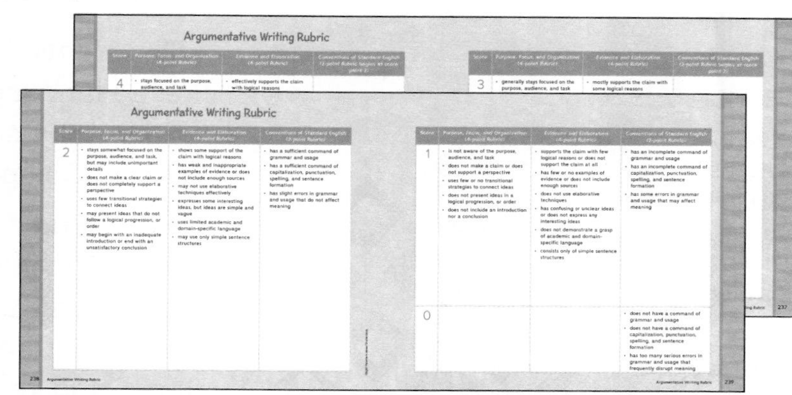

For the full Argumentative Writing Rubric, see **Reading/Writing Companion,** pages 236–239.

English Language Learners

Use the following scaffolds with **Evidence and Elaboration**.

Beginning

Review with students that precise language expresses ideas clearly. Read the highlighted bullet in the rubric with them and explain the meaning. Say: *Precise language is saying exactly what you mean. This makes your ideas clear to readers.* Encourage students about experiences when they did not say exactly what they meant and discuss if there was confusion. Help partners describe using the following: Precise language says exactly what you mean. Precise language makes the writer's ideas clear to readers.

Intermediate

Review the concept of precise language with students. Discuss how using precise language helps the writer. He or she can say his or her ideas clearly so that readers understand. Read the highlighted bullet in the rubric together. Have partners describe how precise language helps writers and readers: Precise language helps writers communicate ideas clearly so readers know exactly what they mean.

Advanced/Advanced High

Have students describe how precise language relates to the communication of ideas. Read the highlighted bullet in the rubric with them. Discuss how vocabulary relates to precise language. Then have partners identify two vocabulary words with different meanings. Have partners discuss how each word has a precise meaning when it is used to say exactly what the writer means.

ELL NEWCOMERS

To help students develop their writing, display the **Newcomer Cards** and **Newcomer Online Visuals**, and ask questions to help them discuss the images. Provide sentence starters. For example: What do you see? I see a/an ___. What are they doing? They are ___. Have students point to the image as they ask and answer. Then have them write the sentences in their notebooks. Throughout the extended writing project, help students develop their writing by adding to and revising their sentences.

FORMATIVE ASSESSMENT

STUDENT CHECK-IN

Have partners share their responses. Then ask them to reflect using the Check-In routine

LEARNING GOALS

We can identify precise language.

OBJECTIVES

Explain how an author uses reasons and evidence to support particular points in a text, identifying which reasons and evidence support which point(s). Identify the author's claim.

Write opinion pieces on topics or texts, supporting a point of view with reasons and information.

Introduce a topic or text clearly, state an opinion, and create an organizational structure in which ideas are logically grouped to support the writer's purpose.

Provide logically ordered reasons that are supported by facts and details.

Demonstrate command of the conventions of standard English grammar and usage when writing or speaking.

Analyze models to understand how to use precise language to express ideas coherently.

ELA ACADEMIC LANGUAGE

- *precise, coherent, unnecessary*
- Cognates: *preciso, coherente, innecesario*

DIGITAL TOOLS

Student Model Sources

Purpose of Argumentative Writing

Precise Language

Express Ideas Clearly

Tell students that using precise language means using the exact right words. Precise language helps writers express their ideas clearly and keep the writing coherent, or easy to follow. Read aloud the paragraph on **Reading/ Writing Companion** page 87 and point out the highlighted language.

Think Aloud I see that the paragraph is about something called a quipu. The writer states that the quipu is an invention of the Incas that was maybe used to keep track of data. The word *invention* helps me understand what the quipu is and who made it. The writer also describes that the quipu has strings and knots. These strings and knots may have been used to keep track of crops in the Inca Empire. The exact words used by the writer help me understand the quipu and its purpose. Since this is something I've never heard of before, the precise language helps me follow these ideas.

Have partners talk about how other precise language in the paragraph helps readers to understand what a quipu is.

For additional practice, reread the first paragraph on **Literature Anthology** page 54. Ask: *What precise language does the writer use to describe the benefits of public transportation?* ("inexpensive" and a "comfortable alternative") Point out some examples of language that are not precise, such as "best ways" and "better for."

Delete Unnecessary Ideas

Discuss how a well-written essay does not contain unnecessary ideas. Each idea in the essay supports the author's claim. To improve sentences, writers should not repeat unnecessary words or phrases in a sentence. Reread the second paragraph on Literature Anthology page 54. Ask: *What sentence contains ideas that do not support the author's claim?* (Planes and buses use a fair amount as well.)

Explain that repetitive information or unnecessary details can confuse readers or stop them from continuing to read.

Analytical Writing Have students reread the paragraph on Reading/Writing Companion page 87 and revise it by crossing out unnecessary words. ("by the Incas" can be deleted; ", and the strings and knots" can be replaced by "that"; the "perhaps" in the final sentence could be eliminated) Ask volunteers to read aloud their revised paragraphs.

Apply

For more practice, have partners read the three student model sources in the **Online Writer's Notebook** and identify examples of precise language.

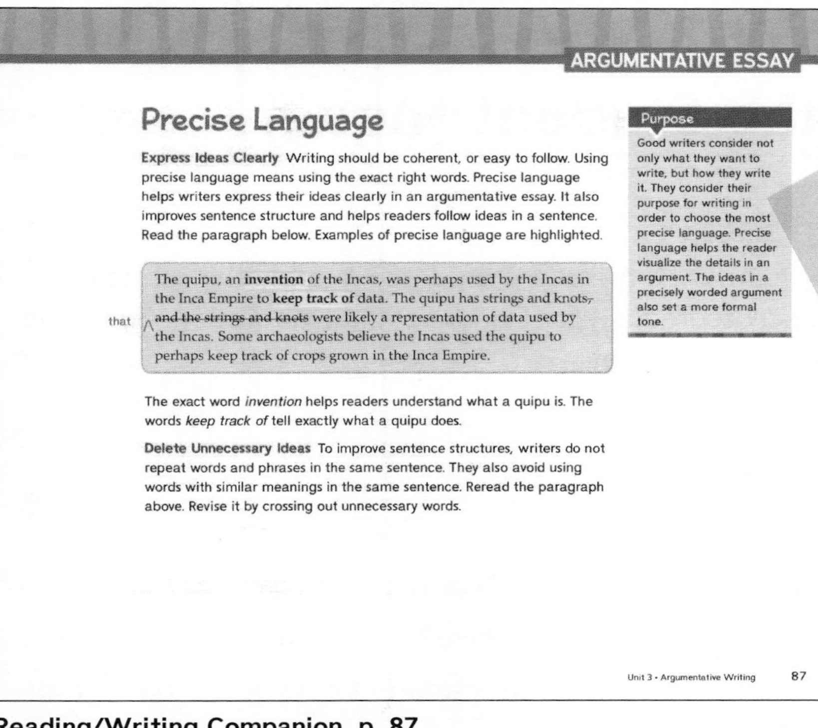
ARGUMENTATIVE ESSAY

Precise Language

Express Ideas Clearly Writing should be coherent, or easy to follow. Using precise language means using the exact right words. Precise language helps writers express their ideas clearly in an argumentative essay. It also improves sentence structure and helps readers follow ideas in a sentence. Read the paragraph below. Examples of precise language are highlighted.

The quipu, an **invention** of the Incas, was perhaps used by the Incas in the Inca Empire to **keep track of** data. The quipu has strings and knots, ~~and the strings and knots~~ [that] were likely a representation of data used by the Incas. Some archaeologists believe the Incas used the quipu to perhaps keep track of crops grown in the Inca Empire.

The exact word *invention* helps readers understand what a quipu is. The words *keep track of* tell exactly what a quipu does.

Delete Unnecessary Ideas To improve sentence structures, writers do not repeat words and phrases in the same sentence. They also avoid using words with similar meanings in the same sentence. Reread the paragraph above. Revise it by crossing out unnecessary words.

Purpose

Good writers consider not only what they want to write, but how they write it. They consider their purpose for writing in order to choose the most precise language. Precise language helps the reader visualize the details in an argument. The ideas in a precisely worded argument also set a more formal tone.

Unit 3 • Argumentative Writing 87

Reading/Writing Companion, p. 87

Purpose

Precise language can help a writer of an argumentative essay present ideas clearly and formally. It also helps readers to visualize details. As students reread the paragraph on the quipu, ask: *How does precise language help the reader to understand what a quipu is?* (It provides descriptions about what the quipu looks like, who used it, and what it was probably used for.) Discuss how the use of precise language set a formal tone.

English Language Learners

Use the following scaffolds with **Express Ideas Clearly.** For additional support, see the **ELL Small Group Guide**.

Beginning

Review that using precise language means using the exact right words. Remind students that precise language helps writers express their ideas clearly. Read each sentence in the paragraph on page 87 aloud together. Help students to pick out a precise word or phrase from each sentence: The quipu is an invention. The strings and knots were a representation of data. The quipu was used to keep track of crops. Discuss how the precise words helped readers follow ideas.

Intermediate

Review the description of precise language with students. Read the paragraph on page 87. Have students discuss how the highlighted words are precise and discuss how this helps readers understand the writing. Then ask partners to identify other precise language: The quipu has strings and knots, and the strings and knots were likely a representation of data used by the Incas. This data is described to perhaps keep track of crops grown in the Inca Empire.

Advanced/Advanced High

Read the paragraph on page 87. Have partners describe how each sentence in the paragraph uses precise language to express ideas clearly. Ask students to identify examples of language that is not as precise in the essay and discuss how language precision affects readers' understanding. Have them suggest other language choices that would be more precise as substitutes.

FORMATIVE ASSESSMENT

STUDENT CHECK-IN

Have partners share their responses. Then have them reflect using the Check-In routine.

LEARNING GOALS

We can use a rubric to evaluate a student model.

OBJECTIVES

Analyze multiple accounts of the same event or topic, noting important similarities and differences in the point of view they represent.

Explain an author's perspective, or point of view, toward a topic in an argumentative text.

Explain how an author uses reasons and evidence to support particular points in a text, identifying which reasons and evidence support which point(s).

Identify the author's claim.

Analyze a model and apply a rubric to understand the elements of an effective argumentative essay.

ELA ACADEMIC LANGUAGE

- *transition, immersion, claim, conclusion*
- Cognates: *transición, inmersión, conclusión*

DIGITAL TOOLS

 Student Model Sources

Analyze the Student Model

10 mins

Argumentative Essay

Students will read and analyze a student model and apply the rubric to explain why Joe's essay scored a 4 for Evidence and Elaboration. Complete the routine below for Joe's prompt.

ANALYZE THE PROMPT ROUTINE

Read aloud the prompt.

Identify the purpose. *Is the purpose to inform or persuade?*

Identify the audience. *Who is the audience?*

Identify the type of writing the prompt is asking for. *What is the prompt asking the writer to do?*

At the completion of the routine, students should understand that Joe's purpose is to persuade, his audience is the students in his class, and the prompt is to develop an argument on the best way to learn a language.

Discuss the Student Model

As you read Joe's model with students, ask them to look for relevant evidence and ways that Joe uses precise language and a logical progression of ideas. Have students note interesting words and any questions they have as they read.

Paragraph 1 Remind students that an argumentative essay contains a claim in its first paragraph. The claim answers the prompt and identifies the writer's perspective on the topic. Precise language is used to express ideas that will help to support the claim. Ask: *What is Joe's claim?* (Students learn more in a classroom setting.) Have students write their response on page 88. Ask: *How do the highlighted examples of precise language support the claim?* (They help describe the type of learning experience Joe supports, which is classroom immersion, and what it will prepare students for, which is the future.)

Paragraph 2 Ask: *What source does Joe use in this paragraph?* (an article called "Language Classes") *What details does Joe use from the article to support his claim?*

Think Aloud I see that the article Joe uses states that, in an immersion class, students are taught many different subjects using a foreign language. The article provides an example of immersion classes where students are learning Chinese while also studying the culture and environment of China. Have students identify and circle transitional phrases on pages 88–89 that

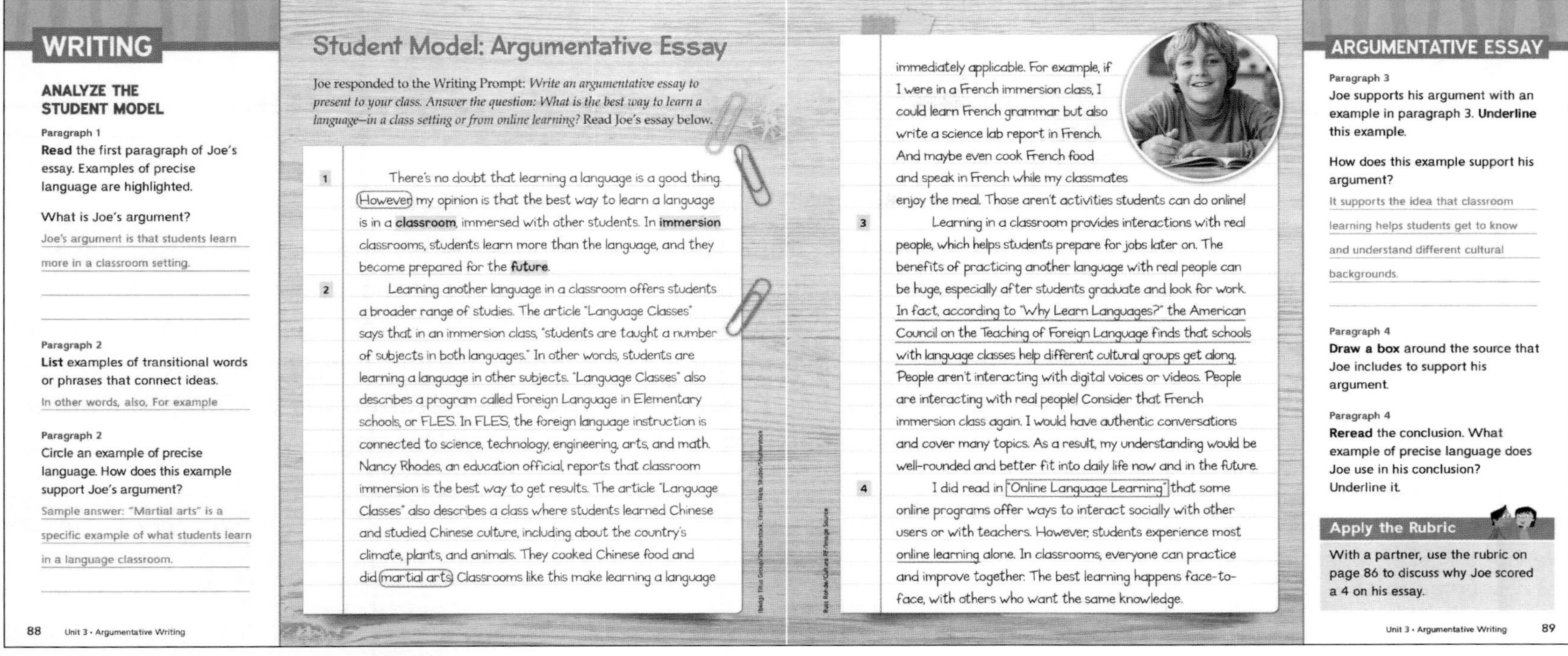

WRITING

ANALYZE THE STUDENT MODEL

Paragraph 1
Read the first paragraph of Joe's essay. Examples of precise language are highlighted.

What is Joe's argument?
Joe's argument is that students learn more in a classroom setting.

Paragraph 2
List examples of transitional words or phrases that connect ideas.
In other words, also, For example

Paragraph 2
Circle an example of precise language. How does this example support Joe's argument?
Sample answer: "Martial arts" is a specific example of what students learn in a language classroom.

88 Unit 3 • Argumentative Writing

Student Model: Argumentative Essay

Joe responded to the Writing Prompt: *Write an argumentative essay to present to your class. Answer the question: What is the best way to learn a language–in a class setting or from online learning?* Read Joe's essay below.

1 There's no doubt that learning a language is a good thing. However, my opinion is that the best way to learn a language is in a **classroom**, immersed with other students. In **immersion** classrooms, students learn more than the language, and they become prepared for the **future**.

2 Learning another language in a classroom offers students a broader range of studies. The article "Language Classes" says that in an immersion class, "students are taught a number of subjects in both languages." In other words, students are learning a language in other subjects. "Language Classes" also describes a program called Foreign Language in Elementary schools, or FLES. In FLES, the foreign language instruction is connected to science, technology, engineering, arts, and math. Nancy Rhodes, an education official, reports that classroom immersion is the best way to get results. The article "Language Classes" also describes a class where students learned Chinese and studied Chinese culture, including about the country's climate, plants, and animals. They cooked Chinese food and did martial arts. Classrooms like this make learning a language immediately applicable. For example, if I were in a French immersion class, I could learn French grammar but also write a science lab report in French. And maybe even cook French food and speak in French while my classmates enjoy the meal. Those aren't activities students can do online!

3 Learning in a classroom provides interactions with real people, which helps students prepare for jobs later on. The benefits of practicing another language with real people can be huge, especially after students graduate and look for work. In fact, according to "Why Learn Languages?" the American Council on the Teaching of Foreign Language finds that schools with language classes help different cultural groups get along. People aren't interacting with digital voices or videos. People are interacting with real people! Consider that French immersion class again. I would have authentic conversations and cover many topics. As a result, my understanding would be well-rounded and better fit into daily life now and in the future.

4 I did read in "Online Language Learning" that some online programs offer ways to interact socially with other users or with teachers. However, students experience most online learning alone. In classrooms, everyone can practice and improve together. The best learning happens face-to-face, with others who want the same knowledge.

ARGUMENTATIVE ESSAY

Paragraph 3
Joe supports his argument with an example in paragraph 3. **Underline** this example.

How does this example support his argument?
It supports the idea that classroom learning helps students get to know and understand different cultural backgrounds.

Paragraph 4
Draw a box around the source that Joe includes to support his argument.

Paragraph 4
Reread the conclusion. What example of precise language does Joe use in his conclusion? Underline it.

Apply the Rubric
With a partner, use the rubric on page 86 to discuss why Joe scored a 4 on his essay.

Unit 3 • Argumentative Writing 89

Reading/Writing Companion, pp. 88–89

connect the ideas in this paragraph. (*In other words, also, For example*)

Have students circle one example of precise language. (martial arts) Ask them to discuss how this example supports Joe's argument. Have them write their responses on page 88.

Paragraph 3 Read the first sentence. Point out that Joe is presenting an argument about how language immersion could prepare students for the future. Read the rest of the paragraph with students.

COLLABORATE Have partners underline an example in this paragraph that supports Joe's claim. Ask: *How does this example support his claim?* (It shows that immersion classes help communities and students understand cultural backgrounds, so there are benefits in the real world.) Have students answer the question on page 89.

Paragraph 4 Read the concluding paragraph. Ask: *What source does Joe include to support his argument?* ("Online Language Learning") Ask: *What example of precise language does Joe use in his conclusion?* (online learning)

Apply the Rubric

COLLABORATE Have partners discuss what may need improvement in Joe's essay and why it scored a 4 for Evidence and Elaboration. Have them use the rubric on page 86 and these sentence starters:

Joe supports his claim by using . . .

His essay could be improved by . . .

TEACH IN SMALL GROUP

● **English Language Learners** For support with reading the student model and analyzing the three sources, see **ELL Small Group Guide**.

CLASSROOM CULTURE

We inspire confident writers. To create a classroom where confident writers flourish, have students analyze the connection between reading and writing. Have them refer to the Student Model. Ask: *How did the student writer support his claim and use precise language? How can I make sure my writing is similar to what I've just read?*

FORMATIVE ASSESSMENT

STUDENT CHECK-IN

Have partners share their responses to Apply the Rubric on Reading/Writing Companion page 89. Then ask them to reflect using the Check-In routine.

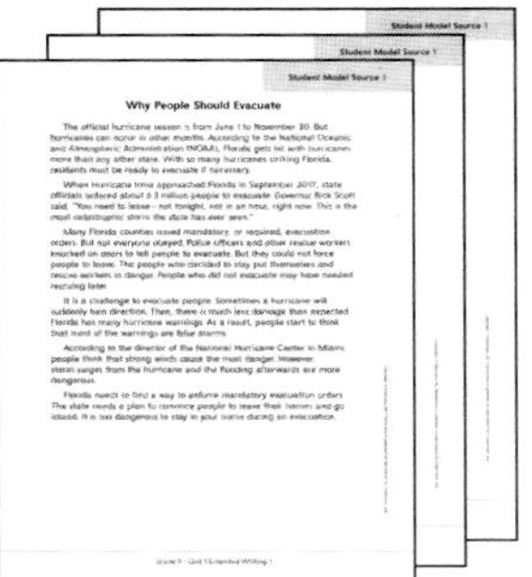

Student Model Sources

LEARNING GOALS

We can analyze student model essay sources.

OBJECTIVES

Quote accurately from a text when explaining what the text says explicitly and when drawing inferences from the text.

Identify the author's purpose.

Determine two or more central, or main, ideas of a text and explain how they are supported by relevant, or key, details; summarize the text.

Analyze multiple accounts of the same event or topic, noting important similarities and differences in the point of view they represent.

Explain an author's perspective, or point of view, toward a topic in an informational text.

Explain how an author uses reasons and evidence to support particular points in a text, identifying which reasons and evidence support which point(s).

Identify the author's claim.

ELA ACADEMIC LANGUAGE

- *quote, article, conclusion, claim*
- Cognates: *artículo, conclusión*

DIGITAL TOOLS

RESOURCE TOOLKIT Evaluate Sources for Relevance

Analyze the Student Model

Analyze the Student Model Sources

Explain that Joe read three sources to write his argumentative essay. Use copies of the online Student Model Sources to show how Joe used precise language from sources to express ideas clearly and support a claim. Remind students that Joe answered this prompt: *Write an argumentative essay to present to your class. Answer the question: What is the best way to learn a language—in a class setting or from online learning?*

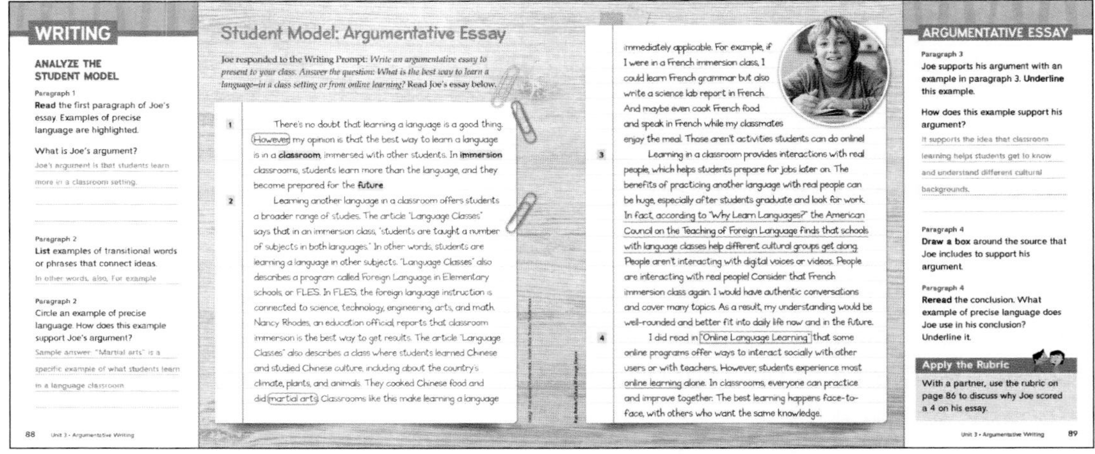

WRITING

ANALYZE THE STUDENT MODEL

Paragraph 1
Read the first paragraph of Joe's essay. Examples of precise language are highlighted.

What is Joe's argument?
Joe's argument is that students learn more in a classroom setting.

Paragraph 2
List examples of transitional words or phrases that connect ideas.
In other words, also, For example

Paragraph 2
Circle an example of precise language. How does this example support Joe's argument?
Sample answer: "Martial arts" is a specific example of what students learn in a language classroom.

88 Unit 3 • Argumentative Writing

Student Model: Argumentative Essay

Joe responded to the Writing Prompt: *Write an argumentative essay to present to your class. Answer the question: What is the best way to learn a language—in a class setting or from online learning?* Read Joe's essay below.

1 There's no doubt that learning a language is a good thing. However, my opinion is that the best way to learn a language is in a **classroom**, immersed with other students. In **immersion** classrooms, students learn more than the language, and they become prepared for the **future**.

2 Learning another language in a classroom offers students a broader range of studies. The article "Language Classes" says that in an immersion class, "students are taught a number of subjects in both languages." In other words, students are learning a language in other subjects. "Language Classes" also describes a program called Foreign Language in Elementary schools, or FLES. In FLES, the foreign language instruction is connected to science, technology, engineering, arts, and math. Nancy Rhodes, an education official, reports that classroom immersion is the best way to get results. The article "Language Classes" also describes a class where students learned Chinese and studied Chinese culture, including about the country's climate, plants, and animals. They cooked Chinese food and did martial arts. Classrooms like this make learning a language immediately applicable. For example, if I were in a French immersion class, I could learn French grammar but also write a science lab report in French. And maybe even cook French food and speak in French while my classmates enjoy the meal. Those aren't activities students can do online!

3 Learning in a classroom provides interactions with real people, which helps students prepare for jobs later on. The benefits of practicing another language with real people can be huge, especially after students graduate and look for work. In fact, according to "Why Learn Languages?" the American Council on the Teaching of Foreign Language finds that schools with language classes help different cultural groups get along. People aren't interacting with digital voices or videos. People are interacting with real people! Consider that French immersion class again. I would have authentic conversations and cover many topics. As a result, my understanding would be well-rounded and better fit into daily life now and in the future.

4 I did read in "Online Language Learning" that some online programs offer ways to interact socially with other users or with teachers. However, students experience most online learning alone. In classrooms, everyone can practice and improve together. The best learning happens face-to-face, with others who want the same knowledge.

ARGUMENTATIVE ESSAY

Paragraph 3
Joe supports his argument with an example in paragraph 3. **Underline** this example.

How does this example support his argument?
It supports the idea that classroom learning helps students get to know and understand different cultural backgrounds.

Paragraph 4
Draw a box around the source that Joe includes to support his argument.

Paragraph 4
Reread the conclusion. What example of precise language does Joe use in his conclusion? Underline it.

Apply the Rubric
With a partner, use the rubric on page 86 to discuss why Joe scored a 4 on his essay.

Unit 3 • Argumentative Writing 89

Reading/Writing Companion, pp. 88–89

SOURCE 1 "Online Language Learning"

After reading Source 1, read aloud Joe's first paragraph. Ask: *Does the information from Source 1 support Joe's argument?* (No, it does not support it.) Read Joe's fourth paragraph. Ask: *How does Joe use information from Source 1 even if it does not support his claim?* (He uses the information that online programs can offer ways to interact socially with other users or teachers. He does this to provide a counterargument.)

COLLABORATE Have partners discuss how Joe may have used information from Source 1 to develop his argument. (Source 1 includes a lot of information about how students can do online learning on their own time. This may have caused Joe to question whether this learning was as good as face-to-face learning. This could have led him to support the perspective that immersion learning is more effective.)

SOURCE 2 "Language Classes"

After reading Source 2, read aloud Joe's second paragraph. Ask: *What information does Joe include from Source 2 that supports his claim?*

Think Aloud I see that Joe uses a quote to describe immersion classes, where "students are taught a number of subjects in both languages." He states that the article describes a program called Foreign Language in Elementary Schools (FLES) and that Nancy Rhodes is an education official who reports that classroom immersion is the best way to get results. He also describes a class where students learn Chinese and study various aspects of Chinese culture. Joe draws the conclusion that these activities help students learn from real life and could not be done online. Explain that giving specific examples and using precise language helps support the writer's claim. Tell students that examples from sources can help them support their claims in their own essay's paragraphs.

Have partners read Source 2 to find more precise language that Joe used to support his claim.

SOURCE 3 "Why Learn Languages?"

After reading Source 3, read aloud Joe's third paragraph. Ask: *What information does Joe include that supports his claim?* (He uses information from Source 3, in which the American Council on the Teaching of Foreign Language states that schools with language classes help different groups get along.)

COLLABORATE Have partners search Source 3 to find precise language that states how language classes can help groups of people. (They can help cultural groups get along.) Have partners discuss how Joe concludes that learning languages can help improve understanding between people and better prepare people for the future. (Joe is saying in his own words that learning languages can allow people to talk to one another directly. This can help people to get along better in a future where there are people from many different cultures living in one place.) Guide students to see how writers can use information from sources and their own words to support their perspectives on a topic in essays.

Synthesize Information

Reread Joe's claim. Explain that Joe developed his argument after reading and thinking about all three sources. Remind students that he also analyzed the prompt and understood his purpose, audience, and task. He supported his claim using precise language so that readers would understand exactly what he meant.

COLLABORATE Have partners search the three sources for precise language that would support Joe's perspective about the best way to learn. Have them look back at their notes and then use their writer's notebook to answer the question *How did Joe develop his claim by synthesizing information from all three sources?* (All sources describe different aspects of language learning. Joe mainly used examples from Sources 2 and 3 to conclude that face-to-face immersion learning would be most effective. He used information from Source 1 to conclude that online learning would not provide as many opportunities for effective learning as immersion learning would.)

TEACH IN SMALL GROUP

Approaching Level Read each online source aloud. Help students identify a claim and precise language in each source.

On Level Read the online sources with students. Have partners work to identify the claim and precise language in each source. Discuss how Joe used the sources to write his essay.

Beyond Level Have students read the online sources. Ask them to pick out different examples of precise language they would use to most effectively support Joe's claim.

English Language Learners Read through one online source with students, stopping after each sentence to summarize its meaning. Focus on identifying the meaning of each precise language word or term. For additional support, see the **ELL Small Group Guide**.

FORMATIVE ASSESSMENT

STUDENT CHECK-IN

Have partners share their responses. Then ask them to reflect using the Check-In routine.

LEARNING GOALS

We can set a purpose for reading sources to answer a prompt.

OBJECTIVES

With guidance and support from peers and adults, develop and strengthen writing as needed by planning, revising, editing, rewriting, or trying a new approach.

Adapt speech to a variety of contexts and tasks, using formal English when appropriate to task and situation.

Follow agreed-upon rules for discussions and carry out assigned roles.

Analyze a writing prompt.

ELA ACADEMIC LANGUAGE

- *prompt, task, analyze*
- Cognate: *analizar*

DIGITAL TOOLS

Skim and Scan for Relevance

Analyze the Prompt

Writing Prompt

Follow the Analyze the Prompt Routine on page T228. Read the writing prompt on **Reading/Writing Companion** page 90 aloud: *Write an argumentative essay to present to your class. Answer the question: Should students participate in study abroad programs?* Guide students to identify the purpose and audience. Then ask: *What is the prompt asking you to do?* (to write an argumentative essay about whether students should participate in study abroad programs)

Anchor Chart Review the features of an argumentative essay with students and add any new ones to the Argumentative Essay anchor chart.

- It provides a claim, or argument, that clearly states the author's opinion on a topic.
- It includes reasons that are supported by relevant evidence.
- It presents ideas in a logical order.

Purpose, Audience, and Task

Remind students that thinking about their purpose and audience will help them plan and organize their writing. Ask students to identify the appropriate purpose of argumentative essays, which is to persuade. Point out that in this writing prompt, the audience is identified. Have them consider who will read what they write, such as the teacher and their classmates. Reread the writing prompt, and then have them think about whether they will use formal or informal language in their essay.

Remind students that the task is the type of writing they are being asked to do. Reread the prompt. Ask: *What words in the prompt tell you about the type of writing?* Have students underline two key words in the prompt on page 90. Ask students to write their responses to the questions.

Set a Purpose for Reading Sources

Tell students that before they write their essays, they will read, annotate, and answer questions about three sources. Encourage them to look at the source on page 91. Read the title aloud. Model skimming the source and asking a question to prepare to read the source, such as: *Why would parents say no to study abroad?* Remind students that when they skim, they don't read every word but read quickly for important ideas and details.

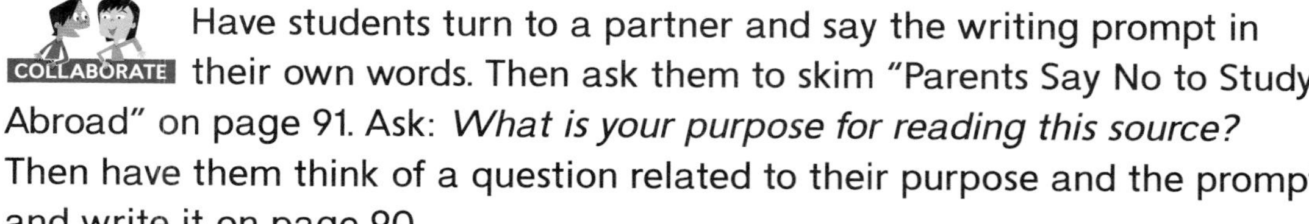

Have students turn to a partner and say the writing prompt in their own words. Then ask them to skim "Parents Say No to Study Abroad" on page 91. Ask: *What is your purpose for reading this source?* Then have them think of a question related to their purpose and the prompt and write it on page 90.

WRITING

My Goal: I can write an argumentative essay.

Analyze the Prompt

Writing Prompt

Write an argumentative essay to present to your class: Answer the question: Should students participate in study abroad programs?

Purpose, Audience, and Task Reread the writing prompt. What is your purpose for writing? My purpose is to ______

Who will your audience be? My audience will be ______

What type of writing is the prompt asking for? ______

Set a Purpose for Reading Sources Asking questions about whether students should participate in study abroad programs will help you figure out your purpose for reading. It also helps you understand what you already know about the topic. Before you read the passage set about study abroad programs, write a question here.

______

90 Unit 3 • Argumentative Writing

Reading/Writing Companion, p. 90

English Language Learners

Use the following scaffolds with **Writing Prompt**. For additional support, see the **ELL Small Group Guide**.

Beginning

Read the prompt with students, and discuss what it means to study abroad. Explain that students sometimes study in other countries for several months. Discuss with students what it would be like to live and study in another country. Help partners describe the prompt using the following: *I will write about whether students* should study abroad *in other countries.*

Intermediate

Read the prompt with students, and discuss what it means. Have students describe what it means to participate in a study abroad program in other countries. Discuss what it would be like to participate in a program where you can live and study in another country. Point to the first part of the prompt and elicit from them that they will write an opinion essay to tell their classmates what they think. Have partners describe the prompt using: *I will write about whether students* should participate in study abroad programs in other countries.

Advanced/Advanced High

Read the prompt with students, and discuss what it means. Explain that the word *abroad* means "in other countries." Have students discuss study abroad programs and what they might be like, to clarify the meaning of the prompt. Point to the first part of the prompt, and discuss the purpose, audience, and task of the prompt. Have partners describe what they will write about for the prompt.

CLASSROOM CULTURE

We respect and value each other's experiences. Working in pairs and small groups not only motivates students but also helps them to value one another. After setting a purpose for reading, ask: *What did you learn from working with your partner? Why is working with a partner a good learning tool?*

FORMATIVE ASSESSMENT

STUDENT CHECK-IN

Have partners share the purpose they set for reading the sources. Then ask them to reflect using the Check-In routine.

LEARNING GOALS

We can take notes to find relevant evidence to answer a prompt.

OBJECTIVES

Draw on information from multiple print or digital sources, demonstrating the ability to locate an answer to a question quickly or to solve a problem efficiently.

Explain how an author uses reasons and evidence to support particular points in a text, identifying which reasons and evidence support which point(s). Identify the author's claim.

Integrate information from several texts on the same topic in order to write or speak about the subject knowledgeably.

Write opinion pieces on topics or texts, supporting a point of view with reasons and information.

Analyze sources to understand the elements of an effective argumentative essay.

ELA ACADEMIC LANGUAGE

- *evidence, opinion, source*
- Cognates: *evidencia, opinión*

TEACH IN SMALL GROUP

Approaching Level Help students find key ideas and details. Complete the questions with the group.

On Level Have partners share their ideas and complete the questions together.

Beyond Level Ask students to share the words they think are important. Discuss how important words help identify claims and supporting details.

ELL For support with reading the sources, see **ELL Small Group Guide.**

Read the following passage set.

SOURCE 1

PARENTS SAY NO TO STUDY ABROAD

1 Parents must consider many factors before allowing their children to study in another country. Because of the requirements, costs, and risks, parents should say no to study abroad.

2 One concern for parents is the **paperwork**. Most students will need a passport and a visa. A visa is a **document** that gives students **permission** to study and live in the country. Students must **apply** for a visa and prove their enrollment, funding, and housing. Students may also need **international** medical insurance, shots, and medications to ensure their health needs are met. Although parents can work with the school to gather information and prepare documents, not all parents and schools have the resources to do so.

3 The second concern is the cost. Traveling to and living in another country for weeks or months can cost more than living and studying at home. Flights, transportation, food, lodging, and tuition can add up. One semester in England, for example, could cost as much as $7,000. Even a less expensive destination could be $4,000 per semester. Consider communication costs, like cell phone service and Internet. There's also the exchange rate. The US dollar is sometimes worth less in other countries, making everyday items expensive.

4 Lastly, parents fear for their children's safety. Even if students travel to safe places, some parents worry that their children will struggle without the comforts, structure, and familiarity of home. A chaperone may be a poor substitute for a knowledgeable parent.

ARGUMENTATIVE ESSAY

FIND TEXT EVIDENCE

Paragraph 1
Underline the claim.

Paragraph 2
Read the highlighted examples of precise language.

How do these examples of precise language make the author's argument more credible?

These examples make the author's argument more credible because they clearly and specifically list what is needed for international travel.

Paragraphs 2–4
Circle the transitional word or phrase in each paragraph that signals the order of reasons listed in paragraph 1.

Take Notes Paraphrase the author's claim, and give examples of supporting details.

Unit 3 • Argumentative Writing 91

Reading/Writing Companion, p. 91

Analyze the Sources

Find Text Evidence As students read the source passages, ask them to note key ideas and details, interesting or unfamiliar words, and any questions they may have in their writer's notebooks. Use the questions below. Remind students to cite text evidence.

"Parents Say No to Study Abroad"

Paragraph 1 *What is the claim?* ("Because of the requirements, costs, and risks, parents should say no to study abroad.")

Paragraph 2 Read aloud the highlighted words. *How do the examples of precise language make the author's claim more credible?* (by clearly and specifically listing what is needed for international travel) *What kind of paperwork do students need?* (a passport and a visa)

Paragraph 3 *What does the author say is the second concern for parents?* (the cost) Have students talk about what costs a lot of money when studying abroad, according to the source.

Paragraphs 2–4 *What transitional words signal the order of reasons in the essay?* (*One, second, Lastly*) *What reason is given in paragraph 4 against studying abroad?* (Students may be unsafe or uncomfortable.)

Analytical Writing **Take Notes** Have students reread the author's claim in paragraph 1 and paraphrase it in their own words. Ask them to use their notes to give examples of supporting details.

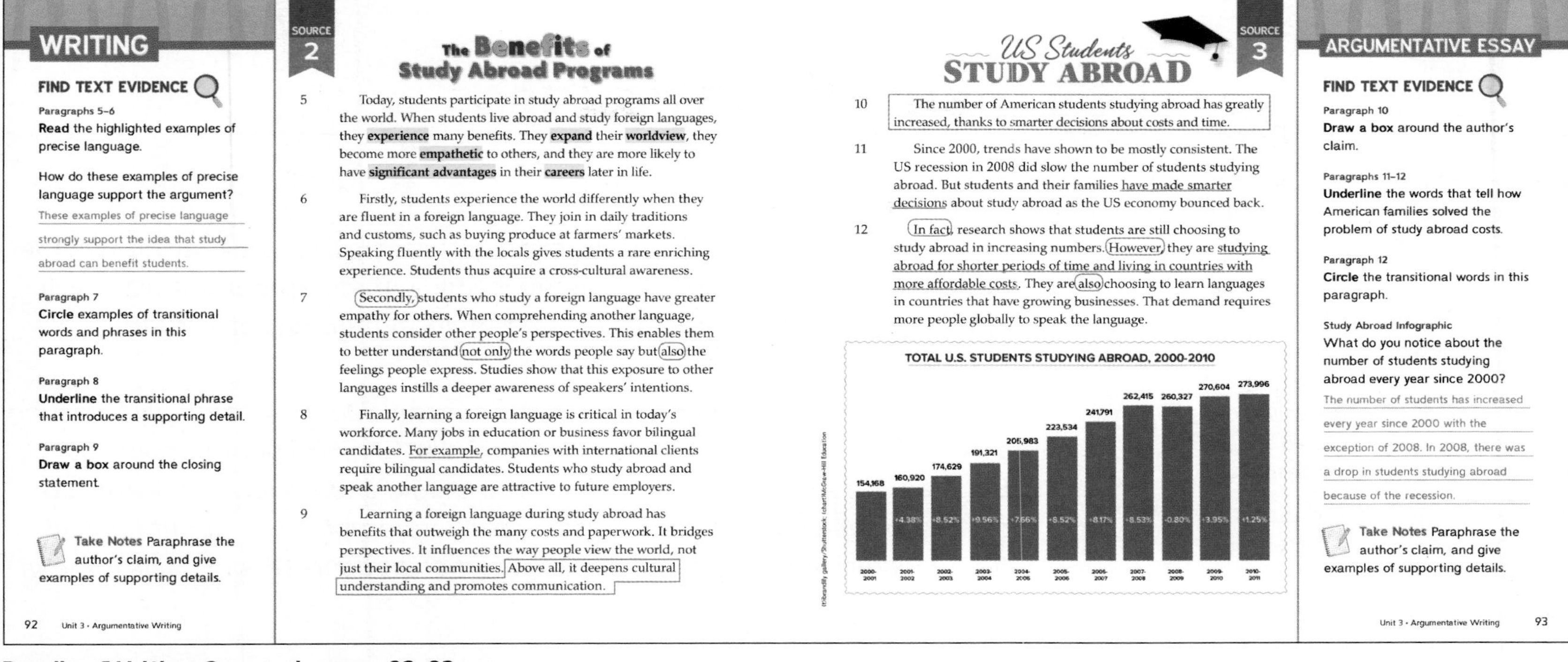

WRITING

FIND TEXT EVIDENCE

Paragraphs 5–6
Read the highlighted examples of precise language.

How do these examples of precise language support the argument?
These examples of precise language strongly support the idea that study abroad can benefit students.

Paragraph 7
Circle examples of transitional words and phrases in this paragraph.

Paragraph 8
Underline the transitional phrase that introduces a supporting detail.

Paragraph 9
Draw a box around the closing statement.

Take Notes Paraphrase the author's claim, and give examples of supporting details.

92 Unit 3 • Argumentative Writing

SOURCE 2

The Benefits of Study Abroad Programs

5 Today, students participate in study abroad programs all over the world. When students live abroad and study foreign languages, they **experience** many benefits. They **expand** their **worldview**, they become more **empathetic** to others, and they are more likely to have **significant advantages** in their **careers** later in life.

6 Firstly, students experience the world differently when they are fluent in a foreign language. They join in daily traditions and customs, such as buying produce at farmers' markets. Speaking fluently with the locals gives students a rare enriching experience. Students thus acquire a cross-cultural awareness.

7 Secondly, students who study a foreign language have greater empathy for others. When comprehending another language, students consider other people's perspectives. This enables them to better understand not only the words people say but also the feelings people express. Studies show that this exposure to other languages instills a deeper awareness of speakers' intentions.

8 Finally, learning a foreign language is critical in today's workforce. Many jobs in education or business favor bilingual candidates. For example, companies with international clients require bilingual candidates. Students who study abroad and speak another language are attractive to future employers.

9 Learning a foreign language during study abroad has benefits that outweigh the many costs and paperwork. It bridges perspectives. It influences the way people view the world, not just their local communities. Above all, it deepens cultural understanding and promotes communication.

SOURCE 3

US Students STUDY ABROAD

10 The number of American students studying abroad has greatly increased, thanks to smarter decisions about costs and time.

11 Since 2000, trends have shown to be mostly consistent. The US recession in 2008 did slow the number of students studying abroad. But students and their families have made smarter decisions about study abroad as the US economy bounced back.

12 In fact, research shows that students are still choosing to study abroad in increasing numbers. However, they are studying abroad for shorter periods of time and living in countries with more affordable costs. They are also choosing to learn languages in countries that have growing businesses. That demand requires more people globally to speak the language.

ARGUMENTATIVE ESSAY

FIND TEXT EVIDENCE

Paragraph 10
Draw a box around the author's claim.

Paragraphs 11–12
Underline the words that tell how American families solved the problem of study abroad costs.

Paragraph 12
Circle the transitional words in this paragraph.

Study Abroad Infographic
What do you notice about the number of students studying abroad every year since 2000?
The number of students has increased every year since 2000 with the exception of 2008. In 2008, there was a drop in students studying abroad because of the recession.

Take Notes Paraphrase the author's claim, and give examples of supporting details.

Unit 3 • Argumentative Writing 93

Reading/Writing Companion, pp. 92–93

SOURCE 2

"The Benefits of Study Abroad Programs"

Paragraphs 5–6 *How do the examples of precise language support the author's argument?* (They stress how studying abroad would be positive.)

Paragraph 7 *What is the reason the author gives for why students should study abroad?* (Students will have greater empathy for others.) Have students circle the transitional word that signals this reason.

Paragraph 8 *What is the transitional phrase that introduces a supporting detail?* (*For example*)

Paragraph 9 *What is the closing statement?* ("Above all, it deepens cultural understanding and promotes communication.")

Take Notes Have students reread the author's claim in paragraph 5 and paraphrase it in their own words. Ask them to use their notes.

SOURCE 3

"US Students Study Abroad"

Paragraph 10 *What is the author's claim?* ("The number of American students studying abroad has greatly increased, thanks to smarter decisions about costs and time.")

Paragraphs 11–12 *How did American families solve the problem of study abroad costs?* (made smarter decisions, students study abroad for shorter periods)

Paragraph 12 *What are the transitional words in this paragraph?* (*In fact, However, also*)

Study Abroad Infographic *What do you notice about the number of students studying abroad every year since 2000?* (It has increased, except in 2008.)

Analytical Writing

Take Notes Have students reread the author's claim in paragraph 10 and paraphrase it in their own words. Ask them to give examples of supporting details.

MULTIMODAL LEARNING

As students read and reread a source, ask them to create a word web of opinions and facts from the source. Students can write a claim in the center circle and then show reasons that support the opinion in circles branching out from the center. Have students share and compare their word webs with a partner.

FORMATIVE ASSESSMENT

STUDENT CHECK-IN

Have partners share their responses. Then ask them to reflect using the Check-In routine.

LEARNING GOALS

We can synthesize information from three sources to plan and organize an argumentative essay.

OBJECTIVES

Introduce a topic or text clearly, state an opinion, and create an organizational structure in which ideas are logically grouped to support the writer's purpose.

Provide logically ordered reasons that are supported by facts and details.

Develop the topic with facts, definitions, concrete details, quotations, or other information and examples related to the topic.

With some guidance and support from adults, use technology, including the Internet, to produce and publish writing as well as to interact and collaborate with others; demonstrate sufficient command of keyboarding skills to type a minimum of two pages in a single sitting.

Produce clear and coherent writing in which the development and organization are appropriate to task, purpose, and audience.

Organize notes from sources to plan an expository essay.

Cite evidence to explain and justify reasoning.

ELA ACADEMIC LANGUAGE

- *synthesize, record*
- Cognate: *sintetizar*

DIGITAL TOOLS

 Model Graphic Organizer

Organizing Notes

Plan: Organize Ideas

Take Notes

Remind students that they will write an argumentative essay telling whether they think students should participate in study abroad programs. They will synthesize information from the sources to form their response to the prompt.

Say: *When you write your argumentative essay, you are not simply restating facts about a topic. You are forming your own opinion about a topic and using reasons and facts to support it. You should choose relevant evidence from each source to craft your answer to the prompt. Think about how all the evidence supports your claim on whether students should participate in study abroad programs.*

Graphic Organizer

Tell students that before writing their argumentative essay, they will organize the notes they took from each source in the graphic organizer on **Reading/Writing Companion** pages 94–95. Some of the graphic organizer has been filled in. Guide students in filling in the graphic organizer.

Claim Remind students that a claim is the main argument of their essay and is presented at the beginning of the essay. It answers the prompt directly and clearly states the author's opinion.

Reasons These statements support the claim in different ways. Students research important information from sources to support the argument.

Relevant Evidence Students record evidence that support the claims. Remind students that strong argumentative essays do not include information unrelated to the claim. Tell students that they may not find evidence from all three sources for each reason listed.

Have students complete the graphic organizer.

Synthesize Information

Explain that when writers synthesize information, they connect details from sources in order to create new understanding. One way to help synthesize information is to ask and answer questions about the topic and the sources. Have partners review their completed graphic organizers and identify answers to the question, What does the evidence tell you about whether students should study abroad or not?

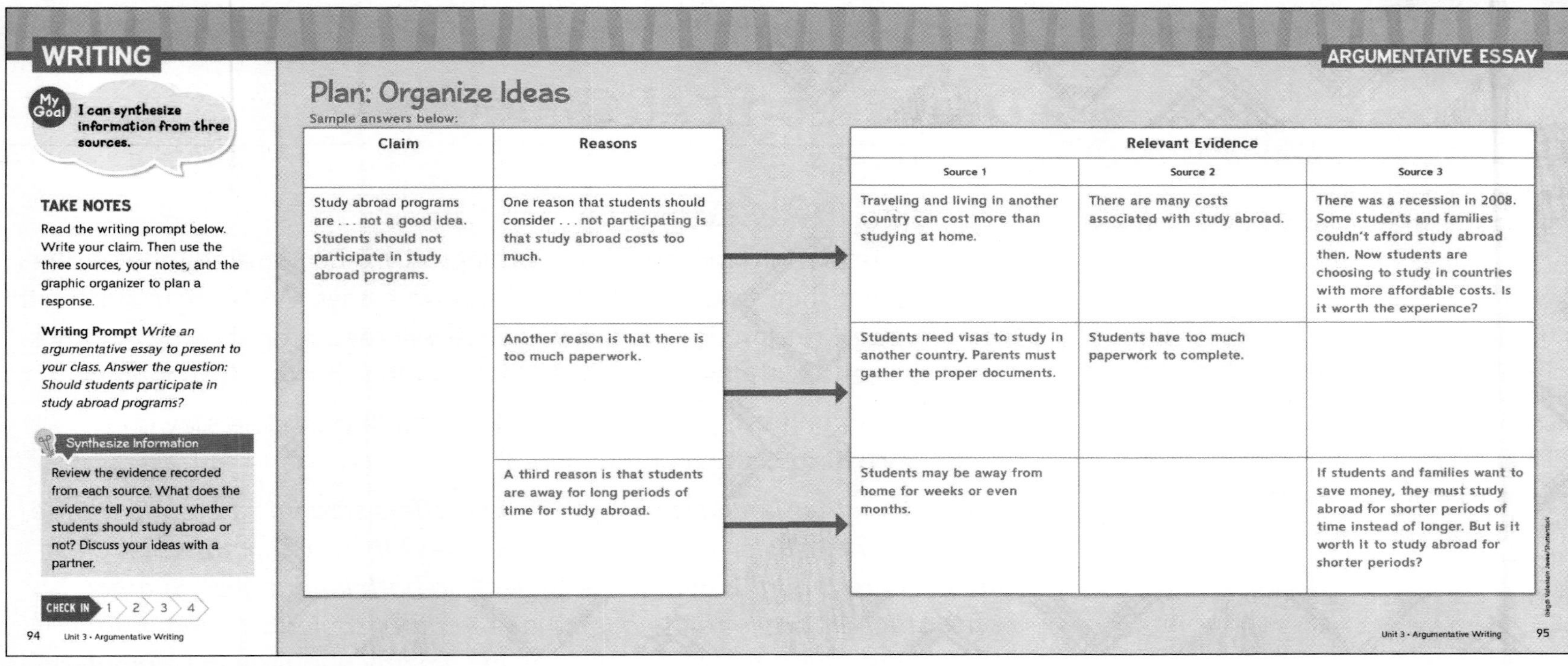

WRITING

ARGUMENTATIVE ESSAY

My Goal: I can synthesize information from three sources.

TAKE NOTES

Read the writing prompt below. Write your claim. Then use the three sources, your notes, and the graphic organizer to plan a response.

Writing Prompt *Write an argumentative essay to present to your class. Answer the question: Should students participate in study abroad programs?*

Synthesize Information

Review the evidence recorded from each source. What does the evidence tell you about whether students should study abroad or not? Discuss your ideas with a partner.

CHECK IN 1 2 3 4

94 Unit 3 • Argumentative Writing

Plan: Organize Ideas

Sample answers below:

Claim	Reasons	Relevant Evidence: Source 1	Relevant Evidence: Source 2	Relevant Evidence: Source 3
Study abroad programs are . . . not a good idea. Students should not participate in study abroad programs.	One reason that students should consider . . . not participating is that study abroad costs too much.	Traveling and living in another country can cost more than studying at home.	There are many costs associated with study abroad.	There was a recession in 2008. Some students and families couldn't afford study abroad then. Now students are choosing to study in countries with more affordable costs. Is it worth the experience?
	Another reason is that there is too much paperwork.	Students need visas to study in another country. Parents must gather the proper documents.	Students have too much paperwork to complete.	
	A third reason is that students are away for long periods of time for study abroad.	Students may be away from home for weeks or even months.		If students and families want to save money, they must study abroad for shorter periods of time instead of longer. But is it worth it to study abroad for shorter periods?

Unit 3 • Argumentative Writing 95

Reading/Writing Companion, pp. 94–95

English Language Learners

Use the following scaffolds with **Graphic Organizer**. For additional support, see the **ELL Small Group Guide**.

Beginning

Help students understand and complete the graphic organizer. Review that the relevant evidence supports the claim. The reasons support the claim. Help students fill in the information. For example, have them look at their notes and find evidence about study abroad programs that support their claim. Help partners describe their claim: *Study abroad programs are* good/bad *for students. They* help students learn a foreign language/cost too much money.

Intermediate

Discuss how the graphic organizer is organized with students. Point out that the relevant evidence supports the reasons and reasons support the claim. For an example, have students fill in the first row. Have them find the information from their notes. Help them describe their claim: *Study abroad programs have* benefits for students/lots of paperwork. *Study abroad programs* help with careers/can cost thousands of dollars.

Advanced/Advanced High

Discuss how the graphic organizer is organized with students, and fill in the first row with them for an example. Have them find the information from their notes. Have them describe their claim and information they can use to support it.

FORMATIVE ASSESSMENT

STUDENT CHECK-IN

Have partners share their graphic organizer on Reading/Writing Companion pages 94-95. Ask them to use the Check-In routine to reflect and fill in the bars.

LEARNING GOALS

We can use our graphic organizer to write a draft.

OBJECTIVES

Introduce a topic or text clearly, state an opinion, and create an organizational structure in which ideas are logically grouped to support the writer's purpose.

Provide logically ordered reasons that are supported by facts and details.

With guidance and support from peers and adults, develop and strengthen writing as needed by planning, revising, editing, rewriting, or trying a new approach.

ELA ACADEMIC LANGUAGE

- *logical, order, chronology*
- Cognates: *lógico, orden, cronología*

DIFFERENTIATED WRITING

Approaching Level Review students' drafts for logical order.

On Level Partners can review each other's drafts for logical order.

Beyond Level Partners can make suggestions for ordering ideas more logically.

ELL For support on writing a draft, see **ELL Small Group Guide**.

DIGITAL TOOLS

 Student Model Draft

Draft: Logical Order

Organize Ideas Logically

Tell students that organizing their ideas logically is one strategy that writers use to present their evidence in argumentative essays. Writers can start with their strongest reason first, so the audience will read it right away. Another option is to end with their strongest reason so that it has a lasting impact.

Read this section from paragraph 2 of Joe's student model essay on **Reading/Writing Companion** page 88:

Learning another language in a classroom offers students a broader range of studies. The article "Language Classes" says that in an immersion class, "students are taught a number of subjects in both languages." In other words, students are learning a language in other subjects. "Language Classes" also describes a program called Foreign Language in Elementary Schools, or FLES. In FLES, the foreign language instruction is connected to science, technology, engineering, arts, and math.

Explain that, in this paragraph, Joe presents a strong reason to support his claim that the best way to learn a language is in a classroom. Say: *First, he starts with this reason: Learning in a classroom "offers students a broader range of studies." Then he presents evidence in a logical order to back up his reason.* Point out that this is Joe's first reason in his essay. Say: *He presents this reason with evidence first because it is strong and is most convincing to the audience at the beginning of the essay.*

Read aloud the paragraph on page 96. Ask: *What is the author's claim?* (that the quipu is a language) Ask: *Which sentences show the strongest evidence for this?* (the third and fourth sentences) Have students use the paragraph as a model to write a claim for their essay.

COLLABORATE Have partners read their paragraphs aloud. Have them describe how the first sentence states the claim and how the rest of the paragraph includes evidence to support the claim. Then have partners discuss: *What evidence will come last to have the strongest impact?*

Draft

Have students write an argumentative essay on whether students should participate in study abroad programs. Have students review the rubric on page 86, the evidence they recorded in the graphic organizer, and the notes they took in their writer's notebook.

Remind students that one feature of a strong argumentative essay is precise language. Encourage them to organize their ideas logically so that their claim is strongly supported.

Make sure students write their drafts legibly in print or cursive or type accurately on-screen in their writer's notebook. Check their progress.

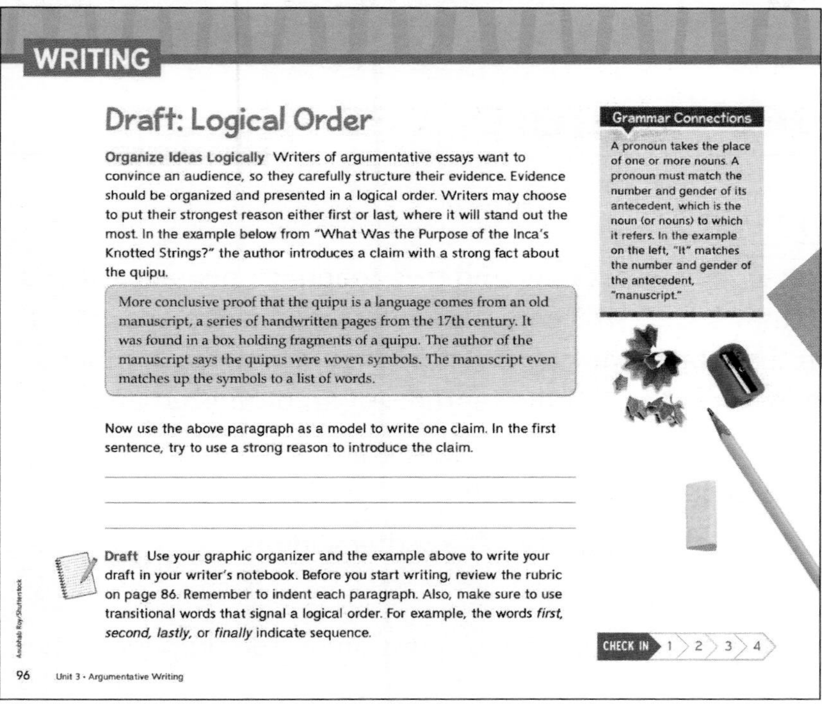

WRITING

Draft: Logical Order

Organize Ideas Logically Writers of argumentative essays want to convince an audience, so they carefully structure their evidence. Evidence should be organized and presented in a logical order. Writers may choose to put their strongest reason either first or last, where it will stand out the most. In the example below from "What Was the Purpose of the Inca's Knotted Strings?" the author introduces a claim with a strong fact about the quipu.

More conclusive proof that the quipu is a language comes from an old manuscript, a series of handwritten pages from the 17th century. It was found in a box holding fragments of a quipu. The author of the manuscript says the quipus were woven symbols. The manuscript even matches up the symbols to a list of words.

Now use the above paragraph as a model to write one claim. In the first sentence, try to use a strong reason to introduce the claim.

Draft Use your graphic organizer and the example above to write your draft in your writer's notebook. Before you start writing, review the rubric on page 86. Remember to indent each paragraph. Also, make sure to use transitional words that signal a logical order. For example, the words *first, second, lastly,* or *finally* indicate sequence.

Grammar Connections

A pronoun takes the place of one or more nouns. A pronoun must match the number and gender of its antecedent, which is the noun (or nouns) to which it refers. In the example on the left, "It" matches the number and gender of the antecedent, "manuscript."

CHECK IN 1 2 3 4

96 Unit 3 • Argumentative Writing

Reading/Writing Companion, p. 96

Grammar Connections

Students can use online **Grammar Handbook** page 463 to review and practice using pronouns and ensure pronoun-antecedent agreement. When writers use the right pronouns to refer to the antecedent, readers can more easily keep track of the writers' ideas. This helps create a logical progression and clear organization.

ELL English Language Learners

Use the following scaffolds with **Organize Ideas Logically**.

Beginning

Review with students that writers present evidence to support their reasons in a logical order. Explain that writers might use their strongest reason first or last so that it stands out. Reread the paragraph on page 96 with students. Say: *The first sentence introduces the author's claim with a strong reason. Restate the author's claim using the sentence frame*: The author's claim is that quipu is a language. *What does the rest of the sentences in the paragraph present?* The rest of the sentences presents evidence to support the claim.

Intermediate

Review with students that writers present evidence for their reasons in a logical order. Read the paragraph on page 96 with them, and have students point out how the author's claim is introduced with a strong reason. Encourage partners to restate the claim to each other: The author's claim is that quipus is a language. Then have them discuss what the rest of the sentences in the paragraph presents using: The rest of the sentences presents evidence to support the claim.

Advanced/Advanced High

Have students explain why evidence for a reason should be presented in a logical order. Have them identify the author's claim in the paragraph on page 96. Point out the strong reason introduces the claim. Then have partners discuss which sentences show the strongest evidence for the claim.

TEACHER CONFERENCES

As students draft, hold teacher conferences with individual students.

Step 1: Talk About Strengths
Point out strengths in the essay: *The claim is clear and tells what you think and feel about the topic.*

Step 2: Focus on Skills
Give feedback on how the student uses relevant evidence: *This evidence does not support your argument. Add evidence that is relevant to your opinion.*

Step 3: Make Concrete Suggestions
Provide specific direction to help students revise: *Make sure that you use precise language to express your position clearly.* Have students meet with you to review progress.

FORMATIVE ASSESSMENT

STUDENT CHECK-IN

Have partners share their draft. Then have them use the Check-In routine to reflect and fill in the bars on Reading/Writing Companion page 96.

LEARNING GOALS

We can revise our writing to make it stronger.

OBJECTIVES

Link ideas within and across categories of information using words, phrases, and clauses (e.g., *in contrast, especially*).

With guidance and support from peers and adults, develop and strengthen writing as needed by planning, revising, and editing.

Engage effectively in a range of collaborative discussions (one-on-one, in groups, and teacher-led) with diverse partners, building on others' ideas and expressing their own clearly.

Follow agreed-upon rules for discussions and carry out assigned roles.

Use knowledge of language and its conventions when writing, speaking, reading, or listening.

ELA ACADEMIC LANGUAGE

- *feedback, conference*
- Cognate: *conferencia*

DIFFERENTIATED WRITING

Check student progress at this stage during Small Group time.

Approaching Level Review students' drafts for precise language and logically ordered claims.

On Level Partners can focus on logically ordered claims as they read each other's drafts.

Beyond Level As students review each other's drafts, they can identify places where precise language can be used to better convince the audience.

ELL For support with revising the drafts, see **ELL Small Group Guide**.

Revise: Peer Conferences

Review a Draft

Explain to partners that they will review and give feedback on each other's drafts. Remind them that a well-written argumentative essay begins with a focused introduction that states the claim. Before they review each other's drafts, remind them to think about some features of an organized and focused essay:

- Evidence and facts that support the claim
- Precise language that clearly expresses the writer's ideas
- Logically ordered reasons, or claims
- Varied sentence structure, starting with a question or adding punctuation for emphasis

Review with students the routine for peer review of writing.

- Step 1: Listen carefully as the writer reads his or her work aloud.
- Step 2: Avoid calling attention away from or interrupting the writer.
- Step 3: Ask questions to help you make sense of anything that is unclear.
- Step 4: Take note of the things you liked about the writing.

Model using sentence starters on **Reading Writing Companion** page 97. Say: *This word is a great example of precise language because* . . . and finish the sentence. Discuss the steps of the peer conferencing routine. Ask: *Why is it important to listen actively?* (to show respect and to comment on the writing) *Why should we take notes about what was effective and what was difficult to follow?* (to show the writer that his or her facts and details were relevant to the topic and supported the claim; to ask the writer to clarify how ideas are connected)

COLLABORATE Circulate and observe as partners review and give feedback on each other's drafts. Ensure that partners are following the routine and the agreed-upon rules of listening actively and taking notes. Remind them to consider replacing generic language with precise language, using clear transitions between ideas, and adding facts and specific details that are relevant to the topic. Have students reflect on partner feedback and write on page 97 which suggestion they found most helpful.

Revision

Review the features of the Revising Checklist on page 97 and the rubric on pages 236–239. Explain that this is a rubric with scores that add up to a maximum of 10. Point out the score in the left column and the three categories in the right column. Have students use the rubric to score their essays on page 97.

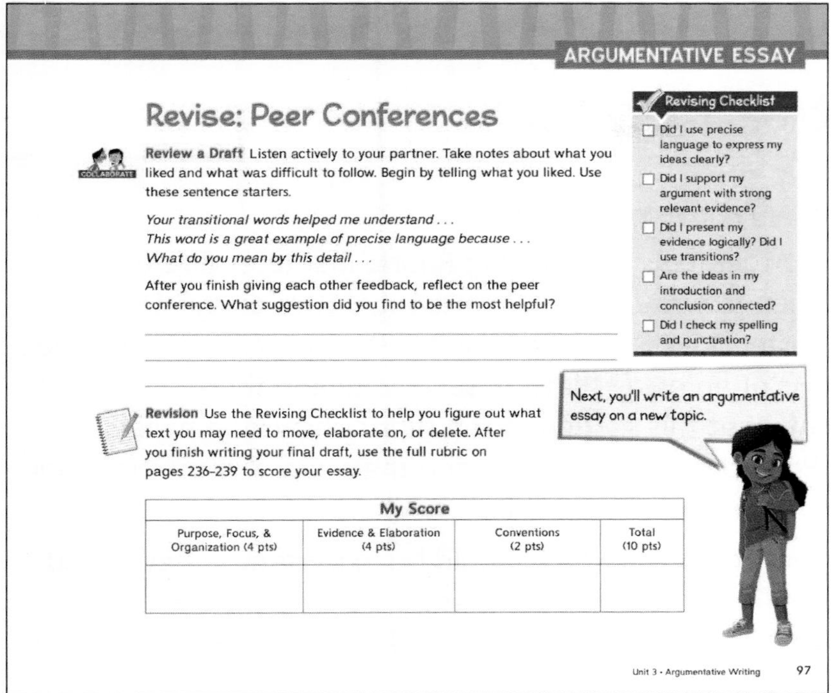

ARGUMENTATIVE ESSAY

Revise: Peer Conferences

COLLABORATE

Review a Draft Listen actively to your partner. Take notes about what you liked and what was difficult to follow. Begin by telling what you liked. Use these sentence starters.

Your transitional words helped me understand . . .
This word is a great example of precise language because . . .
What do you mean by this detail . . .

After you finish giving each other feedback, reflect on the peer conference. What suggestion did you find to be the most helpful?

Revising Checklist

- ☐ Did I use precise language to express my ideas clearly?
- ☐ Did I support my argument with strong relevant evidence?
- ☐ Did I present my evidence logically? Did I use transitions?
- ☐ Are the ideas in my introduction and conclusion connected?
- ☐ Did I check my spelling and punctuation?

Revision Use the Revising Checklist to help you figure out what text you may need to move, elaborate on, or delete. After you finish writing your final draft, use the full rubric on pages 236–239 to score your essay.

My Score			
Purpose, Focus, & Organization (4 pts)	Evidence & Elaboration (4 pts)	Conventions (2 pts)	Total (10 pts)

Unit 3 • Argumentative Writing 97

Reading/Writing Companion, p. 97

ELL English Language Learners

Use the following scaffolds with **Review a Draft**. For additional support, see the **ELL Small Group Guide**.

Beginning

Pair students with more proficient readers. Have students ask for clarification and provide feedback using the following: *Can you reread ____? What does the claim ____ mean? I like ____.* Students may need to see the draft as well as hear it. Have partners complete the partner feedback on page 97. Help students check their drafts for the last two items on the Revising Checklist and help them revise using transitional words to show logical order.

Intermediate

Pair students with more proficient speakers. Have students ask for clarification and provide feedback, using the following: *Can you explain ____? I like the part about ____.* Have partners complete the partner feedback on page 97. Have students use the last three items on the Revising Checklist to identify the revisions they want to make. Have them use transitional words to show a logical order. Check their revisions and provide feedback as needed.

Advanced/Advanced High

Have partners provide feedback using the sentence starters on page 97 and then read each other's responses to check that their partner understood them correctly. Have students use the Revising Checklist to identify the features that appear in their writing.

TEACHER CONFERENCES

As students revise, hold teacher conferences with individual students.

Step 1: Talk About Strengths
Point out strengths in the essay: *The purpose of your essay is clear. Your introduction is strong.*

Step 2: Focus on Skills
Give feedback on how the student uses logical order: *This sentence presents information that doesn't support this claim. Reorder the information so that the claim and evidence follow a logical order.*

Step 3: Make Concrete Suggestions
Provide specific direction to help students revise, such as using transition words or strengthening the conclusion. Have students revise and then meet with you to review progress.

DIGITAL TOOLS

Revised Student Model

Revise Checklist (Argumentative); Revise Conferencing Checklist (Argumentative); Peer Conferencing (Collaborative Conversations Video)

FORMATIVE ASSESSMENT

STUDENT CHECK-IN

Have partners share their drafts and give feedback. Ask them to reflect using the Check-In routine and rubric on Reading/Writing Companion page 97.

LEARNING GOALS

We can use a rubric to understand what makes a strong argumentative essay.

OBJECTIVES

Provide logically ordered reasons that are supported by facts and details.

Provide a concluding statement or section related to the opinion presented.

With guidance and support from peers and adults, develop and strengthen writing as needed by planning, revising, and editing.

Analyze a rubric used to evaluate argumentative essays.

ELA ACADEMIC LANGUAGE

- *progression, logical, introduction, conclusion*
- Cognates: *progresión, lógico, introducción, conclusion*

Analyze the Rubric

Argumentative Writing Rubric

Students will use the Argumentative Writing Rubric first to evaluate a student model and then to write their own argumentative essays. Explain that a rubric helps writers know what to include. Students can also use the rubric to identify parts of an essay that are successful and those that need work. Remind students that this section of the rubric shows the highest scores and criteria. Point out each category and the score of 4 on the rubric on **Reading/Writing Companion** page 98.

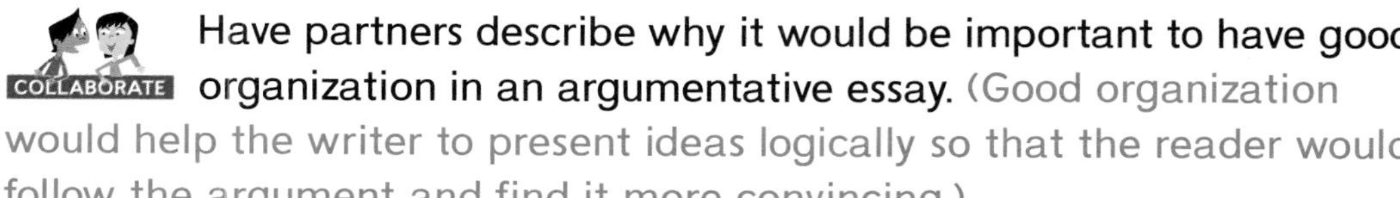

COLLABORATE Have partners describe why it would be important to have good organization in an argumentative essay. (Good organization would help the writer to present ideas logically so that the reader would follow the argument and find it more convincing.)

Purpose, Focus, and Organization

Remind students that an effective essay must have a clear purpose, focus, and organization. Effective organization of an essay includes a strong introduction and conclusion. Students will analyze the fifth bullet in the rubric. Understanding this bullet will help students with the conclusion in their essays. Remind students that a conclusion occurs at the end of an essay. Ask: *Why does a writer need to include a conclusion in an* argumentative *essay?* (to restate the evidence for the claim and give the essay closure)

Analytical Writing Ask: *What is a strong conclusion?* (A strong conclusion tells about the most important ideas and makes the reader agree with the writer's argument) Have students write their response on Reading/Writing Companion page 98. It summarizes the important ideas in the essay that support the claim. Students will examine the conclusion in a student model and then develop their own.

Evidence and Elaboration

Remind students that a strong essay must include evidence and elaboration. This part of the rubric identifies how evidence and elaborative techniques should be incorporated and accomplished using language, vocabulary, and sentence structure. Read all the bullets with students. Have students reread the third bullet. Ask: *What does the word* elaborative *mean?* (very detailed)

Analytical Writing Reread the fourth and sixth bullets. Ask: *What is the connection between expressing ideas clearly and using different sentence structures?* (When you express ideas clearly and vary sentence structure, your reader is excited to continue reading more of your work.) Have students write their responses on page 98. Remind students that using varied sentence structure can add interest to an essay and keep readers engaged in the topic.

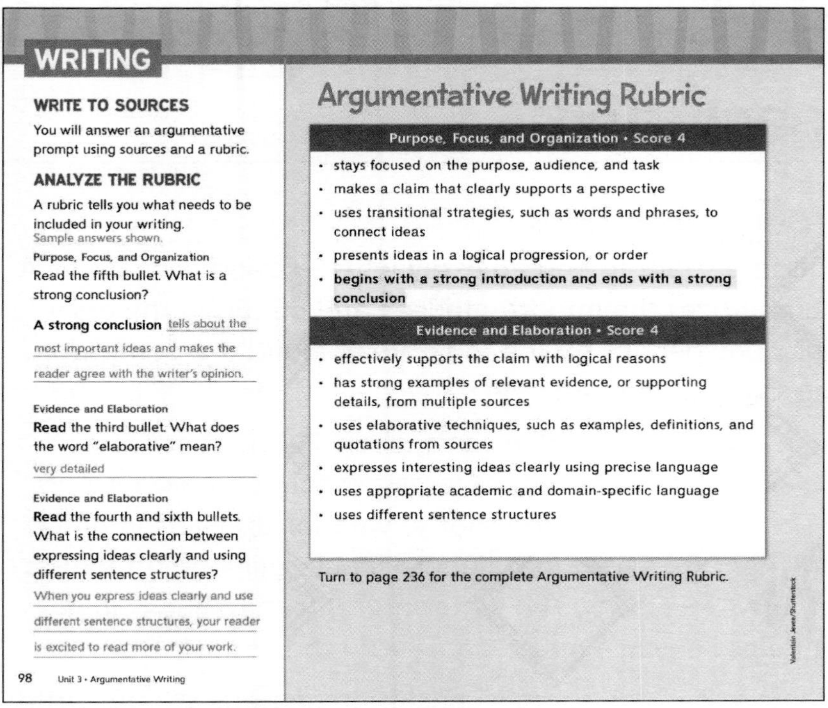

WRITING

WRITE TO SOURCES

You will answer an argumentative prompt using sources and a rubric.

ANALYZE THE RUBRIC

A rubric tells you what needs to be included in your writing.
Sample answers shown.

Purpose, Focus, and Organization
Read the fifth bullet. What is a strong conclusion?

A strong conclusion tells about the most important ideas and makes the reader agree with the writer's opinion.

Evidence and Elaboration
Read the third bullet. What does the word "elaborative" mean?

very detailed

Evidence and Elaboration
Read the fourth and sixth bullets. What is the connection between expressing ideas clearly and using different sentence structures?

When you express ideas clearly and use different sentence structures, your reader is excited to read more of your work.

Argumentative Writing Rubric

Purpose, Focus, and Organization • Score 4

- stays focused on the purpose, audience, and task
- makes a claim that clearly supports a perspective
- uses transitional strategies, such as words and phrases, to connect ideas
- presents ideas in a logical progression, or order
- **begins with a strong introduction and ends with a strong conclusion**

Evidence and Elaboration • Score 4

- effectively supports the claim with logical reasons
- has strong examples of relevant evidence, or supporting details, from multiple sources
- uses elaborative techniques, such as examples, definitions, and quotations from sources
- expresses interesting ideas clearly using precise language
- uses appropriate academic and domain-specific language
- uses different sentence structures

Turn to page 236 for the complete Argumentative Writing Rubric.

98 Unit 3 • Argumentative Writing

Reading/Writing Companion, p. 98

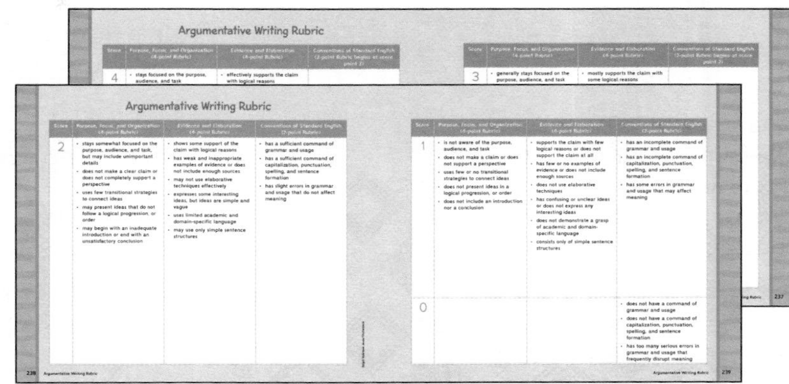

For the full Argumentative Writing Rubric, see **Reading/Writing Companion,** pages 236–239.

English Language Learners

Use the following scaffolds with **Purpose, Focus, and Organization**.

Beginning

Read the highlighted rubric with students. Say: *Put ideas in an argumentative essay in a logical order from the introduction to the conclusion. The introduction is at the beginning, and the conclusion is at the end.* Discuss with students how they make introductions and conclusions satisfying and effective. Help partners describe using the following: An introduction is at the beginning of an essay. Ideas follow in a logical order, then a conclusion is at the end.

Intermediate

Review the concepts of a satisfying introduction and conclusion with students. Discuss how an introduction tells the writer's claim at the beginning of the essay and a conclusion summarizes the claim at the end. Then read the highlighted rubric with them, and have partners discuss what makes introductions and conclusions satisfying with each other. Have partners describe using the following: An introduction states the writer's claim at the beginning of the essay. A conclusion restates the writer's claim at the end of the essay.

Advanced/Advanced High

Have students describe how an introduction and a conclusion help to organize and reinforce ideas in the essay. Read the highlighted rubric with them. Have partners discuss how a writer creates a satisfying introduction at the beginning of the essay and conclusion at the end.

ELL NEWCOMERS

To help students develop their writing, display the **Newcomer Cards** and **Newcomer Online Visuals**, and ask questions to help them discuss the images. Provide sentence starters. For example: What do you see? I see a/an ___. What are they doing? They are ___. Have students point to the image as they ask and answer. Then have them write the sentences in their notebooks. Throughout the extended writing project, help students develop their writing by adding to and revising their sentences.

FORMATIVE ASSESSMENT

STUDENT CHECK-IN

Have partners share their responses. Then ask them to reflect using the Check-In routine.

LEARNING GOALS

We can identify a strong conclusion.

OBJECTIVES

Analyze multiple accounts of the same event or topic, noting important similarities and differences in the point of view they represent.

Explain how an author uses reasons and evidence to support particular points in a text, identifying which reasons and evidence support which point(s).

Explain an author's perspective, or point of view, toward an argumentative text.

Provide logically ordered reasons that are supported by facts and details.

Provide a concluding statement or section related to the opinion presented.

With guidance and support from peers and adults, develop and strengthen writing as needed by planning, revising, and editing.

Analyze models to understand how to write a strong conclusion.

ELA ACADEMIC LANGUAGE

- *summarize, communicate, argument, formal, informal, assert*
- Cognates: *comunicar, argumento, formal, informal*

DIGITAL TOOLS

Student Model Sources

Purpose of Argumentative Writing

Strong Conclusion

End with a Strong Statement

Tell students that it is important to end an essay with a strong conclusion. A strong conclusion summarizes the important ideas and details in the essay as well as the author's perspective on the topic. Read aloud the paragraph on **Reading/Writing Companion** page 99.

Think Aloud I see that the paragraph presents a conclusion about forests. The writer states his or her perspective that forests should be preserved for everyone's benefit. The writer tells nations not to wait for disasters in order to save forests. The writer also states that people should think about forests in a global way, not just a local way. The writer presents these ideas in a clear way, and that helps convince me to agree with the writer's claim.

Have students reread the sample conclusion on page 99 and write a sentence that tells why this sample is a strong conclusion.

Strong Language

Discuss how strong words can help to communicate a writer's argument. Have students look at the highlighted words in the sample. Ask: *What makes these words strong?* (The words demand that people do things; they do not just make suggestions about what could be done.)

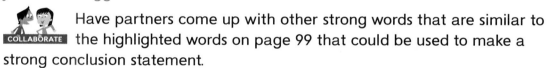

COLLABORATE Have partners come up with other strong words that are similar to the highlighted words on page 99 that could be used to make a strong conclusion statement.

Turn to **Literature Anthology** page 221 and reread the concluding paragraph of the essay, which discusses the ancient city of Machu Picchu.

Think Aloud I see that the paragraph presents a conclusion about how Machu Picchu was used. Some evidence shows that it was used as a royal retreat. Other evidence shows that it was used as an observatory. This conclusion summarizes the main ideas of the essay.

Have students use the sample conclusion on Reading/Writing Companion page 99 as a model to write a strong conclusion about the uses of Machu Picchu based on what they read on **Literature Anthology** page 221. Tell students to be sure to use strong language. Have students write their response on page 99.

Apply

For more practice with reviewing strong conclusions, have partners read the three student model sources in the online **Writer's Notebook** and discuss what makes the conclusion strong in one or more sources.

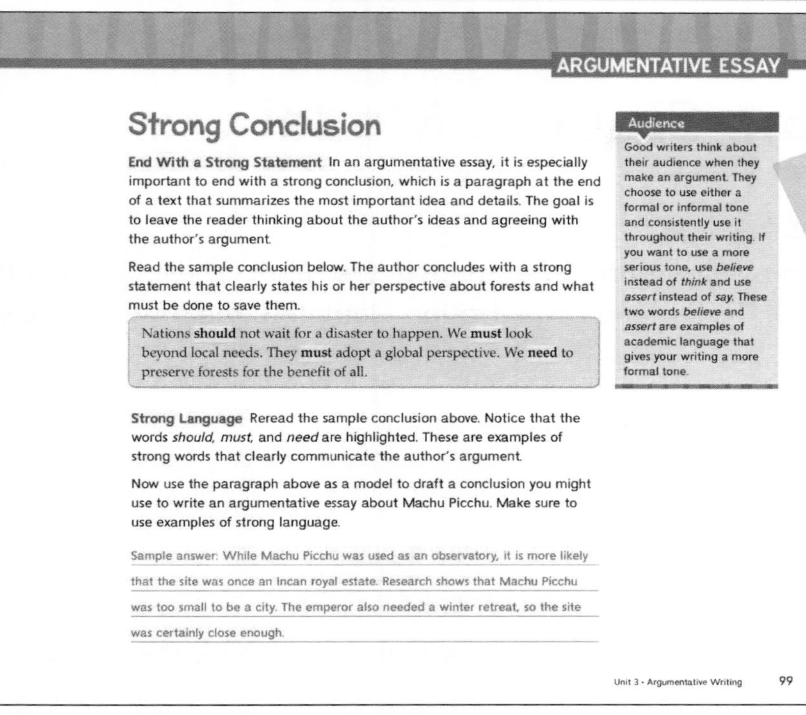

ARGUMENTATIVE ESSAY

Strong Conclusion

End With a Strong Statement In an argumentative essay, it is especially important to end with a strong conclusion, which is a paragraph at the end of a text that summarizes the most important idea and details. The goal is to leave the reader thinking about the author's ideas and agreeing with the author's argument.

Read the sample conclusion below. The author concludes with a strong statement that clearly states his or her perspective about forests and what must be done to save them.

> Nations **should** not wait for a disaster to happen. We **must** look beyond local needs. They **must** adopt a global perspective. We **need** to preserve forests for the benefit of all.

Strong Language Reread the sample conclusion above. Notice that the words *should, must,* and *need* are highlighted. These are examples of strong words that clearly communicate the author's argument.

Now use the paragraph above as a model to draft a conclusion you might use to write an argumentative essay about Machu Picchu. Make sure to use examples of strong language.

Sample answer: While Machu Picchu was used as an observatory, it is more likely that the site was once an Incan royal estate. Research shows that Machu Picchu was too small to be a city. The emperor also needed a winter retreat, so the site was certainly close enough.

Audience

Good writers think about their audience when they make an argument. They choose to use either a formal or informal tone and consistently use it throughout their writing. If you want to use a more serious tone, use *believe* instead of *think* and use *assert* instead of *say*. These two words *believe* and *assert* are examples of academic language that gives your writing a more formal tone.

Unit 3 • Argumentative Writing 99

Reading/Writing Companion, p. 99

Audience

Strong writers think about their audience when making an argument. Based on the topic they are discussing, they choose to use either a formal or an informal tone. Writers may use more informal words, such as *think* and *say*, when the topic is less serious. They may use more formal words, such as *contemplate* or *assert*, when the topic is more serious. Ask: *What words in the sample make the tone more formal?*

English Language Learners

Use the following scaffolds with **Strong Language**. For additional support, see **ELL Small Group Guide**.

Beginning

Review with students how strong words communicate the strong feelings of the writer. Read the paragraph on page 99 with students. Help them describe how the words *should, must,* and *need* express a sense of urgency or importance using: Each word tells something that the writer thinks we have to do. We have to act before a disaster happens. We have to think globally. We have to take care of forests for everyone.

Intermediate

Review strong language such as *should, must,* and *need,* and discuss why these words are important to use in conclusions. Then read the paragraph on page 99 together. Have students describe how the strong words convey the writer's argument with a sense of urgency using: Nations need to act before there are disasters. We have to think about what is happening around the world, not just around us. We have to take care of forests for everyone around the world.

Advanced/Advanced High

Read the paragraph on page 99, and have students identify the strong words. Discuss with them how strong words in conclusion convey the writer's argument with a sense of urgency. Then have partners draft a strong conclusion statement about whether forests should be preserved or not.

STUDENT CHECK-IN

Have partners share their responses. Then have them reflect using the Check-In routine.

LEARNING GOALS

We can use a rubric to evaluate a student model.

OBJECTIVES

Analyze multiple accounts of the same event or topic, noting important similarities and differences in the point of view they represent.

Explain an author's perspective, or point of view, toward a topic in an informational text.

Explain how an author uses reasons and evidence to support particular points in a text, identifying which reasons and evidence support which point(s).

Explain an author's perspective, or point of view, toward an argumentative text.

With guidance and support from peers and adults, develop and strengthen writing as needed by planning, revising, and editing.

Analyze a writing prompt.

Analyze a model and apply a rubric to understand the elements of an effective argumentative essay.

ELA ACADEMIC LANGUAGE

- *rubric, transition, persuade*
- Cognates: *rúbrica, transición, persuadir*

DIGITAL TOOLS

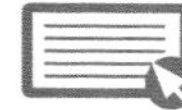
Student Model Sources

Analyze the Student Model

10 mins

Argumentative Essay

Students will analyze a student model and apply the rubric to explain why it scored a 4 for Purpose, Focus, and Organization. Complete the routine below.

ANALYZE THE PROMPT ROUTINE

Read aloud the prompt.

Identify the purpose. *Is the purpose to inform or persuade?*

Identify the audience. *Who is the audience?*

Identify the type of writing the prompt is asking for. *What is the prompt asking the writer to do?*

After the routine, students should understand that Suze's purpose is to persuade, her audience is people at school who would see the bulletin board, and the prompt is to develop a claim about who created the spheres.

Discuss the Student Model

As you read Suze's model with students, ask them to look for relevant evidence and ways that Suze uses examples, definitions, and quotations. Have students note interesting words and questions they have as they read.

Paragraph 1 Remind students that an argumentative essay contains an opinion that answers the prompt and reveals the perspective of the writer. Have students underline Suze's claim on **Reading/Writing Companion** page 100. (However, most scientists and archaeologists agree that the spheres were made by the ancient Diquis people.) Ask: *What is a detail from her introduction that caught your attention?* Have students write their responses on page 100.

Paragraph 2 Remind students that argumentative essays use sources to support the claim. Ask: *What source does Suze use in this paragraph?* (an article) *What are the details that Suze uses from this source?*

Think Aloud I see that the article Suze uses states that the stone spheres were discovered by a fruit company in the 1930s. There are about three hundred spheres, and the largest weighs 16 tons. The article states that a professor says that they were made by the Diquis people. There were marks on the spheres from stone hammers. The professor also states the spheres were made without help from "metal tools, laser beams, or alien life-forms."

COLLABORATE Have partners circle the detail that tells them that the anthropologist is a reliable source. (a leading expert on the Costa Rican spheres) Ask: *How does this source support Suze's claim?* (It says there

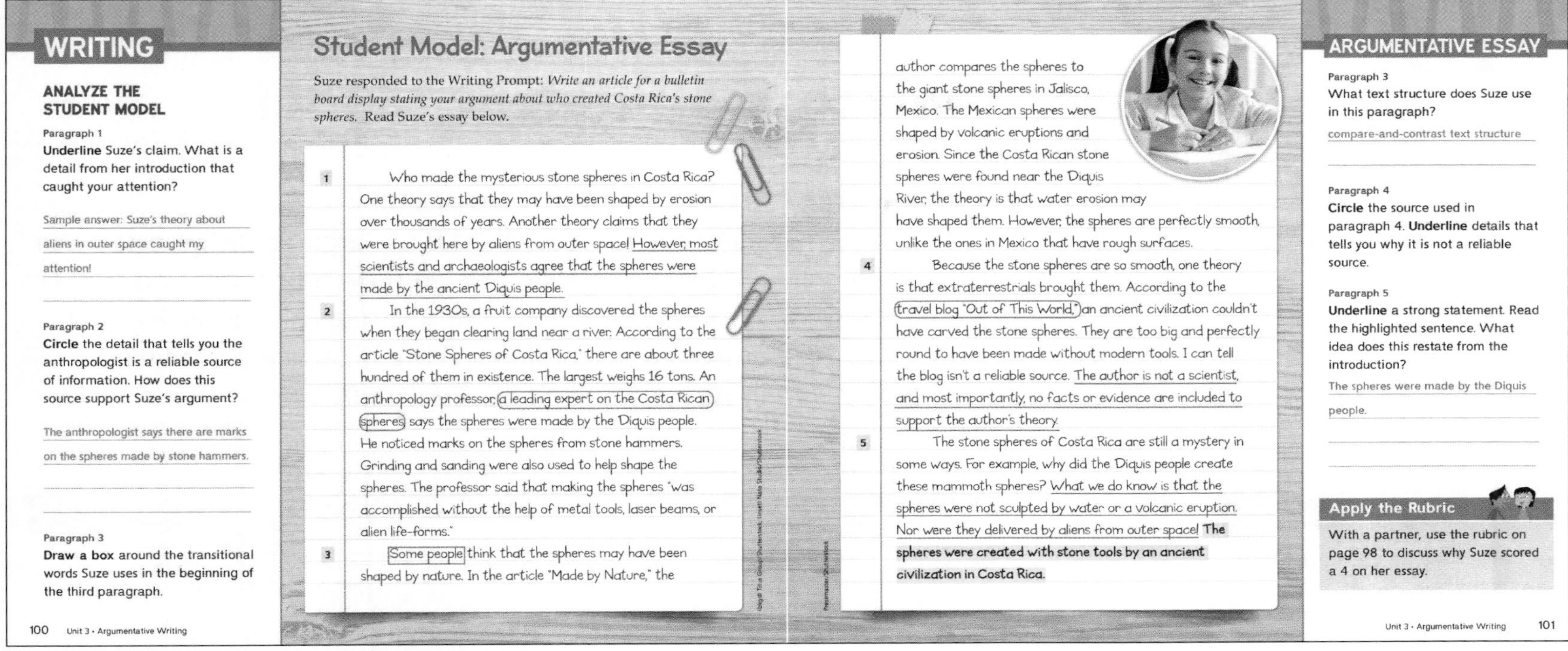

WRITING

ANALYZE THE STUDENT MODEL

Paragraph 1
Underline Suze's claim. What is a detail from her introduction that caught your attention?

Sample answer: Suze's theory about aliens in outer space caught my attention!

Paragraph 2
Circle the detail that tells you the anthropologist is a reliable source of information. How does this source support Suze's argument?

The anthropologist says there are marks on the spheres made by stone hammers.

Paragraph 3
Draw a box around the transitional words Suze uses in the beginning of the third paragraph.

100 Unit 3 • Argumentative Writing

Student Model: Argumentative Essay

Suze responded to the Writing Prompt: *Write an article for a bulletin board display stating your argument about who created Costa Rica's stone spheres.* Read Suze's essay below.

1 Who made the mysterious stone spheres in Costa Rica? One theory says that they may have been shaped by erosion over thousands of years. Another theory claims that they were brought here by aliens from outer space! However, most scientists and archaeologists agree that the spheres were made by the ancient Diquis people.

2 In the 1930s, a fruit company discovered the spheres when they began clearing land near a river. According to the article "Stone Spheres of Costa Rica," there are about three hundred of them in existence. The largest weighs 16 tons. An anthropology professor, a leading expert on the Costa Rican spheres, says the spheres were made by the Diquis people. He noticed marks on the spheres from stone hammers. Grinding and sanding were also used to help shape the spheres. The professor said that making the spheres "was accomplished without the help of metal tools, laser beams, or alien life-forms."

3 Some people think that the spheres may have been shaped by nature. In the article "Made by Nature," the author compares the spheres to the giant stone spheres in Jalisco, Mexico. The Mexican spheres were shaped by volcanic eruptions and erosion. Since the Costa Rican stone spheres were found near the Diquis River, the theory is that water erosion may have shaped them. However, the spheres are perfectly smooth, unlike the ones in Mexico that have rough surfaces.

4 Because the stone spheres are so smooth, one theory is that extraterrestrials brought them. According to the travel blog "Out of This World," an ancient civilization couldn't have carved the stone spheres. They are too big and perfectly round to have been made without modern tools. I can tell the blog isn't a reliable source. The author is not a scientist, and most importantly, no facts or evidence are included to support the author's theory.

5 The stone spheres of Costa Rica are still a mystery in some ways. For example, why did the Diquis people create these mammoth spheres? What we do know is that the spheres were not sculpted by water or a volcanic eruption. Nor were they delivered by aliens from outer space! **The spheres were created with stone tools by an ancient civilization in Costa Rica.**

ARGUMENTATIVE ESSAY

Paragraph 3
What text structure does Suze use in this paragraph?

compare-and-contrast text structure

Paragraph 4
Circle the source used in paragraph 4. **Underline** details that tells you why it is not a reliable source.

Paragraph 5
Underline a strong statement. Read the highlighted sentence. What idea does this restate from the introduction?

The spheres were made by the Diquis people.

Apply the Rubric

With a partner, use the rubric on page 98 to discuss why Suze scored a 4 on her essay.

Unit 3 • Argumentative Writing 101

Reading/Writing Companion, pp. 100–101

are marks on the spheres made by hammers.) Have students write their answer on page 100.

Paragraph 3 Read the first sentence. Have students draw a box around the transitional words Suze uses at the beginning of this third paragraph. (*Some people*) Read the rest of the paragraph with students. Ask: *What does the author of the source "Made by Nature" discuss that relates to Costa Rica's stone spheres?* (giant stone spheres in Jalisco, Mexico) Ask: *What text structure does Suze use in this paragraph?* (compare-and-contrast text structure)

Have partners reread and answer the question on page 101.

Paragraph 4 Have students circle the source used in this paragraph. Then have students underline details that would indicate why it is not a reliable source. Ask: *Why would the writer include a source that is not reliable?* (It helps support the writer's opinion that the stone spheres were made by ancient peoples and not by aliens because the source that presents the alien theory cannot be trusted.)

Paragraph 5 Read the conclusion with students. Have them underline a strong statement. Read the highlighted sentence with students. Ask: *What idea does this restate from the introduction?* (The spheres were made by the Diquis.)

Apply the Rubric

COLLABORATE Have pairs discuss why Suze's essay scored a 4 for Purpose, Focus, and Organization and what needs to be improved. Have them use the rubric on page 98 and these sentence starters:

Suze supports her argument by using . . .

Her conclusion is . . .

TEACH IN SMALL GROUP

ELL For support with reading the student model and analyzing three sources, see **ELL Small Group Guide**.

CLASSROOM CULTURE

We inspire confident writers. Exploring exemplary models reinforces students' understanding of the connection between reading and writing. Analyzing how writers craft essays in the assigned genre will help you create a classroom where students feel more confident as they plan, draft, and revise their own writing in that genre.

FORMATIVE ASSESSMENT

STUDENT CHECK-IN

Have partners share their responses to Apply the Rubric on Reading/Writing Companion page 101. Then ask them to reflect using the Check-In routine.

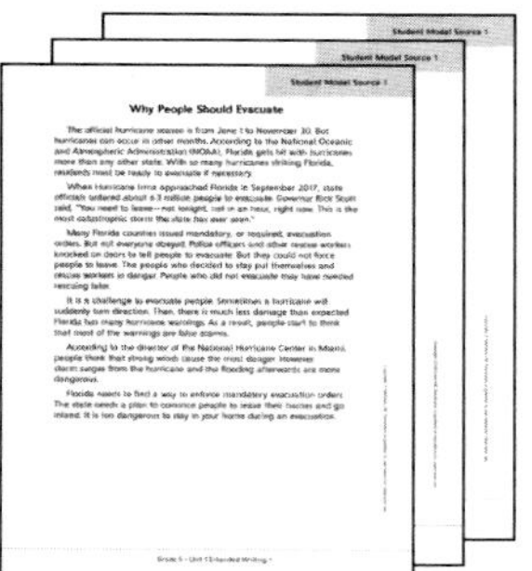

Student Model Sources

LEARNING GOALS

We can analyze student model essay sources.

OBJECTIVES

Explain how an author uses reasons and evidence to support particular points in a text, identifying which reasons and evidence support which point(s).

Explain an author's perspective, or point of view, toward an argumentative text.

Read grade-level text with purpose and understanding.

With guidance and support from peers and adults, develop and strengthen writing as needed by planning, revising, and editing.

Analyze sources to understand the elements of an effective argumentative essay.

Cite evidence to explain and justify reasoning.

ELA ACADEMIC LANGUAGE

- *explanation, claim, conclusion, synthesize*
- Cognates: *explicación, conclusión*

DIGITAL TOOLS

Take Notes

Analyze the Student Model

Analyze the Student Model Sources

Explain that Suze read three sources to write her argumentative essay. Use copies of the online Student Model Sources to show how Suze used details from sources to support her claim and craft a strong conclusion. Remind students that Suze answered this prompt: *Write an article for a bulletin board display stating your opinion about who created Costa Rica's stone spheres.*

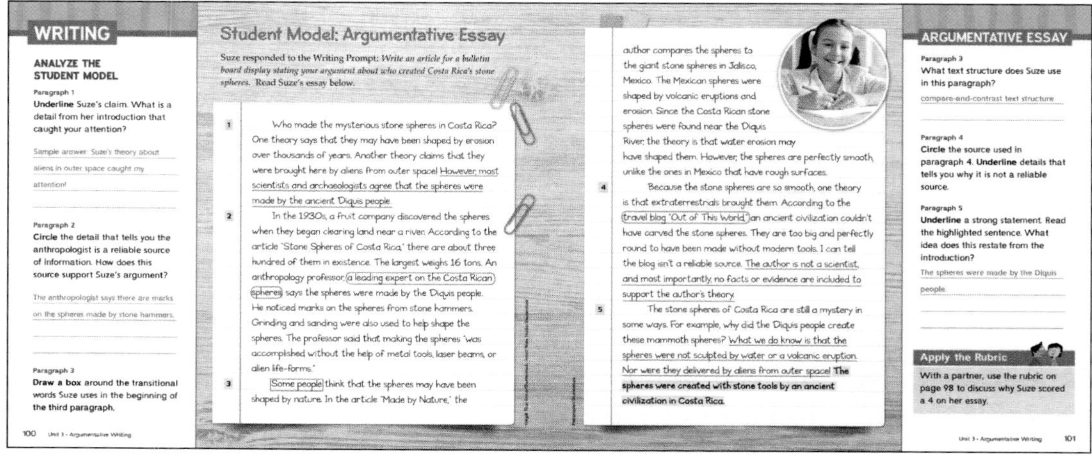

WRITING

ANALYZE THE STUDENT MODEL

Paragraph 1
Underline Suze's claim. What is a detail from her introduction that caught your attention?

Sample answer: Suze's theory about aliens in outer space caught my attention!

Paragraph 2
Circle the detail that tells you the anthropologist is a reliable source of information. How does this source support Suze's argument?

The anthropologist says there are marks on the spheres made by stone hammers.

Paragraph 3
Draw a box around the transitional words Suze uses in the beginning of the third paragraph.

100 Unit 3 • Argumentative Writing

Student Model: Argumentative Essay

Suze responded to the Writing Prompt: *Write an article for a bulletin board display stating your argument about who created Costa Rica's stone spheres.* Read Suze's essay below.

1 Who made the mysterious stone spheres in Costa Rica? One theory says that they may have been shaped by erosion over thousands of years. Another theory claims that they were brought here by aliens from outer space! However, most scientists and archaeologists agree that the spheres were made by the ancient Diquis people.

2 In the 1930s, a fruit company discovered the spheres when they began clearing land near a river. According to the article "Stone Spheres of Costa Rica," there are about three hundred of them in existence. The largest weighs 16 tons. An anthropology professor, a leading expert on the Costa Rican spheres, says the spheres were made by the Diquis people. He noticed marks on the spheres from stone hammers. Grinding and sanding were also used to help shape the spheres. The professor said that making the spheres "was accomplished without the help of metal tools, laser beams, or alien life-forms."

3 Some people think that the spheres may have been shaped by nature. In the article "Made by Nature," the author compares the spheres to the giant stone spheres in Jalisco, Mexico. The Mexican spheres were shaped by volcanic eruptions and erosion. Since the Costa Rican stone spheres were found near the Diquis River, the theory is that water erosion may have shaped them. However, the spheres are perfectly smooth, unlike the ones in Mexico that have rough surfaces.

4 Because the stone spheres are so smooth, one theory is that extraterrestrials brought them. According to the travel blog "Out of This World," an ancient civilization couldn't have carved the stone spheres. They are too big and perfectly round to have been made without modern tools. I can tell the blog isn't a reliable source. The author is not a scientist, and most importantly, no facts or evidence are included to support the author's theory.

5 The stone spheres of Costa Rica are still a mystery in some ways. For example, why did the Diquis people create these mammoth spheres? What we do know is that the spheres were not sculpted by water or a volcanic eruption. Nor were they delivered by aliens from outer space! **The spheres were created with stone tools by an ancient civilization in Costa Rica.**

ARGUMENTATIVE ESSAY

Paragraph 3
What text structure does Suze use in this paragraph?

compare-and-contrast text structure

Paragraph 4
Circle the source used in paragraph 4. **Underline** details that tells you why it is not a reliable source.

Paragraph 5
Underline a strong statement. Read the highlighted sentence. What idea does this restate from the introduction?

The spheres were made by the Diquis people.

Apply the Rubric

With a partner, use the rubric on page 98 to discuss why Suze scored a 4 on her essay.

Unit 3 • Argumentative Writing 101

Reading/Writing Companion, pp. 100–101

SOURCE 1 "Out of This World"

After reading Source 1, read aloud Suze's first paragraph. Ask: *Does the information from Source 1 support Suze's argument?* (No, it does not support it.)

Skip ahead and read Suze's fourth paragraph with students. Ask: *What details from Source 1 does Suze use in this paragraph?* (She uses statements that extraterrestrials brought the stones, because "they are too big and perfectly round to have been made without modern tools.")

COLLABORATE Have partners discuss why Source 1 is not a reliable source. (The author does not appear to be a scientist. The author states what scientists believe about the spheres, but comes up with an alternative theory based on no facts or evidence.)

SOURCE 2 "Made by Nature"

After reading Source 2, read aloud Suze's third paragraph. Ask: *How does Suze use details from this article to discuss how the Costa Rican stone spheres were formed?*

Think Aloud I see that Suze uses details about similar spheres that were found in Mexico to discuss how the Costa Rican spheres were formed. She uses information that explains how the Mexican spheres were shaped by volcanic eruptions and erosion. The source tells that the Costa Rican spheres were found near the Diquis River so that water erosion could have shaped them. The source also tells that the Costa Rican spheres are perfectly smooth, while the ones in Mexico have rough surfaces.

COLLABORATE Have partners read Source 2 together to find one detail that Suze did not use in this paragraph. (Sample response: "According to archaeologists, the ancient Diquis people found the rocks near the river and then chipped away at them until they became perfectly round and smooth.") Discuss how Suze could have incorporated this detail into her essay.

SOURCE 3 "Stone Spheres of Costa Rica"

Read Source 3. Have students scan Suze's essay for facts and details from Source 3. Ask: *Where does Suze use facts and details from Source 3?* (second paragraph) Ask: *What quote does Suze include that supports her claim?* (She uses a quote from an anthropology professor, who states that making the spheres "was accomplished without the help of metal tools, laser beams, or alien life-forms.")

COLLABORATE Have partners search Source 3 to find another detail that could be used to support Suze's claim. (Sample response: The anthropology professor is an expert on ancient cultures in Central and South America; the anthropology professor believes that other stones were used to grind and hammer the stone spheres into shape.)

Synthesize Information

Reread Suze's claim, underlined on **Reading/Writing Companion** page 100. Explain that Suze developed her argument after reading and thinking about all three sources. She supported her claim using details from the sources. She also used strong words from the sources in her claim and conclusion.

COLLABORATE Have partners search among the three sources for similarities. Have partners look back at their notes and then use their writer's notebook to answer the question *How did Suze develop her claim by synthesizing information from all three sources?* (All sources tell about the shape and location of the spheres. All sources discuss the Diquis people, who lived in the area and could have carved the spheres. Sources 2 and 3 give evidence to support the idea that the Diquis people made the spheres. Source 1 provides an alternative theory from an unreliable source. Pointing out that the source is unreliable helps strengthen Suze's argument.)

TEACH IN SMALL GROUP

Approaching Level Read each online source aloud. Help students identify the claim and supporting details in each source.

On Level Read the online sources with students. Have partners work to identify the claim and supporting details in each. Discuss how Suze used the sources to write her essay.

Beyond Level Have students use the online sources to identify the supporting details Suze used in her essay.

ELL Help students understand what Suze's task was. Then read one online source and work with students to identify supporting details. For additional support, see the **ELL Small Group Guide**.

FORMATIVE ASSESSMENT

STUDENT CHECK-IN

Have partners share their responses. Then ask them to reflect using the Check-In routine.

LEARNING GOALS

We can set a purpose for reading sources to answer a prompt.

OBJECTIVES

Provide logically ordered reasons that are supported by facts and details.

Introduce a topic or text clearly, provide a general observation and focus, and group related information logically; include formatting (e.g., headings), illustrations, and multimedia when useful to aiding comprehension.

Use precise language and domain-specific vocabulary to inform about or explain the topic.

With guidance and support from peers and adults, develop and strengthen writing as needed by planning, revising, editing, rewriting, or trying a new approach.

Follow agreed-upon rules for discussions and carry out assigned roles.

Analyze a writing prompt.

Analyze appropriate voice and tone.

ELA ACADEMIC LANGUAGE

- *argumentative, claim, topic*
- Cognate: *tópico*

DIGITAL TOOLS

Paraphrase the Idea

Analyze the Prompt

Writing Prompt

Follow the Analyze the Prompt Routine on page T246. Read the writing prompt on **Reading/Writing Companion** page 102 aloud: *Write an argumentative essay to present to your class. Answer the question: Why is it important to treat archaeological sites with respect?* Guide students to identify the purpose and audience. Then ask: *What is the prompt asking you to do?* (to write an argumentative essay about why it is important to treat archaeological sites with respect)

Anchor Chart Review the features of an argumentative essay with students and add any new ones to the Argumentative Essay anchor chart.

- It begins with an argument that clearly states the author's claim.
- It includes relevant evidence that is supported by credible sources.
- It uses a variety of sentence structures.

Purpose, Audience, and Task

Explain that thinking about their purpose and audience will help students plan and organize their writing. Ask them to identify a typical purpose of argumentative essays: to persuade. Have them consider who will read what they write, such as a teacher, classmates, or family members. Point out that in this writing prompt, the audience is identified. Reread the writing prompt and ask: *Who are you writing this* argumentative *essay for?* (my classmates)

Remind students that the task is the type of writing they are being asked to do. Reread the prompt. Ask: *What words in the prompt tell you about the type of writing?* Have students underline three key words in the prompt on **Reading/Writing Companion** page 102. Then have them think about whether they will use formal or informal language in their essay. Ask students to write their responses to the questions.

Set a Purpose for Reading Sources

Tell students that before they write their essays, they will read, annotate, and answer questions about three sources. Encourage them to look at the source on page 103, read the title, and skim the text. Remind students that when they skim, they do not read every word. They read quickly for the central ideas and important details.

Have students turn to a partner and say the writing prompt in their own words. Then ask them to skim "Remember St. Helena's Role" on page 103. Tell students to think of a question that will help them with their essay, and have them write the question on page 102. If students need help thinking of a question, ask: *What does respect mean to you? What is an example of not treating a place with respect?*

WRITING

My Goal I can write an argumentative essay.

Analyze the Prompt

Writing Prompt

Write an argumentative essay to present to your class. Answer the question: Why is it important to treat archaeological sites with respect?

Purpose, Audience, and Task Reread the writing prompt. What is your purpose for writing? My purpose is to ______

Who will your audience be? My audience will be ______

What type of writing is the prompt asking for? ______

Set a Purpose for Reading Sources Asking questions about why it is important to treat archaeological sites with respect will help you figure out your purpose for reading. It also helps you understand what you already know about the topic. Before you read the passage set about archaeological sites write a question here.

______

102 Unit 3 • Argumentative Writing

Reading/Writing Companion, p. 102

English Language Learners

Use the following scaffolds with the **Writing Prompt**. For additional support, see the **ELL Small Group Guide**.

Beginning

Read the prompt with students and discuss its meaning. Explain that a *site* is a place and *archaeological sites* are places where there are buildings or objects from a very long time ago. Have students discuss why it is important to treat these places with respect. Talk about ways that they can treat the sites with respect. Explain that they can walk only where they are allowed and not take anything from the sites. Help partners describe the prompt using the following: *I will write about why it is* important *to treat archeological* sites *with* respect.

Intermediate

Read the prompt with students and discuss its meaning. To reinforce the meaning of the prompt, have students discuss reasons why it is important to treat archaeological sites with respect and brainstorm ways they can do that. Point to the first sentence in the prompt and elicit that they will write an argumentative essay. Have partners describe the prompt using: *I will write about why* it is important to treat archaeological sites with respect.

Advanced/Advanced High

Discuss the prompt with students. To clarify the meaning of the prompt, have students discuss why they should treat archaeological sites with respect and give examples of how people treat the sites respectfully. Then have partners discuss the purpose and audience for their writing.

CLASSROOM CULTURE

We respect and value one another's experiences.

A classroom where students can work in pairs and small groups not only motivates them but also helps them learn to value one another. After partner work, ask: *What did you learn from working with your partner? Why is working with a partner a valuable learning tool?*

FORMATIVE ASSESSMENT

STUDENT CHECK-IN

Have partners share the purpose they set for reading the sources. Then ask them to reflect using the Check-In routine.

LEARNING GOALS

We can take notes to find relevant evidence to answer a prompt.

OBJECTIVES

Analyze multiple accounts of the same event or topic, noting important similarities and differences in the point of view they represent.

Explain how an author uses reasons and evidence to support particular points in a text, identifying which reasons and evidence support which point(s). Explain an author's perspective, or point of view, toward an argumentative text.

Read grade-level prose and poetry orally with accuracy, appropriate rate, expression, and automaticity on successive readings.

Engage effectively in a range of collaborative discussions with diverse partners, building on others' ideas and expressing their own clearly.

ELA ACADEMIC LANGUAGE

- *conclude, example, statement, claim, supporting detail*
- Cognates: *concluir, ejemplo, detalle*

TEACH IN SMALL GROUP

Approaching Level Help students find words and phrases that relate to the author's opinion. Complete the questions.

On Level Have partners note phrases relevant to their essay and complete the questions.

Beyond Level Ask students to identify the information they will be able to use in their essays. Have them locate details about treating sites with respect.

ELL For support with reading the sources, see **ELL Small Group Guide**.

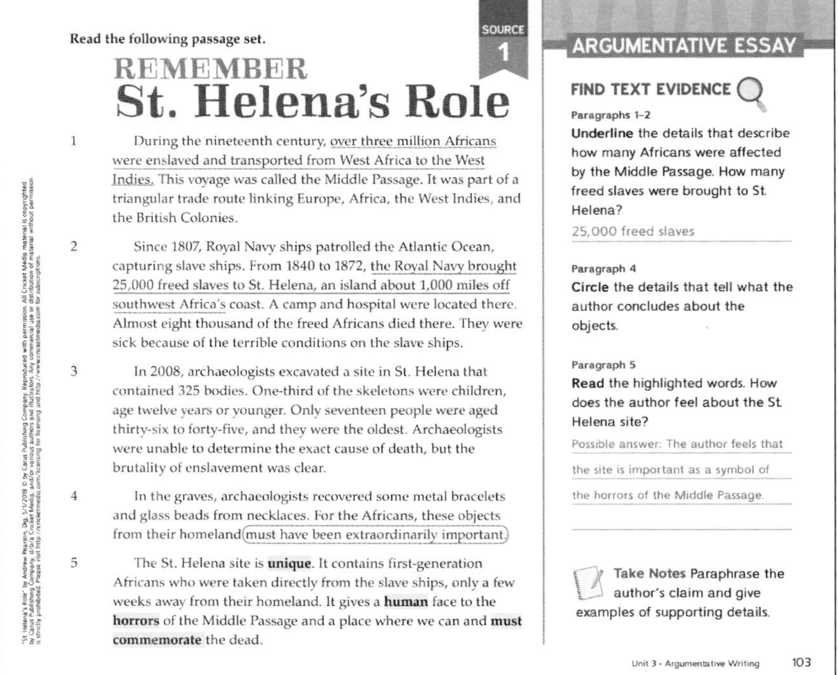

Read the following passage set.

SOURCE 1

REMEMBER St. Helena's Role

1 During the nineteenth century, over three million Africans were enslaved and transported from West Africa to the West Indies. This voyage was called the Middle Passage. It was part of a triangular trade route linking Europe, Africa, the West Indies, and the British Colonies.

2 Since 1807, Royal Navy ships patrolled the Atlantic Ocean, capturing slave ships. From 1840 to 1872, the Royal Navy brought 25,000 freed slaves to St. Helena, an island about 1,000 miles off southwest Africa's coast. A camp and hospital were located there. Almost eight thousand of the freed Africans died there. They were sick because of the terrible conditions on the slave ships.

3 In 2008, archaeologists excavated a site in St. Helena that contained 325 bodies. One-third of the skeletons were children, age twelve years or younger. Only seventeen people were aged thirty-six to forty-five, and they were the oldest. Archaeologists were unable to determine the exact cause of death, but the brutality of enslavement was clear.

4 In the graves, archaeologists recovered some metal bracelets and glass beads from necklaces. For the Africans, these objects from their homeland must have been extraordinarily important.

5 The St. Helena site is **unique**. It contains first-generation Africans who were taken directly from the slave ships, only a few weeks away from their homeland. It gives a **human** face to the **horrors** of the Middle Passage and a place where we can and **must commemorate** the dead.

ARGUMENTATIVE ESSAY

FIND TEXT EVIDENCE

Paragraphs 1–2

Underline the details that describe how many Africans were affected by the Middle Passage. How many freed slaves were brought to St. Helena?

25,000 freed slaves

Paragraph 4

Circle the details that tell what the author concludes about the objects.

Paragraph 5

Read the highlighted words. How does the author feel about the St. Helena site?

Possible answer: The author feels that the site is important as a symbol of the horrors of the Middle Passage.

Take Notes Paraphrase the author's claim and give examples of supporting details.

Unit 3 • Argumentative Writing 103

Reading/Writing Companion, p. 103

Analyze the Sources

Find Text Evidence

As students read the source passages, ask them to note important ideas and details, interesting or unfamiliar words, and any questions they may have in their writer's notebooks. Use the questions below. Remind students to cite text evidence.

SOURCE 1 "Remember St. Helena"

Paragraphs 1–2 *How did the freed slaves get to St. Helena?* (They were taken there by the Royal Navy, which was capturing slave ships in the Atlantic Ocean.) *What did St. Helena have that was meant to help the freed Africans?* (a camp and a hospital)

Paragraphs 3–4 *What was one likely cause of the freed Africans' deaths?* (the way they were treated on the slave ships) *What did archaeologists find in the graves at this site?* (metal bracelets and collections of glass beads from necklaces) Have students circle the details that tell what the author concludes about these objects.

Paragraph 5 *What would the author like people to do if they visit St. Helena?* (remember and think about the people who died there)

Take Notes Have students paraphrase the author's claim and give examples of supporting details.

SOURCE 2 "Collaboration at Angel Mounds"

Paragraphs 6–7 *What is Angel Mounds?* (a Native American archaeological site in southwest Indiana) *What is it an example of?* (a collaboration between archaeologists and the descendants of the people who lived there) *How many people once lived there?* (about a thousand)

WRITING

FIND TEXT EVIDENCE

Paragraphs 6–7
Draw a box around the details that tell you what the Angel Mounds site is comprised of. Why is the site important?

Angel Mounds is a well-preserved archaeological site where we can learn about the Mississippian culture.

Paragraph 8
Underline why Thompson's elders approved of her working at Angel Mounds. What are the Native Americans protecting?

They're protecting their ancestors' graves.

Paragraph 9
Read the highlighted examples of strong language in paragraph 9. **Circle** the statement that expresses the author's perspective about Native American sites.

Take Notes Paraphrase the author's claim, and give examples of supporting details.

104 Unit 3 • Argumentative Writing

SOURCE 2

Collaboration at ANGEL MOUNDS

6 Angel Mounds is a Native American site in southwest Indiana. It is one of the best-preserved archaeological sites in North America. It is also an example of collaboration between archaeologists and tribes who are the descendants of the people who made the site, says Ashleigh Thompson. She is a member of the Red Lake Band of Ojibwe and a college-level archaeologist working at Angel Mounds.

7 The site contains four large platform mounds, smaller earthen mounds, and hundreds of structures. About one thousand people once lived there. They are descended from the Mississippian culture. The Mississippian people lived from about 800 C.E. to 1600 C.E. They are known as mound-builders.

8 When Thompson chose to work at Angel Mounds, her elders approved. They believed that a Native American archaeologist would protect their artifacts and remains. However, Thompson points out that many archaeologists do collaborate with tribes. They ask permission to research Native American sites. They follow laws that help tribes protect their ancestors' graves. In fact, she remembers when her lead archaeologist listened to Native Americans' concerns about the human remains and respected their wish to bury them.

9 Thompson **asserts** that **cooperation** between archaeologists and tribes ensures that both parties are heard and helps everyone learn. A **successful collaboration** at Angel Mounds can be a model for other Native American archaeological sites. It shows that people can work together and keep their values intact.

SOURCE 3

No Digging Allowed

10 Throughout history, archaeologists have disrupted many Native American sites. They studied sites without asking Native Americans' permission. They took artifacts to study or donate to museums. They dug up graves and took Native Americans' ancestors' human remains.

11 What these archaeologists did has made many Native Americans upset. According to Native American tribal teachings, their ancestors shouldn't be disturbed. To restore this balance, they requested that museums return their ancestors' remains and artifacts. They protested and wrote letters to elected officials. Their requests were mostly ignored.

12 After much convincing, Congress passed the Native American Graves Protection and Repatriation Act in 1990. As a result, museums have returned much of what they took.

13 But many Native Americans lost part of their living culture when their artifacts were taken. They believe that their life journey isn't complete until their human remains reside in the earth where they once lived. In August 2007, Apache artifacts were returned to Arizona in shipping crates with breathing holes for the artifacts inside. Apache leaders buried them in sacred sites where they believe the spirits live.

14 Today, it is illegal to buy and sell Native American artifacts. But it may also be a crime to remove them from the dirt, bottoms of rivers, or anywhere else, however unknowingly. Native American tribal members believe that sites shouldn't be disturbed at all. Now the law is on their side.

ARGUMENTATIVE ESSAY

FIND TEXT EVIDENCE

Paragraph 10
Underline the claim. What do the supporting details tell you about how archaeologists felt about Native American beliefs?

The details tell me that the archaeologists didn't respect Native American beliefs.

Paragraph 11
Circle the ways Native Americans made their perspectives known.

Paragraphs 12–13
What effect did the Native American Graves Protection and Repatriation Act have?

Museums had to return what they had taken. Native Americans were able to rebury their artifacts.

Paragraph 14
Draw a box around what Native Americans believe.

Take Notes Paraphrase the author's claim and give examples of supporting details.

Unit 3 • Argumentative Writing 105

Reading/Writing Companion, pp. 104–105

Paragraph 8 *What is Ashleigh Thompson's first example of archaeologists treating an archaeological site with respect?* (asking permission to research Native American sites) *What is her second example?* (following laws that help tribes protect their ancestors' graves)

Paragraph 9 *According to Thompson, how does everyone benefit from cooperation between archaeologists and tribes?* (Both parties are heard, and everyone learns.) *What is the author's perspective about Native American sites?* (It is important for tribes and archeologists to work together.)

Take Notes Have students paraphrase the author's claim and give examples of supporting details.

SOURCE 3

"No Digging Allowed"

Paragraphs 10–11 *How did archaeologists often fail to respect Native American archaeological sites?* (They studied sites without asking permission, took artifacts to study or donate to museums, and dug up graves and took Native Americans' ancestors' human remains.) *Why were many Native Americans upset by this?* (They believe their ancestors should not be disturbed.)

Paragraphs 12–13 *Why did Apache leaders rebury the artifacts that museums returned to them?* (They believe a person's life journey isn't complete until his or her human remains reside in the earth where they once lived.) Have students talk about what they know about Native American traditions.

Paragraph 14 What do Native American tribal leaders believe? (They believe sites shouldn't be disturbed at all.) *How are Native American artifacts protected today?* (It is illegal to buy and sell Native American artifacts. It may also be a crime to remove them from anywhere.)

Take Notes Have students paraphrase the author's claim and give examples of supporting details.

MULTISENSORY LEARNING

Distribute red and blue index cards or squares of paper to students and explain that red represents "Respect" and blue represents "Disrespect." As students read and reread the sources, ask them to note words, phrases, and ideas that show respect or disrespect for archaeological sites on the appropriately colored card or square. Remind students also to write the source on each card or square. Have them read their cards to a partner, arrange the cards in two columns ("Respect" and "Disrespect"), and review the cards together.

FORMATIVE ASSESSMENT

STUDENT CHECK-IN

Have partners share their responses. Then ask them to reflect using the Check-In routine.

LEARNING GOALS

We can synthesize information from three sources to plan and organize an argumentative essay.

OBJECTIVES

By the end of the year, read and comprehend informational texts, including history/social studies, science, and technical texts, at the high end of the grades 4–5 text complexity band independently and proficiently.

Introduce a topic or text clearly, state an opinion, and create an organizational structure in which ideas are logically grouped to support the writer's purpose.

Provide logically ordered reasons that are supported by facts and details.

Recall relevant information from experiences or gather relevant information from print and digital sources; summarize or paraphrase information in notes and finished work, and provide a list of sources.

Organize notes from sources to plan an argumentative essay.

ELA ACADEMIC LANGUAGE

- *complete, source, reason, relevant, evidence, synthesize*
- *Cognate: completar, razón relevante, evidencia*

DIGITAL TOOLS

Model Graphic Organizer

How to Create an Outline

Plan: Organize Ideas

Take Notes

Remind students that they will write an argumentative essay about why it is important to treat archaeological sites with respect. They will synthesize information from each source to form their response to the prompt.

Say: *When you write your argumentative essay, stay focused on your topic and include relevant details and examples from the sources to support your ideas. Think about how the details and examples in the sources will help your readers understand why it is important to treat archaeological sites with respect.*

Graphic Organizer

Tell students that before writing their argumentative essay, they will organize the notes they took from each source in the graphic organizer on **Reading/Writing Companion** pages 106–107. Some of the graphic organizer has been filled in. Guide students in filling in the graphic organizer.

Claim Remind students that the claim is the main argument of their essay and is presented at the beginning of the essay. This essay will present a claim about why it is important to treat archaeological sites with respect.

Reasons Explain that this part of the essay supports the writer's perspective on the topic. Students should include at least three reasons in their essay. Remind students that they will find support for each reason in the sources.

Relevant Evidence Remind students that they should support their claims with evidence from the sources. They don't have to use evidence from all three sources for every reason, but they should use evidence from at least one source for each reason. Remind students that each time they use evidence from a source, they should name the source.

Have students complete the graphic organizer.

Synthesize Information

Remind students that synthesizing information means using details from different sources to form a new understanding. One way writers can synthesize information is by organizing the information into categories. For example, for this essay, information can be organized into two categories: "respect for archaeological sites" and "disrespect for archaeological sites." Have partners share the Relevant Evidence section of their completed graphic organizers and discuss which category each piece of evidence belongs in. Encourage them to label each with an *R* (Respect) or a *D* (Disrespect).

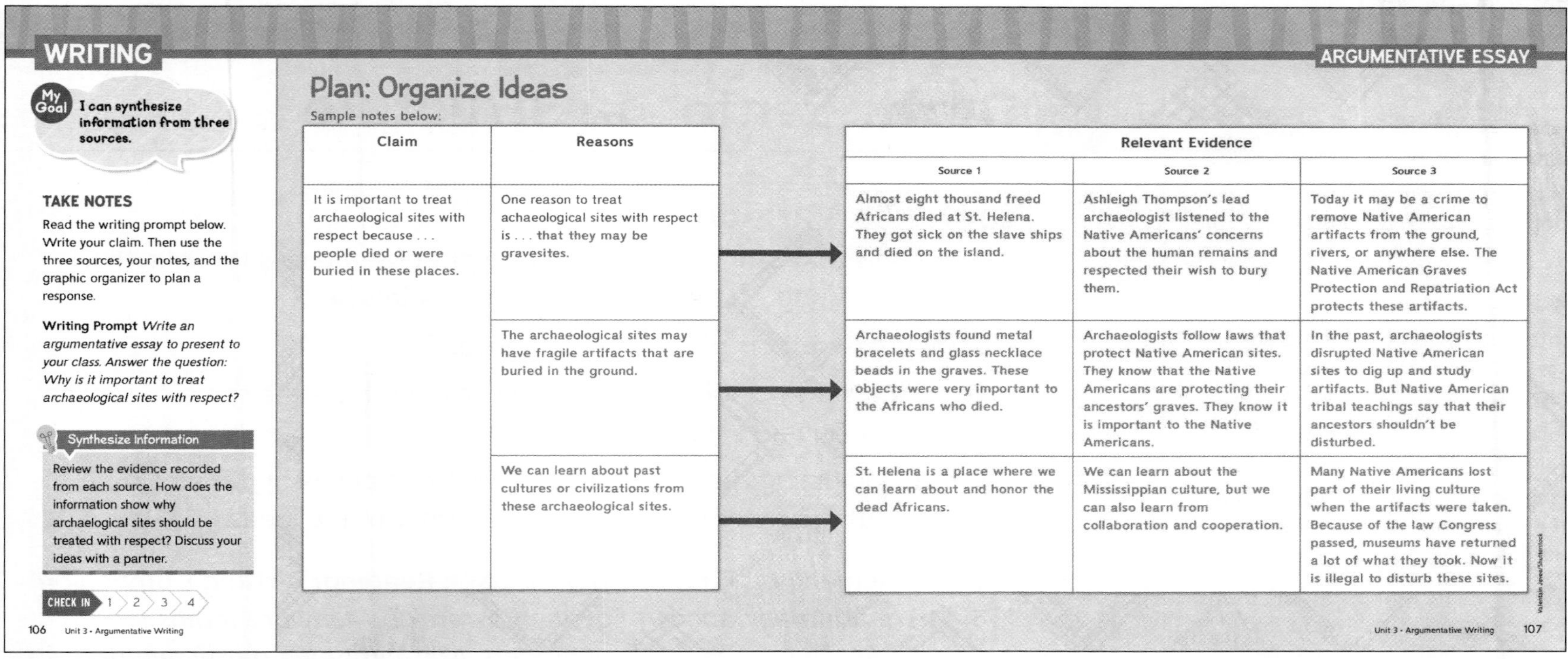

WRITING

ARGUMENTATIVE ESSAY

My Goal: I can synthesize information from three sources.

TAKE NOTES

Read the writing prompt below. Write your claim. Then use the three sources, your notes, and the graphic organizer to plan a response.

Writing Prompt *Write an argumentative essay to present to your class. Answer the question: Why is it important to treat archaeological sites with respect?*

Synthesize Information

Review the evidence recorded from each source. How does the information show why archaeological sites should be treated with respect? Discuss your ideas with a partner.

CHECK IN 1 2 3 4

Plan: Organize Ideas

Sample notes below:

Claim	Reasons	Relevant Evidence: Source 1	Relevant Evidence: Source 2	Relevant Evidence: Source 3
It is important to treat archaeological sites with respect because . . . people died or were buried in these places.	One reason to treat achaeological sites with respect is . . . that they may be gravesites.	Almost eight thousand freed Africans died at St. Helena. They got sick on the slave ships and died on the island.	Ashleigh Thompson's lead archaeologist listened to the Native Americans' concerns about the human remains and respected their wish to bury them.	Today it may be a crime to remove Native American artifacts from the ground, rivers, or anywhere else. The Native American Graves Protection and Repatriation Act protects these artifacts.
	The archaeological sites may have fragile artifacts that are buried in the ground.	Archaeologists found metal bracelets and glass necklace beads in the graves. These objects were very important to the Africans who died.	Archaeologists follow laws that protect Native American sites. They know that the Native Americans are protecting their ancestors' graves. They know it is important to the Native Americans.	In the past, archaeologists disrupted Native American sites to dig up and study artifacts. But Native American tribal teachings say that their ancestors shouldn't be disturbed.
	We can learn about past cultures or civilizations from these archaeological sites.	St. Helena is a place where we can learn about and honor the dead Africans.	We can learn about the Mississippian culture, but we can also learn from collaboration and cooperation.	Many Native Americans lost part of their living culture when the artifacts were taken. Because of the law Congress passed, museums have returned a lot of what they took. Now it is illegal to disturb these sites.

106 Unit 3 • Argumentative Writing

Unit 3 • Argumentative Writing 107

Reading/Writing Companion, pp. 106–107

English Language Learners

Use the following scaffolds with **Graphic Organizer**. For additional support, see the **ELL Small Group Guide**.

Beginning

Review with students that the author's claim tells the writer's main idea and it appears in the first column of the chart. Discuss how the columns for reasons and relevant evidence support the author's claim. Help students fill in information in the correct parts of the chart. Have them look at their notes for facts about archaeological sites. Help partners describe the first reason using: *We should treat archaeological sites with respect because they are* important places *that teach us about the* past.

Intermediate

Review how the graphic organizer is organized with students. Help them write the author's claim and use their notes to fill in the chart. Have partners complete the first reason using the following: *One reason to treat archaeological sites with respect is because* they are places where people once lived and are buried. Have partners write relevant evidence for the reason with information from a source.

Advanced/Advanced High

Have students tell you how the graphic organizer is organized. Monitor students as they complete the chart with the author's claim, reasons, and relevant evidence from sources. Have partners discuss and choose information from their notes to write relevant evidence.

FORMATIVE ASSESSMENT

STUDENT CHECK-IN

Have partners share their graphic organizer on Reading/Writing Companion pages 106–107. Ask them to reflect using the Check-In routine to fill in the bars.

LEARNING GOALS

We can use our graphic organizer to write a draft.

OBJECTIVES

Introduce a topic or text clearly, state an opinion, and create an organizational structure in which ideas are logically grouped to support the writer's purpose.

Provide logically ordered reasons that are supported by facts and details.

With guidance and support from peers and adults, develop and strengthen writing as needed by planning, revising, editing, rewriting, or trying a new approach.

Use punctuation to separate items in a series.

Use a comma to separate an introductory element from the rest of the sentence.

ELA ACADEMIC LANGUAGE

- *strategy, sentence structure, revise, combine*
- Cognates: *estrategia, revisar, combinar*

DIGITAL TOOLS

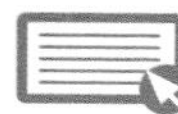
Student Model Draft

Outline to Draft

Approaching Level Review drafts for sentence variety.

On Level Partners can review drafts for sentence variety.

Beyond Level Partners can make suggestions about sentence combining and variety.

ELL For support revising the drafts, see **ELL Small Group Guide.**

Draft: Sentence Structure

Sentence Variety

Tell students that authors use different types of sentences to make their writing interesting. Share with students the points below.

- Sometimes authors write short sentences.
- Sometimes they combine short sentences that have the same or similar ideas into longer sentences.
- When combining short sentences, it might be necessary to eliminate words that are repeated or change the order of the ideas.

Read the sentences in the text box on page **Reading/Writing Companion** 108: *There are many ancient Egyptian pyramids. Many are tombs for pharaohs. Many have multiple chambers.* Ask: *What word is eliminated twice when these sentences are combined?* (*many*) Ask: *Why is this word eliminated?* (Because *many* refers to the pyramids in all three sentences, and we use it only once in the new sentence.)

Have students reread paragraph 5 from Suze's essay on page 101. Have students look at the different lengths of the sentences and identify how the writer combined ideas into longer sentences. Point out the use of commas as well as the different end punctuation, which also adds variety.

Have partners rewrite the following sentences as one sentence: *Archaeological sites tell us about the past. They are fascinating places to visit. They can be found all over the world.* (Archaeological sites tell us about the past, are fascinating places to visit, and can be found all over the world). *Scientists study archaeological sites. Students learn from them. Authors write about these places.* (Archaeological sites are places that scientists study, students learn from, and authors write about.)

Draft

Have students write an argumentative essay that answers this question: *Why is it important to treat archaeological sites with respect?* Have students review the rubric on page 98, the information they recorded in their graphic organizer, and the notes they took in their writer's notebook. Remind students that one feature of a strong argumentative essay is a strong conclusion that summarizes the essay's most important ideas, leaves the reader thinking about the topic, and persuades the reader to agree with the author's opinion. Also, remind students that their essay should include a variety of sentences.

Have students write their drafts legibly in print or cursive or type accurately on-screen. If students choose to write their essays in cursive, guide them to produce legible works within the same timeframe as they would for writing in print. Circulate to check their progress.

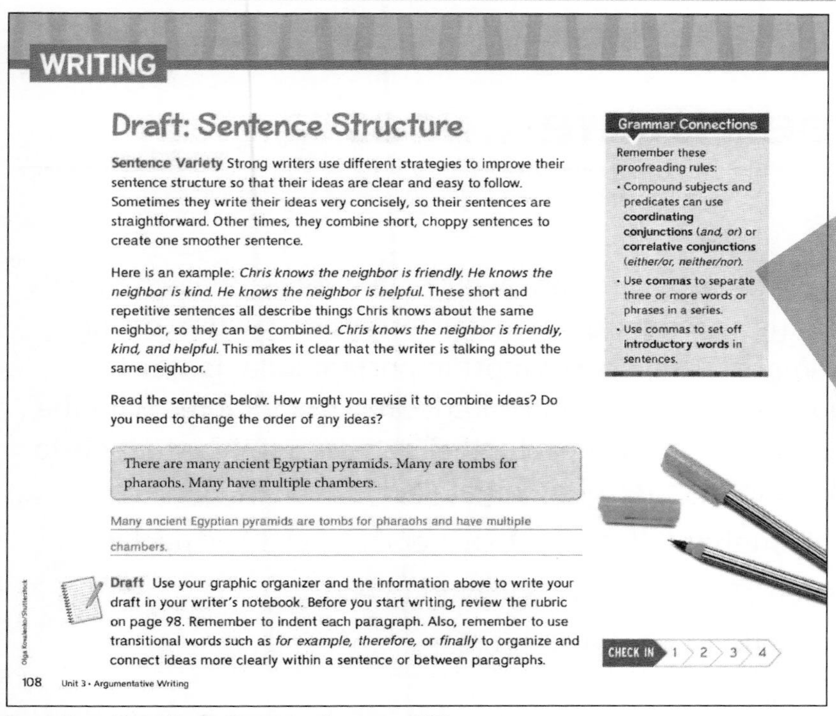

WRITING

Draft: Sentence Structure

Sentence Variety Strong writers use different strategies to improve their sentence structure so that their ideas are clear and easy to follow. Sometimes they write their ideas very concisely, so their sentences are straightforward. Other times, they combine short, choppy sentences to create one smoother sentence.

Here is an example: *Chris knows the neighbor is friendly. He knows the neighbor is kind. He knows the neighbor is helpful.* These short and repetitive sentences all describe things Chris knows about the same neighbor, so they can be combined. *Chris knows the neighbor is friendly, kind, and helpful.* This makes it clear that the writer is talking about the same neighbor.

Read the sentence below. How might you revise it to combine ideas? Do you need to change the order of any ideas?

There are many ancient Egyptian pyramids. Many are tombs for pharaohs. Many have multiple chambers.

Many ancient Egyptian pyramids are tombs for pharaohs and have multiple chambers.

Draft Use your graphic organizer and the information above to write your draft in your writer's notebook. Before you start writing, review the rubric on page 98. Remember to indent each paragraph. Also, remember to use transitional words such as *for example, therefore,* or *finally* to organize and connect ideas more clearly within a sentence or between paragraphs.

Grammar Connections

Remember these proofreading rules:

- Compound subjects and predicates can use **coordinating conjunctions** (*and, or*) or **correlative conjunctions** (*either/or, neither/nor*).
- Use **commas** to separate three or more words or phrases in a series.
- Use commas to set off **introductory words** in sentences.

CHECK IN 1 2 3 4

Olga Kovalenko/Shutterstock

108 Unit 3 • Argumentative Writing

Reading/Writing Companion, p. 108

Grammar Connections

Students can use online **Grammar Handbook** page 479 to review using commas. Students will use a comma after introductory words or phrases at the beginning of a sentence. For example, "After their research, the scientists shared their results." Students will also use commas to separate three or more items in a series. For example, "She packed her supplies, clothes, and shoes in a bag."

English Language Learners

Use the following scaffolds with **Sentence Variety**.

Beginning

Review with students that good writers use sentences of different lengths in their writing. Explain that combining short sentences into longer sentences can make the text more interesting. Discuss with students that when we combine short sentences, we use commas and remove words that repeat. Help students combine these sentences: *At the archaeological site, we found necklaces. We found bracelets at the archaeological site. We found pots at the archaeological site.* At the archaeological site, we found necklaces, bracelets, and pots.

Intermediate

Review with students that when they combine short sentences, they should use commas to separate the ideas. Have partners rewrite to combine these sentences: *At the archaeological site we found necklaces. We found bracelets at the archaeological site. We found pots at the archaeological site.* (At the archaeological site, we found necklaces, bracelets, and pots.)

Advanced/Advanced High

Remind students that when they combine short sentences, they should use commas to separate the ideas. Explain they may take out or replace words, too. Have partners work together to combine these sentences to form one longer sentences: *At the archaeological site the researchers found necklaces. The researchers found bracelets. The researchers found arrows, too.*

TEACHER CONFERENCES

As students draft, hold teacher conferences with individual students.

Step 1: Talk About Strengths
Point out strengths in the essay: *You have used a varied sentence structure with simple, compound, and complex structures to help keep your writing interesting.*

Step 2: Focus on Skills
Give feedback on how the student uses language: *Try using more scientific terms in your essay.*

Step 3: Make Concrete Suggestions
Provide specific direction to help students: *Make sure your conclusion restates your opinion.* Have students meet with you to review progress.

FORMATIVE ASSESSMENT

STUDENT CHECK-IN

Have partners share their draft. Then have them reflect using the Check-In routine to fill in the bars on Reading/Writing Companion page 108.

LEARNING GOALS

We can revise our writing to make it stronger.

OBJECTIVES

Provide logically ordered reasons that are supported by facts and details.

Provide a concluding statement or section related to the information or explanation presented.

Follow agreed-upon rules for discussions and carry out assigned roles.

Review the key ideas expressed and draw conclusions in light of information and knowledge gained from the discussions.

Adapt speech to a variety of contexts and tasks, using formal English when appropriate to task and situation.

Demonstrate command of the conventions of standard English grammar and usage when writing or speaking.

ELA ACADEMIC LANGUAGE

- *feedback, reflect, checklist, delete*
- *Cognate: reflejar*

DIFFERENTIATED WRITING

Check student progress at this stage during Small Group time.

Approaching Level Review students' drafts for sentence variety in Small Group time.

On Level Partners can focus on sentence variety as they review each other's drafts.

Beyond Level As students review each other's drafts, they can determine whether the writer has included a variety of sentences and suggest possible revisions.

ELL For support with revising their drafts, see **ELL Small Group Guide**.

Revise: Peer Conferences

Review a Draft

Explain to partners that they will review and give feedback on each other's drafts. Remind them that strong argumentative essays end with a strong conclusion that summarizes the essay's most important idea, leaves the reader thinking about the topic, and encourages readers to agree with the author's opinion. Before they review each other's drafts, remind students to think about the following features of an organized and focused essay:

- A clearly stated claim that tells the author's opinion and perspective
- A logical progression of ideas from beginning to end
- Relevant evidence with references to sources
- Varied sentence structure
- Strong language that persuades the reader

Review with students the routine for peer review of writing.

- **Step 1:** Listen carefully as the writer reads his or her work aloud.
- **Step 2:** Avoid calling attention away from the writer.
- **Step 3:** Ask a question that will help you understand anything that is unclear.
- **Step 4:** Take note of things you liked about the writing.

Model using the sentence starters on **Reading/Writing Companion** page 109. Say: *Your conclusion was convincing because . . .* and finish the sentence. Discuss the steps of the peer conferencing routine. Ask: *Why is it important to avoid calling attention away from the writer?* (to show respect for the writer and to be sure you are focused on the writing) *Why should you take notes as you listen?* (to remember things you liked about the writing and to keep track of suggestions you want to make)

COLLABORATE Circulate and observe as partners review and give feedback on each other's drafts. Ensure that partners are following the routine and the agreed-upon rules. Remind students to think about and listen for a clearly stated claim, a logical progression of ideas, varied sentence structure, and a strong conclusion. Have them reflect on partner feedback and write on page 109 about how they intend to use the feedback.

Revision

Review the Revising Checklist on page 109 and the features of the rubric on pages 236–239. Explain that this is a rubric with scores that add up to a maximum of 10. Point out the score in the left column and the categories in the three middle columns. Have students score their essays using My Score on page 109.

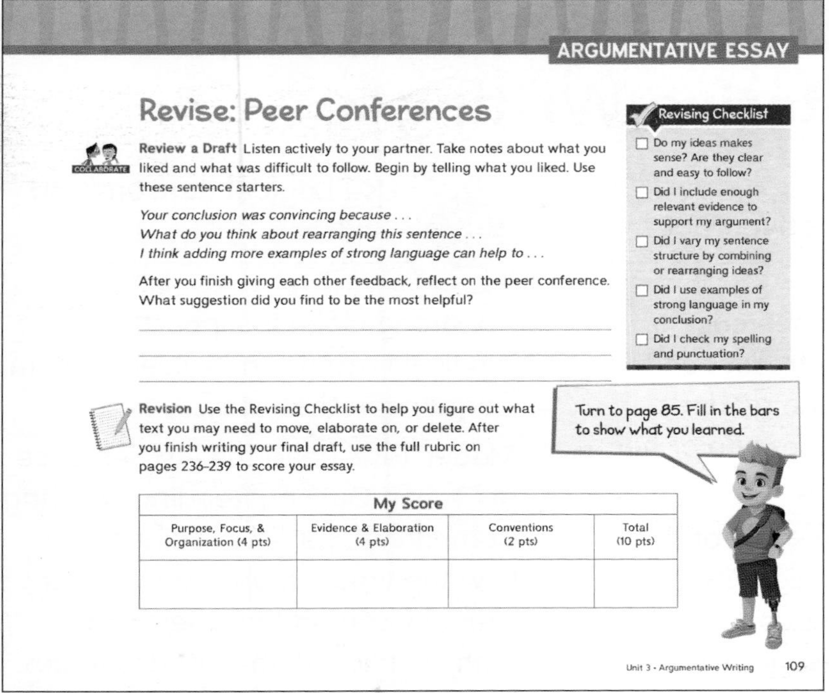

ARGUMENTATIVE ESSAY

Revise: Peer Conferences

Review a Draft Listen actively to your partner. Take notes about what you liked and what was difficult to follow. Begin by telling what you liked. Use these sentence starters.

Your conclusion was convincing because . . .
What do you think about rearranging this sentence . . .
I think adding more examples of strong language can help to . . .

After you finish giving each other feedback, reflect on the peer conference. What suggestion did you find to be the most helpful?

Revising Checklist

- ☐ Do my ideas makes sense? Are they clear and easy to follow?
- ☐ Did I include enough relevant evidence to support my argument?
- ☐ Did I vary my sentence structure by combining or rearranging ideas?
- ☐ Did I use examples of strong language in my conclusion?
- ☐ Did I check my spelling and punctuation?

Revision Use the Revising Checklist to help you figure out what text you may need to move, elaborate on, or delete. After you finish writing your final draft, use the full rubric on pages 236-239 to score your essay.

Turn to page 85. Fill in the bars to show what you learned.

My Score			
Purpose, Focus, & Organization (4 pts)	Evidence & Elaboration (4 pts)	Conventions (2 pts)	Total (10 pts)

Unit 3 • Argumentative Writing 109

Reading/Writing Companion, p. 109

English Language Learners

Use the following scaffolds with **Review a Draft**.

Beginning

Pair students with more proficient readers. Have partners ask for clarification using: *Can you explain ___?* and provide feedback using: *I liked ___ because ___.* Students may need to see the draft as well as hear it. Have students complete the Partner Feedback on page 109. Help students check their draft for the third and fourth items on the Revising Checklist, and help them revise to strengthen their conclusion or vary sentence structures by combining short sentences.

Intermediate

Pair students with more proficient speakers. Have partners ask for clarification using: *What did you mean by___? Does ___ have evidence?* and provide feedback using: *I liked ___ because ____.* Have students complete the Partner Feedback on page 109. Have students use the last three items on the Revising Checklist to identify revisions. Have them check to see that their ideas are clear, sentences vary, and their evidence supports their argument.

Advanced/Advanced High

Have partners provide feedback using the sentence starters on page 109 and read each other's responses to check that their partner understood them correctly. Have students review the Revising Checklist with their partner to be sure they have addressed these elements in their essay and to identify possible revisions. Have them check that they have enough relevant evidence and they varied sentence structures.

TEACHER CONFERENCES

As students revise, hold teacher conferences with individual students.

Step 1: Talk About Strengths
Point out strengths in the essay: *Your claim is clearly stated, and your reasons are easy to follow.*

Step 2: Focus on Skills
Give feedback on sentence variety: *In this paragraph, you have a lot of short sentences. Try combining the sentences that express related ideas.*

Step 3: Make Concrete Suggestions
Provide specific direction to help students revise. *Make sure your conclusion summarizes your argument.* Have students revise and then meet with you to review progress.

DIGITAL TOOLS

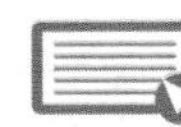
Revised Student Model

Revise Checklist (Argumentative); Peer Conferencing Checklist (Argumentative); Peer Conferencing (Collaborative Conversations Video)

MY GOALS ROUTINE

What I Learned

Review Goals Have students turn back to page 85 of the Reading/Writing Companion and review the first goal.

Reflect Have students think about the progress they've made toward the goal. Review the key, if needed. Then have students fill in the bars.

LEARNING GOALS

We can build skills to improve our writing.

OBJECTIVES

Introduce a topic or text clearly, state an opinion, and create an organizational structure in which ideas are logically grouped to support the writer's purpose.

With guidance and support from peers and adults, develop and strengthen writing as needed by planning, revising, editing, rewriting, or trying a new approach.

Recall relevant information from experiences or gather relevant information from print and digital sources; summarize or paraphrase information in notes and finished work, and provide a list of sources.

Use appropriate voice and tone when speaking or writing.

FLEXIBLE MINILESSONS

Use these minilesson flexibly, in any order, based on the needs of your students. The minilessons can be used separately or in tandem with the Argumentative Writing lessons on pages T224–T259.

Use students' Check-In reflections and your observations to decide which students are ready to independently apply the lesson focus to their own writing. Use the tips in the Conferring Toolkit to provide additional guidance as you confer with students or meet with them in small groups.

FORMATIVE ASSESSMENT

STUDENT CHECK IN

After the Guide activity in each lesson, have students reflect on their understanding of the lesson focus. Have them reflect using the Check-In routine.

Argumentative Writing

Write Effective Hooks

A hook is a catchy sentence or paragraph in an introduction that "hooks" or grabs the reader's attention and entices him or her to continue reading.

Model Text Review some of the strategies students might use to grab a reader's attention: ask a question that makes the reader think about the topic; tell an interesting example or anecdote that relates to the topic; use a quotation relevant to the topic. Read the first paragraph of *Are Electronic Devices Good for Us?* on **Reading/Writing Companion**, page 65. Ask: *Why is the first sentence an effective hook?* (It asks a question about media and electronic devices directly to the reader.)

Guide Have partners turn to "Tuned Out" on page 66 of the Reading/Writing Companion and determine the effectiveness of the hook in the first paragraph. Have them rewrite the paragraph using a different hook.

Apply Have students review their argumentative essays and rewrite the introduction with a strong hook.

Use Logical Reasons and Evidence

A strong claim is supported by logical reasons and evidence in an argumentative essay.

Model Text Read the last sentence of "Tuned Out" on **Reading/Writing Companion**, page 66. Point out how the writer supports his or her claim by stating that there are many studies on the disadvantages of electronic devices for young people. Discuss how this reason is logical, or sensible. Go on to read the second paragraph and point out the evidence given to support the writer's claim.

Guide Write the following example of a claim with an illogical reason: *A lot of people have phones so electronic devices can't be good for kids.* Have partners identify and discuss the issue with the provided reason. Then have them revise the claim with a logical, evidence-based reason.

Apply Have partners exchange argumentative essays and read one another's claims for logical reasons and supporting evidence.

Conferring Toolkit

Write Effective Hooks Students may need support writing strong hooks. Ask students to reflect on the type of introductions that make them want to keep reading an argumentative essay. Review examples as necessary.

Use Logical Reasons and Evidence Point out the student's claim, and discuss whether the reason given makes sense. Guide students in using logical reasons and supporting evidence to strengthen their essays.

Outline Information

Writers use outlines to help them to organize and present information in a logical order.

Model Text Tell students that strong argumentative essays can be divided into three main sections: introduction, body, and conclusion. Turn to pages 66 and 67 of the **Reading/Writing Companion** and point out how "Tuned Out" follows this basic structure and presents information in a logical order. Then begin a class outline about the benefits of recess. Point out that the introduction should include a hook and a strong claim and that the body paragraphs should include strong reasons and factual evidence to support the claim.

Guide Have partners copy the class outline into their writer's notebooks and finish filling it out. Have students share what they added.

Apply Have students create a short outline for an essay based on one of these prompts: *What I Would Change If I Were Principal; Laptops Are Important in the Classroom; Playing Video Games Is Educational.*

Use Parallel Structure

When writers use parallel structure, they use the same pattern of words or grammatical structure in a sentence.

Model Write the following sentence: *Last night, Pedro did his homework, played video games, and cooking dinner with his Dad.* Underline the action verbs and tell students that for the sentence to have a parallel structure, every part of the sentence needs to have the same kind of grammatical structure. Point out that *did* and *played* are past tense verbs, but that *cooking* is present tense. Rewrite the sentence to show parallel structure: *Last night, Pedro did his homework, played video games, and <u>cooked</u> dinner with his Dad.*

Guide Have partners revise the following sentence to have parallel structure: *Jane enjoys playing baseball, running marathons, and to read novels.*

Apply Have students complete these sentences using parallel structure:

My favorite activities are...

Every morning before school, I...

Choose Persuasive Words

Choosing persuasive words or phrases can help convince a reader to agree with an opinion. Persuasive words can be verbs, adjectives, nouns, or adverbs.

Model Discuss how argumentative writers must persuade their readers to agree with their position on a topic. Explain that using persuasive words can help strengthen their argument and clarify their purpose. Model using persuasive language with the class: *The <u>most popular</u> restaurants in town are...* Point out the words *most popular* and discuss the impact of its persuasiveness on the sentence.

Guide Write these sentences and have partners underline the persuasive words and discuss the impact of the word choice:

A major <u>disadvantage</u> of trucks is that they put <u>harmful</u> pollutants into the air.

The <u>advantages</u> of learning another language are <u>endless</u>.

Apply Have students review their argumentative essays and rewrite at least one paragraph using persuasive words.

ELL **Outline Information** Encourage students to think of an outline as a useful organizational tool. Ask: *Does it make sense to introduce your opinion or state your reasons and evidence first? Why?*

Use Parallel Structure Point out any sentences that do not have parallel structure. Say: *Let's reread this sentence together. Does every part of the sentence have the same grammatical structure?*

ELL **Choose Persuasive Words** Help students identify and use persuasive words in their argumentative essays. Ask: *What word could you add to this sentence to convince your readers to agree with you?*

LEARNING GOALS

We can build skills to improve our writing.

OBJECTIVES

Introduce a topic or text clearly, state an opinion, and create an organizational structure in which ideas are logically grouped to support the writer's purpose.

With guidance and support from peers and adults, develop and strengthen writing as needed by planning, revising, editing, rewriting, or trying a new approach.

Recall relevant information from experiences or gather relevant information from print and digital sources; summarize or paraphrase information in notes and finished work, and provide a list of sources.

Explain the function of conjunctions, prepositions, and interjections in general and their function in particular sentences.

FLEXIBLE MINILESSONS

Use these minilesson flexibly, in any order, based on the needs of your students. The minilessons can be used separately or in tandem with the Argumentative Writing lessons on pages T224–T259.

Use students' Check-In reflections and your observations to decide which students are ready to independently apply the lesson focus to their own writing. Use the tips in the Conferring Toolkit to provide additional guidance as you confer with students or meet with them in small groups.

FORMATIVE ASSESSMENT

STUDENT CHECK IN

After the Guide activity in each lesson, have students reflect on their understanding of the lesson focus. Have them reflect using the Check-In routine.

Argumentative Writing

Brainstorm Ideas

Brainstorming is a prewriting activity in which the writer writes anything he or she can think of about a topic without paying attention to grammar or spelling. Brainstorming or free writing about a topic can help a writer establish a point of view.

Model Have students give you an opinion topic and model brainstorming about the topic. After writing nonstop for a minute or two, point out how you wrote without paying attention to grammar or spelling. Underline or circle the most important details or reasons you wrote down and discuss how this can help you determine your topic.

Guide Have students brainstorm about the best kind of pet for two minutes and share what they wrote with a partner.

Apply Have students brainstorm about whether it's better to work on a project independently or as a team. Ask volunteers to share their opinions and reasons.

Integrate Sources

Writers often use certain phrases to introduce sources, such as *an analysis of, studies show,* and *to cite one report.*

Model Text Read aloud the first paragraph of "Tuned Out" on **Reading/Writing Companion,** page 66. Have students read along. Point out how the writer integrated information from a source by using the phrase, "An alarming report states...."

Guide Ask partners to read through the second paragraph of "Tuned Out" and discuss how the writer integrated sources.

Apply Have students review their argumentative essays and revise their sentences to integrate sources smoothly. Have them share their revisions with a partner.

Conferring Toolkit

Brainstorm Ideas Encourage students to brainstorm ideas in preparation for writing an essay. If students struggle, remind them that they can write anything that comes to mind and not worry about making mistakes in this early stage. Tell them they can even draw a picture if it helps!

Integrate Sources Students may have difficulty identifying where they can make revisions and integrate sources. Point out sentences that do not indicate where the source information is from and guide them in adding an introductory phrase.

Use Formal or Informal Language

Formal and informal language differ in choice of words, sentence structure, and tone. Use formal language when writing academic essays and research reports. Use informal language to express personal feelings in a friendly letter, journal, or personal email.

Model Write these sentences:

It is important to do many different activities when you are young.

It's a big deal to do a lot of stuff when you're a kid.

Point out the use of formal and informal language in these two sentences. Ask: *With whom would you use informal language?*

Guide Write this sentence:

Do you want to come get dinner with me?

Ask partners to rewrite the sentence using formal language.

Apply Have students write three sentences of an e-mail to a friend and three sentences of an e-mail to a teacher. Share with a partner.

Add Strong Transitions

Tell students that writers use transitions to help link ideas together. Strong transitions help to make argumentative essays flow more smoothly.

Model Write examples of transition words and explain how they can be used to state your claim: *In my opinion; I believe.* To present your reasons: *First; one reason.* To give examples: *For example; for instance.* To state your conclusion: *In conclusion; as you can see.*

Guide Point out that writers use many different transitions to link ideas and information. Have partners read the last two paragraphs from Online Student Model Source 3, *Why Learn Languages?* and discuss how the transitions support the author's claim.

Apply Have students add strong transitions to their argumentative essays.

Use Conjunctions and Commas

Explain that conjunctions are words that join words, phrases, and sentences together. They help to connect ideas and thoughts and complete the meaning of a sentence. Commas are often used with conjunctions.

Model Point out that the most commonly used conjunctions are *and, or,* and *but.*

Write this sentence:
I like ice cream, but I get a stomachache if I have too much.

Circle the comma and explain that commas are used before conjunctions when you are combining two complete sentences together.

Guide Write these sentences and ask students to use conjunctions and commas to combine them.

My family is going on a vacation. We are going to visit my aunt.

We can have dinner at home tonight. We can eat at a restaurant.

Apply Have students use conjunctions and commas to write a short paragraph about a vacation.

ELL Use Formal or Informal Language For students who are struggling with formal and informal language, prompt them with a question. Ask: *What would you say to your friend? How would you say the same thing with different words to a teacher?*

Add Strong Transitions Point out a sentence where students can use a transition to link ideas or state their claim. Say: *Instead of simply listing your reasons here, let's introduce them with a strong transition like "One reason..." or "For instance..."*

ELL Use Conjunctions and Commas If students struggle with where to place commas, guide them in identifying the conjunction that combines the two complete sentences. Refer to the models sentences again, as necessary.

Action Verbs

LEARNING GOALS

We can identify and use action verbs.

OBJECTIVES

Demonstrate command of the conventions of standard English grammar and usage when writing or speaking.

Explain the function of nouns, pronouns, verbs, adjectives, and adverbs in general and their functions in particular sentences.

Ensure subject-verb and pronoun-antecedent agreement.

DAILY LANGUAGE ACTIVITY

Use the online review for grammar, practice, and usage.

TEACH IN SMALL GROUP

You may wish to use the Talk About It activities during Small Group time.

Approaching Level, On Level, and **Beyond Level** Pair students of different proficiency levels.

ELL According to their language proficiency, students should contribute to the discussion by using short phrases, asking questions, and adding relevant details.

Teach

Introduce Action Verbs

Present the following:

- A **verb** shows what the subject does or is. An **action verb** expresses action. *The bus driver drives us to school.*
- Some common action verbs are *eat, run, walk, work, put,* and *talk. The boy eats cereal. They put the books on the shelf. We talked for many hours.*
- Commonly misused verbs include *lie/lay, sit/set,* and *rise/raise.* **Incorrect:** *I will lay on the bed.* **Correct:** *I will lie on the bed.* **Correct:** *Omar will set the book down. Liz will sit on the floor.* **Correct:** *Jake rises early in the morning. Ana raised her hand.*

See **Practice Book** page 121 or online activity.

Teach

Review Action Verbs

Ask students to describe what an action verb is. Have them use *lie/lay, sit/set,* and *rise/raise* in sentences.

Introduce Subject-Verb Agreement

- A verb must agree with its subject. A singular subject takes a singular verb. A plural subject takes a plural verb. This rule applies to simple, compound, and complex sentences.
- Add *-s* or *-es* to most verbs in the present tense if the subject is singular. *Kelly plays video games.*
- A plural subject has a plural verb. Don't add *-s. The bells ring loudly.*
- **Collective nouns** identify a group and take a singular verb when they refer to the group as a whole. *The swarm of bees buzzes.* Prepositional phrases (like "of bees") do not change the verb.

See **Practice Book** page 122.

Use Action Verbs

Ask partners to use action verbs to talk about things you might do if you visited another country. Students might discuss different sports or activities people do in another country. As they talk, students should listen for action verbs.

Draw It!

Have each student in a small group write 3 action verbs on 3 index cards and place them in a pile. Students take turns selecting an index card and drawing a picture that represents the verb. The rest of the group guesses the verb.

FORMATIVE ASSESSMENT

STUDENT CHECK-IN

After completing each Practice Book page, have partners share. Ask them to reflect using the Check-In routine.

Mechanics and Usage

Subject-Verb Agreement

- A verb must agree with its subject, regardless if the sentence in which the verb or verbs appear is simple, compound, or complex.
- A singular subject takes a singular verb: *Lonnie practices soccer every day.*
- A plural subject takes a plural verb: *The students eat lunch at 11:30.*
- A compound subject takes a plural verb. *My best friend and I like math.*

Read the sentences aloud. Have students choose the correct verb.

- My shoes ______ my coat. (match/matches) (match)
- The boy ______ his pet birds. (feed/feeds) (feeds)
- May and Lexie ______ each other everything. (tell/tells) (tell)

See **Practice Book** page 123 or online activity.

Proofread and Write

Proofread

Have students correct errors in these sentences:

1. The students returns their books to the library. (return)
2. Lisa wait for the bus with her sister. (waits)
3. Marcus talk to his friend on the phone every day. (talks)
4. Jeri and Gina walks home from school. (walk)
5. The troop of scouts earn badges for camping. (earns)

Write

Have students find a piece of their own writing in their writer's notebook and correct subject-verb agreement errors, including those with collective nouns, prepositional phrases, and their influence on subject-verb agreement.

See **Practice Book** page 124.

Assess and Reteach

Assess

Use the Daily Language Activity and **Practice Book** page 125 for assessment.

Rubric Use your online rubric to record student progress.

Reteach

Use the online **Grammar Handbook** pages 458–459 and **Practice Book** pages 121–124 for additional reteaching. Remind students that it is important to use action verbs correctly as they speak and write.

Check students' writing for use of the skill and listen for it in their speaking. Assign grammar revision assignments in their writer's notebook as needed.

Replace The Verbs

Have small groups write three compound sentences about cultural activities they enjoy. Then have students read the sentences aloud, substituting new action verbs in each. Students should keep the verb tense the same.

Role-Play A Scene

Display a list of action verbs. Have students create and act out a scene, using at least four of the verbs. Students can act out a story they already know or imagine a new story. As other students watch, have them listen for the verbs.

Story Time

Have small groups sit in a circle and tell a story using action verbs. Each student adds a sentence to the story as it goes around the circle. Before students start, have them brainstorm topics that involve a lot of action.

LEARNING GOALS

We can identify and use verb tenses.

OBJECTIVES

Demonstrate command of the conventions of standard English grammar and usage when writing or speaking.

Use verb tense to convey various times, sequences, states, and conditions.

Recognize and correct inappropriate shifts in verb tense.

Proofread sentences.

DAILY LANGUAGE ACTIVITY

Use the online review for grammar, practice, and usage.

TEACH IN SMALL GROUP

You may wish to use the Talk About It activities during Small Group time.

Approaching Level, On Level, and **Beyond Level** Pair students of different proficiency levels.

ELL According to their language proficiency, students should contribute to the discussion by using short phrases, asking questions, and adding relevant details.

FORMATIVE ASSESSMENT

STUDENT CHECK-IN

After completing the Practice Book page, have partners share. Ask them to reflect using the Check-In routine.

Verb Tenses

Teach

Introduce Verb Tenses

- The tense of a verb tells when an action takes place.
- A **present tense** verb tells what is happening now.
- To form the present tense of most verbs in the third person, add *-s*: *sees.* Add *-es* to verbs that end in *s, ss, ch, sh, x,* or *zz*: *pushes, buzzes. Juan sees the ball. The lady pushes the cart. The bee buzzes nearby.*
- If a verb ends with a consonant and the letter *y*, change *y* to *i* before adding *-es*: *carries. Ming carries his books to class.*
- The **present progressive tense** shows action that is continuing. *Shanae is eating.*

See **Practice Book** page 133 or online activity.

Teach

Review Present Tense

Review verb tenses with students. Have them form and use past and present tense verbs in a sentence.

Past and Future Tenses

- **Past tense** verbs tell about actions in the past. Add *-ed* to most verbs to show past tense.
- If a verb ends in *e*, just add *-d*: *hiked.* If a verb ends in a vowel and consonant, double the consonant and add *-ed*: *dropped.* If a verb ends in a consonant and *y*, change *y* to *i* and add *-ed*: *tried. We hiked through the forest. She dropped her pen. Carlo tried to sleep on the bus.*
- **Future tense** verbs are formed with the helping verb *will. I will go.*
- The past and future progressive tenses show action that was or will be continuing. *She was running. Alex will be studying.*

See **Practice Book** page 134.

Pick A Verb

Write some action verbs on the board. Have partners each write two sentences for the verb they pick: one in the present tense and one in the present-progressive tense. Ask volunteers to share their sentences.

Use Action Verbs

Display a list of action verbs. Have partners take turns choosing a verb. Partner A chooses the verb, and Partner B makes a sentence using a progressive form of the verb. Partners switch roles.

Mechanics and Usage

Avoid Shifting Tenses

- When talking or writing about the past, present, or future, always use the correct verb tense.
- Take care not to mix verb tenses when describing the same incident. For example: *In the beginning of the story, Clara* *is* *happy, but by the end, she* *is* *sad.* The verbs should both be in the present tense (is) or in the past tense (was).

See **Practice Book** page 135 or online activity.

OPTION

Proofread and Write

Proofread

Have students correct errors in these sentences:

1. Paul sat the glass on the table as he set down. (set/sat)
2. Mrs. Green goes to the store tomorrow. (will go)
3. Nolan stopped walking and looks down the street. (1: stopped/looked; 2: stops/looks)
4. Cora watches yesterday's game eagerly, but her team still lost. (watched)

Write

Have students find a piece of their own writing in their writer's notebook and correct errors in shifting verb tenses.

See **Practice Book** page 136.

OPTION

Assess and Reteach

Assess

Use the Daily Language Activity and **Practice Book** page 137 for assessment.

Rubric Use your online rubric to record student progress.

Reteach

Use the online **Grammar Handbook** pages 458–459 and **Practice Book** pages 133–136 for reteaching. Remind students that it is important to use verb tenses correctly as they speak and write.

Check students' writing for use of this skill and listen for it in their speaking. Assign grammar revision assignments in their writer's notebook as needed.

Picture Practice

Display a picture showing a nature scene with a lot of action. Have partners describe the picture to each other, using action verbs to tell what is happening. Remind them not to shift tenses.

Where Am I?

Have partners take turns using action verbs to describe a place that has, had, or will have a lot of action going on. For example, students might describe a football game or a supermarket. The listening partner guesses the location.

Rewrite A Scene

Have groups rewrite a favorite scene from a story the class has read but with a twist: students must use either the past tense or the future tense as they rewrite the scene. Remind students to use many action verbs and the correct tense.

LEARNING GOALS

We can identify and use main and helping verbs.

OBJECTIVES

Demonstrate command of the conventions of standard English grammar and usage when writing or speaking.

Form and use the perfect (e.g., *I had walked; I have walked; I will have walked*) verb tenses.

Use verb tense to convey various times, sequences, states, and conditions.

Use contractions and apostrophes correctly.

Proofread sentences.

DAILY LANGUAGE ACTIVITY

Use the online review for grammar, practice, and usage.

TEACH IN SMALL GROUP

You may wish to use the Talk About It activities during Small Group time.

Approaching Level, On Level, and **Beyond Level** Pair students of different proficiency levels.

ELL According to their language proficiency, students should contribute to discussions by using short phrases, asking questions, and adding relevant details.

FORMATIVE ASSESSMENT

STUDENT CHECK-IN

After completing each Practice Book page, have partners share. Ask them to reflect using the Check-In routine.

Main and Helping Verbs

Teach

Introduce Main and Helping Verbs

Present the following:

- The **main verb** shows what the subject does or is. *The marble rolled across the table.* The main verb *rolled* tells what the marble did.
- A **helping verb** helps the main verb show an action or make a statement. Some helping verbs include *has, had, am, is, are, and were. I am walking with my sister to school.* The helping verb *am* helps the action verb *walking.*
- Sentences can be in the active or passive voice. In the active voice, the subject is doing something. In the passive voice, the subject is the object of an action. *Mia bought the book.* (active) *The book was bought by Mia.* (passive)

See **Practice Book** page 145 or online activity.

Teach

Review Main and Helping Verbs

Ask students to explain the difference between main verbs and helping verbs.

Introduce Participles and Perfect Tense

- The present progressive tense takes a form of the verb *be* and a **present participle**. *I am walking.*
- **Past participles** for regular verbs take the same form as the past tense: *trapped.* Irregular verbs have irregular past participles: *swum, caught. I have swum for three years.* When you use the irregular verb *swum,* you must also use *has, have,* or *had.*
- The three **perfect tenses** (present, past, future) show a completed action. *I have walked. I had walked. I will have walked.*

See **Practice Book** page 146.

Use Helping Verbs

Display 12 helping verbs. Have students take turns using one of the helping verbs and a main verb of their choice in a sentence. Listeners should check that the speaker uses a helping verb and a main verb correctly.

Pick a Pair

Write helping verbs and action verbs on index cards and organize them into two piles. Have students choose a word from each pile and use them in a sentence. For example: *Nancy and Rita are playing checkers.*

Mechanics and Usage

Special Helping Verbs; Contractions; Troublesome Words

- Special helping verbs can express mood through possibility or obligation. They include the principal modal verbs *can, may,* and *must*.
- A contraction, a shortened form of two words, can be formed from a helping verb and the word *not*: *isn't* comes from *is not*. Contractions can also come from a pronoun and a verb: *he's* comes from *he is*. An apostrophe (') indicates the missing letter.
- Avoid confusing *its* with *it's* and *your* with *you're*. Remember the apostrophe takes the place of a letter. When you see *it's*, think "it is." When you see *you're*, think "you are." Be sure the meaning fits with the sentence.

See **Practice Book** page 147 or online activity.

Proofread and Write

Proofread

Have students correct errors in these sentences:

1. We going to the mall tomorrow. (are)
2. Lin willn't visit Big Bend National Park this year. (won't)
3. You are play that game now. (may)
4. Dexter running very fast today. (is)
5. Your playing well. (You're)
6. Its my turn to pick a book. (It's)
7. Marla had catched the fish with her new fishing rod. (caught)
8. Dad will has finished work soon. (have)

Write

Have students find a piece of their own writing in their writer's notebook and correct their use of main and helping verbs. See **Practice Book** page 148.

Assess and Reteach

Assess

Use the Daily Language Activity and **Practice Book** page 149 for assessment.

Rubric Use your online rubric to record student progress.

Reteach

Use the online **Grammar Handbook** pages 460–461 and **Practice Book** pages 145–148 for additional practice with perfect verb tenses, helping verbs, and participles. Remind students that it is important to use grammar correctly as they speak and write.

Check students' writing for use of these skills and listen for them in their speaking. Assign grammar revision assignments in their writer's notebook as needed.

Twenty Questions

Ask each student to think of an object. Have partners ask up to 20 questions using modal verbs to determine the object. For example: *Could you eat it? Can I see it in this room?* Then have partners reverse roles.

What Time Is It?

Write a time on the board. Have students describe their actions using present participles as if it were the time on the board. For example: *It's 3:00 P.M., and I am sitting on the bus.*

Have You?

Display a list of action verbs. Have partners ask and answer questions using *have* and the past participle of one of the verbs. For example: *Have you played soccer? No, I have not played soccer.*

Linking Verbs

LEARNING GOALS

We can identify and use linking verbs.

OBJECTIVES

Demonstrate command of the conventions of standard English grammar and usage when writing or speaking.

Explain the function of nouns, pronouns, verbs, adjectives, and adverbs in general and their functions in particular sentences.

Use underlining, quotation marks, or italics to indicate titles of works.

Proofread sentences.

DAILY LANGUAGE ACTIVITY

Use the online review for grammar, practice, and usage.

TEACH IN SMALL GROUP

You may wish to use the Talk About It activities during Small Group time.

 **Approaching Level, On Level,** and **Beyond Level** Pair students of different proficiency levels.

● **ELL** According to their language proficiency, students should contribute to discussions by using short phrases, asking questions, and adding relevant details.

FORMATIVE ASSESSMENT

STUDENT CHECK-IN

After completing each Practice Book page, have partners share. Ask them to reflect using the Check-In routine.

Teach

Introduce Linking Verbs

Present the following:

- A **linking verb** links the subject of a sentence to a noun or an adjective. It tells what the subject is, was, or will be.
- Common linking verbs are *am, is, are, was, were,* and *will be. Tony is a good player*. The verbs *seem, feel, appear, look,* and *taste* can also be linking verbs in any tense. *It feels cold! The game was yesterday. The apple looks juicy. The lemonade tastes sweet.*
- Subjects and linking verbs must agree. *The photo is beautiful. The dress will be ready on time.*
- In compound sentences, both subjects and verbs must agree. *My older sisters are talkative, but I am a little shy.*

See **Practice Book** page 157 or online activity.

Teach

Review Linking Verbs

Ask students to describe what a linking verb is and give a few examples.

Introduce How Linking Verbs Work

- A linking verb links the subject of a sentence to a noun or an adjective in the predicate. *Miho feels excited. The soup is hot. Tomorrow will be rainy.*
- A noun that follows a linking verb renames or identifies the subject. *My uncle is a doctor. The honored guest will be an actor. The thief appears to be a raccoon.*
- An adjective that follows a linking verb describes the subject. *Everyone was tired after the long hike. My knee seems swollen. The fabric feels rough.*

See **Practice Book** page 158 or online activity.

OPTION **Talk About It** MULTIMODAL

Action or Linking Verb?

Display the verbs *seem, feel, appear,* and *look*. Partner A should use one of the verbs in a sentence. Partner B should tell whether the verb is used as an action or linking verb. Partners then switch roles.

Use Linking Verbs

Display a list of linking verbs. Have students in small groups take turns making sentences with each verb and adding an adjective. Ask each group to share two or three examples with the class.

Mechanics and Usage

Punctuating Titles and Product Names

- The title of a book or newspaper always begins with a capital letter: *The New York Times*. Don't use a capital letter for articles, conjunctions, and prepositions in titles: *Snow White and the Seven Dwarves*. Underline or italicize book or newspaper titles in text: Where the Mountain Meets the Moon; *Where the Mountain Meets the Moon*.
- Underlining or italics can also be used to show emphasis: Do not forget the date July 2. I am *so* exhausted.
- Use capital letters for the names of products: *Big Blast Hair Dryer, Cozy Feet Slippers, Seal and Stick Glue*

See **Practice Book** page 159 or online activity.

Proofread and Write

Proofread

Have students correct errors:

1. I read sun times news every morning. (*Sun Times News;* Sun Times News)
2. Our neighbors is very friendly. (are)
3. The laughing children looks happy. (look)
4. The weather seem nice. (seems)
5. My favorite book is superfudge. (*Superfudge;* Superfudge)
6. I read the mystery of the missing cat. (*The Mystery of the Missing Cat;* The Mystery of the Missing Cat)

Write

Have students in their writer's notebook correct the use of linking verbs, titles, emphasis, and product names. Remind students that both subjects and verbs should agree in compound sentences.

See **Practice Book** page 160.

Assess and Reteach

Assess

Use the Daily Language Activity and **Practice Book** page 161 for assessment.

Rubric Use your online rubric to record student progress.

Reteach

Use the online **Grammar Handbook** pages 461 and 475 and **Practice Book** pages 157–160 for additional reteaching. Remind students that it is important to use linking verbs correctly as they speak and write.

Check students' writing for use of the skill and listen for it in their speaking. Assign grammar revision assignments in their writer's notebook as needed.

Dictate Sentences

Have partners dictate sentences to each other that include the title of a book. Partners should check to make sure the titles are written correctly. Then have partners describe the setting and characters using linking verbs.

Teamwork

Have students in small groups take turns describing an example of teamwork. Encourage students to use both linking verb + adjective and linking verb + noun. For example: *My soccer team is hardworking.*

My Favorite Meal

Have partners take turns describing a favorite meal, using the linking verbs *taste, feel, smell, be,* and *seem.* If necessary, prompt partners to ask each other questions to elicit information: *How does it taste? What does it smell like?*

Irregular Verbs

LEARNING GOALS

We can identify and use irregular verbs.

OBJECTIVES

Demonstrate command of the conventions of standard English grammar and usage when writing or speaking.

Form and use the perfect (e.g., *I had walked; I have walked; I will have walked*) verb tenses.

Form and use regular and irregular verbs.

DAILY LANGUAGE ACTIVITY

Use the online review for grammar, practice, and usage.

TEACH IN SMALL GROUP

You may wish to use the Talk About It activities during Small Group time.

Approaching Level, On Level, and **Beyond Level** Pair students of different proficiency levels.

ELL According to their language and proficiency, students should contribute to discussions by using short phrases, asking questions, and adding relevant details.

Teach

Introduce Irregular Verbs

- An **irregular verb** is a verb that does not add *-ed* to form the past tense.
- Some irregular verbs include *begin/began, bring/brought, catch/caught, choose/chose, do/did, drink/drank, eat/ate, fall/fell, fight/fought, get/got, go/went, keep/kept, know/knew, leave/left, make/made, read/read, run/ran, say/said, speak/spoke, think/thought, win/won,* and *write/wrote.*
- These examples show the incorrect and correct use of irregular verbs.

Incorrect: Aliya eated lunch.

Correct: Aliya ate lunch.

Incorrect: The dog catched the ball.

Correct: The dog caught the ball.

See **Practice Book** page 169 or online activity.

Teach

Explain that there is no pattern or set of rules for forming irregular verbs, so it is important to remember their spellings.

More About Irregular Verbs

- Some irregular verbs have special endings when used with the **helping verbs** *have, has,* or *had.* For example, *begun, brought, chosen, drunk, eaten, fallen.* These are **past participles**.
- These examples show incorrect and correct use of a helping verb with an irregular verb.

Incorrect: Steve had bringed lunch.

Correct: Steve had brought lunch.

Incorrect: We have saw the rainbow.

Correct: We have seen the rainbow.

See **Practice Book** page 170.

Tell About the Past

Display a list of irregular verbs in the present tense. Ask students to choose a verb and tell their partner a past tense sentence about archaeology or discovering the past. Then have partners switch roles.

When Did It Happen?

Display two irregular verbs. Have partners make up a sentence in the past that shows one action happening before the other (e.g., *write + go = She had written about ancient Rome before she went to Italy*). Ask volunteers to share their sentences. Repeat with new verbs.

FORMATIVE ASSESSMENT

STUDENT CHECK-IN

After completing each Practice Book page, have partners share. Ask them to reflect using the Check-In routine.

Mechanics and Usage

Correct Verb Usage

- A verb shows action or states a condition.
- Use the present tense if the action or condition is happening now.
- Use the past tense to show an action that has been completed in the past.
- Some verbs do not take *-ed* to show the past tense.
- Discuss the verb tense used in each of the following sample sentences, including the use of an irregular verb:

1. Ella *writes* a thank you to her aunt. (present tense)
2. May *jumped* across the puddle. (past tense)
3. Eddie *kept* his bike in the garage. (past tense; irregular form of keep)

See **Practice Book** page 171 or online activity.

Proofread and Write

Proofread

Have students correct errors in these sentences:

1. We eaten popcorn and drinked juice after school. (1: ate; 2: drank)
2. Our team fighted hard and winned the game. (1: fought; 2: won)
3. Maya has chose a topic for her paper. (chosen)
4. Kyle writes his paper last night but have leaves it at home. (1: wrote; 2: has left)

Write

Have students find a piece of their own writing in their writer's notebook and correct verb tenses.

See **Practice Book** page 172.

Assess and Reteach

Assess

Use the Daily Language Activity and **Practice Book** page 173 for assessment.

Rubric Use your online rubric to record student progress.

Reteach

Use online **Grammar Handbook** page 462 and **Practice Book** pages 169–172 for additional reteaching. Remind students that it is important to use irregular verbs correctly as they speak and write.

Check students' writing for use of the skill and listen for it in their speaking. Assign grammar revision assignments in their writer's notebook as needed.

Sort Verbs

Create a T-chart: *Present* and *Past*. Ask students to write a sentence using a past or present verb. Have students post their sentences in the chart. Challenge students to use and identify irregular verbs.

It Happened In the Past

Have partners use at least three irregular verbs to tell each other about an ancient culture. Ask volunteers to share with the class what their partners said. Have students identify the irregular verbs as they listen.

Word Search

Have partners scan a text about archaeology or history for irregular verbs and make a list. Then have them take turns using one of the verbs to make a sentence in the past tense. Ask each pair to share a sentence with the class.

LEARNING GOALS

We can read, sort, and use spelling words with open syllables.

OBJECTIVES

Spell grade-appropriate words correctly, consulting references as needed.

DIFFERENTIATED SPELLING

Go online for Dictation Sentences for differentiated spelling lists.

On Level and **ELL**

minus	profile	decent
loser	local	linen
humor	comet	legal
closet	vacant	panic
recent	punish	smoky
student	cavern	tyrant
equal	shiver	

Review valley, fifteen, culture
Challenge fatigue, fugitive

Approaching Level

minus	hero	legal
loser	local	linen
humor	comet	decent
closet	parade	amaze
camel	punish	fancy
student	human	tyrant
equal	shiver	

Beyond Level

relevant	profile	decent
separate	bayonets	tirade
license	comet	biceps
rehearse	vacant	panic
recent	punished	smoky
utensil	caverns	tyrant
vinyl	stamen	

FORMATIVE ASSESSMENT

STUDENT CHECK-IN

After completing each Practice Book page, have partners share. Ask them to reflect using the Check-In routine.

Open Syllables

Assess Prior Knowledge

Read the spelling words aloud, drawing out the vowel sound in each open syllable.

Point out the open syllable pattern in *recent*. Draw a line between each syllable: *re/cent*. Say each syllable, then point out the open syllable *re* and the closed syllable *cent*.

Demonstrate sorting the spelling words by pattern under the key words *local* and *panic*. Sort a few words. Point out that when the vowel sound is short, the syllable usually ends after the consonant. When the vowel sound is long, the syllable ends after the vowel.

Use the Dictation Sentences from Lesson 5 to give the pretest. Say the underlined word, read the sentence, and repeat the word. Have students write the words and then check their papers.

See **Practice Book** page 126 for a pretest.

Spiral Review

Review the closed syllables in *valley, fifteen,* and *culture*. Read each sentence below, repeat the review word, and have students write the word.

1. Our house is in a valley between hills.
2. We had fifteen minutes to take the quiz.
3. Mikal is studying the culture of Japan.

Have partners check their spellings.

Challenge Words Review this week's open syllable patterns. Read each sentence below, repeat the challenge word, and have students write the word.

1. I felt fatigue after raking the leaves.
2. The fugitive was caught quickly.

Have students check their spellings and write the words in their writer's notebook.

Word Sorts

MULTIMODAL

OPEN SORT

Have students cut apart the **Spelling Word Cards** in the Online Resource Book and initial the back of each card. Have them read the words aloud with partners. Then have partners do an open sort. Have them record their sorts in their writer's notebooks.

PATTERN SORT

Complete the pattern sort from Lesson 1 by using the boldfaced key words in the Spelling Word Cards. Point out the open syllable patterns. Partners should compare and check their sorts. See **Practice Book** pages 127, 127A, and 127B for differentiated practice.

Word Meanings

Have students copy the three statements below into their writer's notebook. Say the sentences aloud and ask students to fill in each blank with a spelling word.

1. An antonym for *plus* is ____. (minus)
2. An antonym for *winner* is ____. (loser)
3. An antonym for *illegal* is ____. (legal)

Challenge students to create statements about antonyms for their other spelling, review, or challenge words. Have students post their statements on the board.

See **Practice Book** page 128 or online activity.

Proofread and Write

Write these sentences on the board. Have students circle and correct each misspelled word. Then have them use a print or a digital dictionary to check their spellings of the words.

1. Megan put the clean linnen sheets in the clozet. (linen, closet)
2. I started to schiver from being in the cold cavurn. (shiver, cavern)
3. The stoodent was interviewed for the locul paper. (student, local)
4. Ten mineus four does not equall five. (minus, equal)

Error Correction Remind students that spelling a lengthy word is easier when you break it into syllables and to focus on one chunk of the word at a time.

Apply to Writing Have students correct a piece of their own writing.

See **Practice Book** page 129.

Assess

Use the Dictation Sentences for the posttest. Have students list misspelled words in their writer's notebook. Look for students' use of these words in their writings.

See **Practice Book** page 126 for a posttest. Use page 130 for review.

Dictation Sentences

1. What is forty minus fourteen?
2. The loser has to start all over.
3. He has a silly sense of humor.
4. My coat is hanging in the closet.
5. We found a recent picture of her.
6. There is a new student in class.
7. Twelve inches is equal to one foot.
8. I recognized Ashley's profile.
9. Most kids go to the local school.
10. The comet left a bright streak.
11. She parked in a vacant lot.
12. They might punish us for lying.
13. Their fort looked like a cavern.
14. The cold made the children shiver.
15. Albert seems like a decent man.
16. Carol ironed her linen shirt.
17. The legal age to vote is eighteen.
18. Remain calm and don't panic.
19. The air began to turn smoky.
20. People thought he was a tyrant.

Have students self-correct their tests.

SPEED SORT

Have partners do a speed sort to see who is fastest. Then have them do a word hunt in this week's readings to find words with the suffixes found in this week's words. Have them record the words in their writer's notebook.

BLIND SORT

Have partners do a blind sort: one reads a Spelling Word Card; the other tells under which open syllable (V/V) pattern it belongs. Then have partners use their cards to play Go Fish with the spelling words, using open syllable (V/V) patterns as the "fish."

LEARNING GOALS

We can read, sort, and use spelling words with open syllables.

OBJECTIVES

Spell grade-appropriate words correctly, consulting references as needed.

DIFFERENTIATED SPELLING

Go online for Dictation Sentences for differentiated spelling lists.

On Level and ELL

video	ruin	casual
poet	diet	trial
riot	patriot	fuel
piano	fluid	meteor
diary	rodeo	diameter
radio	cruel	meander
ideas	genuine	

Review recent, closet, minus
Challenge situation, variety

Approaching Level

video	ruin	casual
poet	diet	trial
riot	giant	fuel
piano	dial	science
diary	rodeo	quiet
radio	cruel	prior
ideas	lion	

Beyond Level

dialect	ruined	casual
grueling	glorious	trials
riot	patriot	variety
radiance	fluidity	meteor
calcium	evaluate	diameter
pioneers	cruelly	meander
ideas	genuine	

FORMATIVE ASSESSMENT

STUDENT CHECK-IN

After completing each Practice Book page, have partners share. Ask them to reflect using the Check-In routine.

Open Syllables (V/V)

Assess Prior Knowledge

Read the spelling words aloud, drawing out the vowel sound in each open syllable.

Point out the spelling pattern in *poet* and draw a line between the syllables: *po/et*. Explain that the word *poet* has an open syllable, which means it has a syllable that ends in a vowel. It is followed by a syllable that starts with a vowel. This is the V/V pattern. Pronounce *poet* and draw a line under the two vowels to show the V/V pattern.

Demonstrate sorting the spelling words by pattern under the various V/V patterns: *ea, eo, ia, ie, io, oe, ua, ue,* and *ui*. Sort a few words. Point out the open syllable in each word.

Use the Dictation Sentences from Lesson 10 to give the pretest. Say each word, read the sentence, and repeat the word. Have students write and check the words.

See **Practice Book** page 138 for a pretest.

Spiral Review

Review the open syllable patterns in *recent, closet,* and *minus*. Read each sentence below, repeat the review word, and have students write the word.

1. His most recent book is excellent.
2. Put your jacket in the hall closet.
3. Sixty minus fifty is ten.

Have partners check their spellings.

Challenge Words

Review this week's open syllable (V/V) patterns. Read each sentence below, repeat the challenge word, and have students write the word.

1. We heard about the dangerous situation on the news.
2. It's healthy to eat a variety of foods.

Have students check their spellings and write the words in their writer's notebook.

Word Sorts

OPEN SORT

Have students cut apart the **Spelling Word Cards** in the Online Resource Book and initial the back of each card. Have them read the words aloud with partners. Then have partners do an open sort. Have them record their sorts in their writer's notebook.

PATTERN SORT

Complete the pattern sort from Lesson 6. Point out words with the open-syllable V/V pattern. Partners should compare and check their sorts. Alternatively, have partners use **Practice Book**, page 139. See Practice Book, pages 139A and 139B for differentiated practice.

Word Meanings

Have students copy the three cloze sentences below into their writer's notebook. Say the sentences aloud. Ask students to fill in the blanks with a spelling word.

1. Vamsi drinks plenty of ____ before he runs a race. (fluids)
2. Jeans and a T-shirt are too ____ for the awards ceremony. (casual)
3. Alex turned on the ____ to hear the emergency broadcast. (radio)

Challenge students to create cloze sentences for their other spelling, review, or challenge words. Have students post their cloze sentences on the board.

See **Practice Book** page 140 or online activity.

Proofread and Write

Write these sentences on the board. Have students circle and correct each misspelled word. Have students use a print or a digital dictionary to check and correct their spellings of the words.

1. We watched a great vidio of a peano concert. (video, piano)
2. Donna, a poet, writes her best idees in her diery. (ideas, diary)
3. The man was put on tryal for his crule crimes. (trial, cruel)
4. Too many sweets will ruine a healthy dyet. (ruin, diet)

Error Correction Remind students not to confuse the order of the vowels in the open syllable V/V pattern. They must carefully pronounce each syllable before spelling it.

Apply to Writing Have students correct a piece of their own writing.

See **Practice Book** page 141.

Assess

Use the Dictation Sentences for the posttest. Have students list misspelled words in their writer's notebook. Look for students' use of these words in their writings.

See **Practice Book** page 138 for the posttest. Use page 142 for review.

SPEED SORT

Have partners do a speed sort to see who is fastest. Then have them compare their sorts. They should brainstorm other words with the open syllable (V/V) pattern. Have them record the words in their writer's notebook.

BLIND SORT

Have partners do a blind sort: one reads a Spelling Word Card; the other tells under which open syllable (V/V) pattern it belongs. Then have partners use their cards to play Go Fish with the spelling words, using open syllable (V/V) patterns as the "fish."

Dictation Sentences

1. Our class watched a video.
2. The poet likes to play with words.
3. Gold fever almost caused a riot.
4. Mrs. Park gave a piano recital.
5. He wrote about it in his diary.
6. Carmen listened to the radio.
7. Esther had strong ideas.
8. Nothing could ruin her plan.
9. A healthy diet includes vegetables.
10. The patriot loves his country.
11. Water is the only fluid I drink.
12. There was a crowd at the rodeo.
13. He cannot tolerate cruel acts.
14. His apology was genuine.
15. Wear casual clothes to the picnic.
16. A judge will oversee the trial.
17. They used wood for fuel.
18. The meteor fell outside of town.
19. The hole is 100 feet in diameter.
20. My little brother likes to meander when we go for walks.

Have students self-correct their tests.

LEARNING GOALS

We can read, sort, and use spelling words with vowel team syllables.

OBJECTIVES

Spell grade-appropriate words correctly, consulting references as needed.

DIFFERENTIATED SPELLING

Go online for Dictation Sentences for differentiated spelling lists.

On Level and **ELL**

footprint	grownup	faucet
fairground	encounter	caution
although	grouchy	boundary
laughter	flawless	doubting
appoint	lawyer	southern
coastal	entertain	roughness
bleachers	applause	

Review poet, radio, fuel
Challenge nowadays, distraught

Approaching Level

footprint	grownup	faucet
fairground	counter	laundry
although	grouchy	caution
August	flawless	boundary
appoint	lawyer	doubting
coastal	entertain	southern
bleachers	applause	

Beyond Level

footprint	faucet	causeway
fairground	encounter	caution
although	bountiful	boundary
allowance	doubting	applause
appoint	flawlessly	southern
laughter	lawyer	roughness
bleachers	entertainment	

FORMATIVE ASSESSMENT

STUDENT CHECK-IN

After completing each Practice Book page, have partners share. Ask them to reflect using the Check-In routine.

Vowel Team Syllables

Assess Prior Knowledge

Read the spelling words aloud, drawing out the vowel sound in each syllable.

Point out the two vowels that make one vowel sound in *footprint* and in *coastal*. Draw a line under these vowels as you say the sounds. Explain that in a vowel team syllable, two vowels work together to make one vowel sound.

Demonstrate sorting the spelling words by pattern under the key words *entertain, applause,* and *southern*. Sort a few words. Point out the vowel team syllable in each word as it is sorted.

Use the Dictation Sentences from Lesson 5 to give the pretest. Say the underlined word, read the sentence, and repeat the word. Have students write the words.

See **Practice Book** page 150 for a pretest.

Spiral Review

Review the open syllable (V/V) pattern in *poet, diet,* and *fuel*. Explain that digraphs are two letters that form one sound, such as *ue* in *fuel*. Read each sentence, repeat the review word, and have students write the word.

1. My sister wants to be a poet.
2. I believe in a healthy diet.
3. We need to get fuel for the car.

Have students trade papers and check their spellings.

Challenge Words

Review this week's vowel team syllable pattern. Read each sentence, repeat the word, and have students write the word.

1. Most people use e-mail nowadays.
2. The distraught child cried.

Have students check their spellings and write the words in their writer's notebook.

OPEN SORT

Have students cut apart the **Spelling Word Cards** in the Online Resource Book and initial the back of each card. Have them read the words aloud with partners. Then have partners do an open sort. Have them record their sorts in their writer's notebook.

PATTERN SORT

Have students complete the pattern sort from Lesson 1 by using the boldfaced key words in the Spelling Word Cards. Point out the vowel team syllables. Partners should compare and check their sorts. See **Practice Book** pages 151, 151A, and 151B for differentiated practice.

Word Meanings

Have students copy the definitions below into their writer's notebook. Say the definitions aloud. Ask students to write the spelling word that matches each definition.

1. an adult person (grownup)
2. perfect; without any faults (flawless)
3. along the seashore (coastal)
4. not happy; grumpy (grouchy)

Challenge students to create definitions for their other spelling, review, or challenge words. Have partners share their definitions and guess the words.

See **Practice Book** page 152 or online activity.

Proofread and Write

Write these sentences on the board. Have students circle and correct each misspelled word. Then have them use a print or a digital dictionary to check and correct their spellings of the words.

1. The sound of lafter and applawse filled the air. (laughter, applause)
2. Althow Jed played well, his performance was not flawliss. (Although, flawless)
3. The crowd filled the bleechers at the fareground. (bleachers, fairground)
4. The loyer advised cawtion to his grouchy client. (lawyer, caution)

Error Correction Remind students that two vowels that make one sound have vowel team spellings. Review any vowel team spellings students frequently misspell.

Apply to Writing Have students correct a piece of their own writing.

See **Practice Book** page 153.

Assess

Use the Dictation Sentences for the posttest. Have students list misspelled words in their writer's notebook, especially errors in digraphs. Look for students' use of these words in their writings.

See **Practice Book** page 150 for a posttest. Use page 154 for review.

Dictation Sentences

1. I saw a footprint in the sand.
2. The circus is at the fairground.
3. Although I wasn't hungry, I still ate.
4. Their laughter was contagious.
5. We must appoint a leader.
6. Mike lives in a coastal town.
7. We sat in the bleachers.
8. My dad is a grownup.
9. That was a close encounter.
10. She was grouchy after a bad day.
11. The diamond was flawless.
12. The lawyer returned from court.
13. My mom loves to entertain.
14. The applause was thunderous.
15. The faucet is leaking.
16. Proceed with caution.
17. The tree marks the boundary.
18. She was doubting what she heard.
19. I always take the southern route.
20. I felt the roughness of the rock.

Have students self-correct their tests.

SPEED SORT

Have partners do a speed sort to see who is fastest. Then have them brainstorm other words with vowel team syllables. Have them record the words in their writer's notebook.

BLIND SORT

Have partners do a blind sort: one reads a Spelling Word Card; the other tells under which key word it belongs. Have them take turns until both have sorted all their words. Then have students explain how they sorted the words.

Consonant + *le* Syllables

LEARNING GOALS

We can read, sort, and use spelling words with consonant +*le* syllables.

OBJECTIVES

Spell grade-appropriate words correctly, consulting references as needed.

DIFFERENTIATED SPELLING

Go online for Dictation Sentences for differentiated spelling lists.

On Level and **ELL**

stable	beetle	label
saddle	kettle	vocal
table	eagle	journal
noble	royal	medal
cattle	cripple	several
stumble	hospital	sample
terrible	legal	

Review entertain, encounter, southern
Challenge impossible, people

Approaching Level

stable	beetle	label
saddle	kettle	vocal
table	eagle	journal
noble	royal	medal
cattle	cripple	pickle
tumble	hospital	sample
terrible	legal	

Beyond Level

unstable	beetle	label
saddle	kettle	fundamental
illegally	eagle	journalists
noble	royal	monumental
chronicle	cripple	several
stumble	hospital	castle
maternal	nocturnal	

FORMATIVE ASSESSMENT

STUDENT CHECK-IN

After completing the Practice Book page, have partners share. Ask them to reflect using the Check-In routine.

Assess Prior Knowledge

Read the spelling words aloud, segmenting the words by sound.

Point out the spelling patterns in *stable* and *beetle* and draw a line between the syllables: *sta/ble, bee/tle*. Say each syllable. Draw a line under the spelling patterns as you say the sounds. Explain that in most words that end in *-le*, the final syllable includes a preceding consonant.

Demonstrate sorting the spelling words by pattern under the key words *stable, royal,* and *label*. As words are sorted, point out the syllable that demonstrates the consonant + *le* sound in each word.

Use the Dictation Sentences from Lesson 10 to give the pretest. Say the underlined word, read the sentence, and repeat the word. Have students write the words.

See **Practice Book** page 162 for a pretest.

Spiral Review

Review the vowel team syllables in *entertain, encounter* and *southern*. Read each sentence below, repeat the review word, and have students write the word.

1. Malika loves to <u>entertain</u> others.
2. I had an <u>encounter</u> with a deer.
3. James followed the <u>southern</u> trail.

Have partners check their spellings.

Challenge Words

Review this week's consonant + *le* syllable spelling pattern. Explain that the pattern is a final stable syllable that always ends with the sound /əl/. Read each sentence, repeat the challenge word, and have students write the word.

1. Fixing the tire was <u>impossible</u>.
2. More than one thousand <u>people</u> came to see the show.

Have students check their spellings and write the words in their writer's notebook.

OPEN SORT

Have students cut apart the **Spelling Word Cards** in the Online Resource Book and initial the back of each card. Have them read the words aloud with partners. Then have partners do an open sort. Have them record their sorts in their writer's notebook.

PATTERN SORT

Have students complete the pattern sort from Lesson 6 by using the boldfaced key words in the Spelling Word Cards. Point out the vowel team syllables. Partners should compare and check their sorts. See **Practice Book** pages 163, 163A, and 163B for differentiated practice.

Word Meanings

Have students copy the groups of words below into their writer's notebook. Say the words aloud. Ask students to write the related spelling word that belongs to each group.

1. couch, dresser, chair (table)
2. letter, newspaper, book (journal)
3. trip, stagger, slip (stumble)
4. awful, horrible, bad (terrible)

Challenge students to create groups of related words for their other spelling, review, or challenge words. Have students write their groups of related words in their writer's notebook.

See **Practice Book** page 164 or online activity.

Proofread and Write

Write these sentences on the board. Have students circle and correct each misspelled word. Then have them use a print or a digital dictionary to check and correct their spellings of the words.

1. I put the saddel on the horse in the stabel. (saddle, stable)
2. Pip's journle has severel tales of royal families in it. (journal, several)
3. Faye won a medle for her vocul performance. (medal, vocal)
4. The eagal gave a terribal cry as it dove through the air. (eagle, terrible)

Error Correction Remind students that *-le* has the same sound as *-al* and *-el*, so they should take care when spelling words with these endings.

Apply to Writing Have students correct a piece of their own writing.

See **Practice Book** page 165.

10 Assess

Use the Dictation Sentences for the posttest. Have students list misspelled words in their writer's notebook. Look for students' use of these words in their writings.

See **Practice Book** page 162 for the posttest. Use page 166 for review.

Dictation Sentences

1. The horses are in the <u>stable</u>.
2. The woman sat high in her <u>saddle</u>.
3. My family eats at the kitchen <u>table</u>.
4. Singh came from a <u>noble</u> family.
5. I see <u>cattle</u> grazing outside.
6. Be careful not to <u>stumble</u>.
7. We saw a <u>terrible</u> rain storm.
8. Gina observed a <u>beetle</u> and a fly.
9. Grandpa put on the tea <u>kettle</u>.
10. The <u>eagle</u> flew over the river.
11. The <u>royal</u> family wore crowns.
12. The cold can <u>cripple</u> your feet.
13. The nurse is at the <u>hospital</u>.
14. Stealing is not <u>legal</u>.
15. The directions are on the <u>label</u>.
16. A <u>vocal</u> group will sing tonight.
17. I wrote about it in my <u>journal</u>.
18. She won a gold <u>medal</u> in track.
19. I ran in <u>several</u> events for my team.
20. Here is a <u>sample</u> of my artwork.

Have students self-correct their tests.

SPEED SORT

Have partners do a speed sort to see who is fastest. Then have them do a word hunt in this week's readings to find words with consonant + *le* syllables. Have them record the words in their writer's notebook.

BLIND SORT

Have partners do a blind sort: one reads a Spelling Word Card; the other tells under which key word it belongs. Have them switch roles. Then have students use one set of cards to play Word Match. Two cards with the same pattern make a match.

LEARNING GOALS

We can read, sort, and use spelling words with *r*-controlled vowel syllables.

OBJECTIVES

Spell grade-appropriate words correctly, consulting references as needed.

DIFFERENTIATED SPELLING

Go online for the Dictation Sentences for differentiated spelling lists.

On Level and ELL

perform	labor	professor
gentler	peddler	shatter
scissors	error	governor
founder	crater	vapor
director	pillar	equator
danger	splendor	fonder
saucer	margin	

Review terrible, legal, journal
Challenge refrigerator, remainder

Approaching Level

perform	labor	professor
gentler	silver	shatter
doctor	error	governor
margin	crater	vapor
director	pillar	actor
danger	neighbor	slobber
saucer	peddler	

Beyond Level

binocular	laborer	professor
gentler	marvelous	stagger
scissors	dimmer	governor
founder	charter	vapor
director	pillar	equator
remainder	splendor	fonder
semester	peddler	

FORMATIVE ASSESSMENT

STUDENT CHECK-IN

After completing each Practice Book page, have partners share. Ask them to reflect using the Check-In routine.

r-Controlled Vowel Syllables

Assess Prior Knowledge

Read the spelling words aloud, placing emphasis on the *r*-controlled vowel syllable.

Point out the spelling patterns in *labor, crater,* and *perform.* Underline each *r*-controlled vowel sound and model blending each one.

Demonstrate sorting spelling words by *r*-controlled vowel sound. Sort a few words, pointing out the different *r*-controlled vowel spellings as each word is placed.

Use the Dictation Sentences from Lesson 5 to give the pretest. Say the underlined word, read the sentence, and repeat the word. Have students write the words and then check their papers.

See **Practice Book** page 174 for a pretest.

Spiral Review

Review the consonant + *le* syllable patterns in *terrible, legal,* and *journal.* Read each sentence below, repeat the review word, and have students write the word.

1. A terrible storm struck the city.
2. John signed the legal papers.
3. Maxine keeps a journal every day.

Have partners trade papers and check their spellings.

Challenge Words Review this week's *r*-controlled vowel syllable spellings. Read each sentence below, repeat the challenge word, and have students write the word.

1. Put the milk in the refrigerator.
2. Kara ate the remainder of the eggs.

Have students check and correct their spellings and write the words in their writer's notebook.

OPEN SORT

Have students cut apart the **Spelling Word Cards** in the Online Resource Book and initial the back of each card. Have them read the words aloud with partners. Then have partners do an open sort. Have them record their sorts in their writer's notebook.

PATTERN SORT

Complete the pattern sort from Lesson 1. Point out the *r*-controlled vowel syllables. Partners should compare and check their sorts. Alternatively, have partners use **Practice Book** page 175. See Practice Book pages 175A and 175B for differentiated practice.

OPTION LESSON 3 Word Meanings

Have students copy each word below into their writer's notebook. Say each word aloud. Then ask students to write words with the same base word for each one.

1. governor (govern, government)
2. gentler (gentle, gentleness, gentlest)
3. director (direct, direction, directive, indirect)

Challenge students to write words that share the same base word for their other spelling, review, or challenge words. Encourage them to write words that are different parts of speech in their writer's notebook.

See **Practice Book** page 176 or online activity.

OPTION LESSON 4 Proofread and Write

Write these sentences on the board. Have students circle and correct each misspelled word. Have students use a print or a digital dictionary to make corrections.

1. Hot vaper escaped from the cracks in the crator. (vapor, crater)
2. The foundir of the school became its first directer of curriculum. (founder, director)
3. The professer eventually became governer. (professor, governor)
4. George was fondar of that soap because it was gentlur on his skin. (fonder, gentler)

Error Correction Model for students how to segment the word syllable by syllable and spell one syllable at a time. They can use print or electronic resources to help check or correct their spellings.

Apply to Writing Have students correct a piece of their own writing.

See **Practice Book** page 177.

LESSON 5 Assess

Use the Dictation Sentences for the posttest. Have students list the misspelled words in their writer's notebooks. Look for students' use of these words in their writings.

See **Practice Book** page 174 for a pretest. Use page 178 for review.

Dictation Sentences

1. Sugar gives me energy to perform.
2. This soap is gentler on my skin.
3. Jonah used the scissors.
4. I'm the founder of the science club.
5. Mr. Wu is the director.
6. Beware of danger!
7. I placed the cup on the saucer.
8. Mrs. Lopez paid me for my labor.
9. The peddler went door to door.
10. I corrected the spelling error.
11. A meteorite made that crater.
12. The pillar blocked my view.
13. Stars are shining in splendor.
14. Be sure to set the left margin correctly.
15. The professor gave a lecture.
16. That delicate vase could shatter.
17. Who is the governor of our state?
18. A foul vapor filled the air.
19. Water is warmer along the equator.
20. I am fonder of chocolate.

Have students self-correct their tests.

SPEED SORT

Have partners compete in a speed sort to see who is fastest, then compare and discuss their sorts. Then have them do a word hunt in this text set's readings to find words with *r*-controlled vowel syllables. Have them record the words in their writer's notebook.

BLIND SORT

Have partners do a blind sort: one reads a Spelling Word Card; the other tells under which *r*-controlled vowel syllable it belongs. Have students compare and discuss their sorts. Then have students write a reflection of how they sorted the words in their writer's notebook.

From Good to Great

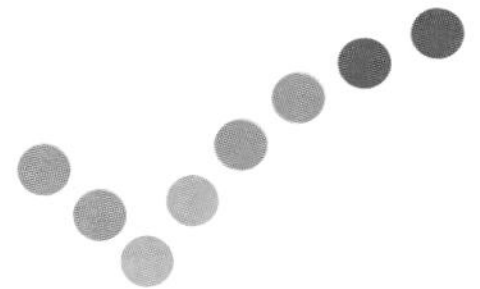

OBJECTIVES

Engage effectively in a range of collaborative discussions (one-on-one, in groups, and teacher-led) with diverse partners on grade 5 topics and texts, building on others' ideas and expressing their own clearly.

Pose and respond to specific questions by making comments that contribute to the discussion and elaborate on the remarks of others.

Review the key ideas expressed and draw conclusions in light of information and knowledge gained from the discussions.

Report on a topic or text or present an opinion, sequencing ideas logically and using appropriate facts and relevant, descriptive details to support main ideas or themes; speak clearly at an understandable pace.

Adapt speech to a variety of contexts and tasks, using formal English when appropriate to task and situation.

Expand, combine, and reduce sentences for meaning, reader/listener interest, and style.

DIGITAL TOOLS

To help students improve their writing, use the Online Grammar Handbook, Digital writing activities, and Writing Center Activity Cards.

PORTFOLIO CHOICE

Ask students to select one finished piece of writing from their writing portfolio. Have them consider a piece that they would like to improve.

Teacher Conference Choose students to conference with, or have them talk with a partner about their writing to figure out one thing that can be improved. As you conference with each student:

- ✓ Identify at least one or two things you like about the writing. *The descriptive details you included in the first paragraph help me visualize _____.*
- ✓ Focus on how the student uses the writing trait. *The supporting details you used help me understand _____.*
- ✓ Make concrete suggestions for revisions.
- ✓ Have students work on their writing and then meet with you to review their progress.

Use the following strategies and tips to provide specific direction to help focus writers.

✓ Purpose, Focus, and Organization

- Read the writing and target one sentence for revision. *Rewrite this sentence to make your claim clearer.*
- Underline a section that needs to be revised. Provide specific suggestions. *The ideas in these sentences are not related to the claim. How can you revise this section to include more relevant evidence to support the claim?*
- Have students reread their writing and think of a stronger way to conclude their essay. *Is the conclusion as strong as it could be? What can you revisit from the essay that will help persuade the reader to agree with your opinion?*
- Ask students to consider the order of their claims. *Can you reorder your claims and reasons for a more logical progression of ideas?*

Have students choose two or three short sentences with related ideas and read them aloud. *Is there a way you can combine these sentences to make one sentence?*

✓ Evidence and Elaboration

- Point out places where evidence could be more relevant to a claim. *Your support for this claim could be more relevant. Reread the sources and find evidence that is more closely related to your claim that _____.*

- Circle a detail that could be stronger. Provide specific suggestions. *You use this detail as an example of ______. Can you think of a better example? Look through the sources again to see if there is a better example, or you can think of a better example from your own experience.*
- If a student misrepresents evidence or a detail from a source, point it out and underline it. *Is this what the source really says? Check the source and compare what it says with what you've written.*
- If the student repeats a detail, say: *The essay already says this. Does this need to be repeated?*
- Read the writing and target one sentence for revision. *This sentence provides evidence, but the essay doesn't name the source the evidence comes from.*

Help students determine relevance. *Why is this evidence relevant or connected to this claim? Why is this evidence not relevant or not connected to this claim?*

✓Conventions

- Underline a run-on sentence. Read it aloud with the student. *This sentence is a run-on sentence because _____. How can you rewrite the sentence so that it's correct?*
- Circle a word that has incorrect capitalization. *Take another look at this word. Did you use the correct capitalization? How can you write this word so that it has the correct capitalization?*
- Read the writing and target a missing or an incorrect comma. *Did you use commas correctly in this sentence? What should you do instead?*

Have students listen as you read their writing. Help them identify run-on sentences. *I hear two sentences here. Where do you think the first sentence ends? What punctuation should there be at the end of a sentence?*

✓ Apply the Rubric

COLLABORATE Have students apply the rubric as they revise their writing. Ask them to read their writing to a partner. Use these sentence starters to focus their discussion:

I like the language because . . .

I think you could make the conclusion stronger by . . .

HABITS OF LEARNING

I write to communicate.

Revising and editing are important steps in the writing process. These steps allow writers to reread and improve their writing to ensure it is clear and focused. Have students ask themselves: *How does revising and editing my work help me communicate effectively?*

Notes

EXTEND, CONNECT, AND ASSESS

Extend

Reading Digitally
Reader's Theater
Level Up with Leveled Readers

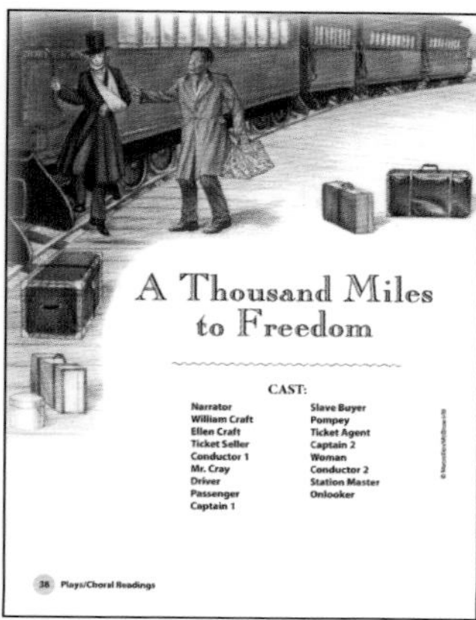

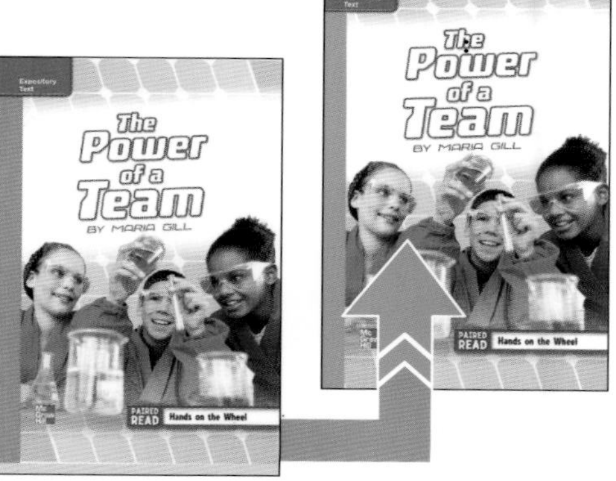

Connect

Connect to Social Studies
Connect to Science
Content Area Reading Options

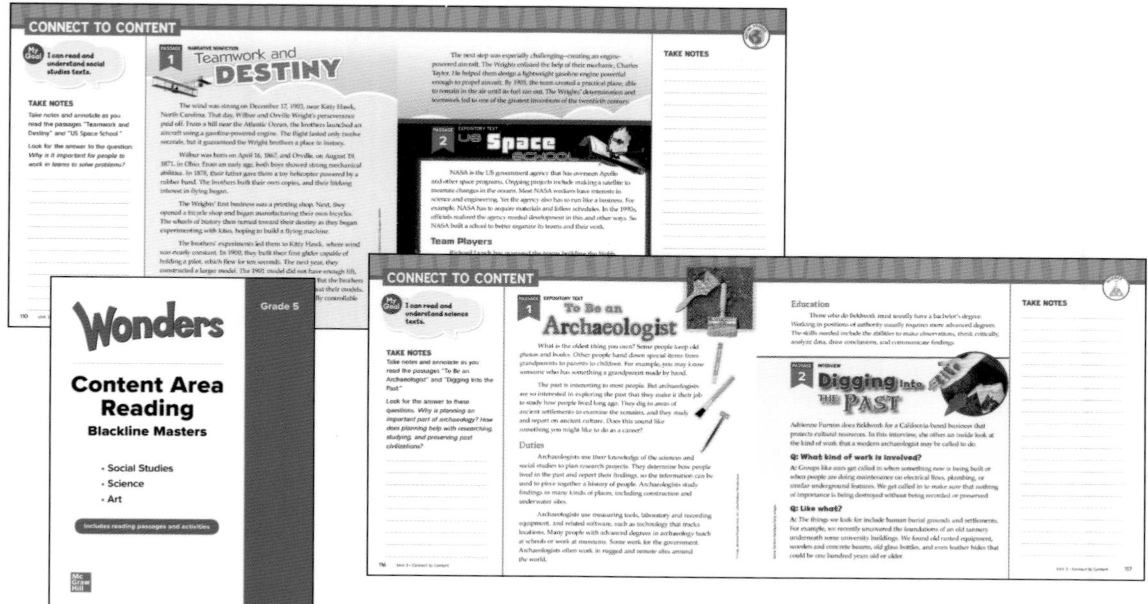

Assess

Reflect on Learning
Unit Assessment
Fluency Assessment

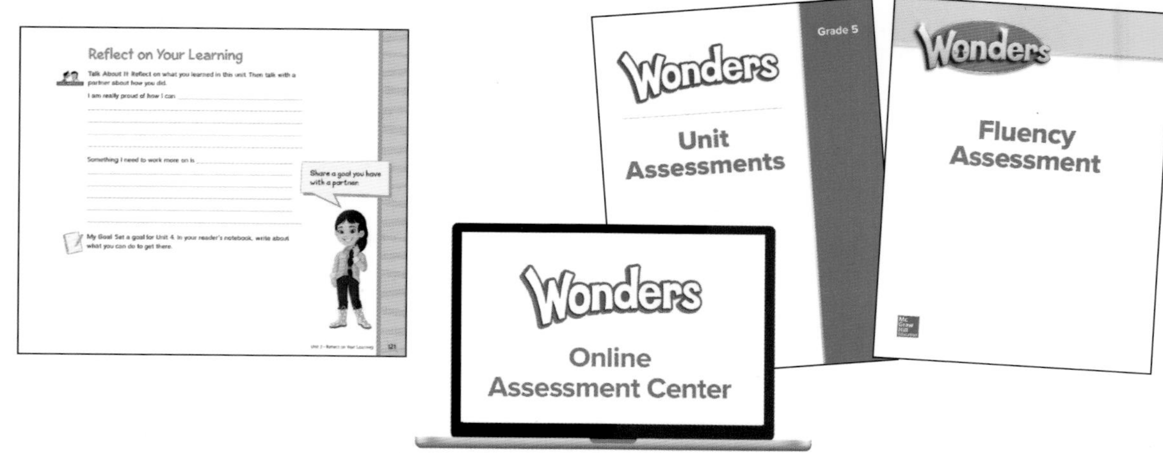

Presentation Options Reader's Theater, Inquiry Space, Writing

Student Outcomes

✓ Tested in *Wonders* Assessments

FOUNDATIONAL SKILLS

Fluency

- Read grade-level texts with accuracy, appropriate rate, expression, and automaticity

READING

Reading Informational Text

✓ Explain how text features contribute to the understanding of a text
✓ Explain how text structures contribute to the overall meaning of texts
✓ Explain how relevant, or key, details support the central, or main, idea(s), implied or explicit
- Read and comprehend texts in the grades 4–5 text complexity band
- Summarize a text to enhance comprehension
- Write in response to texts

Compare Texts

- Compare and contrast how authors present information on the same topic or theme

COMMUNICATION

Writing

Write to Sources

✓ Write an argumentative essay supporting a claim with logical reasons and relevant evidence from sources, while using a variety of sentence structures
- With guidance and support from peers and adults, develop and strengthen writing as needed by planning, revising, and editing

Speaking and Listening

- Report on a topic or text or present an opinion, sequencing ideas; speak clearly at an understandable pace

ELL Scaffolded supports for English Language Learners are embedded throughout the lessons, enabling students to communicate information, ideas, and concepts in English Language Arts and for social and instructional purposes within the school setting.

Researching

- Conduct short research projects that build knowledge through investigation of different aspects of the topic

Creating and Collaborating

- Add audio recordings and visual displays to presentations when apppropriate
- With some guidance and support from adults, use technology to produce and publish writing

VOCABULARY

Academic Vocabulary

- Acquire and use grade-appropriate academic vocabulary

Vocabulary Strategy

✓ Use context clues and/or background knowledge to determine the meaning of multiple-meaning and unknown words and phrases, appropriate to grade level

CONTENT AREA LEARNING

Scientists, Science History, and Community

- Connect grade-level-appropriate science concepts with the history of science, science careers, and contributions of scientists. **Science**

Earth Systems, Patterns, and Interdependence

- Describe how and why, when the environment changes, some animals and plants survive in place and others move or die. **Science**

Discoveries, Innovations, and Community

- Examine how transportation and communication have changed and improved over time. **Social Studies**

Extend, Connect, and Assess

Extend

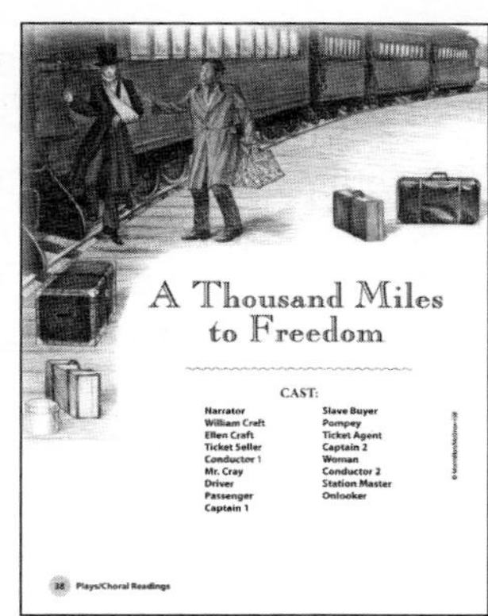

TIME KIDS

Reading Digitally

"Animal Survivors"
Genre: Online Article

Reader's Theater

A Thousand Miles to Freedom
Genre: Play

Connect

Social Studies

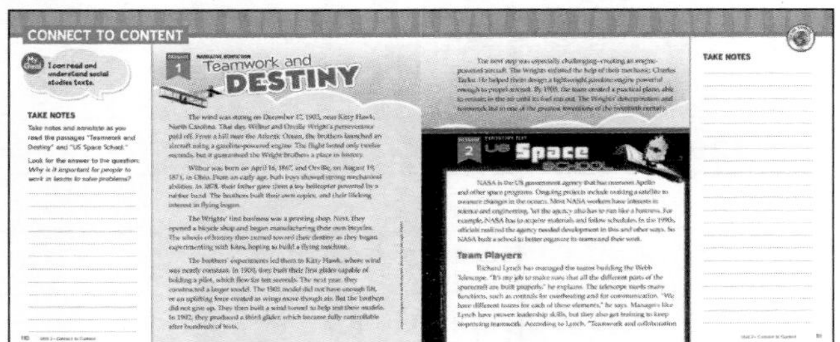

Reading/Writing Companion pp. 110–115

- "Teamwork and Destiny"
- "US Space School"
- Compare the Passages, Share and Reflect, Make a Teamwork Poster

Science

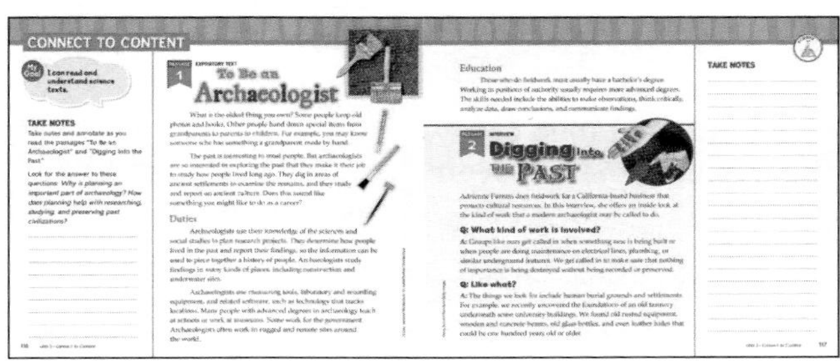

Reading/Writing Companion pp. 116–120

- "To Be an Archaeologist"
- "Digging Into the Past"
- Compare the Passages, Make Observations of Footprints

Assess

Unit Assessments

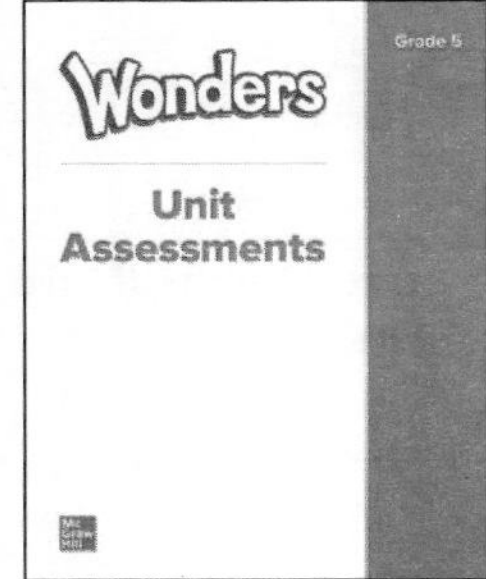

Unit 3 Test

Unit 3 Test Online

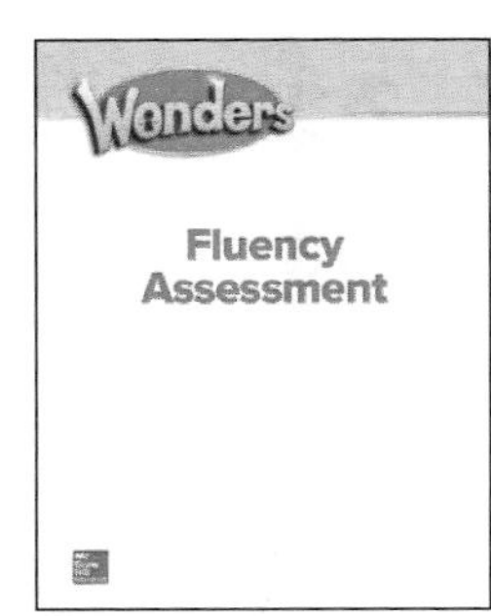

Fluency

EVALUATE STUDENT PROGRESS

Use the *Wonders* online assessment reports to evaluate student progress and help you make decisions about small-group instruction and assignments.

Self-Assess Have students complete Reflect on Your Learning and note any areas where they need improvement.

Planner

Customize your own lesson plans at
my.mheducation.com

Reading
Suggested Daily Time: 60+ mins

READING LESSON GOALS

- **I can read and understand social studies text.**
- **I can read and understand science text.**

SMALL GROUP OPTIONS The designated lessons can be taught in small groups. To determine how to differentiate instruction for small groups, use Formative Assessment and Data Dashboard.

Writing
Suggested Daily Time: 30+ mins

WRITING LESSON GOALS

- **I can write an argumentative essay.**
- **I can synthesize information from three sources.**

	Lesson 1	Lesson 2
Reading	**Reading Digitally, T288–T289** Read "Animal Survivors" TIME KIDS **Reader's Theater, T290–T291** *A Thousand Miles to Freedom* Read the Play and Model Fluency **Connect to Content: Social Studies, T292–T293** Read "Teamwork and Destiny," "US Space School"	**Reading Digitally, T288–T289** Reread "Animal Survivors" TIME KIDS **Reader's Theater, T290–T291** *A Thousand Miles to Freedom* Assign Roles and Practice the Play **Connect to Content: Social Studies, T294–T295** Compare the Passages, Share and Reflect, Make a Teamwork Poster
Writing	**Extended Writing 2: Argumentative Essay, T250–T251** Analyze the Prompt	**Extended Writing 2: Argumentative Essay, T252–T253** Analyze the Sources
	Writing Lesson Bank: Craft Minilessons, T262–T263	
	Teacher and Peer Conferences	

SMALL GROUP

Teacher-Led Instruction

Level Up with Leveled Readers
Approaching Level to On Level, T308
The Power of a Team

Level Up with Leveled Readers
On Level to Beyond Level, T309
The Power of a Team

Level Up with Leveled Readers
ELL Level to On Level, T310
The Power of a Team

Independent/Collaborative Work

Reading

Comprehension
- Book Talk

Fluency
- Reader's Theater

Independent Reading

Reader's Theater Card 39

Book Talk Card 42

Writing

Extended Writing 2: Argumentative Essay

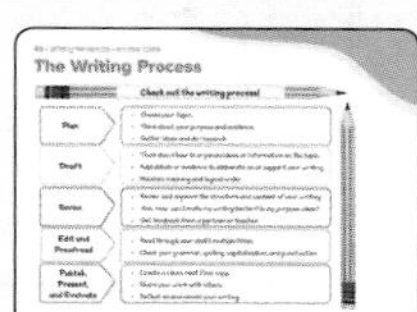
Writing Process Card 43

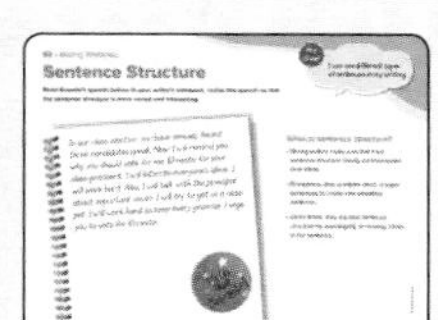
Sentence Structure Card 60

Get Ready for Assessment

Before administering the unit assessment, identify any gaps in students' understanding using the Data Dashboard. Use resources from the unit or your own resources to differentiate Small Group Teacher-Led Instruction and to provide Independent/Collaborative Work options.

Reading		
Reader's Theater, T290–T291 *A Thousand Miles to Freedom* Practice the Play and Extend **Connect to Content: Science, T296–T297** Read "To Be an Archaeologist," "Digging Into the Past"	**Reader's Theater, T290–T291** *A Thousand Miles to Freedom* Perform and Reread the Play **Connect to Content: Science, T298–T299** Compare the Passages, Make Observations of Footprints	**Unit Wrap Up, T300–T301** Make Connections Reflect on Your Learning **Presentation Options, T302–T307** Speaking and Listening Publish and Present Inquiry Space Present Writing **Summative Assessment and Next Steps, T312–T314**
Writing		
Extended Writing 2: Argumentative Essay, T254–T255 Plan	**Extended Writing 2: Argumentative Essay, T256–T257** Draft	**Extended Writing 2: Argumentative Essay, T258–T259** Revise: Peer Conferences
Writing Lesson Bank: Craft Minilessons, T262–T263		
Teacher and Peer Conferences		

Level Up with Leveled Readers
Beyond Level to Self-Selected Trade Book, T311
The Power of a Team

Level Up Writing
From Good to Great, T284–T285
- Purpose, Focus, and Organization
- Evidence and Elaboration
- Conventions
- Apply the Rubric

English Language Learners
See ELL Small Group Guide, pp. 136–137

Content Area Connections

Content Area Reading
- Science, Social Studies, and the Arts

Inquiry Space
- Options for Project-Based Learning

LEARNING GOALS

We can use interactive features to read an online text.

OBJECTIVES

Draw on information from multiple print or digital sources, demonstrating the ability to locate an answer to a question quickly or to solve a problem efficiently.

Integrate information from several texts on the same topic in order to write or speak about the subject knowledgeably.

Review the key ideas expressed and draw conclusions in light of information and knowledge gained from the discussions.

Describe how and why, when the environment changes, some plants and animals survive in place and others move or die.

ELA ACADEMIC LANGUAGE

- *interactive, features, elements*
- Cognate: *elementos*

DIFFERENTIATED READING

Approaching Level and **ELL** Read the text with students. Have partners work together to complete the graphic organizers and summarize the text orally.

On Level and **Beyond Level** Have students read the text and access the interactive features independently. Complete the Reread activities during Small Group time.

TIME for KIDS

Animal Survivors

Before Reading

Introduce the Genre Discuss the features of an online article. Scroll through "Animal Survivors" at my.mheducation.com. Clarify how to navigate the article. Point out the interactive features, such as **hyperlinks, pop-up windows,** and **slideshows**.

Close Reading Online

Read

Take Notes Scroll back to the top. As you read the article aloud, ask questions to focus students on how humans are helping endangered animals. Have them take notes on the central idea and relevant details using **Graphic Organizer 7**. After each section, have partners paraphrase the central ideas, giving text evidence. Make sure students understand domain-specific terms, such as *endangered, habitat,* and *conservation*.

Access Interactive Features Help students access the interactive features. Discuss what information these elements add to the text.

Summarize Review students' graphic organizers. Model using the information to summarize "Animal Survivors." Ask students to write a summary of the article, stating the problem and the actions people took to solve it. Partners should discuss their summaries.

Reread

Craft and Structure Have students reread parts of the article, paying attention to text structure and author's craft. Discuss these questions.

- What text structure does the author use to organize the information?
- For what purpose did the author add the hyperlink?

Author's Perspective Tell students they will now reread to help them support this statement: *According to the author, some animal species would not be here today if not for the work of Jane Goodall and other dedicated people.* Have students skim the text and cite evidence the author uses to support this idea. Have partners share findings and discuss whether they agree with the author's perspective, or point of view.

Integrate

Make Connections

Text Connections Have students discuss the types of experiences that can lead to discoveries such as cultural exchanges, teamwork, and looking at the past. Then have them compare the discoveries they have read about in this unit.

Research Online

Navigate Links to Information Point out that online texts may include **hyperlinks**, colored or underlined text on a Web page that connects to another Web page with related information. Model using a hyperlink to jump to another Web page. Discuss information on the new Web page related to the question *What can people do to help endangered animals?* Remind students to verify information they find online by using at least one other source.

Finding Relevant Information Point out that Web sites may contain information that is irrelevant to their research. Ask a student for a question related to endangered animals. Work with students to navigate to a Web site and point out how it answers the question. Encourage students to scan the site and identify the relevant and irrelevant details.

Paraphrasing Remind students that paraphrasing means using their own words to retell information. Using the Web site that you found above, have students practice paraphrasing important details.

Inspire Action

Saving Endangered Animals Have students research and write about the following question: *How do humans endanger animals?* Encourage students to take notes and make an outline of their main idea and ideas or facts that support it. For example:

- Chimpanzees have been endangered due to hunting and loss of habitat.
- Condors have been poisoned by lead.

As students write, remind them to cite sources used and to end with a strong conclusion. You may also have groups discuss, to spark ideas.

Independent Study

Choose a Topic Students should brainstorm questions related to the article. They might ask: *What can I do to help endangered animals?* Then have students choose a question to research. Help them narrow their question.

Conduct Internet Research Review how to find relevant information by scanning a source and trying to answer a question. Encourage students to ignore irrelevant information and paraphrase information they find.

Present Have groups share what they learned about how they can help endangered animals.

ELL ENGLISH LANGUAGE LEARNERS

Author's Perspective Read the question with students and elicit the information they need to answer. As needed, help students confirm the meanings of challenging sentences in the paragraphs or subtitles. For example: *What clue in the next sentence helps explain the meaning of* on the road? (travels around the world) Jane Goodall travels 300 days a year.

READERS TO WRITERS

Encourage students to think about how they might use interactive features, such as hyperlinks to other relevant Web pages, in their own writing. Students should first make sure any interactive features they include are relevant to their topic.

FORMATIVE ASSESSMENT

STUDENT CHECK-IN

Have partners share something they learned using an online interactive feature. Then have them reflect using the Check-In routine.

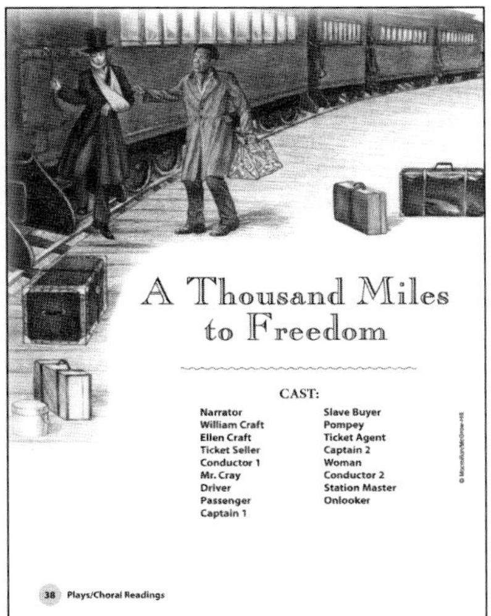

We can read fluently to perform a play.

OBJECTIVES

By the end of the year, read and comprehend literature, including stories, dramas, and poetry, at the high end of the grades 4–5 text complexity band independently and proficiently.

Read grade-level text with purpose and understanding.

Read grade-level prose and poetry orally with accuracy, appropriate rate, expression, and automaticity on successive readings.

Use context to confirm or self-correct word recognition and understanding, rereading as necessary.

TEACH IN SMALL GROUP

You may wish to teach the Reader's Theater lesson during Small Group time and then have groups present their work to the class.

A Thousand Miles to Freedom

Introduce the Genre

Explain that *A Thousand Miles to Freedom* is a play set in 1848 about a real-life couple, Ellen and William Craft, who escaped from slavery. It shows the dangers many enslaved people faced on the road to freedom. Distribute the Elements of Drama handout and scripts from the **Reader's Theater** pages 2–3, 14–31.

- Review the features of a play.
- Review the cast of characters and setting. Explain that, prior to the Civil War, slavery was legal in the South. Before it was abolished in 1865, many enslaved people risked their lives to escape to freedom in the North.
- Point out that the narrator's lines replace most stage directions.

Read the Play and Model Fluency

Model reading the play as students follow along in their scripts. As you read each part, state the name of the character and read the part, emphasizing the appropriate phrasing and expression, or prosody.

Focus on Vocabulary Stop and discuss any vocabulary words that students may not know. You may wish to teach:

- foliage
- steamer
- fidelity
- perilous
- bondage

Monitor Comprehension As you read, check that students are understanding the characters, setting, and plot.

- After reading the narrator's part, have students identify information the role gives.
- After reading each character part, ask partners to note the character's traits. Model how to find text evidence that tells them about the characters.

Assign Roles

You may wish to split the class into two groups. If you need additional roles, you can assign the parts of the narrator, William, and Ellen to two students.

Practice the Play

Allow students time to practice their parts. Pair fluent readers with less fluent readers. Pairs can echo read or chorally read their parts. Work with less fluent readers to mark pauses in their scripts using one slash for a short pause and two slashes for longer pauses. Throughout the week, have students work on **Reader's Theater Center Activity Card 39**.

Once students have practiced reading their parts several times, allow students time to practice performing the script. Remind them that nonverbal communication is an important part of portraying a character and provide examples.

Act It Out

A Thousand Miles to Freedom is a suspenseful play. Assign each student a character in the play and have them perform one of the character's scenes. Ask students to think about what happens in the scene and how their character might feel and react as a result. Students should consider their character's physical traits, personality, and situation. Have students change their volume and tone of voice and use gestures to convey their character's emotions to the audience.

Perform the Reader's Theater

- At the end of the week, have students perform the play in small groups or for the whole class.
- As a class, discuss how performing a play aloud is different from reading it silently. Have partners discuss what they liked about performing the play and what they found difficult. Have students interpret both the verbal and nonverbal messages they saw during the play.
- Lead a class discussion about ways that groups could make their performances more enjoyable for the audience. Consider how props, costumes, and scenery can add to a performance. Encourage students to make personal and emotional connections to the story and its characters.

Reread the Play

A lot can happen during a journey of a thousand miles. The Crafts experience many suspenseful moments along the way. Reread *A Thousand Miles to Freedom.* Then discuss these questions.

1. Why do the Crafts decide to run away? What is their plan?
2. Name each stop on the route from Macon to Philadelphia.
3. Describe one unforeseen obstacle the Crafts face. How do they overcome it?
4. Name one character who helps William and Ellen. What does he or she do to help?
5. What do we learn about the Crafts from the narrator's lines at the end of the play?

ELL ENGLISH LANGUAGE LEARNERS

Review the features of a play with Beginning students: characters, setting, dialogue, stage directions. As students practice their parts, have them ask questions about the play to clarify meaning, for example, *What does it mean when the character says ___?* Have them read aloud the lines for their roles and record them. With each student, listen to the recording as the student silently reads along his or her part in the play.

FORMATIVE ASSESSMENT

STUDENT CHECK IN

Have partners reflect on how fluently they read their lines.

"Teamwork and Destiny"
"US Space School"

LEARNING GOALS

We can apply skills and strategies to understand social studies texts.

OBJECTIVES

Quote accurately from a text when explaining what the text says explicitly and when drawing inferences from the text. Identify the author's purpose.

Determine two or more central, or main, ideas of a text and explain how they are supported by relevant, or key, details; summarize the text.

Compare and contrast the overall structure (e.g., chronology, comparison, cause/effect, problem/solution) of events, ideas, concepts, or information in two or more texts.

Draw on information from multiple print or digital sources, demonstrating the ability to locate an answer to a question quickly or to solve a problem efficiently.

 Examine how transportation and communication have changed and improved over time.

CONNECT TO CONTENT

My Goal: I can read and understand social studies texts.

TAKE NOTES

Take notes and annotate as you read the passages "Teamwork and Destiny" and "US Space School."

Look for the answer to the question: *Why is it important for people to work in teams to solve problems?*

PASSAGE 1 NARRATIVE NONFICTION

Teamwork and DESTINY

The wind was strong on December 17, 1903, near Kitty Hawk, North Carolina. That day, Wilbur and Orville Wright's perseverance paid off. From a hill near the Atlantic Ocean, the brothers launched an aircraft using a gasoline-powered engine. The flight lasted only twelve seconds, but it guaranteed the Wright brothers a place in history.

Wilbur was born on April 16, 1867, and Orville, on August 19, 1871, in Ohio. From an early age, both boys showed strong mechanical abilities. In 1878, their father gave them a toy helicopter powered by a rubber band. The brothers built their own copies, and their lifelong interest in flying began.

The Wrights' first business was a printing shop. Next, they opened a bicycle shop and began manufacturing their own bicycles. The wheels of history then turned toward their destiny as they began experimenting with kites, hoping to build a flying machine.

The brothers' experiments led them to Kitty Hawk, where wind was nearly constant. In 1900, they built their first glider capable of holding a pilot, which flew for ten seconds. The next year, they constructed a larger model. The 1901 model did not have enough lift, or an uplifting force created as wings move though air. But the brothers did not give up. They then built a wind tunnel to help test their models. In 1902, they produced a third glider, which became fully controllable after hundreds of tests.

110 Unit 3 • Connect to Content

Reading/Writing Companion, p. 110

Take Notes Tell students they will be reading two passages about how people solve problems. The passages will help them build knowledge about topics introduced earlier. Explain that they will read using the Close Reading Routine. Remind them to annotate the text, making notes in the side columns.

For students who need more support, use the Read prompts to help them understand the text and the Reread prompts to analyze the text, craft, and structure of each passage.

Read

Ask and Answer Questions DOK 1

Why did the Wright brothers build a wind tunnel? (They built a wind tunnel so they could test their gliders.)

Reread

Author's Craft: Figurative Language DOK 2

What does the author mean by the metaphor "the wheels of history" on page 110? (The author means time passing and events happening.)

Access Complex Text

Specific Vocabulary

"Teamwork and Destiny" includes specialized vocabulary. Review strategies for finding the meaning of unfamiliar words, such as using context clues. Point out the words *perseverance,*

FORMATIVE ASSESSMENT

STUDENT CHECK-IN

Have partners share important ideas from each text about advancements in air and space travel. Then have them reflect using the Check-In routine.

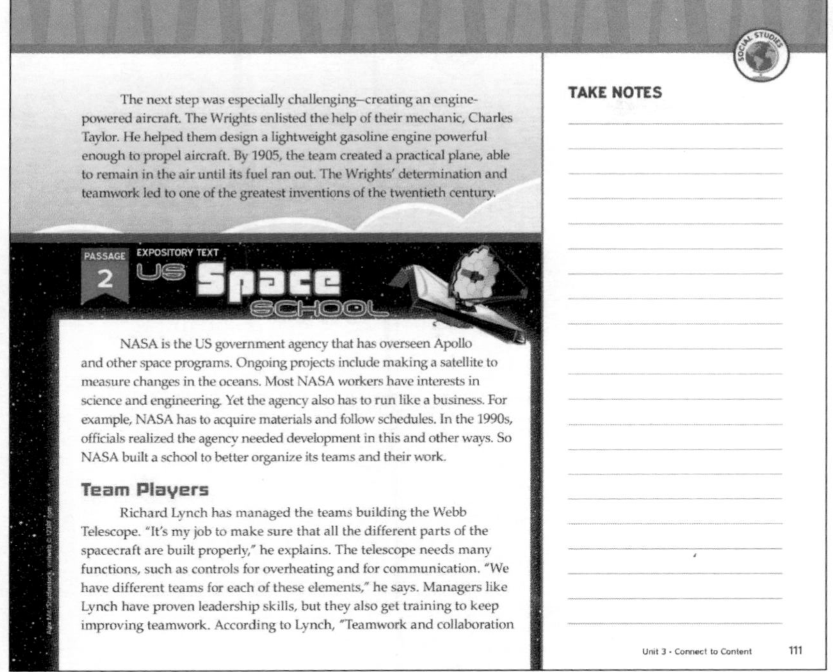
The next step was especially challenging—creating an engine-powered aircraft. The Wrights enlisted the help of their mechanic, Charles Taylor. He helped them design a lightweight gasoline engine powerful enough to propel aircraft. By 1905, the team created a practical plane, able to remain in the air until its fuel ran out. The Wrights' determination and teamwork led to one of the greatest inventions of the twentieth century.

TAKE NOTES

PASSAGE 2 EXPOSITORY TEXT

US Space School

NASA is the US government agency that has overseen Apollo and other space programs. Ongoing projects include making a satellite to measure changes in the oceans. Most NASA workers have interests in science and engineering. Yet the agency also has to run like a business. For example, NASA has to acquire materials and follow schedules. In the 1990s, officials realized the agency needed development in this and other ways. So NASA built a school to better organize its teams and their work.

Team Players

Richard Lynch has managed the teams building the Webb Telescope. "It's my job to make sure that all the different parts of the spacecraft are built properly," he explains. The telescope needs many functions, such as controls for overheating and for communication. "We have different teams for each of these elements," he says. Managers like Lynch have proven leadership skills, but they also get training to keep improving teamwork. According to Lynch, "Teamwork and collaboration

Unit 3 • Connect to Content 111

Reading/Writing Companion, p. 111

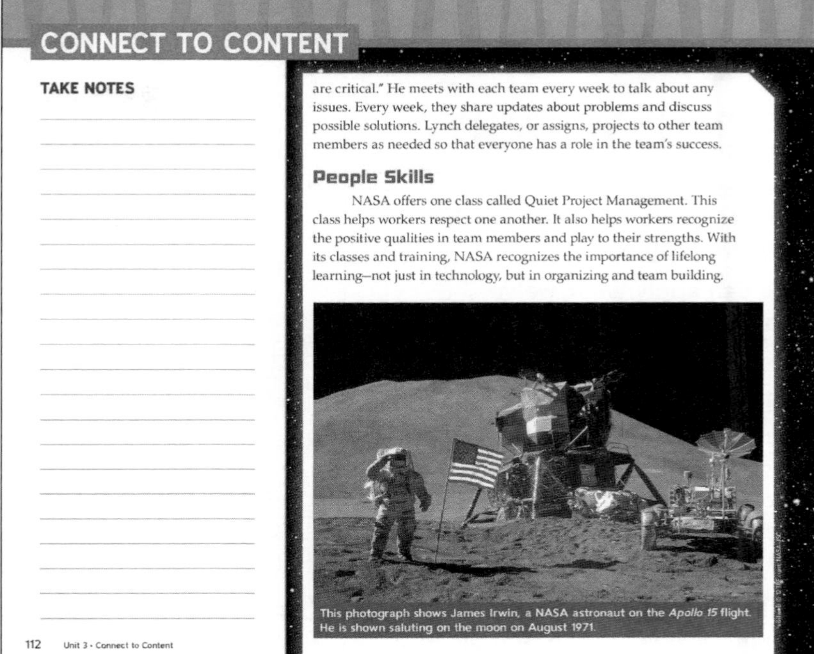
CONNECT TO CONTENT

TAKE NOTES

are critical." He meets with each team every week to talk about any issues. Every week, they share updates about problems and discuss possible solutions. Lynch delegates, or assigns, projects to other team members as needed so that everyone has a role in the team's success.

People Skills

NASA offers one class called Quiet Project Management. This class helps workers respect one another. It also helps workers recognize the positive qualities in team members and play to their strengths. With its classes and training, NASA recognizes the importance of lifelong learning—not just in technology, but in organizing and team building.

This photograph shows James Irwin, a NASA astronaut on the *Apollo 15* flight. He is shown saluting on the moon on August 1971.

112 Unit 3 • Connect to Content

Reading/Writing Companion, p. 112

Read

Central Idea and Relevant Details DOK 2

How did Charles Taylor help the Wright brothers? (He built a lightweight but powerful engine for their glider.)

Read

Author's Perspective DOK 2

What is the author's perspective, or point of view, on the way people like Richard Lynch work with others at NASA? (The author respects the way Richard Lynch and many other people at NASA work together as a team.)

Reread

Author's Purpose DOK 2

What is the author's purpose in writing "US Space School"? (The author's purpose is to show the importance of teamwork and team building for workers at NASA and other places.)

manufacturing, glider, wind tunnel, and *propel.* Help students use strategies to define each word.

- *What is another word for* manufacturing*?* *(making)*
- *What propels an aircraft?* (an engine)

ELL ENGLISH LANGUAGE LEARNERS

"Teamwork and Destiny"
Preteach vocabulary: *destiny, mechanical, model, capable, practical, determination* (Cognates: *destino, mecánico, modelo, capaz, práctico, determinación*). Then guide students to find key details: *What were the Wright brothers' first businesses?* (printing and making bicycles) *What did they do experiments with?* (kites and gliders) *What was the brothers' great invention?* (the airplane)

"US Space School"
Preteach vocabulary: *satellite, collaboration, critical* (Cognates: *satélite, colaboración, crítico*). Then guide students to find key details: *How does Richard Lynch help his teams succeed?* (He meets with them to discuss issues each week and assigns projects to team members.) *How does the Quiet Project Management class help NASA workers?* (It helps workers respect team members, recognize positive qualities, and work with their strengths.)

LEARNING GOALS

- **We can compare two texts about people working together to solve problems.**
- **We can apply what we've learned to make a poster.**

OBJECTIVES

Analyze multiple accounts of the same event or topic, noting important similarities and differences in the point of view they represent.

Explain an author's perspective, or point of view, toward a topic in an informational text.

Draw on information from multiple print or digital sources, demonstrating the ability to locate an answer to a question quickly or to solve a problem efficiently.

Integrate information from several texts on the same topic in order to write or speak about the subject knowledgeably.

Summarize a written text read aloud or information presented in diverse media and formats, including visually, quantitatively, and orally.

ELA ACADEMIC LANGUAGE

- *compare, effectively, reflection*
- Cognates: *comparar, beneficio, reflexión*

FORMATIVE ASSESSMENT

STUDENT CHECK-IN

Compare Have partners share their Venn Diagrams and responses on Reading/Writing Companion page 113.

Make a Teamwork Poster Have partners share their posters.

Ask students to use the Check-In routine to reflect and fill in the bars.

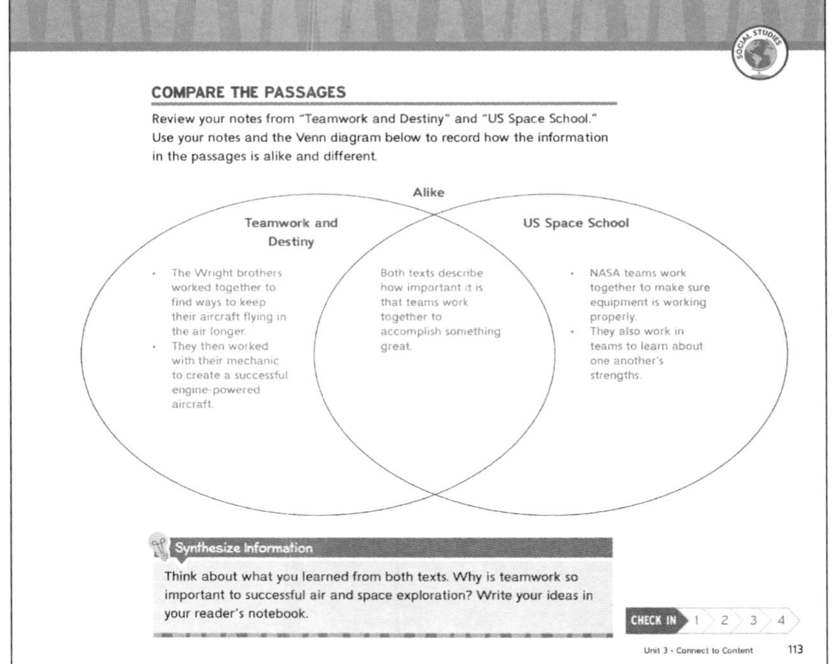

COMPARE THE PASSAGES

Review your notes from "Teamwork and Destiny" and "US Space School." Use your notes and the Venn diagram below to record how the information in the passages is alike and different.

Alike

Teamwork and Destiny
- The Wright brothers worked together to find ways to keep their aircraft flying in the air longer.
- They then worked with their mechanic to create a successful engine-powered aircraft.

Both texts describe how important it is that teams work together to accomplish something great.

US Space School
- NASA teams work together to make sure equipment is working properly.
- They also work in teams to learn about one another's strengths.

Synthesize Information

Think about what you learned from both texts. Why is teamwork so important to successful air and space exploration? Write your ideas in your reader's notebook.

CHECK IN 1 2 3 4

Unit 3 · Connect to Content 113

Reading/Writing Companion, p. 113

Compare the Passages

Explain Remind students that one of the passages they read is narrative nonfiction and the other is expository text, but both give information about how people work together to solve problems. Tell students they will complete a Venn diagram to show how the two passages are alike and different.

Talk About It Have students work in small groups or with a partner to talk about the two texts and their similarities and differences. Have them review the characteristics of each genre. Partners or group members should share ideas with one another about the different ways each text presents information about how people work together to solve problems.

Apply Have students use the notes they made on **Reading/Writing Companion** pages 110–112 and their Talk About It discussion to complete the Venn diagram and answer the Synthesize Information question on page 113.

Synthesize Information — DOK 3

Explain Remind students that when they tell how the passages are alike they are synthesizing information. Students can use the middle of the Venn diagram to understand how information from both passages tells how people work together to solve problems.

Model Point out the last paragraph of "Teamwork and Destiny" on page 111. Then have students reread the "People Skills" section of "US Space School" on page 112. Both paragraphs explain why teamwork is important.

Apply Have students cite evidence from both passages that helps them understand the benefits of working together. They can record their evidence in the center of the Venn diagram.

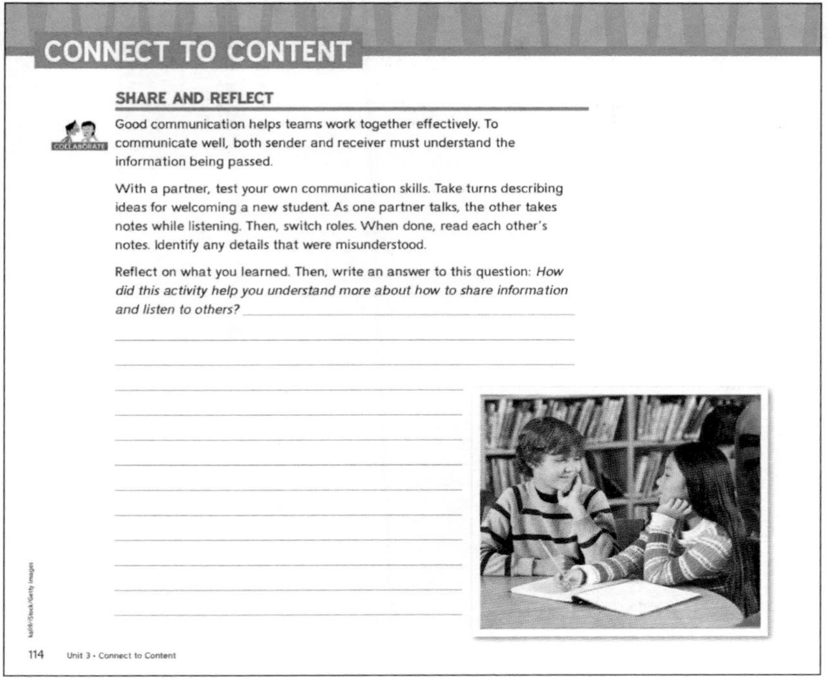
CONNECT TO CONTENT

SHARE AND REFLECT

Good communication helps teams work together effectively. To communicate well, both sender and receiver must understand the information being passed.

With a partner, test your own communication skills. Take turns describing ideas for welcoming a new student. As one partner talks, the other takes notes while listening. Then, switch roles. When done, read each other's notes. Identify any details that were misunderstood.

Reflect on what you learned. Then, write an answer to this question: *How did this activity help you understand more about how to share information and listen to others?*

114 Unit 3 • Connect to Content

Reading/Writing Companion, p. 114

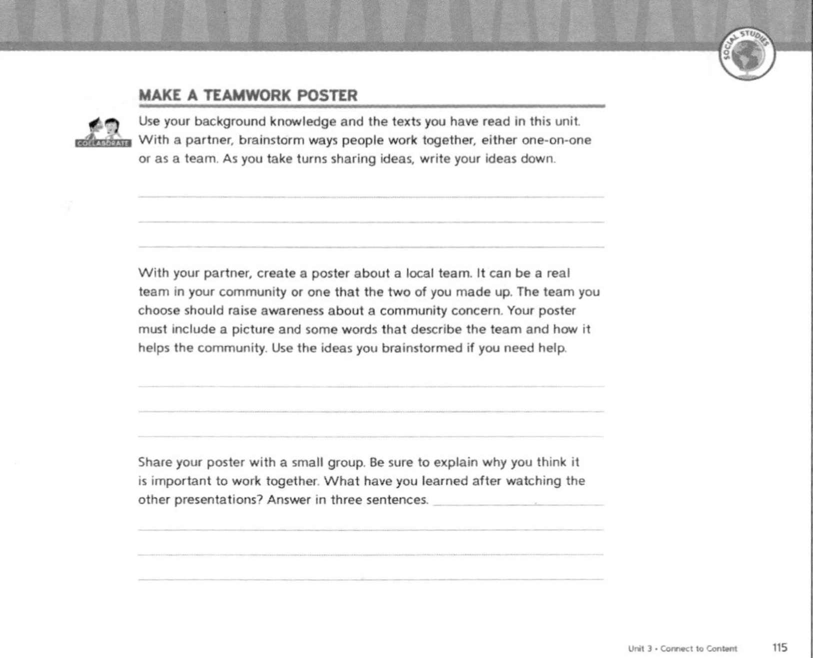
MAKE A TEAMWORK POSTER

Use your background knowledge and the texts you have read in this unit. With a partner, brainstorm ways people work together, either one-on-one or as a team. As you take turns sharing ideas, write your ideas down.

With your partner, create a poster about a local team. It can be a real team in your community or one that the two of you made up. The team you choose should raise awareness about a community concern. Your poster must include a picture and some words that describe the team and how it helps the community. Use the ideas you brainstormed if you need help.

Share your poster with a small group. Be sure to explain why you think it is important to work together. What have you learned after watching the other presentations? Answer in three sentences.

Unit 3 • Connect to Content 115

Reading/Writing Companion, p. 115

Share and Reflect

Explain and Model Explain to students that they will be testing their communication skills by sharing ideas and listening to a partner. The topic of their conversation will be welcoming a new student.

COLLABORATE **Talk About It** Have partners review and discuss their understanding of the directions for the activity on **Reading/Writing Companion** page 114. Have them predict how accurately they can communicate and record ideas.

Apply Have partners take turns sharing their ideas and recording their partner's ideas. Then have them complete the reflection on page 114 to analyze how they share information and listen to others.

Make a Teamwork Poster

Explain Tell students that they will be working with a partner to create a poster about a team that works in your community. Their poster should include both written and visual information about the team.

COLLABORATE **Guided Practice** Have students work in pairs to brainstorm ways people work together. They may wish to use the passages for inspiration. Have students record their ideas on page 115. Circulate and provide help as needed.

Analytical Writing **Apply** Have partners make their poster together, using the ideas they brainstormed. Then have them present their poster to a small group and explain why it is important to work together.

ELL ENGLISH LANGUAGE LEARNERS

Synthesize Information
Provide sentence frames for students to share text evidence they used to synthesize information. In "Teamwork and Destiny," we read about how the Wright brothers Wilbur and Orville worked together. First, they made a glider. Their mechanic Charles Taylor helped the team with the engine for the first airplane. In "US Space School," we read about manager Richard Lynch and his teams. We also learned how Quiet Project Management helps NASA workers learn to respect and work better with teammates.

Make a Teamwork Poster, Apply
Discuss strategies to help students work together making their posters. Suggest that students politely ask for clarification. For example, guide students to clarify by saying, *Please repeat that. Could you explain again? I think you said . . . Is that right?*

"To Be an Archaeologist"
"Digging Into the Past"

LEARNING GOALS

We can apply skills and strategies to understand science texts.

OBJECTIVES

Determine two or more central, or main, ideas of a text and explain how they are supported by relevant, or key, details; summarize the text.

Draw on information from multiple print or digital sources, demonstrating the ability to locate an answer to a question quickly or to solve a problem efficiently.

Summarize a written text read aloud or information presented in diverse media and formats, including visually, quantitatively, and orally.

Connect grade-level-appropriate science concepts with the history of science, science careers, and contributions of scientists.

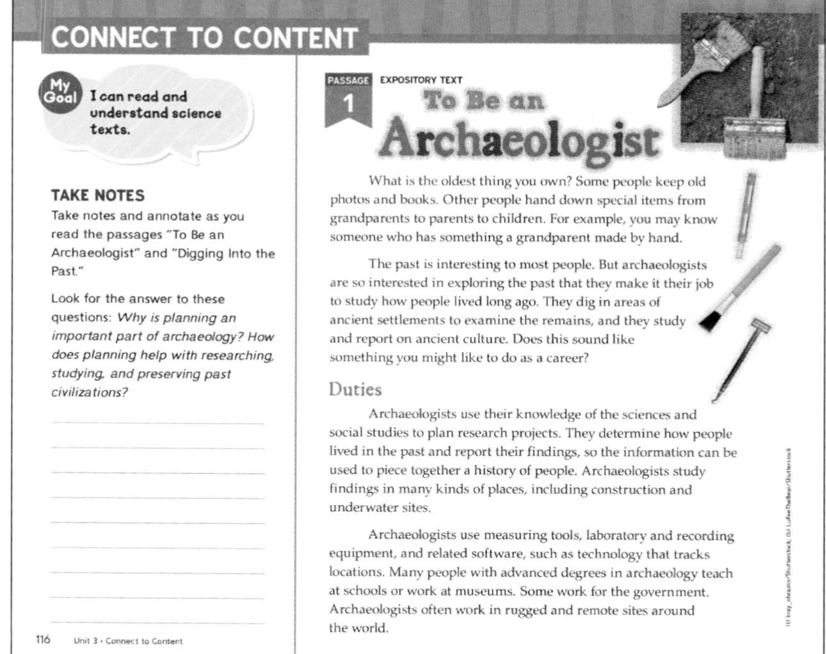

CONNECT TO CONTENT

My Goal I can read and understand science texts.

TAKE NOTES

Take notes and annotate as you read the passages "To Be an Archaeologist" and "Digging Into the Past."

Look for the answer to these questions: *Why is planning an important part of archaeology? How does planning help with researching, studying, and preserving past civilizations?*

116 Unit 3 • Connect to Content

PASSAGE 1 EXPOSITORY TEXT

To Be an Archaeologist

What is the oldest thing you own? Some people keep old photos and books. Other people hand down special items from grandparents to parents to children. For example, you may know someone who has something a grandparent made by hand.

The past is interesting to most people. But archaeologists are so interested in exploring the past that they make it their job to study how people lived long ago. They dig in areas of ancient settlements to examine the remains, and they study and report on ancient culture. Does this sound like something you might like to do as a career?

Duties

Archaeologists use their knowledge of the sciences and social studies to plan research projects. They determine how people lived in the past and report their findings, so the information can be used to piece together a history of people. Archaeologists study findings in many kinds of places, including construction and underwater sites.

Archaeologists use measuring tools, laboratory and recording equipment, and related software, such as technology that tracks locations. Many people with advanced degrees in archaeology teach at schools or work at museums. Some work for the government. Archaeologists often work in rugged and remote sites around the world.

Reading/Writing Companion, p. 116

Take Notes Tell students they will be reading two passages that tell about exploring our past. Explain that they will read independently using the Close Reading Routine. Remind them to annotate the text as they read and use the side columns for notes.

For students who need more support, use the Read prompts to help them understand the text and the Reread prompts to analyze the text, craft, and structure of each passage.

Read

Central Idea and Relevant Details DOK 2

What do all the details in the "Duties" section on page 116 have in common? (They all describe the work that archaeologists do.)

Reread

Genre: Expository Text DOK 1

What expository text features does the author include in "To Be an Archaeologist"? (The author includes headings that tell what each section is about.)

ACT Access Complex Text

Specific Vocabulary

"To Be an Archaeologist" and "Digging Into the Past" both include domain-specific vocabulary that students may not know. Review strategies for finding the meaning of unfamiliar words, such as using context clues, word parts, or a dictionary.

FORMATIVE ASSESSMENT

STUDENT CHECK-IN

Have partners share important ideas from each text about studying the past. Then have them reflect using the Check-In routine.

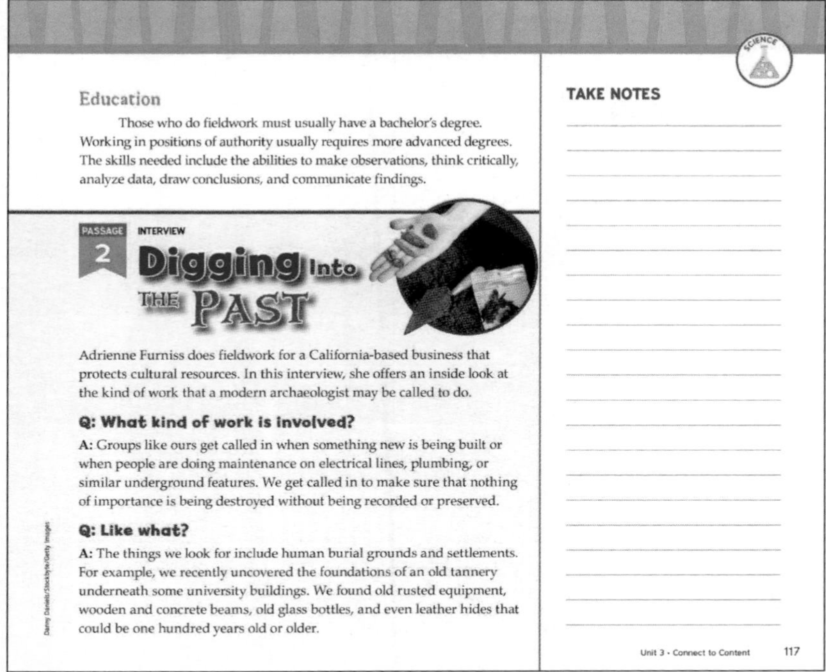

Education

Those who do fieldwork must usually have a bachelor's degree. Working in positions of authority usually requires more advanced degrees. The skills needed include the abilities to make observations, think critically, analyze data, draw conclusions, and communicate findings.

PASSAGE 2 INTERVIEW

Digging Into THE PAST

Adrienne Furniss does fieldwork for a California-based business that protects cultural resources. In this interview, she offers an inside look at the kind of work that a modern archaeologist may be called to do.

Q: What kind of work is involved?

A: Groups like ours get called in when something new is being built or when people are doing maintenance on electrical lines, plumbing, or similar underground features. We get called in to make sure that nothing of importance is being destroyed without being recorded or preserved.

Q: Like what?

A: The things we look for include human burial grounds and settlements. For example, we recently uncovered the foundations of an old tannery underneath some university buildings. We found old rusted equipment, wooden and concrete beams, old glass bottles, and even leather hides that could be one hundred years old or older.

TAKE NOTES

Unit 3 • Connect to Content 117

Reading/Writing Companion, p. 117

CONNECT TO CONTENT

TAKE NOTES

Q: What are the challenges?

A: The work is very hard physically. You have to be able to carry buckets of soil that can weigh up to 60 pounds. You help move large amounts of equipment. We use all kinds of digging tools to remove soil from sites, so our arms can get tired.

We also have to use our minds. For example, we study the smallest differences in soil color and composition. These differences can be clues that something was once there, and the clues can help us plan the best steps to take.

Q: What do you like about the work?

A: History stops being abstract. It's not just read about in a book.

I love using my own two hands to help make discoveries that have been lost to time. You are connecting with the past, touching things that people used on a daily basis. It's almost like having a time machine.

118 Unit 3 • Connect to Content

Reading/Writing Companion, p. 118

Read

Central Idea and Relevant Details DOK 2

What details in "Digging Into the Past" support the idea that being an archaeologist is hard work? (You have to move a lot and carry heavy soil and equipment. You have to use your mind to study tiny differences.)

Read

Summarize DOK 2

Summarize why Adrienne Furniss likes archaeology. (It allows her to connect with the past in a way that uses her senses, especially the sense of touch.)

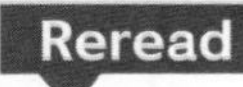

Reread

Genre: Interview DOK 1

How does the author show that "Digging Into the Past" is an interview? (The author includes questions labeled *Q* and answers from Adrienne Furniss labeled *A*.)

Point out the words *archaeologist, fieldwork, settlements,* and *sites.* Have students use strategies to define each word. Ask: *What does an archaeologist do? Which strategies can you use to define archaeologist?* (An archaeologist digs for and studies the remains of human cultures from the past.)

ELL ENGLISH LANGUAGE LEARNERS

"To Be an Archaeologist" Preteach vocabulary: *determine, software, rugged, bachelor's degree* (Cognate: *software*). Then guide students to find key details. *What does an archaeologist do?* (study how people lived in the past) *What tools do they use?* (measuring and recording tools) *What is the last section about?* (It is about the education a person needs to become an archaeologist.)

"Digging Into the Past" Preteach vocabulary: *tannery, composition, abstract* (Cognates: *composición, abstracto*). Then guide students to find key details. *In "Digging Into the Past," what is the interview about?* (the work a modern-day archaeologist does) *Who is being interviewed and what does she talk about?* (archaeologist Adrienne Furniss; she likes to connect with the past using her senses) *What do the capital letters* Q *and* A *stand for?* (*Q* stands for "question," and *A* stands for "answer.")

LEARNING GOALS

- **We can compare two texts about studying the past.**
- **We can apply what we've learned to make observations of footprints.**

OBJECTIVES

Draw on information from multiple print or digital sources, demonstrating the ability to locate an answer to a question quickly or to solve a problem efficiently.

Summarize a written text read aloud or information presented in diverse media and formats, including visually, quantitatively, and orally.

ELA ACADEMIC LANGUAGE

- *interview, observations, evidence, interpret, models*
- Cognates: *observación, evidencia, interpretar, modelo*

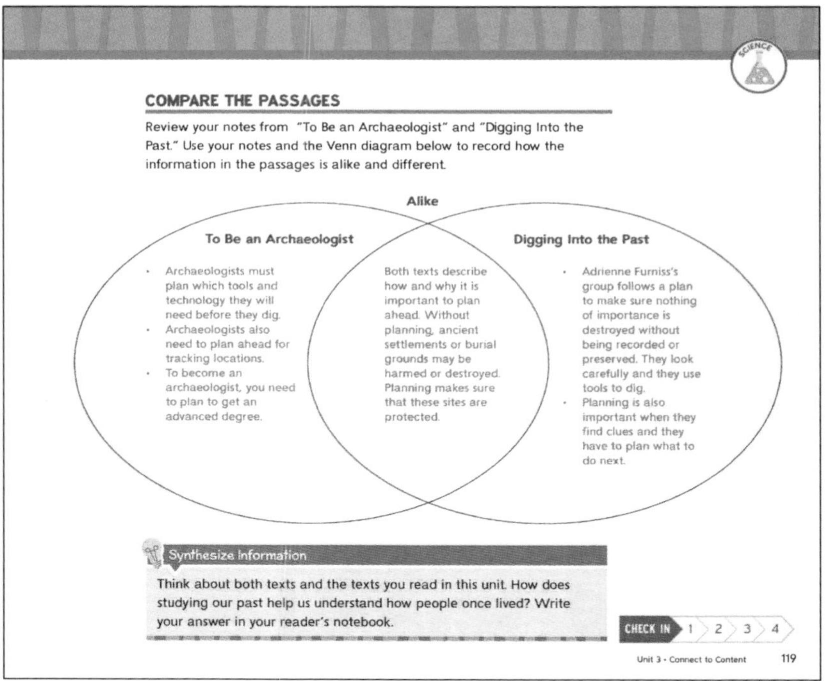

COMPARE THE PASSAGES

Review your notes from "To Be an Archaeologist" and "Digging Into the Past." Use your notes and the Venn diagram below to record how the information in the passages is alike and different.

Synthesize Information

Think about both texts and the texts you read in this unit. How does studying our past help us understand how people once lived? Write your answer in your reader's notebook.

CHECK IN 1 2 3 4

Unit 3 • Connect to Content 119

Reading/Writing Companion, p. 119

Compare the Passages

Explain Remind students that one of the passages they read is an expository text and the other is an interview, but both give information about exploring our past. Tell students they will complete a Venn diagram to show how the two passages are alike and different.

COLLABORATE **Talk About It** Have students work in small groups or with a partner to talk about the two texts and their similarities and differences. Have them review the characteristics of each genre. Partners or group members should share ideas with one another about the different ways each text presents information about how exploring our past helps us understand how people once lived.

Apply Have students use the notes they made on **Reading/Writing Companion** pages 116–118 and their Talk About It discussion to complete the Venn diagram and answer the Synthesize Information question on page 119.

Synthesize Information — DOK 3

Explain Readers can think about information from two passages and connect the ideas to provide the answer to a question.

Model *I can use information from both passages to understand how studying the past helps us understand how people once lived.* Have students reread the "Duties" section of "To Be an Archaeologist" on page 116. Then have them reread the answer to the question "Like what?" in "Digging Into the Past" on page 117.

Apply Have students cite more evidence from both passages that helps them understand how people learn about past civilizations.

FORMATIVE ASSESSMENT

STUDENT CHECK-IN

Compare Have partners share their Venn Diagrams and responses on Reading/Writing Companion page 119.

Make Observations Have partners share their models.

Ask students to use the Check-In routine to reflect and fill in the bars.

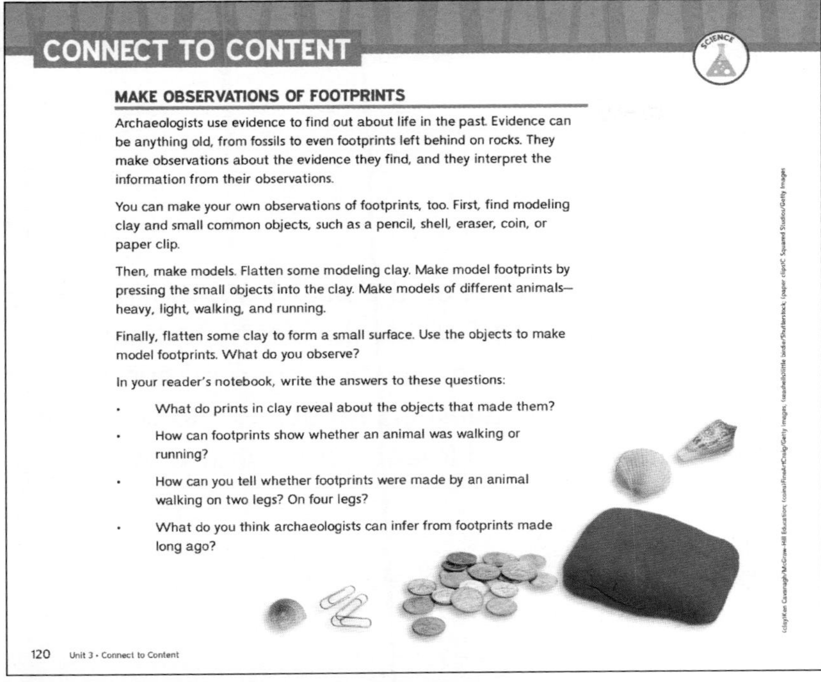
CONNECT TO CONTENT

MAKE OBSERVATIONS OF FOOTPRINTS

Archaeologists use evidence to find out about life in the past. Evidence can be anything old, from fossils to even footprints left behind on rocks. They make observations about the evidence they find, and they interpret the information from their observations.

You can make your own observations of footprints, too. First, find modeling clay and small common objects, such as a pencil, shell, eraser, coin, or paper clip.

Then, make models. Flatten some modeling clay. Make model footprints by pressing the small objects into the clay. Make models of different animals—heavy, light, walking, and running.

Finally, flatten some clay to form a small surface. Use the objects to make model footprints. What do you observe?

In your reader's notebook, write the answers to these questions:

- What do prints in clay reveal about the objects that made them?
- How can footprints show whether an animal was walking or running?
- How can you tell whether footprints were made by an animal walking on two legs? On four legs?
- What do you think archaeologists can infer from footprints made long ago?

120 Unit 3 • Connect to Content

Reading/Writing Companion, p. 120

Make Observations of Footprints

Explain and Model Tell students that they will be creating and interpreting model animal footprints in clay. Sketch several kinds of footprints on the board (two and four feet), heavy and light, and describe them to students.

COLLABORATE **Talk About It** Have partners or small groups of students discuss what kinds of footprints they want to make, what materials they plan to use, and how they plan to use those materials to achieve their desired effects.

Apply After their discussions, have students record the answers to the questions on **Reading/Writing Companion** page 120 in their reader's notebook.

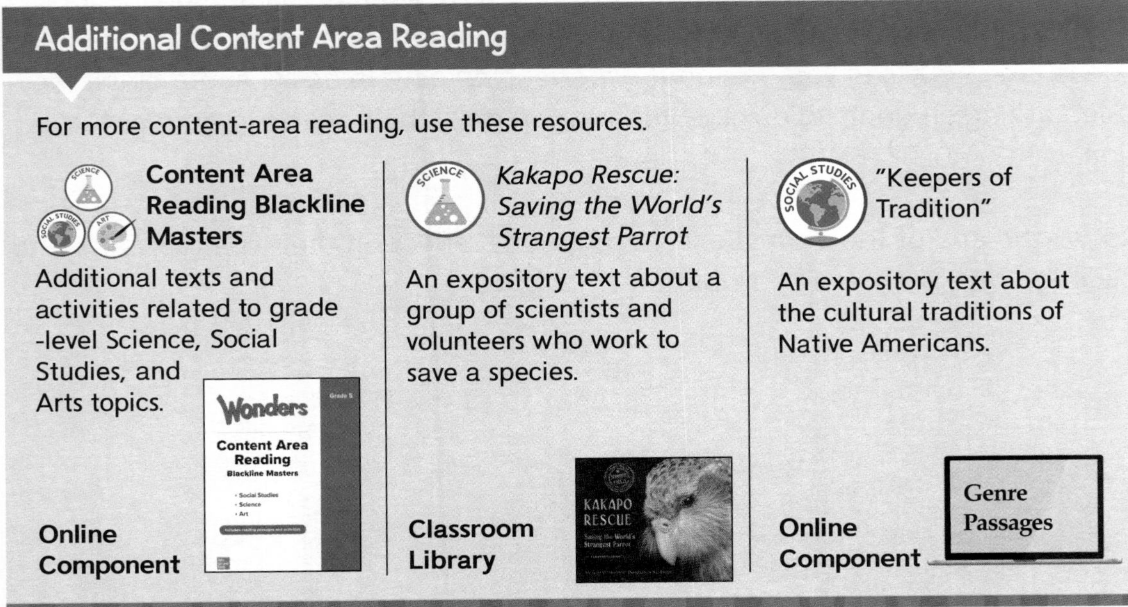
Additional Content Area Reading

For more content-area reading, use these resources.

Content Area Reading Blackline Masters

Additional texts and activities related to grade -level Science, Social Studies, and Arts topics.

Online Component

Kakapo Rescue: Saving the World's Strangest Parrot

An expository text about a group of scientists and volunteers who work to save a species.

Classroom Library

"Keepers of Tradition"

An expository text about the cultural traditions of Native Americans.

Online Component

ENGLISH LANGUAGE LEARNERS

Make Observations of Footprints, Apply List adjectives that students might use to describe the footprints and the animals that made them: *heavy, light, deep, shallow, large, small, narrow, wide, fast,* and *slow.* Then have students use these adjectives in sentences in their answers to the questions on page 120 of the **Reading/Writing Companion**. Provide sentence frames such as: *This animal was* heavy. *I can tell because the footprints are* deep. *This animal hopped on* two feet. *I can tell because the footprints are* together.

LEARNING GOALS

We can synthesize information from multiple texts.

OBJECTIVES

Integrate information from several texts on the same topic in order to write or speak about the subject knowledgeably.

By the end of the year, read and comprehend literature at the high end of the grades 4-5 text complexity band independently and proficiently.

By the end of the year, read and comprehend informational texts at the high end of the grades 4-5 text complexity band independently and proficiently.

Engage effectively in a range of collaborative discussions with diverse partners on grade 5 topics and texts, building on others' ideas and expressing their own clearly.

Come to discussions prepared, having read or studied required material; explicitly draw on that preparation and other information known about the topic to explore ideas under discussion.

Review the key ideas expressed and draw conclusions in light of information and knowledge gained from the discussions.

Follow agreed-upon rules for discussions and carry out assigned roles.

FORMATIVE ASSESSMENT

STUDENT CHECK-IN

Have students reflect on how well they synthesized the unit's information. Then have them reflect using the Check-In routine.

Make Connections

Connect to a Big Idea

COLLABORATE **Text to Text** Write this Big Idea question on the board: *What kinds of experiences can lead to new discoveries?* Divide the class into small groups. Each group will compare the information that they have learned during the course of the unit in order to answer the Big Idea question. Model how to compare this information by using examples from the Leveled Readers and what they have read in this unit's selections.

Collaborative Conversations Have students review their class notes and completed graphic organizers before they begin their discussions. Have each group pick one student to take notes. Explain that each group will use an Accordion Foldable® to record their ideas. You may wish to model how to use an Accordion Foldable® to record comparisons of texts.

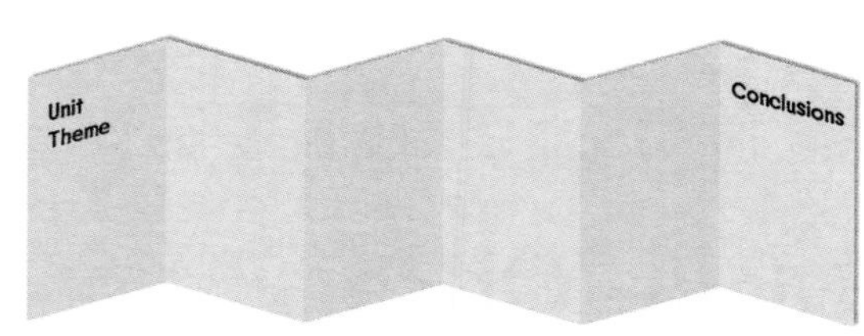

Present Ideas and Synthesize Information When students finish their discussions, ask for a volunteer from each group to read their notes aloud. After each group has presented their ideas, ask: *What are the five most important things we have learned about new experiences and discoveries?* Lead a class discussion and list students' ideas on the board. Have students share any personal or emotional connections they felt with the texts they read and listened to over the course of the unit.

Building Knowledge Encourage students to continue building knowledge about the Big Idea. Display the online Unit Bibliography and have students search online for articles and other resources related to the Big Idea. After each group has presented their ideas, ask: *How can you go about experiencing new things?* Lead a class discussion asking students to use the information from their charts to answer the question.

Reflect At the end of the discussions, have groups reflect on their collaboration and acknowledge one another's contributions.

Reflect on Your Learning

COLLABORATE **Talk About It** Reflect on what you learned in this unit. Then talk with a partner about how you did.

I am really proud of how I can ______

Something I need to work more on is ______

Share a goal you have with a partner.

My Goal Set a goal for Unit 4. In your reader's notebook, write about what you can do to get there.

Unit 3 • Reflect on Your Learning 121

Reading/Writing Companion, p. 121

Reflect on Your Learning

Talk About It

COLLABORATE Remind students that one meaning of *reflect* is to think carefully about something you have done. Give students time to reflect on what they have learned in Unit 3. Ask: *How did the skills and strategies you learned help you with reading and writing in this unit? How can the things you learned help you do other things?* Have partners answer these questions together, using their reader's and writer's notebooks to support their discussion.

Then guide partners to discuss what they did in Unit 3 that made them feel proud and what they need to continue working on. Have students complete the sentence starters on page 121 of the **Reading/Writing Companion**. Encourage them to review their work and feedback they received throughout the unit. They can also review their completed My Goals bars on pages 11, 37, 63, and 85 of the Reading/Writing Companion.

Review students' reflections and guide them in forming a plan to continue developing skills they need to work on.

Set a Unit 4 Goal

Have students set their own learning goal for the next unit. Have partners or small groups flip through Unit 4 of the Reading/Writing Companion to get an idea of what to expect. Pairs can discuss their goals and plans for achieving them. Point out that sharing goals with others can help us achieve them. Then have students record their goal and plan in their reader's notebook.

LEARNING GOALS

We can reflect on our learning and set our own learning goals.

OBJECTIVES

Engage effectively in a range of collaborative discussions (one-on-one, in groups, and teacher-led) with diverse partners, building on others' ideas and expressing their own clearly.

Reflect on learning.

HABITS OF LEARNING

I am a part of a community of learners.

Ask students to reflect on the unit's Habit of Learning and connect the habit to their life outside of school. Ask:

- Why is it important to be able to share information with others?
- How are out-of-school activity groups, such as sports teams or scouting groups, also "communities of learners"?
- Why is it important to listen actively and build on others' thoughts as a member of one of those groups?

FORMATIVE ASSESSMENT

STUDENT CHECK-IN

Have students share one thing they are proud of learning. Then have them reflect using the Check-In routine.

LEARNING GOALS

- **We can use effective speaking strategies.**
- **We can use effective listening strategies.**

OBJECTIVES

Pose and respond to specific questions by making comments that contribute to the discussion and elaborate on the remarks of others.

Report on a topic or text or present an opinion, sequencing ideas logically and using appropriate facts and relevant, descriptive details to support main ideas or themes; speak clearly at an understandable pace.

Summarize the points a speaker or media source makes and explain how each claim is supported by reasons and evidence. identify and analyze any logical fallacies.

Adapt speech to a variety of contexts and tasks, using formal English when appropriate to task and situation.

DIGITAL TOOLS

Students may use these tools:

How to Give a Presentation (Collaborative Conversations Video)

Presentation Checklist (PDF)

FORMATIVE ASSESSMENT

STUDENT CHECK-IN

Speaking Have students use the Presentation Rubric to reflect on their presentations.

Listening Have partners share key ideas they heard during presentations.

Have students reflect using the Check-In routine.

TEACHER CHOICE

As you wrap up the unit, invite students to present their work to small groups, the class, or a larger audience. Choose from among these options:

✓ **Reader's Theater:** Have students perform the play on page T290.

✓ **Research and Inquiry Projects:** Small groups can share their completed projects. See page T26, T102, and T182.

✓ **Inquiry Space:** Students can give multimodal presentations of the work that they developed using Inquiry Space. See page T304.

✓ **Publishing Celebrations:** Have students share one of the pieces of writing they worked on throughout the unit. See page T306.

Use the Speaking and Listening minilessons below to help students prepare.

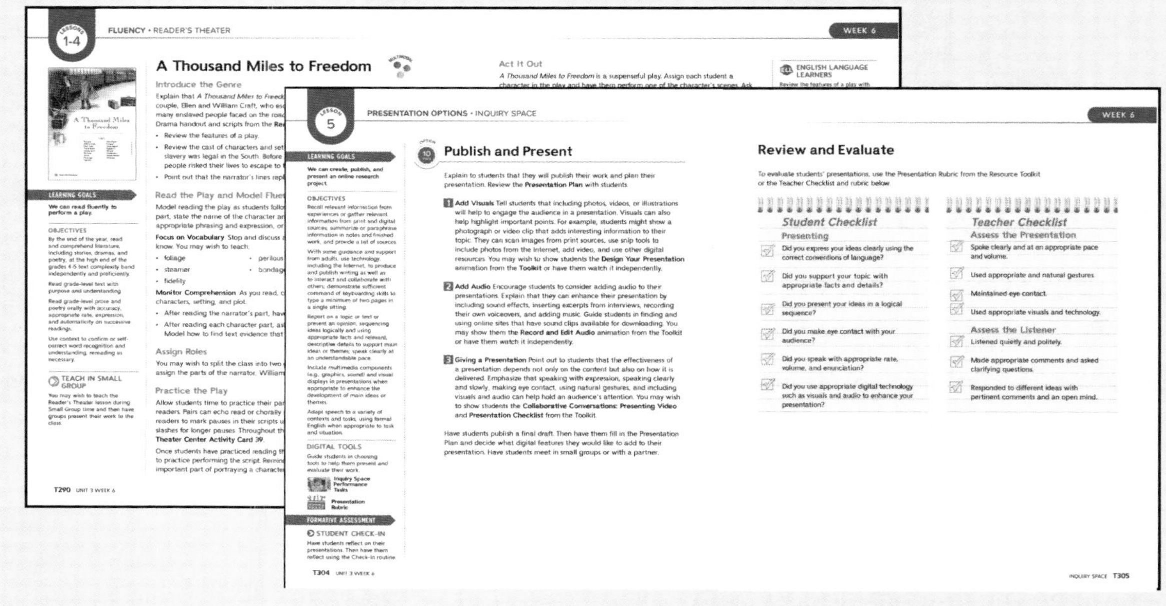

FLUENCY • READER'S THEATER

A Thousand Miles to Freedom

PRESENTATION OPTIONS • INQUIRY SPACE

Publish and Present

Review and Evaluate

Speaking

Explain to students that when orally giving a formal presentation to a large audience, such as a whole class, they should remember these strategies:

- Rehearse the presentation in front of a friend and ask for feedback.
- Speak slowly, clearly, and with speaking rate, volume, enunciation, and conventions of language.
- Emphasize points so that the audience can follow important ideas.
- Make appropriate eye contact with people in the audience.
- Use hand gestures naturally when appropriate.

Remind students to time themselves during practice sessions to allow enough time for questions from the audience following the presentation.

Listening

Remind students that an effective listener

- listens for facts and key ideas about the topic.
- stays focused on the speaker's presentation and ignores distractions.
- listens without interruption but is prepared to ask relevant questions and make pertinent comments after the presentation is finished.
- articulates thoughts clearly and builds upon the ideas of others.

After the presentation, guide a discussion, asking some students to paraphrase or summarize the key ideas.

ELL ENGLISH LANGUAGE LEARNERS

Use the strategies to encourage participation and develop oral proficiency:

- Give students ample time to present and respond.
- Give positive confirmation. Repeat correct response in a clear loud voice and at a slower pace to motivate students.
- Repeat responses to model the proper form for incorrect grammar or pronunciation.

Presentation Rubric

4 Excellent	3 Good	2 Fair	1 Unsatisfactory
• presents the information clearly • includes many facts and details • presents ideas in a logical sequence • includes sophisticated observations	• presents the information adequately • provides adequate facts and details • sequences ideas adequately • includes relevant observations	• attempts to present information • offers few or vague facts and details • struggles with sequencing ideas • includes few or irrelevant observations	• shows little grasp of the task • presents irrelevant information • demonstrates extreme difficulty with research or presentation

LEARNING GOALS

We can create, publish, and present an online research project.

OBJECTIVES

Recall relevant information from experiences or gather relevant information from print and digital sources; summarize or paraphrase information in notes and finished work, and provide a list of sources.

With some guidance and support from adults, use technology, including the Internet, to produce and publish writing as well as to interact and collaborate with others; demonstrate sufficient command of keyboarding skills to type a minimum of two pages in a single sitting.

Report on a topic or text or present an opinion, sequencing ideas logically and using appropriate facts and relevant, descriptive details to support main ideas or themes; speak clearly at an understandable pace.

Include multimedia components (e.g., graphics, sound) and visual displays in presentations when appropriate to enhance the development of main ideas or themes.

Adapt speech to a variety of contexts and tasks, using formal English when appropriate to task and situation.

DIGITAL TOOLS

Guide students in choosing tools to help them present and evaluate their work.

Inquiry Space Performance Tasks

Presentation Rubric

FORMATIVE ASSESSMENT

STUDENT CHECK-IN

Have students reflect on their presentations. Then have them reflect using the Check-In routine.

Publish and Present

Explain to students that they will publish their work and plan their presentation. Review the **Presentation Plan** with students.

1 **Add Visuals** Tell students that including photos, videos, or illustrations will help to engage the audience in a presentation. Visuals can also help highlight important points. For example, students might show a photograph or video clip that adds interesting information to their topic. They can scan images from print sources, use snip tools to include photos from the Internet, add video, and use other digital resources. You may wish to show students the **Design Your Presentation** animation from the **Toolkit** or have them watch it independently.

2 **Add Audio** Encourage students to consider adding audio to their presentations. Explain that they can enhance their presentation by including sound effects, inserting excerpts from interviews, recording their own voiceovers, and adding music. Guide students in finding and using online sites that have sound clips available for downloading. You may show them the **Record and Edit Audio** animation from the Toolkit or have them watch it independently.

3 **Giving a Presentation** Point out to students that the effectiveness of a presentation depends not only on the content but also on how it is delivered. Emphasize that speaking with expression, speaking clearly and slowly, making eye contact, using natural gestures, and including visuals and audio can help hold an audience's attention. You may wish to show students the **Collaborative Conversations: Presenting Video** and **Presentation Checklist** from the Toolkit.

Have students publish a final draft. Then have them fill in the Presentation Plan and decide what digital features they would like to add to their presentation. Have students meet in small groups or with a partner.

Review and Evaluate

To evaluate students' presentations, use the Presentation Rubric from the Resource Toolkit or the Teacher Checklist and rubric below.

Student Checklist

Presenting

- [x] Did you express your ideas clearly using the correct conventions of language?
- [x] Did you support your topic with appropriate facts and details?
- [x] Did you present your ideas in a logical sequence?
- [x] Did you make eye contact with your audience?
- [x] Did you speak with appropriate rate, volume, and enunciation?
- [x] Did you use appropriate digital technology such as visuals and audio to enhance your presentation?

Teacher Checklist

Assess the Presentation

- [x] Spoke clearly and at an appropriate pace and volume.
- [x] Used appropriate and natural gestures.
- [x] Maintained eye contact.
- [x] Used appropriate visuals and technology.

Assess the Listener

- [x] Listened quietly and politely.
- [x] Made appropriate comments and asked clarifying questions.
- [x] Responded to different ideas with pertinent comments and an open mind.

LEARNING GOALS

- **We can use effective strategies to present our writing.**
- **We can use effective strategies to listen to presentations.**

OBJECTIVES

Analyze how visual and multimedia elements contribute to the meaning, tone, or beauty of a text.

With some guidance and support from adults, use technology, including the Internet, to produce and publish writing as well as to interact and collaborate with others; interact and collaborate with others.

Report on a topic or text or present an opinion, sequencing ideas logically and using appropriate facts and relevant, descriptive details to support main ideas or themes; speak clearly at an understandable pace.

Include multimedia components and visual displays in presentations when appropriate to enhance the development of main ideas or themes.

Adapt speech to a variety of contexts and tasks, using formal English when appropriate to task and situation.

TEACH IN SMALL GROUP

You may wish to arrange groups of various abilities to complete their presentations, evaluate each other's work, and discuss portfolio choices.

FORMATIVE ASSESSMENT

STUDENT CHECK-IN

Presenting Have partners share reflections on their writing presentations.

Listening Have partners share one important idea they learned.

Have students reflect using the Check-In routine.

Present Writing

Select the Writing

Now is an opportunity for students to share one of the pieces of writing that they have worked on through the unit. Have them review their writing and select one piece to present. You may wish to invite their parents or students from other classes to the Publishing Celebrations.

Preparing for Presentations

Tell students that they will need to prepare in order to best present their writing. Allow students time to rehearse their presentations. Encourage them to reread their writing a few times. This will help them become more familiar with their pieces so that they won't have to read word by word as they present.

Students should consider any visuals or digital elements that they may want to use to present their writing. Discuss a few possible options with students.

- Do they have photos they want to share in order to help the audience visualize important details?
- Are there charts, tables, maps, or graphs that would give the audience additional information about the topic?
- Is there a video they can project that contains facts or details that support their topic?

Students can practice presenting to a partner in the classroom. They can also practice with family members at home, or in front of a mirror. Share the following checklist with students to help them focus on important parts of their presentation as they rehearse. Discuss each point on the checklist.

Speaking Checklist

Review the Speaking Checklist with students as they practice.

- ☐ Have all of your notes and visuals ready.
- ☐ Take a few deep breaths.
- ☐ Stand up straight.
- ☐ Look at the audience.
- ☐ Speak clearly and slowly, particularly when communicating complex information.
- ☐ Speak loud enough so everyone can hear.
- ☐ Speak with enthusiasm to generate interest.
- ☐ Use appropriate, natural gestures.
- ☐ Hold your visual aids so everyone can see them.
- ☐ Point to relevant details on your visual aids as you speak.

Listening to Presentations

Remind students that they will be part of the audience for other students' presentations. A listener serves an important role. Review with students the following Listening Checklist.

Listening Checklist

DURING THE PRESENTATION

- ☐ Listen carefully to the speaker.
- ☐ Pay attention to how the speaker organizes ideas logically.
- ☐ Notice how the speaker supports the topic with relevant, descriptive details.
- ☐ Take notes on one or two things you liked about the presentation.
- ☐ Write one question about the topic for which you need clarification.

AFTER THE PRESENTATION

- ☐ Summarize and explain the speaker's main points and how each is supported.
- ☐ Tell why you liked the presentation.
- ☐ Ask a relevant question or share a pertinent comment you have based on the information presented.
- ☐ If someone else makes the same comment first, elaborate on that person's response.

Portfolio Choice

Ask students to select one finished piece of writing, as well as two revisions, to include in their writing portfolio. As students consider their choices, have them use the questions below.

FINISHED WRITING	WRITING ENTRY REVISIONS
Does your writing	**Do your revisions show**
• clearly state your opinion about the topic? • organize and connect your ideas clearly? • use the correct voice (formal or informal) based on the audience? • have few or no spelling or grammatical errors? • demonstrate neatness when published? • demonstrate legible cursive writing skills, if handwritten?	• a consistent voice? • connotative words? • additional evidence that clearly supports your main idea? • ideas that transition naturally? • only information that supports the topic? • improved cursive writing, if handwritten, so that it can be read easily by others?

Explain that students will also have the opportunity to improve their finished writing. Use the suggestions on the Level Up Writing lesson on pages T284–T285 to meet students' individual needs.

Leveled Reader

OBJECTIVES

Explain the relationships or interactions between two or more individuals, events, ideas, or concepts in a historical, scientific, or technical text based on specific information in the text.

Determine the meaning of general academic and domain-specific words and phrases in a text relevant to a grade 5 topic or subject area.

By the end of the year, read and comprehend informational texts, including history/social studies, science, and technical texts, at the high end of the grades 4–5 text complexity band independently and proficiently.

Review the key ideas expressed and draw conclusions in light of information and knowledge gained from the discussions.

Approaching Level to On Level

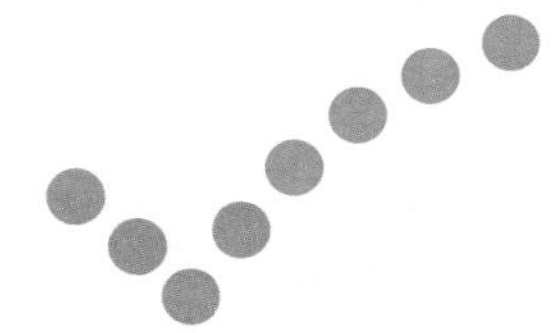

The Power of a Team

Preview Discuss what students remember about how scientists around the world work together in teams to answer difficult questions and solve problems. Tell them they will be reading a more challenging version of *The Power of a Team.*

Vocabulary Use the Visual Vocabulary Cards and routine to review.

Specific Vocabulary Review with students the following content and academic words that are new to this title. Model how to use word parts or context clues to determine the meanings of *expertise, detected, cues, intrigued, unreliable,* and *perfected.* You may also want to point out the contextual meaning of the multiple-meaning word *fields* on page 3. Ask: *How does the author help you understand which meaning is correct?* (The author includes the phrase "or areas of knowledge" to indicate the correct meaning.)

Connection of Ideas Students may find it challenging to link the different ideas in each section and sidebar and connect them to the central idea that scientists can achieve more by working as a group. Walk students through the table of contents on page 1, discussing what the repeated use of the word *New* in each chapter title might indicate. Then have students read the sidebar on page 3 and think more about why Florey chose scientists with different areas of expertise to research the use of penicillin. Ask: *How does this help you understand what the author says in the main text above the sidebar?* (It describes a specific example of how people from different fields produce powerful results when they collaborate.) Continue by exploring how collaborating helped both the Bell Lab scientists and the scientists from Princeton University (pages 9–10).

Sentence Structure Students may need help understanding questions posed to the reader within the text. Chorally read the first paragraph on page 2 with students and ask them to state what the paragraph is about. Ask: *Is a scientist asking the question or is the author?* (The author is asking the question.) *Why does the author include this question?* (She wants to get readers to think about the main topic before presenting the details.) Repeat these steps for the question in the sidebar on page 16, guiding students to see that the questions are posed by the scientist profiled in the sidebar.

Ask students to complete the Respond to Reading on page 18. Have students complete the Paired Read and hold Literature Circles.

On Level to Beyond Level

The Power of a Team

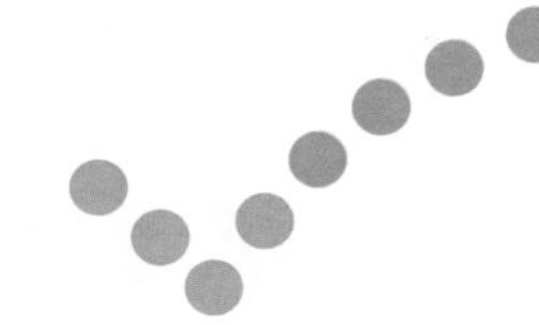

Leveled Reader

Preview Discuss what students remember about how scientists around the world work together in teams to answer difficult questions and solve problems. Tell them they will be reading a more challenging version of *The Power of a Team.*

Vocabulary Use the Visual Vocabulary Cards and routine to review.

▶ **Specific Vocabulary** Review with students the following content and academic words that are new to this title. Model how to use word parts or context clues to determine the meaning of *infectious, evaluate, robotic, experimental, monitoring, crowded, convinced,* and *eliminate.*

▶ **Connection of Ideas** Students will at times need to infer in order to connect the ideas in each section and sidebar to the central idea that scientists can achieve more by working in a group. Have students read the sidebar on page 3. Ask: *What do you learn about Howard Florey's approach to solving problems?* (I learn that Florey decided that he would accomplish more if he worked with other scientists to figure out how to treat infectious diseases.) *What does this tell you about Florey?* (It makes me think that Florey is a team player and is happy to succeed as part of a team rather than on his own.) Repeat these steps for other descriptions of teamwork, including how Marc Buoniconti's father was motivated to raise money for spinal research (page 13).

▶ **Sentence Structure** Students may be challenged by more complex sentences at this level, including those containing colons. Remind students that a colon can be used to separate two independent clauses in which the second clause provides more information about the first. Have students read the last sentence of the first paragraph on page 6. Ask: *How does the part of the sentence after the colon provide more information about the first part of the sentence?* (It describes what the team did to keep the rover going.) Repeat with other sentences containing colons on pages 5 and 16.

Ask students to complete the Respond to Reading on page 18. Have students complete the Paired Read and hold Literature Circles.

OBJECTIVES

Determine two or more central, or main, ideas of a text and explain how they are supported by relevant, or key, details; summarize the text.

Explain the relationships or interactions between two or more individuals, events, ideas, or concepts in a historical, scientific, or technical text based on specific information in the text.

Determine the meaning of general academic and domain-specific words and phrases in a text relevant to a grade 5 topic or subject area.

By the end of the year, read and comprehend informational texts, including history/social studies, science, and technical texts, at the high end of the grades 4–5 text complexity band independently and proficiently.

Use context (e.g., cause/effect relationships and comparisons in text) as a clue to the meaning of a word or phrase.

Leveled Reader

OBJECTIVES

Determine two or more central, or main, ideas of a text and explain how they are supported by relevant, or key, details; summarize the text.

Explain the relationships or interactions between two or more individuals, events, ideas, or concepts in a historical, scientific, or technical text based on specific information in the text.

Determine the meaning of general academic and domain-specific words and phrases in a text relevant to a grade 5 topic or subject area.

By the end of the year, read and comprehend informational texts, including history/social studies, science, and technical texts, at the high end of the grades 4–5 text complexity band independently and proficiently.

Form and use the perfect (e.g., *I had walked; I have walked; I will have walked*) verb tenses.

Use context (e.g., cause/effect relationships and comparisons in text) as a clue to the meaning of a word or phrase.

English Language Learners to On Level

The Power of a Team

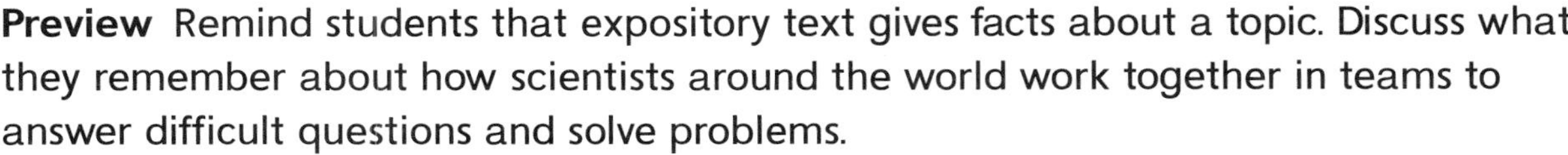

Preview Remind students that expository text gives facts about a topic. Discuss what they remember about how scientists around the world work together in teams to answer difficult questions and solve problems.

Vocabulary Use the Visual Vocabulary Cards and routine to review the vocabulary. Point out cognates: *artificial, colaborar, dedicado(a), flexible, función, obstáculos, técnicas.*

▶ **Specific Vocabulary** Show students how to identify context clues that will help them figure out difficult words. Turn to page 9 and have students point out the word *intrigued.* Say: *Scientists are* intrigued *by the mysteries of space. A mystery is something we can't explain. A mystery is interesting because we do not understand it. What does that tell you about the meaning of* intriguing? (Something intriguing is interesting.) Repeat for other words new to the On Level title, including *brainpower* on page 4, *smoothly* and *luckily* on page 5, *dragging* on page 6, and *crushed* on page 13.

▶ **Connection of Ideas** Students will need to make connections between details in the text to understand why Florey's team is a good example of the benefits of collaborating (page 3), why Schwann cells might repair spinal tissue (page 15), and why scientists are studying honeybees to create a new kind of robot (page 16). For example, on page 3, the author says that when people from different fields collaborate, they can produce powerful results. Discuss how the sidebar provides an example of this: The sidebar tells one way that scientists worked together. Together the scientists figured out how to use penicillin to cure illness.

▶ **Sentence Structure** Students may have difficulty with the use of the past perfect tense, such as on page 5. Read the first paragraph on the page and point out the phrase *had already figured out.* Say: *This action happened earlier in the past. The engineers figured out what to do if an air bag blocked the rover before* Spirit *touched down.* Have student describe the order of the events: The engineers solved the air bag problem before it happened to *Spirit.*

Ask students to complete the Respond to Reading on page 18. Have students complete the Paired Read and hold Literature Circles.

Beyond Level to Self-Selected Trade Book

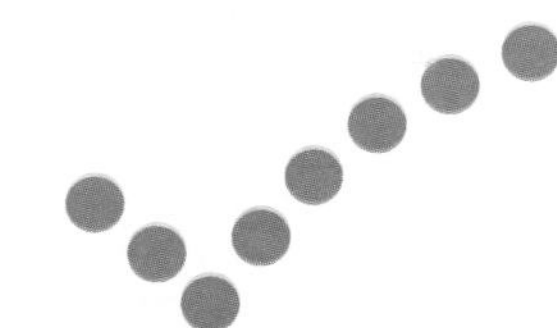

Leveled Reader **Advanced Level Trade Book**

Independent Reading

Together with students identify the particular focus of their reading based on the text they choose. Students who have chosen the same title will work in groups to closely read the selection.

Taking Notes Assign a graphic organizer for students to use to take notes as they read. Reinforce a specific comprehension focus from the unit by choosing one of the graphic organizers that best fits the book.

EXAMPLES	
Fiction	**Expository Text**
Theme	Central Idea and Relevant Details
Graphic Organizer 5	Graphic Organizer 7

Ask and Answer Questions Remind students to ask questions as they read. Have students record their questions on chart paper. As students meet, have them discuss the section that they have read. They can discuss the questions they noted and work together to find text evidence to support their answers. They can record their answers on the chart paper.

EXAMPLES	
Fiction	**Expository Text**
What was a theme of the story? How did the characters' words and actions help you determine it?	Identify important details in the text. What do they have in common? Use them to find the central idea.

Literature Circles Suggest that students hold Literature Circles and share interesting facts or favorite parts from the books they read.

OBJECTIVES

Determine two or more central, or main, ideas of a text and explain how they are supported by relevant, or key, details; summarize the text.

By the end of the year, read and comprehend literature, including stories, dramas, and poetry, at the high end of the grades 4–5 text complexity band independently and proficiently.

By the end of the year, read and comprehend informational texts, including history/social studies, science, and technical texts, at the high end of the grades 4–5 text complexity band independently and proficiently.

Summative Assessment

Unit 3 Tested Skills

COMPREHENSION	VOCABULARY	GRAMMAR	WRITING
• Plot: Characterization • Theme • Central Idea and Relevant Details • Text Structure: Problem and Solution • Text Structure: Compare and Contrast • Author's Claim • Literal and Figurative Language • Comparative Reading	• Latin Roots • Context Clues	• Action Verbs • Verb Tenses • Main and Helping Verbs	• Argumentative Writing Prompt

Additional Assessment Options

Fluency

Conduct assessments individually using the differentiated passages in **Fluency Assessment**. Students' expected fluency goal for this unit is 123–143 words correct per minute (WCPM) with an accuracy rate of 95% or higher.

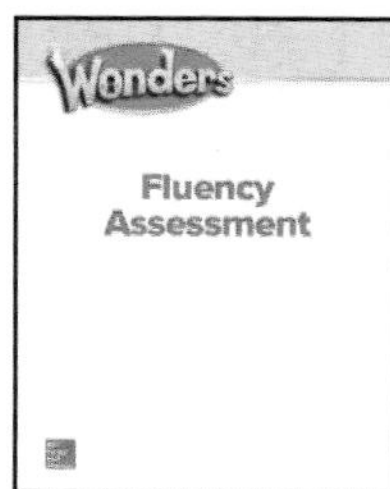

ELL Assessment

Assess English Language Learner proficiency and track student progress using the **English Language Development Assessment**. This resource provides unit assessments and rubrics to evaluate students' progress in the areas of listening and reading comprehension, vocabulary, grammar, speaking, and writing. These assessments can also be used to determine the language proficiency levels for subsequent sets of instructions.

Making the Most of Assessment Results

Make data-based grouping decisions by using the following reports to verify assessment results. For additional student support options refer to the reteaching and enrichment opportunities.

ONLINE ASSESSMENT CENTER

- ***Gradebook***

DATA DASHBOARD

- ***Recommendations Report***
- ***Activity Report***
- ***Skills Report***
- ***Progress Report***
- ***Grade Card Report***

 Assign practice pages online for auto-grading.

TIER 2

Reteaching Opportunities with Intervention Online PDFs

IF STUDENTS SCORE . . .	THEN ASSIGN . . .
below 70% in **comprehension . . .**	tested skills using the **Comprehension PDF**
below 70% in **vocabulary . . .**	tested skills using the **Vocabulary PDF**
below 8 on **writing prompt . . .**	tested skills using the **Writing and Grammar PDF**
0–122 WCPM in **fluency . . .**	tested skills using the **Fluency PDF**

Use the* Phonics/Word Study PDF *and* Foundational Skills Kit *for additional reteaching opportunities.

Enrichment Opportunities

Beyond Level small group lessons and resources include suggestions for additional activities in the following areas to extend learning opportunities for gifted and talented students:

- ***Leveled Readers***
- ***Genre Passages***
- ***Vocabulary***
- ***Comprehension***
- ***Leveled Reader Library Online***
- ***Center Activity Cards***

UNIT 3

Next Steps

NEXT STEPS FOR YOUR STUDENTS' PROGRESS . . .

Interpret the data you have collected from multiple sources throughout this unit, including formal and informal assessments.

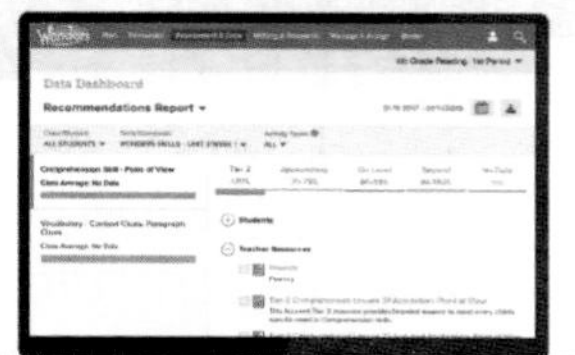
Data Dashboard

Who

Regrouping Decisions

- Check student progress against your interpretation of the data, and regroup as needed.
- Determine how English Language Learners are progressing.
- Consider whether students are ready to Level Up or Accelerate.

What

Target Instruction

- Analyze data from multiple measures to decide whether to review and reinforce particular skills or concepts or whether you need to reteach them.
- Target instruction to meet students' strengths/needs.
- Use Data Dashboard recommendations to help determine which lessons to provide to different groups of students.

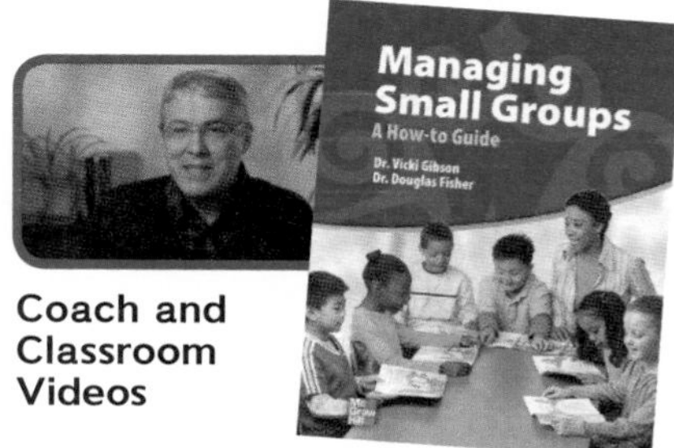

Coach and Classroom Videos

Methodology

How

Modify Instruction

- Vary materials and/or instructional strategies.
- Address students' social and emotional development.
- Provide students with opportunities for self-reflection and self-assessment.

AUTHOR INSIGHT

"It's rare for students to benefit from instruction on what they already know or when it flits from one not-quite-so learned skill to another. Use assessment—including daily observations of kids' learning—to aim instruction at ensuring that they master essential reading skills."
—Dr. Timothy Shanahan

Courtesy of Timothy Shanahan

NEXT STEPS FOR YOU . . .

As you prepare your students to move on to the next unit, don't forget to take advantage of the many opportunities available in your online course for self-evaluation and professional development.

Instructional Routines

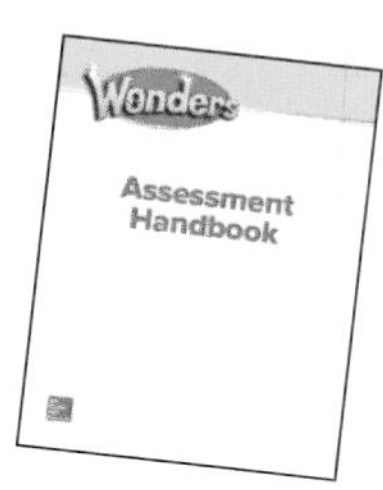

Manage Assessments

Program Author Whitepapers

Research Base

Contents

Program Information

Additional Digital Resources

my.mheducation.com

- Unit Bibliography
- Word Lists
- More Resources

Scope and Sequence

Text Set Focus	Read Aloud	Shared Read	Literature Anthology	Leveled Readers	Vocabulary
Text Set 1: **Weeks 1 and 2** **Essential Question:** How can experiencing nature change the way you think about it? **Genre:** Narrative Nonfiction *Differentiated Genre Passages available*	**Interactive Read Aloud:** "Capturing the Natural World" **Genre:** Narrative Nonfiction	"A Life in the Woods" **Genre:** Narrative Nonfiction **Lexile:** 770L *ELL Scaffolded Shared Read available*	**Anchor Text** *Camping with the President* **Genre:** Narrative Nonfiction **Lexile:** 760L **Paired Selection** "A Walk with Teddy" **Genre:** Autobiography **Lexile:** 910L	**Main Selections** **Genre:** Narrative Nonfiction ● *Save This Space!* **Lexile:** 750L ● *Save This Space!* **Lexile:** 960L ● *Save This Space!* **Lexile:** 730L ● *Save This Space!* **Lexile:** 980L **Paired Selections** **Genre:** Expository Text ● "The Journey of Lewis and Clark" ● "The Journey of Lewis and Clark" ● "The Journey of Lewis and Clark" ● "The Journey of Lewis and Clark"	**Academic Vocabulary:** debris, emphasis, encounter, generations, indicated, naturalist, sheer, spectacular Homographs Prefixes
Text Set 2: **Weeks 3 and 4** **Essential Question:** How do we get the things we need? **Genre:** Realistic Fiction *Differentiated Genre Passages available*	**Interactive Read Aloud:** "Finding a Way" **Genre:** Realistic Fiction	"A Fresh Idea" **Genre:** Realistic Fiction **Lexile:** 760L *ELL Scaffolded Shared Read available*	**Anchor Text** *One Hen* **Genre:** Realistic Fiction **Lexile:** 810L **Paired Selection** "Reading Between the Dots" **Genre:** Personal Narrative **Lexile:** 910L	**Main Selections** **Genre:** Realistic Fiction ● *Parker's Plan* **Lexile:** 680L ● *Can-do Canines* **Lexile:** 790L ● *Can-do Canines* **Lexile:** 570L ● *Cleaning Up the Competition* **Lexile:** 970L **Paired Selections** **Genre:** Expository Text ● "Taking Care of Your Money" ● "You Can Bank on It" ● "You Can Bank on It" ● "Growing Money"	**Academic Vocabulary:** afford, loan, profit, prosper, risk, savings, scarce, wages Context Clues: Sentence Clues Suffixes
Text Set 3: **Week 5** **Essential Question:** What are the positive and negative effects of new technology? **Genre:** Argumentative Text *Differentiated Genre Passages available*	**Interactive Read Aloud:** "Electronic Books: A New Way to Read" **Genre:** Argumentative Text	"Are Electronic Devices Good for Us?" **Genre:** Argumentative Text **Lexile:** 900L *ELL Scaffolded Shared Read available*	**Anchor Text** *The Future of Transportation* **Genre:** Argumentative Text **Lexile:** 870L **Paired Selection** "Getting from Here to There" **Genre:** Technical Text **Lexile:** 890L	**Main Selections** **Genre:** Expository Text ● *What About Robots?* **Lexile:** 740L ● *What About Robots?* **Lexile:** 840L ● *What About Robots?* **Lexile:** 760L ● *What About Robots?* **Lexile:** 990L **Paired Selections** **Genre:** Persuasive Text ● "No Substitute" ● "No Substitute" ● "No Substitute" ● "No Substitute"	**Academic Vocabulary:** access, advance, analysis, cite, counterpoint, data, drawbacks, reasoning Greek and Latin Prefixes

Week 6	Reading Digitally	Fluency	Connect to Content: Science	Connect to Content: Social Studies	Writing	Presentation Options
Extend, Connect, and Assess	**Genre:** Online Article "Take It from Nature"	**Reader's Theater:** *It Couldn't Be Done*	**Passages** **Genre:** Narrative Nonfiction "A Protector of Nature" **Genre:** Narrative Nonfiction "Children Save the Rain Forest" **Genre:** Realistic Fiction "Solutions, Not Complaints" **Activities** Compare the Passages Complete a Map Write an Essay	**Passages** "The NYC Subway: An Interview with a Transit Supervisor" "Solutions, Not Complaints" **Activities** Compare the Passages Write a Letter	**Writing Process** Write to Sources: Argumentative Writing Analyze the Prompt Analyze the Sources: "Honoring Black Women Inventors of the Past," "Morse Code Is Safe and Reliable," "All Aboard on America's Rail System" Plan: Organize Ideas Draft: Elaboration Revise: Peer Conferences	**Reader's Theater** **Inquiry Space** **Writing**

	Comprehension	Phonics and Spelling	Fluency	Writing and Grammar	Research and Inquiry
	Ask and Answer Questions Primary and Secondary Sources Text Structure: Cause and Effect Author's Perspective	**Week 1** Short Vowels **Week 2** Long Vowels *Differentiated Spelling Lists available*	**Week 1** Accuracy and Expression **Week 2** Intonation and Rate	**Respond to Reading** **Writing Process** Write to Sources: Argumentative Writing Analyze the Rubric Rubric Minilesson: Make a Claim Analyze the Student Model **Grammar and Mechanics** **Week 1:** Sentences; Punctuating Sentences **Week 2:** Subjects and Predicates; Commas	**Project:** Experiencing Nature **Product:** Promotional Map **Blast:** "Protecting Our Parks"
	Reread Plot: Conflict and Resolution Plot: Events Text Structure: Chronology	**Week 3** Words with /ū/, /ů/, and /ü/ **Week 4** *r*-controlled Vowels /är/, /âr/, /ôr/ *Differentiated Spelling Lists available*	**Week 3** Expression and Phrasing **Week 4** Rate	**Respond to Reading** **Writing Process** Write to Sources: Argumentative Writing Analyze the Prompt Analyze the Sources: "Landmark Deal Approved!," "Fund Florida Forever!," "Revitalize Florida's Downtowns" Plan: Organize Ideas Draft: Relevant Evidence Revise: Peer Conferences **Grammar and Mechanics** **Week 3:** Compound Sentences; Punctuation in Compound Sentences **Week 4:** Complex Sentences; Commas	**Project:** Meeting Needs **Product:** Compare/Contrast Chart **Blast:** "Clothing, Food, and Shelter"
	Reread Headings and Graphs Author's Claim Author's Purpose	**Week 5** *r*-controlled Vowel /ûr/ *Differentiated Spelling Lists available*	**Week 5** Accuracy and Phrasing	**Respond to Reading** **Writing Process** Write to Sources: Argumentative Writing Analyze the Rubric Rubric Minilesson: Strong Introduction Analyze the Student Model **Grammar and Mechanics** **Week 5:** Run-on Sentences; Correcting Run-on Sentences	**Project:** Technology **Product:** Debate **Blast:** "Riding Technology's Rollercoaster"

Scope and Sequence

Text Set Focus	Read Aloud	Shared Read	Literature Anthology	Leveled Readers	Vocabulary
Text Set 1: Weeks 1 and 2 **Essential Question:** What do good problem solvers do? **Genre:** Expository Text *Differentiated Genre Passages available*	**Interactive Read Aloud:** "The Haudenosaunee Confederacy" **Genre:** Expository Text	"Creating a Nation" **Genre:** Expository Text **Lexile:** 690L *ELL Scaffolded Shared Read available*	**Anchor Text** *Who Wrote the U.S. Constitution?* **Genre:** Expository Text **Lexile:** 760L **Paired Selection** "Wordsmiths" **Genre:** Expository Text **Lexile:** 970L	**Main Selections** **Genre:** Expository Text ● *The Bill of Rights* **Lexile:** 820L ● *The Bill of Rights* **Lexile:** 920L ● *The Bill of Rights* **Lexile:** 840L ● *The Bill of Rights* **Lexile:** 1000L **Paired Selections** **Genre:** Expository Text ● "Having Your Say" ● "Having Your Say" ● "Having Your Say" ● "Having Your Say"	**Academic Vocabulary:** committees, convention, debate, proposal, representatives, resolve, situation, union Context Clues Dictionary and Glossary
Text Set 2: Weeks 3 and 4 **Essential Question:** When has a plan helped you accomplish a task? **Genre:** Folktale *Differentiated Genre Passages available*	**Interactive Read Aloud:** "Lost Lake and the Golden Cup" **Genre:** Folktale	"The Magical Lost Brocade" **Genre:** Folktale **Lexile:** 740L *ELL Scaffolded Shared Read available*	**Anchor Text** *Blancaflor* **Genre:** Folktale **Lexile:** 870L **Paired Selection** "From Tale to Table" **Genre:** Expository Text **Lexile:** 990L	**Main Selections** **Genre:** Folktale ● *The Lion's Whiskers* **Lexile:** 760L ● *The Riddle of the Drum: A Tale from Mexico* **Lexile:** 810L ● *The Riddle of the Drum: A Tale from Mexico* **Lexile:** 570L ● *Clever Manka* **Lexile:** 860L **Paired Selections** **Genre:** Expository Text ● "From Fiber to Fashion" ● "Make a Drum" ● "Make a Drum" ● "From Bee to You"	**Academic Vocabulary:** assuring, detected, emerging, gratitude, guidance, outcome, previous, pursuit Personification Roots
Text Set 3: Week 5 **Essential Question:** What motivates you to accomplish a goal? **Genre:** Poetry *Differentiated Genre Passages available*	**Interactive Read Aloud:** "How to Make a Friend" **Genre:** Narrative Poetry	"A Simple Plan," "Rescue" **Genre:** Narrative and Free Verse Poetry **Lexile:** NP *ELL Scaffolded Shared Read available*	**Anchor Text** "Stage Fright," "Catching Quiet" **Genre:** Narrative and Free Verse Poetry **Lexile:** NP **Paired Selection** "Foul Shot" **Genre:** Free Verse Poetry **Lexile:** NP	**Main Selections** **Genre:** Realistic Fiction ● *Clearing the Jungle* **Lexile:** 650L ● *I Want to Ride!* **Lexile:** 730L ● *I Want to Ride!* **Lexile:** 600L ● *Changing Goals* **Lexile:** 860L **Paired Selections** **Genre:** Poetry ● "Just for Once" ● "Home Run" ● "Smash!" ● "Today's Lesson"	**Academic Vocabulary:** ambitious, memorized, satisfaction, shuddered **Poetry Terms:** narrative, repetition, free verse, rhyme Homographs

Week 6	Reading Digitally	Fluency	Connect to Content: Science	Connect to Content: Social Studies	Writing	Presentation Options
Extend, Connect, and Assess	**Genre:** Online Article "The Long Road"	**Reader's Theater:** *A Boy Named Abe*	**Passages** "Popover! The Ultimate Baked Bubble" "Cooking with Electricity" **Activities** Compare the Passages Make Observations Explain Your Observations	**Passages** "Searching for Freedom" "Supporting Religious Liberty" **Activities** Compare the Passages Make a Timeline	**Writing Process** Write to Sources: Expository Writing Analyze the Prompt Analyze the Sources: "Going Above and Beyond," "The Turtle Lady of Juno Beach," "Community Bird Scientist" Plan: Organize Ideas Draft: Transitions Revise: Peer Conferences	**Reader's Theater** **Inquiry Space** **Writing**

Unit 2

	Comprehension	Phonics and Spelling	Fluency	Writing and Grammar	Research and Inquiry
	Reread Headings and Timelines Text Structure: Problem and Solution Print and Graphic Features	**Week 1** Variant Vowel /ô/; Diphthongs /oi/, /ou/ **Week 2** Plurals *Differentiated Spelling Lists available*	**Week 1** Accuracy and Rate **Week 2** Accuracy and Expression	**Respond to Reading** **Writing Process** Write to Sources: Expository Writing Analyze the Rubric Rubric Minilesson: Central Idea Analyze the Student Model **Grammar and Mechanics** **Week 1:** Kinds of Nouns; Capitalizing Proper Nouns **Week 2:** Singular and Plural Nouns; Forming Plural Nouns	**Project:** Founders Solve Problems **Product:** Multimedia Slideshow **Blast:** "Meet Me in the Middle"
	Make Predictions Plot: Setting Theme Text Structure: Sequence	**Week 3** Inflectional Endings **Week 4** Contractions *Differentiated Spelling Lists available*	**Week 3** Expression and Phrasing **Week 4** Rate	**Respond to Reading** **Writing Process** Write to Sources: Expository Writing Analyze the Prompt Analyze the Sources: "Benjamin Franklin's Bifocals," "Margaret Knight, Engineer and Inventor," "Henry Ford and the Model T" Plan: Organize Ideas Draft: Elaboration Revise: Peer Conferences **Grammar and Mechanics** **Week 3:** More Plural Nouns; Plural Forms and Appositives **Week 4:** Possessive Nouns; Adding *-s* or *-'s*	**Project:** Accomplishing a Task **Product:** Illustrated Food Web **Blast:** "Stand by Your Plan"
	Repetition and Rhyme Narrative and Free Verse Theme Form and Line Breaks	**Week 5** Closed Syllables *Differentiated Spelling Lists available*	**Week 5** Expression and Phrasing	**Respond to Reading** **Writing Process** Write to Sources: Expository Writing Analyze the Rubric Rubric Minilesson: Academic Language Analyze the Student Model **Grammar and Mechanics** **Week 5:** Prepositional Phrases; Punctuating Titles and Letters	**Project:** Achieving Goals **Product:** Comic Strip **Blast:** "Reaching a Goal"

Scope and Sequence

Text Set Focus	Read Aloud	Shared Read	Literature Anthology	Leveled Reader	Vocabulary
Text Set 1: Weeks 1 and 2 **Essential Question:** What can learning about different cultures teach us? **Genre:** Realistic Fiction *Differentiated Genre Passages available*	**Interactive Read Aloud:** "Foods for Thought" **Genre:** Realistic Fiction	"A Reluctant Traveler" **Genre:** Realistic Fiction **Lexile:** 770L *ELL Scaffolded Shared Read available*	**Anchor Text** *They Don't Mean It!* **Genre:** Realistic Fiction **Lexile:** 870L **Paired Selection** "Where Did That Come From?" **Genre:** Expository Text **Lexile:** 940L	**Main Selections** **Genre:** Realistic Fiction ● *All the Way from Europe* **Lexile:** 690L ● *Dancing the Flamenco* **Lexile:** 790L ● *Dancing the Flamenco* **Lexile:** 510L ● *A Vacation in Minnesota* **Lexile:** 950L **Paired Selections** **Genre:** Expository Text ● "A Sporting Gift" ● "Flamenco" ● "Flamenco" ● "The Scandinavian State?"	**Academic Vocabulary:** appreciation, blurted, complimenting, congratulate, contradicted, critical, cultural, misunderstanding Context Clues: Cause and Effect Adages
Text Set 2: Weeks 3 and 4 **Essential Question:** What benefits come from people working as a group? **Genre:** Expository Text *Differentiated Genre Passages available*	**Interactive Read Aloud:** "Teamwork in Space" **Genre:** Expository Text	"Gulf Spill Superheroes" **Genre:** Expository Text **Lexile:** 860L *ELL Scaffolded Shared Read available*	**Anchor Text** *Winter's Tail* **Genre:** Expository Text **Lexile:** 940L **Paired Selection** "Helping Hands" **Genre:** Expository Text **Lexile:** 1040L	**Main Selections** **Genre:** Expository Text ● *The Power of a Team* **Lexile:** 740L ● *The Power of a Team* **Lexile:** 900L ● *The Power of a Team* **Lexile:** 800L ● *The Power of a Team* **Lexile:** 1010L **Paired Selections** **Genre:** Expository Text ● "Hands on the Wheel" ● "Hands on the Wheel" ● "Hands on the Wheel" ● "Hands on the Wheel"	**Academic Vocabulary:** artificial, collaborate, dedicated, flexible, function, mimic, obstacle, techniques Latin Roots Similes and Metaphors
Text Set 3: Week 5 **Essential Question:** How do we explain what happened in the past? **Genre:** Argumentative Text *Differentiated Genre Passages available*	**Interactive Read Aloud:** "Stonehenge: Puzzle from the Past" **Genre:** Argumentative Text	"What Was the Purpose of the Inca's Knotted Strings?" **Genre:** Argumentative Text **Lexile:** 920L *ELL Scaffolded Shared Read available*	**Anchor Text** *Machu Picchu: Ancient City* **Genre:** Argumentative Text **Lexile:** 990L **Paired Selection** "Dig This Technology!" **Genre:** Expository Text **Lexile:** 970L	**Main Selections** **Genre:** Expository Text ● *The Ancestral Puebloans* **Lexile:** 820L ● *The Ancestral Puebloans* **Lexile:** 920L ● *The Ancestral Puebloans* **Lexile:** 840L ● *The Ancestral Puebloans* **Lexile:** 990L **Paired Selections** **Genre:** Persuasive Text ● "The Ancestral Puebloans Were Astronomers" ● "The Ancestral Puebloans Were Astronomers" ● "The Ancestral Puebloans Were Astronomers" ● "The Ancestral Puebloans Were Astronomers"	**Academic Vocabulary:** archaeologist, era, fragments, historian, intact, preserved, reconstruct, remnants Sentence Clues

Week 6	Reading Digitally	Fluency	Connect to Content: Social Studies	Connect to Content: Science	Writing	Presentation Options
Extend, Connect, and Assess	**Genre:** Online Article "Animal Survivors"	**Reader's Theater:** *A Thousand Miles to Freedom*	**Passages** **Genre:** Expository Text "Teamwork and Destiny" "U.S. Space School" **Activities** Compare the Passages Share and Reflect Make a Teamwork Poster	**Passages** **Genre:** "To Be an Archaeologist" "Digging into the Past" **Activities** Compare the Passages Make Observations of Footprints	**Writing Process** Write to Sources: Argumentative Analyze the Prompt Analyze the Sources: "Remember St. Helena's Role," "Collaboration at Angel Mounds," "No Digging Allowed" Plan: Organize Ideas Draft: Sentence Structure Revise: Peer Conferences	**Reader's Theater** **Inquiry Space** **Writing**

Unit 3

Comprehension	Phonics and Spelling	Fluency	Writing and Grammar	Research and Inquiry
Summarize Plot: Characterization Theme Author's Purpose	**Week 1** Open Syllables **Week 2** Open Syllables (V/V) *Differentiated Spelling Lists available*	**Week 1** Intonation **Week 2** Expression and Phrasing	**Respond to Reading** **Writing Process** Write to Sources: Argumentative Writing Analyze the Rubric Rubric Minilesson: Precise Language Analyze the Student Model **Grammar and Mechanics** **Week 1:** Action Verbs; Subject-Verb Agreement **Week 2:** Verb Tenses; Avoid Shifting Tenses	**Project:** Learning About Different Cultures **Product:** Pamphlet **Blast:** "A Special Day"
Ask and Answer Questions Text Structure: Problem and Solution Central Idea and Relevant Details Literal and Figurative Language	**Week 3** Vowel Team Syllables **Week 4** Consonant + *le* Syllables *Differentiated Spelling Lists available*	**Week 3** Accuracy and Rate **Week 4** Rate	**Respond to Reading** **Writing Process** Write to Sources: Argumentative Writing Analyze the Prompt Analyze the Sources: "Parents Say No to Study Abroad," "The Benefits of Study Abroad Programs," "U.S. Students Study Abroad" Plan: Organize Ideas Draft: Logical Order Revise: Peer Conferences **Grammar and Mechanics** **Week 3:** Main and Helping Verbs; Special Helping Verbs; Contractions; Troublesome Words **Week 4:** Linking Verbs; Punctuating Titles and Product Names	**Project:** Working Together **Product:** Television Segment **Blast:** "Two Heads Are Better Than One"
Summarize Text Structure: Compare and Contrast Author's Claim Figurative Language	**Week 5** *r*-controlled Vowel Syllables *Differentiated Spelling Lists available*	**Week 5** Accuracy and Rate	**Respond to Reading** **Writing Process** Write to Sources: Argumentative Writing Analyze the Rubric Rubric Minilesson: Strong Conclusion Analyze the Student Model **Grammar and Mechanics** **Week 5:** Irregular Verbs; Correct Verb Usage	**Project:** Investigating the Past **Product:** Multimedia Presentation **Blast:** "Remnants of the Past"

Scope and Sequence

Text Set Focus	Read Aloud	Shared Read	Literature Anthology	Leveled Reader	Vocabulary
Text Set 1: Weeks 1 and 2 **Essential Question:** What can people do to bring about a positive change? **Genre:** Biography *Differentiated Genre Passages available*	**Interactive Read Aloud:** "Fighting for Change" **Genre:** Biography	"Frederick Douglass: Freedom's Voice" **Genre:** Biography **Lexile:** 830L *ELL Scaffolded Shared Read available*	**Anchor Text** *Rosa* **Genre:** Biography **Lexile:** 860L **Paired Selection** "Our Voices, Our Votes" **Genre:** Expository Text **Lexile:** 920L	**Main Selections** **Genre:** Biography ● *Jane Addams: A Woman of Action* **Lexile:** 700L ● *Jane Addams: A Woman of Action* **Lexile:** 910L ● *Jane Addams: A Woman of Action* **Lexile:** 710L ● *Jane Addams: A Woman of Action* **Lexile:** 1000L **SS.5.C.2.5** **Paired Selections** **Genre:** Expository Text ● "Gus García Takes on Texas" ● "Gus García Takes on Texas" ● "Gus García Takes on Texas" ● "Gus García Takes on Texas"	**Academic Vocabulary:** anticipation, defy, entitled, neutral, outspoken, reserved, sought, unequal Prefixes and Suffixes Hyperbole
Text Set 2: Weeks 3 and 4 **Essential Question:** What can you discover when you give things a second look? **Genre:** Drama *Differentiated Genre Passages available*	**Interactive Read Aloud:** "The Mystery Riddle" **Genre:** Drama (Mystery Play)	"Where's Brownie?" **Genre:** Drama (Mystery Play) **Lexile:** NP *ELL Scaffolded Shared Read available*	**Anchor Text** *A Window Into History: The Mystery of the Cellar Window* **Genre:** Drama (Mystery Play) **Lexile:** NP **Paired Selection** "A Boy, a Horse, and a Fiddle" **Genre:** Legend **Lexile:** 950L	**Main Selections** **Genre:** Drama ● *The Mysterious Teacher* **Lexile:** NP ● *The Unusually Clever Dog* **Lexile:** NP ● *The Unusually Clever Dog* **Lexile:** NP ● *The Surprise Party* **Lexile:** NP **Paired Selections** **Genre:** Realistic Fiction ● "The Case of the Missing Nectarine" ● "The Gift Basket" ● "The Gift Basket" ● "The Clothes Thief"	**Academic Vocabulary:** astounded, concealed, inquisitive, interpret, perplexed, precise, reconsider, suspicious Adages and Proverbs Synonyms and Antonyms
Text Set 3: Week 5 **Essential Question:** How do you express something that is important to you? **Genre:** Poetry *Differentiated Genre Passages available*	**Interactive Read Aloud:** "I'm a Swimmer" **Genre:** Free Verse Poetry	"How Do I Hold the Summer?," "Catching a Fly," "When I Dance" **Genre:** Lyric and Free Verse Poetry **Lexile:** NP *ELL Scaffolded Shared Read available*	**Anchor Text** "Words Free as Confetti," "Dreams" **Genre:** Free Verse and Lyric Poetry **Lexile:** NP **Paired Selection** "A Story of How a Wall Stands" **Genre:** Free Verse Poetry **Lexile:** NP	**Main Selections** **Genre:** Realistic Fiction ● *Tell Me the Old, Old Stories* **Lexile:** 650L ● *From Me to You* **Lexile:** 810L ● *From Me to You* **Lexile:** 580L ● *Every Picture Tells a Story* **Lexile:** 990L **Paired Selections** **Genre:** Poetry ● "Family Ties" ● "Dear Gina" ● "Sssh!" ● "The Eyes of a Bird"	**Academic Vocabulary:** barren, expression, meaningful, plumes **Poetry Terms:** lyric, alliteration, meter, stanza Similes and Metaphors

Week 6	Reading Digitally	Fluency	Connect to Content: Social Studies	Connect to Content: Science	Writing	Presentation Options
Extend, Connect, and Assess	**Genre:** Online Article "Droughtbusters"	**Reader's Theater:** *The Golden Door*	**Passages** "Cesar Chavez: Hero at Work" "Army of Helpers" **Activities** Compare the Passages Analyze a Quote Create a Brochure	**Passages** "Colorful Chameleons" "Changing Their Look" **Activities** Compare the Passages Research Mimicry	**Writing Process** Write to Sources: Expository Writing Analyze the Prompt Analyze the Sources: "A Life in Color," "The Federal Art Project," "William Bartram: One with Nature" Plan: Organize Ideas Draft: Strong Conclusion Revise: Peer Conferences	**Reader's Theater** **Inquiry Space** **Writing**

Unit 4

Comprehension	Phonics and Spelling	Fluency	Writing and Grammar	Research and Inquiry
Summarize Photographs and Captions Author's Perspective Text Structure: Chronology	**Week 1** Words with Final /əl/ and /ən/ **Week 2** Prefixes *Differentiated Spelling Lists available*	**Week 1** Expression **Week 2** Accuracy and Rate	**Respond to Reading** **Writing Process** Write to Sources: Expository Writing Analyze the Rubric Rubric Minilesson: Relevant Evidence and Sources Analyze the Student Model **Grammar and Mechanics** **Week 1:** Pronouns and Antecedents; Pronoun-Antecedent Agreement **Week 2:** Kinds of Pronouns; Quotation Marks in Dialogue	**Project:** Positive Change **Product:** Plaque **Blast:** Liberty and Justice for All
Visualize Play Character Perspective Similes and Metaphors	**Week 3** Homographs **Week 4** Words with /chər/ and /zhər/ *Differentiated Spelling Lists available*	**Week 3** Phrasing **Week 4** Accuracy and Expression	**Respond to Reading** **Writing Process** Write to Sources: Expository Writing Analyze the Prompt Analyze the Sources: "Building a Better World," "The Power of Words," "A War at Home and Abroad" Plan: Organize Ideas Draft: Strong Introduction Revise: Peer Conferences **Grammar and Mechanics** **Week 3:** Pronoun-Verb Agreement; Abbreviations **Week 4:** Possessive Pronouns; Apostrophes, Possessives, and Reflexive Pronouns	**Project:** A Second Look **Product:** Formal Letter **Blast:** A Second Glance
Stanza and Meter Lyric and Free Verse Theme Imagery	**Week 5** Suffixes *-ance* and *-ence* *Differentiated Spelling Lists available*	**Week 5** Expression and Rate	**Respond to Reading** **Writing Process** Write to Sources: Expository Writing Analyze the Rubric Rubric Minilesson: Logical Text Structure Analyze the Student Model **Grammar and Mechanics** **Week 5:** Pronouns and Homophones; Punctuating Poetry	**Project:** What Is Important to You? **Product:** Timeline **Blast:** Expressions of Freedom

Scope and Sequence

Text Set Focus	Read Aloud	Shared Read	Literature Anthology	Leveled Reader	Vocabulary
Text Set 1: Weeks 1 and 2 **Essential Question:** How can scientific knowledge change over time? **Genre:** Expository Text *Differentiated Genre Passages available*	**Interactive Read Aloud:** "The Sun: Our Star" **Genre:** Expository Text	"Changing Views of Earth" **Genre:** Expository Text **Lexile:** 910L *ELL Scaffolded Shared Read available*	**Anchor Text** *When Is a Planet Not a Planet?* **Genre:** Expository Text **Lexile:** 980L **Paired Selection** "The Crow and the Pitcher" **Genre:** Fable **Lexile:** 640L	**Main Selections** **Genre:** Expository Text ● *Mars* **Lexile:** 700L ● *Mars* **Lexile:** 900L ● *Mars* **Lexile:** 700L ● *Mars* **Lexile:** 970L **Paired Selections** **Genre:** Science Fiction ● "Zach the Martian" ● "Zach the Martian" ● "Zach the Martian" ● "Zach the Martian"	**Academic Vocabulary:** approximately, astronomical, calculation, criteria, diameter, evaluate, orbit, spheres Greek Roots Thesaurus
Text Set 2: Weeks 3 and 4 **Essential Question:** How do shared experiences help people adapt to change? **Genre:** Historical Fiction *Differentiated Genre Passages available*	**Interactive Read Aloud:** "Starting Over" **Genre:** Historical Fiction	"The Day the Rollets Got Their Moxie Back" **Genre:** Historical Fiction **Lexile:** 900L *ELL Scaffolded Shared Read available*	**Anchor Text** *Bud, Not Buddy* **Genre:** Historical Fiction **Lexile:** 950L **Paired Selection** "Musical Impressions of the Great Depression" **Genre:** Expository Text **Lexile:** 990L	**Main Selections** **Genre:** Historical Fiction ● *The Picture Palace* **Lexile:** 710L ● *Hard Times* **Lexile:** 830L ● *Hard Times* **Lexile:** 520L ● *Woodpecker Warriors* **Lexile:** 900L **Paired Selections** **Genre:** Expository Text ● "The Golden Age of Hollywood" ● "Chicago: Jazz Central" ● "Chicago: Jazz Central" ● "A Chance to Work"	**Academic Vocabulary:** assume, guarantee, nominate, obviously, rely, supportive, sympathy, weakling Idioms Puns
Text Set 3: Week 5 **Essential Question:** How do natural events and human activities affect the environment? **Genre:** Argumentative Text *Differentiated Genre Passages available*	**Interactive Read Aloud:** "Dams: Harnessing the Power of Water" **Genre:** Argumentative Text	"Should Plants and Animals from Other Places Live Here?" **Genre:** Argumentative Text **Lexile:** 930L *ELL Scaffolded Shared Read available*	**Anchor Text** *The Case of the Missing Bees* **Genre:** Argumentative Text **Lexile:** 950L **Paired Selection** "Busy, Beneficial Bees" **Genre:** Expository Text **Lexile:** 980L	**Main Selections** **Genre:** Expository Text ● *The Great Plains* **Lexile:** 760L ● *The Great Plains* **Lexile:** 910L ● *The Great Plains* **Lexile:** 830L ● *The Great Plains* **Lexile:** 1020L **Paired Selections** **Genre:** Persuasive Text ● "Save the Great Plains Wolves" ● "Save the Great Plains Wolves" ● "Save the Great Plains Wolves" ● "Save the Great Plains Wolves"	**Academic Vocabulary:** agricultural, declined, disorder, identify, probable, thrive, unexpected, widespread Root Words

Week 6	Reading Digitally	Fluency	Connect to Content: Science	Connect to Content: Social Studies	Writing	Presentation Options
Extend, Connect, and Assess	**Genre:** Online Article "Is Anybody Out There?"	**Reader's Theater:** *Jane Addams and Hull House*	**Passages** "Sir Isaac Newton" "Gravity" **Activities** Compare the Passages Investigate Newton's Laws Record Your Data	**Passages** "Wind in the Great Plains" "Dusting Off with Humor" **Activities** Compare the Passages Write a 1-2-3 Report on Environment	**Writing Process** Personal Narrative Revise: Strong Conclusion Peer Conferencing Edit and Proofread Publish, Present, and Evaluate	**Reader's Theater** **Inquiry Space** **Writing**

Unit 5

Comprehension	Phonics and Spelling	Fluency	Writing and Grammar	Research and Inquiry
Ask and Answer Questions Diagrams Central Idea and Relevant Details Imagery	**Week 1** Suffixes **Week 2** Homophones *Differentiated Spelling Lists available*	**Week 1** Expression **Week 2** Accuracy and Phrasing	**Respond to Reading** **Writing Process** Research Report Expert Model Plan: Relevant Evidence Draft: Elaboration **Grammar and Mechanics** **Week 1:** Clauses; Appositives **Week 2:** Complex Sentences; Commas with Clauses	**Project:** Scientific Knowledge Grows **Product:** Podcast **Blast:** "A Better World with Satellites"
Make, Confirm, and Revise Predictions Plot: Characterization Plot: Conflict Text Structure: Compare and Contrast	**Week 3** Prefixes **Week 4** Suffixes *-less* and *-ness* *Differentiated Spelling Lists available*	**Week 3** Rate **Week 4** Accuracy	**Respond to Reading** **Writing Process** Research Report Revise: Sentence Structure Peer Conferencing Edit and Proofread Publish, Present, and Evaluate **Grammar and Mechanics** **Week 3:** Adjectives; Capitalization and Punctuation **Week 4:** Adjectives That Compare; Using *More* and *Most*	**Project:** Supporting One Another **Product:** Collage **Blast:** "Shared Experiences"
Ask and Answer Questions Charts and Headings Author's Perspective Puns	**Week 5** Suffix *-ion* *Differentiated Spelling Lists available*	**Week 5** Accuracy and Rate	**Respond to Reading** **Writing Process** Personal Narrative Expert Model Plan: Sequence Draft: Description **Grammar and Mechanics** **Week 5:** Comparing with *Good* and *Bad*; Irregular Comparative Forms	**Project:** Environmental Changes **Product:** Mock Blog Report **Blast:** "Leaving a Trace"

Scope and Sequence

Text Set Focus	Read Aloud	Shared Read	Literature Anthology	Leveled Reader	Vocabulary
Text Set 1: **Weeks 1 and 2** **Essential Question:** How do different groups contribute to a cause? **Genre:** Historical Fiction *Differentiated Genre Passages available*	**Interactive Read Aloud:** "Hope for the Troops" **Genre:** Historical Fiction	"Shipped Out" **Genre:** Historical Fiction **Lexile:** 810L *ELL Scaffolded Shared Read available*	**Anchor Text** *The Unbreakable Code* **Genre:** Historical Fiction **Lexile:** 640L **Paired Selection** "Allies in Action" **Genre:** Expository Text **Lexile:** 870L	**Main Selections** **Genre:** Historical Fiction ● *Mrs. Gleeson's Records* **Lexile:** 730L ● *Norberto's Hat* **Lexile:** 770L ● *Norberto's Hat* **Lexile:** 640L ● *The Victory Garden* **Lexile:** 900L **Paired Selections** **Genre:** Expository Text ● "Scrap Drives and Ration Books" ● "The Bracero Program" ● "The Bracero Program" ● "Gardening for Uncle Sam"	**Academic Vocabulary:** bulletin, contributions, diversity, enlisted, intercept, operations, recruits, survival Homophones Literal and Figurative Language
Text Set 2: **Weeks 3 and 4** **Essential Question:** How are living things adapted to their environment? **Genre:** Expository Text *Differentiated Genre Passages available*	**Interactive Read Aloud:** "Bacteria: They're Everywhere" **Genre:** Expository Text	"Mysterious Oceans" **Genre:** Expository Text **Lexile:** 980L *ELL Scaffolded Shared Read available*	**Anchor Text** *Survival at 40 Below* **Genre:** Expository Text **Lexile:** 990L **Paired Selection** "Why the Evergreen Trees Never Lose Their Leaves" **Genre:** Pourquoi Story **Lexile:** 850L	**Main Selections** **Genre:** Expository Text ● *Cave Creatures* **Lexile:** 760L ● *Cave Creatures* **Lexile:** 900L ● *Cave Creatures* **Lexile:** 750L ● *Cave Creatures* **Lexile:** 1010L **Paired Selections** **Genre:** Pourquoi Story ● "Why Bat Flies at Night" ● "Why Bat Flies at Night" ● "Why Bat Flies at Night" ● "Why Bat Flies at Night"	**Academic Vocabulary:** adaptation, agile, cache, dormant, forage, frigid, hibernate, insulates Context Clues: Paragraph Clues Sound Devices
Text Set 3: **Week 5** **Essential Question:** What can our connections to the world teach us? **Genre:** Poetry *Differentiated Genre Passages available*	**Interactive Read Aloud:** "The Beat" **Genre:** Lyric Poetry	"To Travel!," "Wild Blossoms" **Genre:** Lyric and Narrative Poetry **Lexile:** NP *ELL Scaffolded Shared Read available*	**Anchor Text** "You Are My Music (Tú eres mi música)," "You and I" **Genre:** Lyric and Narrative Poetry **Lexile:** NP **Paired Selection** "A Time to Talk" **Genre:** Lyric Poetry **Lexile:** NP	**Main Selections** **Genre:** Realistic Fiction ● *Your World, My World* **Lexile:** 730L ● *Flying Home* **Lexile:** 790L ● *Flying Home* **Lexile:** 610L ● *Helping Out* **Lexile:** 940L **Paired Selections** **Genre:** Poetry ● "Do I Know You?" ● "Tell Me, Show Me" ● "Fun and Play" ● "A Journalistic Journey"	**Academic Vocabulary:** blares, connection, errand, exchange **Poetry Terms:** personification, assonance, consonance, imagery Personification

Week 6	Reading Digitally	Fluency	Connect to Content: Social Studies	Connect to Content: Science	Writing	Presentation Options
Extend, Connect, and Assess	**Genre:** Online Article "The Tortoise and the Solar Plant"	**Reader's Theater:** *'Round the World with Nellie Bly*	**Passages** "Sarah Winnemucca: Word Warrior" "Sequoyah's Gift" **Activities** Compare the Passages Research Historical Information Write About a Memory	**Passages** "Wonders of the Water Cycle" "An Ocean of Adaptations" **Activities** Compare the Passages Observe Water Molecules in Action	**Writing Process** Narrative Poem Revise: Concrete Words and Sensory Language Peer Conferences Edit and Proofread Publish, Present, and Evaluate	**Reader's Theater** **Inquiry Space** **Writing**

Unit 6

	Comprehension	Phonics and Spelling	Fluency	Writing and Grammar	Research and Inquiry
	Summarize Plot: Flashback Theme Print and Graphic Features	**Week 1** Words with Greek Roots **Week 2** Words with Latin Roots *Differentiated Spelling Lists available*	**Week 1** Expression and Phrasing **Week 2** Intonation	**Respond to Reading** **Writing Process** Historical Fiction Expert Model Plan: Characters Draft: Develop Plot **Grammar and Mechanics** **Week 1:** Adverbs; Capitalization and Abbreviations in Letters and Formal E-mails **Week 2:** Adverbs That Compare; Using *good, well; more, most; -er, -est*	**Project:** World War II **Product:** Cause/Effect Chart **Blast:** "Outstanding Contributions"
	Ask and Answer Questions Maps Text Structure: Cause and Effect Character Perspective	**Week 3** Words from Mythology **Week 4** Number Prefixes *uni-*, *bi-*, *tri-*, *cent-* *Differentiated Spelling Lists available*	**Week 3** Accuracy and Rate **Week 4** Expression and Phrasing	**Respond to Reading** **Writing Process** Historical Fiction Revise: Dialogue and Pacing Peer Conferences Edit and Proofread Publish, Present, and Evaluate **Grammar and Mechanics** **Week 3:** Negatives; Correct Double Negatives **Week 4:** Sentence Combining; Commas and Colons	**Project:** Animal Adaptations **Product:** Slideshow **Blast:** "Blending In"
	Assonance and Consonance Lyric and Narrative Point of View and Perspective Imagery	**Week 5** Suffixes *-ible*, *-able* *Differentiated Spelling Lists available*	**Week 5** Expression and Phrasing	**Respond to Reading** **Writing Process** Narrative Poem Expert Model Plan: Characters, Setting, and Plot Draft: Figurative Language **Grammar and Mechanics** **Week 5:** Prepositional Phrases; Pronouns in Prepositional Phrases	**Project:** Connections **Product:** Email **Blast:** "Be Nice"

Social Emotional Development

	KINDERGARTEN  GRADE 1
Emotional Self Regulation Maintains feelings, emotions, and words with decreasing support from adults	 As the child collaborates with a partner, the child uses appropriate words calmly when disagreeing. 
Behavioral Self Regulation Manages actions, behaviors, and words with decreasing support from adults	
Rules and Routines Follows classroom rules and routines with increasing independence	Transitioning from one activity to the next, the child follows established routines, such as putting away materials, without disrupting the class. 
Working Memory Maintains and manipulates distinct pieces of information over short periods of time 	 
Focus Attention Maintains focus and sustains attention with minimal adult support	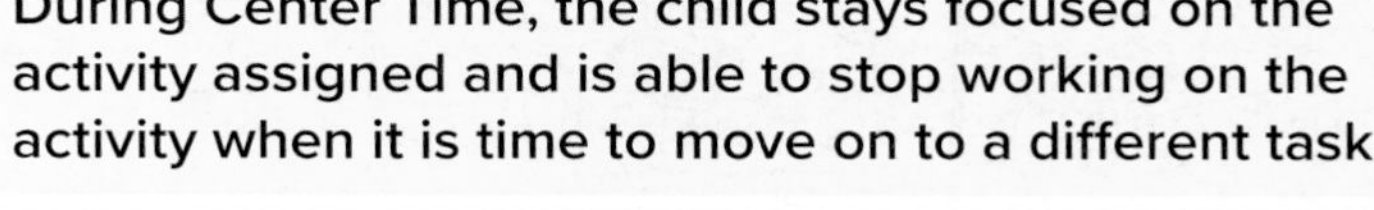 During Center Time, the child stays focused on the activity assigned and is able to stop working on the activity when it is time to move on to a different task.
Relationships and Prosocial Behaviors Engages in and maintains positive relationships and interactions with familiar adults and children 	
Social Problem Solving Uses basic problem solving skills to resolve conflicts with other children 	
Self Awareness Recognizes self as a unique individual as well as belonging to a family, community, or other groups; expresses confidence in own skills	
Creativity Expresses creativity in thinking and communication	
Initiative Demonstrates initiative and independence 	When working independently, the child understands when to ask for help and gets the help needed. 
Task Persistence Sets reasonable goals and persists to complete the task	
Logic and Reasoning Thinks critically to effectively solve a problem or make a decision	
Planning and Problem Solving Uses planning and problem solving strategies to achieve goals 	
Flexible Thinking Demonstrates flexibility in thinking and behavior	

Throughout the grades, students continue to progress in each aspect of their social emotional growth.

GRADE 2 GRADE 3 GRADE 4 GRADE 5

During class discussions, the child can wait until called upon to provide a response, without shouting out.

When responding to a text, the child can identify text evidence from notes previously recorded.

The child willingly works with any other child in the class on partner or group activities that are assigned.

When working on a project in a small group, the child negotiates roles and cooperates with others to complete the task.

In class discussion, the child is not fearful of sharing a unique perspective while respecting the opinions of others.

The child finds a creative way to gather information needed for a writing assignment.

When assigned to read a difficult text, the child applies routines or strategies learned to complete the reading.

Through logic and reasoning, the child is able to figure out how the author's choices of words and structures affect the communication of ideas.

When working on a long-term research project, the child can think through how to complete the different parts of the assignment over a period of time.

As the child struggles with an activity, the child can determine a different way to complete the activity successfully.

Text Complexity Rubric

In *Wonders*, students are asked to read or listen to a range of texts within a text set to build knowledge. The various texts include:

- Interactive Read Alouds
- Shared Reads
- Anchor Texts
- Paired Selections
- Leveled Readers
- Differentiated Genre Passages

Understanding the various factors that contribute to the complexity of a text, as well as considering what each student brings to the text, will help you determine the appropriate levels of scaffolds for students. Quantitative measures, such as Lexile scores, are only one element of text complexity. Understanding qualitative factors and reader and task considerations is also important to fully evaluate the complexity of a text.

At the beginning of each text set in the *Wonders* Teacher's Edition, information on the three components of text complexity for the texts is provided.

Qualitative The qualitative features of a text relate to its content or meaning. They include meaning/purpose, structure, language, and knowledge demands.		
Low Complexity	**Moderate Complexity**	**High Complexity**
Meaning/Purpose The text has a single layer of meaning explicitly stated. The author's purpose or central idea of the text is immediately obvious and clear.	**Meaning/Purpose** The text has a blend of explicit and implicit details, few uses of multiple meanings, and isolated instances of metaphor. The author's purpose may not be explicitly stated but is readily inferred from a reading of the text.	**Meaning/Purpose** The text has multiple layers of meaning and there may be intentional ambiguity. The author's purpose may not be clear and/or is subject to interpretation.
Structure The text is organized in a straightforward manner, with explicit transitions to guide the reader.	**Structure** The text is largely organized in a straightforward manner, but may contain isolated incidences of shifts in time/place, focus, or pacing.	**Structure** The text is organized in a way that initially obscures meaning and has the reader build to an understanding.
Language The language of the text is literal, although there may be some rhetorical devices.	**Language** Figurative language is used to build on what has already been stated plainly in the text.	**Language** Figurative language is used throughout the text; multiple interpretations may be possible.
Knowledge Demands The text does not require extensive knowledge of the topic.	**Knowledge Demands** The text requires some knowledge of the topic.	**Knowledge Demands** The text requires siginifcant knowledge of the topic.

Quantitative

Wonders provides the Lexile score for each text in the text set.

Low Complexity	Moderate Complexity	High Complexity
Lexile Score Text is below or at the lower end of the grade-level band according to a quantitative reading measure.	**Lexile Score** Text is in the midrange of the grade-level band according to a quantitative reading measure.	**Lexile Score** Text is at the higher end of or above the grade-level band according to a quantitative reading measure.

Reader and Task Considerations

This component of text complexity considers the motivation, knowledge, and experiences a student brings to the text. Task considerations take into account the complexity generated by the tasks students are asked to complete and the questions they are expected to answer.

In *Wonders*, students are asked to interact with the texts in many different ways. Texts such as the Shared Reads and Anchor Texts are read over multiple days and include tasks that increase in difficulty. The complexity level provided for each text considers the highest-level tasks students are asked to complete.

Low Complexity	Moderate Complexity	High Complexity
Reader The text is well within the student's developmental level of understanding and does not require extensive background knowledge.	**Reader** The text is within the student's developmental level of understanding, but some levels of meaning may be impeded by lack of prior exposure.	**Reader** The text is at the upper boundary of the student's developmental level of understanding and will require that the student has background knowledge of the topic.
Task The questions and tasks provided for all texts are at various levels of complexity, ensuring that all students can interact with the text in meaningful ways.		

Index

A

Key 1 = Unit 1

B

C

Key 1 = Unit 1

Key 1 = Unit 1

D

E

Key 1 = Unit 1

F

G

Key 1 = Unit 1

H

I

L

Key 1 = Unit 1

M

N

Key 1 = Unit 1

R

Key 1 = Unit 1

S

Key 1 = Unit 1

T

Key 1 = Unit 1

U

V

Key 1 = Unit 1

Key 1 = Unit 1